LIBERTY OR DEATH

PETER McPHEE

LIBERTY
OR
DEATH

THE FRENCH REVOLUTION

YALE UNIVERSITY PRESS
NEW HAVEN AND LONDON

Published with assistance from the Annie Burr Lewis Fund

For information about this and other Yale University Press publications, please contact:

U.S. Office: sales.press@yale.edu   yalebooks.com
Europe Office: sales@yaleup.co.uk   yalebooks.co.uk

Typeset in Adobe Caslon Regular by IDSUK (DataConnection) Ltd
Printed in Great Britain by TJ International Ltd, Padstow, Cornwall

Library of Congress Cataloging-in-Publication Data

McPhee, Peter, 1948- author.
Liberty or death : the French Revolution, 1789-1799 / Peter McPhee.
New Haven : Yale University Press, 2016.
LCCN 2015040677 | ISBN 9780300189933 (cloth : alk. paper)
LCSH: France—History—Revolution, 1789-1799.
LCC DC148.M4535 2016 | DDC 944.04—dc23
LC record available at http://lccn.loc.gov/2015040677

A catalogue record for this book is available from the British Library.

10 9 8 7 6 5 4 3 2 1

For Kit

CONTENTS

List of Maps   ix

Introduction   x

1 Patchworks of Power and Privilege: France in the 1780s   1

2 A World of Intellectual Ferment   23

3 Mismanaging Crisis, 1785–88   39

4 The People's Revolution, 1789   58

5 Regenerating the Nation, 1789–90   81

6 The Revolution Triumphant, 1790   102

7 Fracturing Christ's Family: Religious Schism and the King's Flight, 1790–91   119

8 Fear and Fury, 1791–92, and a Second Revolution   142

9 Republicans at the Crossroads, 1792–93   164

10 Liberty or Death: Choosing Sides in Violent Times, 1793   188

11 'Terror until the peace', July–October 1793   205

12 Saving a Republic of Virtue, October 1793–April 1794   228

13 Terror, Victory and Collapse, April–July 1794   252

14 Settling Scores: The Thermidorian Reaction, 1794–95   274

15 Men with a Stake in Society, 1795–97   297

16 The Great Nation and its Enemies, 1797–99   321

17 The Significance of the French Revolution   342

Chronology   371
The Revolutionary Calendar   380
Notes   381
Select Bibliography   434
Index   455
Illustration Credits   469

Maps

1 French provinces in the eighteenth century. xiv
2 Revolutionary Paris. xv
3 *Départements* of France, 1800. xvi
4 Zones of conflict, 1793–94. xvii

INTRODUCTION

IN THE YEARS AFTER 1789, FRENCH REVOLUTIONARIES SOUGHT to remake their world on the basis of the principles of popular sovereignty, national unity and civic equality. This was an awesome challenge in a large, diverse kingdom hitherto based on absolute monarchy, entrenched privilege and provincial exemptions. Other people, both French and foreign, took up arms in an attempt to destroy a revolution seen to be inimical to established practices of social hierarchy, religious belief and authority.

Contemporaries were polarized in their assessment of what the Revolution achieved. For all of the vicissitudes of the revolutionary decade, all the strength of the reaction against revolutionary excesses both real and imagined, it left an unforgettable, durable image of the possibilities of civic emancipation. The German philosopher Immanuel Kant, aged seventy-four, concluded in 1798 that

> such a phenomenon in the history of the world will never be forgotten, because it has revealed at the base of human nature a possibility for moral progress which no political figure had previously suspected. Even if we must return to the Old Régime, these first hours of freedom, as a philosophical testimony, will lose nothing of their value.[1]

Victoire de Froulay de Tessé, Marquise de Créquy, was twenty years older than Kant. In contrast, she was vitriolic about what she saw around her at the same time:

In the towns you see only insolent or evil people. You are spoken to only in a tone which is brusque, demanding or defiant. Every face has a sinister look; even children have a hostile, depraved demeanour. One would say that there is hatred in every heart. Envy has not been satisfied, and misery is everywhere. That is the punishment for making a revolution.[2]

Historians, like those who lived through those years, have agreed on the unprecedented and momentous nature of the great acts of revolution in the months between May and October 1789. They have never agreed, however, about why what came to be called the *ancien régime* was overthrown with such widespread support, or about why the Revolution took its subsequent course, or about its outcomes. The consequences of the events of 1789 were so complex, violent and significant that reflection and debate on their origins and course show no signs of concluding. The Revolution continues to fascinate, perplex and inspire. Indeed, the two great waves of revolutionary change since the 1980s—the overthrow of regimes in eastern and south-eastern Europe and the 'Arab spring'—have served to revivify our interest in the world-changing upheavals of the late eighteenth century.[3]

The drama, successes and tragedies of the Revolution, and the scale of the attempts to arrest or reverse it, have attracted scholars to the subject for more than two centuries.[4] By the time of Napoleon Bonaparte's seizure of power in November 1799, the first historians of the Revolution had begun to outline their narratives of these years and their judgements about the origins and consequences of revolutionary change. Why and how did an apparently stable regime collapse in 1789? Why did it prove to be so difficult to stabilize a new order? Did the political turmoil of these years disguise a more fundamental social and economic continuity? Was the French Revolution a major turning point in French—even world—history, or instead a protracted period of violent upheaval and warfare that wrecked millions of lives? This book seeks to answer those questions.

Like all major revolutions, the French Revolution had many episodes of heroism and horror, civic sacrifice and slaughter. When commenting in 1927 on peasant uprisings in Hunan province, Mao Tse-Tung famously wrote that a revolution is not a dinner party, or writing an essay, or painting, or doing embroidery; it cannot be so refined, so leisurely and gentle, so temperate, kind, courteous, restrained and magnanimous. A revolution is an insurrection, an act of violence by which one class overthrows another.[5]

Mao was then thirty-four years of age, the same age as a French revolutionary, Maximilien Robespierre, when he responded in November 1792 to the taunts of his political opponents that he had blood on his hands: 'Citizens, did you want a revolution without revolution?' The Parisians who had overthrown Louis XVI in August 1792 and slaughtered hundreds of his guards were, Robespierre insisted, acting for all patriots: 'to make a crime of a few apparent or real misdemeanours, inevitable during such a great upheaval, would be to punish them for their devotion'.[6]

Most general histories of the French Revolution have been written as if it was purely Parisian, and imposed on a recalcitrant, increasingly hostile, countryside. Paris made the Revolution; the provinces reacted to it.[7] In contrast, the underlying approach of this book is that the Revolution is best understood as a process of negotiation and confrontation between governments in Paris and people across the country, in cities, towns and villages. So readers of this book will find much about how the ordinary people of town and country made, opposed and experienced revolutionary change as well as about the history of political struggle in Paris.

It is true that Paris was the epicentre of revolution, but only approximately one French person in forty—about 650,000 of more than 28 million—lived in Paris in the 1780s. This was a land of villages and small towns. The men who governed France through a decade of revolution were overwhelmingly of provincial origin and brought to their nation-building the perspectives that their constituents communicated to them in waves of correspondence. The book will investigate the ways in which the lived experience of legislative, cultural and social change in France from 1789 to 1799 challenged and transformed assumptions about power and authority across provincial society. How did rural and small-town men and women adopt, adapt to and resist change from Paris? The results are surprising.

As a turbulent, violent crisis in a predominantly visual and oral culture, the Revolution generated a vast quantity of visual representations designed to make sense of what had happened and to pour vituperation or mockery on one's enemies. It also produced a mass of ephemera: objects such as entry cards for political clubs, cartoons, or the revolutionary banknotes known as *assignats*. It certainly generated extensive plans to memorialize what it had achieved in monumental architecture, but these were never realized in a context of instability, war and privation. Few physical vestiges remain of a revolution that has shaped contemporary France.[8]

In identifying some of the few signs that survive in the built environment, I received particular assistance from Bernard Richard, who shared his vast knowledge of the physical objects commemorating the Revolution, such as the Bastille stone in the village of Saint-Julien-du-Sault. I have benefited directly from conversations over many years with fine historians, among them David Andress, Michel Biard, Stephen Clay, Ian Coller, Suzanne Desan, Alan Forrest, Paul Hanson, Lynn Hunt, Colin Jones, Peter Jones, Hervé Leuwers, Marisa Linton, Jean-Clément Martin, John Merriman, Noelle Plack, Timothy Tackett, Charles Walton, and generations of my students. Heather McCallum, Candida Brazil and Rachael Lonsdale of Yale University Press and their readers have offered encouragement and wisdom; Richard Mason and Samantha Cross applied their professional expertise to copy-editing and design respectively. Mira Adler-Gillies helped me locate some of the illustrations that are so important to this volume, while Julie Johnson produced the index. Other specific assistance was offered by Juliet Flesch, Kit McPhee, Jeremy Teow and Aurore Mulkens. Most important, I am deeply grateful to my partner Charlotte Allen for her engaged, insightful readings of drafts.

A book of this type inevitably owes a profound debt of scholarship, in this case to the many hundreds of historians who have probed questions about the French Revolution over the past 225 years. For all the polemics that divide them, they have made the quality of research and writing about the Revolution one of the jewels in the crown of historical scholarship, as befits an historical period of such profound importance. The service provided by the staff of French archival repositories has underlined my good fortune in being the historian of a country of great archival guardianship. When the Archives Départementales in Nancy were closed for refurbishment, its staff went so far as to open them solely to enable me to work there.

Parts of Chapter 4 are reproduced with the publisher's permission from my chapter in David Andress (ed.), *The Oxford Handbook of the French Revolution*, ch. 10 (Oxford University Press, 2015). Sections of Chapter 17 are reproduced with the publisher's permission from Peter McPhee (ed.), *A Companion to the French Revolution*, ch. 27 (Blackwell Publishers, 2013).

1 French provinces in the eighteenth century.

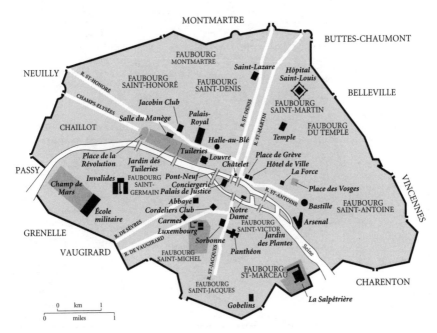

MONTMARTRE

BUTTES-CHAUMONT

NEUILLY

FAUBOURG
MONTMARTRE

Saint-Lazare

Hôpital
Saint-Louis

FAUBOURG
SAINT-HONORÉ

FAUBOURG
SAINT-DENIS

BELLEVILLE

R. ST-HONORÉ

CHAMPS-ELYSEES

Jacobin Club

Palais-
Royal

FAUBOURG
SAINT-MARTIN

FAUBOURG
DU TEMPLE

Salle du Manège

R. ST-DENIS

R. ST-MARTIN

CHAILLOT

Halle-au-Blé

Temple

Tuileries

Louvre

Place de la
Révolution

Jardin des
Tuileries

Châtelet

Place de Grève

Hôtel de Ville

PASSY

Invalides

FAUBOURG
SAINT-
GERMAIN

Pont-Neuf

Conciergerie

Palais de Justice

La Force

Champ de
Mars

R. ST-ANTOINE

Place des Vosges

VINCENNES

École
militaire

Abbaye

Cordeliers Club

Notre
Dame

Bastille

FAUBOURG
SAINT-ANTOINE

Carmes

R. DE SÈVRES

Luxembourg

FAUBOURG
SAINT-VICTOR

Arsenal

GRENELLE

R. DE VAUGIRARD

Sorbonne

Jardin
des Plantes

VAUGIRARD

FAUBOURG
SAINT-MICHEL

R. ST-JACQUES

Panthéon

Seine

CHARENTON

FAUBOURG
ST-MARCEAU

FAUBOURG
SAINT-JACQUES

La Salpêtrière

Gobelins

0   km   1

0   miles   1

2 Revolutionary Paris.

3 *Départements* of France, 1800.

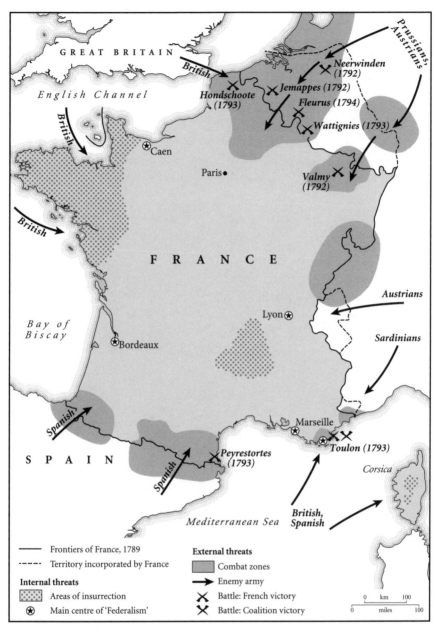

4 Zones of conflict, 1793–94.

CHAPTER ONE

PATCHWORKS OF POWER AND PRIVILEGE

FRANCE IN THE 1780S

L OUIS XVI MADE HIS CEREMONIAL ENTRANCE INTO REIMS FOR HIS coronation in June 1775 in a massive new carriage weighing one and a half tonnes and costing at least 50,000 *livres*, about seventy times the annual stipend of most parish priests. The panels of the carriage were decorated with the lily symbol of the Bourbon family (the *fleur de lys*), the coats of arms of France and Navarre, and gold statuettes, as befitted the *Rex Christianissimus*.[1] The governor of the province of Champagne, the Duc de Bourbon, presented Louis with the keys to the city. Dressed in purple velvet and ermine, he was anointed in the cathedral with drops of the holy oil used in Reims in 496 to baptize Clovis, the first king of the Franks (Fig. 1). Louis swore to protect the Church and to exterminate heretics; in turn the archbishop enjoined him to give charity to the poor, to set an example to the rich, and to keep the peace. The twenty-year-old king was later joined by Queen Marie-Antoinette, aged nineteen, and laid hands on 2,400 sufferers from scrofula (a tuberculous disease of the lymph glands in the neck) who came forward to be cured of the 'king's evil' by his touch.

Across eight centuries the Bourbon monarchy had stitched together a huge kingdom, the largest in Europe outside Russia. It was a patchwork of privilege, everywhere marked by the accretions of history and custom. From the languages spoken by the king's subjects to the laws and courts that regulated their behaviour, from the systems of provincial administration to the structures of the Church, from levels of taxation to systems of weights and measures, every dimension of public life bore the imprint of eight centuries of state-building and compromise with newly incorporated provinces. Privilege was endemic. Not only did particular towns and provinces enjoy privileged status, for example, in levels of taxation, but across the kingdom the corporate privileges of the Church and nobility determined how their members were taxed and judged, and in turn how they taxed and judged others.

The two most important characteristics the inhabitants of eighteenth-century France had in common were that 97 per cent of them were Catholic and all were subjects of Louis XVI, 'by the grace of God, King of France and of Navarre'. The awe-inspiring palace at Versailles, with its seven hundred rooms and garden facade of 575 metres largely completed under Louis XIV by 1710, was redolent of the might of a monarch with absolute powers and responsible to God alone for the well-being of his people. His successors Louis XV and Louis XVI continued the display of majesty.

But France in the 1780s was a society in which people's deepest sense of identity was attached to their particular province or *pays*. While Louis' distant predecessor Francis I had required through the 1539 edict of Villers-Cotterêts that all Church records and legal and administrative documents be kept in French, the reality was that in daily life only a minority of the monarch's subjects used a form of French that would have been intelligible to him. Across most of the country French was the daily language only of those involved in administration, commerce and the professions. Members of the clergy also used it, as well as Latin, although they commonly preached in local dialects or languages. Several million people in Languedoc spoke variants of Occitan; Flemish was spoken in the north-east; German in Lorraine. There were minorities of Basques and Catalans along the Spanish border, and perhaps one million Celts in Brittany. When the Abbé Albert, from Embrun in the southern Alps, travelled westwards through the Auvergne, he noted:

> I was never able to make myself understood by the peasants I met on the road. I spoke to them in French, I spoke to them in my native *patois*, I even tried to speak to them in Latin, but all to no avail. When at last I was tired of talking to them without their understanding a word, they in their turn spoke to me in a language of which I could make no more sense.[2]

Even in the northern half of France, local dialects of French—'parlers' or, more pejoratively, 'patois'—varied between regions.

France was characterized by diversity and contrast in every way. Topographically it ranges from the highest mountains in Europe—Mont

Blanc at 4,800 metres and the Pyrenees at 3,000 metres—to the broad, flat plains of the Paris basin, and the rugged landscape of the Massif Central (Map 1). Agricultural practices were equally diverse, as were the habitats of the mass of people, from the tightly clustered villages and small towns, or *bourgs*, of the south to the isolated hamlets and scattered farms in the west and north-west. The regional diversity of landscape, architecture and produce so loved by tourists today was then far more marked and complex. It was within this diversity that the drama of the decade after 1789 was to be enacted.

More than twice as many people now live in France as in the eighteenth century. But the countryside of the 1780s would have seemed very crowded to us, for this was predominantly a rural society in which most people tilled the soil and consumed its produce directly. Ten times as many people worked the land as do today. Only two persons in ten lived in towns with a population of more than 2,000. Instead, most people inhabited the 40,000 rural communities or parishes with, on average, a population of about 600.[3]

It was this rural population that underwrote the costs of the three pillars of authority and privilege in eighteenth-century France: the monarchy, the Catholic Church (or 'First Estate' of the realm) and the nobility (the 'Second Estate'). The taxes of the royal state, the tithes paid to the Church, and the feudal dues levied by seigneurs together amounted to anywhere between 15 and 40 per cent of peasant produce, depending on the region. And more people were seeking to extract a living from the soil than ever before. Despite the ever-present threat of harvest failure, after 1750 a long series of adequate harvests disturbed the demographic equilibrium of births and deaths: the population increased from perhaps 24.5 million to 28 million by the 1780s.[4]

Most of rural France was characterized by subsistence polyculture: that is, a system of family labour that sought to produce a wide range of plant- and animal-based foodstuffs and clothing. Only in fertile regions close to large cities—for example, the Brie and Beauce near Paris—could owners or renters of substantial farms concentrate their enterprise on a single commodity such as wheat. Most communities had complex economies that mixed production for a local urban centre with subsistence agriculture for local needs.

Two contrasting communities at opposite ends of the kingdom typify this complexity. In the small village (population 280) of Menucourt, just twenty miles north-west of Paris, the large estate of the seigneur Chassepot de Beaumont was used to grow cereal crops for the city. The peasants in Menucourt were also involved in working wood from the chestnut trees to the south of the village into wine-barrels and stakes; others quarried stone for new buildings in Rouen and Paris. This market-oriented activity was supplemented by a subsistence economy on small plots of vines, vegetables, fruit trees (apple, pear, plum, cherry) and walnut trees, the gathering in the forest of chestnuts and mushrooms, and the milk and meat of sheep and cows. As in villages everywhere in France, people plied several trades: for example, Pierre Huard ran the local inn and sold bulk wine in Menucourt, but he was also the village stonemason.[5]

Different in almost every way was the village of Gabian, thirteen miles north of Béziers, near the Mediterranean coastline of Languedoc. Indeed, most people in Gabian could not have communicated with their fellow subjects in Menucourt for, like most Languedociens, they spoke Occitan in daily life. Gabian was a large (770 inhabitants) and important village, with a constant supply of fresh spring water, and since 988 its seigneur had been the Bishop of Béziers. He spent little time there, but extracted a maze of seigneurial dues from the community, including one hundred *setiers* (a *setier* was here about eighty-five litres) of barley, twenty-eight *setiers* of wheat, 880 bottles of olive oil, eighteen chickens, four pounds of beeswax, four partridges and a rabbit. Reflecting Gabian's ancient role as a market centre between the mountains and coast, its inhabitants also had to pay the bishop one pound of pepper, two ounces of nutmeg and two ounces of cloves. Whereas Menucourt was linked to wider markets by its cropping, timber and quarrying industries, Gabian's cash economy was based on extensive vineyards and the wool of one thousand sheep, which grazed on the stony hillsides that ringed the village. A score of weavers of the sheeps' wool worked for merchants from the textile town of Bédarieux to the north.[6]

A personal insight into this rural world is provided by Nicolas Restif de la Bretonne, born in 1734 in the village of Sacy, on the border of the provinces of Burgundy and Champagne. Restif, who moved to Paris and became notorious for his ribald stories in *Le Paysan perverti* (1775), later wrote down his recollections of Sacy in *La Vie de mon père* (1779). He recalled the happy marriage his relative Marguerite had made to Covin, 'a great joker, well-built, a vain country-bumpkin, the great local story-teller':

> Marguerite had about 120 *livres* worth of arable land, and Covin had
> 600 *livres* worth, some in arable land, some under vines, and some fields

dispersed in the grasslands; there were six parts of each type, six of wheat, six of oats or barley, and six fallow . . . . as for the woman, she had the profit of her spinning, the wool of seven or eight sheep, the eggs of a dozen hens, and the milk of a cow, with the butter and cheese she could extract from it. . . . Covin was also a weaver, and his wife had some domestic work; her lot in consequence must have been pleasant enough.

The simple term 'paysan'—like its English equivalent 'peasant'—disguises the complexities of rural society that would be revealed in the varied behaviour of rural people during the Revolution.[7] The peasantry made up about four-fifths of the 'Third Estate' or 'commoners', but across the country it owned only about one-third of the land outright. In areas of large-scale agriculture, like the Île-de-France around Paris, farm labourers were as much as half the population. In most regions, however, the bulk of the population were owners or renters of small farms, or sharecroppers, and many of them were also reliant on practising a craft or on waged work. In all rural communities there was a minority of farmers, often dubbed the *coqs du village*, who were tenant farmers or owners of large farms. Large villages also had a minority of people—priests, artisans, textile workers—who were not peasants at all, but who commonly owned some land, such as the vegetable garden belonging to the priest. The heart of textile manufacturing was also to be found in rural France through peasant women's part-time work linked to provincial towns, such as sheepskin gloves in Millau, ribbons in St-Étienne, lace in Le Puy, cottons in Elbeuf and Rouen, woollens in Amiens, Abbeville and Bédarieux, and silk in Lyon and Nîmes.

The backbreaking work performed in town and country to satisfy the needs of the household was the bedrock of the entire social order. A rural world in which households engaged in a complex strategy to secure their own subsistence could inevitably expect only low yields for grain crops grown in unsuitable or exhausted soil. The dry and stony soils of a southern village like Gabian were no more suited to growing grain crops than were the heavy, damp soils of Normandy: in both places, however, a large proportion of arable land was set aside for grain to meet both local needs and the requirements of seigneurial exactions and tithes. Consequently, most rural communities had restricted 'surpluses' that could be marketed to cities. Far more important to most peasants were nearby *bourgs*, whose regular market fairs were as much an occasion for the collective rituals of local cultures as for the exchange of produce.

While every provincial town and province had its specific history and institutions, they were all part of a kingdom based on 'corporations'. Individual occupations, towns, provinces, and in particular the Church and nobility, had corporate 'rights' and 'privileges' with which the monarchy in Versailles was in perpetual negotiation. In theory, French society mirrored a medieval model in which the three social orders had obligations to pray, to fight and (for the 99 per cent in the Third Estate) to work. The monarchy had long recognized the privileged status of the Church and nobility through, most importantly, separate law codes for their members and tax exemptions. The Church paid only a voluntary contribution (*don gratuit*) to the state, usually no more than 5 per cent of its estimated annual income of 250 million *livres*, by decision of its governing synod. Across the century, however, the monarchy had to grapple with the increasing costs of international warfare and empire, and had succeeded in imposing a series of tax levies—the *capitation, dixième* and *vingtième*—on the property of nobles. By the 1780s these universal taxes were bringing in more than the *taille*, the main direct tax on property.[8] But taxation remained variable across regions and social orders: in Languedoc, for example, noble landowners were now paying 8–15 per cent of their annual revenues in direct taxes, as much as commoners in some areas. In general, however, commoners paid higher rates, and a range of other taxes besides.[9]

Rural communities consumed so much of what they produced that towns and cities faced chronic problems of food supply and in return there was a limited rural demand for their manufactures. Although only 20 per cent of French people lived in urban communities, in a European context France was remarkable for the number and size of its cities and towns. There were eight cities with more than 50,000 people (Paris was easily the largest, with perhaps 650,000 people, then Lyon with 145,000, Marseille, Bordeaux, Nantes, Lille, Rouen and Toulouse), and another seventy with 10,000–40,000. These cities and towns all had some large-scale manufacturing, but most were dominated by artisan-type craftwork for the needs of the urban population itself and the immediate hinterland, and by a range of administrative, judicial, ecclesiastical and policing functions. They were provincial capitals: only one person in forty lived in Paris, and communication between the capital Versailles and the rest of the kingdom was usually slow and uncertain.

The size and topography of the country were a constant impediment to the rapid dissemination of instructions and laws and movement of goods, even if improvements to roads after 1765 meant that no city in France was more than ten days' travel from Versailles. Coaches travelling at sixty miles per day could in five days take people the 290 miles from Paris to Lyon, France's second largest city. It took five days to reach Strasbourg or Nantes from Paris, six to reach Bordeaux, and eight to arrive at Toulouse or Marseille.[10]

Paris was the centre of both an elaborate road network and a convergence of rivers into the Seine (the Yonne, Aube and Marne), together enabling, for example, 141,400,000 gallons of wine to arrive yearly, with 400,000 sheep, 185,000 head of cattle and 40,000 pigs. But cereal crops were the most important foodstuff of the city's population, in particular wheat. Like many other cities, Paris was ringed by a wall for the collection of customs duties on goods imported into the city. Within the walls the *faubourgs* ('suburbs') each had their distinctive mix of a migrant population and its trades. In the sprawling *faubourg* Saint-Antoine in the east of the city, for example, labourers worked in the textile, building and furniture trades. Some made good. The patriarch of the Damoye family had arrived in the *faubourg* as an adolescent from near Beauvais in 1733, and subsequently he and his children had rapidly climbed the ranks of the carriage-building trade, then real estate, to a point where in 1790 their wealth was estimated at 250,000 *livres*.[11]

In the western neighbourhoods of Paris, the building industry was booming as the well-to-do constructed imposing residences away from the teeming medieval quarters of the city's centre. However, most Parisians continued to live in congested streets in central neighbourhoods near the river, where the population was vertically segregated in tenement buildings: often, wealthy bourgeois or even nobles would occupy the first and second floors above shops and workplaces, with their domestic servants, artisans and the poor inhabiting the upper floors and garrets. Paris was typical of France's major cities in its occupational structure. It was dominated by skilled, artisanal production despite the emergence of a number of large-scale industries: in the *faubourg* Saint-Antoine, Réveillon's wallpaper factory employed 350 people while the brewer Santerre had 800 workers.

In skilled trades, a hierarchy of masters controlled the entry of journeymen, who had qualified by presenting their masterpiece (*chef d'oeuvre*) on completion of their *tour de France* through provincial centres specializing in their trade. The 40,000 guild-masters and mistresses who enjoyed their own corporate privileges were among those participating enthusiastically in the booming consumer culture of Louis XVI's Paris.

Their skilled workers were identified as much by their trade as by whether they were masters or workers. Contemporaries referred to the working people of Paris as the 'common people' (*menu peuple*): they were not an industrial working class. Nevertheless, frustrations between workers and their masters were evident in trades where entry to a mastership was difficult, such as building and printing; in some industries the introduction of new machines was threatening the skills of journeymen and apprentices. There were frequent labour disputes, particularly in the printing trades, where qualified artisans were militantly opposed to attempts to employ workers who had not completed an apprenticeship. In 1776 skilled wage-earners had rejoiced at the prospect of the Controller-General or Finance Minister Turgot's abolition of guilds and the chance of establishing their own workshops, but the project was not completed; then in 1781 a system of *livrets*, or workers' pass-books recording their conduct, was introduced, strengthening the hand of masters at the expense of fractious employees.[12]

As in rural communities, the Catholic Church was a presence everywhere in Paris: there were 140 convents and monasteries and 1,200 parish clergy. The Church owned a quarter of the city's property. The number of parish priests in France had halved across the eighteenth century, a trend accelerating after 1750, but in the fifty-two parishes of Paris there was still one parish clergyman for every 750 people. However, more secular attitudes were sapping some of the vitality from clerical culture: by the 1780s, probably fewer than half of Parisians regularly took communion. One reason was that the sprawling new *faubourgs* were poorly served by the Church: the large church of Sainte-Marguerite in the east of the city could hold as many as 3,000 worshippers, but this was just a fraction of the parish population of 42,000.[13]

The *faubourgs* ringing the old heart of Paris were incorporated inside the new customs wall of the General Tax Farm in 1785–87, causing profound resentment at increased taxes and prices. On the 'margins' just outside the city walls gathered many of the poorest recent arrivals to the metropolis, eking out an existence between Paris and the farming villages. For the countryside was close by. When Maximilien Robespierre from the northern town of Arras was a scholarship boy in the 1770s at the kingdom's finest secondary school, the Lycée Louis-le-Grand opposite the Sorbonne, he joined with his classmates in the group outings that occurred for one half-day most weeks, under the watchful eye of the masters. Inner Paris was perceived to be full of temptation and danger, so most of the outings were to the countryside through the city walls, just a short walk south: there the regulations instructed the boys to avoid 'anything that may lead to tumult or complaint, such as chasing after game, entering vineyards, trampling in wheat fields, etc.'.[14]

The lives of urban workers were mostly lived out in public. Large cities like Paris, Lyon and Marseille were characterized by tightly packed, medieval centres where most families occupied no more than one or two rooms: the majority of the routines associated with eating and leisure were public activities. Men in skilled trades found their own solidarities in *compagnonnages*, illegal but tolerated brotherhoods of workers that acted to protect work routines and wages and to provide leisure outlets after working days of fourteen to sixteen hours. There were other, female spaces used by working women to settle domestic disputes as well as issues over rents and food prices, such as at the Saint-Germain market in Paris, where forty-eight of the fifty-seven stalls were held by women.[15] Less fortunate were the estimated 25,000 prostitutes in the city who, like one in ten of the population, eked out a fragile existence on the margins.

But far more typical of urban France were inland provincial centres such as Arras, capital of the northern province of Artois that was incorporated into the kingdom after the Treaty of the Pyrenees with Spain in 1659.[16] The town's population was only about 22,500, but it was a swirl of activity. Despite its compactness—it could be traversed on foot in fifteen minutes—it was a tapestry of small neighbourhoods: the well-to-do parishes of noble and bourgeois families; the crowded streets of the poor along the polluted arms of the River Scarpe; the army 'citadelle'; and a separate quarter in which clustered the fine edifices of the royal administration, the Church and the judiciary. Around Arras the nobility owned perhaps 30 per cent of the land, and the bishopric, cathedral chapter and abbeys another 20 per cent. The province was flourishing through its wealth as a grain and textile producer, and Arras was at the centre of that long boom, as home to one of the largest grain markets in the kingdom.

The gothic bell tower of this 'city of a hundred steeples' dominated its flat hinterland, with a cathedral and eleven parish churches, the great Abbey of Saint-Vaast (to which accrued some 555,000 *livres* of rents annually), as well as eleven convents and seven monasteries. In all, 4 per cent of the town's population were composed of religious: priests, nuns and monks were prolific in the public spaces.[17] So too were members of the fifty great noble families resident in Arras, who drew their wealth from their rural estates and from the feudal dues they levied in their *seigneuries* and then expended in the town. They and the successful middle-class professional and merchant families had begun erecting the elegant town houses whose facades—carefully restored after their destruction by bombs in 1915—continue to give Arras its distinctive Flemish-Baroque architectural style today.

A few smaller, industrial north-eastern centres had sprung up around large iron foundries and coal mines, such as at Le Creusot (Burgundy), Niederbronn (Alsace) and Anzin (Flanders), where 4,000 workers were employed. In 1787 Louis XVI ennobled the Bavarian migrant Christophe-Philippe Oberkampf, who had established a printed-fabrics factory at Jouy, near Versailles, with more than one thousand workers. These new industries were rare. It was rather in the Atlantic ports that a booming colonial trade with the Caribbean colonies was developing a capitalist economic sector in shipbuilding and in processing colonial goods, as for example in Bordeaux, where the population expanded from 67,000 to 110,000 between 1750 and 1790 (Fig. 2). Bordeaux and its hinterland was the most dramatic example of the emergence of a dual economy. In the maritime ports (such as Bordeaux, Le Havre, Nantes and Marseille), the great river ports (Rouen, Paris, Lyon) and their hinterlands, a flourishing economy based on overseas trade, luxury-goods consumption and agricultural specialization was in stark contrast to an 'internal' economy based on long-established cycles of agricultural production and local market fairs.

The great merchants and financiers felt confident in their success. Marseille, with 120,000 inhabitants in 1789, was dominated economically by three hundred trading families. They were the force behind rich intellectual life in the city as well as its economic growth; said one of them in 1775: 'The trader of whom I am speaking, whose status is not incompatible with the most ancient nobility or the most noble sentiments, is the one who, superior by virtue of his views, his genius, and his enterprise, adds his fortune to the wealth of the state . . .'.[18] However, most middle-class families drew their income and status from more traditional forms of activity, such as the law and other professions, working for the royal administration, and from investment in property. The term 'bourgeois' (literally 'town-dweller') could be used to denigrate middle-class pretensions, but carried with it claims of merit and status. To be a 'bourgeois de Paris', and benefit from its minor but prestigious rights and exemptions, one had to be resident in the city, pay taxes there, and not be involved directly in agriculture, but increasingly the term was used just to mean someone living from investments or property rather than manual work or a trade.[19]

The nobility dominated the most prestigious positions in the royal administration, but its lower ranks were staffed by the middle classes. The administration at Versailles was tiny, with only about 670 employees, but across a network of provincial cities and towns it employed many thousands more in courts, public works and government. For bourgeois who had substantial means, there were no more attractive and respectable investments than low-return, secure government bonds or land and seigneurialism. The latter, in particular, offered the hope of social status and even marriage into the nobility. By the 1780s as many as one-fifth of the seigneurs in the countryside around the western town of Le Mans in Maine were of bourgeois background. Among the choicest objects of bourgeois acquisition were about 70,000 venal offices, positions sold by the state to raise revenue, and upwards of 4,200 of which conferred nobility on their owners. Among the most sought-after, the position of 857 'king's secretaries' carried no duties but bought nobility. But, while ennoblement was the ambition of the wealthiest bourgeois, the Second Estate's *recherches de noblesse*, set up to investigate claims to noble status, guarded the boundaries closely against *parvenus*.[20]

Town and country were interdependent. In provincial towns, bourgeois owned extensive rural property from which they drew rents from peasant farmers; in turn, domestic service for bourgeois families was a major source of employment for young rural women. Less fortunate girls worked as prostitutes or in charity workshops. Another important link between town and country involved the practice of working women in cities such as Lyon and Paris sending their babies to rural areas for wet-nursing, often for several years. Babies had a greater chance of survival in the countryside, but even so one-third would die while in the care of the wet nurse.[21] A human trade of another kind involved scores of thousands of men from highland areas with a long 'dead season' in winter who migrated to towns seasonally or even for years at a time to look for work. The men left behind a 'matri-centric' society, where women tended livestock and produced textile fabrics.

The most important link of all between urban and rural France was the supply of foodstuffs, particularly grain. This was a link that was often strained by competing demands between urban and rural consumers. Even in normal times urban workers spent about half their wages on large, heavy loaves of bread. As prices rose during years of shortage, so did the tension between urban populations dependent on cheap and plentiful bread and the poorer sections of the rural community, threatened by local merchants seeking to export their grain to lucrative urban markets. Twenty-two of the years between 1765 and 1789 were marked by food riots, either in urban neighbourhoods where women in particular sought to impose *taxation populaire* to hold prices at customary levels, or in rural areas where peasants banded together to prevent scarce supplies being sent away to market.[22]

Eighteenth-century France was a land of mass poverty in which most people were vulnerable to harvest failure. Very high birth rates (about 4.5 per hundred people) were almost matched by high mortality rates (about 3.5 per hundred). Men and women married late: men usually married aged between twenty-six and twenty-nine, women between twenty-four and twenty-seven. Especially in devout areas, where couples were less likely to avoid conception by *coïtus interruptus*, fertile women conceived as often as once every twenty months. Across much of the country, as many as one-half of all children died of infantile diseases and malnutrition before the age of five. In Gabian, for example, there were 253 deaths in the 1780s, 134 of them being children younger than five. While old age was not unknown—in 1783 three octogenarians and two nonagenarians were buried in the village—the average life expectancy of those who survived infancy was just fifty years.[23]

The clergy were omnipresent. In all, there were about 140,000 of them: 0.5 per cent of the population. Their calling divided them between the 81,500 'regular' clergy (monks and nuns) in religious houses and the 59,500 'secular' clergy (priests or *curés* and curates or *vicaires*) who ministered to the spiritual needs of lay society.[24] The Church drew its wealth largely from a tithe (usually 8–10 per cent) imposed on farm produce at harvest, bringing in an estimated 150 million *livres* each year, and from extensive landholding by religious orders and cathedrals. From this was paid in most dioceses a *portion congrue*, or stipend, to parish clergy, which they supplemented by the charges they levied for special services such as marriages and masses said for departed souls. Although the minimum annual salaries of priests and curates were raised to 750 and 300 *livres* respectively in 1786, such stipends made them little more comfortable than most of their parishioners. In addition, the First Estate owned between 6 and 10 per cent of the land in France, and as much as 40 per cent in the northern region of Cambrésis, while the harvest dues and rents it levied accounted for up to 130 million *livres* annually. The Church was also a major urban property owner: it owned three-quarters of the western town of Angers in Anjou, for example. Here, as elsewhere, the Church was a major source of local employment, meeting the needs of the six hundred clergy resident in this town of 34,000 people: servants, clerks, carpenters, cooks and cleaners depended on the clergy, as did the lawyers who ran the Church's fifty-three legal courts for the prosecution of rural defaulters on tithes and rents on its vast estates.[25]

Many male religious houses were moribund by the 1780s: the recruitment of monks had declined steadily and Louis XV had closed more than 450 religious houses (with a total of just 509 monks and nuns). Female orders were stronger, such as the Sisters of Charity in Bayeux who provided food and shelter to hundreds of impoverished women working as lacemakers. Throughout rural France, it was the parish clergy who were at the heart of the community: as a source of spiritual comfort and inspiration, as counsellors in time of need, as dispensers of charity, as employers, and as a source of news from the outside world.

During the winter months it was the parish priest who provided the rudiments of an education, although perhaps only one man in ten and one woman in fifty could have read the Bible. North of a line from Saint-Malo in Brittany to Geneva more than 50 per cent, and in some regions more than 90 per cent, of men could at least sign their marriage certificates. About 40 per cent of women could. In the western and southern two-thirds of the kingdom only 20–40 per cent of men and 10–30 per cent of women were able to. In Paris, by contrast, there was a primary school for every 1,200 people, and most men and women could actually read.[26]

The theology to which the faithful were exposed was marked by a 'Tridentine' mistrust of worldly pleasures, by emphasis on priestly authority, and by powerful imagery of the punishments awaiting the lax when they passed beyond the grave. Yves-Michel Marchais, the *curé* of a devout western parish, preached that 'everything that might be called an act of impurity or an illicit action of the flesh, when done of one's own free will, is intrinsically evil and almost always a mortal sin, and consequently grounds for exclusion from the Kingdom of God'. Once excluded, sinners were left in no doubt about the punishments that awaited them, as expressed by preachers such as Father Bridaine, a veteran of 256 missions to the flock:

> Cruel famine, bloody war, flood, fire . . . raging toothache, the stabbing pain of gout, the convulsions of epilepsy, burning fever, broken bones . . . all the tortures undergone by the martyrs: sharp swords, iron combs, the

teeth of lions and tigers, the rack, the wheel, the cross, red-hot grills, burning oil, melted lead . . .

However, while 97 per cent of French people were nominally Catholic, levels of both religiosity (the external observance of religious practices, such as attendance at Easter mass) and spirituality (the importance that individuals accorded to such practices) varied across the country. The essence of spirituality is, of course, largely beyond the reach of the historian; however, the decline in faith in some areas at least is suggested by increasing numbers of brides who were pregnant (from 6 to 10 per cent across the century) and a decline in priestly vocations (the number of new recruits declined by 23 per cent across the years 1749–89).[27]

Catholicism was strongest in the west and Brittany, along the Pyrenees, and in the southern Massif Central, regions characterized by a strong clerical recruitment of boys from local families well integrated into their communities and cultures. These were areas of scattered farms and hamlets, where it was at Sunday mass that the inhabitants of outlying farms and hamlets felt a sense of community. Parishioners and clergy decided on the full range of local matters after mass in tiny theocracies governed by priests. Everywhere the most devout parishioners were more likely to be older, female and rural.

Protestants who wished to worship needed to abjure their faith, at least in public, until 1788. There were approximately 700,000 Protestants in parts of the east and the Massif Central. Memories of the religious wars and intolerance following the revocation of the Edict of Nantes in 1685 remained powerful: the people of Pont-de-Montvert in the Cévennes, in the heartland of the Protestant Camisard rising in 1700, had an army garrison (the Knights of Malta) and a Catholic seigneur to remind them daily of their subjection.[28] In Paris there was far greater accommodation between Catholics and Protestants, perhaps because of the city's turbulent religious history. In November 1787, Louis XVI signed the Edict of Toleration, largely the work of a former government minister, Lamoignon de Malesherbes, and a Protestant pastor from Nîmes, Jean-Paul Rabaut Saint-Étienne, which effectively restored to Protestants the right to openly practise their religion as well as their legal and civil status, including the right to contract marriages without having to convert to Catholicism. But this freedom was not extended to Jews, and Catholicism remained the state religion.[29]

Like Protestants, the geographically segregated Jewish communities, in all 40,000 people, preserved a strong sense of identity in Bordeaux and Bayonne, the Comtat-Venaissin region around Avignon, and Alsace-Lorraine. In the south-west Sephardi descendants of refugees from Spain had long enjoyed royal recognition of specific 'rights' and took some pride in their degree of acceptance. This recognition was far less the case among the Askenazi Jews of eastern France, although after 1770 the 'privileges' accorded to Jews in the local capital of Nancy had broadened. In 1788 they were permitted to build a synagogue, with a cemetery and hospital. Most of the forty extended families in Nancy were poor but others, such as the Berr and Cerfberr families, were very wealthy both here and in Strasbourg. Despite their long presence in these towns, however, there were periodic outbursts of anti-Semitism, as in Nancy in February 1788, when the Cerfberrs' grain store was pillaged and other Jewish homes were attacked.[30]

The most lucrative positions as heads of religious orders (often held *in absentia*) and as bishops and archbishops were dominated by the nobility. Whereas nine commoners had become bishops in the first half of the century, there had been only one since, the brilliant preacher Abbé de Beauvais, named to Senez in south-eastern France, one of the smallest and most isolated dioceses in the kingdom, in 1773. However, although the archbishops and bishops were united by noble origin, they were divided by wealth and status, for example, between the extremes of the Cardinal de Rohan, Archbishop of Strasbourg, who had a stipend of 450,000 *livres* per year, and the 20,000 *livres* of the Bishop of Apt in the Alps.[31]

At the pinnacle of every form of privilege—legal, fiscal, occupational—was the noble elite of the first two Estates or orders. The ancient and immensely wealthy noble families at the summit of power shared a conception of social and political authority which they expressed through ostentatious display in their dress, dwellings and consumption of luxuries. This was a tiny elite, perhaps no more than 25,000 noble families or 125,000 individual nobles, about 0.4 per cent of the population. As an order, the nobility drew on several sources of corporate wealth and power: fiscal and seigneurial privileges, the status that went with insignia of eminence, and exclusive appointment to a range of official positions.[32] The entry of a son into a military academy and the promise of a career as an officer was one of the favoured ways in which provincial nobles preserved status and economic security. Their standing within the army was buttressed by the 1781 Ségur ordinance requiring four generations of nobility for army officers. Only sixteen of the 211 lieutenant-generals were of commoner origin, and more than 90 per cent of the total officer corps were noble.[33]

Like the other Estates, the nobility was characterized by great internal diversity. In Paris, for example, there were perhaps 6,000 nobles, concentrated in the *faubourgs* of Saint-Honoré and Saint-Germain, in the Marais and on the Île Saint-Louis. Louis XVI's cousin, the Duc d'Orléans, had an income of two million *livres* per year, and another close relative, the Prince de Conti, twice as much. There were another one hundred noble families in Paris with incomes of 50,000–300,000 *livres* and three or four hundred more with 10,000–50,000 *livres*.[34] In contrast, the poorest provincial nobles (referred to dismissively as *hobereaux*) on their country estates had little in common with the Parisian elite, the several thousand courtiers at Versailles (*les Grands*), or the magistrates of the high courts and senior administrators. It rankled that their noble status was usually far more ancient than that of those who had been ennobled for their administrative services (*noblesse de robe*) or who had simply bought a title.

Within the elite of the nobility, social relations were further fractured by intricate hierarchies of status and prerogative; for example, between those who had been formally presented at court, those permitted to sit on a footstool in the queen's presence, and those even permitted to ride in her carriage. These were not empty symbols: the family of the queen's favourite the Duchesse de Polignac received 438,000 *livres* in pensions and salaries. Sometimes these were not enough. The Prince and Princesse de Rohan-Guéméné, he being the Grand Chamberlain and she the governess of royal children and closely related to the Cardinal de Rohan, declared a bankruptcy of 33 million *livres* in 1783.

Even for lesser nobles, the cost of keeping up appearances appropriate to family status could be high: the court family of Saulx-Tavanes spent annually 20,000 *livres*, one-third of the duke's revenues from estates in Burgundy, on clothing and other accessories. One of the most eminent nobles, Charles Maurice de Talleyrand-Périgord—who entered the priesthood rather than the army because of a congenital limp, and was ordained a bishop just ten years later, in January 1789—described the nobility as 'a cascade of contempt'.[35] What all nobles had in common, however, was a vested interest in a system of social elitism and hierarchy from which came material privilege, status and preferment.

Most nobles drew a significant proportion of their wealth from the ownership of property, particularly in the countryside. The Second Estate owned outright perhaps one-third of the land in France, and exerted seigneurial 'rights' over most of the rest, a relic of a medieval conception of social order in which all land had an overlord ('nulle terre sans seigneur'), in return for which the lord had obligations for the well-being of the community. The most important of these 'rights' was regular payment of a proportion of the harvest (known as the *champart, censive* or *tasque*) of the major crops produced on all land within the *seigneurie*; the levy was normally between one-twelfth and one-sixth, but up to one-quarter in parts of central France. It was often bolstered by other significant rights, such as a monopoly (*banalité*) over the village oven, grape and olive presses, and mill; financial levies on land transfers and even on marriages; and the requirement of unpaid labour by the community on the lord's lands at harvest time. It has been estimated that the value of such dues was as much as 70 per cent of noble income in the province of Rouergue in Auvergne where the *champart* took one-quarter of peasant produce, and as low as 8 per cent in the neighbouring region of the Lauragais to the south.[36]

The model of obligations and privileges in a traditional society of 'orders' was sharply at odds with changing social realities and the polarities of wealth and status within every order. Rather than understanding eighteenth-century France as based on social orders in which everybody 'knew their place', the relative stability of the social and political system is better explained by viewing it as in 'flexible equilibrium', in which tensions were held in check by an elaborate system of privileges and exemptions, and the threat of exemplary force. The exercise of monarchical authority was pivotal to the equilibrium.

The body of established practice and precedent by which the king governed France was customary, not a written constitution. The royal line was Catholic and passed only through the eldest sons, according to the medieval Salic Law. As head of the executive authority the king appointed ministers, diplomats and senior officials, and had the power to declare war and peace. In practice, however, the king manoeuvred rather than dictated. In particular, since the highest courts (the *parlements*) had the responsibility of registering the king's decrees, they had increasingly assumed the right to do more than simply vet them for legalistic correctness; instead, they insisted that their 'remonstrances' could also defend subjects against violations of their privileges and customary rights.

The ruling elite of late eighteenth-century France—Louis XVI and his court, and the noble elite that dominated landed wealth, the administration,

Church and judiciary—were held together by countervailing tensions. Relations between the privileged orders and the monarch were based on mutual dependence and negotiation: this was an uneasy equilibrium of power. Since Louis''Declaration of the Clergy of France' in 1682, the king was head of the Gallican Church, which claimed a measure of autonomy from Rome in matters of ecclesiastical authority and organization, but in turn the king was dependent on the goodwill of the clergy for celebrating the legitimacy and majesty of monarchy. In return the Catholic Church enjoyed a monopoly of public worship and moral codes. Similarly, in return for the obedience and deference of his fellow nobles, the king accepted that they would be at the pinnacle of every institution, from the Church to the armed forces, from the judiciary to his own administration. Jacques Necker, a Genevan banker who was Finance Minister between 1777 and 1781 and Chief Minister from June 1788, was Louis XVI's only non-noble minister.

The symbolic authority of the monarchy was majestic, but its bureaucracy was both small in size and limited in function to the control of public order, foreign policy and trade. There were only six named ministries, and three of them were devoted to Foreign Affairs, War and the Navy; the others were concerned with Finances, Justice and the Royal Household. Much of the collection of taxes was 'farmed-out' to private *fermiers-généraux* rather than being the responsibility of state tax-collectors. These tax-farmers were the largest employers in the kingdom after the armed forces, and two-thirds of their 30,000 employees constituted a paramilitary force that was widely loathed and feared. One of the most famous of the tax-farmers was Antoine Lavoisier, who combined fastidious collection with brilliant chemistry in his private laboratory with his young wife Marianne, and agricultural improvement on his estate at Fréchines near Blois on the River Loire.[37]

The reality of the monarchy's administration reflected centuries of compromise with newly incorporated territories, for everywhere the monarchy needed to respect the particular customs and privileges of the thirty-nine provinces and their noble and clerical elites (Map 1). The provinces were grouped for administrative purposes into thirty-six *généralités*, to which the king appointed *intendants*. There were significant differences in their size and autonomy, reflecting the date and circumstances of their incorporation into France. They were still being added to, most recently Lorraine (centred on Nancy, in 1766), Corsica (Bastia, 1768), Gascony (Auch, 1776), Labourd (Bayonne, 1784) and Béarn (Pau, 1784). The powers which the king's *intendants* could exercise in his provinces varied considerably. Some of the *généralités*, known as the *pays d'état* (such as Artois, Brittany, Languedoc and Burgundy), claimed a broad measure of autonomy, for example, in the apportionment of taxation to their populations, which other areas, the *pays d'élection* (such as Normandy and Auvergne) could not.

Ecclesiastical boundaries reflected the Church's own history. The 136 dioceses and eighteen archdioceses ranged in size and wealth from the sprawling archdiocese of Paris to the 'évêchés crottés' ('muddy bishoprics'), tiny sees that were the result of political agreements in earlier centuries, particularly in the south during the fourteenth-century exile of the papacy in Avignon. Some of these southern cathedrals—such as Rieux, Saint-Papoul, Vabres and Senez—were located in what were little more than large villages. The kingdom even included an extensive enclave—Avignon and the surrounding Comtat-Venaissin—which had continued to belong to the papacy since its exile.

Different again were the boundaries of the highest courts in the kingdom, the thirteen *parlements* and four *conseils souverains*. The *parlement* of Paris exercised power over half the country, whereas the *conseils souverains* of Arras and Perpignan had only a tiny local jurisdiction. The centres of royal administration, the archdiocese and the judicial capital were often located in different towns within the same province. The legal systems of eighteenth-century France were further complicated, for not only did members of the two privileged orders enjoy their own law codes for most cases, but across the kingdom legal systems reflected the weight of history and custom. There was an ancient division between the written or Roman law of the south and the customary law of the north, and on either side of this divide lay tens of local law codes.

The treatment of subjects in a court of law depended both on their position in the social order and on where they lived. Punishments for commoners—particularly the poor—were severe and designed to be exemplary. In 1783, for example, a defrocked Capuchin monk accused of sexually assaulting a boy and stabbing his victim seventeen times was 'broken on the wheel' (his limbs smashed with iron rods) and burned alive in Paris. Two beggars from the Auvergne were broken on the wheel in 1778 for making armed threats towards their victim. In all, 19 per cent of the cases before the Prevotal Court in Toulouse in the period 1773–90 resulted in public execution (reaching 31 per cent in 1783), and as many again in life imprisonment in naval prisons.[38]

Those involved in trade and the professions complained of the difficulties created for their work by the complexity of legal codes. Further obstacles were posed by the numerous systems of currency, weights and measures—there were no common measures of size or volume across the kingdom—and by internal customs barriers. Nobles and towns imposed their own tolls (*péages*) as produce was transported along rivers and canals. In 1664 much of northern France had formed a customs union; but there were customs houses between the north and the rest of the country, though not always between border provinces and the rest of Europe: it was easier for eastern provinces to trade with Prussia than with Paris.

The compromises that successive French monarchs had had to make in order to guarantee the acquiescence of newly acquired provinces were also evident in the complicated tax arrangements across the country. The main direct tax on property, the *taille*, varied in scale between provinces, and some towns had managed to buy their way out of it entirely. The major indirect tax, the *gabelle* on salt, varied from over 60 *livres* per 72 litres to just 1 *livre* 10 *sous* for the same amount. So stark were these contrasts that contemporaries described bands of ostensibly pregnant women smuggling salt from Brittany, the lowest taxed area, eastwards into areas of high taxation in order to profit from clandestine sales. In just one area near Angers, almost 3,500 men, women and children were sentenced for salt-smuggling during the period 1780–83; many more were not caught or were acquitted.[39]

So France was an intricately hierarchical society in which the weight of authority guaranteed relative obedience and stability. The people of the small towns and villages of rural France inhabited a world in which the spiritual, legal and material power of the Church and nobility was reinforced by the daily routines of community life, from the marking of time and the seasons by the Church to respect for the seigneur's control of communal ovens and presses. Across the centuries, too, the privileged orders had etched their eminence onto the physical landscape through the construction of châteaux and churches, recalling the duties of commoners to labour and defer to their betters.

While seigneurs were less likely to reside on their country estates by the 1780s than earlier in the century, preferring to live in Paris or other major cities, they continued to exercise a maze of prerogatives reinforcing the community's subordinate position, whether by reserving a pew in the parish church, wearing a weapon in public or naming the village officials in the 1770s and 1780s. We cannot know the extent to which the deference on which they insisted was a sincere recognition of their eminence; certainly, however, there were repeated instances of peasant animosity that outraged members of the elite.

Paradoxically, while France appeared to be the most stable of realms, protest was in fact endemic, most commonly in the form of food-rioting or of complaints about the presumptions of the privileged. This was protest within the system, against threats to idealized ways in which the system was believed to have once worked. Indeed, during the most extensive popular unrest in the years prior to 1789—the 'Flour War' in northern France in 1775—rioters shouted that they were lowering the price of bread to its customary price of 2 *sous* per pound 'in the name of the king', tacit recognition of the king's responsibility to God for his people's well-being.

But there is evidence of a change in the tenor of protest in some regions. On the lowlands of Languedoc, for example, young men in particular were more commonly contesting the authority of seigneur, priest and local officials, and exhibiting a contrariness denounced as a 'republican spirit' by the authorities. For example, in a village south-east of Carcassonne, a day labourer commented to others as the seigneur passed: 'If you would do as I do we'd soon put to rights this young ___ of a seigneur'. Later he had continued to a blacksmith, 'If you would all do as I do, not only would you not raise your hats when you pass in front of them, but you wouldn't even recognize them as seigneurs, because as for me I've never and will never in my life raise my hat, they're a huge load of scum, thieves, young ___'. Those described by priests, nobles and the local well-to-do as 'libertins' and 'séditieux' were overwhelmingly young peasant men, and three-quarters of the incidents in which they were involved concerned their refusal to make 'signs of submission'.[40]

Members of the local elite at the time were sure that social relations were changing. In 1776, towards the end of his forty-eight years as Bishop of Carcassonne, Armand Bazin de Bezons warned his superiors at Versailles:

> for some time the spirit of revolt and the lack of respect for one's elders has become intolerable . . . no remedies avail since people believe themselves to be free; this word 'liberty' known even in the most isolated mountains has become an unchecked license . . . I hope that this

impunity does not lead to and produce in the end some very bitter fruits for the government.[41]

Was the bishop's lament simply that of an old man regretting the perceived collapse of idealized patterns of behaviour or was there substance to his belief that the spirit of 'liberty' was eroding deference?

CHAPTER TWO

A WORLD OF INTELLECTUAL FERMENT

IN 1780 THE LAWYER CHARLES DOMINIQUE DE VISSERY DE BOIS-VALÉ constructed a gigantic lightning conductor on his house in Saint-Omer, a small town near the English Channel in the northern province of Artois. The conductor was a physical expression of his 'enlightened' contempt for those who understood lightning as an expression of God's anger. According to one report:

> This contraption consisted of a gilded sword-blade, screwed onto an iron rod of sixteen feet in length: at the point where the rod joins the sword-blade mentioned above, there is a weathercock in the shape of a globe decorated with lightning darts pointing in different directions; the lower part of this rod plunges into a funnel made of tin, with a plate of the same metal, pierced by several holes at the end and terminating in a 57 feet-long pipe, also of tin, which goes down the wall of the neighbouring house . . .

The towering apparatus had alarmed neighbours to the point where they had obtained a court order to have it dismantled. Vissery objected, and they resorted to throwing stones, singing and chanting. The court order was confirmed by the local magistrate's court.[1]

Vissery refused to be defeated: he appealed to the Council of Artois, the highest court in the provincial capital of Arras, and charged the lawyer Antoine Buissart with preparing his defence. Buissart was a passionate amateur scientist, nicknamed 'the barometer' by locals. He wrote a voluminous report to brief a brilliant young friend, Maximilien Robespierre, who had returned to Arras to practise law in 1781 after twelve years of study in Paris. Drawing on this work done by his mentor, Robespierre, aged twenty-five, was able in June 1783 to have the ruling overturned in a context of references to enlightenment triumphing over 'obscurantism' (Fig. 3). 'Gentlemen,' he pleaded to the Council, 'you must defend Science':

> you are to defend a sublime invention which is rapturously admired: the fact that the whole of Europe is watching this case will ensure that your decision will be as well-known as possible. . . . Paris, London, Berlin, Stockholm, Turin, St Petersburg will hear almost as soon as Arras of this mark of your wisdom and enthusiasm for scientific progress.[2]

Robespierre's success in the case emboldened him to send a copy of his court address to Benjamin Franklin, resident in Paris since 1776 as Commissioner for the new United States of America and long famous for his experiments with electricity. In his accompanying letter of 1 October 1783, Robespierre noted that it was Franklin's discovery he was defending and hoped that 'the desire to assist in uprooting the prejudices which stood against its progress in our province' would merit 'the honour of earning the approbation of a man whose least virtue is that of being the most famous man of science in the universe'.

On 27 August 1783, Franklin had been excited to witness the world's first hydrogen balloon flight, launched from the Champ de Mars (now the site of the Eiffel Tower). The following week, on 3 September, he was flushed with the success of signing the Peace of Paris, formally ending the American War of Independence and recognizing the new United States. Robespierre was only one of many among France's educated elite who lionized Franklin before his departure for home in July 1785.[3]

Franklin was feted not simply because he was the representative of the courageous colonists who had brought France's old enemy to its knees and had created a new republic, but because, as Robespierre saw it, Franklin was a man of science and 'progress'. Their cause was reason and 'enlightenment', their sphere the 'republic of letters' that was populated by people of any land who were free of prejudice. To be 'enlightened' meant sharing a common language about individuals and their relationship to authority: that legitimate political authority rested on recognition of the public sphere and that individual liberties were 'rights' rather than 'privileges'.

Educated contemporaries like them understood themselves within a trans-Atlantic 'republic of letters' bonded by the certainty voiced by Voltaire in his *Idées républicaines* (1765) that the 'community of men' were capable of 'governing themselves' rather than suffering under 'despotism'. In actuality, the 'republic of letters' extended not just from Italy to Scotland and Philadelphia, for its correspondents ranged from Latin America to eastern and south-eastern Europe and south Asia.[4] But its epicentre was France, and there was an essential connection between the major themes of the new philosophy and the society it was challenging. The vibrant intellectual life of the second half of the eighteenth century was a product of that society: the chief and linked targets of critical writing were royal absolutism and theocracy. In the words of Denis Diderot in 1771:

> Every century has its own characteristic spirit. The spirit of ours seems to be liberty. The first attack against superstition was violent, unchecked. Once people dared in whatever manner to attack the barrier of religion, this barrier which is the most formidable as well as the most respected, it was impossible to stop. From the time when they turned threatening looks against the heavenly majesty, they did not fail the next moment to direct them against the earthly power. The rope which holds and represses humanity is composed of two strands: one of them cannot give way without the other breaking.[5]

From 1751 to 1772, Diderot was preoccupied with editing the *Encyclopédie*, or 'universal dictionary of arts, sciences and trades', with his fellow editor Jean d'Alembert, an opus finally comprising twenty-eight volumes, with 71,818 articles and 3,129 illustrations. Its contributors included the great names—Voltaire, Rousseau, Turgot, Holbach, Quesnay—although the Protestant polymath Louis de Jaucourt wrote one-quarter of all the articles. (The elderly Jaucourt, born in 1704, had earlier lost the result of twenty years' work, the manuscript of a six-volume dictionary of medicine, in a shipwreck.) Diderot's comment in the *Encyclopédie* that 'the revolution which has been made in people's minds' would change the world, echoed his sentiments in a letter to his lover Sophie Volland of 26 September 1762:

> What characterizes philosophy and distinguishes it from the everyday is that nothing is accepted without proof, that it never accedes to dubious notions, and that it questions what are the limits of the certain,

the probable and the doubtful. In time this work will surely produce a
revolution in people's minds, and I hope that tyrants, oppressors, fanatics
and the intolerant will lose. We will have served humanity.[6]

The liberation of public life would necessarily also encourage the unleashing
of creativity in economic life: for 'physiocrats' such as Turgot and Quesnay,
worldly progress lay in unleashing the initiative to allow free enterprise
and free commerce (*laissez-faire, laissez-passer*). By removing obstacles to
economic freedom—such as guilds, which restricted entry to professions,
internal tolls and controls on the grain trade—and by encouraging agricultural improvement and enclosures, the economic wealth would be created
that would underpin the progress of civil liberties and humanity in general.[7]

The limited but dramatic expansion of capitalist enterprise in industry,
agriculture in the Paris hinterland and above all colonial commerce, was
generating forms of wealth, behaviour and values discordant with the institutional bases of absolutism, an ordered society of corporate privilege,
landed property, and the claims to authority of aristocracy and Church. The
certainty that economic freedoms were inseparable from civic freedoms
and greater prosperity was paralleled by a 'consumer revolution'. The number
of 'bourgeois' in France increased from about 700,000 in 1700 to perhaps
2.3 million in 1780. Even among petit-bourgeois—shopkeepers, master
craftsmen, minor officials—a distinctive 'consumer culture' was thriving,
apparent in the taste for writing-tables, mirrors, clocks and umbrellas.[8] If
markers of status were now becoming fashionable clothes and luxury goods
which those with money could purchase, how could nobles continue to
mark their distance from commoners?

A civic discourse of 'virtue' underpinned a shift in the meaning of
'nobility' itself, for side by side with the continued language of birth, privilege and obligation emerged a broader use of the term to indicate civic and
moral excellence. In the increasingly commercial world of the late eighteenth century, nobles and others debated whether abolishing laws of *déro-
geance* (derogation) to permit nobles to engage in trade would resuscitate
the 'utility' of the nobility in the eyes of commoners.[9]

These changing values were evident in the magazines of the time. The
decades after 1750 were remarkable for an expansion of written communication. The number of periodicals in France increased from fifteen in 1745
to eighty-two in the 1780s, with perhaps 70,000 copies sold, and each copy
would have been read by many people. But these were for the educated

elite: one of the most important was the *Gazette de Leyde*, produced in the Netherlands by Protestants and with 4,200 subscribers who could afford the 36 *livres* per year, well beyond the reach of wage-earners. In the 1780s the *Journal de santé* and other periodicals devoted to hygiene and health were launched, calling for schemes to wash the streets and to circulate air: the heavy mix of sweat and perfume of bewigged courtiers was as intolerable as the 'stench' of the urban poor and peasantry. Heightened sensitivity towards the body ranged from concern for cleanliness to outrage at torture. The increasing use of terms such as 'public opinion', 'citizen' and 'nation' in political commentary was reflected in the popularity of the *Courrier de l'Europe*, printed in Boulogne-sur-Mer on the English Channel, which translated columns from London newspapers reporting on debates in the British Parliament.[10]

The Enlightenment was a self-conscious cultural movement reflected, for example, in the desire to own books. In 1700 estate inventories in Paris showed that books were owned by 13 per cent of wage-earners, 32 per cent of magistrates and 26 per cent of nobles of the sword; by the second half of the century the respective figures were 35, 58 and 53 per cent. In the *faubourg* Saint-Marcel the wealthy tanner Nicolas Bouillerot left seventy-three books, all of them about religion, when he died in 1734; in contrast, another tanner, Jean Auffray, who died in 1792, was less wealthy but left five hundred books, including works of history and Latin classics, and a number of maps and pamphlets. Rather than simply the literary tastes of two individuals, the cases typify changing values and interests among bourgeois for whom the Enlightenment was 'a way of life'.[11]

The 1770s and 1780s were a great age of international interest in philosophy, the sciences and travel among European elites. Sales boomed of travel books produced both legally and as pirated editions by a publishing house, the Société Typographique, across the Swiss border in Neuchâtel; 87,000 volumes were sold in France alone.[12] Some of these travellers, collectors and scholars were 'cosmopolitan' in the sense of seeing themselves as 'citizens of the world', who dreamed of the possibilities of humanity united under a single benevolent government. Many more were impelled by a desire for knowledge that knew no bounds, geographically or intellectually. They relished accounts of new discoveries, whether tales of the South Pacific by Cook and Bougainville or serious studies of the volcanoes in the Auvergne by Faujas de Saint-Fond and Lamoignon de Malesherbes.[13] Never before had so many books been sold. Not surprisingly, established authorities were troubled by books suggesting that volcanoes taught one that the earth was very old or that participation in the thirteenth-century Crusades did not justify fiscal immunity in perpetuity.

Perhaps the most corrosive shift in educated discourse was the assumption that 'rights' were universal and inherent in human beings. The 'rights' that the privileged orders valued—to bear arms in public, to be exempt from common obligations, to levy harvest dues on peasants—had been accorded by the monarchy. Instead, prominent public intellectuals such as Voltaire, Diderot and Rousseau—dubbed *philosophes*—understood 'rights' rather to be intrinsic to human existence, and incontrovertible. The special outrage of torture, as expressed most trenchantly by the Italian jurist Cesare Beccaria in *On Crimes and Punishments* (1764), was that the individual body, the vessel of inalienable rights and dignity, was violated.[14]

If individuals were born with rights and the sensibilities needed to experience emotions, then the 'public sphere' was where they could exercise these rights and capacities by participating in political culture. This was not just in the sense of claiming rights to know about public affairs and even to influence them, but extended into all the 'spaces' in which ideas were articulated and contested. For example, at variance with the corporate, privileged world of the aristocratic royal academies were the more open, free-thinking Masonic lodges, a form of bourgeois, male sociability that proliferated remarkably after 1760. Despite injunctions from several popes (which did not prevent four hundred French priests from joining), there were some 210,000 members in 600 lodges in the 1780s. The lodges were not overtly political, but there was something about the fraternal camara-derie and the choice of office-bearers based on merit that appealed to educated, busy men.[15]

This expansion of freemasonry was part of the expression of a distinc-tive bourgeois culture outside the norms of the aristocratic elite. Even the thirty-five prestigious royal academies, dominated by nobles, were drawn into discussion of fundamental questions about religious freedom, poverty and judicial reform.[16] Certainly, these were masculine spaces, but there were other places where intellectually engaged women could gather: in particular, the world of the *salon* in Paris and other cities was one in which women played a central role in the creation of spaces that were both femi-nized and 'free-thinking'.[17]

One of the watchwords of enlightened society was 'utility', whether for useful objects of consumption, reforms that might improve agriculture and manufacturing or as a critique of the claims of the privileged, which were based on custom. Everything from hereditary privilege, venality of office and trade monopolies to formal gardens, court pomp and book censorship was seen as anathema to reason, simplicity and liberty. A powerful dimension of the discourse of 'utility' was the contrast drawn between useful, even 'patriotic' commerce and aristocratic luxury. In 1788, Jean-Baptiste Rougier de la Bergerie, a prominent agronomist, contrasted the cultivator, who is 'always useful, always virtuous, always honest, always beneficent, always attached to his *patrie*, to his king', with the aristocrat corrupted by money and luxury. In his *Essai sur les privilèges* (1788) the Abbé Emmanuel Sieyès, the son of a tax-collector who had become a canon in the cathedral at Chartres, similarly identified nobles as peculiarly prone to corruption, 'because the prejudice of their superiority inflames them ceaselessly to overdo their expenditure'.[18] The great dramatic hit of the century was Beaumarchais' comedy *The Marriage of Figaro*, which attracted 97,000 people to its first seventy-three performances in 1784. The climax of the play was Figaro's denunciation of his employer, the Comte d'Almaviva:

'Because you are a great lord, you think yourself a great genius! Nobility, wealth, rank, positions, all this makes you so proud! What have you done for so much? You gave yourself the trouble of being born, that's all. Otherwise you are pretty ordinary.'[19]

Despite the arrows aimed at the pillars of society—the traditional nobility, the Church (particularly the upper clergy and the contemplative orders), and even the monarchy itself—members of the privileged orders were attracted to the new ideas and some were even among its leading thinkers. In Artois, for example, the most prominent nobleman of the province, Ferdinand Dubois de Fosseux, was a man passionate about enlightened discussion who, as secretary of the Royal Academy of Arras, wrote no fewer than 21,000 letters to his 1,200 correspondents across the kingdom in the five years after 1785. When his *protégé* Robespierre was elected Director of the Academy in 1786, he spoke to his learned audience for almost two hours on the legal discrimination suffered by children born outside wedlock, perhaps in pointed reference to the jibes that he himself had been conceived well before his parents' marriage.[20] The Marquis de Girardin, an army officer with 100,000 *livres* in rents and 800 hectares at

Ermenonville, north-east of Paris, established a 'natural' or 'English' garden there, contrasting its natural contours and local plants (and a mock charcoal-burner's cabin for peasant simplicity) with the geometric severity of Versailles. The marquis welcomed Jean-Jacques Rousseau to his estate, where the *philosophe* was buried in 1778 on the 'Isle of Poplars' in a landscape dedicated to the ideals of nature.[21]

Just as the Enlightenment was not a unified intellectual crusade that alone undermined the fundamental assumptions of the status quo, so the Catholic Church was not a monolith that always shored up the power of the monarchy. Some of the most prominent *philosophes* were themselves clerics by training: Mably, Condillac, Raynal and Turgot, for example. In particular, there were long-term religious consequences of Protestant and Jansenist notions of political liberty and challenges to ecclesiastical hierarchy. While Jansenism—based on the works of the seventeenth-century Flemish theologian Cornelius Jansen—on one level was a rigorous form of Catholicism emphasizing original sin, human depravity and the dangers of laxity, on another it was subversive to established order in its insistence that the synod of the French Church was superior to the Pope and that God alone is sacred.[22] Despite the suppression of Jansenism across the century, its values survived among the 'Richerists', followers of a seventeenth-century canon lawyer who had argued that Christ had commissioned not only the twelve Apostles as 'bishops' but also the seventy-two disciples or 'priests' mentioned in Luke's Gospel.

The 'Enlightenment' was an umbrella-term for divergent attitudes, particularly about politics and social change. The *philosophes* were not revolutionaries. The extent of their social critique was limited by what they saw as the ignorance and superstition of the masses: most intellectuals turned to enlightened monarchs as the best way of ensuring liberalization of public life. Similarly, despite their dismissal of what they called 'superstition', the majority of intellectuals accepted the social value of parish priests as guardians of public order and morality.

Rather different to most of his peers was Rousseau, fundamentally democratic in motivation and convinced that virtuous citizens could be created by more child-centred education, representative government and civic-minded legislators. Above all, Rousseau insisted that the European world had been led to perdition by the extremes of wealth and poverty. As he described injustice most powerfully in *A Discourse on the Origins of Inequality* (1755):

The great inequality in manner of living, the extreme idleness of some, and the excessive labour of others ... The too exquisite foods of the wealthy which overheat and fill them with indigestion, and, on the other hand, the unwholesome food of the poor, often, bad as it is, insufficient for their needs ... the innumerable pains and anxieties inseparable from every condition of life ... these are fatal proofs that the greater part of our ills are of our own making.[23]

Rousseau's solution, elaborated in his two great works published in 1762, *Émile, or on Education* and *On the Social Contract*, was a radically egalitarian society in which the civic virtues were inculcated to create a citizenry motivated by the 'general will':

Therefore the social contract is the basis of every civil society, and ... can be summed up in this formula: *Each of us puts his goods, his person, his life, and all his power in common under the supreme direction of the general will, and we as a body accept each member as a part indivisible from the whole.*[24]

What did people want to read in the late eighteenth century? The history of publishing—an economic as much as a cultural behaviour—is particularly revealing about the cultural changes of the 1770s and 1780s. The popularity of conventional books about theology and law was challenged by books about travel, scandal, court cases and history. At a time when there were no best-seller lists, and the censors employed by the monarchy and the Church controlled the production of 'legal' books, the clandestine, illegal book trade reveals what the reading public also wanted. In a regime of tight censorship, the cheap pirated editions of the *Encyclopédie* smuggled in from Switzerland sold an estimated 25,000 sets during the period 1776–89. While the state authorities tolerated the trade in cheap editions of works ranging from the *Encyclopédie* to the Bible, it was the underground trade in other banned books that is most revealing: a whole network of people from printers, booksellers, pedlars and mule-drivers risked imprisonment in order to profit from public demand.[25]

The outstanding best-seller on the Société Typographique de Neuchâtel list was Louis-Sébastien Mercier's *L'An 2440*, which went through at least twenty-five editions after it was first published in 1771. The novel was utopian, describing a Paris without poverty, prostitutes or beggars; without a standing army since there would be universal peace; without slavery; and even without trade, since the ideal France would be rural and self-sufficient. Most boldly, it was a society in which a populist monarch had expunged the memory of Louis XIV, and had had the Bastille prison fortress demolished. It was a future without prelates, monks and priests; instead there was a Rousseauist religion of virtue overseen by benevolent pastors.[26]

The Swiss catalogues offered readers at every level of urban society a socially explosive mixture of philosophy and obscenity: the finest works of Voltaire, Rousseau, Helvétius and Holbach jostled with titles such as *Vénus dans le cloître, ou la religieuse en chemise* and *La Fille de joie*. In the land of Rabelais and Molière there was nothing new about sharp sexual satire; what was new, however, was that it was widely circulated. The 1779 play *Les Amours de Charlot et Toinette* began with a description of the queen masturbating and of her affairs with her brother-in-law, and it ridiculed the king:

> It is very well known that poor Sire
> Three or four times condemned ...
> For complete impotence
> Cannot satisfy Antoinette.
> Of this misfortune we are sure
> Given that his 'match'
> Is not fatter than a straw
> Always soft and always curved ...

The subversive tone of these books and pamphlets was paralleled in popular songs. A clerk in the department responsible for regulating the book trade called on his superior to impose more severe censorship: 'One observes that the songs sold in the street for the amusement of the populace instruct them in the system of liberty. Rabble of the most vile sort, mistaking themselves for the Third Estate, no longer respect the high nobility.'[27]

The ribald yet moralistic tone of these publications and songs mocked the Church, nobility and the royal family itself for their decadence and sexual impotence, questioning both the mystique of those born to rule as well as their right to do so. Joy at the royal marriage in 1770—and sympathy for the fifteen-year-old prince and his fourteen-year-old Austrian bride—dissipated into ribald mockery of the king's presumed impotence after his accession to the throne in 1774. Already in the spring of 1776 a song amused Parisians:

Everyone asks himself beneath his breath:
Can the King do it? Or can't he?
The wretched Queen despairs of it.
Some say he cannot get it up,
Others that he cannot get it in,
That he is a transverse flute.

The birth of a daughter in 1778 was cause for further satire. *Les Amours de Charlot et Toinette* implied that the king's brother Artois ('Charlot') was the father, since the queen's 'most majestic husband was bad at fucking'. Only the birth of a male heir in October 1781 could provoke a popular rejoinder:

If the King is everyone's father,
The Queen's our mother too;
Rejoice, boys, let's rejoice
To see a little brother given to us.[28]

Even in provincial towns dominated in every way by the privileged orders, such as Toulouse, Besançon and Troyes, the *Encyclopédie* and the ribaldry of the literary underground found a ready market.

Public attitudes towards the monarchy were shifting, and contemporaries were talking of a new space they called 'public opinion'.[29] Working people in Paris also became more involved in this public debate, not because the writings of intellectuals filtered down to them but as a response to what they felt to be the arbitrary rule of the monarchy and moribund claims to privilege. One of these workers, Jacques-Louis Ménétra, recalled later in life his apprenticeship as a glazier before the Revolution, in a rebellious milieu of *compagnons* who relished obscene pranks, casual sex and ritualized violence with other brotherhoods. However, Ménétra also claimed to have read Rousseau's *Social Contract*, *Émile* and *La Nouvelle Héloïse*, and even to have met their author.[30] Nor was Rousseau's perspective the only radical critique of luxury and unchecked property, for Paris in particular was bubbling with small religious and secular groups that fulminated against wealth and individualism in the name of self-sacrifice and civic virtue.[31]

When middle-class boys—and a tiny minority of girls—attended schools, they were instructed in church history through the bishops and theologians Jacques-Bénigne Bossuet and François Fénelon. But the classics saturated the curriculum: the boys were immersed in classical Rome and its language to the point where it became more familiar than recent French history. Aristotle's *Ethics* was a key text, teaching that pride, jealousy, licentiousness and greed were the antithesis of wisdom, justice, temperance and knowledge, and that discipline, humility and piety could lead the weak to a state of virtue. In addition, a recent French translation of Plutarch's *Parallel Lives* was the perfect text for expanding interest in the lessons of history. But this was a curriculum dominated by Latin: indeed, that was the language used for the teaching of philosophy. From texts by Horace, Virgil and especially Cicero, and digests of other writers, such as Tacitus, Livy and Sallust, the boys learnt ancient history and politics, particularly of late republican and Augustan Rome.[32]

The civic virtues were described in the classics as patriotism and love of liberty, austerity and industry, self-sacrifice and courage, integrity and justice—a stark contrast with the vices of luxury, greed, conspiracy and corruption the authors saw all around them. A key text was Cicero's account of the Catiline conspiracy, when he had acted decisively and uncompromisingly against a plot to seize power in first-century-BC Rome by Catilina's aristocratic faction. Maximilien Robespierre's schoolmate Camille Desmoulins would later recall 'how many times . . . did I embrace Cicero, my eyes wet with tears'. Cicero's account emphasized the conspirators' immoral behaviour and their use of sex and bribery to achieve their ends:

> All foreign affairs are tranquillized. . . . Domestic war alone remains. The only plots against us are within our own walls, the danger is within, the enemy is within. . . . For on the one side are fighting modesty, on the other wantonness; on the one chastity, on the other uncleanness; on the one honesty, on the other fraud; . . . on the one honour, on the other baseness; on the one continence, on the other lust . . .[33]

The heroic contest between the vices and virtues, the latter under conspiratorial threat, seems to have become embedded in the way of thinking of Maximilien and many other boys.

The language of 'morality' and 'virtue' also applied to art and architecture. The author of *Sur la peinture* (1782) attacked conventional painting and the decadence of the social elite, exhorting art critics to engage 'considerations which are moral and political in character'. This was exemplified in the public reception of Jacques-Louis David's *Oath of the Horatii* in 1785, with its celebration of civic behaviour perceived as virtuous. The critic in the *Journal de Paris* felt that it, 'to use an expression of J. J. Rousseau, has something poignant about it that attracts one ... one believes oneself transported to the earliest days of the Roman Republic'.[34] Its subject matter resonated among middle-class audiences schooled in the classics. At the Paris Salon of 1787 the new United States ambassador Thomas Jefferson, who had succeeded Benjamin Franklin in 1785, found that 'the best thing is the Death of Socrates by David, and a superb one it is'.[35]

Reform-minded young men like Robespierre looked with admiration towards the aristocratic Jean-Baptiste Mercier-Dupaty, President of the Parlement of Bordeaux and renowned for his critiques of judicial error. His most famous case, in 1777, had concerned the defence of seven men condemned by the Metz Parlement in 1769 to the death penalty or life in the galleys. Perhaps his acolytes were unaware that Mercier-Dupaty had been born into a very wealthy La Rochelle merchant family and had used the wealth generated from the colonial and slave trade to purchase his advocate-general position in the Bordeaux Parlement for 84,000 *livres*.[36]

The liberties trumpeted by the Enlightenment were to be for Europeans alone: most *philosophes*, from Voltaire to Helvétius, rationalized plantation slavery as the natural lot of inferior peoples. There were, however, exceptions to such views. In Amsterdam in 1772 the Abbé Raynal published the *Histoire philosophique et politique des établissemens et du commerce des Européens dans les deux Indes*, in ten volumes. Among the contributors were prominent 'enlightened' writers such as Holbach and Diderot. The *Histoire philosophique* was initially banned and burned in France, and was not published there until 1780.

The colonial trade—and with it the slave trade—was at the heart of the growth in the French economy and the global clash of European empires during the eighteenth century. This was an imperial competition, particularly with Britain, which was ultimately to be fatal for those who ruled France. The Treaty of Paris at the end of the Seven Years War (1756–63) had sharply reduced France's colonial power: only 'confetti', as it was called, was left in North America from an empire that had included Canada and the vast, fertile lands along the Ohio valley. In India only five trading *comptoirs* were maintained, including Pondichéry; in the Caribbean the French kept Sainte-Lucie, Guadeloupe, Martinique and, most importantly, the west of Saint-Domingue. But France's overriding concern in 1763 was to protect its Caribbean empire: Québec may have been dispensable, but Saint-Domingue was not.

Despite the French losses, an economic boom continued in the great ports, especially on the Atlantic coast where a triangular trade linked France with its Caribbean colonies and Africa through commerce in slaves, wines and spirits, sugar, coffee, cotton and indigo.[37] One leg of the trade involved scores of purpose-built slave-ships that carried a human cargo from the west coast of Africa to the Caribbean colonies. In Saint-Domingue, 31,000 whites ruled 465,500 slaves according to the 'Code noir' of 1685, which forbade 'ill-treatment' but denied slaves any legal rights and deemed their children to be the slave-owner's property. Saint-Domingue was the jewel in the colonial crown, generating about 40 per cent of all overseas exports to France by the 1770s, and producing more sugar than Jamaica. The slave population of Saint-Domingue in the 1780s made up most of the 700,000 slaves in French colonies. By then the slave trade was reaching its apogee: 54,000 Africans were transported to the French colonies in 1790.[38] Almost all of the slaves in the Caribbean colonies were from west Africa, where Gorée and Saint-Louis-du-Sénégal were major bases for the trade. There were also slaves on Martinique, Guadeloupe and elsewhere in the Caribbean, and on the Île Bourbon (Réunion) and the Île de France (Mauritius) in the Indian Ocean.[39]

In the period 1716–89 the volume of French colonial trade through the great Atlantic ports grew fourfold. Growth was as high as 4 per cent per annum in Bordeaux, sustaining large shipbuilding, ropemaking, tobacco, sugar and glassmaking enterprises: the population of the city doubled to 110,000 across the century.[40] The slave trade was integral to this growth. In 1785 there were 143 ships actively engaged in the trade from French ports: forty-eight of them from Nantes, thirty-seven each from La Rochelle and Le Havre, and others from Bordeaux, Marseille, Saint-Malo and Dunkerque. Across the century from 1707 these slave-ships had made more than 3,300 voyages, subsidized by a state bonus of 40 *livres* per ton for every slave-ship: the royal treasury furnished about half the slavers' profits.[41]

More than two-fifths of the slave expeditions were mounted from Nantes where, as in Bordeaux, the mercantile class had prospered mightily across the century. The slave trade represented 20–25 per cent of the traffic to and from the port in the 1780s. Nantes had about 90,000 inhabitants, among whom were around four hundred merchant families. The slave trade returned about 10 per cent net profit annually, and had never been more profitable than in the 1780s. As in Bordeaux, an imposing, neo-classical stock-exchange building erected in the heart of Nantes symbolized this confidence in the virtues of enterprise. A remarkable eighteenth-century variant of a 'gated community' launched in the 1720s had just reached completion in the 1780s: this Isle of Feydeau was constructed as an ensemble of magnificent town houses for one hundred families from the merchant elite, cordoned off by water from the insalubrious and menacing popular neighbourhoods. In Nantes in particular, Africans were a common sight, as the great merchants chose particular individuals to be servants rather than send them on to the plantations; others worked in the city as artisans and labourers.[42]

France in 1780 may have seemed to contemporaries the most powerful and stable realm on the continent, whatever the scandals that titillated the fancies of the literate. But there were past and present instances of violent upheavals that menaced all governments. The classical world was replete with examples in which French middle-class boys were inculcated. The Greek and Roman examples and that of the English Revolution formed the essential mental framework for those who pondered upheaval: Oliver Cromwell's name was familiar as the symbol of military usurpation. But there was a later example, too, one even closer to home, where Corsicans had proclaimed a constitutional republic in 1755. Genoa sold its last bastions on Corsica to France in 1767, and France had crushed Corsican resistance by 1769. The Corsican example remained present in the minds of French reformers, even if the resistance leader Pasquale Paoli had found welcoming refuge as an exile in the heart of the old enemy in London.

But it was the consequences of the Seven Years War that were most explosive. From a wider perspective, Anglo-French rivalry in North America was a spectacular instance of a global competition for commercial empire by European powers—France, Britain, Spain, Portugal—and the mounting costs of the warfare to expand and protect it.[43] For example, an average-sized naval vessel with seventy-four cannon required 2,800 century-old oak trees for its construction, and forty-seven such vessels (as well as thirty-seven frigates) were built in France in the 1780s.[44] The war had hit France hard. The British East India Company was returning more than three times its expenses in the 1780s; its French equivalent was only breaking even.[45]

The humiliations France had suffered at England's hands in 1763 in India, Canada and the Caribbean were assuaged by successful intervention in the war of independence of Britain's North American colonies after 1779. The intervention of 8,000 troops under the Comte de Rochambeau and the Marquis de Lafayette would be pivotal in General Cornwallis's surrender at Yorktown in 1781. The final peace treaty was signed in Paris and Versailles between Britain, the new United States and France on 3 September 1783 (Fig. 4).

The United States Constitution of 1787, with its historic compromise between states that were for and against the abolition of slavery, sparked the establishment of anti-slavery societies: Sharp and Clarkson's Society for the Abolition of the Slave Trade in London in 1787 and Jacques-Pierre Brissot and Étienne Clavière's Société des Amis des Noirs (Society of the Friends of the Blacks) in Paris in 1788. The most important lesson from the American War of Independence, however, was the republican revolution embedded in the new nation's constitution. Its framers asserted that the balance of social forces—monarch, aristocracy, commons—that preserved liberty in the British Parliament could be replicated in the United States by electing commoners to the roles of president, senators and representatives. In other words, the commons could govern themselves, and further continue to protect their freedoms by separating the powers of executive, legislature and judiciary. Brissot was an enthusiast for the new United States as well as an energetic member of the Société des Amis des Noirs. 'People governed by a free constitution are naturally grave and deliberate,' he wrote; 'they prefer in everything they use goodness to elegance, what is solid to that which is subject to the caprices of fashion.'[46]

French participation in the American War of Independence had partly avenged the loss of empire on the North American mainland in 1763. But the intellectual ferment created by the colonists' victory had sharpened social and political critique at home, and the war had cost the monarchy over one billion *livres*, more than twice the usual annual revenue of the state. The monarchy was confronted with the imperative of increasing taxes and cutting costs at the same time as public scandals provided new barbs for those convinced that the highest authorities had lost the respect of public opinion.

CHAPTER THREE

MISMANAGING CRISIS, 1785–88

O N 15 AUGUST 1785, CARDINAL DE ROHAN, ARCHBISHOP OF Strasbourg and a prince of the Holy Roman Empire, was to officiate at the Feast of the Assumption in front of the royal family and court. Before he could do so, he was taken before the king, the queen, the 'garde des sceaux' or Minister of Justice, the Marquis de Miromesnil, and the Minister of the Court, the Baron de Breteuil. The cardinal was charged with using the queen's name to procure an extraordinarily expensive diamond necklace, and taken to the Bastille. The 'Diamond Necklace Affair' erupted in a torrent of political and sexual innuendo. The highest court of the kingdom, the Parlement of Paris, found that a self-styled princess, the Comtesse Jeanne de la Motte, and others had deceived Rohan by forgeries and impersonations into believing that Marie-Antoinette herself wished him to use his credit to obtain the necklace for her, as a way of then stealing it. The cardinal was acquitted, but was later exiled by the king, using his powers of arbitrary punishment through the use of a *lettre de cachet*. Despite Rohan's inordinate wealth (estimated at 400,000 *livres* annually) and casual attitude to his spiritual duties, popular support for him and jubilation at his release by the Parlement in May 1786 also indicated popular support for the *parlements* as protection against what was dubbed 'ministerial despotism'.

The acquittal was humiliating for Marie-Antoinette. At the horse races at Longchamp the season's preferred colours were hats and ribbons *à la Cardinal*, the red and yellow symbolizing a cardinal on the straw of the Bastille. A popular chant celebrated how

The Holy Father made him red
The King and Queen made him black
Parlement has made him white
Hallelujah.

Jeanne de la Motte was not so fortunate, being whipped and branded a thief with a hot iron before her imprisonment. After her escape to London she poured invective on her former lovers, whom she claimed included both the cardinal and the queen herself.[1]

The Diamond Necklace Affair coincided with a very different type of judicial scandal, in which the Parlement of Paris made a contrasting finding. In October 1785 a labourer and two horse and cattle traders were sentenced to die *roué* (that is, by strangulation after having their limbs broken with steel bars while stretched across a wheel) for violent assault and theft at a farmhouse near Troyes in the Champagne region in January 1783. The judicial delays, bungled and fabricated evidence, and final cruelty of the sentence decreed by the Parlement had already aroused indignation when Jean-Baptiste Mercier-Dupaty took up the case. Mercier-Dupaty, president of the Parlement of Bordeaux, was by then well known as a critic of the legal system and its punishments. His long 'mémoire justificatif' on what had become known as the scandal of the 'Trois Roués' castigated the judicial system as 'barbaric'. In response the Parlement of Paris ordered copies of his *mémoire* to be burned and one of its senior members inveighed against people like him, 'those citizens, foreigners in their own land ... reformers solely occupied with overthrowing our laws under pretext of bringing them closer to the code of nature'. But Mercier-Dupaty triumphed and the three accused were exonerated and released in December 1787, almost five years after the crime.[2] His brilliant intervention saved three, probably innocent, men and directly contributed to judicial reform launched by the new 'garde des sceaux', the Minister of Justice, Chrétien-François de Lamoignon.

The avid public interest in the affair, and its successful depiction as an example of systemic barbarity rather than an isolated miscarriage of justice, demonstrates the acute nature of the crisis of authority in the 1780s and the challenge for the monarchy. It was a crisis of legitimacy, often played out in agitated public controversy about scandal and injustice. Lawyers, self-consciously the guardians of expertise and probity, catered for the lively taste for scandal by publishing trial briefs (*mémoires*) of *causes célèbres*, to publicize their clients' interests and claims and to raise funds for legal costs. In the 1770s these *mémoires* sold in runs of up to 10,000 in Paris, and in the 1780s up to twice as many. Nicolas Toussaint des Essarts, himself a lawyer, compiled an astonishing series of 196 volumes of them. The *mémoires* demonstrate a powerful and increasingly frequent repudiation of a traditional aristocratic world depicted as violent, feudal and immoral, and as opposed to enlightened values of citizenship, rationality and utility.[3]

Public interest in the scandals was an illustration of how changes in social attitudes were undermining the legitimacy of absolute monarchy and aristocracy. Barristers were a key group within 'public opinion', jostling for fame with their calls for reform and their critique of privilege. They were the most visible members of a nationwide subculture of legal men both enmeshed in the system and yet naturally in opposition because of their judicial role in the courts.[4]

The *raison d'être* of aristocratic society was also eroded by attacks from some of its most prominent members and greatest beneficiaries. The Comte de Mirabeau, Lepeletier de Saint-Fargeau and the Comte de Montlosier were among wealthy nobles who castigated what they saw as the puerile excesses of the court and even the inequities of seigneurialism. Montlosier later recalled that in the 1780s he shared the popular view that 'feudalism was a barbarous institution, the rights of justice a usurpation of royal authority, and the system of the *censive* [dues payable on freehold land] a usurpation of the rights of the people'. The aristocrats had been 'veritable brigands'.[5]

As the royal state lurched into financial crisis after 1783, these changes in social attitudes conditioned conflicting responses to Louis XVI's pleas for assistance in reforming his system. The increasing costs of war, maintaining an expanding court and bureaucracy, and servicing a massive debt impelled the monarchy to seek ways of eroding the immunity from taxation of nobles and ending the capacity of *parlements* to resist royal decrees enforcing change.[6] But the monarchy and its fractured noble elite mismanaged the challenge.

In 1775 the French state could rely on about 377 million *livres* in taxes and other revenues, while out goings were about 411 million *livres*. About 35 million of that was spent on the court alone, which sustained almost the entire economy of the 50,000 inhabitants of Versailles. Some 154 million *livres* of the expenditure was to cover debt repayments, and about 35 million per year in interest were added to that total. Involvement in the American War of Independence saw the gap between revenue and expenditure balloon to about 160 million *livres*. The cost of running the navy's 165 frigates and ships had quadrupled by the end of the war, and spending on the navy now had to be curtailed.

From today's perspective, the financial crisis of the monarchy seems not so much the scale of the deficit—the debt to revenue ratio—as the structure of public finances. Rather than a consolidated public debt open to scrutiny and skilled management, the monarchy's finances were characterized by complexity and diversity, with loans at comparatively high rates of interest (4.8 to 6.5 per cent, almost twice the British rate through the national Bank of England) being secured for the state by private financiers, many of them international.[7]

The monarchy had already embarked on a sweeping reform of provincial administration designed to make it more uniform and to reduce the capacity of holders of venal office and its perquisites to reject reform, especially to taxation. In 1778 and 1779 the king had allowed members of the three Estates to participate in provincial assemblies where these existed, then, in 1787, required assemblies to be elected at provincial, district and parish level in *pays d'élection*. The results were unanticipated. On the one hand, holders of venal offices expressed outrage at the threat to their privileges, especially seigneurial: office-holders in Rethel in Champagne complained that rural municipalities were just 'assemblies of tenant farmers whose learning is still ... strongly circumscribed by the tilling of the fields'. On the other hand, those involved for the first time in representative elections saw the defence of tradition against 'ministerial despotism' for what it was. An alternative model of administration—based on uniformity and ability—would become more attractive.[8]

Overshadowing all administrative reform, and coinciding with the demoralizing Diamond Necklace Affair and other scandals, was the financial crisis that confronted the Vicomte de Calonne, Controller-General of Finances since November 1783. Calonne was a hard-headed and astute, even unscrupulous figure, with long experience as the king's administrator (*intendant*) in Metz and Lille, and an intimate knowledge of power and privilege. In February 1787 he sought to convince an assembly of 144 'Notables', fewer than ten of whom were non-noble, of the need for a universal land-tax, the reduction of the *taille* and *gabelle*, and the abolition of internal customs barriers to encourage commerce. To put pressure on the privileged orders Calonne published a pamphlet in March in tandem with his proposals and urged priests to read it from the pulpit:

We will be paying more! ... No doubt, but who? Only those who were not paying enough: they will pay what they owe according to a just proportion, and nobody will be overburdened.

Privileges will be sacrificed! ... Yes: justice demands it, need requires it. Would it be better to put further burdens on the unprivileged, the people?

There will be a great outcry! ... That was to be expected. Can general good be done without bruising a few individual interests? Can there be reform without some complaints?[9]

On 17 April 1787 the king read a speech, written by Lamoignon, that promised sweeping judicial reforms to undermine the power of the *parlements*. But Calonne's proposals to increase productive investment, rein in expenses and increase taxes foundered on the resentments and manoeuvrings of the privileged, in particular on the principle of the uniform land-tax. After Calonne's fall in April and the collapse of hopes in the Assembly of Notables, Louis resorted to frequent hunting to deal with his depressed mood. The Austrian ambassador, the Comte de Mercy-Argenteau, wrote to Joseph II that the king's 'returns from hunting are followed by such immoderate meals that there are occasional lapses of reason and a kind of brusque thoughtlessness which is very painful for those who have to endure it'.[10] Louis was then thirty-two years old.

Following Calonne's dismissal, his successor Loménie de Brienne, Archbishop of Toulouse, failed to convince the Notables of similar proposals, and they were dismissed at the end of May. Brienne pursued his wide-ranging programme of reforms; this time, in July, it was the Paris Parlement that refused to register a uniform land-tax. Tension between crown and aristocracy came to a head in August, with the exile of the Parlement to Troyes; such was the popular and elite support for the Parlement, however, that the king was forced to recall it. On 28 September 1787 its members re-entered Paris amid popular celebrations. 'Ministerial despotism' had been defeated.

The debates about the escalating debt triggered by involvement in the American War of Independence came to a head when the consequences of debt left France unwilling to intervene in the Netherlands to protect reformers against Prussian and Orangist repression in 1787. At the same time as the crisis between crown and *parlements* was reaching a climax in September, news arrived that Prussian troops had crossed the border to support the Hohenzollern Princess of Orange against the 'patriot' party in the Dutch Republic. Assumptions that French intervention to support the patriots was imminent were dashed when the government announced that the military were unprepared, a casualty of the parlous state of French finances. By 1788 there were 1,500 refugee Dutch families in France. Many more were in the Belgian principality of Liège, which had its own, very different, political agitation, in this case hostility to the centralization policies of Joseph II of Austria. As the royal state stumbled further into debt, it was simple for the privileged to blame the ministry for the swelling deficit and its own elite for its pampered profligacy. The Foreign Minister, the Comte de Vergennes, and the Finance Minister, Jacques Necker, had been able to finance and conduct a successful war in North America without raising taxes, they insisted; now the French people had to stand by while Prussian troops overran the Dutch Republic because the Foreign Minister, the Comte de Montmorin, admitted that intervention would be too costly.[11]

The resistance of the *parlements* was increasingly expressed through calls for a meeting of the Estates-General, an advisory body composed of representatives of the three Estates, which had last been consulted in 1614. In November 1787, Lamoignon made a speech to a royal sitting of the Parlement of Paris in which, as a former president of the Parlement, he reminded his peers of Louis XVI's pre-eminence by dismissing their call for such a meeting:

> These principles, universally accepted by the nation, testify that sovereign power in his kingdom belongs to the king alone;
>
> That he is accountable only to God for the exercise of supreme power;
>
> That the link that unites the king and the nation is by nature indissoluble;
>
> That the reciprocal interests and duties of the king and his subjects ensure the perpetuity of this union;
>
> That the nation has a vested interest that the rights of its ruler remain unchanged;
>
> That the king is the sovereign ruler of the nation, and is one with it;
>
> Finally that legislative power resides in the person of the sovereign, depending upon and sharing with no-one.
>
> These, sirs, are the invariable principles of the French monarchy.

'When our kings established the *parlements*,' he reminded them, 'they wished to appoint officers whose duty it was to administer justice and to maintain the edicts of the kingdom, and not to build up in their bodies a power to rival royal authority.'[12] Lamoignon's resounding statement of the principles of the French monarchy did not intimidate the king's most eminent subjects into submission.

Entrenched noble interests were even couched in the language of the *philosophes*: the Parlement of Toulouse asserted that 'the natural rights of municipalities, common to all men, are inalienable, imprescriptible, as eternal as nature which forms their basis'. This language of opposition to the royal state, appeals to traditional autonomy in provincial centres such as Bordeaux, Rennes, Toulouse and Grenoble, and the vertical bonds of economic dependency, generated an alliance against 'ministerial despotism' between local *parlements* and those dependent on them for employment. In May 1788 the Brienne ministry issued six edicts aimed at undermining the judicial and political power of the *parlements*, provoking rioting in Rennes: the *intendant* of Brittany, Bertrand de Moleville, was forced to flee the city. After the closing of the Paris Parlement, the audience attending an historical play interrupted it to insist that an actor repeat some lines which resonated with its imagined reference to current events:

The tyrant's plan is everywhere well proven,
See this palace that the guards surround
Accomplices of schemes that have been woven
Where exile, terror, punishment abound.

When the Parlement of Grenoble was exiled in May for its defiance towards the ministry's strike at noble judicial power, royal troops were driven from the city by popular rebellion on 7 June, the 'Day of the tiles', as supporters of the Parlement rained down roof-tiles on royal troops. In July boatmen on the River Isère in Dauphiné refused to carry the *intendant* crossing the Rhône to Valence to install the new court following the suppression of the Parlement.[13]

While the battles between monarchy and *parlements* stemmed from the desperate, self-destructive attempts of most of the nobility to cling to privilege and fiscal immunity in the face of the state's financial crisis, there was also a powerful current for reform within the elite of the nobility. There was apparent acceptance by some of the removal of most, if not all, fiscal exemptions; the problem, it was argued by the Assembly of Notables, was that the proposed land-tax was too high. But the common argument among nobles was that the real cause of the crisis was court profligacy and 'ministerial despotism', and these easy targets were widely accepted in the fevered months of dispute during 1787–88.

In arguing that an Estates-General alone could resolve the issues, and that the crux of the problem was abuse of power and fiscal inefficiency, the Notables were confident that the popular support apparent in the battles over the *parlements'* rights would strengthen their standing and power at the expense of a weak monarch. But the demand for an Estates-General would be fatal to their cause for, in the process, they accentuated political discussion across French society.

The self-interest behind noble appeals to 'natural law', 'inalienable rights' and the 'nation' ensured that the alliance of *parlementaires* and people could not last. From a meeting of local notables in July 1788 at the banker Claude Périer's recently acquired château at Vizille came a call from 500 representatives of the Three Orders who demanded the full return of the *parlements*, a provincial assembly or Estates for the Dauphiné, and an Estates-General— but this time for the Third Estate to have double the representation of the other orders in recognition of its importance in the life of the nation.[14]

By August 1788 the state needed 240 million *livres* in short-term borrowings and was effectively bankrupt. The king sought two solutions. One was to recall Necker as Chief Minister, who was popularly if incorrectly believed to have left the state in surplus when he had been dismissed in 1781. Necker promptly repudiated Lamoignon's proposed judicial reforms and was able to borrow sufficient funds to avoid immediate bankruptcy of the state.[15] The other solution was that, on 8 August, Louis decided he would, after all, convoke an Estates-General for May 1789, and Lamoignon and Brienne resigned. Jean-Jacques Duval d'Eprémesnil, a militant defender of the prerogatives of the *parlements*, had been exiled to an island in the Mediterranean in May; four months later he was released, and returned a hero.

In September 1788 the English agronomist Arthur Young found himself in the Atlantic port of Nantes just six weeks after Louis XVI had announced the convening of the Estates-General. A keen observer and recorder, Young noted in his journal:

> Nantes is as *enflammée* in the cause of liberty, as any town in France can be; the conversations I witnessed here prove how great a change is

effected in the minds of the French, nor do I believe it will be possible for the present government to last half a century longer, unless the clearest and most decided talents be at the helm.[16]

Nantes was a bustling port that had boomed due to the rapid growth of the colonial trade with the Caribbean throughout the eighteenth century. The merchants with whom Young conversed had convinced him of the rights of the 'talented' to participate more fully in public life. Their enthusiasm for reform reveals how much further the crisis of absolutist France now went beyond friction between nobles and monarch.

In September 1788, less than a year after Mercier-Dupaty's triumph in the case of the 'Trois Roués', the young Arras lawyer Maximilien Robespierre heard of the death of the great man, aged just forty-two. Robespierre had written to him when a student in 1777. Now his eulogy was striking for his self-perception as part of a generation that had begun to break the bounds of cruelty and superstition, and for his assumed role, like Mercier-Dupaty's, as 'the virtuous citizen who watches over the execution of the law within its walls and keeps order and harmony there':

> He who aspires to the glory of being useful to his fellow citizens, who makes such great and sublime use of his capacities, who dares to say to the powerful of this world, 'You have committed an injustice,' and thus raises himself above other men, must, no doubt, expect to have dangerous enemies: he must believe that hatred and vengefulness will join with envy to bring him down. This has ever been the fate of great men.[17]

But Robespierre went far further than an effusive eulogy to a man of principle setting an example to the legal profession. In attacking 'barbarous prejudices' and 'the outrages to which humanity has been subjected', Robespierre highlighted the vulnerability of the 'poor and unknown, unfortunate victims of our criminal laws'. 'Do you know why there are so many indigents?' he asked,

> It's because you hold all the wealth in your greedy hands. Why are this father, this mother, these children exposed to all the rigours of the weather, without a roof over their heads, suffering all the horrors of hunger? It's because you inhabit sumptuous houses to which your gold attracts everything which can serve your flabbiness and occupy your

idleness. It's because your luxury devours the sustenance of a thousand men in a single day.[18]

Nor was this political and social indignation limited to elites. Popular interest in political gossip and scandal was by no means new, but the language used was changing, as recorded by Louis-Sébastien Mercier, an acute observer of the Paris of the 1780s, in compiling twelve volumes of 'scenes'. Early in the decade he was sure that 'dangerous rioting has become a moral impossibility in Paris', not only because of the close watch of the authorities but because, unlike Londoners, 'the citizen of the capital has never given a thought to his political importance. . . . the little more liberty he might obtain is not worth fighting for'. An outbreak of violent protest such as the recent Gordon Riots in London was simply 'unimaginable'.[19] But such was the febrile atmosphere in Paris by 1787 that Mercier could note in his chronicle that 'in each building there is always someone known as "the philosopher"; if a merchant's shop-boy or a solicitor's clerk utters a few striking propositions beyond the ordinary run of ideas, he becomes "the philosopher"'.[20] The Parisian cobbler Joseph Charon recalled similarly in his memoirs that before the disturbances of August–September 1788 political ferment had descended:

> from men of the world of the highest rank to the very lowest ranks through various channels . . . people acquired and dispensed enlighten-ment that one would have searched for in vain a dozen years earlier . . . and they have acquired notions about public constitutions in the past two or three years.[21]

Even the popular songs sung in the streets and taverns of Paris were becoming more worrisome for the authorities, with openly political content and strident, moralistic choruses.[22]

The dilemma for the privileged was that, as the monarchy previously had successfully imposed direct levies on the nobility through the *capitation*, *dixième* and *vingtième* in the name of the universal obligation to contribute, how could exemption from the *taille* and other levies be justified? And how could provincial variations negotiated through centuries be maintained? If the king's ministers could contract expensive loans in the name of the public, should not the public have the right to be involved in their negotiation? An anonymous pamphlet from Normandy vented commoner spleen:

The clergy is too rich . . . : its exemptions are the cause of the surcharge on the people . . . . The nobles that we call seigneurs have great possessions and great exemptions. These privileges make my blood boil! . . . Are not all citizens equally the subjects of the king? . . . All children should be treated by their father the same way.[23]

So the king's calling of the Estates-General in May 1789 facilitated the expression of tensions at every level of French society, and revealed social divisions that challenged the idea of a society of 'orders'. The remarkable vibrancy of debate in the months before May was in part a function of the suspension of press censorship. It has been calculated that 1,519 pamphlets on political issues were published between May and December 1788; in the first four months of 1789 they were followed by a flood of 2,639 titles. This war of words was fuelled by Louis' indecision about the procedures to be followed at Versailles. Torn between a loyalty to the established corporate order of rank and privilege on the one hand, and the exigencies of fiscal crisis on the other, the king vacillated on the crucial political question of whether the three Estates would meet separately, as in 1614, or in a common chamber. In September 1788 the Parlement of Paris had decreed that tradition would be followed in this matter; then Louis' decision on 27 December to double the size of the Third Estate representation served to highlight further the crucial issue of political power, because he remained silent on how voting would occur. The issue was vital, for it would decide the advice Louis would receive from his Estates at Versailles: from the two privileged orders against the commons, or from a single assembly where the commons comprised the majority.

The calling of the Estates-General fractured the opposition to 'ministerial despotism' because it opened up the broadest questions of power and reform in a freer public space. Some of the most prominent people in the kingdom took to gathering at the home of a magistrate in the Paris Parlement, Adrien Duport. They included peers and senior magistrates, and prominent figures ranging from the Marquis de Lafayette, the Duc d'Aiguillon, Louis de Noailles, the Lameth brothers, La Rochefoucauld-Liancourt, Mirabeau and Dupont de Nemours, to the young Bishop of Autun, Talleyrand, and the *philosophe* mathematician, the Marquis de Condorcet. The gathering came to be known as the Society of Thirty (although there were at least twice that number of members) and, although most of them were noblemen, they articulated a sweeping programme of dismantling privilege, including support for doubling Third Estate representation and the vote by head in a common assembly.[24] The aristocratic elite was fracturing.

This fracturing was apparent when a new Assembly of Notables had convened in November–December 1788. But the recalcitrant were in the ascendancy. In considering the form the Estates-General should take in May 1789, only thirty-three voted in favour of doubling the Third Estate representation; 111 voted against. No one spoke out in favour of a vote by head in a common assembly. Louis XVI's younger brother, Louis-Stanislas, Comte de Provence, was prepared to countenance increased representation for the Third Estate, but his youngest brother, Charles-Philippe, Comte d'Artois, and the 'princes of the blood' made their recalcitrance and fear known in a 'memoir' to the king in December:

> Who can say where the recklessness of opinions will stop? The rights of the throne have been called into question; the rights of the two orders of the State divide opinions; soon property rights will be attacked; the inequality of fortunes will be presented as an object for reform; the suppression of feudal rights has already been proposed, as has the abolition of a system of oppression, the remains of barbarism . . .
>
> May the Third Estate therefore cease to attack the rights of the first two orders; rights which, no less ancient than the monarchy, must be as unchanging as its constitution; that it limit itself to seeking the reduction in taxes with which it might be burdened; then the first two orders, recognizing in the third citizens who are dear to them, will, by the generosity of their sentiments, be able to renounce those prerogatives which have a financial interest, and consent to bear public charges in the most perfect equality.[25]

The monarchy ruled over patchworks of privilege in which groups differentiated by social and occupational background jostled for preferment, and adopted the language of 'rights' as the basis of their claims. The imperative of compromise and reform now collapsed into self-interest and recrimination. In Lille, for example, the privileges accorded to the merchant guilds were used as the basis to contest the 'despotism' of the nobility and the municipal bureaucracy. Who was to represent the commons at the Estates-General? The battles over the organization of the elections in the province brought this question to a head. The Third Estate of Lille declared: 'the municipal magistrates want to be US; they want that we only have civil existence in THEM. They want to be deputies for US, they conspire in silence against the most precious of our rights.'[26]

The establishment of the provincial Estates in 1787 was now seized on by the nobility as their opportunity to take the political initiative against the alleged 'despotism' of a monarchy bent on eroding fiscal privilege. In provinces like Provence it fed into a centuries-old conflict over noble and commoner land and fiscal privilege, and the nobility's objectives were increasingly contested. When the Estates of Provence opened on 25 January 1789 the Third Estate refused to accept the legitimacy of the gathering because it deemed it unrepresentative. It received powerful support from Mirabeau, who argued that the Third Estate deputies were 'the veritable representatives of the Nation'—and was promptly expelled from the noble delegation for his treachery. This tension occurred against a background of economic privation due to a poor harvest and an extremely cold winter, when urban riots targeted the 'reves' (municipal tolls on foodstuffs), municipal officers and seigneurialism, which together represented for the common people the interests of a privileged oligarchy.[27]

The provincial assemblies often met with the best of intentions, as in Lower Normandy where its president, the Duc de Coigny, insisted in 1788 that the aim was 'the happiness of the people' and its duty was 'to distribute taxes equitably': 'the burden on the rich man would be proportioned to his fortune'. In practice, however, such enlightened principles became mired in manoeuvring to preserve special treatment in the name of the defence of 'traditional liberties'. In Normandy itself the Parlement accused an 'inquisitorial regime' of unleashing 'terror' by instigating a search for property titles and sources of wealth.[28]

The shift in popular support away from the *parlements* was rapid and striking. By January 1789 a Genevan journalist of French Huguenot background, Mallet du Pan, editor of the *Mercure de France*, observed:

Public debate has changed its aspect. It no longer troubles itself except secondarily with the king and despotism, or with the constitution: it has become a war between the third estate and the two other classes, against whom the court has stirred up the towns. The Parlement was an idol six months back; now everyone detests and insults it: d'Eprémesnil, the avenger of the nation, the Brutus of France, is vilified everywhere.[29]

The change in mood is apparent also in the correspondence of the Parisian Nicolas Ruault, a Left Bank bookseller who had known and published Voltaire. He regretted in his letters to his brother, a parish priest in the town of Évreux in Normandy, 'the stranglehold of intolerance' in the Church (with which his brother agreed). Ruault was scathing about the 'brute' Louis, the queen, and how the English aristocracy was 'on top of us; they are crushing us as hard as they can'. In August 1787 he had bemoaned the fact that 'we have a king so inadequate for his century and his nation! Everyone knows of his private life, his total incapacity in the art of government, and his wife's conduct.' By early 1789, however, Ruault had decided instead that it was the king's advisers and leading nobles ('Huns' and 'Vandals') who were to blame and looked forward to a form of monarchy 'more suited to the customs and the condition of the French'.[30]

At times the agitated war of words even spilled over into serious violence. This first occurred in Brittany where, in the context of sharp economic privation, open hostilities erupted over the opposition of the nobility and upper clergy to any changes to the powers and privileges of the local Estates and whether guarantees should be sought of the autonomies within the Breton 'constitution' negotiated in its union with France in 1532. On 26–27 January 1789 up to 1,500 armed supporters of the privileged—many of them in their domestic employ—clashed with pro-reform law students in Rennes, leaving three dead and sixty wounded.[31]

The same month, the Abbé Emmanuel Sieyès contributed the most remarkable of his several pamphlets, titled *What is the Third Estate?*[32] Castigating the nobility's obsession with its 'odious privileges', Sieyès issued a ringing declaration of commoner capacity. To be sure, Sieyès was no democrat—he noted that women and the poor could not be entrusted with political responsibilities—but his challenge articulated a radical intransigence:

We have three questions to ask ourselves.

1. What is the Third Estate?—everything.
2. What has it been until now in the political order?—nothing.
3. What is it asking?—to be something . . .

Who thus would dare to say that the Third Estate does not contain everything that is needed to make up a complete nation? It is a strong and robust man who still has one arm in chains. If the privileged orders were removed, the nation would not be worse off for it, but better. So, what is the Third? Everything, but a fettered and oppressed everything. What would it be without the privileged order? Everything, but a free and flourishing everything ... the fear of seeing abuses reformed inspires more fear in the aristocrats than the desire they feel for liberty. Between it and a few odious privileges, they have chosen the latter. ... Today, they dread the Estates-General that they once called upon with such fervour.

Sieyès' pamphlet resonated with the language of patriotism: that the nobility were too selfish to be committed to a process of national 'regeneration' and could therefore be excluded from the body politic. Significantly, too, Sieyès wrote of just one privileged order, evidently assuming that the clergy, too, were irrevocably divided between noble elite and commoner parish priests. His image of proud, dignified commoners appealed to men such as Jérôme Pétion, a lawyer from Chartres already known for his trenchant critiques of priestly celibacy and the system of primogeniture favouring first-born sons. In February 1789, Pétion described the regenerated citizen needed to lead France to virtue:

> The free man does not walk with his head bent; nor is his gaze haughty or disdainful, but rather assured; his walk is proud; ... he sees no one around him of whom he need be afraid and before whom he might have to abase himself. His joy is pure, it is honest, his affections are gentle and good. ... Make man free if you desire his happiness, if you wish to see him handsome, strong, and virtuous.[33]

Pétion's language reflected an urban, bourgeois sensibility. There is no evidence at all that the reading matter peddled through the countryside by *colporteurs* (pedlars) was imbued with 'Enlightened' precepts. In rural areas, the major sources of the printed words that the few literate people occasionally read aloud to their evening gatherings (*veillées*) were the Bible, popular almanacs of festivals and seasons, and cheap paperbacks with tales of the supernatural, lives of saints and magic (Fig. 5).[34] Nevertheless, rural France was in crisis. In many regions peasant farmers struggled with increases in rents in the 1780s, and they were hit by harvest failure in 1785. A free-trade treaty with England negotiated by the Foreign Minister Vergennes in September 1786, part of Calonne's ambitious proposals, was designed to benefit French agriculture, but in the short term cheap English imports were a body blow to the rural textile industry in the north.

In some parts of the kingdom at least, seigneurs were employing experts *(feudistes)* to check or tighten the exaction of dues as a way of increasing income in a time of inflation. For example, in 1786, the family of Saulx-Tavanes in Burgundy used their elevation to a dukedom to double all dues for a year, resurrecting a practice not employed since the thirteenth century. Their investment in farm improvements, never more than 5 per cent of their receipts, shrank to nothing in the late 1780s while rents were doubled as the nobles attempted to pay off their debts. A tax official travelling through the south-west of France in 1779 was astonished to find nobles enforcing 'rights and dues unknown or forgotten', such as an extraordinary *taille* exacted by a noble magistrate in the Toulouse Parlement every time he bought land:

> How can people protect themselves against parchments they cannot read and cannot have explained to them for want of cash? Seigneurs' archives are full of unknown dues which are successively brought out from the dust to be returned only if an abuse of power or chicanery has not succeeded in making them worthwhile.[35]

This tightening of seigneurial exactions occurred in the context of long-term inflation, whereby grain and fuel prices had outstripped labourers' wages, and short-term harvest failures in 1774 and 1785 that doubled grain prices. Taken together, they explain the escalation of conflict in the countryside: some three-quarters of 4,400 recorded collective protests in the years 1720–88 occurred after 1765, mostly in the form of food riots and anti-seigneurial incidents.[36]

Then, in 1788, a ruinous harvest crisis hit most of the kingdom. The summer had been characterized by long, dry periods, followed by wild storms. Thomas Blaikie, a famous Scottish gardener employed by Louis-Philippe-Joseph d'Orléans (Louis XVI's cousin) on his 800-acre estate ten miles east of Paris at Le Raincy, noted how huge hailstones had sliced through branches and killed 'hares, partridges and many other things'.[37] At the southern extreme of the kingdom, in the Corbières, hail and rain swelled the River Verdouble to a point where it carried away part of the bridge at Rouffiac, ruined hundreds of acres of millet and beans, and washed away 1,200 hay-ricks, in all about half the year's produce. Then an unusually hard winter exacerbated the suffering. In the diocese of Narbonne in Languedoc an estimated 100,000 olive trees died; in Lagrasse alone, where there had been 14,400 trees in 1754, the frosts left over 6,200 of them dead and another 3,000 damaged. The Canal du Midi had frozen to a depth of ten centimetres.[38] Across the kingdom, especially in the north, there were acute grain shortages and prices escalated.

Increasingly, the seigneurial system and its maze of privileges appeared as little more than a cash-racket rather than the backbone of the social order. Looking back from the mid-nineteenth century, Alexis de Tocqueville argued that, by the 1780s, seigneurial dues could no longer be legitimized as the price the non-privileged paid for poor relief, protection and assistance from seigneurs who were rarely present in the community. Tocqueville came from an eminent Norman aristocratic family with ancestors who had participated in the Battle of Hastings in 1066. His father was an officer of Louis XVI's Guard; his mother was from the equally esteemed Lepeletier de Rosanbo family, relatives of Lamoignon and of Louis XIV's great military engineer Vauban. Despite his long aristocratic heritage, Tocqueville concluded in *The Ancien Régime and the Revolution* (1856) that an increasingly intrusive and powerful monarchical state had rendered the nobility 'dysfunctional' by undermining the theoretical justification of its privileges.[39]

The entrenched hostility of most nobles towards fiscal and social reform was generated by two long-term factors: first, as Tocqueville concluded, the pressures of royal state-making, exacerbated by the costs of empire, which threatened to reduce further the nobility's privileges; and, second, the challenge from a wealthier, larger and more critical bourgeoisie and an openly disaffected peasantry to aristocratic conceptions of property, hierarchy and social order. The French social and political system was in a state of crisis in the 1780s: never before had there been such a deep-seated crisis of legitimacy facing the monarchy and its noble elite; never before had criticism across society been so trenchant and fundamental.

The panoply of power enjoyed by the monarchy and its nobility had been shredded by interrelated economic, social and cultural shifts, evident in the changing material and political 'cultures' of eighteenth-century France: that is, the objects and practices of economic life, and changing assumptions being made about legitimacy and public opinion. The emergence of concepts such as 'despotism', 'patriotism', 'public opinion' and 'nation' paralleled the rise of a commercial and consumer culture which, if not a direct cause of the crisis, informed the political culture through which it was expressed.

This material culture was inextricably linked to an expanding Atlantic economy of trade in colonial produce, French manufactures and wine, and slaves. The importance of the Atlantic trade, and the involvement of French armed forces in the American War of Independence, led to the ruinous expenditure that prompted the calling of the Estates-General in May 1789.

Asking how the regime of Louis XVI came to be mired in fiscal crisis to the point of collapse is not the same question as asking whether there were revolutionary pressures or impulses. There was no self-conscious class of bourgeois with a political programme for the Third Estate.[40] The various occupational groups that made up the bourgeoisie did not define themselves as members of a 'class' united across the country by similar socio-economic roles and interests. Indeed, some of those ambitious young bourgeois who were to be most distinguished in the forefront of militant anti-noble initiatives after 1789 found it desirable at times to add a noble prefix or suffix to their plebeian names: hence Jacques-Pierre Brissot added the suffix de Warville to his name. The wealthiest bourgeois sought to buy noble offices and titles, for they brought with them wealth as well as status in their society. This is hardly surprising, for these bourgeois were seeking eminence in a world that they never imagined would end. For example, the aforementioned Claude Périer, a wealthy banker from Grenoble, who also had a sugar plantation in Saint-Domingue, paid one million *livres* for several *seigneuries* and the huge château of Vizille in 1780, where he constructed a new textile factory. It was there that he hosted the Third Estate meeting in July 1788. But the elite of the bourgeoisie was seeking entry into the aristocratic world at the same time as it was subverting that world. Even where the well-to-do among the bourgeoisie pinned their hopes and fortunes on entry into the nobility, they were necessarily still 'outsiders': not only were their claims to eminence based on different grounds of achievement, but their very success subverted the *raison d'être* of noble status. In turn, nobles who emulated the bourgeoisie by seeking to appear 'progressive', for example, by joining a Freemasons, lodge, were undermining the exclusivity of their order.

The crisis of the regime was the result of three linked causes: the increasing costs of empire; the failure of ruling elites to deal with the financial crisis emanating from involvement in the American War of Independence; and changes in political culture and social assumptions that were undermining the legitimacy of absolute monarchy and aristocracy.[41] Different social groups within the Third Estate—from those in commerce and the professions to the rural poor—had their own reasons for responding enthusiastically to the opportunities presented by the greater political liberties that accompanied the calling of the Estates-General of May 1789.

But regimes are in crisis far more often than they are overthrown. A revolution was neither foreseen nor planned in France in 1788–89. The royal state may have been under critical financial and political pressures, and foundering in a crisis of public confidence, but its overthrow was the outcome of a contingent political crisis that the government failed to manage.

CHAPTER FOUR

THE PEOPLE'S REVOLUTION, 1789

Louis XVI's decision on 27 December 1788 to double the size of Third Estate representation had served only to highlight the issue of political power, because he remained silent about how voting would occur at Versailles in the Estates-General of May 1789. The popular expectation of reform that now erupted revealed how much deeper the crisis went than confrontation between intransigent nobles and the monarch. The crisis was a national one, concerning people everywhere. An Estates-General had not been convened since 1614, during the regency of Marie de Médicis, widow of the assassinated Henry IV and mother of the young Louis XIII. Now Louis XVI, 175 years later, had summoned his subjects to articulate their grievances, elect their representatives, and suggest remedies for his financial crisis. His summons was responded to with alacrity.

The political ferment was aggravated by the sharp winter of 1788–89, which was one of hunger and misery in cities as well as the countryside. Contemporaries spoke of 80,000 unemployed in Paris, and half or more of the looms lay idle in textile towns such as Amiens, Lyon, Carcassonne, Lille, Troyes and Rouen. The conviction that they were living in extraordinary times convinced two working women from the parish of Saint-Paul in the town of Orléans to begin diaries. Jeanne-Victoire Delzigue was a twenty-year-old apprentice dressmaker; Marie-Anne Charpentier, who decided to keep a diary of 'only what I see with my own eyes' was probably a little older but also from an artisan background. So these precious and rare accounts tell us more about marketplaces and public contention than they do about male spaces such as electoral assemblies and municipal council meetings. Both accounts begin with events that impressed another diary-keeper, the

wine-barrel maker Billard of Saint-Denis-en-Val, located in Orléans's food
bowl just across the River Loire: the summer hailstorms in July 1788 that
devastated crops across northern France. Then a bitterly cold winter was
followed by torrential rains that fractured the ice into devastating blocks,
which smashed the river defences at Saint-Denis in January 1789, inun-
dating the lowlands, drowning livestock and flooding the textile works.
Jeanne-Victoire Delzigue headed her first page '1789, a year of sadness
everywhere'.[1]

The coincidence of unprecedented political tension and economic crisis
generated desperate hopes for the Estates-General among the working
poor, mixed with equally fevered rumours of grain hoarding and conspiracy.
On 21 March 1789 posters in Marseille urged protest by workers excluded
from voting for delegates on the basis of insufficient wealth: 'if you have
courage, show it now'. Two days later the homes of a tax-collector and the
intendant were attacked, and crowds ransacked warehouses storing fish
and flour, shouting 'Vive le Roi!' as if they were rioting in the king's name.
There was a similar mix of subsistence and politics in violent protests
in March and April in many other towns and cities, including Cambrai,
Valenciennes, Vannes, Besançon and Alençon.[2]

As the bitter winter dragged into spring, the sharp edge of hunger and
anxiety accentuated the expectation occasioned by Louis' calling of the
Estates-General. People in small towns and villages as well as cities began
behaving and voicing attitudes that challenged the structures of their world
in resolute and illegal ways. Peasants were refusing to pay taxes or dues or
were seizing food supplies in parts of the Cambrésis and Hainaut regions in
the north-east, the Franche-Comté, and the Paris basin, perhaps in expectation of royal recognition of their plight. Indeed, at times they claimed that
the king had promised an end to dues and tithes.[3]

Now they had the perfect pretext for bolder actions than ever before.
The easing of controls on public debate and open friction about the
form and function of the Estates-General opened up a moment in
which boundaries of obedience could be tested. In many regions there were
reports of opposition to the seigneurial system itself, in particular to hunting
and grazing restrictions. In Provence the châteaux of Solliès and Besse
were ransacked and in many parishes communal herds were driven onto
seigneurs' lands. East of Gap, three villages banded together in April against
their seigneur d'Espraux, a councillor in the Parlement of Aix, and seized
back the grain they had paid as harvest dues in 1788. In Artois peasants

from a dozen villages banded together to kill the Comte d'Oisy's game and proclaimed that they would pay no more dues.[4]

The acts of rebellion during the winter were sporadic and local, but everywhere across the kingdom anxiety over food supplies now coincided with unprecedented opportunities to participate in political life. The royal letter convening the Estates-General in May was issued on 24 January, setting out its objectives in 'surmounting all our financial difficulties and . . . the welfare of our subjects and the prosperity of our kingdom'. To that end Louis requested that he hear 'the wishes and the grievances of our people' through *cahiers de doléances* (lists of grievances) from every community.[5] The electoral provisions were broad, at least in the countryside: adult male taxpayers were eligible to attend special parish meetings that were to agree on the content of their *cahier*. Millions of households that had hitherto experienced the structures of power and privilege as constraints to be obeyed, sidestepped or occasionally contested were now requested to suggest remediation for their grievances.[6] The drawing up of the *cahiers* in the context of political anticipation and a subsistence crisis was for rural people the first episode in a decade of revolution. Of course, they would know that only in hindsight.

At least on the surface, the *cahiers* of all three Estates showed a remarkable level of agreement. They were replete with expressions of gratitude towards the king, while at the same time expressing the view that the meeting of the Estates-General should become regular: in other words, some form of parliamentary regime and elected assembly should become elements of government. The *cahiers* also agreed that the fiscal crisis was the result of the inefficiency and wastefulness of the king's ministers: the Estates-General (often called the 'nation assemblée') should in future have control over expenditures and taxes. The *cahiers* expressed agreement that the Church was in urgent need of reform to improve the position of the parish clergy and to check abuses, such as multiple office-holding and absenteeism among its elite. People across the social spectrum urged the Estates-General to undertake reform of the legal system, to achieve greater uniformity, humanity and efficiency. At least on the surface, the privileged orders also seemed to recognize the need for tax reform, although such recognition was often qualified to ensure that specific interests were protected. But the political question of voting procedures at Versailles was intractable; so, for example, the Second Estate of the province of Berry meeting in Bourges expressed its delight at 'the spirit of unity and agreement' between the three orders, while noting that there was a gulf separating them on 'the question of voting by head'.[7]

Despite the goodwill, there were fundamental divisions evident between most of the nobility, or Second Estate, on the one hand and the Third Estate on the other. While recognizing, at least in principle, the need for reform of 'abuses', the *cahiers* of the provincial nobility in particular articulated an idealized world view where nobles were accorded the social esteem they merited and where the king assigned them a distinct role in government. There could be no question of surrendering the maze of seigneurial exactions on the peasantry, which were at the heart of the social order as well as the income of most nobles.

Parish priests and religious orders similarly voiced a vision of the future that was an idealized image of the past, in which members of the clergy and their flocks were reunited in their commitment to a reinvigorated faith. They reasserted the Church's privileged position as the official faith of the kingdom. The First Estate of Bourges asserted that 'The apostolic and Roman Catholic religion is the only true religion', and it called on 'His Majesty'

> to order that all those who, through their writings, seek to spread the poison of incredulity, attack religion and its mysteries, discipline and dogmas, be seen as enemies of the Church and the State and severely punished; that printers be once again forbidden to print books contrary to religion.[8]

There were, nevertheless, ominous signs of division over the need for reforms within the Church itself (in particular, opening up senior positions to commoners, men and women, of unimpeachable conduct and ability) and, most importantly, over taxation. The parish clergy were likely to express particular sympathy for the claims of the Third Estate to a uniform tax regime on wealth. So the clergy of Troyes insisted on the traditional distinction of the three orders meeting separately, but they made a crucial exception on the matter of taxation; on this issue they urged a common assembly to adopt a tax 'proportionately borne by all individuals of the three orders'.[9]

The town *cahiers* of professional men, merchants and landowners articulated an ideal of 'careers open to talent', of the end of the family name as the basis of entitlement to a position. They insisted that the king's financial problems could only be solved by an equal sharing of tax burdens across all social orders, but placed that within a bolder ideal of equal rights and individual responsibilities. Just as striking in their *cahiers* was an insistence on the dignity of the commons, that its deputies show resolve by refusing to meet in a separate chamber once at Versailles.[10] The *cahiers* repeatedly articulated a reform of the social and political order while in effect demanding its abolition.

Most urban workers were too poor to be eligible to participate in the meetings of guilds and parishes where *cahiers* were formulated. The views of master craftsmen—and occasionally women—who were wealthy enough revealed a commonality of outlook with their middle-class neighbours over questions of privilege and taxation, but often parted company on economic reform, expressing hostility to mechanization and the free market in essential goods. 'Let us not call the rich capitalists egoists: they are our brothers,' conceded the hatters and furriers of the city of Rouen, before calling for the 'suppression of machinery' so 'there will be no competition and no problems about markets'. East of Rouen, the *cahier* of the textile-producing village of Vatimesnil, similarly, called on 'His Majesty for the good of the people to abolish spinning machines because they do great wrong to all poor people'.[11] In contrast, in the nearby textile town of Elbeuf, the manufacturers, merchants and professional men who formulated the *cahier* on 28 March had other targets:

> the inefficient administration of finances ... these constraints, these impediments to commerce: barriers reaching to the very heart of the kingdom; endless obstacles to the circulation of commodities ... representatives of manufacturing industries and Chambers of Commerce totally ignored and despised; an indifference on the part of the government towards manufacturers ...[12]

Theirs was a radical vision of a national free market, with uniform commercial regulations and laws, and recognition of their own value to the kingdom.

The 40,000 peasant *cahiers* ranged in length from many pages of detailed criticisms and proposals to the three sentences written in a mixture of French and Catalan from the tiny village of Serrabone in the stony foothills of the Pyrenees. In many areas model *cahiers* were circulated through the countryside from towns, although they were frequently added to at a village level.[13] And although in theory all male taxpayers over twenty-five years of age were eligible to participate in the process of drawing up the *cahiers*, their compilation was often assumed by the better-off minority of villagers.[14] Occasionally, the exclusion of poorer peasants resulted in overt friction: for example, at Beignon, near Ploërmel in Brittany, after a gathering of twenty-six of the well-to-do had formulated a placatory *cahier* on 5 April 1789, eighty-six others met two days later in protest, writing their own *cahier* to attack the seigneur, in particular for felling 860 trees.[15]

The peasant *cahiers* were replete with references to the past, ranging from evocations of an imaginary golden age to specific dates when arrangements with seigneurs had been codified. But such historic references jostled with new and startling claims about national representation, privilege and control of resources. More than three-quarters of the village *cahiers* criticized seigneurialism in some way, but an even more common target of peasant anger in 1789 was state taxation, hardly surprising given the purported recipient of the *cahiers*. The issues were closely linked, however, for what rankled most with commoners was the privileged fiscal treatment of the noble elite, whether as seigneurs or as bishops and abbots within the Church. Hostility to seigneurial exactions tended to go together with criticism of the tithes, fees and practices of the Church; they were seen as interdependent within the seigneurial system.[16] Typical in this regard was the *cahier* of the parish of Sagy, situated between the Seine and Oise rivers north of Paris. Its chief targets were the burden of state taxes on commoners, and hunting by nobles and their other privileges: the parishioners wanted 'to pay taxes in proportion to their capacity, with the clergy and nobility, and to enjoy in freedom the cultivation of their land without being troubled by any form of servitude'.[17] There were frequent criticisms of other 'rights', such as the seigneurial monopoly (*banalité*) over the village oven, grape and olive press, and mill; the attempts by lords to exert the right of 'triage' to assume ownership of part of the common lands; and the unpaid labour required from the community on the lords' lands. In stark contrast, 84 per cent of *cahiers* issued by nobles were simply silent about seigneurial dues.[18]

Equally striking in the *cahiers* was their tone of resolute optimism, common across the kingdom. Most rural people spoke a language other than French in daily life, such as Breton, Basque, Flemish or Occitan, and many lived in provinces such as Lorraine or Roussillon only recently incorporated into the kingdom. Despite their lively expression of regional difference, however, their *cahiers* communicated an assumption of French citizenship within a regenerated kingdom.[19] Words like 'patrie', 'nation' and 'citoyen' were studded throughout the *cahiers*, which were imbued with assumptions of a secular citizenship as the basis of a regenerated public realm. Peasant attitudes had been a long time in the moulding.

Some assemblies were so brave as to criticize their seigneur's position explicitly. In the south-western corner of the kingdom, the few lines submitted from the tiny community of Périllos were unreservedly hostile to the system under which they claimed the seigneur treated them 'like slaves'.[20] Much further north, in the impoverished little village of Erceville, north of Orléans, the parish assembly was presided over by the local judge employed by the seigneur, a prominent member of the Parlement of Paris whose personal holdings covered most of the parish. Not surprisingly, his tenants decided to stay away from the meeting, but those peasants, labourers and artisans who did attend to draw up the *cahier* were bold and blunt. They required the judge to write articles stipulating that, 'without any distinction of title or rank, the said seigneur be taxed like them' and—clearly aware of the looming political issue of whether the three orders would deliberate separately or jointly at Versailles—that all taxes should require 'the consent of the whole Nation assembled in Estates-General'.[21]

The longing for national 'regeneration' was balanced by a lively concern for local issues. Nowhere was this more acute than in Brittany, where the survival of the local rental regime of *domaine congéable* (very long-term leases in which the tenant owned the buildings as well as the produce) rankled with farmers. The *cahier* of the peninsula of Rhuys at the mouth of the Gulf of Morbihan insisted that it be abolished as a form of 'servitude', giving tenants ownership. Rhuys was unusual among Breton communities in recommending the destruction of Brittany's unique privileges and even its language, which formed 'a wall separating half of Brittany from the rest of France': elsewhere many Bretons insisted on guarding their unique degree of autonomy from the rest of the kingdom, whereby the union with France in 1532 had guaranteed certain rights, such as exemption from the salt-tax.[22]

Men long used to the exercise of power in the countryside were unsettled by the boldness of some rural communities and the confident new language with which the charged political context of early 1789 had invested their grievances. From the village of Pont-sur-Seine in the Champagne region a seigneur's agent wrote to his master:

In vain I've done everything I can to exclude from the *cahier* the articles
on the abolition of *banalités*, of the right to hunt, and other seigneurial
dues. . . . The intention and the tenacity of the people are immovable on
this question and it is impossible to dissuade them, because they have
been given the right to express their grievances.[23]

In themselves, the *cahiers* were not explicitly revolutionary: no one in
France in the early spring of 1789 knew that they were about to live through
what became in hindsight 'the Revolution of 1789'. But the divisions over
the key issues of political power, seigneurialism and claims to corporate
privilege were already irreconcilable by the time the deputies arrived in
Versailles for the May Estates-General. Most obviously of all, nobles and
commoners could not agree on arrangements for voting at the Estates-
General. Demands for a periodic assembly with real powers over taxation
were virtually unanimous across the *cahiers*. But the vagueness of the nobility
on equality of taxation, and its intransigence on seigneurial rights and the
status of the Second Estate, were starkly exposed by the issue of the vote.
Again and again, in contrast, the *cahiers* of the Third Estate had made
demands for a regular meeting of a representative body such as the Estates-
General, equality of taxation and opportunity, and the end of seigneurialism.
Consciously or not, these demands taken together presupposed the end of
the social and political system.

After drawing up their *cahiers*, parish assemblies elected two delegates
for the first one hundred households and one more for each extra hundred;
these delegates in turn chose deputies for each of the 234 district constituencies and consolidated parish *cahiers* into a single one for their district.
Participation at the parish level was generally high everywhere, but it varied
sharply: for example, in parishes around Béziers in Languedoc it ranged
from 5 to 83 per cent, near Vitré in Brittany from 6 to 96 per cent, and
in Artois from 14 to 97 per cent. In what was to become a common feature
of the revolutionary period, such variations were a reflection either of
levels of enthusiasm or of the extent to which voters shared a common view
about who should or would be elected, that is, whether it was worth voting
at all.[24]

The district assemblies in local town centres were often confused and
stormy occasions, for many urban bourgeois dismissed parish complaints
about seigneurial rights and other specific grievances as private, petty
matters between them and their seigneur, provoking indignation from their

rustic fellows. Despite the experience of municipal office of many delegates, at the *bailliage* (bailiwick) level there was lack of clarity about what was being decided: at times peasant delegates seem to have assumed that they were deliberative gatherings of the sovereign people. Desmé de Daubuisson, lieutenant-general of the *bailliage* of Saumur on the Loire river, complained:

> What is really tiresome is that these assemblies that have been summoned have generally believed themselves to be invested with some sovereign authority and that when they came to an end the peasants went home with the idea that henceforward they were free from tithes, hunting prohibitions and the payment of seigneurial dues.[25]

It was at these district assemblies that provincial representatives were chosen to attend the Estates-General scheduled for 4 May. The elections were complex and often hotly contested, and some were not complete until July. The elections to the Estates-General brought animosities out into the open, as the nobility sought to use the municipal bodies they dominated as the vehicle for selecting Third Estate deputies. In Artois, Robespierre was narrowly elected one of eight deputies only after five months of vitriolic debate about the attempts of the noble municipal elite to control the elections. His opponents were furious with his brother Augustin's open campaigning for votes in the countryside.[26]

The voting procedures and eligibility requirements for Third Estate deputies reinforced deeply ingrained assumptions about education, wealth and capacity, and ensured that virtually all of the 604 Third Estate deputies finally certified were lawyers, officials and property-owners, men of substance and repute in their town or region.[27] The deputies were all educated men, and with few exceptions materially comfortable, even wealthy. There were even sixty nobles among them, and several Protestants, including Rabaut Saint-Étienne and two Parisian bankers. The Abbé Sieyès was chosen as a representative of the Third Estate of Paris. But there were no artisans or shopkeepers, and the forty-three deputies with agricultural backgrounds were substantial landowners or lease-holders: there were only two deputies who identified themselves as peasants through their dress, the Bretons Michel Gérard and Corentin Le Floc'h. The deputies were also experienced in local affairs and mostly middle-aged: 52 per cent were over forty-five years of age, and the largest age cohort was forty-five to forty-nine years.[28]

Most of the 278 noble deputies were also well known in their districts. But in their attitudes they were a world away from those like Lafayette, Condorcet, Mirabeau, Talleyrand and others active in the reformist Society of Thirty in Paris, who were wealthy and worldly enough to accept the importance of surrendering at least some of their order's fiscal privileges. More than 220 of the noble deputies were serving or retired army and navy officers; recent cutbacks to the armed forces added to the resentment they felt towards the regime for its failure to guarantee privileges.[29]

The composition of the First Estate would be of crucial importance. Louis had approved voting regulations for the clerical deputies that advantaged the parish clergy: they were all eligible to attend district assemblies and vote for their deputies, while the cathedrals could send only one delegate for every ten canons, and monasteries one sole representative. The king's advisers knew that the parish clergy were most likely to pressure the nobility and the elite of their own order to make major fiscal concessions. 'As *curés* we have rights,' exclaimed a parish priest from Lorraine, Henri Grégoire, son of a tailor: 'such a favourable opportunity to enforce them has not occurred, perhaps, for twelve centuries .... Let us take it.'[30] Indeed, about three-quarters of the 330 deputies were from the lower clergy, and only 46 of the 176 bishops were chosen as deputies.

Excitement about the opening of the Estates-General did not end the recourse to angry protest. Only one in five Parisians over twenty-five years of age was eligible to vote for delegates to the Estates-General, and there had been months of angry mutterings and pamphlets expressing the ire of wage-earners at their exclusion from the political process. An offhand (and misreported) remark about high wages by the wealthy wallpaper manufacturer Réveillon at a Third Estate meeting in Paris on 23 April triggered a riot in the *faubourg* Saint-Antoine during which, echoing Sieyès' *What is the Third Estate?*, shouts of 'Long live the Third Estate! Liberty! We will not give way!' were heard. The riot was ruthlessly suppressed by troops, at the cost of about three hundred lives (some estimates were as high as nine hundred), the bloodiest event of 1789.[31] The bloodshed fuelled the expectant, nervous atmosphere building for the meeting of the Estates-General due in a fortnight. The priest Antoine Caillot, confessor to several prominent noblewomen, was struck that 'even women were attacked by this political contagion; and no lover could hope to keep his mistress if he didn't adopt her opinions and support her party'.[32] For other noblewomen, this was the moment when their insouciance turned to anxiety. One of them was the nineteen-year-old relative of the Archbishop of Narbonne, Lucy Dillon, who in 1787 had married Frédéric de La Tour du Pin, son of one of the senior military men of the realm. The seriousness of the situation only began to hit home for her when, on returning from horse races at Vincennes, her entourage was caught up in the riot at the Réveillon factory. She remained convinced that the riot, and those that were to follow, were orchestrated and financed by hidden hands.[33]

Anger about shortages and prices also prompted violent scenes in the provinces. A massive food riot in Orléans on 24–25 April lasted thirty hours and resulted in the demolition of the house belonging to a merchant called Rime. Finally troops were sent in with orders to suppress the riot without mercy, which they did, killing an estimated ninety-six people.[34] The very day the Estates-General opened in Versailles, on 4 May 1789, about eight hundred people in the southern town of Limoux forced officials to seal the granaries, demanded an end to dues and indirect taxes, then ransacked the tax-collector's offices and threw records into the River Aude.

Protracted elections meant that only about 800 of the 1,200 deputies elected from the three orders were actually present at the opening of the Estates-General on 4 May. Like many other deputies, Robespierre had to make a frantic dash from Arras to be there. But when he arrived at Versailles he was exhilarated that, despite differences of language, the bourgeois deputies articulated a common outlook, insistent on their dignity and responsibility to 'the Nation'. The deputies Le Chapelier and Lanjuinais founded the fervently pro-reform Breton Club in the Café Amaury, a short walk from the palace. They were soon joined by non-Bretons such as Sieyès, Duport, Barnave, the Lameth brothers and Robespierre himself. The excitement and expectation were palpable.

At the opening of the Estates-General the First and Second Estates were to wear the costume and decorations appropriate to their particular rank within their order, whereas the Third Estate deputies were to dress uniformly in coats and stockings of black cloth. In the words of an English doctor then in Paris, their attire was 'even worse than that of the inferior sort of gownsmen at the English universities'. 'A ridiculous and bizarre law has been imposed upon our arrival,' fumed one deputy, 'by the grand-master of court puerilities.'[35] Once inside, the pressing issue remained that of voting procedures. Louis XVI's opening speech urged the deputies of all three orders to contemplate bold reforms, but he also requested them to proceed to their separate chambers to verify their deputies' elections and to commence deliberations.

The king's lack of procedural boldness at the opening of the Estates-General was his greatest mistake. But he was in an intractable situation: how could he support the demands of the Third Estate, which may have solved his financial problems but at the cost of collapsing the pillars of a system of which he was the greatest beneficiary? Louis' profound desire for reform was matched by his reticence and timidity: his brother Louis-Stanislas, the Comte de Provence, remarked that trying to pin down his views was like trying to hold two oiled billiard balls together.[36] In private, Louis stated to his senior courtiers that he supported verification in a common assembly, but he followed the wish of the nobility (by 188 votes to 46) to vote separately, supported by the clergy (but only after vigorous debate and a vote of 133 to 114). Louis' capacity to manage a fractious situation was further undermined by the tragic death at seven years of age of Louis Joseph, the Dauphin, on 4 June. To the king's confusion and anxiety was now added grief.

The Revolution was latent. Ultimately, the king's acquiescence in the nobility's demand for voting to be in three separate chambers galvanized the outrage of the Third Estate deputies. They refused to begin formal discussions. The political stand-off was remarkable for their degree of agreement about the radical changes they believed necessary. In this they were encouraged by a trickle of defections from the privileged orders of individuals convinced of the need for reform. On 13 June three *curés* from Poitou joined the Third Estate, followed by six others, including Grégoire, the next day. On 17 June deputies of the Third Estate made a revolutionary claim, that 'the interpretation and presentation of the general will belong to it . . . . The name National Assembly is the only one which is suitable . . .'.

A turning point in the political stand-off was the vote to join the Third Estate taken by 149 clerical deputies against 137, on 19 June. A key reason for their decision was anger at the gulf in attitudes between them and their episcopal elite. The Abbé Barbotin wrote home to a fellow priest in Prouvy, Picardy:

> Upon arriving here I was still inclined to believe that bishops were also pastors, but everything I see obliges me to think that they are nothing but mercenaries, almost Machiavellian politicians, who mind only their own interests and are ready to fleece—perhaps even devour—their own flocks rather than to pasture them.[37]

On 20 June, finding themselves locked out of their usual meeting place during preparations for a royal plenary session on 23 June, the deputies moved to an indoor royal tennis court and, under the elected presidency of the astronomer Jean-Sylvain Bailly, insisted by oath on their 'unshakeable resolution' to continue their proceedings to establish a written constitution. It was a stunning claim to legitimacy:

> The National Assembly, whereas it is called on to lay down the constitution of the kingdom, implement the regeneration of public order, and maintain the true principles of the monarchy, declares that nothing can stop it from continuing its deliberations in whatever place it may be obliged to establish itself, and that finally, anywhere its members are gathered together, that is the National Assembly.[38]

There was only one dissenting voice, that of Martin Dauch, elected from Castelnaudary in Languedoc. The Third Estate deputies had made a revolutionary stand, in essence insisting that France would henceforth be governed by a representative parliament and a constitutional monarch. This was an act of extraordinary boldness and risk, a revolutionary challenge to the core elements of the political system.

Louis now compounded the problem caused by his indecision about a common assembly. At his plenary session on 23 June he insisted again that the three orders should deliberate separately. His master of ceremonies, the Marquis de Dreux-Brézé, informed Bailly and the National Assembly of the king's wishes, but Mirabeau sprang to his feet and allegedly retorted: 'Go tell your master that we are here by the will of the people, and that we shall retire only at the point of the bayonet.'[39] Later that day Louis then issued a 'Declaration of Intentions' which conceded that the Estates-General would be a permanent feature of political life with the power to impose or rescind taxes. He announced his desire for onerous taxes such as the *gabelle* to be abolished and for the privileged to accept a common system of taxation, while guaranteeing tithes and all 'feudal and seigneurial rights and duties'. Had he presented this reform agenda at the opening of the Estates-General he might just have succeeded; now it was too late.

The Third Estate was unmoved, and their resolve was strengthened by the arrival at their assembly the next day of forty-seven liberal nobles, led by Louis' own cousin, the Duc d'Orléans. By 27 June, Louis now seemed to accept a *fait accompli* and ordered the remaining noble deputies to join their fellows. Despite their apparent victory, however, the commoner deputies and their allies were soon confronted by a counter-attack from the court. Jacques Necker, the one non-noble minister, had chosen not to attend the royal session on 23 June and an indignant Louis dismissed him on 11 July. Paris, thirteen miles from Versailles and seething with enthusiasm for the cause of the Third Estate, was invested with 20,000 troops. Rumours were rife of preparations for a military crackdown.

The soldiers might simply have occupied and dispersed the National Assembly. The deputies were saved from summary dismissal not only by Louis' profound desire to avoid confrontation and bloodshed, but also by a collective action by thousands of Parisian working people convinced that the court was preparing a coup against the heroic Third Estate deputies. Sustaining this anger in Paris was an escalation in the price of a 4lb loaf of bread from 8 to 14 *sous*, up to 70 per cent of workers' wages, an increase widely assumed to be the result of a deliberate withholding of supplies by noble landowners. Parisian disturbances had hitherto been intimidating rather than violent: early in July, for example, crowds up to 10,000-strong freed fourteen soldiers who had been imprisoned for insubordination.[40] But the fate of Necker tipped food-rioting and protest into violent rebellion. The Paris bookseller Sébastien Hardy, whose diaries are an unparalleled source for the early months of the Revolution, noted that people were saying 'that the princes were hoarding grains deliberately in order to more effectively trip up M. Necker, whom they are so keen to overthrow'.[41] Necker's dismissal on 11 July confirmed these suspicions.

A first target was the new ring of customs houses around Paris, which had been the object of sarcasm and resentment as much for their architectural grandeur as for their function. Begun in 1785, fifty-four of fifty-five customs houses in a sixteen-mile wall had been constructed by July 1789. Between 7 and 17 July forty of them would be damaged or destroyed, with the exception of those along the northern edge.[42] Protestors were urged on by street orators such as Camille Desmoulins, who harangued the crowd from a table at the Café de Foy at the Palais Royal. Political insurrection began on 13 July on the Place de Grève, the huge square outside the Hôtel de Ville where labourers assembled each morning in the hope of a day's work, where others went on strike and demonstrated, where the great fireworks show—'the fires of St-Jean'—attracted revellers in June, and where criminals were executed in spectacularly public fashion. Now in July 1789 it was where insurgents swarmed (Map 2). The wealthy men who comprised the electoral assembly of the Third Estate of Paris created a citizens' militia in an attempt to preserve order. They were powerless to do so. The abbey of Saint-Lazare was searched for arms; popular suspicions that the nobility were trying to starve the people into submission were confirmed when stocks of grain were also discovered there. Arms and ammunition were also seized from gunsmiths and the Invalides military hospital.

The ultimate target was the Bastille fortress in the *faubourg* Saint-Antoine, both for its supplies of arms and gunpowder and because this powerful fortress dominated the popular neighbourhoods of eastern Paris. It was also an awesome symbol of the arbitrary authority of the monarchy. On 14 July up to 8,000 armed Parisians laid siege to the fortress (Fig. 6). The governor, the Marquis de Launay, refused to surrender and, as crowds forced their way into the courtyard, ordered his soldiers to open fire, killing about one hundred insurgents. Only when two detachments of Gardes Françaises sided with the crowd and trained their cannon on the main gate did he surrender. The most prominent *vainqueurs de la Bastille* were later celebrated for their bravery. On one list of 662 survivors compiled by a *vainqueur*, Stanislas Maillard, there were a score of bourgeois, including manufacturers and merchants, and seventy-six soldiers. The rest were typical of the *menu peuple*: tradesmen, artisans and wage-earners from about thirty different trades, notably forty-nine joiners, forty-eight cabinet-makers, forty-one locksmiths, twenty-eight cobblers, eleven wine-merchants, and ten hairdressers and wig-makers.[43] Those celebrated for the taking of the Bastille were all men, apart from one Marie Charpentier. But there were others involved, like Marguerite Pinaigre who

> worked equally hard [alongside her wounded husband] with all her might . . . . It is she who ran to several wineshops to fill her apron with bottles, both broken and unbroken, which she gave to the authorities to be used as shot in the cannon used to break the chain on the drawbridge of the Bastille.[44]

The seizure of the Bastille on 14 July 1789 was a political earthquake. It saved the National Assembly and legitimized a sharp shift in power. Paris was now controlled by a new city government under an elected mayor, Bailly, inaugural president of the National Assembly, and a civil militia commanded by the French hero of the American War of Independence, the Marquis de Lafayette, and staffed by men of means. Early on the morning of 17 July, Louis' youngest brother, the Comte d'Artois, and Marie-Antoinette's favourite, the Duchesse de Polignac, left France in disgust at the collapse of respect evident among commoners. A steady trickle of disgruntled courtiers would join Artois in his *émigré* court in Turin. On the same day, however, Louis took advice to go to Paris to reassert his position after the symbolic defeat of 14 July and announced the withdrawal of troops and the recall of Necker. On 17 July the king was welcomed, 'with solemn severity', at the Hôtel de Ville, where Bailly, on behalf of the electors, presented him with a tricolour cockade, now a common symbol of the insurgents. By placing it in his hat, Louis asserted his unity with his people—and inaugurated a national emblem.[45] The revolutionary tricolour cockade—the white of the Bourbons fused with the red and blue of Paris, perhaps Lafayette's idea—was born in the symbolism of a king inseparable from the people of Paris.

The storming of the Bastille also confronted revolutionaries with a dilemma they found distressing and intractable. The insurrection had been decisive in the triumph of the Third Estate and the National Assembly; however, some in the exultant crowd who took the Bastille had exercised violent retribution by killing with great cruelty the governor of the fortress, Launay, and six of his troops. Later that day the elderly Jacques de Flesselles, the *prévôt des marchands* (effectively mayor) of Paris was killed in retribution for his alleged deviousness in avoiding arming the insurgents, his head paraded through the streets with Launay's. Some felt that these were understandable—indeed justifiable—acts of popular vengeance on men whose decisions had resulted in the deaths of one hundred of the assailants. Others saw them as the actions of a crowd too used to the spectacular punishments meted out by the authorities in the violent society that the Revolution would reform. And to some they were simply inexcusable acts of barbarity, the antithesis of all for which the Revolution should stand.

More was to come. On 22 July the royal governor of Paris since 1776, Louis Bertier de Sauvigny, was caught as he tried to flee Paris. He and his father-in-law Joseph Foulon, who had been appointed to the ministry after Necker's removal, were battered to death and decapitated, their heads paraded through Paris, in retribution for supposedly conspiring to worsen the long hunger through which Parisians had lived in 1788–89. Foulon had allegedly stated that if the poor were hungry they should eat straw. In one of the new newspapers that rushed to report on the unprecedented events, the *Révolutions de Paris*, a young journalist from Bordeaux, Elysée Loustallot, reported that the 'frightening and terrible' day was now marked by horror and despair (Fig. 7). After Foulon had been decapitated,

> A handful of hay was in his mouth, a striking allusion to the inhuman sentiments of this barbarous man ... the revenge of a justifiably furious people! ... A man ... O God! The barbarian! pulls (Bertier's) heart from its palpitating entrails. ... What a horrible sight! ... I sense, my fellow citizens, how these revolting scenes afflict your soul; like you, I am struck by it; but think how ignominious it is to live as a slave. ... Never forget, however, that these punishments outrage humanity, and make Nature shudder.[46]

From Paris to the smallest hamlet, the summer and autumn of 1789 saw an unprecedented collapse of the royal state.[47] In cities, noble councillors were forced from office; in villages and small towns the vacuum of authority was filled by municipal bodies chosen by popular mandate. This seizure of power was accompanied everywhere by a rejection of the claims of the state, seigneurs and Church over the payment of taxes, dues and tithes. As royal troops openly fraternized with civilians in the exultation of the people's power, the judiciary seemed powerless to enforce the law.

News of this unprecedented challenge to the might of the state and nobility was rapidly transmitted across a countryside suffused with an explosive atmosphere of anticipation, menace and fear. The desperate hopes invested in the National Assembly were caught by Arthur Young, on his third tour of France, while talking on 12 July with a peasant woman in Lorraine who recounted her family's poverty:

> Walking up a long hill, to ease my mare, I was joined by a poor woman, who complained of the times, and that it was a sad country. ... It was said, at present, that something was to be done by some great folks for such poor ones, but she did not know who nor how, but God send us better, *car les tailles & les droits nous écrasent* ('because property taxes and feudal dues are crushing us'). This woman, at no great distance, might have been taken for sixty or seventy, her figure was so bent, and her face so furrowed and hardened by labour—but she said she was only twenty-eight.[48]

As news of the seizure of the Bastille spread, fear of the aristocracy's revenge replaced such hopes. The bands of people made destitute by economic crisis and who were roaming country roads were the focus of suspicion as anxious, hungry peasants waited for the new crops to ripen: were they possibly in the employ of vengeful nobles conspiring to destroy peasants' crops as punishment for the boldness of the Third Estate? During the second half of July villages formed popular militias in anticipation of external menace, armed with farm implements and tools. Hope, fear and hunger made the countryside a tinder-box ignited by imagined sightings of 'brigands' in the pay of nobles. Panic fanned out almost simultaneously from sparks in six different parts of the country as tales of suspicious behaviour by 'outsiders' became magnified into fearful accounts of armed brigands destroying crops. The rumours travelled like bushfires from village to village, and affected every region except Brittany and the east. While many local incidents took the form of compelling vulnerable members of the privileged orders or their agents to surrender food and drink, there were at times two new elements: the seizure and destruction of feudal registers, and the public humiliation of seigneurs or their stewards (Fig. 8).

This unprecedented panic and its effects came to be known as the 'Great Fear' of the summer of 1789. What happened in the village of Silly-en-Multien, twenty miles north-east of Paris, was typical. From 1771, Pierre-Louis-Nicolas Delahaye, the schoolteacher and parish clerk, kept a diary of 'remarkable and curious events' in the village, including the suffering during the hard winter of 1788–89. In late June 1789 he recorded that 'we are in frightful distress, all we hear is talk of revolts and massacres everywhere. There is no more wheat to be found.' The ripening harvest of 1789 promised an end to hunger. Then, in the anxious, expectant atmosphere after news arrived of the taking of the Bastille on 14 July, the villagers acted on the rumour that harvesters working for vengeful nobles were cutting the crops prematurely: 'the alarm was sounded and the priest ran through the village to gather all the men and boys, all armed, a few with rifles, the others with forks, spits, axes, pitchforks, with whatever they could, then left with the priest at their head, wearing his cockade'.[49]

After the drawing up of the cahiers de doléances, this was the second great act of revolution in which masses of rural people were involved. Unlike the meetings that had produced the cahiers, when parishes hid radical demands behind protestations of fealty to the king, this time those involved in this frontal assault on the seigneurial system were well aware of the consequences of what they were doing. Rural communities in the mountain regions of Bresse and Bugey east of Lyon were already menacing châteaux before news of the taking of the Bastille reached the local capital Bourg on 19 July. Once the threat of revenge by the nobility had passed, peasants in many rural communities in Bresse seized and burned feudal registers on the basis of the popular belief that 'il n'y a nul seigneur sans titre' ('there is no seigneur without a title'). The region became an epicentre of the fears and rumours sweeping across the country. Most spectacularly, on 25 July up to eight hundred peasants from twelve villages attacked the abbey at Saint-Sulpice near Bourg, forcing the monks to burn the registers and plundering the abbey's cellar. The following day they erected a gibbet in the middle of the cloister, ostensibly to hang the monks, who were allowed finally to flee in terror into the surrounding forest before the insurgents set fire to the buildings.[50]

In late July châteaux were pillaged and burned in the valley of the Saône, including Senozan (belonging to the Marquis de Talleyrand, the Bishop of Autun and already a prominent figure in the National Assembly). Levies of food, drink and money were exacted from the wealthy and clergy, and feudal registers were burned. The abbey of Cluny, a major landowner and holder of seigneurial rights, was a particular target. Some 160 'brigands'—winegrowers, labourers, village artisans, beggars—were later arrested. Most insisted that they were 'swept up' by the crowd and meant no harm; a few admitted that the intention was 'to burn and raze the abbey', 'to destroy the abbey and the town' or to ensure 'the end of tithes and seigneurial dues'. So frightened were the 'patriots' and so determined were they to re-impose order that emergency committees were established to mete out justice: in the end, twenty-seven men were hanged in Cluny, Mâcon and Tournus.[51]

In some places the 'Great Fear' unleashed actions that targeted other objects of hatred. In Alsace, Jewish homes were pillaged in several villages.[52] Further north, on the eastern border of Lorraine, the people of Sarreguemines celebrated the news of the fall of the Bastille at a mass on 22 July, then on 28 July they forced the tax-collectors to flee. Tensions over taxes, in particular on salt, continued for months, with the hope expressed in a pamphlet titled 'Das Nationalische Vatter unser der vereinigten Frantzosen' ('Our national father of the reunited French people') that Louis would abolish the tax office.[53] In the little Norman town of Mortagne-au-Perche, near Alençon, François Lamberdière led a crowd of men, women and children to the tax office, where they seized and burned the registers, then imposed 'taxation populaire' to lower prices of grains, tobacco and salt. For several days the local authorities were powerless to resist the intimidation, but they would not forget.[54]

Just as some rural communities had 'believed' they were doing the king's will in refusing to pay dues in the winter of 1788–89, so in July 1789 others claimed a new authorization for disobedience. According to an official in Ploërmel, Brittany:

> all the peasants around here and in my area generally are refusing their quota of sheaves to the tithe-collector and say quite openly that there will be no collection without bloodshed on the senseless grounds that as the request for the abolition of these tithes was included in the *cahiers* of this district, such an abolition has now come into effect.[55]

The collapse of authority encouraged peasants to abandon well-practised tactics of dissembling and duplicity against authority and instead to be explicit about their grievances. In particular, they coopted the language of the Third Estate revolt to their own ends. From Montmartin, to the northeast of Paris, the steward of the estate of the Duke of Montmorency wrote to his master on 2 August that 'approximately three hundred brigands from all the lands associated with the vassals of Mme the Marquise de Longaunay have stolen the titles of rents and allowances of the seigneurie, and demolished her dovecotes'; they then gave a receipt for the theft signed 'The Nation', a dramatic and confident flourish.[56]

Actions during the Great Fear amounted to a revolutionary confrontation, and the noble, clerical and bourgeois deputies of the National Assembly were well aware of its import. In an atmosphere of terror and exhilaration a series of nobles mounted the rostrum on 4 August to respond to the crisis in the countryside. The legislators' original intention—to quieten peasant insurrection by reducing or abolishing particular seigneurial dues—was overwhelmed by the panic-stricken surrender of a maze of other privileges in an 'electric whirlwind' of generosity, as Mirabeau put it. In the succeeding week, however, sobered legislators made a distinction between instances of 'personal servitude' (serfdom, dovecotes, seigneurial and royal hunting privileges and unpaid labour), which were abolished outright, and 'property rights' (seigneurial dues payable on harvests) for which peasants would have to pay compensation before ceasing payment:

> Article 1. The National Assembly completely destroys the feudal regime. It decrees that rights and duties . . . deriving from real or personal mortmain, and personal servitude . . . are abolished without compensation; all

the others are declared redeemable, and the price and the manner of the redemption will be set by the National Assembly. Those of the said rights that are not abolished by this decree will continue nonetheless to be collected until settlement.

The equivocation over total abolition would fuel continuing anger in the countryside.

The decree responded to a core grievance expressed in the *cahiers* by abolishing tax exemptions. Seigneurial courts were also abolished: in future, justice was to be provided free of charge according to a uniform set of laws. The August Decree was based on the assumption that henceforth all individuals in France were to enjoy the same rights and be subject to the same laws: the age of privilege and exception was over.

> Article X ... all special privileges of the provinces, principalities, counties, cantons, towns and communities of inhabitants, be they financial or of any other nature, are abolished without compensation, and will be absorbed into the common rights of all French people.

Tithes and property taxes were to be replaced by more equitable ways of funding the Church and state; in the meantime, however, they would continue to be paid, just like harvest dues.[57] Despite such hesitation, the boldness of the changes was exhilarating. In his newspaper the *Révolutions de Paris*, Louis-Marie Prudhomme felt 'as though a new day was breaking in France.... Everywhere there were feelings of fraternity, sweet fraternity.'[58]

The National Assembly's Constitutional Committee had concluded on 27 July that a Declaration of Rights was a necessary foundation for the regenerated nation. However, as reports flooded in to the Assembly of the extent of peasant revolt and of bloodshed, those opposed to such a notion were emboldened. Influential deputies such as the Baron Malouet, Mirabeau and Champion de Cicé (the Archbishop of Bordeaux) argued that such 'rights' would be misinterpreted by the ignorant, who would fail to understand the limits that the law would necessarily impose. 'Why, then, begin by transporting him to the summit of a high mountain, and showing him his empire without limits,' asked Malouet, 'when he must descend to find them with every step he takes?' Others, such as the Duc de Lévis and senior clergy, felt that it was essential that any such declaration be accompanied by a statement of duties. Their proposal was defeated, but only by 570 votes to 433.[59]

On 26 August the Assembly approved the Declaration of the Rights of Man and Citizen, without duties. After asserting that 'ignorance, forgetfulness, or contempt of the rights of man are the sole causes of public misfortune', the Declaration pronounced:

Article I. Men are born and remain free and equal in rights. Social distinctions may only be based on common usefulness.

II. The goal of every political association is the preservation of man's natural and imprescriptible rights. These rights are liberty, property, security, and resistance to oppression.

III. The principle of all sovereignty resides essentially in the nation. No body, or individual may exercise authority that does not expressly emanate from it.

The Declaration asserted the essence of liberalism, that 'liberty consists of the power to do whatever is not injurious to others'; accordingly, it guaranteed rights of free speech and association, of religion and opinion, limited only by 'the law'.

Together with the August Decree, the Declaration marked the end of the absolutist, seigneurial and corporate structure of eighteenth-century France. They were also a revolutionary proclamation of the principles of a new golden age, to be founded on an equality of rights, responsibilities and civic dignity. This was to be a land in which all were to be equal in legal status, and subject to the same public responsibilities: it was an invitation to become citizens of a nation instead of subjects of a king. The social order would no longer be based on a hierarchy of birth and status but on capacity, in which citizens would choose their leaders on the basis of merit. A land of corporate privilege and provincial exemptions would henceforth treat its citizens as equal in the eyes of the law, with equal rights and responsibilities. These rights would extend to freedom of religion. The 'dream of freedom' was that of inclusion, an invitation to all—whatever their social or linguistic background—to become citizens of the nation, enjoying freedoms limited only by the obligations to obey the law and to respect the rights of others.

While universal in its language, and resounding in its optimism, the Declaration was ambiguous. In particular, its distinction between 'men' and 'citizens' was the basis on which it proclaimed that the law applied equally to all while political rights were reserved to those designated 'citizens'. That is, while proclaiming the universality of rights and the civic equality of all citizens, it was vague on whether the propertyless, slaves and women would have political as well as legal equality, and silent on how the means to exercise one's talents could be secured by those without education or property. As a women's *cahier* from the Pays de Caux region north of Paris had posed the question in the spring of 1789: 'we are told there is talk of freeing the Negroes; the people, almost as enslaved as them, is recovering its rights. . . . Will men persist in wanting to make us victims of their pride or injustice?'[60]

As the blueprint for a regenerated France, the seventeen articles of the Declaration may also be read as a mirror for how most deputies saw the past. It was an uncompromising repudiation of a political and social order based on hierarchical appointment, corporate privilege and special arrangements. In this rupture with the past it was in stark contrast with its sister revolution across the Atlantic. The American Revolution was profoundly radical in its republicanism but institutionally was a regeneration of existing British structures by which the people would govern themselves through an elected president, Senate and House of Representatives rather than a system in which were balanced monarchy, lords and commons. From the outset of the French Revolution, in contrast, the social and political function of the nobility as a counterweight between monarchy and people was repudiated: the people's representatives were to govern in harmony with a people's king.

The demands of elements of the Third Estate—whether bourgeois, urban working people or peasants—were inherently and incipiently revolutionary months, even years, before the massive revolt of July–August 1789. From late 1788 their grievances, as expressed in collective protest and the *cahiers*, could not have been accommodated within the structures of what was now referred to as the former (*ancien*) regime.[61] The causes of the Revolution are best understood as originating deep in French society, as well as being the result of elite political mismanagement. History is replete with examples of regimes that have collapsed because of their own failure or inability to respond to crisis; it is much rarer that such collapses result in a revolutionary shift in who holds power and for what purposes. France in 1789 was one of those rare occasions.

CHAPTER FIVE

REGENERATING THE NATION, 1789–90

REVOLUTIONARY ELATION AND ANXIETIES WERE ON SHOW IN THE art exhibition at the Paris Salon of 1789. The sculptor Jean-Antoine Houdon exhibited a bust of Thomas Jefferson completed just before the envoy returned to the United States in September. Jacques-Louis David exhibited *The Lictors bringing Brutus the Bodies of his Sons*, in which the Roman consul receives the dead bodies of two sons who had conspired with the Tarquins against the Roman Republic. David had long smarted at what he took to be repeated slights on his talents from aristocratic patrons and juries, and his classical allegories took on—or were imputed—a bolder political edge. David had also just completed a portrait of the brilliant chemist Antoine Lavoisier and his wife Marie-Anne, for which the noble tax-collector scientist had paid him 7,000 *livres*. But when Lavoisier, a government Commissioner for Gunpowder, was almost lynched as a rumour swept Paris in August that gunpowder stocks were being removed, it was felt prudent not to exhibit the portrait.[1]

In this febrile, exhilarated atmosphere, those seeking stability through a strong monarch and an English-style Parliament went on the offensive: wealthy, influential nobles such as Mirabeau, the Marquis de Lally-Tollendal, the Comte de Clermont-Tonnerre and Baron Malouet, supported by influential commoners such as Jean-Joseph Mounier, and the Genevan journalist Mallet du Pan.[2] These 'Monarchiens' pushed for a House of Lords on the English model but, such was the mistrust the nobility had earned across 1789, plus the suspicion of many provincial nobles that the House would be dominated by the Versailles elite, that the proposal was crushed by 849 votes of the 1,060 present on 10 September. Sovereignty would not be divided.

Mounier and the Monarchiens had more success on the question of the powers of the king. The Estates-General had been summoned to offer Louis advice on the state of his kingdom: did his acceptance of the existence of a 'National Assembly' require him to accept its decisions? What would his powers be in the new order? A compromise to give him a suspensive veto (enabling him to hold up particular legislation for three two-year terms) was accepted by 673 votes to 325 on the second ballot. The latter represented the pinnacle of vestigial support for absolute monarchy. Among the 673 were 220 (including Sieyès, Robespierre and Pétion) initially opposed to any veto at all.[3]

At the heart of the revolutionaries' optimism was the certainty of 'regeneration'. Now a life of liberty lived with respect for the freedoms of others would unchain the goodness that nature had inscribed in every heart. A new age of social harmony had dawned. The prejudice, corruption and misery all around them would dissipate in the blaze of virtue. In the fervour of August 1789 it seemed self-evident that the wisdom of all men of goodwill would express that virtue, and that those who warned of the folly of 'rights' were either unenlightened or malevolent. The recalcitrance of so many of the nobles, and their open contempt for the liberals from their own ranks, fed commoner assumptions that their claims for special treatment were specious or worse.

But civic regeneration needed to be prompted. The Protestant pastor Jean-Paul Rabaut Saint-Étienne, elected as a deputy from Nîmes, urged that the French people 'must be renewed, rejuvenated, transformed through their institutions to change their ideas, changed in their laws to change their morals. Everything must be destroyed, yes destroyed, since everything must be recreated.' He described the existing framework of institutional jurisdictions, privileges and exemptions as 'a monstrous and contradictory pile of inequalities, that time, hazard, abuse, privilege, and the favour of despotism have composed out of chaos'. In the National Assembly on 18 August he referred to the Declaration of the Rights of Man and Citizen under discussion as

> an alphabet for children, to be taught in the schools. With such a patriotic education, a strong and vigorous race of men can be born, and know well how to defend the liberty that we have won for them: always armed with reason, they will know how to resist despotism.[4]

Rabaut Saint-Étienne's imperative of regeneration was underscored by the anxiety that the mendacious would use the new liberties to thwart progress.

Denunciation of abuses and of the wicked would also play a part in national renewal. Revolutionaries knew from the lessons of classical antiquity engraved in their schoolboy hearts that transparency was the gauge of probity. At the same time these men had grown up in a world where the king's desire to be his people's father was perverted by conniving ministers and plotting courtiers. Conspiracy and dissimulation were the weapons of the malevolent. From the outset, they knew that self-interest was a fearsome obstacle. As early as 28 July, Adrien Duport, who had abandoned the Second Estate to join the National Assembly in June, warned that 'plots are being mounted against the well-being of public affairs (*la chose publique*), we can be in no doubt of that. . . . Let our vigilant eye be turned in every direction.'[5] In an atmosphere fraught with expectation and uncertainty, denunciation was seen as a virtue, with legal protections the guarantee of individual liberty. From the outset of the Revolution there was always enough evidence of duplicity to make such suspicions self-evidently true.[6]

But these were heady days in the National Assembly, and indeed across the entire nation. Among those transfixed by the convocation of the Estates-General and its transformation into the National Assembly was the mathematics teacher Gilbert Romme, private tutor to the young Russian noble Pavel Stroganoff, whom he had spent seven years tutoring in Russia. He took Pavel to observe the Estates-General as 'a sublime school of public law'; there Romme became acerbic in describing the noble deputies' insistence on 'fastidious distinctions' instead of 'speaking the language of patriotism'.[7] Another enthusiast in Paris was the fifteen-year-old student Edmond Géraud, who wrote to reassure his mother in Bordeaux that he prayed to the 'Supreme Being' morning and night, but was delighted to attend lectures at the Collège de France by the priest Gournand, in which Gournand had his students study Rousseau's *Social Contract*: 'He launches bitter and satirical gibes at the upper clergy . . . and he always comes back to the marriage of priests and then he really warms up.'[8]

This highly charged atmosphere of debate and reform was fuelled by anxiety about the price and availability of foodstuffs, and not just in Paris. At the time of the elections to the Estates-General in April, river-workers on the Loire had invaded Orléans, smashing windows and menacing grain merchants. Now, on 12 September, royal troops escorting grain through the

Place du Martroi, in the heart of the town, were attacked with stones and flower-pots thrown from windows. A huge crowd from villages south of the river then converged on Orléans but were forced back. One of the rioters was summarily tried and hanged on the Place du Martroi as troops restored order. Near Saint-Étienne hardware artisans went to Furet-la-Valette and destroyed an establishment using new machines to produce hardware such as cutlery in large quantities.[9]

In Paris itself, popular anxiety and suspicion focused on why the abundant harvests of July had not resulted in lower prices, but here there was a sharp political edge to the anger. Louis XVI had not yet pronounced on the August Decree and the Declaration. Claims multiplied of open contempt for the Revolution on the part of aristocrats: for example, after a banquet at Versailles on 1 October for the officers of new troops, newspapers reported that the new national cockade had been besmirched by drunken noble officers. For the second time, the *menu peuple* of Paris intervened to safeguard a revolution they assumed to be theirs. This time, however, it was particularly the women of the markets: in the words of the observant bookseller Hardy, 'these women said loudly that the men didn't know what it was all about and that they wanted to have a hand in things'.[10] On 5 October up to twenty thousand women marched to Versailles; among their spontaneous leaders were Stanislas Maillard, a *vainqueur* of 14 July, and a woman from Luxembourg, Anne-Josephe Terwagne, who would become known as Théroigne de Méricourt. They were belatedly followed by the National Guard commanded by Lafayette.

On the morning of 5 October the Comte de Saint-Priest, effectively Louis' minister for Paris, tried to inform the king of the march on Versailles, but Louis had already left to go shooting (rather than hunting; this was his concession to political tensions, since he would be easier to contact if not in full hunt). Louis' diary for that day records that he 'shot at the Porte de Châtillon. Killed 81 head. Interrupted by events.' He was back at Versailles by three in the afternoon. It was the last time he would have freedom to choose between hunting and shooting.[11]

Once at Versailles the women invaded the Assembly. A deputation of them was then presented to the king, who promptly agreed to sanction the decrees. The king kept going to the balcony at Versailles with the intention of appeasing the crowd but was too overwrought to be able to say anything. He may have recalled a similar incident when new to the throne in 1775, when he had authorized sweeping repression. It soon became apparent this time, in contrast, that the women would be satisfied only if the royal family returned to Paris; on 6 October it did so, the Assembly in its wake. The road to the city took the crowd and its king seven hours. Paris was now to be the centre of the Revolution and the capital of the nation.[12]

This was a decisive moment in the Revolution of 1789. The National Assembly owed its existence and success once again to the armed intervention of the people of Paris. Some of the women claimed to have brought with them the royal family as 'the baker and his wife, and the baker's apprentice', making explicit the ancient assumption of royal responsibility to God for the provision of food. The mayor of Paris, Jean-Sylvain Bailly, recalled that, when the women returned to Paris on 6 October, they were singing 'vulgar ditties which apparently showed little respect for the Queen'. Marie-Antoinette was profoundly unpopular because of the Diamond Necklace Affair, her extravagant expenditure, and her allegedly scandalous private life.[13]

Convinced now that the Revolution was complete and secure, and determined that never again would the common people of Paris exercise such power, the Assembly ordered an inquiry into the 'crimes' of 5–6 October, and gave authorities the power to declare martial law. One of those interviewed was Madelaine Glain, a forty-two-year-old cleaner, who was open about the link assumed between assent to the decrees, the supply of bread, and Louis' presence in Paris:

> ... she went with the other women to the hall of the National Assembly, where they entered in great numbers; that some of these women having demanded 4 pound bread for 8 sols, and meat for the same price, the witness ... came back with Mr Maillard and two other women to the Paris town hall, bringing the decrees that were given to them in the National Assembly.[14]

Most of the deputies were delighted that the hold of the court over Louis had been ruptured, but their anxiety about their vulnerability to popular unrest was expressed in the proclamation of temporary martial law on 21 October. The same day a labourer from the Bastille district was hanged for inciting 'sedition'.[15]

Members of the former privileged elite were horrified by another manifestation of rebellion, the collapse of deference from their social inferiors. For this they blamed the Jacobin Club, founded by radical Breton deputies as the Society of the Friends of the Constitution in late 1789, and soon known by the Parisian name given to the Dominican order from whom it rented a monastery for its meetings.[16] The court painter Élisabeth Vigée-Lebrun decided to leave France for Rome with her daughter at the time of the October Days. In their coach, she recalled:

> there also sat a mad Jacobin from Grenoble, about fifty years old, with an ugly, bilious complexion, who each time we stopped at an inn for dinner or supper made violent speeches of the most fearful kind. At all of the towns a crowd of people stopped the coach to learn the news from Paris. Our Jacobin would then exclaim: 'Everything is going well, children! We have the baker and his wife safe in Paris. A constitution will be drawn up, they will be forced to accept it, and then it will be all over.' There were plenty of ninnies and fatheads who believed this man as if he had been an oracle.[17]

The key decrees now sanctioned, and the court party in disarray, the Revolution's triumph seemed assured. Elsewhere in Europe and across the Atlantic, most people were excited by the dramatic events of France's revolutionary summer. The Declaration of the Rights of Man and Citizen appeared in translation in the *Saint Petersburg Gazette* and the *Magyar Kurir* in Budapest. Elsewhere the news revivified hopes of the Dutch 'Patriots' crushed by the Prussian army in 1787 and of Belgians seeking independence from Austria.[18] Among the crowned heads of Europe, only Catherine the Great of Russia and the kings of Sweden and Spain were hostile from the outset; others took pleasure from the temporary incapacity of France in international power politics. Everywhere, ordinary people responded to the news from France as a promise of humanity's future of peace and freedom. While Edmund Burke in England was dismayed by the alacrity with which custom and tradition were abandoned, and others were sceptical about the decision not to follow the English model of a House of Lords, most welcomed the Revolution as producing a new, more democratic example of the reformist spirit. Poets such as Wordsworth, Burns, Coleridge, Southey and Blake joined with musicians, writers and poets on the continent (among them Beethoven, Goethe, Fichte, Hegel, Hölderlin, Kant and Herder) in celebrating a revolution seen as a high point in the history of humanity.

Revolutionaries were mindful of their intellectual and military heritage. Lafayette sent one of the keys of the Bastille to George Washington as 'a tribute which I owe as a son to my adoptive father, as an aide-de-camp to my general, and as a missionary of liberty to its patriarch'. In turn, Washington, who had been elected six months earlier as the first President of the United States, wrote to his envoy in France, Gouverneur Morris, on 13 October: 'the revolution which has been effected in France is of so wonderful a nature, that the mind can hardly recognize the fact. If it ends as ... [I] predict, that nation will be the most powerful and happy in Europe.'[19] Morris was less enthusiastic.

Louis made apparently sincere efforts to behave like a constitutional monarch, for example, making an impromptu visit to congratulate the Assembly on its work on 4 February 1790. There his supporters argued successfully for the continued opulence of the court. 'Do you not wish that your king be the most magnificent of kings, as you are the greatest of nations?', asked the Committee on Finances in June. The Assembly accepted Louis' request for a 'civil list' of twenty-five million *livres*, with another four million for Marie-Antoinette, but the scale of the king's civil list and the size and luxury of the royal household would become symbolic of the jarring incompatibility of the old and new. A request to make the royal palaces at Versailles, Fontainebleau, Saint-Cloud, Rambouillet and elsewhere his personal property was never granted.[20] Louis' reluctant consent to revolutionary change was only thinly explained by the fiction that his obstinacy was solely due to the malign influence of his court.

Jostling with the potent sense of euphoria and unity in the autumn and winter of 1789 was the realization of how revolution had been achieved and of the magnitude of what remained to be done. While the Declaration proclaimed the universality of rights and the civic equality of all citizens, it was ambiguous about the meaning of political and social equality. With the Assembly's prevarication on the full abolition of seigneurial dues, these ambiguities and silences were to underpin ongoing uncertainty and confrontation in town and country. Most important of all, the revolutionaries' declaration of the principles of the new regime presupposed that every aspect of public life would be reshaped. To that enormous task they now turned.

The impulse to 'regenerate' the kingdom was personified by Bertrand Barère, one of the deputies from the Gascon-speaking Bigorre region of the western Pyrenees. Barère was a successful lawyer in the Parlement of Toulouse; indeed, he liked to call himself Barère de Vieuzac after a small fief his family owned south of Lourdes. Like so many professional men across the country, however, he saw the mass of exemptions, privileges and local practices of his ancient province as remnants of a moribund feudal order rather than as living survivals of a unique past. Indeed, when the National Assembly turned its attention to reforming the ancient map of provinces, each with their distinctive 'rights', Barère insisted on the need 'to efface all traces of history, all prejudices resulting from communities of interest or origins. Everything in France must be new and must date from today.'[21] So in 1789–90, Bigorre lost its ancient meeting of Estates, which had decided on levels of taxation, and became an administrative area called Hautes-Pyrénées after its high mountains, and uniform in every way with eighty-two other departments (Map 3).

Most of the men of the Constituent or National Assembly shared Barère's desire to 'regenerate' the kingdom by a sweeping overhaul of every aspect of public life. For two years until September 1791, the 1,200 members of the clergy, nobility and commons who had previously convened for the Estates-General in May 1789, minus those deputies from the privileged orders who had gone home in disgust, threw themselves into the task with extraordinary energy on the Assembly's thirty-one committees. Their work was facilitated by abundant harvests in 1789 and 1790, and above all by a deep reservoir of popular goodwill.[22]

The remaking of France was based on a belief in the common identity of French citizens whatever their social or geographic origin. This was a fundamental change in the relationship between the state, its provinces and the citizenry. In every aspect of public life—administration, the judiciary, the armed forces, the Church, policing—traditions of corporate rights, appointment and hierarchy now gave way to civil equality, accountability and elections within uniform national structures. The institutional structure of the *ancien régime* had been characterized by the recognition of extraordinary provincial diversity controlled by a network of royal appointees. Now this was reversed: at every level officials were to be elected, but the institutions in which they worked were everywhere to be the same.

The 44,000 new 'communes', based on the parishes of the *ancien régime*, were to be the bedrock of an administrative hierarchy of cantons, districts and departments. The eighty-three departments announced in February 1790 were designed to facilitate the accessibility of administration, for each capital was to be no more than a day's ride from any commune. The creation of this new map of France was designed to give reality to two of the keywords of the 'patriots' in the National Assembly: to 'regenerate' the nation while cementing its 'unity'. There was usually a valid geographic rationale to each department; but they also represented a victory of the new state over the resurgent provincial identities expressed since 1787. Their very names, drawn from rivers, mountains and other natural features, undercut claims to other provincial and ethnic loyalties: so the Basque country would be 'Basses-Pyrénées', not the 'Pays Basque'; there would not be any institutional recognition of regions such as Artois, Brittany or Languedoc.

Article 11 of the August Decree had abolished all provincial exemptions and privileges in the name of a commonality of rights, obligations and institutions across the new kingdom. The article ended the treaty of 1532 between the Duchy of Brittany and France, for example, and with it special arrangements for fiscal and judicial autonomy. Brittany's fiscal privileges—Necker had estimated that Bretons paid 12 *livres* 10 *sous* per head in taxes, against Languedoc's 22 *livres* 15 *sous* and about 64 *livres* in the Île-de-France—would now disappear. The consequences for Brittany of the vision of a kingdom of French subjects equal in rights and responsibilities were not lost on the Breton deputies, even those hitherto in the vanguard of change. They would find an ally in the staunchly counter-revolutionary Abbé Maury, who argued in November that the National Assembly had no right to abrogate a formal treaty without the consent of Brittany itself.[23]

Provincial capitals bore the brunt of institutional change. In Toulouse the Parlement aristocracy made up 5 per cent of the population of 60,000 but controlled 44 per cent of the city's wealth, employing a mass of clerks, servants and artisans. Now Toulouse would be reduced to a departmental capital from its proud history as capital of the vast region of Languedoc.[24] Such was the rivalry between towns that had benefited from the complex, diffused institutional structures of the *ancien régime* that occasionally a compromise had to be reached: so Laon had seen off the campaign of its rival Soissons to be the capital of the new department of Aisne, thereby keeping its administrative and judicial functions, but at the price of losing the bishopric to its rival.[25] Yet such a compromise was rare.

The department capitals were to administer laws, elections, the collection of taxes and every other public function in precisely the same way. But revolutionary legislation from Paris was often interpreted and adapted to local needs. In this process, the million or more men who were elected to local government, the judiciary, National Guard and administrative positions played the key role in the gulf that existed between the Assembly's national programme and the exigencies of the local situation. Where particular legislation was unpopular, especially that concerning tax collection and the redemption of seigneurial dues, the commitment of these officials to the law could also earn them isolation and contempt. Often they had to deal with chaotic situations as the poorest peasants refused to pay taxes, felled trees, or cleared common land in the hope of appropriating a small plot.

The abolition of seigneurs' hunting monopolies in the August 1789 decree unleashed a massacre of wildlife. As the English agronomist Arthur Young travelled between Avignon and Aix, he recorded that 'I have been pestered with all the mob of the country shooting; one would think that every rusty gun in Provence is at work, killing all sorts of birds; the shot has fallen five or six times in my chaise and about my ears.'[26] In his diary, the schoolteacher of Silly-en-Multien, north of Paris, detailed with glee the unchecked killing of the Prince de Conti's game and the delight of his fellow villagers that they could hunt as they wished, 'just as the Prince used to'. Well into winter the teacher was recording that 'hunting is still going on; we're hunting everywhere'. Fish were sought after, too. The elderly and acerbic Marquise de Créquy was caustic about the damage done to one of her ponds on her estate in the Gâtinais near Orléans. On the pretext that the Assembly had abolished the hunting privileges of the nobility and the feudal rights of the Church, instead of buying her fish 'four or five bands of people from roundabout, led by their mayors in their tricolour sashes' forced her guards to take refuge and 'everyone helped themselves to our fine fish and carted off what they could. It had been sixty years since this pond had been drained. . . . All of them went off gaily, shouting . . . "Vive la nation! Vive Necker! Vive l'Assemblée nationale!"'[27]

The sweeping changes legislated in 1789, and the gulf in understanding them that existed between legislators and rural people, highlighted the necessity of rapid, uniform communication as never before. In pre-revolutionary France the dominant concerns of royal authorities had been record-keeping and policing in the interests of ensuring that peasants paid their taxes, fulfilled their obligations and obeyed the law. All these constraints were filtered through a maze of local practices and laws. Now the new citizens were the focus of a revolutionary agenda aimed at reforming an entire institutional system on the basis of uniformity and rights. On 21 November 1789 the deputy Rabaut Saint-Étienne reported that many villages in his home region around Nîmes had still not received the crucial August Decree on feudalism: little wonder that peasants were imagining its content as they wished. The postal service in particular became of crucial importance.[28]

The decrees despatched from the National Assembly soon became voluminous and impenetrable. The Abbé Grégoire's inquiry of 1790 was sobering for legislators. Only fifteen departments, with three million people, were identified as purely French speaking. In the Gascon-speaking department of Lot-et-Garonne in the south-west, for example, priests complained of peasants falling asleep during the reading of decrees from the Assembly, 'because they do not understand a word, even though the decrees are read in a loud and clear voice and are explained'. In consequence, successive assemblies encouraged the translation of decrees into local languages.[29]

The overarching aim of the National Assembly was the formulation of France's first written constitution, and it would be September 1791 before the complexities of constitutional monarchy could be settled. In the meantime, the Assembly had to address the urgent necessity of fundamental reform in several areas: fiscal reform to implement the Assembly's commitment to the principle of uniform, proportional taxation; administrative reform to establish the practice of popular sovereignty within reformed institutional structures; reforms to the justice system; religious freedoms; and measures to resolve the ambiguities concerning feudalism within the August legislation.

The first problem was fiscal. The Assembly had inherited the monarchy's bankruptcy, further aggravated by popular refusal to pay taxes, and by its own measures to abolish the *gabelle* and unpopular indirect taxes on leather, iron, soap and oils, and finally wine. Revenue from indirect taxes fell from 52 million *livres* in 1788 to less than 14 million in 1790. The Assembly took several measures to meet this crisis. Across the country, people responded to calls for 'patriotic contributions' or donations, to be paid in three instalments amounting to 25 per cent of direct taxes, in the April of 1790, 1791 and 1792. For example, in the eastern town of Nancy one part of the parish of Saint-Pierre was thereby levied 1,492 *livres* in sums of 673, 413 and 406. As elsewhere, the outcome was more modest: only 618 *livres* were finally paid, in instalments of 380, 122 and 116.[30]

Most importantly, prominent commoner deputies had begun to identify church property as offering a solution. On 10 October, just four days after the Assembly had shifted its meetings from Versailles to the Manège riding-school in the gardens of the Tuileries Palace in Paris, Talleyrand, the Bishop of Autun, proposed that church property be nationalized and sold as a way of dealing with the national debt and underwriting better salaries for parish clergy. The upper clergy were outraged by what they saw as an act of betrayal by one of their own. But Talleyrand had caught the mood of the commoner deputies and on 2 November church property was 'placed at the disposal of the nation' by 510 votes to 346. Royal property was also made 'national'. The predominance of clerical deputies among the opposition indicated just how rapidly they had become disenchanted with change. The wording of the motion was deliberately vague, but the majority soon made it plain that it meant sale by auction.[31]

Church property, 6–10 per cent of the wealth of the kingdom, was mostly of prime quality, and was sold in large lots by auction. In all, there were up to 700,000 purchasers: at least one family in eight bought some land, but it was purchased mainly by urban and rural bourgeois—and many nobles.[32] The greatest densities of church land sales by area and value were in the richest agricultural zone: the north-east, the Paris basin, Alsace and Mediterranean Languedoc. The property of the abbey of Fontfroide in the district of Narbonne alone was valued at 805,000 *livres* (one-fifth in seigneurial rights), including huge estates (and 119 beehives) at Bizanet, Boutenac and Ornaisons.[33] Similarly, in the district of Grasse, in Provence, where about 7 per cent of land changed hands, it was local bourgeois who dominated the auctions. Three-quarters of the property sold was bought by one-quarter of the buyers; 28 of the 39 largest purchasers were merchants from Grasse itself.[34] In the north-east around Laon, eighty-five groups of up to one hundred people formed 'associations' to buy up property. Nevertheless, here too the sales were dominated by the wealthier land-owners, tenant-farmers and grain merchants.[35] The value of sales exceeded pre-sale estimates of the worth of church land and buildings, but the eager purchasers were often the object of recrimination, whether as rich 'outsiders' expanding their wealth or as those who were 'stealing' the kitchen gardens once used by parish priests.

On the basis of the anticipated sales of 400 million *livres* worth of 'national lands', and the patriotic contributions, the Assembly decided in December 1789 to issue paper certificates or bonds (*assignats*) to that value in 1,000-*livre* notes, carrying 5 per cent interest (Fig. 9). They were supposed to be withdrawn and destroyed as cash from land sales was received, but the collapse of tax revenue and the huge sums necessary to compensate former office-holders for redundant positions in the new institutional structure led the Assembly to treat *assignats* as paper money and to print far more in lower denominations. By September 1790 there were 1,200 million *livres* worth in circulation. The *assignats* were crucial in meeting pressing financial needs for the Assembly, but the mounting reliance on printing paper money would mean that the trade-off with inflation would become increasingly unbalanced. Use of the money also became a litmus test for confidence in the Revolution, as farmers in particular were unwilling to accept *assignats* for their produce.[36]

A new and universal taxation system took far longer to implement. On 25 September 1789 the Assembly had decreed that the nobility, clergy, and others who so far had had fiscal immunity would now have to pay a proportionate share of direct taxes, backdated to cover the second half of 1789. The difficulties of completing new tax registers and assessments for every community were time-consuming, however, and resulted in the Assembly having to continue the *ancien régime* tax system for 1790, including the tithe. However, the August Decree was interpreted by communities across France as meaning that there seemed little reason to pay taxes or tithes in the meantime. Communes objected to paying the tithe at all, and brought in crops without waiting for the tithe-collector. Finally a new system of taxation, based on the estimated value of and income from property, was introduced from the beginning of 1791. The new taxes were considerably higher than under the *ancien régime* and, for tenant-farmers, were often added to rents. In Brittany, the Revolution substantially increased the burden of taxation without meeting tenant-farmers' demands for greater security of tenure. For most peasants, however, the 15–20 per cent increase in state taxes was more than offset by the ending of tithes and, ultimately, of seigneurial dues.

The second pressing question was the concrete meaning to be given to 'popular sovereignty'. The Declaration had defined this as the right of 'all citizens or their representatives' to participate in the formulation of the laws, but where was the line of direct participation to be drawn? Ultimately, the Assembly excluded all women and about two-fifths of adult men, those too poor to pay taxes to the value of three days' labour. Both were deemed to be too 'dependent' to exercise an individual choice, and would be 'passive' rather than 'active' citizens. Elections to the next parlement would also be indirect: that is, voters would choose electors who in turn would choose deputies from about fifty thousand men who paid the 'silver mark' (fifty-four days' worth of labour) in property taxes. In his newspaper the *Révolutions de France et de Brabant*, Camille Desmoulins denounced the new 'aristocratic system': 'But what is this much repeated word *active citizen* supposed to mean? The active citizens are the ones who took the Bastille.'[37]

The Assembly had made a crucial compromise in its definition of formal citizenship rights.

On 14 December 1789 a law on municipal government extended Calonne's 1787 reforms so that mayors, municipal officers and 'notables' (councillors) were directly elected by 'active' citizens. For the first time, seigneurs no longer had the right of appointment: mayors would be the people's choice. Participation rates in the municipal elections of January 1790 were often very high. In Orléans, a city of almost 45,000 inhabitants, 1,778 of the 2,050 eligible voters (almost 90 per cent) elected the new council. The voter turnout at local elections was rarely so high in small communities and neighbourhoods where it was well known who would win because choices had already been made in public, in the marketplace, in taverns or after church.[38]

The municipal law placed a huge burden of responsibility on villagers; they were now responsible for apportioning and collecting direct taxes, carrying out public works, supporting the poor, providing for the material needs of churches and schools, and maintaining law and order. In very small communities these were awesome, even impossible, responsibilities. In the west, where priests and their vestries had governed their communities, the local government law created a puzzling separation of municipality and vestry, and excluded many men and all women used to discussing parish matters after mass. Few communes had the resources of Paris, where textile workshops were set up in 1790 for people without means, in eleven former convents. Those assisted worked twelve-hour days and were given two bowls of soup as well as payment by piece.[39]

The principle of popular sovereignty also applied in the citizens' National Guard, where as many as 500,000 volunteers elected their officers. However, while officer positions in the armed forces were now opened to non-nobles, the Assembly stopped short of applying popular sovereignty to their election. Could troops be trusted to elect the best rather than the most likeable officers?

Third, the complex set of royal, aristocratic and clerical courts and their regional variations was replaced by a uniform, national judicial system deliberately made more accessible and egalitarian. Liberal reform to punishments was spearheaded by the prominent and wealthy noble Louis-Michel Lepeletier, a lawyer in the former Parlement of Paris, who pushed for consistent, proportionalte and humane sentencing. In particular, the introduction of elected justices of the peace in every canton was immensely popular for its provision of cheap and accessible justice for rural communities formerly subject to the vagaries and costs of the seigneur's court.[40]

The abrupt shift in the ultimate source of judicial authority—from the king to the nation—was also to be expressed in the design of courtrooms themselves. Two deputies who had been eminent lawyers in the *ancien régime parlements*, Jacques Guillaume Thouret and Guy-Jean Target, were instrumental in composing a circular of 22 January 1791 to the 547 new district tribunals explaining how they should arrange their courtrooms. Rather than the *ancien régime* diamond-shaped courtroom with the king or his representative at the corner apex, the new space was to be circular, with one small semicircle for the elected judges opposite two other semicircles for the parties involved. In Thouret's words, these were to be 'a simple composition without showiness. This befits the character of the gentle, pacific functions of civil justice. But they are imbued with the majesty of the constitution from which they arise and the majesty of the law they serve.'[41]

For centuries executions had been public, protracted and spectacular, designed to awe observers into obedience. Reformers had long campaigned for fewer and simpler deaths, both because of their horror at the outrages committed on the human body and because the behaviour of crowds suggested that the public enjoyed (and were thus perverted by) such spectacles. Subsequent to brilliant debates on capital punishment in May 1791, when the Assembly decided not to abolish it entirely, a new criminal code was enacted on 6 October. The number of capital offences was dramatically reduced, and *ancien régime* 'crimes' such as sodomy were decriminalized by being passed over in silence.[42] Joseph-Ignace Guillotin, a Parisian physician and deputy, proposed changes to criminal trials that would overturn centuries of differential punishment: 'The same crimes will be punished by the same penalty, regardless of the rank and estate of the guilty party. . . . The criminal will have his head severed.' Guillotin's reform appealed because it would execute in a way that was public and awe-inspiring on the one hand but rapid on the other. Executions would be as quick and humane as possible, but would be performed on the principal public square of each town.[43]

The guillotine would not be used for the first time until 25 April 1792, to execute Nicolas-Jacques Pelletier, who had been convicted of the violent theft of 800 *livres* in *assignats* in October 1791. While officials in Paris were delighted that the execution was over 'in the blink of an eye', and orders were received to construct a machine for each of the eighty-three departments, the speed of the execution seems to have disappointed those in the crowd used to spectacular and protracted suffering. The *Courrier extraordinaire* reported that they were startled by the sight of Pelletier in his red shirt, then disappointed by the lack of spectacle:

> The people seemed to call for M. Sanson [the executioner] to return to the *ancien régime*, and said to him:
>
> Give me back my wooden gallows,
>
> Give me back my gallows.[44]

The fourth area requiring immediate reform of 'abuses' was religious freedom. The Declaration of the Rights of Man and Citizen had already held out the promise that henceforth all citizens would share equal rights to freedom of conscience and the external practice of their faith. By the end of 1789 full citizenship had been granted to France's 400,000 Protestants and, by January 1790, to the Sephardi Jews of Bordeaux and Avignon (but only by 374 votes to 280). The situation of Ashkenazi Jews in the east was different, despite the longevity of their communities. There were anti-Semitic complaints in some local *cahiers* in the region, and the Bishop of Nancy opposed their emancipation with the same vehemence with which he opposed mooted changes to the Catholic Church.[45] Some deputies from Alsace, such as Jean-François Reubell from Colmar, expressed open anti-Semitism at the same time as he campaigned for the rights of 'people of colour'. This prompted a spirited rejoinder from eastern Jews in January 1790:

> France must, for justice and interest, grant them the rights of citizenship, in that their home is in this empire, that they live there as subjects, that they serve their fatherland through all the means that are in their power, that they contribute to the maintenance of the public force like all the other citizens of the kingdom, independently of the onerous, degrading, arbitrary taxes that ancient injustices, ancient prejudices, supported by the old regime, accumulated on their head: they say, there can only be two classes of men in a State; citizens and foreigners; to prove that we are not foreigners is to prove that we are citizens.[46]

At Metz in the north-east Abraham Goudchaux Spire, the son of the rabbi, produced a newspaper, just a few pages, written in Hebraic script in German in 1789–90. It was essentially a pro-revolutionary catalogue of events, but he expressed his dismay that the deserved recognition of the rights of Sephardi Jews in the south in November 1789 was not extended to those of the east. Some of the inhabitants of Alsace and Lorraine, he regretted, 'are looking for any means to damage the holy people, to proscribe them without pity. We have to place our trust in reason and the passage of time to terminate such odious opinions which outrage humanity.' His hope in 'divine providence' would only be realized in September 1791, when the eastern Jews were granted full civic equality.[47]

A final area of urgent need concerned seigneurialism. From the outset of the Revolution, the National Assembly had been caught between the radical demands of peasants determined not to pay further seigneurial dues and the insistence of seigneurs that they be compensated for their losses. The feudal legislation of 4–11 August 1789 was fraught with ambiguities concerning the extent to which seigneurialism had been abolished. But peasants only accepted without question the opening phrase of the August Decree, that 'the National Assembly completely destroys the feudal regime'.

Disappointment that the National Assembly's putative abolition of feudalism would not reform the rental system of *domaine congéable* caused a surge of peasant protest in Upper Brittany in January 1790. Already in October 1789 the *recteur* of the parish of Coëtbugat in the diocese of Vannes had warned the National Assembly of 'the murmurings of discontent in our countryside'. 'Our peasants are coarse,' he added, 'but sensitive as well.'[48] During the four months after December 1789 peasants from 330 parishes in the triangle between Montauban, Rodez and Périgueux in the south-west invaded over one hundred châteaux to protest against the requisite payment of harvest dues, among the highest in France. These 'wild federations' appeared spontaneously during the winter as bands of villagers armed themselves after church and went to neighbouring villages to join in the destruction of weathercocks and other symbols of the *ancien régime* before lighting a bonfire with pews from the church and erecting and dancing around a maypole ('mai'). Often the pole would be decorated with slogans that would have seemed contradictory to the Assembly, such as 'Long live the Nation, the Law, the King' and 'Woe to he who pays his rent!' A peasant from Allassac added: 'We don't need bourgeois or gentlemen any more.'[49] Here, as in all revolutions, popular ideologies fused ancient resentments with new assumptions about power and rights. From near Cahors, the farmer Michel Célarié described how,

on 26 January 1790, we the inhabitants of Bégoux, Peyrat and Cavaniès,
made a revolution against M. Calméjanne, the seigneur of Cavaniès . . . .
In the end, it was marvellous to see in the courtyards of all sorts of
property-owners the poles planted by their vassals and all the weathercocks pulled down. The people of Quercy did not invent these revolutions. . . . The town of Paris set the example for the rest of the kingdom
and it sped from village to village, from town to town, just like a fire
catching from one branch to the next.[50]

Similar protests, whether by violent action or non-compliance, occurred in
most parts of the countryside, often through spontaneous celebrations around
improvised 'liberty trees'.[51] Faced with open challenges in rural areas to the
lack of finality in the 1789 decree on feudalism, the Assembly acted in March
1790 to clarify what had been abolished (unpaid labour for seigneurs, and
seigneurial *triage* rights over commons, control over communal ovens and
the pressing of grapes and olives), and the compensation that would need to
be paid to redeem dues payable on harvests. The compensation was set in
May at twenty times the annual total if paid in cash or twenty-five times if
in kind. Villagers from Thuellin east of Lyon complained to the Committee
on Feudalism that 'not only is redemption impossible for poor landowners,
but it would be so disadvantageous that even the better-off would not undertake it'. Villagers elsewhere did not bother to express similar feelings except
by refusal to pay, for the costs of contesting the former seigneurs' legal rights
were prohibitive. In any case, courts required only the evidence drawn from
'the statutes, customs and rules observed up until the present'. In other words,
the burden of proof rested with those who paid.[52]

Despite such frustrations, the impulse for 'regeneration' was expressed
in a mission of extraordinary boldness. Not only were French people to
be citizens rather than subjects, but their relationship to all the markers of
identity was to be transformed. The ancient patchwork of provincial institutions, practices and privileges was to be cast aside for a new cloth of unity
and uniformity. The overlay of public institutions—from laws and taxes
to administration and public order—was radically refashioned from the
ground up. The traditional markers of institutional space, from parishes to
provinces, were swept aside; citizens now inhabited communes within
districts and departments. The intricacies of local exemptions and practices,
the prerogatives of privileged corporations, towns and occupations were to
be replaced by simple, uniform and rational structures.

The Assembly removed internal customs houses and controls on the grain trade, in the interests of encouraging a national market and stimulating economic initiative. From May 1790, eminent philosophers and scientists, including the Marquis de Condorcet, Pierre-Simon Laplace, Adrien-Marie Legendre and Antoine Lavoisier were appointed to a Commission of Weights and Measures to investigate a new, rational, metric system of weights and measures, in Condorcet's words, 'for all people for all time'. Initially, Thomas Jefferson was also involved, but United States participation failed to receive the backing of Congress. The Commission's report in March 1791 advocated detailed work on a decimal system for distance and volume, and the Academy of Sciences was requested to design and implement it.[53]

Not surprisingly, those whose identity had been wedded to the markers and practices of the past were outraged by change. Men who had made careers within the outmoded structures—such as the lawyers and their clerks—fretted about their futures. Others were appalled at the repudiation of history and custom: 'They renamed my province after a stream,' sniffed the nonagenarian Marquise de Créquy from her estate near Orléans, now in the department of Loiret.[54]

As the outlines of the new France took shape, thoughts turned to commemorating its triumphs. It was not until June 1790 that the besiegers of the Bastille were formally honoured. While the National Assembly went about its work of reconstruction, Pierre-François (now nicknamed 'Patriot') Palloy oversaw a massive work of destruction of the fortress.[55] While most of the work to demolish the Bastille was completed by the end of the year, it would finally take one thousand workers two years, a task plagued by accidents, conflict and unhappy neighbours. At the same time it became a place of revolutionary pilgrimage, with guided tours, official balls and improvised celebration. Palloy himself was the great beneficiary, making a fortune from organizing guided tours and selling off the stonework as carved statuettes and medals. Each of the eighty-three departments received a free carving of the Bastille made from one of its foundation stones.

Increasing awareness that large numbers of fellow citizens, particularly among the old elites, did not share the same revolutionary elan as patriots, sparked gatherings of growing numbers of supporters of the Revolution, led by National Guards, in a 'federation movement'. From humble beginnings along the Loire valley in 1789, this movement spread across the nation. In May 1790 about 3,500 delegates from well over one hundred nearby towns and villages assembled on 9 May south of Orléans to take oaths. As they returned to the city, municipal officers had to rescue a noble who had refused to respond to requests to shout 'Vive Le Roi! Vive la Nation!', and had to imprison him for his own safety as crowds sought to seize and hang him.[56] The gathering at Lille on 6 June was attended by about 100,000 people, with its mayor overjoyed at 'a population of friends' animated by 'reciprocal joy'.[57] On 13 June about 75,000 patriots converged on Strasbourg, on the newly designated Champ de la Confédération, to pledge support for the new constitution. Here the protracted festivities were held with one eye across the Rhine, where German princes and French *émigrés* were muttering menacingly about military intervention.

These movements were deeply emotional responses to anxiety about the possibility of harmonious change. Their ceremonies were often religious and marked by the presence of clergy, as at Bordeaux, where a huge ceremony linking the city with Toulouse reminded the officiating priest of 'the unity and fraternity' preached by Christ. The 'federations' culminated in the formalities of 14 July 1790, when as many as 44,000 delegates from the provinces would attend the great Festival of Federation to commemorate the taking of the Bastille a year earlier. The festival was held in the rain on the Champ de Mars, which had been levelled by voluntary labour. Louis XVI, Talleyrand (former Bishop of Autun) and Lafayette proclaimed the new order in front of 300,000 Parisians (Fig. 10). The king took an oath 'to use the power given to me by the constitutional law of the State, to maintain the Constitution as decided by the National Assembly and accepted by myself, and to enforce the laws'.[58] It was a solemn oath that would haunt the rest of his days.

Never again would there be such a resolutely peaceful, spontaneous surge of solidarity: the Revolution was at its pinnacle. Popular songs celebrated the new era of peace and harmony:

> On this place where I am dancing,
> You used to hear nothing but grievances,
> People feared this king whom I love;
> Oh, love is worth more than fear,
> We all will create sweet concerts
> Where once people were in chains.[59]

On the eve of 14 July 1790 in Paris 2,000 people, including the deputies, shared a 'patriotic meal' at the Palais Royal; after another huge public banquet, 5,000 poor were allowed in to eat the leftovers.[60]

This ceremony occurred all over France, the most dramatic, unified example of the use of festivals as an element of revolutionary political culture. On 14 July the peals of celebration from church steeples in villages and towns were deafening.[61] Liberty trees were planted everywhere: just one may still be standing, in distant Tamniès, north of Sarlat (Figs 11 and 12). In a society rich in religious rituals and displays of royal splendour, ceremonies celebrating revolutionary unity drew on the old for style if not for substance or imagery. The colliers of Montminot adapted a traditional festival by swearing on 'the axe always raised in order to defend, at the risk of their lives, the finest edifice that ever was, the French Constitution'. In Laon the festival was a joyful occasion, capped by the wedding at the altar of the homeland of a 'poor and virtuous girl' to a soldier in the National Guard. The altar thus received 'the double vow of conjugal union of these happy spouses, and the fraternal union of all citizens'.[62] At Beaufort-en-Vallée, in the Loire valley in western France, eighty-three women slipped away during the festivities and returned costumed as the new departments. For fashion-conscious, well-to-do women the Parisian *Journal de la mode et du goût* was full of recommended dresses for the new age, self-consciously simpler, often in the colours of the tricolour, and with patriotic motifs such as patterns of tiny liberty caps.[63]

CHAPTER SIX

THE REVOLUTION
TRIUMPHANT, 1790

THE DECLARATION OF THE RIGHTS OF MAN AND CITIZEN WAS universalist in its claims, but 'patriots' were well aware that they were standing on the shoulders of great predecessors. On learning of Benjamin Franklin's death in April 1790, the National Assembly declared three days of mourning. The loss was widely felt. Augustin and Charlotte Robespierre wrote from Arras to their brother Maximilien in Paris that they had donned mourning clothes.[1] The same month the Assembly welcomed the Corsican Pasquale Paoli, a living symbol of liberty and self-government. From 1755 until its conquest by the armies of Louis XV in 1768, Corsica had had a popularly elected constitutional republic, albeit under Paoli's tutelage. He had since lived in exile in England. The National Assembly had passed a decree incorporating Corsica into the new France in November 1789, but now granted amnesty to exiles, and Paoli embarked immediately for his native island.[2]

The celebrations on 14 July 1790 for the first anniversary of the seizure of the Bastille marked a high point of cosmopolitanism as well as patriotism. On 19 June the Prussian noble Jean-Baptiste du Val-de-Grâce, the Baron de Cloots, had led thirty-six foreigners to the bar of the National Assembly: the minutes of the Assembly noted the presence of 'Arabs, Chaldeans, Prussians, Poles, English, Swiss, Germans, Dutchmen, Swedes, Italians, Spaniards, Americans, Syrians, Indians, Brabançons, Liégois, Avignonnais, Genevans, etc.' The delegation of 'foreign nations resident in Paris' asked for the right to participate on 14 July. Even though their request was attacked by royalist deputies, the general response to the delegation was warm, with regret expressed for France's subjugation of foreign nations. To mark this high point of optimism about the future of humankind, the enthusiastic session concluded with the abolition of noble titles.[3] Titles such as Marquis, Comte, Baron and Chevalier were defunct and so too, it was assumed, were the nobility's claims to a culture of status, privilege and 'honour'.

The foreigners' request was granted and, on 14 July, Cloots, now a Jacobin enthusiast, was accorded a marquee for as many as one thousand foreigners. The English writer Helen Maria Williams, aged thirty-one, was there and enthused that 'it was the triumph of human kind; it was man asserting the noblest privileges of his nature; and it required but the common feelings of humanity to become in that moment a citizen of the world'.[4] Cloots would be dubbed 'the orator of the human race' and subsequently take the name 'Anarcharsis' from a popular 1788 novel about a descendant of the sixth-century BC Scythian philosopher.

Prominent Jacobins within the National Assembly took the lead in seeking other formal ways of marking what had been achieved. One of the prominent members of the Paris Club was Jacques-Louis David, who in September 1790 was commissioned to paint the collective portrait of the Third Estate deputies taking their oath on the Versailles tennis court on 20 June 1789. The commission was massive—72,000 *livres*—and the painting was to be commensurate: 23 by 33 feet. Aware of the rupture in the nature of government and administration in 1789, and cognizant of its importance, the National Assembly decided on 12 September 1790 to create the Archives Nationales, 'the repository of all the acts which establish the Constitution of the Kingdom, its public statutes, its laws, and their distribution to the departments'. It chose as its first archivist Armand Gaston Camus, a prominent Third Estate deputy and one of the Assembly's first presidents in 1789. Camus spoke more than anyone else in the Assembly—six hundred times in its two years—largely because of his deep knowledge of church law. One month later, in October 1790, the Assembly created the Commission on Monuments to conserve artistic objects among nationalized property.[5]

European responses to news from France were overwhelmingly optimistic, even euphoric. Before the Revolution, refugees had been accorded refuge or sanctuary by 'the king's Grace'. Now the universalism embedded in the Declaration generated a key transition to a generalized right of asylum. There were many political exiles in Paris only too eager to spread the revolutionary message into their own lands, particularly the thousands of Belgian, Dutch and Liégois refugees. The Swedish poet Johan Henrik Kellgren wrote to his brother: 'tell me, was there ever anything more sublime in History, even in Rome or Greece? I wept like a child, a man, at the story of this great victory.' In Russia, Count Stroganov enthused in similar terms that 'the best day of my life will be that when I see Russia regenerated by such a Revolution'. Even the Austrian emperor Leopold II wrote that 'infinite happiness will result from this everywhere, the end of injustice, wars, conflicts and arrests, and it will be one of the most useful fashions introduced by France into Europe'. That enthusiasm did not stop him the next year taking advantage of division and disorder in the new 'United States of Belgium', proclaimed on 10 January 1790, to invade and reimpose Austrian control by the end of the year.[6]

In Hamburg a wealthy merchant organized a meeting of tricolour-cockade-wearing enthusiasts who celebrated the first anniversary of the fall of the Bastille and heard the poet Friedrich Klopstock recite an ode:

> Had I a hundred voices, they would not suffice to sing
> The freedom of Gaul ...
> Alas, my Fatherland, it was not thou who scaled
> The peaks of Freedom and gave to all the peoples round
> The shining example! It was France.[7]

In Switzerland, while news of the Revolution electrified public debate in cities like Geneva, Fribourg and Basel, there was less resonance in the rural areas. One exception was in the French-speaking Bas-Valais—the lower valley of the Rhône at the eastern end of Lake Geneva. Here there were resentments against the tax regime and political dominance by the German-speaking Haut-Valais and the prince-bishop of Sion. In September 1790 the administrator of the Bas-Valais, Hildebrand Schiner, was forced to flee his château in the village of Monthey before it was pillaged. But by the end of the year order had been restored.[8]

News of the Declaration of the Rights of Man and Citizen and of the new constitutional and representative government provoked polarized responses in the colonies. When news of the Revolution reached Pondichéry, Chandernagore and other French trading posts (*comptoirs*) in India in February 1790, it legitimized the expression of grievances against royal officials. In Pondichéry mixed-race *topas*—often descended from unions of Portuguese with Indians—pushed successfully for recognition as French citizens on the grounds of their free, property-owning status alongside the more readily accepted *métis*, children of French fathers and Indian mothers.[9]

In Sénégal mixed-race traders in produce and slaves hoped for an end to the trade monopoly of the Compagnie des Indes. Planters in the Caribbean, too, initially saw in the promise of the Declaration the opportunity for free trade with other European empires rather than the menace of freedom for the slaves who made their wealth. They were mistaken. Skilled leaders such as Julien Raimond and Vincent Ogé, both wealthy slave-owners on Saint-Domingue, began arguing for full citizenship rights for both 'free men of colour' and mixed-race men like themselves, but not for the abolition of slavery.[10]

No French city was more dependent on the slave trade and its privileged trading relationship (*l'exclusif*) with Saint-Domingue than the Atlantic port of La Rochelle. Here the Revolution of 1789 was enthusiastically welcomed, especially by Protestants, who comprised only about 7 per cent of the city's 18,000 people but who dominated the economy. After 1789 they also moved into political power. Nine of the twelve men on the first municipal council of La Rochelle were merchants, and five of them were Protestants. The merchants constructed a Protestant church with remarkable speed, and gave material support to the new nation. Daniel Garesché, owner of six slave-ships (*négriers*), and mayor in 1791–92, gave 17,000 *livres* initially, then 50,000 more, as his 'contribution patriotique'.

The Rochelais merchants' support for the Revolution was as pragmatic as it was enthusiastic. They were able to reconcile their principles with their self-interest with seeming self-assurance. Their *cahier* of the Third Estate of La Rochelle in March 1789 was an eloquent plea for liberty and humanity: the use of the whip on slaves was condemned as contrary to humanity, as 'irreconcilable with the enlightenment and humanity which distinguish the French nation'. However, the slave trade itself was not mentioned, even though the merchants knew that Africans were human beings wishing to live freely: there were forty-four free blacks living in the city in 1777 (there were hundreds of others in Paris and Nantes).

But the question of the applicability of the Declaration of the Rights of Man and Citizen to the French colonies could not simply be set aside. In the National Assembly a trenchant debate pitted the colonial lobby (the Club Massiac) against the Société des Amis des Noirs, which included Jacques-Pierre Brissot and the Abbé Grégoire. One of La Rochelle's observers at the Estates-General, Pierre-Samuel Demissy, was caught up in the enthusiasm for change and made the mistake of joining the Amis des Noirs and calling for the abolition of slavery in 1789. By the following year he had come to agree with his fellow observer Jean-Baptiste Nairac, who always hoped that 'the political aspects which are so important will triumph over moral considerations'. When the Assembly supported the arguments of Antoine Barnave on behalf of the colonial lobby, and in its decree of 8 March 1790 deferred to the interests of the planters, Nairac was exultant: 'Without giving things their real names, it maintains the slave-trade, slavery, the exclusive régime.'[11]

An unsigned statement from 'Nantes commerce' made it clear that, in its view, 'neither the Creole nor the Frenchman sent to our colonies will ever consent to see sitting next to him in primary assemblies, and thus become his equal' men who had been slaves. The slave bore 'the ineradicable imprint of his parents' slavery ... a vile and bastard race'. Even the most civilized people ever to grace the earth, the Greeks and Romans, had agreed: it was a fact of life. 'Free people of colour' in the colonies were 'vulgar, ignorant and with the debauched and violent passions of their mothers'. In the near future they would take power in the colonies and force the whites to 'flee lands given up to all the horrors of anarchy', and would then offer up the fertile lands of the colonies to the first foreign power that appealed to their greed.[12]

Despite the racial panic the Nantais merchants expressed with such disarming honesty, the Revolution remained overwhelmingly popular. Most of the mercantile class of the great colonial trading ports, Bordeaux, Nantes and La Rochelle, was staunchly in support of the Revolution. Certainly, the dramatic reorganization of institutional structures had meant that many thousands of middle-class officials and lawyers lost their positions, venal or not; however, not only did they succeed in being elected to positions in the new structures, but they were also compensated for their lost offices. The final cost of paying compensation to owners of venal offices was more than 800 million *livres*, necessitating massive issues of *assignats* and precipitating inflation. The compensation was received at an ideal time for investment in the vast amounts of church property thrown onto the market from November 1790.

The Revolution was altering radically every dimension of public life throughout France, from the judicial system and economic regulation to the processes and structures of local administration. Scores of thousands of officials, lawyers and beneficiaries of privilege had had to scramble for compensation and new positions, offset by an equal number for whom the new institutions offered employment as well as a sense of participation and equality. There were many individuals who regretted the collapse of the *ancien régime* because it threatened their livelihoods. Elsewhere, resentment towards the Revolution stemmed from the loss of status following administrative reorganization, as in Vence, near Nice, where an agitated campaign failed to retain its bishopric, now relocated in nearby Saint-Paul. Saint-Papoul, near Castelnaudary, home of an imposing Benedictine abbey, had been elevated to a bishopric in 1317, and a flourishing little town had fattened on the estates and privileges of its clergy. Stripped of its bishopric in 1790, it quickly became no more than the village it is today, and peasants helped themselves to the stonework and marble from the cloister. This was only the most dramatic of many instances where the rationalization of the number of bishoprics from 135 down to 83 turned the smallest of the sees into sleepy small towns seething with resentment at change. The location of departmental, district and cantonal capitals (*chefs-lieux*) swamped legislators with a flood of complaints and rivalries from those who lost out, which could call into question support for the Revolution in towns formerly sustained by the presence of the maze of courts and offices of the Bourbon regime.[13]

Those who moved in to fill the power vacuum left by the collapse of the *ancien régime* and those who were among the major initial beneficiaries of the Revolution were bourgeois: particularly professional men and property-owners. Other social groups instrumental in bringing the *ancien régime* to an end did not have all their needs and aspirations met. Among them were the wage-earners of Paris and other cities, whose demand for full political rights was made the more agitated by some of the Assembly's economic reforms. The Declaration of the Rights of Man and Citizen had been silent on economic matters, but from 1789 the Assembly passed a series of measures revealing its commitment to economic liberalism.

The August 1789 decree had abolished all corporations as privileged bodies incompatible with the principles of liberty and equality. The full consequences of this principle were explosive for the world of labour. If guilds were to be abolished as impediments to the principle of the freedom of economic initiative and individual contracts, how could the quality of produce be assured? Following the Allarde law of March 1791, on 1 April a new system of occupational licences (*patentes*) came into effect, whereby individual professionals, artisans and shopkeepers simply paid a tax to be entitled to practise. There were immediate concerns—meat from diseased and dead animals was found to have been sold in Paris in May—but the pre-revolutionary world of guild controls was dead. The logical consequence

of the legislation was that the ancient *compagnonnages* of workers in particular trades were also abolished.[14]

In the countryside, frustration at having to pay existing taxes coincided
with continuing anger at the unresolved question of seigneurial dues.
Across most of the country the compromise legislation of March and May
1790 had encountered stubborn and at times violent resistance. This action
took two forms. First, since the 1789–90 legislation treated seigneurial
exactions as a legal form of rent that peasants could only terminate by
compensating the seigneur, many communities decided to take legal action
to force seigneurs to submit their feudal titles for legal verification. This
legal challenge was often connected with an illegal, second type of action,
the abrupt refusal to pay feudal dues. In the Corbières region of Languedoc,
for example, at least 86 of the 129 communes were involved in legal action
against former seigneurs or openly refused to pay dues during the period
1789–92.[15]

Such confrontations were intensely personal and even fatal. The enormous *seigneurie* of Le Peletier de Rosanbo, near Lannion in Brittany,
included 820 individual leases and brought in 70,000 *livres* annually in
rents. Rosanbo, a senior judge in the Paris Parlement, had only visited his
estates and massive château once, in 1780. He was fashionably liberal;
indeed, his wife, whose father was Lamoignon de Malesherbes, Louis XVI's
reformist minister in 1787, would become famous as 'la quêteuse citoyenne', raising funds for the families who had fallen at the Bastille. Out on
the estate, however, their manager was being intimidated by tenants into
dispersing food and money, and he wrote to Rosanbo that 'I don't know
what to do or say to avoid upsetting the people'.[16] Others paid a high price
for not knowing. In October 1790 the villagers of Varaize, in the western
department of Charente-Inférieure, stabbed to death their mayor Latierce,
the manager of the Comtesse d'Amelot's estates, in the streets of the nearby
town of Saint-Jean-d'Angély. Latierce was apparently held upright so that
his neighbours could all have the opportunity to join in this violent act, as
if symbolically expelling him from the community.[17]

The Assembly was equally concerned about seizures of rural land and
forest resources belonging to the state and to seigneurs. In late 1789 news
of widespread forest incursions prompted royal proclamations warning that
all such infractions would be punished. There were environmental concerns
as well. From Carcassonne the chief administrator of the department of
Aude expressed his anxieties about the rough hillsides (*garrigues*) formerly

controlled by seigneurs and used for grazing sheep. Poorer villagers were now insisting that these were common lands (*vacants*) and that they had a right to their share:

> people are complaining on all sides about the misguided greed of peasants who are spending every day clearing the woods and the uncultivated land on mountain-sides, without realising that this soil will only be productive for a year or two. . . . This pernicious clearing has accelerated since the destruction of the feudal régime because the people of the countryside imagine that the communes have become the owners of the *vacants*, that the former seigneurs were stripped of them at the same time as they were of judicial power . . .[18]

It was already obvious, the administrator noted, that gravel and stones were being washed down into streams, congesting their beds and causing them to spill over onto the best land. But local authorities and successive revolutionary assemblies seemed powerless to halt extensive felling in forests and illegal land clearances. The municipality of Grospierres, near the valley of the River Ardèche, despaired that its requests to divide up common lands between its families had been ignored and that people had taken matters into their own hands: 'the woods have continued to be ravaged, to such a point that there is no longer anything to be found there'.[19]

The paradox was that the Assembly's vision of a regenerated France based on citizenship and rights had facilitated the expression of demands and behaviours which were uncomfortable for the new regime itself. Already apparent well before 1789, new assumptions about the legitimate bases of local power were the most corrosive—and contested—cultural change of the revolutionary period. For example, in the tiny community of Fraïsse, south-west of Narbonne, the mayor had once described the terror of his fellow villagers at the behaviour of the seigneur, the Baron de Bouisse, and his nephews, 'possessors of imposing physique and walking about with four-pound sticks'. By 1790, the eighty-six-year-old baron was in turn horrified by the behaviour of formerly 'peaceful' peasants at Fraïsse: people had refused outright to pay seigneurial dues or the tithe. The Baron despaired:

> I have cherished and I still cherish the people of Fraïsse as I have cherished my own children; they were so sweet and so honest in their way,

but what a sudden change has taken place among them. All I hear now is 'corvée, lanternes, démocrates, aristocrates', words which for me are barbaric and which I can't use. . . . the former vassals believe themselves to be more powerful than Kings.[20]

Certainly the 'former vassals' embraced the possibilities of participation in local politics. While village council elections were straightforward, however, those at other levels were time-consuming, and required travel from 'active' citizens. The forty-five eligible voters from Silly-en-Multien north-east of Paris had a short walk to Nanteuil for the canton elections in April 1790, but were expected to stay several days. The schoolteacher Delahaye recorded in his diary how the unprecedented event was organized:

> This assembly was held upstairs in the granary, which was decorated at the end near the chestnut-trees with a rostrum raised on two steps, covered with a rug on which there were an armchair and table. Behind the armchair was attached to a large cloth the list of the fourteen or fifteen parishes which make up this canton, with the names of all the active citizens, numbering 768. Beneath the rostrum was a large table covered with a rug on which were two vases to put the ballot papers, inkwells, pens, sand and so on.

The president, seated in the armchair, was the oldest man, aged eighty-three or eighty-four, with the three next eldest appointed scrutineers of the 231 votes cast, 'most having left, some to take some air, others to do other things'.[21]

Electoral participation was only one part of this new political culture. Another was the extraordinary volume of unofficial correspondence that criss-crossed the country. This travelled both vertically, to and from constituents and their deputies in Paris, and horizontally, in particular between the Jacobin clubs (or Societies of Friends of the Constitution). One of the common activities in thousands of Jacobin clubs and other popular societies was the exchange of letters with similar gatherings.[22] Whereas Jacobin clubs were normally limited to 'active' citizens, in Paris and elsewhere alternative forums of revolutionary sociability developed for the 'passive'. In Paris, the Cordelier Club, led by Georges Danton and Jean-Paul Marat, welcomed all-comers. From the insistence that all citizens constituted the sovereign people slowly developed an understanding that 'democracy' was an entire political system rather than, as in Britain, only one arm of government balanced by an upper house and monarchical executive power. 'Patriots' increasingly referred to themselves as 'democrats'.[23]

Women were welcome at some clubs. In Paris the Fraternal Society of Citizens of Both Sexes, animated by a schoolteacher named Claude Dansard, gathered up to eight hundred men and women at its sessions, and deliberately integrated women into office-holding. The rights of women were also advocated by individual activists such as Olympe de Gouges, Théroigne de Méricourt, the Dutch feminist Etta Palm d'Aelders and the Marquis de Condorcet; and the Cercle Social urged the vote for women, the availability of divorce, and the abolition of inheritance laws favouring the first-born son. The last of these demands, at least, was quickly recognized, although more with a view to breaking the power of great noble patriarchs than to strengthening the economic position of women. On 15 March 1790 the Assembly decreed 'that all inheritances ... will be, without regard for the ancient noble quality of possessions and persons, shared between heirs according to the laws, statutes and customs that regulate distributions between all citizens'.[24] The legislation was to have a dramatic impact in those regions (for example, most of the south and Normandy) where inheritance laws had favoured first-born sons; in western regions such as Maine and Anjou, on the other hand, partible inheritance was already the norm.

Debate and division engulfed women as much as men, despite the exclusion of women from formal politics. Well-to-do and talented women hosted *soirées* where men and occasionally other women gathered to network, negotiate and socialize. The more elite of these *soirées*—such as those of Louise de Kéralio, Germaine de Staël and Sophie de Grouchy (Condorcet's wife)—resembled the exclusive *salons* of the *ancien régime*. The gatherings hosted by a brilliant couple from Lyon, Marie-Jeanne and Jean-Marie Roland, were less formal, but also by invitation. The core of the group were close allies from the Jacobins: the three provincial lawyer deputies Buzot, Pétion and Robespierre, the journalist Brissot and Étienne Clavière, a Swiss banker involved in the short-lived Genevan Republic crushed by French troops in 1782.[25]

Most 'patriotic' women were content to lend their active support to their newly empowered menfolk. No doubt the chests of the active male citizens of Orléans swelled with pride as a deputation of women offered their support on 14 July 1790. Even if 'we are without the knowledge accorded only to the men who govern us . . . ; if the weakness of our sex prevents us from sharing in the noble works of our brave and generous defenders . . . we still promise to instill deep in the hearts of our children the courage of our liberators . . .'.[26]

But the contradiction between the inclusive, universal promises of the Declaration of the Rights of Man and Citizen and the exclusions enshrined in subsequent legislation was not lost on women activists. In 1791 Olympe de Gouges published a draft social contract for marriage arrangements concerning children and property and a Declaration of the Rights of Women and Citizenesses, dedicated to Marie-Antoinette:

> First Article: Woman is born free and remains equal to man in rights. Social distinctions can only be founded on common utility . . .
>
> VI: The law must be the expression of the general will; all female and male Citizens must assist personally, or through their representatives, in its formation; it must be the same for all: all female and all male Citizens, being equal in its eyes, must also be eligible for all public dignities, positions and employments according to their abilities, and without any distinction other than that of their virtues and their talents.[27]

Such participation by men and women in public life through clubs and elections was only one of the means through which the Revolution was expressed. In early 1789 there were perhaps eighty newspapers in the whole country; over the next few years about 2,000 others were launched. The newspaper-reading public perhaps trebled within three years. The listening public increased far more, for the newspapers that circulated from urban centres through the countryside, and that were a new presence in village taverns or at peasant 'veillées', were read aloud, often after translation into the local language or dialect. In Paris alone there were 515 new newspapers in these years. Even taking account of how ephemeral many were—357 (69 per cent) lasted fewer than three months, and 21 per cent appeared only once—the contrast is striking with London. There a larger city, of over one million inhabitants, had just twenty-two periodicals.[28] In contrast, in France the publication of new books declined: 216 new novels were printed in 1788, but only 103 in 1791.

The new political culture was expressed just as commonly through song as in print. Historians have identified 116 new political songs in 1788 but

308 in 1791, including the 'Ça ira!' ('It'll be fine!'), apparently first sung as the Champ de Mars was prepared for the Festival of Federation in 1790:

> Ah! It'll be fine, it'll be fine, it'll be fine,
> The aristocrat says *Mea culpa!*
> The clergy regrets its wealth,
> The nation, with justice, will have it.
> Thanks to prudent Lafayette,
> Everyone will calm down.

Later versions of the song would not be so polite.

This was a society in which the most vibrant expressions of opinion were conveyed through the spoken and sung word, or through the thousands of cheap engraved illustrations that circulated throughout the country popularizing images of what the Revolution had achieved. 'Patriots' enjoyed improvising display to mock those to whom they had been constrained to defer. At about the same time as the Festival of the Federation in July 1790, for example, 'funeral rites for the aristocracy' were held as a comic farce on the Champ de Mars:

> A log had been bizarrely dressed as a priest: band, calotte, short coat, everything was there. A long line of mourners followed this black cortège, from time to time raising their hands to heaven and repeating in hoarse, yapping voices, sobbing *Mori! . . . Mori!*[29]

Through such vehicles of expression, millions of people learned the language and practice of popular sovereignty in an intense period of political activity, and they came to question the most deeply ingrained assumptions about the sanctity of monarchy, the moral authority of the Church, the honour of the nobility, and their own place in the social hierarchy.

The new revolutionary culture touched everyone and everything. In April 1791 the actor François-Joseph Talma, who had made his name in Marie-Joseph Chénier's patriotic tragedy *Charles IX*, left the Théâtre Français to set up a new company. Its repertoire would be, he felt, more in keeping with the new patriotic ethic being practised in the visual arts by his friend Jacques-Louis David. Already in 1791 there was greater leniency about who could submit to the Salon, and more than 180 artists (including twenty-one women) submitted more than eight hundred paintings. The greater openness of the art world posed problems for one of the most prestigious portraitists, Adélaïde Labille-Guiard, who had stayed in Paris, unlike her peer Élisabeth Vigée-Lebrun, but who now had to compete with many more aspiring professional painters at a time when some of her best clients had fled. Labille-Guiard responded by painting fourteen of the leading figures of the Assembly, including Robespierre, Talleyrand, the Duc d'Orléans, Adrien Duport, Barnave and Alexandre de Lameth.[30]

From the outset, children were the object of the regenerating project and even the poorest of parents expressed hope. Abandoned children left at religious establishments were now less likely to be given only a saint's name and more likely to be given a name taken from the patriotic ribbon left on them by mothers hoping one day to collect them. Among the children left at the Hôtel-Dieu in the western town of Niort were 'Prosper Red Ribbon', 'Philippe Blue Cockade', 'Jean-Marie Blue Band' and 'Unfortunate Marie White Ribbon'.[31] More fortunate middle-class children might be bought an 'enlightened' version of the traditional snakes-and-ladders board game whereby players had to work their way to the prize of the new constitution in the making by landing on squares with ladders (such as the emancipation of Jews and Protestants) and avoiding those with snakes (such as the *parlements*).

The rapidity of change in 1789 convinced revolutionaries of their sublime mission. From the outset patriotic language expressed a fervour for the possibilities of regeneration, which had quasi-religious overtones of redemption and rebirth. The men of the National Assembly had been socialized into a world saturated with Christian theology and royal claims to divine authority, and then educated in a curriculum rich in epic tales from the classical world. At the same time, the place of 'conspiracy' in understanding opposition drew on a long tradition of court intrigue in politics, and a deep Christian assumption about good and evil—but also the desire in 1789 for a radical break with the past to effect regeneration.

Those less enamoured of the urgency of sweeping change were suspected of still being mired in the old world of privilege, favour and perquisite. The temptation to understand opposition as the result of malevolence, even conspiracy, was due in large measure to the political culture of the court, where the favours of the powerful were disseminated through a network of influence, and where disadvantage was assumed to be the result of self-interested cabals preventing the king from knowing of his subjects' plight. It was also due to the scale of securing change in a large nation characterized by difficulty of communication created by geography and linguistic diversity. As local power-holders deliberately or unwittingly misinterpreted news from Paris, it became a simple matter to blame obstacles to progress on plots.[32]

In any case, from the outset of the Revolution there had been real as well as imagined conspiracies. One of the earliest and most notorious was that of Thomas de Mahy, Marquis de Favras, who had made a career as an army officer in the regiment of Louis XVI's brother, the Comte de Provence. A detailed pamphlet published in December 1789 outlined the plot whereby Paris would be invested with 30,000 loyal royalist troops and Bailly, Necker and Lafayette assassinated. Provence, who would supposedly fund the coup, quickly disavowed it, but an armed attempt to free Favras from prison seemed to confirm his guilt, and he was hanged on the Place de Grève in February 1790.[33]

Another fervent defender of the traditional powers of altar and throne was François Froment, former collector of revenues for the cathedral chapter in Nîmes, who played a leading role in stoking the fires of civil war in Languedoc, where Protestant merchants and manufacturers had assumed control of local politics in key towns. Already in January 1790 he had visited the king's youngest brother, the Comte d'Artois, in Turin, where Froment had been assured of arms and contacts for an anti-revolutionary and anti-Protestant uprising. While he was bitter that the material support was never forthcoming, Froment and his allies were able to aggravate resentment against Protestants in Nîmes, Montauban and the villages of the southern Massif Central, where the Revolution had brought them civil equality and a share of political power. Early in 1790 the Society of the Friends of the Constitution in Nîmes had 417 members, of whom 355 were Protestants.[34] The Assembly's refusal to proclaim Catholicism the state religion in April 1790 provided the pretext for large-scale violence. While five Protestants were killed in Montauban, the sectarian violence in Nîmes would result in many more Catholic deaths, when bands of Protestant peasants from the nearby regions of the Cévennes and Vaunage marched on the city. The violence in Nîmes was to become known as the brawl or *bagarre de Nîmes*, a misnomer for four days of fighting that left three hundred Catholics dead, but few Protestants.

Others sought more covert ways of ending revolutionary upheaval. Already the object of suspicion across the Assembly, by July 1790 Mirabeau was advising the king and queen about the desirability of civil war to halt the Revolution and restore monarchical power and military discipline.

Marie-Antoinette's adviser, the Austrian ambassador Mercy-Argenteau recorded on 31 July that 'M foresees civil war; he thinks that is more to be welcomed than feared despite the ills it will engender …'. Indeed, Mirabeau advised Louis directly a fortnight later that civil war was 'certain and perhaps necessary'. Louis, looking desperately for means to halt the Revolution without bloodshed, was horrified.[35] But Mirabeau continued to confer about ways of attenuating change with the Comte de Montmorin, Minister for Foreign Affairs since 1787 and who then replaced Necker as Chief Minister in September 1790.

Louis was in an invidious position, often immobilized by his distress at the changes bubbling around him and his own distaste for the intricacies of government. Whatever his benevolent predisposition, he continued to flounder in a volatile situation largely of his own making but well beyond his capacities. The clash between Louis' formation as an absolute king and the imperative that he should behave as if he had been 'regenerated' into a constitutional monarch was latent in his dealings with the National Assembly. For his son, Louis-Charles, Duc de Normandie, born in 1785, such a clash was to be avoided. Heir to the throne since the death of his older brother in 1789, the little boy's education was a matter for earnest debate in the Assembly, for he offered the possibility of being a king educated into constitutionality.[36]

The Revolution was as much a cause for celebration and optimism—and some dread—outside France as within. From the outset of the Revolution, however, there had been apprehension about the malevolence of Europe's crowned heads. The emigration of the Comte d'Artois to Savoy, then Turin and Trier, linked the two. By 1790 a new slogan 'Vivre libre ou mourir' ('Live free or die') was starting to appear, especially on National Guard flags for 14 July 1790. Despite the Assembly's insistence that wars would be inconceivable between fraternal peoples, unlike kings, there was widespread suspicion that France would not be left free to pursue its own revolution. News in May 1790 that Spanish forces had seized English ships in Nootka Sound on the west coast of Vancouver Island provoked heated debate. Was the new regime in France obliged to support the *pacte de famille* with Bourbon Spain, which had been openly hostile to change in France? The incident prompted the National Assembly in May 1790 to proclaim that 'the French nation renounces the undertaking of any war of conquest and will never use its forces against the liberty of any people'. When Spain and England reached an accommodation in October, many Jacobins were convinced that this was proof of their determination to destroy the Revolution, in league with the French court. 'All courts are conspiring against the French constitution,' declared Camille Desmoulins in his newspaper the *Révolutions de France et de Brabant*, 'Vienna, Turin, Madrid, Naples, and the cabinets of St. James and St. Cloud.'[37]

The potent mix of revolutionary zeal and anxiety about military invasion created widespread insubordination in the armed forces. The army and navy were wracked by internal conflict between noble officers and soldiers over control of regimental funds and the role of the army in repressing civilian protests.[38] There were serious rebellions in the fleets at Toulon in December 1789 and Brest in September 1790. In June 1790 the garrison in Perpignan rebelled against its militant royalist commander, Mirabeau's brother the Vicomte de Mirabeau, a colonel in the Touraine regiment, and he was briefly imprisoned by the municipal council. (The assertively counter-revolutionary Mirabeau was popularly known as Mirabeau-Tonneau, or 'Barrel Mirabeau', because of his penchant for drink.) The most serious unrest was in the army garrison at Nancy in August 1790. The commander, the Marquis de Bouillé, a relative of the commander of the National Guard, Lafayette, refused to negotiate with insurrectionary soldiers but rather decided to use his garrison from Metz and National Guards to punish the mutineers. This led to about ninety deaths and the punishment of many others: one was broken on the wheel, twenty-two were hanged and forty-one sent to the galleys, all from the Châteauvieux regiment, only one of three regiments involved.[39] Desperate to enforce stability, the majority in the Assembly endorsed Bouillé's actions. For others such as Élysée Loustallot of the newspaper *Révolutions de Paris*, already despondent over the violence that had continued since July 1789, the news of the massacre was intolerable:

> How can I narrate with a leaden heart? How can I reflect when my feelings are torn with despair? I see them there, these corpses strewn about the streets of Nancy .... Await rascals, the press that uncovers all crimes and dispels all errors will deprive you of your joy and your strength: how sweet it would be to be your last victim!

Loustallot died shortly thereafter, at just twenty-nine years; his funeral oration was delivered by another prominent journalist and revolutionary, Camille Desmoulins.[40]

From the outset of the Revolution in the spring of 1789, its life force had been an irresistible combination of regenerative idealism and violent retribution. Like all great revolutions, the French Revolution drew its energy from an inspiring vision of a new society based on equality and freedom, but there was a constant impulse that its leaders found difficult to control which sought also to punish the guilty and intimidate the recalcitrant. At the same time, the National Assembly was treading a fine line between those who were frustrated by the lack of more sweeping change and those who felt it had descended into intolerable innovation. Whose revolution was this?

But the Revolution seemed triumphant at the time of the great celebrations of July 1790. In the same way that 'regeneration' was a profound hope in 1789, so 'fraternity' became the highest aspiration in the year of reform that followed. Fraternity embraced all peoples, in the words of the Abbé Grégoire, 'whatever their opinions, the colour of their skin, their homelands'.[41] The reforms introduced or initiated in the first year of the Revolution were as ambitious as they were radical. Every dimension of public life was reworked according to the core principles of equality, popular sovereignty, efficiency and humanity. The reforms are unparalleled in history for the scale and speed of such change. Just two days before the euphoric festivals of 14 July 1790, however, the Assembly had passed legislation that was to turn the euphoria to recrimination and to shatter the national unity which had inspired the hopes for rebirth.

CHAPTER SEVEN

FRACTURING CHRIST'S FAMILY
RELIGIOUS SCHISM AND THE KING'S
FLIGHT, 1790–91

NOBLES AND THEIR ENTOURAGES WHO HAD DECIDED THAT THE
Revolution was intolerable fled into an exile that was seething with
resentments, but hardly threatening to the success of the Revolution. Adèle
d'Osmond, Comtesse de Boigne, a member of the inner court at Versailles,
was only ten years old in 1791 but later recalled the rancour that festered
among *émigré* noblewomen now having to work for a living: 'the mix of
ancient pretensions and recent slights was disgusting'. When Lucy de La
Tour du Pin went to Switzerland for a fortnight with her aunt in 1791, she
too was shocked by the self-indulgence and arrogance of the *émigré*
community: 'they all brought the airs and the insolence of Paris society . . .
they mocked everything'. Their valour consisted of sending snide letters to
fellow nobles who had not resigned army commissions and white feathers
to relatives who had chosen to retreat to country estates inside France.[1]

The scale and intensity of opposition to the Revolution were transformed by the National Assembly's reforms to the Church. The rift was
unforeseen and unintended. Among the most common grievances voiced in
the *cahiers* of 1789 was the need for sweeping ecclesiastical reform, and the
Assembly moved quickly to the task. There was widespread agreement on
core issues, such as improving the lot of the parish priests and pruning the
perquisites of the high clergy. In particular, there was no question of separating Church and State: the public functions of the Church were assumed
to be integral to daily life, and the Assembly accepted that public revenues
would support the Church after the abolition of the tithe in August 1789.

Ancien régime monarchs, as heads of the Gallican Church, had directly
intervened in ecclesiastical administration, for example closing religious

houses deemed to be moribund. Louis XV had closed hundreds of them. It was therefore assumed that the new regime of the National Assembly had the right to reform the Church's temporal organization. Three months after nationalizing church property, the Assembly resolved on 13 February 1790 that all convents and monasteries, except those involved in educational and charity work, were to be closed; contemplation alone was inadequate justification for public subsidy. The choice of religious to leave or to seek to stay in their institution was painful, and depended on factors such as age and the leadership of the order. For example, while many of the sixty-one religious in the six institutions in the district of Sarrebourg in Lorraine would have wished to stay on, almost all of the fifteen Dominican women at Rinting— mostly comparatively young, aged from twenty-six to forty-six—were happy to leave. In contrast, all twenty-four women in the Saint-Élisabeth convent at Vézelise—half of them older than fifty-four—expressed a wish to stay.[2] Similarly, only a minority of the two hundred religious in the fourteen institutions in the town of Nancy intimated they would be happy to leave. In the large Carmelite monastery only one of the thirty-one monks wanted to re-enter the secular world. For the district of Nancy as a whole, there were more than 620 still in their orders in November 1791, all having to be paid.[3] No doubt there were many members of religious orders for whom an end to cloistered life was welcome, but others would have agreed with those from the cathedral chapter of Orléans who announced in October 1790 that 'it is from obedience and not choice, but rather from *force majeure* that they are acquiescing [*s'immolent*]'.[4]

Equally troubling for the Church was the Assembly's commitment to denominational equality, symbolized in the election of the Protestant pastor Rabaut Saint-Étienne as its president on 15 March 1790. The same month, as 'patriots' in Avignon won control of the city and sought to integrate the papal territories into France, the Pope condemned the Declaration of the Rights of Man and Citizen: popular sovereignty was dangerous, he insisted, because it implied that people would only obey laws to which they had consented. Worried by the radical reforms to the place of the Catholic Church, on 14 April the Carthusian monk and deputy Dom Gerle asked the Assembly to decree that Catholicism was not only the state religion but 'the only public and authorized one'. Although the vote against considering his proposal was decisive—903 votes to 297—one-third of the noble deputies supported him and 144 of the 300 clerical votes were also for a Catholic monopoly. The split with the bourgeois deputies of the former

Third Estate, more than 90 per cent of whom rejected the idea of Catholic monopoly, was ominous.[5]

The widespread agreement in the *cahiers* on the need for reform guaranteed that the Assembly had been able to push through the nationalization of church lands, the closing of contemplative orders, and the granting of religious liberty to Protestants and Sephardi Jews by January 1790. Mounting clerical opposition to these changes ultimately focused on the Civil Constitution of the Clergy, which was approved by the Assembly on 12 July 1790 and which mapped out sweeping reforms to the Church.

Many of the provisions in the Civil Constitution reflected popular grievances in the *cahiers* of 1789, where the most common demands were for the abolition of the 'casuel' (fees charged for particular services) and the tithe, and for bishops to be chosen on merit and required to reside in their dioceses. Most priests were advantaged by a new salary scale, and only the upper clergy would have regretted that bishops' stipends were dramatically reduced. However, the Assembly redrew diocesan and parish boundaries, radically reducing the number of parish churches in line with commune boundaries. There was a torrent of complaints from villages and hamlets deemed too small to be communes and which would now lose their parish church. There were many like the parishioners of Pocé-les-Bois, just outside Vitré in Brittany, who petitioned the National Assembly that they 'be allowed to place into your bosom their sorrows, their worries, and their demands', because the distance to the nearest church would now create problems in poor weather and for small children.[6]

In towns and cities, too, closure of churches in the name of efficiency was a wrench for the faithful. In towns there would be one parish church for every 6,000 people, so Paris would lose nineteen of its fifty-two parishes, Rouen twenty-one of thirty-two, Bourges eleven of fifteen and Angers nine of seventeen. All but two of the twelve tiny parishes on the 'plateau' (high town) of Laon in Picardy were closed; this and the collapse of the Church's wealth—it had owned 28 per cent of the region's land, and many seigneurial titles—would ravage the town as surely as it benefited substantial rural landowners who bought the property.[7] In Toulouse, members of the clergy were one in fifteen of the population: apart from the cathedral and basilica, there were more than fifty convents and monasteries, and church property covered one-third of the town. Now this property was to be sold, 'surplus' parish churches were shut, the religious orders would slowly close, and there would be consequent unemployment.[8]

Most contentious, however, was the issue of how the clergy were to be appointed in future. To the trenchant objections from clerical deputies in the Assembly that the Church hierarchy was based on the principle of divine authority and appointment by superiors, deputies such as the prominent lawyer and one of Rabaut's successors as president of the Assembly, Jean-Baptiste Treilhard, retorted that this had resulted in nepotism. Only the people could choose their priests and bishops: 'Far from undermining religion, in ensuring that the faithful have the most honest and virtuous ministers, you are paying it the most worthy homage. He who believes that this would be to wound religion, is forming a truly false idea of religion.'[9] In applying the popular sovereignty of 'active' citizens to the choice of priests and bishops, however, the Assembly crossed the narrow line separating temporal from spiritual life. The Assembly thereby excluded women and the poor from the community of the faithful who were to choose their clergy, but in theory included Protestants, Jews and non-believers who were wealthy enough to vote.

Why was the Assembly unwilling to negotiate or compromise? The Church was both so embedded in public life and so suffused with the abuses of the *ancien régime* that it needed to be reformed as an institution—and in accordance with revolutionary principles. The Assembly's imperative to introduce a uniform taxation system and to reform the Church had led it to abolish the tithe as both variable and unfair. The state's bankruptcy had led to the nationalization of church property with the consequence that the clergy would still be dependent on the state in some other way. Hence the few suggestions that the Church should run its own affairs fell on deaf ears. The August 1789 decree had abolished privileged corporations: how could the Assembly negotiate a compromise with the Church when it believed its reforms were simply administrative in nature, and therefore the prerogative of the Assembly alone? A church synod could not be consulted about whether it agreed with reforms voted by the people's representatives. In any case the papacy was equally as intransigent as the Assembly.[10]

In the end, it proved impossible to reconcile a Revolution based on popular sovereignty, tolerance of all faiths and the certainty of earthly fulfilment through secular reason with a Church based on hierarchical appointment, divinely revealed dogma and a certainty of one true faith. Despite the opposition of most clerical deputies, a frustrated majority in the Assembly sought to force the issue by requiring elections of clergy to be held early in

1791, with those elected to swear an oath of loyalty to the law, the nation and the king. This was the moment that fractured the Revolution.

Everywhere the oath faced parish priests with an agonizing choice. The reforms had been sanctioned by the king, but did that remove their anxiety that the oath contradicted loyalty to the Pope and long-established practice? A petition from 105 Breton priests insisted that 'it is the thread of the Apostolic succession which gives life to our powers; if it is broken, our mission ceases to be divine'.[11] Many priests sought to resolve the dilemma by taking a qualified oath, such as the priest of the northern parishes of Quesques and Lottinghen east of Boulogne:

> I declare that my religion does not allow me to take an oath such as the National Assembly requires; I am happy and I even promise to watch over as well as we possibly can the faithful of this parish who are entrusted to me, to be true to the nation and the king and to observe the constitution decreed by the National Assembly and sanctioned by the king in all that is within the competence of his power, in all that belongs to it in the order of purely civil and political matters, but where the government and the laws of the Church are concerned, I recognize no superior and other legislators other than the Pope and the bishops . . .[12]

These qualified oaths were unacceptable to the authorities. Priests had to choose between accepting the Civil Constitution, and with it the Revolution, or the authority of the Pope and their noble bishops.

In the district of Nancy only twenty-eight religious took the oath (nine of them canons who taught at the secondary school), forty refused it, and forty-five sought to take it with conditions.[13] In contrast, there was general acceptance of the church reforms in Orléans, led by the bishop, even though the city's twenty-five parishes were reduced to six. Demands for sweeping reforms to the Church, often couched in 'secularized' tone, had characterized the *cahiers* of the district in 1789; reform not just to hierarchy and taxation privileges but to the status of parish priests. The parish priest of Saint-Hilaire just west of Orléans urged his community to 'be faithful to the Nation, the Law and the King: the Nation is you; the Law is your will; the King is the worthy guardian of the law which guarantees the wellbeing of the French by sowing into his son's heart the precious seeds of Liberty and Patriotism'.[14]

In contrast, the priest of Pithiviers, to the north of Orléans, claimed that, when he explained to his congregation that he could only take a restricted oath, 'everyone was crying, everyone watered the paving-stones or their handkerchiefs with their tears'.[15] François-Pierre Julliot, one of the many priests and religious of Troyes who refused the oath, was outraged by the reported behaviour of active citizens who gathered to elect the bishop:

> The high altar served as a dining-table for the electors when they did not want to interrupt their sessions to take a meal; they took immodesty and sacrilege to a point where they satisfied the call of nature within the choir and sanctuary. The most scandalous utterings carried into the sacred vaults thousands of times.[16]

Across the nation only a handful of bishops and perhaps half the parish clergy took an unqualified oath. Many of those who did subsequently retracted when, on 13 April 1791, the Pope issued the encyclical 'Charitas' to condemn the Civil Constitution and the Declaration of the Rights of Man and Citizen as inimical to a Christian life. Already outraged by the loss of ancient papal territory in and around Avignon, he now counselled the clergy of France to regard the constitutional clergy as heretics:

> Take special care lest you proffer ears to the insidious voices of this secular sect, which voices furnish death, and avoid in this way all usurpers whether they are called archbishops, bishops or parish priests, so that there is nothing in common between you and them, especially in divine matters . . . for no one can be in the Church of Christ, unless he is unified with the visible head of the Church itself . . .[17]

Some 'patriot' clergy were enraged: J.-F. Nusse, a country priest at Chavignon, south of Laon, asked 'how can we believe that the Pope has the right to force us to disown a constitution which is so close to the Gospel, and so necessary for the happiness of the State?' In the end 78 per cent of the priests in his district maintained their oath; elsewhere the proportions were reversed. The Pope's intransigence led many religious to retract their oaths, such as a seminary prior from Orléans who informed the mayor that he was 'no longer being able to resist the cries of my conscience. . . . I prefer indigence and death to the misfortune of being separated from its [the Church's] leader and members.'[18]

The sharp regional contrasts in clerical preparedness to take and maintain the oath reflected not only individual choice or the influence of senior clergy, but also local ecclesiastical culture. The outcomes were to be fundamental to subsequent political choice and division at every level across the revolutionary decade, and beyond. By mid-1791 two Frances had emerged, contrasting the pro-reform areas of the south-east, the Paris basin, Champagne and the centre with the 'refractory' west and south-west, the east, and the southern Massif Central. The strength of refractory clergy in frontier areas fed Parisian suspicions that peasants who could not understand French were weaker prey to the 'superstitions' of their 'fanatical' priests.

The refractory or non-juring clergy saw themselves as servants of God, while the constitutional clergy saw themselves as servants of the people, as 'citizen priests'. To the former, the Civil Constitution was anathema to the corporate, hierarchical structure of the Church and the leadership of the Pope; to the latter, in areas where clergy were accustomed to a weaker temporal role in daily life, the Civil Constitution was the will of the people and it reinforced Gallicanism at the expense of the church hierarchy in Rome.

Shifts in the strength of religiosity were occurring well before the Revolution: between regions and between town and country. These shifts predisposed clerical communities either to reject institutional change or, in more secular areas, to accept their role as constitutional clergy serving their communities as 'citizen-priests'. Across the thirty years before the Revolution the proportion of new clergy born in towns had declined from about 45 per cent to about 27 per cent, but this varied dramatically. In some provinces the decline was far more dramatic, such as in the dioceses of Aix-en-Provence, Orléans and Autun. The overall decline in recruitment—from both town and country—was particularly marked, more than 40 per cent, in regions where oath-taking in 1791 was highest: Paris, Provence, the regions south of Paris (Nivernais, Berry, Bourbonnais, Burgundy), and around Bordeaux and Lyon. In contrast, in parts of the west (Maine, Anjou, Lower Poitou), overall recruitment had actually risen by almost half, especially from rural areas.[19]

The oath fractured both the Church and the Revolution. The constitutional cleric the Abbé Rousselot, from Franche-Comté, insisted that he regarded his position as 'that which conforms to the real principles of our religion and is the most useful to the state. I hold no grudge against our dissident colleagues and I sincerely hope that nothing bad happens to them.'

But he regarded such dissidence as wrong and worried about its effect on the 'good order and peace' he longed for under a reformed, constitutional monarchy.[20] From the pulpit of Notre-Dame in Paris the Abbé Claude Fauchet proclaimed on 4 February 1791:

> The dark shadows in which the universe was hidden must be pierced in this epoch of liberty, equality and general fraternity among all people.... Homage therefore, and immortal glory to the National Assembly of France and the King of the French, who have embraced this regime of general fraternity, universal equality and ecumenical liberty.

In May, Fauchet became constitutional Bishop of Calvados, and subsequently decided on a political career.[21]

The 'patriot' deputies insisted that a sweeping overhaul of ecclesiastical structures was necessary, as was higher remuneration for most parish clergy. But the repudiation of the reforms by most religious—and their damnation by the Pope—gave all those opposed to revolutionary change the certainty that theirs was a righteous cause and not simply self-interest.

The imperative felt by the rational men of the National Assembly to ensure that an institution as central to public life as the Catholic Church, and funded from the public purse, was administered efficiently led them to cut swathes from what they saw as the unnecessary provision of religious services. Thomas Lindet, parish priest of the Norman town of Bernay and deputy for Eure, published a pamphlet in December 1790 addressed to his protesting peers, arguing that the new regime had every right to say 'you are too numerous. Your opulence is bad for the public good.' He reminded them that, just as the old ecclesiastical divisions were creations of the *ancien régime*, so the new divisions should reflect the reforms made by the Revolution.[22]

The imposition of the clerical oath in January–February 1791 sparked more than moral outrage in some places. In Brittany, in particular, the oath was the moment where divisions simmering for two years erupted into open conflict. Hundreds of 'patriots' from there and Anjou gathered at Pontivy in January and February 1790 to express their unity with 'all the French', while others muttered angrily about the abolition of Brittany's distinctive 'constitution' and privileges. The reforms to the Church aggravated tensions immeasurably in a region where priests from local families had often enjoyed high salaries and prominence in their tiny theocracies.

Their status was reflected in the fact that 42 of the 232 elected mayors in Morbihan were priests. On 13 February more than one thousand peasants armed with picks, scythes and some guns from parishes around Vannes marched on the town in support of the non-juror Bishop Amelot. In the words of one, inaction would mean that 'Protestants will be sent in to teach the new laws and there will be no baptism before the age of seven years'. The priest of Sarzeau encouraged them, not least, one suspects, because his unusually high salary of 2,600 *livres* before the Revolution had now been halved. Soldiers from Vannes fought off the peasants at the cost of several lives. The aghast *procureur* (public prosecutor) in Vannes was sure that 'our country brothers are the victims of fanaticism and the pride of the former aristocrats who have made an alliance with the bishops'.[23]

The gulf between urban, bourgeois, 'enlightened' culture and the world of substantial villages bonded by religion and language was nowhere more evident than in Brittany and southern Anjou. Departmental administrators in Vannes were astonished that villagers could not understand that priests and nobles were acting simply from wounded pride and self-interest: 'fanatics of pride' would now have to pay taxes like anyone else.[24] In the *bourg* of Saint-Nolff, north-east of Vannes, the new mayor and public prosecutor were the priest and his curate, two of the five priests ministering to 1,200 people. In early 1790 they had drawn up a list of 'all souls' to pay the 'patriotic contribution' to taxes, but by the end of the year their village council was bemoaning reform of the Church—'we do not want to rebel against our priests'—and accusing the government of 'having promised us fine things'. The five priests fled to Spain and the village refused to pay taxes henceforth.[25]

Very often this was a gulf between urban and rural cultures. After the nuns of Couëts across the River Loire from the city of Nantes refused to allow the constitutional Bishop Minée to enter their convent, a band of women from Nantes went to the village and whipped the nuns. At Vieillevigne, in the *bocage* area south-west of the town, the priest refused to announce the Assembly's decrees. When the mayor went into the church, he was surrounded by women who tore up the decrees and shouted 'Kill! Kill! Bash him! Bash him!', until he found a way to escape. In Nantes' department of Loire-Inférieure there were only 97 oath-takers among the 455 parish priests.[26] Typical of the rejection of 'intruder' priests was the reaction of parishioners in Guémené. Immediately after Easter, on 26 April 1791 the mayor, a supporter of the newly elected constitutional priest, was dragged from a chapel and physically intimidated into resigning by angry men and women; other councillors had to flee. The mayor was targeted with obscene abuse as a scoundrel and far worse. Six months later the sacristy was burgled, apparently to further intimidate the 'intruder'.[27]

A Revolution that had begun with high hopes for the 'regeneration' of the Church now spiralled into reciprocal antagonism. A gulf of incomprehension divided 'patriots' from those opposed to the Revolution, both inside and outside the Church. This was not a simple question of vested interests, of winners and losers. Rather, on opposite sides of the gulf were communions of souls and communities of citizens. The latter found personal identity in participation in the new institutions and in secular notions of personal worth, and found it difficult to tolerate those who preferred existing practices of worship, ritual and authority. For their part, those opposed to the Revolution found the 'patriots' to be wreckers of custom, order and obedience. The consequences of the oath were to make patriots angrily dismissive of what they described as fanaticism and superstition, and to turn defenders of the faith into potential converts to counter-revolution.

Clerical responses were a reflection of the attitudes of the wider community, for only a minority of priests felt sufficiently independent from their communities to flout public opinion. In large cities like Paris, priests who opposed the Civil Constitution risked mockery and rejection. The chronicler of Parisian life and pro-revolutionary Louis-Sébastien Mercier described how the *curé* of the parish of Saint-Sulpice tried to preach against the Assembly's reforms:

> A universal cry of indignation reverberated through the arches of the church.... Suddenly, the majestic organ filled the church with its harmonious music and echoed through every heart the famous tune: *Ah! ça ira! ça ira!* ... the counterrevolutionary instigator was invited to sing *ça ira*. He climbed down from his chair, covered with laughter, shame, and sweat.[28]

In rural France as well the oath became a test of popular acceptance of the Revolution as a whole. In regions such as the south-east and the Paris basin, where public life had long been relatively 'secularized' and priests were seen as providing only a spiritual service, there was broad acceptance of the Civil Constitution as of the Revolution in general. In regions with prominent Protestant minorities, in contrast, such as the Cévennes and

Alsace-Lorraine, the oath-taking and subsequent departures of non-juring clergy aroused wider fears about attacks on a way of life to which Catholic ritual and charity were pivotal. There were many regions where formerly pro-revolutionary parishioners expressed their grief at the departure of a respected cleric or order of nuns, and their irritation at the closure of churches deemed surplus to requirements. Many people felt that the disruption to long-established practices was proof that the Revolution was urban and bourgeois.

The response of many women to the ecclesiastical reforms was particularly visceral and violent as they expressed their dismay, rage and anxiety about changes to familiar patterns of ritual and support. In the small southern towns of Millau and Sommières crowds of poor women and children aimed their anger both at local Protestants and pro-revolutionary Catholic administrators deemed to be complicit in destroying religious and social certainty: at Millau women shouted 'We want to conserve our religion, the religion of Jesus Christ, we want our clergy!'[29] Other, pro-revolutionary women were just as angry in return. On 22 February 1791 a group of *citoyennes* in Paris implored the Cordeliers Club to be militant:

We have consoled ourselves for our inability to contribute to the public good by exerting our most intense efforts to raise the spirit of our children to the heights of free men. But if you deceive our hope ... then indignation, sorrow, despair will impel and drag us into public places.

A fortnight later, on 6 March, Pauline Léon, a twenty-two-year-old chocolate-maker and militant, sent a petition to the National Assembly with three hundred signatures: 'everyone predicts that a violent shock is coming,' she feared, and demanded that women be able to procure 'pikes, pistols, sabres, muskets' and practise with them on the Champ de la Fédération on festival days and Sundays.[30]

A religious schism had caused a broader one, between 'patriots' and their enemies. The counter-revolutionary press thrived on the same freedoms as its enemies. In March 1791 the ultra-royalist *Ami du Roi* summarized the division over the clerical oath in emotive terms:

| The right wing of the National Assembly, The élite of the defenders | The left wing, and the monstrous assembly of the principal enemies of the Church and of the Monarchy, |

| of religion and of the Throne. | Jews, Protestants, Deists. |
| All worthy and virtuous citizens | All the libertines, cheats, Jews and Protestants. |

The newspaper was here referring to one of the most durable innovations of the Revolution's political language: the use of 'left' and 'right', referring to the clusters of like-minded deputies on the benches of the National Assembly.[31]

Particularly trenchant in their opposition to the Revolution were those whose loss of status, certainty and wealth could be blamed on a reversal of fortunes in ancient sectarian hatreds. After the hundreds of Catholic deaths in the *bagarre de Nîmes* in June 1790, François Froment and the mayor of the village of Berrias, Louis-Bastide de Malbosc, had called for a gathering of Catholic royalists on the mountain plateau of Jalès, dominated by the 'commanderie' dating from the Crusades, on the border of the southern departments of Ardèche and Gard, and up to 30,000 people from 180 villages assembled there on 18 August. After their dispersal, Froment returned to Turin, where he received a letter from Louis XVI assuring him that he would be ennobled once absolute monarchy was restored. The next gathering at the Camp de Jalès, on 20 February 1791, also followed violence between Catholics and Protestants, this time in Uzès. The gathering was smaller—perhaps 10,000 strong—and angrily opposed by 'patriots'. Local National Guards were sent to disperse it; the battered body of the militantly royalist Malbosc was found a fortnight later on the banks of the Rhône.[32]

Those opposed to the Revolution did not have to look far to find reasons to be terrified. In December 1790 the firebrand journalist Jean-Paul Marat used his newspaper the *Ami du peuple* to advise patriots that

> A year ago by cutting off five or six hundred heads you would have set yourselves free and happy for ever. Today it would need ten thousand; within a few months perhaps you will need to cut off a hundred thousand, and you will do a fine job; there is no peace for you until you have exterminated the implacable enemies of the *patrie* down to their last member.[33]

The entire nation was polarizing. By 1791 both 'patriots' and royalists were stigmatizing each other and openly describing opponents in violent terms.

The deputy Corbel de Squirio was outraged by 'the atrocious crimes, murders, and poisoning perpetrated by the refractory priests ... in the name of a religion of peace and love'; in contrast, Barnabé Durosoi's royalist *Gazette de Paris* called on 'all the sovereigns of Europe to hasten as rapidly as possible to exterminate' those spreading the revolutionary 'virus'. The author and now revolutionary administrator François de Neufchâteau wrote to his friend Joseph Poullain de Grandprey in May 1791 that Paris 'is calm on the outside, but inside very perilous. The volcano is dormant. There will certainly be terrible eruptions.'[34]

Neufchâteau hoped that the national Constitution, now in its final stages of drafting, would quieten that volcano. The Constitution was a delicate balancing act between the king (with the power to name ministers and diplomats, temporarily block legislation, and declare peace and war) and the legislature (with a single chamber, with powers over finance and legislation). The personal dilemma for Louis was how to interpret the contrasting voices of a sovereign people, hitherto his subjects, who were increasingly divided about the changes the Revolution had wrought and the future direction it should take. He had consented to the Civil Constitution of the Clergy but was outraged when a suspicious crowd prevented him from leaving Paris to celebrate Easter mass with non-juring clergy at his château in Saint-Cloud, west of the capital.

There were many who looked to Louis as the embodiment of stability and a guarantor of the Constitution's promise of peaceful reform against both angry counter-revolutionaries and those demanding more sweeping revolution. In the Mediterranean port of Toulon, a second, more conservative, political club was founded in mid-1791. The new club, pointedly called 'The Friends and *Defenders* of the Constitution', justified its existence by the allegedly 'violent behaviour of a handful of sedition-mongers, who had outraged the sensibilities of the membership with a hypocritical display of patriotism that ... forced many decent citizens to withdraw' from the first club.[35] To the north, near Aix-en-Provence, in the little Provençal town of Éguilles (population 2,000), 104 members of the Amis de la Constitution broke away to form a conservative club with the same name on 22 June. Led by some local notables, they averred in their inaugural session that 'It is for wise and enlightened citizens, and for true patriots, and it is for friends of order to give an example of obedience to the law, without which the liberty which has just been conquered for us will undoubtedly escape us and bury us in a slavery worse than the abyss which we have left.'[36] They could not know that, on the very day they expressed their fervent hope that the Revolution was now both safe and over, that hope was doomed to disappointment as Louis XVI began a humiliating coach trip.

Ever since July 1789 the Assembly had faced a double challenge: how could it protect the Revolution from its opponents? And how far should the Revolution go? These questions came to a head in mid-1791. Outraged by the limitations to his own power and consumed with guilt that he had sanctioned the reforms to the Church, Louis XVI fled Paris with his family on the night of 20–21 June.[37] He left a declaration repudiating the direction the Revolution had taken: 'the only recompense for so many sacrifices is to witness the destruction of the kingdom, to see all powers ignored, personal property violated, peoples' safety everywhere in danger'. He appealed to his subjects to return to the certainties they had once known:

> People of France, and especially you Parisians, inhabitants of a city that the ancestors of His Majesty delighted in calling 'the good city of Paris', be wary of the suggestions and lies of your false friends; come back to your king; he will always be your father, your best friend.[38]

As news of the king's flight swept the city, however, the mood was one of indignation rather than repentance.

The royal family's desperate flight to safety with the Marquis de Bouillé's garrison at Montmédy on the eastern frontier was a series of blunders from the outset. A few miles after Sainte-Menehould the royal coach left the main road to Metz and turned north on a minor road towards Montmédy and the border with Luxembourg. But the king had already been recognized by Jean-Baptiste Drouet, the postmaster at Sainte-Menehould, who dashed to alert people in the next town, Varennes. There Louis and his family were offered protection from a furious, swelling crowd by a village official, the grocer Jean-Baptiste Sauce. The king was effectively under house arrest while troops rushed from Paris.

The return of the royal family to Paris starting on 22 June was slow and humiliating, as crowds gathered in shock and resentment. The Assembly was stunned: Louis was suspended from his position as king, but it was determined to quell any unrest during his return to the capital. 'Whoever applauds the king will be batonned,' it warned, 'whoever insults him will be hanged.' Shows of support for the king were rare and dangerous. One who declared his loyalties was the Comte de Dampierre, an officer in the Quercy regiment who in 1785 had married a relative of the then Minister of War, the Maréchal de Ségur. The Dampierres lived in their *seigneurie* of Hans, just west of Sainte-Menehould. They were not wealthy, and the abolition of many of their privileges had been angrily contested by Dampierre. He had received the Order of Saint-Louis, and made a point of wearing it as the royal coach left Sainte-Menehould. The count's ostentatious saluting of the king as he rode alongside his carriage was the last straw for peasants who knew him only too well. The count was shot dead.[39] The king's last chance to escape was in Châlons-sur-Marne, where local notables cele-brated his presence over a sumptuous dinner on the evening of 22 June, but the crowds of angry commoners outside demanding his departure for Paris convinced Louis to leave for the city the next morning.

Some departmental administrations, such as that of Aisne, east of Paris, were anxious about how news of the king's flight might further agitate popular unrest about subsistence issues, and they persisted in official views that he had been forced to flee against his will. Their populations were not so readily deceived. As the returning cortège traversed the town of Château-Thierry in the south of the department, a crowd ignored official warnings not to insult the king and forced the dauphin to shout 'Vive la Nation!' The municipal council received Louis in silence and the National Guard refused to present arms.[40]

News of the royal flight, first announced in Paris early on Monday 21 June, spread like wildfire across the nation, at five or six miles per hour. At times it was faster: the news reached the western town of Saintes, 310 miles from Paris, in thirty-six hours. It was received in Metz in the east and Nantes in the west by late on Wednesday; after five days, it had trav-elled as far as Perpignan and Toulon on the Mediterranean. Word of the arrest took longer, only arriving in Perpignan one week later. Both events were stunning news. The Jacobin Club of Montmorillon, two hundred miles south-west of the capital in the department of Vienne, had expressed the hope that stability was imminent: 'but the disappearance of the King has crushed all our hopes, and warned us not to count on such a return'.[41]

The king's intention, which had never altered, was to return to the powers of the throne he had held before July 1789, and to dissolve the National Assembly, even if he would not necessarily have unwound all of the Revolution's changes.[42] His failure and capture reinforced the certain-ties of both sides, that the Revolution was imperilled or that the Revolution was itself the peril. There were many people across the country who could not imagine a France without its king. When the royalist *Gazette de Paris* called for 'hostages to the King' to offer themselves in return for Louis' 'freedom', some 4,160 letters were received from volunteers.[43] In contrast the *Père Duchesne*, whose editor Jacques-René Hébert used a deliberately earthy style, had previously supported the king, but now turned on him in vituperative terms: 'You are no longer my king, no longer my king! You are nothing but a cowardly deserter . . . . We will stuff you into Charenton and your whore into the Hôpital. . . . I'll be stuffed with an axe if you get away.'[44] A farmer from Saint-Denis-en-Val across the river from Orléans noted in his diary that 'the King had fled to escape with his wife and children to join his brothers outside France, but it was good fortune for France that he was arrested at Varennes'.[45] News of the arrest of the king arrived in the bustling river-port town of Bergerac (population 11,700) on the River Dordogne on 24 June and was received 'with joy'. But it also triggered increased concerns about a likely war with Spain and England: the popular society reassured citizens that there were 500,000 National Guards ready to defend the frontiers and 'to live in freedom or die'. It decided to contact the Friends of the French Revolution in London to urge them to combat the wicked Prime Minister Pitt.[46]

The king's flight and suspension by the Assembly accentuated social tensions that were already acute in the capital. Many wage-earners were angered by the introduction of a free market in labour by the Le Chapelier law of 14 June 1791 outlawing associations of employers and employees, 'the destruction of all types of corporations of citizens of the same trade and profession being one of the fundamental bases of the French constitution'.[47] Le Chapelier, an ennobled lawyer, had presided over the session of 4 August 1789 in the National Assembly, and was one of the radical Breton deputies who had founded the Jacobin Club. His law, with Pierre-Gilbert d'Allarde's 1791 law abolishing guilds, was decisive in the creation of a *laissez-faire* economy, aimed at the 'counter-revolutionary' practices and privileges of the old world of corporations.

The Le Chapelier law was chiefly aimed at 'coalitions' of Parisian wage-earners, but it was also directed at the waves of strikes by harvesters working on the large commercial wheat-farms in the Paris basin, where prosperous farmers hired up to eighty harvesters at a time. These often violent strikes or 'bacchanals' occurred at times when harvests were plentiful and labour in strong demand, as in the summer of 1791. The administrators of Aisne had to outlaw strikes of up to seven hundred harvesters on farms around

Château-Thierry, and ultimately set maximum rates of pay (in wheat, which the harvesters customarily sold). The free market in grains was also the target of anger: on 20 July there was a stand-off near the village of Totes, north of Rouen, when two hundred soldiers and National Guards from the city were confronted by up to 4,000 people, armed with rifles, led by members of municipal councils wearing their sashes and National Guard units from twenty-two villages, insisting on controls on the grain-trade. Five hundred more soldiers were necessary to disperse them.[48]

The celebration of the second anniversary of the taking of the Bastille on 14 July 1791 lacked the fraternal solidarity and optimism of the previous year. 'Patriot' communities were now more resolute. In Saint-Julien-du-Sault, in Burgundy, a new bell—the 'Marie Jacques', weighing 1,550 kg—was ordered to celebrate 'the Civil Constitution of the Clergy, the suppression of hereditary nobility and social orders, the abolition of taxes of foodstuffs and salt and of servitude and the feudal regime, individual freedoms, equality of taxation, the new administration of finance and justice'. The bell was blessed by the priest Jean Longuet, who was also responsible for securing a stone from the Bastille to be embedded in a tower at the entry to the village, with the inscription: 'This stone was taken from the ruins of the Bastille. Patriotism has found a better use for it by raising it here to give this place the sweet name of Liberty, in the second year of French liberty.' It remains there to this day (Fig. 13).[49]

In Paris the celebration of the second anniversary of the taking of the Bastille was a far more sombre affair than the first. François-Joseph Gossec, the director of the Paris Opera, had composed a celebratory 'Te Deum' in 1790; now he and the poet Marie-Joseph Chénier contributed a militant 'Song of 14 July' one year later:

> God of the people and of kings, of cities, of the countryside,
> Of Luther, of Calvin, the children of Israel . . .
> Remember the times when the sinister tyrants
> Crushed under foot the rights of the French;
> The time, not so long ago, when wicked ministers
> Deceived peoples and kings. . . .
> Princes, nobles, bishops swam in opulence;
> The people shuddered under their wealth;
> Their palaces were cemented with
> The blood of the oppressed, the tears of misery.

Overshadowing the celebrations was the question of the king's fate. During Louis' suspension by the Assembly, Jacobins such as the Abbé Grégoire argued that he should be forced to abdicate:

> The premier public servant abandons his post; . . . he breaks his word, he leaves the French a declaration which, if not criminal, is at the least— however it is envisaged—contrary to the principles of our liberty. He could not be unaware that his flight exposed the nation to the dangers of civil war; and finally, in the hypothesis that he wished only to go to Montmédy, I say: either he wanted to content himself with making peaceful observations to the National Assembly regarding its decrees, and in that case it was useless to flee; or he wanted to support his claims with arms, and in that case it was a conspiracy against liberty.

Nevertheless, despite Louis' humiliating capture and return, the Assembly reinstated him and on 15 July decreed that he had been 'kidnapped' and that the monarchist provisions of the Constitution of 1791 would stand.

For most of the deputies, the issue was clear; in the words of Antoine Barnave, a Protestant lawyer from Grenoble and one of the three deputies sent to escort Louis back to Paris on 23 June:

> any change today would be fatal: any prolonging of the Revolution today would be disastrous. . . . Are we going to end the Revolution, or are we going to start it all over again? . . . if the Revolution takes one more step, it can only be a dangerous one: if it is in line with liberty its first act could be the destruction of royalty, if it is in line with equality its first act could be an attack on property . . . It is time to bring the Revolution to an end. . . . is there still to be destroyed an aristocracy other than that of property?[50]

Barnave was here referring to a wave of strikes and demonstrations by wage-earners and the unemployed in the capital, and to continuing unrest in the countryside. But he also had in mind the violent unrest in Saint-Domingue, on which he had been a powerful advocate for the planters. Louis XVI had therefore become a symbol of stability against the increasingly radical demands of 'passive' citizens, slaves and their supporters.

On 17 July the Cordeliers Club organized a petition demanding Louis' abdication, to be signed at a demonstration on the Champ de Mars, at the same 'altar of the homeland' on which the Fête de la Fédération had been celebrated a year earlier. The substance of the petition was:

> to take into consideration the fact that Louis XVI's crime is proven, that the king has abdicated; to receive his abdication, and to call a new constituent body so as to proceed in a truly national fashion with the judgment of the guilty party, and especially with the replacement and organization of a new executive power.[51]

At the Champ de Mars tensions were acute: two men discovered hiding under the 'altar' were lynched as 'spies'. Lafayette, the commander of the National Guard, was ordered to disperse the petitioners. Perhaps 6,000 of the 50,000 there had signed by the time he ordered the red flag raised as a signal that troops would fire if the crowd did not disperse. As stones were thrown, he ordered the Guard to open fire, killing perhaps fifty of the petitioners (Fig. 14).[52]

'The massacre on the Champ de Mars', as it came to be known, was not the first large-scale bloodshed of the Revolution; however, for the first time, it was the result of open political conflict within the Parisian Third Estate that had secured revolutionary change in 1789. The king's flight and the Assembly's response had divided the country. Several days after the killings, a delegation from Chartres representing the administration of the department of Eure-et-Loir was warmly received into the Assembly. The delegates expressed their delight that the Assembly had decided that Louis would retain his throne and the Constitution was now nearing completion:

> We have come to assure you, with the most exact truthfulness, that this decree that decides the empire's destiny, was received with joy and gratitude by all the citizens of the department; that it has only added to the confidence, the admiration that is due to you on so many grounds. Finally, we have come to repeat at your hands the solemn oath to shed the last drop of our blood for the fulfilment of the law and the upholding of the Constitution. [There is applause.][53]

In contrast, one of those who signed the Champ de Mars petition was a twenty-three-year-old cook, Constance Évrard. When interrogated afterwards for having insulted the wife of a National Guard, Constance said that she had been there with Pauline Léon and her daughter to sign 'like all good patriots ... to have the executive organized differently'. She readily admitted that she read the radical newspapers by Marat, Camille Desmoulins and others. For Robespierre, the blame for the killings lay with 'the most dastardly and corrupt of men', men such as Barnave and Lafayette 'who regard the slightest restlessness, inseparable from any revolution, as the destruction of society, as the overthrow of the universe'.[54]

But most of the members of the National Assembly were concerned to consolidate the state of the Revolution and the Constitution, now nearing completion. More than 260 of the deputies deserted the Jacobin Club for the Feuillants, similarly named after its meeting place in a former convent, leaving perhaps only thirty in a tiny radical minority.[55] The Parisian lawyer Jean-Baptiste Billecocq was one of many who left the Jacobin Club because it had become too 'popular': there were too many foreign refugees and Parisians whose only motive was 'patriotism' instead of 'devotion to the constitution, the hatred of vice and the practice of the virtues'.[56]

Divisions were now all-pervasive and the hopes of moderate constitutional monarchists that the Revolution was over were dashed. Political sensitivities were acute. In 1791 an actor in *Richard, Coeur de Lion* replaced a reference to Richard with the name of Louis: 'Oh, Louis! Oh, my King! With our love we faithfully embrace you'. There was applause from the boxes, but shouts of 'Down with the traitors!' from the pit. The orchestra attempted to diffuse the tensions by playing the 'Ça ira!', but only police intervention quelled the commotion. A few months later an actress provoked an onstage scuffle with spectators by looking directly at Marie-Antoinette when she sang 'Oh, how I love my mistress!' There was similar friction between patrons in private boxes and those on the floor at the Comédie Italienne following the line 'The people should be educated but not misled!' Police were pelted with potatoes as they rushed onto the stage to restore order.[57]

Louis' failed attempt to reach the safety of a foreign land revivified fears that had been present from the outset of the Revolution that the crowned heads of Europe would not stand idly by while France was engaged in revolution. These fears were evident in the letters sent home by the deputy Pierre-François Lepoutre, a prosperous tenant-farmer from the border country north of Lille. He and his wife Angélique exchanged more than five hundred letters during the life of the National Assembly, many of them concerned with her management of the farm from which he had thought he would be absent for just a few weeks in 1789. Shortly after the flight of the 'imbecile king' in June 1791, Pierre-François expressed his concern that 'war is inevitable, that the Prince de Condé together with the Comte d'Artois are going to descend on France with an army of about 5,000 men in black clothes made from the cassocks of non-juring clergy and studded with deaths heads'. Angélique had her own concerns, that 'the democrats and the aristocrats are becoming more and more hot-headed, but it seems to me that they are like dogs on leashes. They know how to bark but not to bite.'[58]

There was plenty of evidence to support the Lepoutres' fears. Louis XVI's younger brother, the Comte d'Artois, moved his *émigré* court from Turin to Coblenz—the capital of his uncle's principality of Trier—in January 1791. There he would be joined a few months later by their other brother, the Comte de Provence, who had succeeded in fleeing as Louis was captured in June 1791, and a stream of noble *émigrés* with their retinues. Further up the Rhine the Prince de Condé set up another *émigré* court in Mainz. Other *émigrés* fled south across the Pyrenees into Spain.[59]

The king's flight convinced many inside France that military conflict was imminent. Meanwhile the threatening Declaration of Padua ('The Padua Circular', 5 July) by Leopold II, Holy Roman Emperor, and the Declaration of Pillnitz (27 August) by both Leopold and Frederick William II of Prussia, though more bluster than substance, provided the proof. In particular, the hostility of Leopold II of Austria exacerbated popular mistrust of his sister Marie-Antoinette. The Assembly was desperate to avoid war, but a precautionary call for volunteers resulted in a rush of 100,000 young men, their revolutionary zeal and blue uniforms in sharp contrast to the white uniforms and habit of obedience of most of the professional line army.

The work of the Assembly had been vast in scope and energy. The foundations of a new social order were laid, underpinned by an assumption of the national unity of a fraternity of citizens. At the same time, the Assembly was walking a narrow path. On the one side lay a growing hostility from nobles and the church elite angered by the loss of status, wealth and privilege, and bolstered in many areas by a disillusioned parish clergy and their parishioners. On the other, the Assembly was alienating itself from the popular base of the Revolution by its compromise on the complete abolition of seigneurial dues, its antipathy to non-juring clergy, its exclusion of the 'passive' from the political process, and its implementation of economic liberalism.

The king's failed flight had accentuated these divisions and fears, since basing the new order on constitutional monarchy sat uneasily with evidence of Louis' hesitation—and the outright opposition of members of his court—towards major revolutionary reform. Louis' own incapacity to manage political upheaval further eroded popular goodwill. The coincidence of political crisis with freedom of the press allowed the old obscene satire of Louis to re-emerge, now charged with unbridled political contempt. The 1779 play mocking the royal couple, *Les Amours de Charlot et Toinette*, was republished seven times within a few months. Royalist writers joined in, blaming Louis' weakness for the revolutionary momentum:

> Our monarch
> Dumber than a dog
> If you notice him
> He's like a king's fart.

One royalist pamphlet compared him with his grandfather Louis XIV, accusing him of drunkenness and imbecility: 'your people have treated you like a child'.[60]

Gendered attacks on the moral stature of the king and queen sapped the monarchy's symbolic standing; Louis, mocked before the Revolution for his supposed impotence, rapidly became the 'pig-king' after his ignominious return from Varennes, gluttonous and incapable of satisfying his emasculating queen. Without her alleged lover, the Swedish Count Axel von Fersen, a satirist had Marie-Antoinette bemoaning 'Alas! Alas! With whom then will I procure the joys of this world? Not with our pig. . . . Now I am surrounded only by Frenchmen and followed around by a *pauvre sire* [bungling wretch].'[61]

From the outset of the Revolution, opposition had been interpreted as evidence of malevolence or, worse, conspiracy to thwart the triumph of justice and the will of the people. But this was not simple paranoia: there had always been actual plots, and the king's perjury was to make opposition to the Revolution a matter of deep suspicion.[62] On several occasions Louis had taken solemn oaths to uphold the future Constitution, all the more resonant in a society of mass illiteracy in which public oath-taking was sacrosanct. At the Festival of Federation, on 14 July 1790, Louis had taken an oath 'to use the power given to me by the constitutional law of the State, to maintain the Constitution as decided by the National Assembly and accepted by myself, and to enforce the laws'.[63] His flight in June 1791 demonstrated that the nation's leader could not be trusted. Public confidence in the king would never recover. Moreover, his perjury was compelling evidence that a public oath was not necessarily a gauge of sincerity. How would people know in future whether oath-taking was a transparent and authentic statement of revolutionary zeal?

CHAPTER EIGHT

FEAR AND FURY, 1791–92, AND A SECOND REVOLUTION

ON 14 SEPTEMBER 1791, LOUIS XVI, REINSTATED BY THE NATIONAL Assembly, promulgated France's first written constitution, which embodied the Assembly's work since 1789. France was to be a constitutional monarchy with power shared between the king, as head of the executive, and a single-chamber assembly elected by a restrictive property franchise. The provisions of the Constitution were an historic achievement, laying the groundwork for a radically different system of government based on popular sovereignty and equality before the law. Whatever its limitations—particularly the lack of explicit political and social rights for women, slaves and the poor—the Assembly had created the most inclusive and participatory system in the world.[1] Fewer than two hundred of the 1,200 deputies who had gathered at Versailles in May 1789 voted against the Constitution's final form. Many were elated, like the scientist and writer Lallemand de Sainte-Croix, who celebrated its proclamation by flying from Paris to Provins on 18 September in a hot-air balloon, scattering copies of the document in the wind as he dined on chicken legs, bread and wine.[2]

The National Assembly was keen to see the completion of its majestic work as fulfilling the promises of the Revolution. The same day that Louis promulgated the Constitution, the Assembly passed a law granting amnesty to people in prison for acts of rebellion and revolution since 1788. Those it benefited included seventeen peasants from Davenescourt, south of Amiens in the department of Somme. In February 1791 they had committed acts of pillage, intimidation and possibly murder at the château belonging to the Comtesse de la Myre, in retribution for a bitter decade of conflict over

1. Antoine-François Callet, *Louis XVI*, c.1778. Callet's formal portrait of the king in his coronation robes was used as a 'prime version' for later copies used as gifts.

2. The Place Royale, Bordeaux, was completed c.1755. The stock exchange at its apex symbolized the wealth and confidence of the city's mercantile élite. A statue of Louis XV in the centre was melted down during the Revolution.

3. The young Louis-Léopold Boilly (b.1761) painted this portrait of the barrister Maximilien Robespierre in 1783 while studying in Arras. Robespierre, aged twenty-five, seems be flushed with his first major court success. He always enjoyed the companionship offered by dogs.

4. This is one of the bas-reliefs on the thirty-metre obelisk erected in 1783 in the Mediterranean town of Port-Vendres to commemorate major port works commissioned by Louis XVI. This one shows Louis assisting American independence; the others lauded him for abolition of serfdom, free trade and a stronger navy.

5. While completed more than a century before the Revolution, Jacques de Stella's *La Veillée à la ferme pendant l'hiver* captures the ambiance of comfortable peasant households gathered for an evening in winter.

6. The storming of the Bastille on 14 July 1789 is here captured by one of the most talented of the revolutionary artists, Jean-Louis Prieur, who contributed 67 of the 144 quasi-official 'Tableaux historiques' series. Prieur, a juror on the Revolutionary Tribunal, was guillotined with Fouquier-Tinville in May 1795, the day after the death of his father.

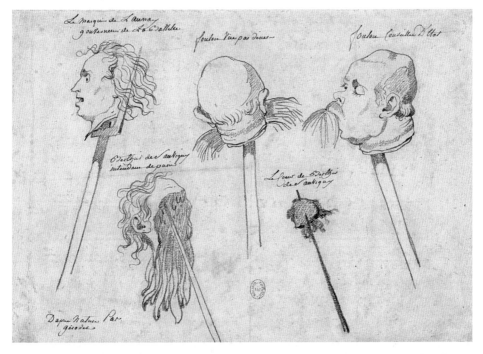

7. Anne-Louis Girodet, a twenty-two-year-old student of Jacques-Louis David, captured his horror at the killings of the royal officials Launay, Foulon and Bertier de Sauvigny in July 1789 before leaving to take up an artistic residency in Rome.

8. There are few visual representations of the Great Fear of July–August 1789. In fact, physical intimidation of seigneurs or their estate managers, and destruction of feudal registers was far more common than the burning of châteaux.

9. The value of the revolutionary banknotes (*assignats*) was backed by the nationalized property of the Church. The later flood of *assignats* and consequent inflation was resented across much of the country.

10. Pierre Gabriel Berthault here captures the scale of the celebrations in Paris for the first anniversary of the seizure of the Bastille. The Festival of Federation of July 1790 was the high point of revolutionary unity and optimism.

11. This barely surviving plane tree was probably planted in the tiny village of Tamniès, north of Sarlat, to mark the first anniversary of the storming of the Bastille. It grows in front of the parish church, from where it was photographed. It is now probably the only living 'liberty tree' from that point of the Revolution.

12. In the tiny southern village of Camps-sur-l'Agly, on the frontier of Languedoc and Roussillon, one Occitan-speaking family decided to mark the significance of the great year by placing a carved stone image of the Bastille as the lintel over their door, and it remains there today.

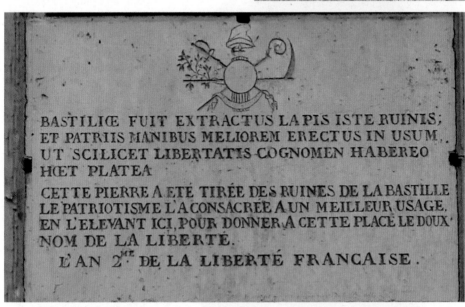

13. After the building entrepreneur Pierre-François Palloy was contracted to demolish the Bastille, he sent carvings of it made from its foundation stones to the eighty-three new departments. This stone was acquired in 1790 by the village of Saint-Julien-du-Sault in Burgundy on 'Liberty Square'. It remains there today. Palloy's certification of authenticity is just discernible along the bottom.

14. The proclamation of martial law at the Champ de Mars on 17 July 1791, here captured by Jean-Louis Prieur, and the subsequent killing of people signing a petition calling for Louis to abdicate, was a violent rupture in revolutionary unity.

15. François Bonneville's 1796 portrait of Jacques-Pierre Brissot, the 'moderate' republican leader and advocate of war executed in October 1793.

16. The capture of the Tuileries Palace in Paris on 10 August 1792 as seen by Jacques Bertaux.

17. The Revolution changed the material objects of daily life, as with this plate marking the nation's unity and resolve in 1792. Household crockery was a particularly common choice for symbolizing support for the Revolution.

18. Charlotte Corday was born in 1768 into a minor noble family at this farm of Les Champeaux, near Écorches in Normandy. A committed Girondin republican, she murdered Jean-Paul Marat on 13 July 1793. She was executed four days later.

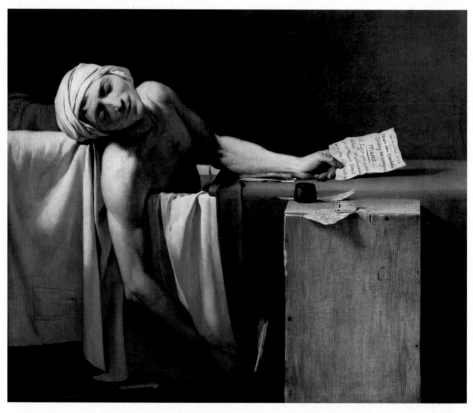

19. Jacques-Louis David's brilliant work of political deification, commemorating Jean-Paul Marat, assassinated by Charlotte Corday in July 1793.

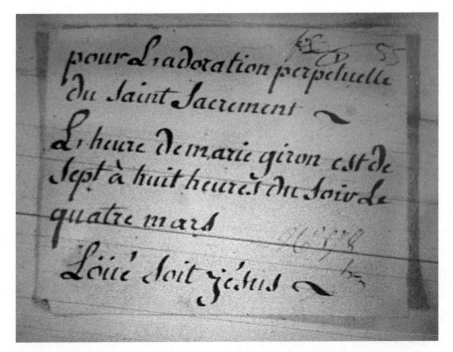

20. In 1793 Revolutionary administrators in Nantes found this note, a call to celebration of the 'holy sacraments', referring also to the role of Marie Giron. The commitment of women to the 'traditional' church was at the heart of the rejection of revolutionary change in the west.

21. Political life after 1789 centred on a small area between the Jacobin Club (lower left), the Rue St-Honoré, where Robespierre and other deputies lived, and the National Convention, housed until 10 May 1793 in the Manège (bottom), then in a theatre within the Tuileries Palace (top). The Committee of Public Safety met on the left-hand side of the Tuileries. Robespierre's life ended on the Place de la Révolution at lower right.

22. A meeting of a 'popular society' or political club in Paris in 1793, by Louis René Boquet, foregrounds a *sans-culottes*, distinguished by his full-length work trousers rather than the culottes of the well-to-do.

23. Members of the Jacobin Club (Société des amis de la constitution) of Mont-Égalité, thirty miles east of Paris, celebrated the credo, 'Unity, indivisibility, fraternity or death', on their membership cards. The village was formerly known as Faremoutiers and known chiefly for its seventh-century Benedictine abbey founded by St Fara.

her monopoly of the mill, her right to plant and fell trees, her successful claim of one-third of the commons, and her punitive revision of the list of seigneurial dues payable to her. But the peasants had the great fortune of sharing a cell in Montdidier with the young revolutionary François-Noël ('Camille') Babeuf, himself in prison for leading a band of squatters from his home town of Roye to seize common land. Babeuf, a brilliant auto-didact, convinced the Minister of Justice that the peasants' act had been a revolutionary, not a criminal, one.[3]

The hope of the National Assembly was that the amnesty of those imprisoned would symbolize that a page was being turned on the violent upheavals of 1789–91. For them, the Assembly had achieved its objectives; the Revolution was over. The disaffected would now use the due processes of law rather than violent protest to prosecute their claims. The deputies dispersed when the Assembly was dissolved on 30 September: many returned home, others decided to stay in the capital. Among the latter was the Protestant pastor from Nîmes, Rabaut Saint-Étienne, who started on a narrative account of the work of the Assembly: 'the bulk of France is settled,' he concluded, 'the Constitution is complete and the moment has come to write the history of the Revolution.'[4]

One who returned home to Arras, uncertain as to whether he would work in local administration or return to the capital, was Maximilien Robespierre.[5] It may be that during his stay in Arras and its region he reread his idol Jean-Jacques Rousseau's *Social Contract*. He would have been reminded of the social equality necessary for democracy: 'laws are always of use to those who possess and harmful to those who have nothing: from which it follows that the social state is advantageous to men only when all have something and none too much'. Even then, however, Rousseau would have reminded Robespierre that the general will and the popular will are not synonymous, for 'the people is often deceived. ... The general will is always in the right, but the judgment which guides it is not always enlightened.' The role of the 'virtuous' and disinterested legis-lator would be paramount, exposing conspiracy and aligning the popular will with its own best interests. The attractions of personal glory or popu-larity were to be shunned. There was no better warning than the case of Mirabeau, who had revelled in his eminence as the Revolution's eloquent mouthpiece while secretly serving the court.[6]

Robespierre took from Rousseau the clear message that republics are not per se virtuous: indeed, Rousseau had insisted that the hallmark of good government was respect for the public interest, and that in that sense a healthy republic—the *res publica* ('public affairs')—could even be achieved under a monarchy. Those who were unsettled by the king's duplicity had alternative views. Jacques-Nicolas Billaud-Varenne, a former lawyer in the Paris Parlement, wrote a trenchant pamphlet titled *L'Acéphocratie*, still under his pre-revolutionary name of Billaud de Varenne, in which he argued for a federated republic along American lines as the best way to ensure genuine popular participation in a populous country. Another who was enamoured of the United States was a prominent writer of travel and political literature, and also of pornography, Jacques-Pierre Brissot. He had travelled there in 1788 and subsequently enthused in a three-volume work published in 1791 about its potential as an example for France to follow, with an elected president within a peaceful, federal Europe (Fig. 15).[7]

Angry divisions within and outside France turned such a utopian vision into a mirage. Inside France violent conflict continued to bubble through the social rifts created by reforms to the Church and unresolved questions about seigneurial dues and the control of resources, such as commons and forests. From 1789 a plethora of reports poured in to Paris of seizures of land belonging to the state and to seigneurs, and of unchecked felling of trees. Marginal, uncultivated land and even forested land was being seized and cleared by the rural poor, desperate for an arable plot. Legislation sought to resolve rural conflict and to protect trees and land belonging to others, but was usually ineffectual and seen as reinforcing the interests of the well-to-do.[8] Often the disappointment at the limits to agrarian reform and anger at changes to the Church came together in a wave of rage. What had rankled with masses of peasants in Lower Brittany, for example, was the system of *domaine congéable*, whereby the landlord owned the land while the tenant or *colon* owned not only the crops but also the buildings. Since many of these leases were very long term, tenants had come to see themselves as owners rather than renters of the property. Tenants felt that any improvements they made to the farm only provided a pretext for landowners to evict them and charge higher rents. Neither the August decrees of 1789 nor later rural legislation on 6 August 1791 addressed the specific problems of the *congéables*—were they tenants or owners?—since that of 1791 only gave the *colons* the right to initiate an end to the lease, and to claim compensation for buildings they had erected. The National Assembly had alienated the crucial group of substantial tenant-farmers, the core of the rural community, already furious about reforms to the Church.

Henceforth they engaged in a long struggle of attrition against both revolutionary governments and local landowners.[9]

The legislators were caught between their commitment to the sanctity of private property, their uneasy awareness of the strength of peasant attachment to collective practices, and their horror at environmental damage in many parts of France. This confusion was evident in two key pieces of legislation passed in late September 1791. First, on 28 September, the National Assembly enacted the Rural Code, in which it tried to balance the rights of individuals to enclose pastures and forests with ancient collective rights, for example, to graze sheep on common or fallow land. The conflict would prove impossible to resolve.[10] Next day the Assembly passed its long-awaited Forest Code, essentially a restatement of the major provisions of Colbert's 1669 code on state control of its forests, but with an insistence that privately owned forests were fully at the owner's disposition, 'to do with as he wishes', whatever the traditional rights of access by peasants.

Peasant landholders and tenant-farmers were not alone in protesting against attenuated change. For generations slaves had manoeuvred for advantage within a plantation system based on systematic violence. Their tactics had ranged from foot-dragging to deception, but only very rarely outright refusal. Now debates about human rights opened up a breach in the ideological wall surrounding slavery. In August 1790 slaves in Saint-Domingue had started burning plantation properties, setting sugar cane alight, and breaking the machines that pulped the cane. They attempted to seize the port of Le Cap, where the colonial assembly was being held, before retreating into the hills. The National Assembly's somewhat feeble response to violent conflict in the colonies, in May 1791, had granted 'active' citizen status to free blacks with free parents and the necessary property, but avoided the issue of slavery: 'the National Assembly decrees that it will never deliberate on the station of people of colour who are not born of free father and mother, without the prior, free and spontaneous wish of the colonies'.[11]

In August 1791 wider slave insurrection erupted on the northern plain of the colony of Saint-Domingue, and insurgents swept once more towards Le Cap where the colonial assembly was again in session. They were unable to take the town, and retreated into the mountains where they established defensive camps against colonial troops. Many of the slaves were veterans of civil wars in the Congo region of central Africa and used to guerrilla tactics. The insurrection was bloodily uncompromising, since the rebels knew that their failure would mean death. By the end of 1791 there were perhaps four hundred deaths of white colonists, but the numbers of deaths among slaves may have been ten times greater.[12]

The rebellion intensified the opposition of the colonial lobby in France to any concessions. In November 1791 alone the mercantile community of Nantes donated almost 120,000 *livres* to assist their peers in Saint-Domingue, buying everything from guns, pistols, ammunition and sabres to biscuits, pear brandy, and Dutch beer and cheese. It was despatched on ships with names such as the *Magnifique* and the *Sage*.[13] The aid was insufficient: widening rebellion pressured the new Legislative Assembly, which convened on 1 October 1791, into extending civil equality to all 'free persons of colour' in April 1792, but the issue of slavery itself was left untouched.

From outside France, monarchs expressed concern for Louis' safety after his capture at Varennes, and fears that the Revolution might spread, while supporters of change looked to France for inspiration. In 1791 the Hungarian guardsman István Batsányi wrote a poem 'On the Changes in France':

> O you still in the slave's collar, that yoke
> which drags you down to the grave!
> And you too! Holy consecrated kings, who
> – though the very earth demands your blood – still
> slay your hapless subjects: turn your eyes to Paris!
> Let France set out the fate of both king and shackled slave.[14]

The young Rotterdam patrician Gijsbert Karel van Hogendorp concluded in 1791 that there was an international struggle going on between those who assumed that power was of 'divine origin and supported by the church' and those for whom it was based on the 'free consent of those who submit to it': 'Church and State' against 'Sovereignty of the People, or Democracy'.[15]

In England a heated pamphlet war pitted Edmund Burke and others against defenders of the Revolution. Burke's *Reflections on the Revolution in France* sold 17,500 copies within months of its publication in November 1790; it was immediately translated into French and sold well. It was contested by Mary Wollstonecraft's *A Vindication of the Rights of Men* (also 1790), and particularly by Thomas Paine's *Rights of Man* (March 1791), the sales of which exceeded 200,000. Paine insisted that 'it is an age of

Revolutions, in which everything may be looked for'. The conflict was not only a war of words. On the second anniversary of the taking of the Bastille, on 14 July 1791, 'Church and King' rioters wrecked the Birmingham home of the scientist Joseph Priestley, a strong defender of the Revolution against Burke. Early in 1792 the London Corresponding Society had 10,000 members and most Scottish towns and cities had a Society of Friends of the People. In Ireland the United Irishmen were inspired to campaign to extend the suffrage to Catholics.[16]

Everywhere the revolutionary challenge encountered societies themselves in a state of flux, and local circumstances determined how the challenge would be absorbed, adapted or rejected. So, for example, in 1792 Ahmed Efendi, the Ottoman Sultan Selim III's private secretary, recorded in his diary his wish: 'may God cause the upheaval in France to spread like syphilis to the other enemies of the empire, hurl them into prolonged conflict with one another, and thus accomplish results beneficial to the Empire. Amen.'[17]

The question of Louis XVI's sincerity encapsulated these debates. From the outset of the Revolution, anxieties about the king's real intentions had jarred with the desire to see him as the 'restorer of French liberty'. His disastrous attempt to flee in June 1791 had reinforced those suspicions, despite the fervent attempts to believe his new protestations of fidelity in proclaiming the Constitution in September of that year.[18] Views were polarized. In December, Charles-Armand, Marquis de la Rouërie launched the Breton Association, calling for a restoration of absolute monarchy and the former rights of his province.[19] In contrast, the Jacobin Club of Marseille wrote to Louis in February 1792 reminding him that 'the people are sovereign and you only a subject'.[20]

On 14 September 1791, the same day as the Constitution was promulgated, the National Assembly voted to incorporate Avignon and its region of Comtat-Venaissin into the new France, ending nearly five hundred years of papal rule. The Assembly had avoided a decisive response in 1790 to popular demands from Avignon and its region for reunification with France in the hope of a rapprochement with the papacy over church reform. The Pope's repudiation of reform in April 1791 removed that constraint. Votes were gathered from the ninety-eight communities in the area, with only nineteen against. Internal political and religious dissensions in Avignon itself, exacerbated by a long drought, erupted on 16 October when a crowd of women claimed that a statue of the Virgin Mary was weeping in dismay at the patriots' sacrileges. One of the prominent Jacobins, Nicolas Lescuyer, was seized and battered to death with chairs and paving stones; his eyes and face were attacked with knitting needles and scissors. In retribution, patriots led by Mathieu Jourdan—nicknamed 'Coupe-tête' for claiming to have beheaded the governor of the Bastille in 1789—rounded up suspects and alleged accomplices and killed sixty of them with swords, iron bars and rifle butts. Their bodies were dumped in a latrine in a tower of the palace known as La Glacière. When commissioners arrived in Avignon from Paris in November they began arresting the perpetrators; the bodies were disinterred and given a civic funeral. But the killers would go free when the Legislative Assembly voted in March 1792 to offer a general amnesty for all crimes committed in Avignon before November 1791.[21]

It was in this highly charged context that the new Legislative Assembly convened in Paris in October 1791. It had been elected in the week after 29 August: the overall participation of about one-quarter of 'active' citizens disguised extremes of 11–12 per cent in Pyrénées-Orientales and only 14 per cent in Paris, compared with about 50 per cent in Alsace and Corsica.[22] The Legislative Assembly was composed of 'new men', following the self-denying ordinance passed by the National Assembly on Robespierre's urging, which disqualified the framers of the Constitution from being those who implemented it. At the outset most of its members sought above all to consolidate the Revolution and constitutional monarchy. These 'Feuillants' were, depending on the vote, between 264 and 334 (35–45 per cent) of the 750 deputies in the new Assembly; 'independents' comprised between 275 and 345 (37–46 per cent) deputies, and Jacobins as few as 136 (18 per cent). Among the Jacobins were Brissot, Condorcet and some brilliant orators from Bordeaux, such as Pierre Vergniaud and Marguerite-Élie Guadet.[23]

Despite the level of consensus in the Assembly among those seeking stability through constitutional monarchy, the Constitution was promulgated amid thunderous rumblings of discontent. European powers threatened France over what they saw as Louis' imprisonment, at the same time as the king's flight had shattered his people's faith in his attachment to them. Half the clergy of the country—and many of their parishioners—had been alienated by the upheavals of the Church. Millions of peasants were locked in an unresolved, bitter stand-off over seigneurial dues. Artisans and labourers in provincial centres had lost employment and custom with the abolition of *ancien régime* institutions and the sale of church property. The richest colony in the empire had just erupted in a civil war to the death.

Anxieties about external hostility played into a nationalist narrative that had developed inside France to explain its increasing diplomatic isolation and decline. Central to the reforming zeal of the National Assembly was the belief that the new nation would be 'regenerated' and return to the international status it had enjoyed before the successive foreign affairs humiliations since 1763.[24] The mounting hostility of opponents of the Revolution inside and outside France focused the deputies' concern on the counter-revolution centred on Coblenz, where Louis' brother the Comte de Provence had joined his other brother, the Comte d'Artois, who had emigrated in July 1789. The officer corps of the royal army began to disintegrate, with over 6,000 noble officers emigrating by December 1791, more than half of all officers.[25]

The increasingly anxious deputies of the Legislative Assembly were swayed by the bellicose rhetoric of a group of Jacobins, led by Brissot, who blamed the Revolution's difficulties on internal conspiracies linked to external enemies. The deputies were well aware of the magnitude of what had been achieved in 1789–91 and readily convinced that the crowned heads of Europe would stop at nothing to prevent the spread of the revolutionary contagion. Once the king attempted to flee in June 1791 and his fellow monarchs felt impelled to voice more bellicose attitudes to the Revolution, rumours of war sharpened the certainty that counter-revolution was more dangerous than it was in actuality.

The real threat of counter-revolution created this obsessive mentality, but there was also a mindset predisposed to believing in a Manichean struggle. The old belief that 'the king is good but his advisers are wicked' survived the Revolution of 1789 and was intrinsic to the vehemence with which Marie-Antoinette was attacked as having emasculated and perverted the king. The power of rumour was magnified by the difficulty of rapid communication to and from Paris, creating a context in which news was delayed and inflated. Rumours of conspiracies to reimpose the *ancien régime* were fuelled by news of actual counter-revolutionary activities and, in regions close to the frontiers, by fear of invasion and war.

The followers of Brissot agitated within the Legislative Assembly. In a debate on the *émigrés*, Vergniaud declared that 'a wall of conspiracy' had been formed around France.[26] It was evident to revolutionaries that the self-interest of the malevolent lay behind the conspiracies that had prevented the universal embrace of the promise of human regeneration expressed in the Declaration of 1789 and now the Constitution of 1791. In

November the Jacobin Claude Basire warned the Assembly that 'we are surrounded by conspirators; everywhere plots are under way and you are continually receiving denunciations of individual facts, which are all connected with the great conspiracy, about whose existence none of us can have any doubt'. This 'great conspiracy' linked the crowned heads of Europe, the aristocracy and the papacy.[27]

Brissot's Jacobins convinced the Feuillants. On 9 November 1791 the Legislative Assembly passed a sweeping law, effectively declaring the *émigrés* outlaws should they not return by the start of the new year: 'they will be prosecuted, and punished with death'.[28] Three days later the king used his suspensive veto to block the legislation. Then Maximin Isnard, a deputy from Provence, insisted that the only solution to the sectarian division in the south was to exile non-juring clergy. On 29 November the Assembly decided that those who refused a new oath would lose their pensions and any right to administer the sacraments. On 19 December, Louis vetoed that decree as well.

By early 1792 such was the combination of anxiety, zeal and fear pervading the Assembly that most deputies convinced themselves that the rulers of Austria and Prussia in particular were engaged in naked aggression towards the Revolution. They were encouraged in their certainty by the urgings of political refugees in Paris who had formed themselves into a force of fifty-four companies of volunteers ready to depart to liberate their homelands. The Brissotins argued that the Revolution would not be safe until the foreign threat was destroyed. A military strike at Austria and Prussia, which would be brief because of the welcome the commoners in those countries would naturally offer to their liberated brothers, especially in Belgium, would also expose internal counter-revolutionaries in the cauldron of armed conflict between old and new Europe.[29]

Like self-deluded leaders before and since, the followers of Brissot found in the appeal of military mobilization a simple solution to complex problems. The costs of their delusion would be terrible. During the push for war in 1791 by Brissot's faction, Robespierre was convinced that internal opponents of the Revolution, especially the court, would welcome a war that would provide the occasion for its enemies to purge France of revolutionary contamination. 'Let us overcome our enemies within and then march against our foreign foes, if any still exist,' Robespierre urged the Jacobins on 18 December. Not only was the Revolution far from complete, but precipitate, ill-prepared war would expose the nation to the danger of military rule: in turbulent times 'army chiefs become the arbiters of the fate of their country and tip the scales in favour of the party they have embraced. If they are Caesars or Cromwells, they grab power themselves.'[30] Brissot responded on the 29 December, insisting that the new nation must declare war 'for its honour, external security, domestic peace, to restore our finances and public credit, to put an end to terror, betrayals and anarchy'. At the Jacobin Club on 2 January 1792, Robespierre repudiated Brissot's analogy with the American War of Independence, for in that case the colonists had fought a defensive war against the English king's army on their own soil.[31] In contrast, 'nobody likes armed missionaries: and the first advice nature gives to prudence is to repel them as enemies. . . . The declaration of rights is not a ray of sunshine which strikes everyone at the same moment.'[32] But very few inside, or outside, the Assembly were convinced by Robespierre's warnings.

The conviction that *ancien régime* Europe would not allow France to make its revolution in peace was accentuated by continued angry and often violent divisions inside France. During the winter of 1791–92 a wave of attacks across the south of the Massif Central targeted non-juring clergy and former seigneurs still seeking to collect feudal dues. The administrators of the district of Aurillac reported on 27 March 1792 that 'everywhere it's the priests, the former nobles, the *émigrés* or those suspected of being their partisans who have been the targets and their victims'.[33] In the department of Gard a band of up to 1,500 men ransacked the huge château at Aubais; those at Gallargues and Aujargues were set ablaze. This was the start of weeks of arson attacks on scores of properties of 'aristocrats', remembered as the 'war on the châteaux'. On 5 April five hundred people invaded the château at Le Mercou, near Le Vigan, and made such an intense bonfire of its furnishings that stone walls cracked. They also felled avenues of chestnuts, laurel trees and an orchard of pear trees. It was weeks before administrators could begin to stifle the people's rage.[34]

Very different, but just as troubling, was an incident thirty miles south-west of Paris on 3 March 1792.[35] Jacques Simonneau, mayor of Étampes, was proprietor of a tannery with about sixty employees, and also a member of his local Jacobin Club. Despite widespread food shortages among wage-earners, he was prepared to impose martial law to protect the free market in foodstuffs against demands for price-fixing (*taxation populaire*). After seven hours of unrest in the markets from locals and peasants from surrounding villages, Simonneau asked the local cavalry officer to have his eighty troops armed and at the ready. The troops refused to load their muskets and fled once shots were fired at Simonneau. Others fired on and battered his dead body before leaving to shouts of 'Vive la Nation!' He was not the first mayor to be killed by his fellow citizens, but the majority in the Legislative Assembly were determined to enforce the rule of law and the freedom of commerce. The Assembly decided to honour Simonneau's courage in upholding the law with a Festival of Law, to be orchestrated by Jacques-Louis David.

David also helped organize another festival. The Jacobin Club had long anticipated a reception to celebrate the arrival of amnestied soldiers from the Châteauvieux regiment who had been summarily punished for mutiny by the Marquis de Bouillé, now an *émigré*, and to whose side the king had tried to flee in June 1791. The soldiers were invited to the Legislative Assembly on 9 April 1792 and David was involved in designing the Jacobins' celebration of their arrival. But he was struggling to complete his commission to commemorate the Oath of the Tennis Court—how could the original sketch be a template when some of its principal actors, such as Bailly, had turned their backs on the Revolution?[36]

Supporters of the Constitution of 1791 dominated the early months of the Legislative Assembly, but their hopes of stability were always trapped in the swirling waters of internal turmoil, mounting international menace, and uncertainty about the king. They too came to see war as a panacea. The dominant Feuillant triumvirate—Antoine Barnave, Adrien Duport, Alexandre Lameth—hoped that a limited military campaign would bolster Louis' standing and, in the process, their own plans for a conservative revision of the Constitution. On the other hand, their rival, the Marquis de Lafayette, embarrassed by the king's flight, looked to a military campaign to boost his own standing as a successful commander and pillar of the Constitution. Desperate members of old elites clinging to receding power— Louis XVI, Marie-Antoinette and the court—joined in the war chorus for the worst of reasons, hoping that massive loss of life, defeat and surrender would restore their personal authority. All were playing a dangerous game, encouraging the people's war that the Brissotins wanted to unleash.[37]

In its decree of 22 May 1790 placing the power to declare war and make peace in the hands of the National Assembly rather than the king, the Assembly had declared that 'the French nation renounces the undertaking of any war with a view to making conquests, and that it will never use its forces against the freedom of any people'. A war would be fought in the name of freedom, not against it. So on 20 April 1792 the Assembly declared war on Austria but insisted that 'the war that it is obliged to support is in no way a war of nation against nation, but the rightful defence of a free people against the unjust aggression of a king'.[38] Prussia joined its ally Austria by declaring war on France on 13 June. The new nation was now at war with its most powerful eastern neighbours.

The conflict may have exposed internal opposition, as the Brissotins hoped, but it was neither limited nor brief. With the Civil Constitution of the Clergy, it was one of the major turning points of the revolutionary period, and would dominate the history of France and Europe for twenty-three years. The stakes were higher than in the dynastic wars of the past: not only was the Revolution itself at stake, but by its decision on 14 September 1791 to incorporate Avignon and the Comtat-Venaissin, the Assembly had made a momentous shift to the principle of self-determination away from dynastic claim: a clear principle, but one that was to become fraught very quickly. Who would decide whether 'the people' wanted self-determination and in what form?[39]

The war destroyed the generous cosmopolitan impulses of the early years of the Revolution and pitted revolutionary France against the monarchies of Europe. It immediately raised the hopes of the counter-revolution, by adding a military and religious mission to the small, embittered *émigré* communities in exile in Europe, particularly at Coblenz. One such *émigré* was the former noble army officer Gabriel-Isidore Blondin d'Abancourt. Jaded by the pettiness of *émigré* life, he was only too pleased when he heard that 'it was war, and joy was written on every face the day we received the order to leave our encampment around Coblenz'.[40] Blaise de Fournas de la Brosse, the brother of four other *émigrés*, who had emigrated in 1791 from near Carcassonne and would never return from Spain, expressed in a poem in 1792 the vengeful resentment that the actions of revolutionaries now inspired in royalists:

People, may suffering break you and consume you
Ungrateful people, you have worn out God's good will
This day full of bitterness has finally arrived
Attracted by your impiety.[41]

While the counter-revolution could now also claim to be fighting a holy crusade to restore religion, inside France the war made the position of non-juring clergy intolerable. On 27 May 1792 they were ordered to leave the country if denounced by twenty citizens, another law vetoed by the king. For all those seeking a ready target to blame for the difficulties the Revolution now faced, the non-juring clergy were the most obvious. Was not the Pope himself blessing the foreign troops who were killing Frenchmen on the frontiers? A former priest who had been saying mass for the school-teaching order of Ursuline nuns in Lille on 29 April was murdered in angry revenge as revolutionary troops retreated after their first, disastrous battle with the Austrians. Within months the Ursulines had been expelled and their order closed; while most slipped across the border into Austrian Flanders, thirteen of them whose sense of duty impelled them to stay were later to be guillotined for counter-revolutionary activity in support of the enemy.[42]

Every division of opinion inside and outside the country now had far graver, even deadly implications. The outbreak of war gave the pretext to European governments to suppress groups that used praise of France to criticize their own rulers. In July 1790 the German poet Klopstock had enthused to a group of admirers:

> What have the enfranchised Gauls not done! They have
> Enchained even war, most horrid of all the monsters![43]

But the group that then formed itself into a Jacobin Club was now closed down. Repression of enemies intensified inside France, too. In the southern town of Alès on 14 July 1792, the third anniversary of the storming of the Bastille was the occasion of horrific scenes, as news of military defeats combined with the recent 'war on the châteaux', memories of the *bagarre de Nîmes* in June 1790 and denominational hatreds. Local authorities and National Guards were insufficient to prevent insurgents from breaking open the doors of the prison at the fort. Shortly afterwards the heads of the Chevalier d'Esgrigny and the Dame Gaillard—he recently returned from exile in Spain, she the activist wife of an organizer of the counter-revolutionary Camp de Jalès—were paraded through the streets.[44]

The war further strengthened the claims of the popular revolution; after the National Assembly had called on 'passive' citizens to volunteer to fight, their political and social demands became more insistent and harder to deny. Among them were women demanding the right to join actively in the war effort. A petition from the Société Fraternelle des Minimes with three

hundred signatures (including that of the activist Pauline Léon) was read
out to the Legislative Assembly:

> Our fathers, husbands and sons may perhaps be the victims of our
> enemies' fury. Could we be forbidden the sweetness of avenging them
> or of dying at their sides? ... We wish only to be allowed to defend
> ourselves. You cannot refuse us, and society cannot deny us this right,
> which is given us by nature, unless it is claimed that the Declaration of
> Rights does not apply to women.[45]

The Assembly did not act on the petition, preferring simply to praise the
value of women's domestic patriotism.

Prominent women found other ways to be patriots. Now that Jean-
Marie Roland was Minister for the Interior, his wife Marie-Jeanne offered
twice-weekly dinners to a dozen or more friends and allies. Gone now
from their circle was a man who had become a dangerous foe, Robespierre.
Instead, they hosted gatherings of leading Brissotins, men such as Étienne
Clavière, Jérôme Pétion, Jean-Baptiste Louvet, Marguerite-Élie Guadet,
Armand Gensonné and Charles Jean-Marie Barbaroux. The prominence
of the guests at an opulent table marked it off from other groups of diners
in the capital. At what point did regular dining become the meeting of a
faction? At what point did political planning become a conspiracy? To
Jacques Hébert, editor of the radical newspaper the *Père Duchesne*, 'the
tender other half of the virtuous Roland now has France on leading strings,
like the Pompadours and du Barrys of the past'.[46]

The initial months of the war were disastrous for revolutionary armies
in a state of disarray consequent to the mass defection of so many officers.
As recriminations and accusations swirled through Paris following news
of defeats, Louis' dismissal of his Brissotin or 'patriot' ministers on 13 June
1792 provoked an angry demonstration in Paris a week later. Among the
placards paraded past the king on 20 June were some carrying slogans
such as 'Tremble tyrants! Here are the *sans-culottes*!', using a new term for
a militant patriot, a social description signifying men of the people who did
not wear the knee-breeches and stockings of the upper classes. In time
radical women of the people, who did not wear petticoats like upper-class
women, became known as *sans-jupons*. It was at this time, too, that the use
of 'citizen' and 'citizeness' became a mark of patriotic zeal. One Jacobin
versifier defined the *sans-culottes* as 'partisans of poverty ... proud warriors

... without hose and without breeches'. Such a sturdy physical image was in stark contrast to the scurrilous mockery of the king and queen. The new man of the Revolution was imagined to be politically and physically virile, the opposite of the mocking image of the aristocracy as morally and physically effete.[47]

This was a time of savage satire and venomous attacks on political opponents, a freedom opened up by the ending of political censorship in 1789. The king and queen were the most vulnerable of targets for revolutionaries. In particular, Marie-Antoinette was relentlessly attacked for her alleged sexual depravities and maleficent political power at a time when her brother Leopold II and, following his death in March 1792, her nephew Francis II, were on the enemy throne of Austria.[48] But it was not only revolutionaries who took advantage of the new freedom. Royalist writers took it to extremes, dismissing Brissot as a great fool (*Bis-sot*) and friend of blacks (*le noir Brissot*), mocking the homosexuality of the pro-revolutionary Marquis de Villette, and lampooning Pétion as 'Pet-hion' (Donkey-fart) and Théroigne de Méricourt as a prostitute whose one hundred lovers a day each paid 100 *sous* in 'patriotic contributions'.[49] The right-wing press had published lists of 'patriots' the Prussians would execute when they reached Paris, coupled with lurid images of the Seine choked with Jacobins and streets red with the blood of *sans-culottes*. But once war broke out, the question of free speech became one of the national interest and potentially deadly, for were not those seen to be advancing the cause of counter-revolution, even of invasion and defeat, guilty of treachery?[50]

Ever since 1789, Louis, now thirty-eight years old in 1792, had struggled with the intractable question of how the scale and intricacies of absolutist splendour could be reconciled with the more mundane and circumscribed expectations of constitutional monarchy. Contact between deputies and members of his court only accentuated discord. One indignant deputy who had been to the court reported back to the National Assembly in February 1792 that 'we were received in an antechamber where one of those men with epaulettes and gold braid mocked us with the most condescending and insulting of smiles'.[51] Louis was caught in a desperate personal conflict between his upbringing as the 'Most Christian King and eldest son of the Church' and the Revolution's determination to make the Church the servant of its people. In 1789 the Chapelle du Roi had had sixty-three clergy, and after June 1790 it became a locus of angry opposition to the Civil Constitution of the Clergy. Even after Louis' ignominious return from Varennes in June 1791, his court continued to use ostentatious periods of mourning to express disapproval of the Revolution. Since 1789 it had been in mourning for 374 days, a rate three times the yearly average beforehand. Even though monarchs were expected to lament each other's losses, Louis' decision to mourn the deaths of France's enemies Leopold II (1 March 1792) and then, after the declaration of war on Austria, his wife Maria Louisa (15 May 1792), was profoundly shocking to the Assembly.[52]

It was all the more shocking because in the summer of 1792 Austrian troops were slicing their way through disorganized French armies in the north-east. Their commander-in-chief Lafayette now made a fatal miscalculation: he left his troops in Maubeuge to return to Paris to confront and threaten the Jacobins, whose radicalism he blamed for dividing the nation. But his speech to the Legislative Assembly on 28 June had the opposite effect, and Robespierre and others rounded on his desertion. Years earlier, Thomas Jefferson, reflecting on Lafayette's brilliance, had noted that his weakness was his 'canine appetite for popularity'; now his vanity had led him to exaggerate his influence.[53]

On 11 July the Assembly was forced to declare publicly to the nation that 'the homeland is in danger' and appealed for total support in a spirit of self-sacrifice:

> Would you allow foreign hordes to spread like a destroying torrent over your countryside! That they ravage our harvest! That they devastate our fatherland through fire and murder! In a word, that they overcome you with chains dyed with the blood of those whom you hold most dear.[54]

In the east, most directly affected by the Austrian and Prussian invasion, the call for volunteers was answered quickly and often in far greater numbers than expected: the department of Haute-Saône raised eight battalions in four days; Meurthe was to provide 2,500 men but enrolled 4,000; the town of Saint-Dié, with a population of about 5,000, was asked for 80 volunteers but sent 181.[55]

The worsening military crisis made the king's position impossible. In using his suspensive veto to block critical pieces of legislation (ending pay for non-juring clergy, ordering émigrés to return and non-juring clergy to leave, seizing émigré property, and calling volunteers to Paris), the king seemed to be acting in the interests of his wife's nephew, the emperor of

Austria. Could not the military defeats since April 1792 be seen as proof of this, as well as, in hindsight, his attempted flight in June 1791? Further proof of the tentacles of conspiracy was evident in armed counter-revolutionary activities. The first two gatherings on the plateau of Jalès in the south of the department of Ardèche had above all been angry musters of Catholics resentful at the civic equality of Protestants and seeking revenge for bloody fights in Nîmes, Uzès and elsewhere. Now a third gathering in July 1792 was openly counter-revolutionary. It was rapidly dispersed by local National Guards: its leader the Comte de Saillans was decapitated by a vengeful crowd at Les Vans on 12 July, and hundreds of others were killed or imprisoned over the following months.[56]

Then, early in August, Parisians learnt of a manifesto issued by the commander-in-chief of the Prussian armies, the Duke of Brunswick. Its language threatened summary justice on the people of Paris if Louis and his family were harmed: 'they will wreak an exemplary and forever memorable vengeance, by giving up the city of Paris to a military execution, and a total destruction, and the rebels guilty of assassinations, to the execution that they have merited'.[57] There had been threatening Declarations in 1791 from foreign rulers and émigré camps at Padua (5 July) and Pillnitz (27 August), but the Brunswick Manifesto was altogether different. Popular broadsheets tried to make fun of it by picturing the manifesto being used for toilet paper, but patriots knew this was no laughing matter. This time the population of Paris was specifically singled out for military punishment, and the manifesto was written when Prussian armies were advancing across French soil.[58]

The threat added to the popular conviction that Louis was complicit in the defeats being suffered by the army. In response, all but one of the forty-eight sections of Paris voted to form a Commune of Paris to organize an army of 20,000 sans-culottes drawn from the newly democratized National Guard in the neighbourhood sections to overthrow the monarchy. While most deputies in the Legislative Assembly hesitated, the move was finally backed by the Cordeliers and most Jacobins. Robespierre's prescient critique of the Brissotins' war had strengthened the ties between the more radical Jacobins and their sans-culotte allies, although he and other Jacobins were reluctant to commit themselves until the insurrection was under way.[59] Joined by fédérés, volunteers from Marseille and Brest on their way to the front, the sans-culottes attacked and seized the Tuileries Palace after a ferocious battle on 10 August (Fig. 16). Among the women involved in the fighting was Théroigne de Méricourt, well known with Pauline Léon for advocating women's right to bear arms. After Louis took refuge in the nearby Assembly, six hundred Swiss Guards, the palace's main defenders, were killed in the fighting or subsequently in bloody acts of retribution.[60]

The crisis of the summer of 1792 had dashed the hopes of those who saw in the Constitution of 1791 the completion of the Revolution. The declaration of war against European powers, and subsequent military defeats, had made Louis' position untenable. The king might have saved his throne had he been willing to accept a more minor role in government or had he been less prone to vacillation. But his downfall was also caused by the intransigence of the noble elites who had dominated the Catholic Church, the armed forces and the administration. Louis had become guilty by association.

By overthrowing the monarchy, the popular movement had effectively issued the ultimate challenge to the whole of Europe. Internally, the declaration of war and overthrow of the monarchy had radicalized the Revolution. The military defeats of the summer of 1792 again confronted priests with the most fundamental of questions about their loyalties. Many had accepted their new role as citizen priests whose task it was to strengthen the resolve of their fellow villagers; however, the position of the non-juring clergy was now impossible. On 23 August the Legislative Assembly required all non-juring clergy to leave the kingdom within seven days, 'considering that the unrest excited in the kingdom by priests who are not under oath is one of the major causes of danger to the homeland'.[61]

The conflict was now an international struggle, evident in the decree of 26 August 1792 granting citizenship to a group of eighteen foreigners seen to embody the Revolution's universalist aspirations—a startling decision at a moment when the king was under arrest, Lafayette had just defected to Austria, and the Prussians had invaded and seized the north-eastern fortress of Longwy in Meurthe-et-Moselle. The foreigners included heroes of the American Revolution and Republic (James Madison, Alexander Hamilton, George Washington, Tom Paine); British and European radicals (William Wilberforce, Jeremy Bentham, Joseph Priestley, the Pole Tadeusz Kosciuszko, the Prussian Anacharsis Cloots); a German and a Swiss educator, respectively Joachim Campe and Johann Pestalozzi: 'those men who, through their writings and through their courage, have served the cause of liberty and prepared the emancipation of peoples, cannot be seen as foreigners by a nation that has been made free by their knowledge and their courage'.[62] Those suspected of being less benevolent were to be subject to closer surveillance. In the early years of the Revolution passports had been abolished in the name of freedom of movement. Then, after the attempted flight of the king in June 1791, the borders were closed for the first time in the resultant panic. After war broke out in April 1792, subsequent decrees gave authorities the right to refuse a passport on political grounds. This was to be a turning point in the history of passports and cross-border movement.

The Legislative Assembly also acted finally to meet the anti-feudal grievances that had been simmering in the countryside. There had been thousands of angry protests across the country after 1789. On 25 August 1792 a motion to end seigneurialism was passed by the Assembly. Harvest dues were abolished without compensation, unless they could be proven to be derived from a concession of land with a legally valid contract.[63] But an attempt a few days later to defuse tensions in the west failed. A law of 27 August satisfied no one in Brittany. It sought to elevate the status of the *colons* to that of de facto owners of the land, while requiring them to pay compensation of twenty times the annual value of the lease. They refused.[64]

On 2 September news reached Paris that the great fortress at Verdun, just 140 miles from the capital, was about to surrender to the Duke of Brunswick's troops. The news generated an immediate, dramatic surge in popular terror and outrage in a city where the duke's menacing manifesto still resonated. Convinced that 'counter-revolutionaries' (whether nobles, priests or common-law criminals) in prisons were waiting to break out and welcome the invaders once the volunteers had left for the front, hastily convened popular courts sentenced to death about 1,200 of the 2,700 prisoners brought before them, including 240 priests. They were killed immediately, mainly by stabbing.[65] Those who 'tried' the prisoners were plainly convinced of the need for, and even justice of, their actions. One young army volunteer wrote home on 2 September that 'necessity has made this execution inevitable. ... It is sad to have to go to such lengths, but it is better (as they say) to kill the devil than to let the devil kill you.' Another of them, who had stolen a handkerchief from a corpse's clothing, was himself put to death by the killers for this 'uncivic act'.[66]

The killings were observed by Restif de la Bretonne, who tried to convince himself that the 'cannibals' were not residents of his beloved city. He found it difficult to describe the death of the Princess de Lamballe, a close confidante of Marie-Antoinette and popularly accused of being in a lesbian relationship with her:

> I saw a woman appear, pale as her underclothing, held up by a counter-clerk. They said to her in a harsh voice: 'Cry out: Long live the nation!' – 'No! no!' she said. They made her climb onto a heap of corpses. . . . They told her again to cry out 'Long live the nation!' She refused disdainfully. Then a killer seized her, tore off her dress and opened her belly. She fell, and was finished off by the others. Never had such horror offered itself to my imagination. I tried to flee; my legs failed. I fainted.

On reflection, Restif was quite clear about 'the true motive for this butchery'; it was not simply because volunteers 'would not leave their wives and children to the mercy of brigands. . . . They only wanted one thing: to get rid of non-juring priests. Some even wanted to get rid of all of them.'[67]

Another who witnessed the massacres was the eighteen-year-old Edmond Géraud, son of a wealthy shipbuilder and merchant from Bordeaux who was studying in Paris. He wrote home of how the Paris municipality's proclamation of 2 September that Verdun was about to fall and that 'the enemy is at the gates of Paris' provoked a rush to volunteer:

> This news was also the sad signal for a horrible massacre of all the criminals in the prisons. . . . At every step you can see the hideous and bloody remains of mutilated bodies in open graves . . . the image of death and massacre is present everywhere in the most terrifying ways.

At the same time Edmond had no doubt of the veracity of the rumours about prison plots among the 'thieves, assassins, Swiss imprisoned after 10 August, well-known conspirators, refractory priests . . . the plan was, on the arrival of the Prussians, to break open all the prisons in the capital, to arm all the brigands inside them, and to pillage and massacre all the residents still in the city'.[68] Similarly, the middle-class Jacobin sympathizer Rosalie Jullien wrote from Paris to her husband on 2 September that the 'most wicked conspiracies' had made the killing necessary:

> The people . . . is taking revenge for three years of cowardly treachery. . . . Martial fury, which has taken hold of all Parisians, is prodigious. . . . An atrocious necessity . . . heads cut off, priests massacred . . . . The

Prussians and kings would have done as much and one thousand times
more.... With what furious ardour our brave volunteers have left Paris!
They are sure to die or to return victorious.[69]

The killings were not confined to Paris. In these weeks there were about
seventy-five separate incidents in thirty-two departments. In every case,
while panic-stricken rage was omnipresent, the trigger was the chance to
mete out revenge and justice on those blamed for the carnage about to
explode. The massacres spread to Versailles, where on 9 September a crowd
attacked fifty royalist prisoners being deported from Orléans to Paris in
chains. Forty-four heads were impaled on the spikes of the gates to the
royal palace.[70] In Orléans itself, on 16 September, a crowd killed a grain
merchant who had shouted 'If you're not happy with the price, go and
eat grass!', and paraded his head through the streets and sacked houses
of merchants, burning their furniture on the Place du Martroi before
merchants agreed to cut the price of a 9lb loaf from 24 to 20 *sous*.[71] In the
second city of the nation, Lyon, open class hatreds between manufacturers
and the business sector and the mass of textile workers was the fuel for
bitter rhetoric in political clubs, but it seems to have been news from Paris
that unleashed massacres. On 9 September crowds of men and women
returning from traditional heavy Sunday drinking burst into a prison using
axes and crowbars, killing eight army officers being held as likely *émigrés*
and three refractory priests.[72]

Another who was shocked to his core by the killings was Nicolas-Joseph
Grain, who had worked as a stonemason, bookbinder and land-surveyor
before becoming secretary to the municipal council of Vadencourt, in the
north-eastern department of Aisne. In August 1792 he was one of the electors chosen to go to Soissons to elect the department's deputies to the
National Convention. When he arrived early in September, the town was
in the grip of panic about the rapidly approaching Austrian soldiers. About
25,000 soldiers and volunteers were camped outside the town, their
numbers regularly swollen by new arrivals from all over the country. The
word spread that one of these new arrivals was in fact soliciting volunteers
to cross to the enemy. Soldiers dragged him through the streets, stabbing
him with their bayonets to cries of 'Long live the *patrie*! Death to the
traitor!' He was taken to the town hall where the council tried in vain to
convince the volunteers to release him. Almost dead, the individual was
forced to kneel, ask forgiveness from the nation, and then decapitated. His

head was presented to the town council on the end of a bayonet, where Grain recalled how 'I recoiled in horror from this sight because there is nothing more horrible to see ['Il n'y a rien d'aussi horrible à voir']. I shuddered to the tips of my fingers. The sight followed me everywhere and I just couldn't forget it.' The cadaver was then hacked into pieces and paraded through the streets.[73]

Never before had the Revolution seen such horrifying bloodshed, but prominent revolutionaries, notably Danton and Marat, excused the killings: thereafter they would be derided by their opponents as 'septembriseurs'. For those hostile to the Revolution—at the time and ever since—the escalation of punitive violence was the result of a revolutionary intolerance and popular bloodlust already discernible in 1789.[74] But it was the real menace of the counter-revolution and the mixed emotions of panic, outrage, pride and fear that it aroused which fostered a willingness to believe that enemies were omnipresent. Then the outbreak of war transformed political divisions into matters of life and death. By the summer of 1792 the stakes being fought for were so high that a thorough purge of their enemies seemed to both sides the only way to secure or overturn the Revolution.

The dominant emotion in France from mid-1791 was fear: of the unknown, of enemies both open and clandestine, of economic instability and hardship, of loss of position and power. Those who were believed to be openly thwarting the promise of the Revolution were at times made to feel other emotions, of terror and humiliation. The September massacres demonstrated the desire of furious crowds to punish their perceived enemies, often in degrading and cruel ways. Where the enemy was an erstwhile friend who had betrayed the people, the punishment could include prolonged, ritualized humiliation, as Nicolas-Joseph Grain had observed at Soissons.

By the autumn of 1792 the Revolution had been transformed by a radical, second revolution. It was now armed, democratic and had overthrown its king. In stark contrast with 1789, however, the exhilarated sense of regeneration and resolve by which these months are characterized was muted by the horrors of September and the desperate military situation that hung over a nation without a king.

CHAPTER NINE

REPUBLICANS AT THE
CROSSROADS, 1792–93

THE HORROR OF THE KILLINGS HUNG OVER THE ELECTIONS FOR THE National Convention early in September 1792. This time, all men aged twenty-one resident in their commune for one year and who lived from their income or work could vote: only domestic servants were excluded. To be eligible to be a deputy one had also to be twenty-five years old. These were still indirect and cumbersome elections, however, where a small number of electors were chosen to make the final decision, one that could take many days. Added to this, other factors—farm work at harvest time, preoccupation with war, and opposition to the church reforms and the overthrow of the monarchy—meant that fewer than 12 per cent of eligible men voted.

As the 749 deputies convened in Paris for the Convention's opening session on 20 September, revolutionary armies won their first great victory, at Valmy, 120 miles east of the capital. The mainly volunteer troops fought under generals Kellermann and Dumouriez against the Duke of Brunswick's 50,000-strong Austro-Prussian army, fresh from victories at Longwy and Verdun. While the invaders retreated rather than being defeated, the news of the victory received in Paris on 22 September was startling, and an auspicious coincidence with the proclamation of the Republic the same day. Might revolutionary armies indeed be capable of defending the Revolution?

Among the Prussian troops was Goethe, earlier an admirer of the Revolution, but now at Valmy with his patron, the Grand Duke Karl August of Saxe-Weimar. The poet reflected that 'from this place and from this day forth commences a new era in the world's history'.[1] Personifying the new era was the presence in the revolutionary armies of Francisco de Miranda, an army officer from the Venezuela Province of the Spanish Empire who had been in Paris lobbying in the interests of the Spanish colonies in the Americas.[2] The Convention's sense that it was at the heart of a struggle of international significance was symbolized by the presence, as elected deputies, of two foreign revolutionaries, Tom Paine and the Prussian Anacharsis Cloots. The Englishman Joseph Priestley was elected in two departments, but declined to take his seat. They were three of the foreigners who had been made honorary French citizens on 26 August.

The victory at Valmy was a dramatic boost for revolutionary hopes. The military crisis was the major issue confronting the deputies, but they also had to decide the fate of Louis and make new constitutional arrangements now that the monarchical Constitution of 1791 was defunct. The deputies were democrats and republicans: on convening, they had abolished the monarchy the following day, 21 September, and proclaimed France a republic the day after that. Across much of the country the news was the occasion of celebration, tempered always by the knowledge of the nation's parlous military position (Fig. 17). In the Breton port of Brest, huge liberty caps were mounted on poop decks while others in wood were raised to mastheads. As on 14 July 1790, liberty trees were planted, this time to celebrate the proclamation of the Republic: six hundred miles south of the capital, the constitutional priest Marcou celebrated the great event by planting a liberty tree opposite his church in the tiny village of Villardebelle, in the high Corbières east of Limoux.[3] It is probably the only one still standing from 1792.

In the closing months of 1792 the 'nation in arms' won another major victory—over Austrian troops at Jemappes near Mons on 6 November—which opened entry into the Austrian Netherlands (present-day Belgium), and it had occupied the Rhineland, Nice and Savoy by Christmas. French troops entered Chambéry in late September 1792 under General Montesquiou, who proclaimed peace and liberty for the people of Savoy, 'year IV of liberty and the first year of equality'. The welcome, from commoners at least, was mostly enthusiastic, and the full range of revolutionary laws was applied in the new French department of Mont-Blanc. Here, as elsewhere, the most divisive reforms were to the Church, and most priests emigrated.[4] Where French troops had military successes across the border, the question was now raised about the 'natural' borders of France. Brissot and Danton were not alone in insisting that there was no more natural frontier in the east than the Rhine, and began voicing the idea of 'sister republics' all the way to Moscow. Popular support for annexation in

Savoy, Mainz (Mayence) and Nice enabled the Convention to claim that this was an act of self-determination; but how was one to rationalize popular rejection of annexation in much of the Rhineland?[5]

The planting of liberty trees was accompanied by crowds singing new songs, among them the army officer Rouget de Lisle's *Chant de guerre pour l'armée du Rhin*. The song had travelled south and been adopted by republican patriots in Montpellier and Marseille, whence soldiers of Marseille brought the song—now known as the 'Marseillaise'—with them to the capital in August. In late September the newspaper *Révolutions de Paris* reported:

> The people's spirits are still extremely good . . . one must see them, one must hear them repeating in chorus the refrain of the war song of the Marseillais, which the singers in front of the statue of Liberty in the Tuileries gardens are teaching them every day with renewed success.

> Forward children of the homeland!
> The day of glory is upon us;
> Against us, the bloody standard
> Of tyranny is raised.
> Do you hear these ferocious soldiers
> Bellowing in the fields?
> They come into your very midst
> To slaughter your sons, your wives!
> To arms, citizens, form your battalions,
> March on, march on,
> That impure blood will water our furrows.[6]

On 21 October the Jews of Metz in eastern France joined with their Gentile neighbours to celebrate the recent victory of French revolutionary armies over Austrian and French royalist troops at Thionville, singing a Hebrew version of the 'Marseillaise' that used biblical imagery to link Jewish emancipation to the Revolution:

> O House of Jacob! You have suffered abundant grief.
> You fell through no fault of your own . . .
> Happy are you, O Land of France! Happy are you!
> Your would-be destroyers have fallen to the dust.[7]

Soldiers in particular enjoyed the mixture of bravado and humour in marching songs. One of the most popular had initially been composed by the noble Chenu de Souchet to scoff at an enthusiastic but poor Jacobin in Auxerre, Guillaume Roussel, nicknamed 'Cadet' as the youngest member of his family. Soldiers adopted the fourteen verses as a rousing satire to chant while marching. The first verse took sardonic pleasure in his poverty, and perhaps their own:

> Cadet Roussel has three houses,
> They have no beams or rafters.
> They give lodging to the swallows,
> What do you say about Cadet Roussel?
> Ah! Ah! Ah! Yes, truly,
> Cadet Roussel is a good lad!

The song also inspired theatrical performances in Paris in 1793.[8]

A few months later the use of Marianne—a common peasant name—to symbolize the Republic started to become widespread. The name was first employed in an Occitan song, 'La Garisou de Marianno' ('Marianne's Cure'), by the Protestant shoemaker and schoolteacher Guillaume Lavabre from the southern village of Puylaurens, near Castres. The song referred both to Joseph Servan, Minister of War, and Jean-Marie Roland, Minister of the Interior:

> Marianne, seriously attacked by a grave illness,
> Was always mistreated and was dying in misery. . . .
> The helpful bloodletting that happened on 10 August,
> Has helped our beloved Marianne rediscover her appetite:
> Bad illnesses disappear quickly when one can rediscover one's appetite:
> A little of Servan's olive oil, a little of Roland's syrup,
> Have certainly cleared her chest:
> Marianne is feeling better.[9]

These songs were only one dimension of a republican revolution in popular culture. In 1791 the old monopolies on theatre licences had been lifted and any citizen was given the right to open a theatre. There, for a few coins, people could participate in the most popular form of urban entertainment. One example of the political ideology that now pervaded the theatre in the autumn of 1792 was written by 'citizen Gamas', *Émigrés in the Austral Lands or the Last Chapter of a Great Revolution, a Comedy*, performed for the first time in the Théâtre des Amis de la Patrie in Paris in November.[10] Gamas' play was redolent of the heady mix of patriotic virtues and hatred for the old Europe of the aristocracy. The noble and clerical *émigrés*, still dressed in their finery and utterly unreconstructed in their prejudices, have to come to terms with life in a state of nature. Oziambo, an idealized Aborigine, is eager to learn from the 'benefactor of humanity' Matthew the ploughman, the hero of the play: 'Love of fellow man, courage, integrity, these are his obligations. There are none more sacred . . . . The idle man is the greatest scourge of any society, and will forever be banished from ours.' The play ended with a rousing song castigating 'the hideous hydra of despotism' and promising that 'our strong arms may set free the universe', sung to the tune of the 'Marseillaise'.

The woollen caps of working men among the *sans-culottes* became fused with the red Phrygian caps, symbolizing liberty in the classical world, into the potent symbol of revolutionary patriotism, the *bonnet rouge*. Another who adopted it was Louis-Michel Lepeletier, formerly the Marquis de Saint-Fargeau, from one of the most distinguished noble families of the *ancien régime*, who as a Second Estate deputy rallied to the Revolution in 1789 and became a prominent advocate of educational reform. At the electoral assembly in the Burgundian town of Sens on 8 September, a report described how 'Monsieur Lepeletier (de St-Fargeau) had just been chosen. He immediately placed on the table the red cap he had on his head, the costume of all the electors, so much so that the electoral assembly looked like a field of poppies.'[11]

The revolution in culture had a more serious dimension, too. If the landed property of *émigrés* and traitors was to be sold off, what should happen to more personal possessions, such as their libraries? Even though in September 1790 the National Assembly had referred to its records as 'national archives', in May–June 1792 the Legislative Assembly had ordered the burning of huge mounds of noble genealogies found in former convents and monasteries in Paris. Some 300,000 books and manuscripts had been seized from *émigrés*; much else was simply destroyed. The royal library, dating back to the reign of Louis XI in the fifteenth century, was now to be their repository, and in September 1792 it became a public library, the Bibliothèque Nationale.[12]

The deputies who took that decision had much in common. They were mostly of bourgeois background: lawyers, landowners and officials, committed to the desirability of economic liberalism and safeguards for private property. There were few former nobles (twenty-three) or Catholic clergy (forty-six) among them, and just a sprinkling of farmers and artisans. The men of the Convention were younger than their predecessors: 46 per cent were younger than forty years (compared with 32 per cent in the National Assembly in 1789). Almost one-quarter were under thirty-five. But they were experienced: although only 258 of the 749 had been deputies previously, no fewer than 86 per cent had held some sort of public office since 1789.[13]

Despite the considerable consensus in the Convention, in the autumn and winter of 1792–93 its 749 members tended to divide into three voting blocs. The Jacobins or 'Montagne', a name deriving from their habit of sitting together on the upper left-hand benches in the Convention, could rely on a minimum of 215 supporters. The supporters of Brissot, now commonly called 'Girondins', could be certain of only 20 per cent of deputies but could, like the Jacobins, call on the support of the large numbers of those on the 'Plain', including the Abbé Sieyès and the Abbé Grégoire, who swung their support depending on the issue. Paris itself was dominated by Jacobins (twenty of its twenty-four deputies) of the stature of Robespierre, Danton, Desmoulins and Marat. Their opponents stigmatized them as a Parisian clique, but they represented a nationwide political tendency. In social and political terms, Jacobins were somewhat closer to the popular movement, and fostered an image of uncompromising republicanism. In contrast, the label 'Girondins' denoted men closer in sympathy to the upper bourgeoisie of provincial cities, particularly Bordeaux, capital of the Gironde, from whence came some of its leaders, such as Pierre Vergniaud, Armand Gensonné and Marguerite-Élie Guadet.

Some of the leading Jacobins elected were quite young men: Robespierre was thirty-four years old, Danton and Desmoulins both thirty-two. Overall, 47 per cent of the under-forties in the Convention were Montagnards, middle-class professional men and officials born between 1752 and 1767 whose careers before 1789 had been slowed by barriers of age, privilege and venality. In contrast, Pierre Faure from Le Havre was at sixty-six years the oldest deputy, and was chosen as the first president. His writings on the navy had inspired the entry 'Marine' in the *Encyclopédie*; he was a committed republican, but despised the Jacobins.[14]

At the centre of the Girondins were Jean-Marie Roland, Minister of the Interior, and his dynamic younger wife Marie-Jeanne ('Manon'); her twice-weekly dinners were the occasion of intense political discussion and both sought after and mistrusted accordingly. Her husband held enormous power and responsibility at a time of war and a new, republican revolution. For both, the September massacres were the occasion of horrified despair. Roland had failed to order armed force to stop the massacres, and his subsequent acquiescence in Girondin attempts to blame Robespierre, Danton and Marat only fuelled their hostility to what they argued were his political uses of a ministry ostensibly above party politics.[15] He resigned as minister in January 1793.

Central to Jacobin ideology was the certainty about the innate goodness of the common people, corrupted by centuries of misery and ignorance and now by the deception, even conspiracy, of those who would prevent them from reaping the revolutionary harvest. The inspiration was Rousseau, now more popular than ever, who in his *Social Contract* had stressed the role of the virtuous legislator in interpreting what was best for the people at a time of lies by those with vested interests. For Jacobins, as for Rousseau, there was no higher duty than that to answer the call of one's country at a time of war.

The Girondins' prime target was Robespierre, an uncompromising advocate of democracy and critic of the war and the alleged backsliding of his opponents. Robespierre may have been particularly attracted to the 'divine' Rousseau because he too had lost his mother after childbirth—both died nine days later, of puerperal fever—and his father had deserted him when young. As for many others, however, it was above all Rousseau's concern with the necessity of 'virtue' in the creation of a healthy body politic with which Robespierre fully identified. Rousseau's premise, that 'the people' are inherently good, however corrupted by poverty and the self-serving behaviour of powerful elites, had become the core principle in Robespierre's understanding of popular sovereignty. He had come to believe that he, too, was 'a virtuous man', called to devote his life to creating a state of virtue to serve and enlighten the people. His friend Rosalie Jullien described him as 'a man who is devoted to the public with the generosity of the greatest men of antiquity. . . . This Robespierre is a real Roman.'[16]

The Girondins attacked the Jacobins as 'anarchists' and 'levellers', and aimed to tar them with the brush of the September massacres. The brilliant journalist and deputy Antoine-Joseph Gorsas used a parody of the 'Marseillaise' as a 'Christmas carol' attacking the Jacobins:

Forward children of anarchy,
The shameful day is upon us . . .
The people blinded by their rage,
Raise the bloody knife.

His ally Vergniaud insisted that 'equality for man as a social being consists solely in the equality of his legal rights'; and Brissot issued an *Appel à tous les républicains de France* in October warning against 'the hydra of anarchy', castigating Jacobins as 'disorganizers who wish to level everything: property, leisure, the price of provisions, the various services to be rendered to society'. While Brissot exaggerated the 'levelling' impulses of the Jacobins, they were certainly more flexible than the Girondins in their willingness to temporarily control the economy, particularly the price of foodstuffs. In late 1792 Robespierre had responded to food-rioting around Chartres by insisting that 'the most fundamental of all rights is the right of existence. The most fundamental law of society is, therefore, that which guarantees the means of existence to every person; every other law is subordinate to this.' Similarly, his young ally, Louis-Antoine Saint-Just, elected to the Convention at age twenty-five from the northern frontier department of Aisne, agreed that 'in a single instant you can give the French people a real homeland, by . . . intimately linking their welfare and their freedom'.[17]

The deputies divided further over the trial of the king. For his defence, Louis XVI turned to Guillaume-Chrétien de Lamoignon de Malesherbes. The distinguished lawyer and former minister, now aged seventy-one, had retreated from public life to his beloved botanical pursuits, in part from disappointment at Louis' inability to make radical reforms before 1789, but he now defended him as best he could.[18] Again and again, as the king's accusers went over the list of crises faced by the Revolution since 1789, such as the killings on the Champ de Mars on 17 July 1791, Louis simply replied, 'What happened on 17 July can have nothing to do with me', and appealed to provisions in the Constitution of 1791:

The king's person is inviolable and sacred; his sole title is *king of the French.* . . . If the King places himself at the head of an army and directs the forces thereof against the nation, or if he does not, by formal statement, oppose any undertaking carried on his name, he shall be deemed to have abdicated the throne.[19]

The deputies agreed on Louis' guilt, and that the Constitution of 1791 was now inoperable. But the Girondins argued during a dramatic and eloquent debate in the Convention that his fate should be decided by referendum, that the king should be sentenced to death or that he should be reprieved. The great strength of the Jacobin argument, in contrast, was that to spare Louis would be to admit his special nature: was not Louis Capet a citizen guilty of treason? Robespierre, Marat and Saint-Just argued initially that, as an outlaw, he should simply be summarily executed: 'the people' had already judged him. However, most Jacobins argued for a full trial on the basis that the king should be tried like any other alleged traitor.

The Catalan Joseph Cassanyes, who had just left his southern frontier department of Pyrénées-Orientales for the first time in his life, recalled that 'I had no more idea of what was a Brissotin, a Girondin or a Montagnard than I did of the Koran. I pushed them all aside and voted according to my conscience.' In the end Cassanyes' conscience would lead him to vote with the Montagnards.[20] Among others in the Convention convinced by the Jacobin argument were the Lindet brothers Thomas and Robert from the Norman town of Bernay. Thomas had studied theology at the Sorbonne before returning to Normandy as a priest. He was elected as a clerical deputy in 1789 and his support for sweeping reform to the Church was one reason why he was elected constitutional bishop of his native department of Eure in 1791. A strong supporter of clerical marriage, he set the example in November 1792 before leaving the priesthood altogether the next year. His brother Robert had worked as a lawyer in Bernay before being elected to the Legislative Assembly in 1791. The Lindets abandoned their former Girondin allies in the debates over the trial of the king, when Robert wrote the case for the prosecution, a litany of Louis' alleged crimes.[21]

The majority who voted for the king's death was 75; only 319 of the 721 deputies present voted for imprisonment, and to the 361 unqualified votes for death have to be added others proposing variations on the timing of execution. Devastated, Malesherbes was incapable of pleading for compassion: 'I have observations to make to you ... will I have the misfortune of losing them if you do not allow me to present them ... tomorrow?' He was not given that chance.[22] The former noble Lepeletier was one who voted for death, and he paid with his life immediately after the vote, stabbed in a Paris café. The Jacobins then successfully defeated the Girondins' final appeal for clemency, by 380 votes to 310. Many people agreed with the

Jacobins: from Bordeaux, capital of the Gironde itself, the Citizenesses' Society of the Friends of Liberty accused Louis of

> protecting factious priests, who sowed trouble and discord in the inte-
> rior . . . he who turns his army against the fatherland! . . . he who orders
> the carnage of his subjects! . . . was reclusion or banishment enough for
> the one who made so much blood flow? . . . No: his head had to fall;
> Representatives, you have fulfilled the wish of the Republic, you have
> been just . . . .[23]

Louis went to the scaffold on 21 January 1793, evidently with great courage. He strode to the edge of the platform and attempted to silence a drum-roll so he could address the crowd. One account recalls him stating 'I die inno-cent. I pardon my enemies. I desire that France . . .'. Although he was so obese that his neck would not fit properly into the guillotine's groove, he died immediately. His final words had been more decisive than his immo-bility in the years of crisis. The *Républicain* reported that 'the execution did not even last eight seconds. But scarcely was the weight of the guillotine detached, when a universal cry of *Vive la République* was heard . . . . The greatest tranquillity reigned in Paris.' A Jacobin deputy from Angers, Pierre-René Choudieu, captured the feelings of many, if by no means all: 'What's it to us? We always wanted him; he never wanted us.'[24]

Within weeks of the execution of the king, France was also at war with England, Spain and the Netherlands. With the creation of a European alli-ance– in hindsight named the First Coalition–the military tables turned. A series of defeats in the south-east, south-west and north-east resulted in foreign forces crossing well into France early in 1793. Emergency measures were necessary. On 21 February, Edmond Dubois-Crancé was elected pres-ident of the Convention. An army lieutenant under the *ancien régime*, he had advocated democratic reform within the army and had refused to serve as an officer under Lafayette. The same day he was elected president he successfully proposed the 'amalgame', a sweeping military reform designed to resolve tensions between professional and volunteer battalions. Now 'demi-brigades' were to be formed by merging two battalions of volunteers with one regular battalion, designed to meld the greater professionalism and obedience of the latter with the patriotism and zeal of the volunteers. Junior officers and non-commissioned officers were to be elected, and differential uniforms and dates of pay would be ended. Ultimately, 196 demi-brigades of infantry were created, each with a company of artillery, as well as cavalry and engineers.[25]

William Eden, Lord Auckland, British ambassador to the Netherlands, wrote to his brother late in 1792 that 'the French troops, however despicable they may be in point of discipline and command, are earnest in support of the wicked and calamitous cause in which they are engaged'.[26] But the officer corps remained a problem. There were many junior noble officers who had welcomed the abolition of special treatment for the most privileged that came with the reforms to the armed forces in the period 1789–91. But the military and political crisis of 1792 shattered these liberal reforms, as continued political upheaval, the overthrow of the monarchy and military chaos disillusioned the officers. Almost all of them had resigned or emigrated by December. Now the new republic had to find fresh sources of the officer corps from among the ranks and from remaining 'patriotic' nobles.[27]

Defections of prominent figures infuriated volunteers. Gilbert and Gilbert-Amable Favier had been twenty-two and eighteen years old respectively when they volunteered in September 1791. They were the sons of a lawyer's widow from the little town of Montluçon (population 5,500) in central France. Gilbert made a rousing speech as they left the town:

> For fourteen hundred years our Estate was crushed by the irons of tyranny, our empire was a vast prison from where our *anthropophages* [blood-suckers] took us out only to suck our blood more easily. The light of freedom pierced the grills of our cages. Our chains have been broken, our slavery is over, our rights have been returned . . .

Gilbert, appointed an officer, was horrified by stories of the massacres of the Swiss in August 1792 and admitted to his mother in a letter that he had his doubts as to whether 'that part of the Paris population which rebelled were sure that they represented the citizens of the other eighty-three departments, in terms of the nation's sovereignty'. But he was also having doubts about the motivations of his general Lafayette, who had emigrated to the Austrian Netherlands on 19 August, and by 17 October was looking forward to the time when 'the French Republic will become the most beautiful nation in the universe'. His letters to his mother spoke also of his own desperate situation in terms of his food and clothing, and his distress at entering villages along the eastern frontier that had been 'totally pillaged and ruined'. 'I abhor unrest and anarchy, but I would die for the Republic.'

Suspicions that the Girondins were incapable of leading the Republic through a war they had unleashed a year earlier were reinforced by the defection of a leading Girondin ally, General Dumouriez, who had been the hero of the first great victories at Valmy and Jemappes. He had led his troops to a bloody defeat against the Austrians and a small contingent of Dutch Republic soldiers at Neerwinden in the Austrian Netherlands on 18 March 1793, before attempting in vain to lead them to Paris to crush 'the licentiousness and anarchy into which we have been plunged'. Dumouriez then fled across the border to the Austrian army on 5 April. Gilbert wrote to his mother from Lille of his outrage that Dumouriez 'has taken off his mask'. Meanwhile he feared further defeats because of 'the indiscipline that reigns in our army, disorder, the most appalling pillage, panic and terror which make our soldiers flee'.[28]

The deteriorating military situation called for desperate measures. In border areas in particular, the Convention's appeal for volunteers was accompanied by the local organization of battalions of volunteers outfitted by local communities. While election of officers was never practised in the professional army, the detachments of volunteers chose their own officers of all levels in patriotic ceremonies. Their revolutionary zeal was not always a substitute for military training. In the south of the department of Aude, from where the fighting with the Spanish army around Perpignan could be heard, the former seigneur turned 'patriot' Antoine Viguier was unimpressed by the volunteers: 'the officers who have been chosen by their companies know no more about military matters than they do the Koran. The soldiers have no experience, they spend the whole day scouting the river-banks for frogs.'[29]

The looming menace and rushed formation of battalions had opened up spaces for women keen to join the ranks. In the northern border village of Mortagne-du-Nord two young women, Félicité and Théophile Fernig, aged twenty-two and seventeen respectively, had dressed as men and joined local forces as Austrian troops menaced the village in the autumn of 1792. The women were accepted by Dumouriez's aide Bernouville, and fought at Valmy and Jemappes. When Dumouriez went into exile in April 1793 they followed him. In contrast, Marie-Thérèse Figueur, aged nineteen, from Talmay near Pontarlier in Burgundy, fought in uniform in 1793 after changing her sympathies from royalism.

The Girondins meanwhile were in a cleft stick. Among them were some of the most consistent and active opponents of slavery and the slave trade, notably Brissot himself, and yet their strongest political bases were in the major provincial centres of trade and commerce, such as Lyon and Bordeaux. Even though the Girondins were effectively in power for about one year, from early 1792, they made no serious attempt to end slavery, for this would have further devastated trade in the Atlantic ports. The war they had so confidently begun in April 1792 with the continental empires to the east had exploded into a more general war that placed the future of the Caribbean colonies themselves at risk. Their attack on Louis XVI in the summer of 1792 threatened to expand the war and so they held back from further provocation by attempting to save his life. Before August 1792 the Girondins had been able to blame Louis for military reverses; but who could they accuse now? So the Jacobins and *sans-culottes* became the scapegoat for instability.

By early 1793, Girondin rhetoric about Parisian radicalism was sounding increasingly hollow in the context of external military crisis, and the deputies of the 'Plain' began to swing in behind the Jacobins' emergency proposals. In particular, the Convention responded to the crisis by ordering a levy of 300,000 conscripts in February. Wealthy farmers complained that a levy on such a scale took labourers from the fields.[30] In most regions the conscription ballot was seen as arbitrary and at best a necessary sacrifice, especially in places where reforms to the Church had alienated many rural communities. In the western region south of the Loire, however, the conscription ballot provoked from March 1793 massive armed rebellion and civil war, known, like the region itself, as 'the Vendée' (Map 4).

Violent opposition in the Vendée to the Revolution could not have been predicted in 1789; the *cahiers* of rural communities shared many of the grievances of those from elsewhere, with two exceptions. First, they were less likely to criticize the Church. The region was characterized by a distinctive *bocage* landscape, where high hedgerows across the undulating landscape kept cattle enclosed and within which most of the population lived on scattered farms and in hamlets outside the central village or *bourg*. It was there on Sundays that the rural community—a communion of souls— gathered to worship and decide local matters, under the tutelage of the parish clergy, typically esteemed local men. Second, opinion-makers in the Vendée tended to be substantial renters of land on long-term tenancies, often frustrated by their subordination to the urban bourgeois who acted as the middlemen between farmers and the religious orders and nobles who owned the land. The Revolution was resented for having destroyed a religious culture inseparable from life itself, without having done anything for those who rented farms and who therefore had few seigneurial obligations.

The Vendée was marked by a deep fissure between 'enlightened' townspeople and the countryside and its priests. In Angers, for example, the new bourgeois administrators had long been characterized by their hostility to clerical power and wealth (the Church owned three-quarters of property in the town). In the district of La Roche-sur-Yon, too, administrators had few hesitations about closing nineteen parish churches (out of a total of fifty-two) deemed to be surplus according to the provisions of the Civil Constitution of the Clergy.[31] This was one of the few regions where the tithe had been paid directly to the local clergy rather than to the diocese, hence facilitating the capacity of priests to minister to all the needs of the parish. Priests' salaries had often been higher than the national salary-scale by which they were now paid. Few parish clergy were prepared to take an oath to the Constitution, exposing constitutional priests elected from outside the parish to humiliation and even physical assault. Revolutionary administration was firmly in the hands of 'patriots', local bourgeois with secular notions of authority and few qualms about imposing the new tax regime or ecclesiastical reforms. It was they who had bought the church property to add to the estates they continued to rent to peasant farmers. In the district of Cholet, for example, nobles bought 23.5 per cent of such land, the bourgeois 56.3 per cent, but peasants only 9.3 per cent. The last straw was that the conscription levy of February 1793 exempted men on local councils, those seen to be the face of the new regime. The rage of rural communities was focused on men it knew only too well, distinguished by their wealth, clothing and loyalties.

Whereas the republicans, or 'blues', were largely bourgeois, including some artisans and shopkeepers, the rebels represented a cross section of rural society. The slogans of the insurgents expressed support for the 'good priests' as the essence of a threatened way of life, and hatred for bourgeois:

You'll perish in your towns
Cursed *patauds* [bourgeois patriots]
Just like caterpillars
Your feet in the air.[32]

Accordingly, the first targets were local officials. On 11 March a band of about 1,500 insurgents overran the small town of Machecoul and across the next six weeks killed at least 160 locals: local officials in particular, but also a range of artisans, shopkeepers and labourers seen as the enemy. The killings later became magnified (they were often reported as eight hundred) and embellished in terms of cruelty.[33]

To the north, up to 6,000 peasants hostile to conscription swept into the little town of La Roche-Bernard near Vannes on 15 March shouting 'Vive le Roi! Vive la bonne religion!' before killing a score of the two hundred republican troops. The next day they turned on the district administrator, Joseph Sauveur, and his deputy. According to Émile Souvestre, a fellow Breton among the soldiers, Sauveur was shot in the mouth but managed to stay erect and took out his republican medal of office. Although then shot in an eye and with his fingers hacked off, he refused to let go. Souvestre described how Sauveur was then burned alive on a pyre made of the liberty tree. Three months later the Convention renamed the town La Roche-Sauveur.[34]

As news reached the Convention of the scale of the insurrection in the west, it passed a sweeping law on 19 March 1793 decreeing rebels who took up arms to be 'hors la loi' (outlaws).[35] The violence and initial success of the rebellion confirmed its resolution to show no mercy. The 'Catholic and Royal Army' established headquarters at Châtillon-sur-Sèvre (today Mauléon), and on 5 July inflicted a heavy defeat on republican troops under the command of François Westermann. Only three hundred of his 7,000 troops survived. Westermann would not forget the need for revenge.

The Vendéan insurrection was a visceral rural rejection of a revolution that had brought nothing but trouble, particularly to parish life, and which was seen as the work of unsympathetic, wealthy townspeople. The leadership of nobles and refractory clergy made it openly counter-revolutionary, but most peasants were unwilling to march on Paris to restore the *ancien régime*. The most common slogan of the rebels was 'Vive le Roi!', but this was a password for the like-minded rather than a clear motive. The terrain of the region suited guerrilla-type ambushes and retreat, facilitating a vicious cycle of killing and reprisals by both sides, each convinced of the treachery of the other. Republican troops were unsettled by the insurgents' fervour. According to one local, 'these men only need a hunk of black bread and some water for their provision. who. who. who .... Led by religious fury, hoping only for a martyr's glory, they fling themselves on our cannon and weapons.'[36] To republicans, the rebels were superstitious and cruel, manipulated in their ignorance by malevolent, 'fanatical' priests and nobles. In the words of the *Révolutions de Paris*, they were 'vindictive lordlings, wild priests, gamekeepers without pity, valets, clerks, and a quantity of fanatic peasants, for whom crime has become an act of virtue. Jesus Christ and the virgin, Louis XVII and his mother, are their war-cries.'[37]

The civil war that raged through much of the west was characterized by the same fury as civil wars before and since, both sides convinced of the malevolent brutality and fanaticism of the other. The massive losses on each side included huge numbers who died slowly and horribly in impro- vised, overcrowded military hospitals.[38] The republican thirst for revenge was typified by Jacques Garnier, known as Garnier de Saintes, a particularly hot-headed Jacobin deputy sent to the army defending the port of La Rochelle in April 1793:

> The great measures that we are taking resemble wind-gusts which make the rotten fruit fall and leave the good fruit on the trees; afterwards you will be able to harvest what's left; it will be ripe and full of flavor, it will give life to the Republic. What use is it to have a lot of branches if they are rotten? It's better that fewer are left, provided they are green and vigorous.[39]

In the regional capital Nantes, members of the political club known as the Société Saint-Vincent now called themselves *sans-culottes* and renamed their club and neighbourhood Vincent-la-Montagne. They prepared for a fight to the death.[40]

Elsewhere the repression meted out by representatives of the belea- guered National Convention seemed disproportionate to local expressions of discontent. The department of Loiret south-west of Paris had been solidly pro-revolutionary but had elected mostly Girondins in September 1792 alongside the Jacobin Léonard Bourdon. In November 1792 the Société Populaire of the department's capital, Orléans, appealed to the National Convention for moderation and order: 'Paris, you believed your- self to be another Rome and you are only the commune of Paris: we are not your allies; we are your brothers, your equals.'[41] Then, on 15 March 1793, three deputies-on-mission were humiliated in the streets of Orléans, with young men climbing onto their carriage to spit at them. The next day Bourdon himself was physically assaulted to shouts of 'go and join Lepeletier!' Sixty people would be arrested and nine of them tried by the

Revolutionary Tribunal and executed in Paris on 13 July, wearing the red shirts of parricides.[42]

Orléans sought to redeem its reputation, but there was always a question mark over the sincerity of its inhabitants. When other deputies-on-mission were in Orléans in April 1793, the one hundred students at the Collège National sent them an address that spoke of their classical education: 'New Tarquins have crossed the Tiber to rejoin Porcenna, and they are threatening their country; may these traitors tremble; Mucius-Scaevola is not dead; a surer and more fortunate, but not less courageous, hand will avenge him.' The colleagues of these deputies, Jacques-Léonard Laplanche and Jean-Marie Collot d'Herbois, were less welcome a week later: while attending a play on 23 April, *L'Honnête Criminel* by Fenouillot de Falbaire, some in the audience took delight in shouting at any line that could be construed against the deputies.[43] On 12 May twenty-nine brave women of Orléans sent a petition to the Convention castigating the controls exercised by the deputies-on-mission, their detention of anyone at all suspect, and the pressure of the *sans-culottes* on the Convention, while at the same time recognizing that the *patrie* was menaced. Alluding to Joan of Arc, they reminded Jacobins that 'if a girl, in similar circumstances, delivered Orléans and France from British oppression, citizenesses, wives and mothers ... would deliver their fellow citizens from proconsular tyranny' exercised by deputies-on-mission.[44]

In other parts of the countryside, the law of 25 August 1792 virtually abolishing feudalism had not ended hostility to former seigneurs. Relations between the Marquis de Sade and his *seigneurie* of Lacoste on the slopes of the Lubéron mountain in Provence had deteriorated from sympathy for a man perceived in 1789 as a victim of despotism to the pillaging of his château in September 1792. Sade had drawn considerable wealth (17,500 *livres* annually) from his *seigneurie*, but was rarely there.[45] In north-eastern France, in contrast, social hatreds were now increasingly turned against the wealthy families of the former Third Estate, particularly large landowners and tenant-farmers.[46] In Saint-Just's home village of Blérancourt, near Soissons, an official alleged in February 1793 that 'the large landowner or farmer is a despot who has no scruples about doing down his neighbour and friend and does not care at all about what might become of a family he has plunged into misery'. The municipality of Neuves-Maisons, just outside Nancy, agreed that the 'hoarders of wheat and the farmers ... are at present more to be feared than despotism; they are more to be feared than the cruelest aristocracy'. At Courville, near Chartres, a crowd estimated at 6,000 strong forced republican officials to sign a document fixing prices on grain, candles, meat, shoes and other essentials.[47]

The war had polarized attitudes both inside and outside France. Once war broke out with France in February 1793, the swelling anti-Jacobin mood in Britain became government policy, with scores of cases of 'seditious libel' against publications seen as inciting civil disobedience. A Scottish convention against war was dispersed and its leaders, including Thomas Muir, were transported to the penal colony of Botany Bay in Australia. Leaders of political societies in Britain supportive of the French Revolution were harassed and arrested.[48] England had been much admired on the continent for its historic defence of its political freedoms, but admiration in France now turned to angry mistrust.[49] From Paris, England was seen to be behind the anti-Jacobin insurrection of April 1793 in Corsica, an island important to the Revolution because of Pasquale Paoli's popularity and its long republican tradition. In 1789 Paoli had been celebrated as a hero by the National Assembly but, with the overthrow of the monarchy and the surge of militant Jacobinism, he became increasingly concerned at the uncompromising nationalism of the National Convention. Corsican society divided between supporters of Paoli and of the Bonaparte clan, the latter forced to flee to the mainland and denounced by the Corsican Assembly as 'traitors and enemies to the fatherland, condemned to perpetual execration and infamy'. Paoli's decision to seek English military protection would result in his damnation in similar terms.[50]

Foreign populations were not uniformly hostile to the Revolution. French sailors and residents across the Mediterranean celebrated events of the Revolution in ways that were welcomed and adapted by those who observed them. On the day of Louis' execution, 21 January 1793, Antoine Fonton, a French administrator in Constantinople, described proudly how an 'enormous crowd of spectators' watched the erection of a liberty tree, listened to a twenty-one-gun salute from a French ship, and heard toasts to 'all the true Patriots, all the friends of Liberty, and the Turks who are the first Nation to have allowed the French to make a public homage to ... their Revolution'.[51] News of the Revolution was interpreted everywhere through the lens of local cultures and arrangements of power. When reports of the overthrow of the monarchy arrived in the Indian port of Pondichéry in March 1793, groups of citizens planted a liberty tree and threw a banquet echoing with cries of *Vive la Nation!* and *Vive la République!* Within three months, however, Pondichéry and the other French *comptoirs* had been overrun by British armed forces.[52]

Inside France attitudes towards foreigners had hardened dramatically since 1791. Under the *ancien régime* foreigners could live freely in France, albeit with restrictions on whether their property could be passed on; after 1789, assumptions about the universality of the rights of man led to an open-door policy. After the declaration of war in 1792, attitudes changed, even more so early in 1793, with sweeping decrees expelling foreigners or placing them under house arrest. The application of these decrees was always subject to political judgement. Just as the decree of 26 August 1792 had recognized prominent foreigners as French citizens (among them James Madison, George Washington, Tom Paine, William Wilberforce, Jeremy Bentham and Joseph Priestley), similarly those active in neighbourhood section meetings or Jacobin clubs, or otherwise useful to the Republic, were untroubled. The Neapolitan Joseph Tosi was even president of the revolutionary committee of the Bonnet Rouge section in Paris; his colleagues included the Milanese Piccini and the Swede Lindberg.[53]

The shifting fortunes of war had a terrible impact, and not just on those who were killed or maimed in the fighting. When the republican General Custine's forces took the city of Mainz in the Rhineland in October 1792, local patriots created a Society of Friends of Liberty and Equality with five hundred members, adapted their own version of the 'Marseillaise', the 'Bürgerlied der Mainzer', and planted a liberty tree. The naturalist and Mainz librarian Georg Forster, who had travelled with his father on Captain Cook's second voyage to the Pacific in 1772–75, flung himself into revolutionary politics in Mainz after its occupation by French troops. Fifty villages in the surrounding area had their own liberty trees. The trees would, however, become easy targets for the disaffected, as in France itself.[54] On 18 March 1793 democrats from about 130 towns in the surrounding Palatinate region proclaimed the 'Republic of Mainz'. But Prussian troops were already occupying the area and laid siege to the city, and French troops in Mainz surrendered on 23 July. Forster had been sent to Paris as an emissary when the town was besieged by the Prussians in April. The misery of being rejected by his wife was compounded in Paris by the realization that the magnitude of the war had created in the National Convention such a powerful patriotism that he would always be a stranger in France as much as he would be a traitor in Prussia. Forster tried in vain to remain positive about his suspicious hosts:

Alongside their deficiencies and faults I also recognize their good aspects—and I see no nation alone as ideal. All nations together make up the whole of the human race, and the French have been chosen . . . to provide martyrs for the good of all, which the Revolution will bring about.[55]

Forster died a broken and disillusioned man in January 1794.

The civil war in the Vendée, military losses on the frontiers, and the increasingly desperate rhetoric of the Girondins pushed the deputies of the 'Plain' into supporting Jacobin proposals for emergency wartime measures. Between March and May 1793 the Convention placed executive powers in a Committee of Public Safety and policing powers in a Committee of General Security, both elected from among the deputies, and it acted to supervise the army through deputies-on-mission. The Convention passed decrees declaring *émigrés* 'civilly dead', providing for public relief, and placing controls on grain and bread prices. It was determined not only to nationalize the Republic's resources, but also to control and centralize the punishment of counter-revolutionaries. Danton justified the establishment of a Revolutionary Tribunal on 9 March 1793 by harking back to the September Massacres:

If a tribunal had then existed, the people, who have been so cruelly reproached for these *journées*, would not have covered them with blood. . . . Let us do what the Legislative Assembly failed to do, let us be terrible so as to save the people from being so. . . . So that the sword of the law weighs over the heads of all its enemies . . . (and) so that all will be avenged.[56]

The fevered atmosphere in the capital infused the Convention's rhetoric and fears. Information and rumour swirled through Paris's 3,000 wine shops and taverns, 600 bakeries and 1,000 groceries where women and men gathered. Military news sometimes spread there through returning army detachments before being announced in the Convention. The capital was a tense and dangerous place, but the *sans-culottes* were far from the drunken, bestial mobs relished by later novelists. Their neighbourhood leaders were those most likely to be men of long-standing substance and repute. In the militant *faubourg* Saint-Antoine in the east of the city, for example, the wealthy carriage-maker and property-owner Antoine-Pierre Damoye had been elected to various positions, had been a deputy to the insurrectionary Commune of 1792, and was a member of the Jacobin Club. The Revolution had also been good to him for the opportunities it created to purchase nationalized property, culminating in 1793 in Damoye's purchase of the château and estate of an *émigré* aristocrat near the village that his father had left on foot for the capital in 1733. There were thousands of men who, like Damoye, were accepted as leaders within neighbourhoods, and who formed the dense framework of Jacobin rule in Paris and other cities. It was they who controlled the section assemblies, dominated the popular societies, organized armed patrols, sought out suspects and supplies, and furnished huge contingents of men for the front. From Paris alone, more than 80,000 volunteers and conscripts left for the front, and 30,000 marched on the Vendée.[57]

The Girondins were frightened by Parisian radicalism. They had been stung by their loss of power in the Convention and the increasing attacks on them by the *sans-culottes*. They countered by seeking to remove parliamentary immunity from and impeach 'the people's friend' Marat in April 1793, by attacking the municipal government of Paris, the Paris Commune, and even by threatening to move the capital to Bourges, in central France. In May 1793 the Jacobin Rosalie Jullien wrote to her son that 'our ship is being battered by the most horrible storms; and our pilots ... give the impression of sailors who are fighting at the very moment where furious waves are about to swamp them'.[58] Unity was impossible. 'I tell you in the name of France,' the Girondin Maximin Isnard warned the *sans-culottes*, 'that if these perpetually recurring insurrections ever lead to harm to the parliament chosen by the nation, Paris will be annihilated, and men will search the banks of the Seine in vain for traces of the city.' In the context of military crisis such threats sounded eerily like the Duke of Brunswick's manifesto of July 1792, and incensed Parisian working people.

Economically, the plight of wage-earners in particular had continued to deteriorate: by June 1793 the purchasing power of the *assignat* had fallen to 36 per cent of its face value. Market-women began the call for a purge of untrustworthy 'people's mandatories': by mid-April thirty-five sections had agreed on a list of Girondins to be expelled from the Convention and established a Central Revolutionary Committee. The Paris Commune ordered the formation of a paid militia of 20,000 *sans-culottes*, which surrounded the Convention at the end of May and intimidated the reluctant deputies to accede to its wishes. Twenty-nine Girondin deputies were arrested.[59] A further seventy-five who signed a protest were incarcerated.

The deputies knew that the violent purging of the Convention was an outrage to the principle of national sovereignty, whatever the harm done to united national resolve by the Girondins' attacks on the Convention's majority. Its subsequent message to the provinces was a hollow attempt to justify the purge of elected deputies. The vulnerability of the Convention to intimidation by Paris militants could not be ignored. Above all, however, the Convention was impelled to meet the threats to a nation in danger of internal collapse and external defeat.

These threats were aggravated by the hostile response of sixty departmental administrations to the purge of the Girondins. The largest provincial cities were taken over by a coalition of conservative republicans and royalists. These so-called 'federalist' revolts were united only by the coincidence of their timing; however, they all drew on proud regional traditions of autonomy. The revolt was particularly powerful in the large cities of the south (Bordeaux, Lyon and Marseille) and in Normandy (Caen).[60] Marseillais, for example, expressed unbounded pride in claiming that the Republic had been born in their city, and articulated a similar ideology to Jacobins elsewhere: popular sovereignty and the right to rebel, hatred of privilege and unearned wealth, love of *patrie* against the aristocracy and counter-revolution. At the same time there was a fierce sense of regional identity and suspicion of Paris that would challenge national unity.[61] Above all, at the heart of federalism was the anger of the upper bourgeoisie, especially those in commercial towns, at the radical direction the Revolution had taken; the purging of their elected representatives was the last straw. The immediate targets of the revolts were local Jacobins and militants, reflecting the class-based nature of local divisions.

Some of the federalist insurrections were either short-lived or were repressed without great bloodshed. In Caen, once it became apparent that Robert Lindet, the deputy-on-mission, was not bent on wholesale reprisals and promised clemency, order was quickly restored. Two thousand Caen federalists set off for Paris on 8 July 1793, but retreated in panic once they encountered republican forces at Brécourt across the River Eure from Évreux. But only about fifty people were arrested.[62]

That was not the case elsewhere. By May 1793 provincial elites in Lyon had also become convinced that the nation's woes were the result of minority Jacobin intimidation of the Convention, and most of the silk-workers had also come to blame the most radical local Jacobins led by Joseph Chalier for the economic instability that added to the fears generated by the war to the east of the city. A Commission was appointed with emergency powers after Chalier's municipal government was overthrown on 29 May. Chalier's execution was popular but disgusted onlookers: the executioner had to sever his head with a knife after four blows from the guillotine failed. As the disparate leaders of the revolt became aware that there was a gulf between their popular rhetoric of resistance and their capacity to mount an armed challenge to the central government, there were desperate attempts to step back.[63] But there would be no forgiveness for armed secession and rebellion at the time of the Republic's greatest crisis.

Such was the hatred directed towards 'Paris'—for its perceived arrogance, despotism, centralism and social menace—that Girondins were even tempted by secession. Edmond Dubois-Crancé, sent as deputy-on-mission to the south-east, reported that departmental administrators had insisted that 'the South could get along without the North'. Manon Roland noted in her memoirs that this had been discussed in some detail. But while the major provincial cities such as Lyon, Marseille and Bordeaux were Girondin bulwarks, the same could not be said of Toulouse, and most of the south was polarized between Jacobins and Girondins, with a minority of royalists. Any open call for secession would have created a Vendéan civil war on a national scale.[64]

In the summer of 1793 the Revolution was facing its greatest crisis, which was at the same time military, social and political. Enemy troops were on French soil in the north-east, south-east and south-west and, internally, the great revolt in the Vendée was absorbing a major part of the Republic's army (Map 4). The international war had spread to the Caribbean, where English and Spanish forces were threatening to seize Saint-Domingue. Federalists had challenged the authority of the Convention in many of the Republic's largest provincial cities. In such a situation every French citizen faced the ultimate challenge of deciding where his or her loyalties lay.

From the outset of the Revolution a potent mix of revolutionary zeal to regenerate the nation and fear of conspiracy had created a political atmosphere simmering with suspicion. There were always enough actual conspiracies to convince patriots that the threat was real. The king's flight in June 1791 and the desertion of Lafayette and Dumouriez in 1792 and 1793 respectively were only the most famous cases of perjury and treason. Who could be trusted? The collapse of the institutional structures of the *ancien régime* and the power of violent popular intimidation added to this atmosphere of fear and mistrust. By the time the military crisis reached its peak in mid-1793, the evidence seemed incontrovertible that counter-revolution and the 'foreign plot' were the two faces of the double-headed monster of the *ancien régime*.[65] In a context of invasion and civil war, this was a question of 'Liberty or Death'.

CHAPTER TEN

LIBERTY OR DEATH
CHOOSING SIDES IN VIOLENT TIMES, 1793

Léon Dufour, just nine years of age when the Revolution began, recalled vividly later in life how political debate in his south-western town of Saint-Sever (population 5,000) 'did not preoccupy only men and their wives; party spirit electrified even children. My Latin classes suffered a lot from this political fever.' By 1793, Léon was leader of his anti-revolutionary political pack among the twelve-year-olds: 'the bravest, the best at using fists, sticks and stones. We battled energetically with the democrats . . .'. But the stakes were higher for his parents in this small centre where there was a revolutionary tribunal and four prisons. His mother, well known as an 'aristocrate', had made sure Léon received his first communion from a refractory priest hiding in the countryside. The family avoided imprisonment or worse only because his father gave free medical care at the hospital and to the poor. Léon confessed that, aged fourteen, he went with friends to see the execution of the elderly father of an *émigré*.[1]

People made individual choices but, as Léon Dufour's story suggests, these were a reflection of family relationships and the family's position in its neighbourhood, especially in a society such as that of eighteenth-century France where the survival and well-being of the entire household were of unquestioned importance to most individuals. By mid-1793, as Léon's parents knew only too well, what had been differences of opinion before the outbreak of war and armed counter-revolution were now matters of life and death.[2]

French people were novices in forging a political life and its institutions on the basis of popular sovereignty and equality before the law, but they had grown up in an environment of power, like all societies. They made choices in 1793 on the basis of how they felt the Revolution had advantaged or disadvantaged them and those close to them, in both material and emotional ways. The key determinants were material—the impact of changes to seigneurialism, career and family fortune—but also affective: the place of the Catholic Church in one's life and the personal resonance of revolutionary ideas. Where revolutionary change had disrupted valued rhythms of spiritual and community life without compensating material improvement, or had caused impoverishment, people were most likely to be opposed to the Revolution or even counter-revolutionary. Where people had a distant or hostile relationship with the Church, and where the Revolution had alleviated the burden of seigneurialism or had opened up new opportunities, the promise of a new social order was most likely to be appealing, even to the point of voluntary military service in the revolutionary armies.

Choices had often already been determined by mid-1793. For example, in the bustling small town of Aubagne, near Marseille, angry divisions had quickly emerged after 1789, based on pre-revolutionary rivalries of family, neighbourhood and control over resources, and then on political choices about revolutionary reform. The outbreak of war would etch these divisions in blood, as deeper divisions were fought out in a smouldering fury over the control of power.[3] There was more room to manoeuvre in the town of Bergerac, up the Dordogne river from Bordeaux. Although the Popular Society there had supported the impeachment of Marat in April 1793, and opposed the expulsion of leading Girondins in June, it soon swung to the Jacobin position and announced on 2 July that the Society 'abhors royalists and federalists; it swears to oppose their destructive actions and to perish, if needs be, for the unity and indivisibility of the Republic'.[4] It was an adroit choice.

The choices people had made by 1793 were a function of individual and family position and outlook, but these were embedded in the particular circumstances of a person's occupation, neighbourhood and region. There were economic and geographic contexts that predisposed regions and communities to welcome or reject the Revolution, and particular types of social relations that created loyalties and hatreds. Memories of the Revolution—whether positive or negative—were so ingrained in households and regions that they would be a critical determinant in later political choices during the political upheavals of the democratic Second Republic of 1848–51. These memories would continue to mark political choices in

France until the 1980s.[5] Nowhere was this the case more than in the west of France where the terrible loss of life during the repression of the insurrection in the Vendée left permanent scars on society and politics. For republicans the uprising was a fratricidal 'stab in the back' at the moment of the Revolution's greatest crisis; for the rebels the repercussions of the insurrection were seen as a slaughter of the faithful.

In rural areas, attitudes were a function of the material gains that peasants had won from the Revolution and of attitudes to church reform. Where the reforms had disrupted local religious life to the point of alienating local clergy, however, not even material advantage could soften resentment. But these choices were also mediated through a complex filter of personal and gender relationships, family ties and the attitudes of the community, whether that community was their neighbourhood, their profession or their faith. The specific nature of family relationships could also mean that its individual members might react in contrary ways.

The Third Estate had been almost unanimous in its enthusiasm and optimism in 1789, a key reason why evidence of increasing hostility to the Revolution was seen as proof of malevolence. But every region—indeed, every community—was divided in its loyalties by 1793, and there were discernible regional variations in the strength of republican and counter-revolutionary commitment.[6] Most strikingly, there was a dominant hostility towards the Revolution in the west and north-west and parts of the southern Massif Central, and majority republican patriotism in much of the centre and Paris basin. But even in these areas there were important minorities with different loyalties. The south and south-east were deeply divided. Everywhere, the most important determinant of political choice was the strength and nature of religious commitment. This was not only a question of community responses to reforms to the Catholic Church, but was also a question of gender and of whether families were among minorities of non-believers, Protestants or Jews. Most members of religious minorities did not waver in their loyalty to a Revolution that had given them religious and civic equality.[7]

Only a minority of people chose the republican side in a great scoop west of a line running from Caen to La Rochelle through Tours. Here, the mass of the rural population in Brittany and Anjou had experienced little but trouble from the Revolution. By early 1793 the coincidence of seething resentments and external invasion was to create the Vendée powder keg ignited by the conscription ballot of February 1793. In most rural communities of the north-west, and even some large towns, 'patriots' were a small and identifiable group, often local bourgeois. Their frustration with the 'malevolence' of the local priests and nobles and the 'fanaticism' of the peasants shines through the surviving village council registers, expressed in the French language which their rural fellows knew little, if at all.

The most striking characteristic of the religious grievances in the *cahiers* of 1789 was the apparent paradox that these were sharpest in the towns of the west around which would erupt the violent rural rejection of the Revolution's demands for conscripts in March 1793. Patterns of clerical recruitment before 1789—where there were strong increases in total recruitment in many western dioceses even though urban recruitment fell sharply—suggest a divergence in attitudes between town and country that would be articulated in the *cahiers*, then reflected in the implementation of the reforms of the Civil Constitution, and finally expressed in violent civil war in 1793. Urban *cahiers* in the west had demanded an end to clerical privileges, and had called for religious toleration and measures to restrict church ownership of property. In other provinces, local authorities sought to mitigate the local impact of church reform, or even manoeuvre around it; in the west, however, urban authorities imposed reforms implacably, even with alacrity. There the authorities found 'all priests tiresome' and welcomed the chance of 'relegating priests to their proper place'; in the small town of Josselin in Brittany they were called 'aristo-calotinocrates' after the *calotte*, the skull-cap worn by priests. The government had to intervene after the flight of the king in June 1791 to secure the release of non-juring clergy from illegal detention in towns such as Angers, Nantes and Saint-Brieuc. This hostility was mirrored in much of the countryside, where 'intruder' priests faced public rejection, aggression and worse. As a local threatened in the village of Montautour, near Vitré in Brittany, 'You holy beggar (*sacré gueux*) of an intruder, I've had a gutful of you, you're on top at the moment but not for long!'[8] Their lives were a misery.

In La Rochelle, on the southern edge of the Vendée, the Revolution had also brought uncertainty and economic difficulty; here, however, violent frustration had very different targets. The port had long prospered thanks to its privileged trading relationship with Saint-Domingue, its commerce in salt, wine and wheat with northern Europe and along the coast, and the slave trade. The war was a disaster for the trade: from twenty-two slave expeditions in 1786, the number fell to just two in 1792. Local sugar refineries closed with the collapse of colonial trade. By June 1792 five of the wealthiest merchants were bankrupt, including Daniel Garesché, the mayor. But La Rochelle was proudly pro-revolutionary, particularly its Protestant mercantile elite, for whom the Revolution had opened the way to religious freedom and municipal power. On 16 January 1793 fifteen boys and girls aged about thirteen years appeared before the municipal council to present clothing for soldiers, which they had bought by pooling their savings. One of them, Nanine Weis, from one of the wealthy Protestant families of the town, explained:

> Citizen magistrates, you see before you a little society of young patriots, often brought together by the need our age has of fun, under the auspices of the friendship which unites our parents. Love of the homeland is already growing in our young hearts and we were worried to learn that the brave volunteers from our department who have leapt to our defence lack some of the necessities of their equipment. We took up a collection among ourselves, using our modest savings; we don't have much to offer. Our efforts have so far only been able to extend to the purchase of 26 pairs of shoes and 29 pairs of socks, that we ask you to send to our generous compatriots on the frontiers. We will not stop offering prayers to Heaven for the success of our arms against the enemies of our Republic.[9]

The Weis family was one of those ruined when, following the execution of Louis XVI in January 1793, the English naval blockade brought the Atlantic trade to a halt.

Just as in Paris and elsewhere during the earlier massacres in September 1792, non-juring clergy were the obvious scapegoats in La Rochelle, and unemployed artisans and dockworkers targeted them and the town's monasteries and convents for their unemployment, uncertainty and, it appears, the sexual frustration they blamed on the hold of priests over their women. The eruption of rebellion to the north, in the Vendée, further focused their anger. The town sent a band of 2,000 volunteers to the Vendée on 19 March 1793, which was quickly routed. As the volunteers straggled back into La Rochelle their supporters found the perfect target for their rage and humiliation. On 21 March four refractory priests were to be moved for their own safety from the city prison to an offshore prison. The priests were surrounded and stabbed to death. Then, reported the justice of the peace, 'the people seized the bodies and after having decapitated them began to parade them through various parts of the town'. This was a sanitized summary of the acts of mutilation committed on the bodies, repeated the next afternoon when two other priests had the misfortune to arrive in the port from the Île de Ré. Their bodies were literally torn to pieces; genitals were brandished on the end of sticks.

The departments of Lower Normandy—such as Calvados, Sarthe, Eure and Orne—were marked by the same general antipathy between town and country as distinguished the *bocage* of the west, but here it was perceived Parisian and Jacobin radicalism that was rejected rather than the Revolution as a whole. Here most districts had Jacobin political clubs in fewer than 10 per cent of communes and the districts were dominated by artisans, shopkeepers and traders (53 per cent), and professional men and officials (22 per cent), rather than by peasants (20 per cent). But this was a republicanism that, while strongly supporting the execution of the king, quickly became hostile to the perceived radicalism of Paris and sympathetic to the Girondins. In January 1793 the Granville Club worried that 'people in Paris are talking of imposing a dictatorship', and those of St-Lô and Périers signed a petition to march on Paris 'to make heads fall'. It was Marat who personified the menace, 'the provoker of murder' who led 'a totally disgusting faction of blood, the cause of all our problems'.[10]

It is not surprising that those who lost most power, privilege and wealth through the changes instituted in the period 1789–91 were quick to shed any illusions in which they had been swept up in 1789. This was the case for graduates of the eleven provincial officer training schools which, with two others in Paris, had been largely for the less wealthy nobility: more than half the boys were on scholarships. Of the 266 officers who graduated from the school at the château of Effiat, near Riom in the Auvergne, between 1771 and 1791, 195 emigrated, and 128 were serving in coalition armies. One group of them wrote to Louis XVI in January 1792, before joining the Prince de Condé in exile, to assure him that they were 'his most faithful servants and subjects, and that we earnestly desire, Sire, to have the chance to prove this to your Majesty, even at the cost of our lives'.[11] These were men bonded by family ties, by deep socialization in the royal training schools that had given them the chance to have a brilliant career, and by the brotherhood of danger. The pressures to conform were both subtle and profound.

While some *émigrés* were intransigent aristocrats and clergy committed to the *ancien régime* as a social and political system, more were primarily motivated by fury at the loss of status, privilege and perquisites. The numbers swelled of former nobles from the officer corps of the army and navy who joined the ranks of the invading armies, and thousands of *émigrés* seeking safety. The Channel island of Jersey, then with a population of about 36,000, was swamped in 1792 by the arrival of over one thousand families from the former nobility of Brittany, Normandy and Poitou. A second wave arrived in 1793, of 2,200 priests and three bishops.[12] There were many religious like the priest François-Pierre Julliot of Troyes, who decided in September 1792 to 'flee far from a country consumed by anarchy, irreligion, blood and carnage'. Julliot and eighty others were searched, threatened, and obliged to pay bribes to reach the Swiss border.[13] *Émigré* nobles fled with extensive funds—what we would today call a 'flight of capital'—often leaving behind a family member to hang on grimly to property while the inferno lasted. But most numerous of all the *émigrés* were commoners from near the borders whose emigration was the result of a calculation about the safest place to be.[14]

Much more surprising are rare examples of members of old privileged elites whose support for the Revolution endured. One of those able to make the right choice at the propitious moment was Thomas-Alexandre Davy de la Pailleterie, the son of a nobleman in Saint-Domingue who took the name of his slave mother, Marie Dumas. Unlike his siblings who were sold into slavery, young Alexandre Dumas was brought to France by his father in 1776, aged fourteen. The towering young mulatto enlisted, aged twenty-four, in 1786; three years later the Revolution would begin to open choices and chances for able young commoners, even the sons of slaves. Dumas' choice was to be a republican and to remain in the army. He was only a corporal in early 1792, but the outbreak of war and the decision to create an 'American Legion' (composed of freed slaves) saw him appointed its lieutenant-colonel. When General Dumouriez deserted in April 1793, Dumas refused to follow him. By September he was named a division general.[15]

Dumas had good reason to be grateful to the Revolution for the opportunities it opened up for a young man who would previously have been stigmatized for life. Others were motivated by a sense of obligation to their country. The young Étienne-Denis Pasquier, born in 1767 to a legal family of *noblesse de robe*, had embarked on a promising career at the Parlement of Paris before the Revolution. Unlike many of his peers, however, he and his family determined to stay on. He was sceptical about the motives for emigration:

for some a question of escaping from danger; for a very small number, a genuine enthusiasm; for many a point of honour, to be accepted without argument; for the great majority, the fashionable thing to do; while for nearly all of them it meant hope sustained by the craziest correspondence and the intrigues of a few ambitious men bent upon making their fortunes.[16]

Women were divided like their menfolk, but they very often felt more keenly the collapse of established forms of religious life and the departure of esteemed religious. Some women may have been drawn to hitherto unimaginable possibilities by the way in which a series of radical laws had changed the status of women, in particular the inheritance law of March 1790 and a liberal divorce law of 20 September 1792.[17] The reforms to family life created greater spaces for women's involvement, but they were divided over these reforms. Marie-Victoire Monnard was twelve years old when the Revolution began, the daughter of a farmer (*laboureur*) from Creil, forty miles north of Paris. Her father's situation was made difficult when his contract from the Church to collect the tithe for the district was made redundant, and in 1790 she was sent to Paris as an apprentice to a linen merchant. After three years' apprenticeship, Marie found work with a widow ('an excellent woman, although a Jacobin') who had just remarried 'à la République' ('in republican fashion'). This marriage consisted of swearing fidelity at an altar of the homeland while wearing a liberty cap and revolutionary cockade:

> It seems that the basis of her republican marriage was not very solid because the attributions of liberty, such as the tricolour cockade, the bonnet rouge and patriotic oaths could not consolidate the hymen of citizen Vachot, who left his republican wife three months later, without needing recourse to divorce, then recognized in law.[18]

In contrast to the views of Monnard, there were at least sixty Jacobin women's clubs in the provinces, some of them in small towns. While the activities of these clubs were mainly born of a self-consciously serious desire to support the Revolution, they were at times also insistent on women's political rights. In 1791 a twenty-two-year-old mother of four named Élisabeth Lafaurie spoke to the men's club in Léon Dufour's south-western town of Saint-Sever, arguing that the denial of the vote was 'unjust, because the mass of women is subject to laws which they have not been able to refuse or approve, which is contrary to their liberty and to the idea that we should have of social conventions'.[19]

The Revolution soured quickly for people who had been dependent on positions in the intricate, complex networks of justice and administration under the *ancien régime* and who now saw much simpler structures concentrated in a rival town. The bitter resentments called into question support for the Revolution in general. In the northern department of Aisne, the victory of Vervins in the battle for district administrative superiority during the reorganization of 1790–91 may well explain its pro-revolutionary stance thereafter in contrast with Guise, which before 1789 had been the centre of an administrative district, with a court, a customs office, military administration and convents.[20] In Laon, the capital of Aisne, the cathedral, religious orders and eleven churches had been a major employer in a town of 7,000 people. The high town ('le plateau') of Laon was now to have only two parishes instead of twelve, and it had lost its cathedral status to Soissons. The new administrators found themselves having to deal with unemployment as they closed churches and orders; professional people employed in the ecclesiastical courts and administration suffered too. The head of the new administration was confronted by the brother of a gardener at the Capuchin monastery who called him 'Judas': 'I used to be your friend, but today I hate you, I detest you as a wicked anti-Christian. I hate and detest equally your district and your department.'[21] The steadfastly pro-revolutionary administrators of Laon recognized that any 'great revolution' would have its attendant problems, but they were acute in this clerical town 'where religious houses and the clergy were the source of almost all wealth ... workers of all types are without work and without bread; the number of beggars used to be excessive, now it is incalculable'. The enemies of the Revolution 'are saying to the people that in the times that they dare to call happy, the worker did not lack work, and the beggar received charity'.[22]

By mid-1793 people had a new and deadlier choice to make. The combination of conscription to meet the terrifying might of military invasion and armed counter-revolution, economic privation and hostility to the political power of Paris and its *sans-culottes* combined with religious disaffection to seduce people in many provincial areas into support for 'federalist' rebellion. The precise motives for and character of these rebellions varied between the provincial centres, but everywhere they shared a suspicion of the Jacobins' claims to act in the national interest, a desire for economic certainty and free trade, and a hostility to popular radicalism and menace.

The conflicts that erupted in mid-1793 were concentrated in and around large provincial cities, with strong commercial ties to their hinterlands and international trade. They were both internal civil wars and wars against Paris. These substantial towns—Lyon, Marseille, Toulon, Bordeaux, Caen—had divided over economic and social self-interest and, for their pro-Girondin leadership, 'Paris' had come to represent lower-class anarchy, a menace to life and property. These and other cities rejected the overarching authority of the capital, and resentments were accentuated by the ancient civic pride of regional capitals. They could draw on the support of fellow townspeople threatened by commercial instability and rural hinterlands used to looking to their provincial capital for leadership.

In the department of Jura in the eastern region of Franche-Comté, disappointment at the failure of the assemblies to resolve grievances over forests and resentment at the monopoly of the wealthy over purchase of church property meshed with political hostility towards the execution of the king and the expulsion of Girondin leaders, seen through the optic of the region's self-identity as a province with special rights. But there were activist Jacobins in Dole bitter at the way Lons-le-Saunier had monopolized institutional power after 1789, and hostile to the political control of well-to-do conservatives. These Jacobins cooperated with the repression overseen by René Dumas, himself from Lons-le-Saunier and now a friend of Robespierre and president of the Revolutionary Tribunal in Paris. The rural response was different in neighbouring Doubs, where about 1,200 men from thirty upland communities were sparked into armed rebellion by pressures to join the army and a rumour that an *émigré* invasion was imminent. Here anger had been simmering since the Civil Constitution of the Clergy. Dubbed 'la petite Vendée' by Montagnards, the rising was quickly and harshly suppressed: five hundred men were arrested, twenty deported, forty-six imprisoned and forty-three executed.[23]

The leadership of the federalist rebellions came from the bourgeois elites of provincial cities, men of success and eminence in the professions and business. François-Antoine Boissy d'Anglas, from a comfortably well-off Protestant family of doctors and lawyers from Ardèche, was destined to be an active Girondin. He was a man of great courage, having personally confronted an angry crowd in Annonay on 16 September 1792 to save five refractory priests. He shared the contempt felt by the federalist and Girondin leadership for angry *sans-culotte* militants. Boissy d'Anglas was also very fortunate that, immediately after the purge of Girondin leaders from the Convention on 2 June 1793, he had managed to scratch out his name on the list of seventy-five names of deputies who protested.[24]

A fundamental element in the choice of which type of republicanism to support was a person's attitude to the economy. Jean-Marie Roland, the Minister of the Interior in 1792, and other Girondins were committed to internal free trade and the application of the rule of law in markets; Jacobins and *sans-culottes* were far more likely to favour intervention and the imperatives of the 'rights to subsistence'.[25] To the young Jacobin Marc-Antoine ('Jules') Jullien, it was Paris that had made the Revolution of 1789, abolished the nobility, chased out the privileged, overthrown the monarchy and now, in 1793, was attacking the inequality of wealth. That was why, he believed, the wealthy urban elites wanted to attack it in return.[26]

On the borders, regional loyalties were more profound because these were provinces more recently incorporated into the kingdom and with their own languages. But ethnic minorities were divided in their political choice, like French people everywhere. In the border region of Lorraine, the centre of much of the fighting against continental powers, victory at Valmy in September 1792 strengthened support for the new regime. Here the Civil Constitution of the Clergy had been massively rejected by priests in the German-speaking border areas (by 97 per cent in the canton of Bitches, and 92 per cent in Sarreguemines), and there was certainly extensive emigration and counter-revolutionary activity, but the province had been part of the kingdom for too brief a time for strong Bourbon loyalty to develop. The Revolution had brought concrete benefits to the mass of the peasantry, and now a foreign coalition was marching across their fields.

There was a radically different response to the crisis of spring 1793 at the farthest extremity from Paris, in the small Pyrenean hill-town of Saint-Laurent-de-Cerdans. Here the Revolution, initially welcomed by an impoverished Catalan majority as promising the end of privilege, had quickly soured for Laurentins with the increased difficulties of legal and illegal trade across the Pyrenees and, especially, with ecclesiastical reforms perceived as an urban, secular outrage against orthodox Catholicism. On 17 April, Laurentins welcomed royal Spanish troops into their village and the local National Guard fired on retreating French volunteers. The Spanish troops were welcomed with a song in Catalan asking them for 'good laws', code for the Catholic Church they had known:

La bonica mozardalla es la dels fusillers bermels,
Ni ha pas en tot França de comparables a els,
Tots volem ser ab vosaltres,
Mentres nos dongueu bonas leys.

What fine soldiers are these red-coated fusiliers!
There are none in all of France who are their equals.
We all want to join with you,
Provided you give us good laws.

Several hundred men volunteered to fight alongside Spanish troops.[27]

The ecclesiastical reforms in particular commonly perplexed communities of ethnic minorities otherwise enthusiastic about their membership of the new nation. Eastwards down the Pyrenees from Saint-Laurent, another Catalan community, the little port and fishing town of Collioure, was one such place, solidly behind a revolution that had removed entrenched privilege but with the religious fervour of fishing populations vulnerable to sudden storms at sea. Collioure's ten religious were unequivocally 'refractory', and from 1791 the town would now have just one priest, an Occitan, for its 2,300 inhabitants. Despite strong support for the Revolution, in particular for the principle of popular sovereignty and for the abolition of the privileges enjoyed by Collioure's elites, the community resented the changes imposed on their religious life by the National Assembly. This resentment was particularly intense among the fishermen, women and sailors of the poorer *faubourg*, used to worshipping in the chapel of a Dominican monastery in their neighbourhood, now up for sale. But the anti-revolutionary attitudes of the priests were to alienate a growing number of their parishioners and, when Spanish troops laid siege to the port in May 1793, most of the townspeople rallied to the side of republican troops.[28]

The experience of military invasion is always harrowing, and was complicated in 1792–93 by ethnicity, for the soldiers who crossed the borders were often speaking the same Flemish, German, Basque or Catalan as the local populations. Caught between invaders who spoke their own language and soldiers from elsewhere in France who could not always be understood, what were locals to do? On the frontiers of the east and south, the ebb and flow of the battles between revolutionary and coalition armies exposed people to the necessity of a choice that could be fatal. So in the eastern department of Meuse after the Prussian invasion of 1792, the mayor of

Romagne was accused of requisitioning for them 'just like brigands', as was the village clerk of Mouzay who selected the houses where supplies were to be seized. In Verdun, a group of young women, dressed in white and decked with flowers, presented the keys of the town to the invading Prussians in 1792; when republican troops retook the city later that year they were found and guillotined. In nearby Dieue four men and three women were accused of 'having chopped up the national cockade ... menaced the patriots ... and shouted "the Nation can get fucked!"'[29]

Explaining the physical and social geography of opinion does not mean that the choices that individuals, families and communities made were either scripted from the outset of the Revolution or fixed. Even Pierre-François Palloy, who had made a career as 'Patriot' Palloy after winning the contract to demolish the Bastille, and who dined on stuffed pig's head with his family on the night of Louis XVI's execution, later regretted his 'youthful stupidities' (although he had been thirty-eight years old at the time). Nor were commitments necessarily profound or explicitly political. Nineteen-year-old Jacques Fricasse, born in a village near Chaumont (Haute-Marne), worked on the estate of the Bernardins of Clairvaux and then for those who bought the monastery in 1791. He volunteered for the army on 24 August 1792: the only reason he gave was that France was losing battles and 'I was burning with impatience to see for myself things which were impossible to believe'.[30]

By 1793 republicans were choosing between alternative ways of saving the Republic, and did so according to personal friendships and antipathies. Those who battled over the implementation of the revolutionary changes worked within pre-existing or newly formed networks of friends and the like-minded. There were others they came to mistrust, even to hate. Particular individuals came to be seen to personify particular phases of the Revolution, and were consequently loved or demonized. Men who at various points were powerful within the Jacobin Club—such as Barnave, Brissot, Pétion, Robespierre and Desmoulins—developed relationships that may have been respectful or even affectionate but ended by becoming venomous and fatal. Rosalie Jullien advised her teenaged son 'Jules', a precocious Jacobin enthusiast, that

> The Revolution has aroused such passions that it is impossible to see the truth about anybody. You must be prudent to avoid the traps of designing men. You must keep a lock on your lips and a key to your mouth, and not let a word escape that can be held against you ...[31]

Rosalie understood that there was a tension between friendship and civic virtue, where personal ties and loyalties could be seen as inimical to the public good. Particularly after the establishment of the Republic in September 1792, the public language of revolutionary leaders was peppered with references to the figures of ancient Greece and Rome and their conspiracies. These were no mere rhetorical embellishments: the educated middle-class men of the revolutionary assemblies assumed the classical world to be a well of wisdom from which directly relevant lessons could be drawn. For the true patriot had to be willing to sacrifice anything for the safety of the *patrie*, even false friends.

By mid-1793 the great internal and external crises of these years left no family untouched by or undecided about the Revolution. Such is the nature of family relationships that bitter division also reached into their heart, as in the Faligant family of Rennes. There had been violent clashes in the town in January 1789 between commoners seeking greater Third Estate representation in the processes leading up to the Estates-General and those intent on preserving the Breton 'constitution', which guaranteed a measure of provincial autonomy and fiscal exemptions. The Civil Constitution of the Clergy had deepened those divisions in this provincial centre of 25,000 people. One of the non-jurors was the Abbé Nicolas-François Faligant, a thirty-six-year-old teacher at the Collège de Rennes. He was arrested on Sunday 4 December 1791 after holding illegal church services for large numbers of people in his home, and for having counter-revolutionary material. After a year of imprisonment, he was transferred in November 1792 to detention at Mont-Saint-Michel. Before he left, he wrote at great length to his father, a master carpenter committed to the Revolution and who had shunned him, warning him that his wilful ignorance of God's will, 'far from excusing you in the eyes of God will only serve to condemn you to eternal suffering':

> I close by beseeching you with tears in my eyes, my hands raised to heaven, to think of your final moments . . . I hope that if you do not wish to see me any more you will at least put aside your scorn and cruelty to the point of deigning to read and reply to me.

His father did reply, also at great length, insisting that the reforms to the Church were merely administrative and that those who opposed them were counter-revolutionaries who were obeying an external power whose will was far from infallible. He defended the constitutional clergy 'who have suffered patiently and without complaining the persecution that you have resolved to inflict on them through a devilish conspiracy'. Echoing his son, he now called on him to 'respond to the tenderness of a father whose only desire is to see you pull back from the precipice'. The Abbé was not persuaded.[32]

Ultimately, self-perception—spiritual, civic, familial—seems to have been crucial in individual choices. Individuals whose profession or family background would have suggested either opposition to or muted support for the Revolution could have particular reasons to make the opposite choice. The first of two examples is Pascal-Antoine Grimaud, fifty-seven years of age in 1789, who became a militant republican by 1793 after a long church career. The son of a merchant family from Clermont-Ferrand, Grimaud had undertaken lengthy ecclesiastical training in Paris, and taught philosophy in the seminary at Saint-Sulpice, before returning to his home town as a poorly remunerated cathedral canon in 1776. Possessing a fractious disposition and being proud of his earlier success in Paris (he continued to sign himself 'Professor of Theology'), Grimaud smarted at the attitudes of his bishop, François de Bonal. In his pastoral letter for Lent in February 1789 the bishop had inveighed against 'the mortal poison of an impious philosophy which is spreading among us'. The calling of the Estates-General, then the Civil Constitution of the Clergy, brought the friction to a head. Grimaud was obviously a sincere enthusiast for the principles of 1789, for the idea that a reformed Church should be integral to a regenerated France, and disillusioned by the 'machinations of those who've sold themselves to the ecclesiastical aristocracy to push aside the patriots and heat up the heads of the wicked'. Grimaud was elected first episcopal vicar in the neighbouring diocese of the Allier in Moulins, before being dismissed by his bishop, presumably for indiscipline, in October 1792. Describing himself as a 'citizen and democrat by taste and on principle', he then became a prominent Jacobin militant in Moulins, notorious for his trenchant attitudes to excessive property and towards suspects.[33]

The second example is Benoît Lacombe, the young son of a powerful bourgeois farming and mercantile family from the south-western town of Gaillac (population 6,000) that on the eve of Revolution had succeeded in its dream of buying a noble title. But whereas his family were conservative and primarily interested in consolidating their local power, Benoît was enthusiastic in his support for the Revolution. This may have been pragmatic—he bought the land and massive buildings belonging to the Abbey of Gaillac—and by 1795 he had spent 252,886 *livres* on nationalized property. But his reasons may also have been personal—his uncle, a priest, had always been snubbed by the clerical establishment in the abbey—and there were personality reasons too, for Benoît's years in Bordeaux in the 1780s had reinforced his idea of himself as enlightened and of Gaillac as a backwater. By 1793 he was effectively the leader of Gaillac's section of 'sans-culottes à piques', and his militancy was a good measure of his probity, despite his wealth.[34]

So the potentially deadly choices of mid-1793 were a matter of individual and family choice based on the perceived desirability of revolutionary change, and therein attitudes to religion were crucial. After 1789 most French people were only beginning their apprenticeship in formal politics, and in any case only men were allowed to be apprentices. Maps of political choice using the elections to the Estates-General, the Legislative Assembly and the National Convention are notoriously difficult to interpret, because there were no political parties in the sense we understand, and only a minority of those eligible to vote did so, for various reasons. The map of priests' decisions whether to accept election according to the provisions of the Civil Constitution of the Clergy is far more helpful, since in most places—but by no means all—there was an affinity between this choice and the views of their parishioners. Everywhere, however, people disagreed and their choices were those of individuals and their families in terms of their perceptions of the Revolution. Only for a minority of people had all of the changes been an unmitigated benefit or disaster. People accepted some changes with relish and opposed or sidestepped others. Everywhere, however, they had made up their minds.

Of course, many—perhaps most—people found choices too painful and opted to keep their heads down. Most nobles did not emigrate and instead sought to shelter from the winds of change by making the necessary concessions, however grudgingly. Most men and women of the Catholic Church re-entered the secular world, many feeling that their vocation had been shattered, but others happily. Masses of peasants welcomed the dramatic revolutionary changes—to seigneurialism, the judicial, fiscal and political system, to their own status—and concentrated on meeting only the strict minimum of what the new state demanded at a time of war.

But no one could avoid choices, and the great crisis of mid-1793 meant ones that would change lives forever. Such choices could be fatal, and not just on the battlefield. In the Breton village of Grand-Champ, north of

Vannes, a local named Villemain had bought extensive church properties, and early in 1794 a band of fifty men wearing white cockades killed him before sacking his house. Three of the band were sentenced to death. While other local patriots in Grand-Champ once felt a commitment to the Revolution to the point of forming surveillance committees, their work of rounding up wives of *émigrés* sapped their ardour to a point where they found excuses not to attend.[35]

By mid-1793 such decisions had become a question of life and death. 'Liberty or death' was now a key revolutionary catch-cry, meaning the freedom for citizens to remake their nation without external interference. Hundreds of thousands of them had volunteered to join the revolutionary armies or had made other commitments to the revolutionary cause in places where this exposed them to ostracism and violence. But their bitter opponents of various hues felt that their options were just as stark. Girondin supporters who found the power of Paris intolerable, men and women of the Church who longed for the freedom to worship where and how they chose, adherents of the *ancien régime* whose 'rights' had been stripped away, all faced a fateful choice about whether possible death was the price to pay for fighting for their freedom.

CHAPTER ELEVEN

'TERROR UNTIL THE PEACE', JULY–OCTOBER 1793

T HE FEDERALISTS WERE NEVER ABLE TO MUSTER A SUFFICIENTLY powerful military force to pose a serious threat to national armies, but the personal threat reached to the heart of the Convention. On 13 July 1793, the same day that nine citizens of Orléans went to the Paris guillotine in the red shirts of parricides for assaulting deputies-on-mission, a Girondin sympathizer from Caen, Charlotte Corday, went to see Jean-Paul Marat in his lodgings in the capital. Earlier, Marat had urged the Convention to repress the revolt in Caen and elsewhere by arming good *sans-culottes* with 'pitchforks, scythes, pikes, guns and sabres ... and crush them without mercy'. For Corday, Marat was the personification of the Revolution's excesses and she had resolved to kill him. She gained access to his room by promising to reveal secrets about counter-revolutionary plots; 'furthermore, I am persecuted in the cause of liberty. I am unhappy. That is sufficient to give me the right to your protection.'[1] Marat suffered from pruritus, and by the summer of 1793 spent much of his life in his bath, seeking relief from his skin ailment. Corday stabbed him to death as he bathed. She was tried by the Revolutionary Tribunal on 17 July and executed the same day (Fig. 18).

Marat formed a triumvirate of revolutionary martyrs with Lepeletier, murdered by a royalist the night the Convention voted for the death of Louis XVI, and Joseph Chalier, the Jacobin leader in Lyon executed by federalists on 17 July. To make the most of the lessons of Marat's death, the Convention turned to Jacques-Louis David, who earlier in 1793 had staged the public funerals for Lepeletier and Claude-François Lazowski, a Polish-born *sans-culotte* hero of 10 August whose funeral eulogy was delivered by

Robespierre. David had wanted Marat's body displayed in his bathtub, but warm weather since 13 July had caused such decay that it was instead placed in damp cloth on a platform. Girls dressed in white and youths carrying branches of cypress and braziers burning perfume were followed by deputies, local delegations and mourners. The procession took six hours.[2] David would then turn his attention to painting Marat's martyrdom (Fig. 19).

The murder of Marat in the heartland of the Revolution seemed stark proof that the new Republic was disintegrating in the face of armed counter-revolution and invasion by foreign armies. The Revolution, indeed France itself, was in danger of falling apart. In desperation the Convention approved a series of draconian measures designed to defeat external and internal military threats, to intimidate the recalcitrant and to forge a new 'patriot' alliance. These included surveillance committees, sweeping powers for the executive committees and deputies-on-mission, preventive detention and other controls on civil liberties deemed necessary to secure the Republic to a point where the new, democratic Constitution of June 1793 could be implemented.[3]

The Constitution, largely the work of Robespierre, was remarkable for its guarantees in a new Declaration of the Rights of Man and Citizen of social rights and popular control over an assembly elected by direct, universal male suffrage:

> Article 21. Public aid is a sacred debt. Society owes subsistence to unfortunate citizens, either by obtaining work for them, or by providing means of existence to those who are unable to work.
>
> Article 22. Instruction is a necessity for all. Society must further the progress of public reason with all its power, and make instruction available to all citizens. . . .
>
> Article 35. When the government violates the rights of the people, insurrection is the most sacred of rights and the most indispensable of duties for the people and for each portion of the people.[4]

The results of a referendum on acceptance of the Constitution (officially 1.8 million 'yes' votes to 11,600 against) were announced at a great festival in Paris on 10 August, the first anniversary of the overthrow of the monarchy, at the Festival of the Unity and Indivisibility of the Republic. The final figure for 'yes' votes was probably closer to two million of the approximately six million eligible males. This was about one-third of adult men, the highest turnout since the municipal elections of 1790, a remarkable figure at a time of invasion and civil war. Participation rates varied from fewer than 10 per cent in much of Brittany to 40–50 per cent along the Rhine and parts of the Massif Central. In many small communities, officials simply noted that all those assembled had voted in favour; and many of those who abstained did so because it was obvious that their commune endorsed the Constitution.

In some places the voting was itself a festival: in the little town of Saint-Nicolas-de-la-Grave, west of Montauban in the department of Tarn-et-Garonne, some of those present, moved into 'transports of the most sublime enthusiasm . . . their eyes swimming with tears of joy, threw themselves into each other's arms to share a fraternal kiss'. Here women insisted on being able to take the civic oath and vote, and the men agreed:

> all citizens and citizenesses intermingled, holding each other by the hand, as a sign of unity forming a single chain, and to the sound of drums, fifes and bells danced a farandole as they went through all the streets of the town, mixing with the sound of the instruments the singing of the holy hymns of Liberty.

At Lamballe, near the English Channel in Brittany, similarly, 'women swarmed into the assembly to offer their assent to the Constitution'; elsewhere, 175 women and 163 children voted at Pontoise north of Paris, and 343 women at Laon.[5]

The active participation of women was at the heart of the strength both of the Republic's response to invasion and of the rising in the Vendée (Fig. 20). They made the survival or destruction of the Revolution a matter of visceral commitment. In town and country, women's work became more important than ever before in keeping the household together, for in the years 1792–94 perhaps one family in ten was economically and emotionally drained by the death or wounding of a husband, son or father.

While there was minimal support within the Convention for formal political participation by women, what was different now was the range of women's political actions and the possibility of women protecting their rights within the household. The inheritance law of March 1790 had called into question the extent of paternal authority by guaranteeing sons and daughters equal inheritance rights. This was accentuated by a radical change in the legal age of independence: until September 1792 men under thirty years of age and women under twenty-five needed parental consent to marry; now both sexes were considered to have reached their 'majority' at twenty-one. A divorce law voted at the last session of the Legislative Assembly, on 20 September 1792, gave women remarkably broad grounds for leaving an unhappy or a meaningless marriage: the couple could agree to separate because of mutual incompatibility or either spouse could initiate divorce on grounds such as the protracted absence or cruelty of their partner.[6]

Questions of family law were at the heart of heated debates about the place of women, including one in August 1793 on the issue of the wife's rights to an equal role in decisions concerning the family's property. Whereas Philippe-Antoine Merlin de Douai argued that 'woman is generally incapable of administration and men, having a natural superiority over her, must protect her', he was countered by Georges Couthon, a wheelchair-bound Jacobin from the Committee of Public Safety: 'Woman is born with as many capacities as man. If she has not demonstrated it until now, it is not the fault of Nature but of our former institutions.' Couthon was supported by Camille Desmoulins, who admitted that 'in support of my opinion is the political consideration that it is important to make women love the Revolution'. They carried the day, but the law was never fully applied.[7]

As at the Festival of Federation on 14 July 1790, the nation's unity was to be personified in Paris on 10 August 1793, at the Festival of the Unity and Indivisibility of the Republic, by the presence of a delegate from every one of the thousands of cantons from the eighty-six departments.[8] To mark this first anniversary of the overthrow of the monarchy, symbols of 'tyranny' were burned on the Place de la Révolution (today the Place de la Concorde). A more formal ceremony was organized by David on the site of the demolished Bastille, where deputies and the oldest of the departments' representatives filed past the Fountain of Regeneration—a model of the Egyptian allegory of nature, Isis, from whose breasts spouted regenerative water to slake the representatives' thirst for virtue. From the statue were then released three thousand doves, each with tiny banners saying 'We are free! Imitate us!' attached to their feet.

The Republic's grandeur was marked symbolically by the foundation of the public museum of the Louvre on the same day, a turning point in the history of museology. After Louis XIV had abandoned the Tuileries Palace for Versailles in 1682, the Louvre had for a century housed the Académie Royale de Peinture et de Sculpture, a maze of ateliers and workshops. In

1791 the National Assembly had decreed it should become instead a museum for the nation's masterpieces. It opened on 10 August 1793 with more than five hundred paintings, mostly from royal collections or property confiscated from the Church. Its early administrators included prominent painters such as Jean-Honoré Fragonard and François-André Vincent. On 3 September an entranced Edmond Géraud wrote home to his father in Bordeaux about the new museum: 'it is one of the thousand and one marvels of the Revolution. All of our works by Lebrun, Lesueur, Gérard Dow, Salvator Rosa, Raphaël, everything is there.'[9] There were private initiatives as well. The Théâtre National opened its doors at the same time with Jean-François Guéroult's *La Journée de Marathon*: the message of the classical allegory of the heroic struggle between Athens and the might of the Persians was not lost on the audience.[10]

Even allowing for the hostility of those for whom the Revolution had become a negative, even life-threatening, experience—certainly a majority of people in the west and Brittany—the Constitution of 1793 and its Declaration of Rights represented the most accurate statement of what most French people aspired to at that time. On 28 August, nevertheless, the Jacobin Bertrand Barère from the Committee of Public Safety argued that the military situation would not allow immediate implementation of the Constitution's requirement for new single-member rather than department-wide constituencies; and when a policy of emergency government 'until the peace' was resolved in late September, the Constitution was suspended, symbolically placed in a chest at the heart of the Convention. The goal was to achieve the military security to enable it to be implemented.

In July 1793 the Republic was at war with most of Europe, and foreign troops were on French soil in the south-west, south-east and north-east. The Vendéan insurrection was unchecked, and major centres of federalism, notably Lyon, were openly at war with the Convention. The international conflict had also spread to the colonies. The military challenge was met by an unrelenting mobilization of the nation's resources, combined with uncompromising repression of opponents. Essential to this challenge was the creation by the Jacobin-dominated government of a new national alliance by a mixture of intimidation, force and policies aimed both to address popular grievances and to place the entire country on a war footing.

This was a period of sweeping governmental measures to win a civil and foreign war, rather than the 'reign of Terror', a descriptor first used only afterwards.[11] It has often been caricatured as a dictatorial, even totalitarian regime imposed by ideologues, particularly Robespierre and Saint-Just, to create a 'virtuous' society based on the violent exclusion of the 'other'. Robespierre, elected to the Committee of Public Safety on 27 July, was indeed the most articulate and admired of the Jacobin leaders (as well as the most despised by opponents), but the Jacobins were a mixed group of republicans applying exceptional laws in extraordinary circumstances as they grappled both to create a republican society and to defend it against its enemies.[12]

It was not a simple task. Perhaps 35,000 soldiers (6 per cent of the total army) had deserted in the first half of 1793, and many others reacted to deficiencies in supplies by theft of local produce. Soldiers complained that 'from first to last we are without shoes, tormented by scabies, and eaten by vermin'. One battalion reported that it was surviving by eating roots; another battalion of volunteers from Argentan in Normandy was reportedly camped on the property of an *émigré* and surviving by felling and selling 'huge quantities of all kinds of trees, walnuts, oaks, elms, alders, plums'.[13] In response Robert Lindet, a key member of the Committee of Public Safety and at forty-seven its oldest, was to play a crucial role in ensuring supplies for the army. Like his fellow Committee members Lazare Carnot, Barère and Robespierre, he lived on the Rue St-Honoré, close to the Convention (Fig. 21). Lindet's responsibilities, shared with Prieur de la Côte-d'Or, included dealing with a large, new bureaucracy in a reformed Subsistence Commission for a nation that seemed to be falling apart as enemy armies advanced, often with the connivance of collaborators. He had to deal with the acute challenges of communication in a large country where news still travelled quickest by horseback, and where the English naval blockade disrupted imports of grain.[14]

The Convention agreed that only total mobilization of rich and poor alike could save the Republic: on 23 August all single males aged eighteen to twenty-five were conscripted by a 'levée en masse':

> The young men will go forth to fight; married men will forge weapons and transport provisions; the women will make tents and uniforms; the old men will be carried to public places to rouse the warriors' courage, to preach hatred for kings and to uphold the unity of the Republic.[15]

In 1792 the French army had numbered about 155,000 men: 113,000 infantry, 32,000 cavalry and 10,000 artillery. The levy of 300,000 in March

1793 had added significantly to that, and was now doubled by the 'levée en masse'. There would be about 700,000 men in the armies within six months.[16] The dramatic expansion in the scale of the army, plus the menace that the war was being fought on French territory, made this an unprecedented case of 'the people under arms'.

National Guard units were charged with hunting down those who evaded conscription or deserted. Conscripts from non-French-speaking regions were given basic instruction in French and scattered through the army to reduce the temptation of collective flight; mass propaganda, such as Jacques-René Hébert's earthy newspaper, the *Père Duchesne*, was distributed; and deputies-on-mission from the Convention threatened retribution to hesitant officers and unwilling rank and file. But the building of a new spirit in the army was not the result of coercion alone: soldiers' letters home are also studded with remarks about their commitment to the *patrie* and the Revolution. The volunteer Pierre Cohin wrote to his family from the Armée du Nord that 'the war which we are fighting is not a war between king and king or nation and nation. It is the war of liberty against despotism. There can be no doubt that we shall be victorious. A nation that is just and free is invincible.'[17]

Frontier departments in particular simmered with anxiety at the proximity of the war. After a major defeat in the north-east at Valenciennes in July, the deputies-on-mission Joseph-Marie Lequinio and Sylvain Lejeune sent to the department of Aisne ordered the detention not only of the families of noble *émigrés*, but of all nobles, whatever their politics. In all, up to five hundred people would be held as 'suspects'. The draconian measure at least succeeded in convincing the population that possible counter-revolution had been averted, and the guillotine would be used only twice there in the following year.[18] This north-eastern front was only two days away from Paris by messenger, but Toulouse and Marseille were eight days away by coach, and the southern battlefront several more days away over difficult terrain. The necessity of coordinating the nation's resources deluged the departments with requests and instructions. During the period 1789–92 more than one hundred notices on average were sent to the district capitals each month, in four to six separate deliveries—already a striking number. In December 1793, however, the number of notices had jumped to three hundred, in thirteen separate deliveries.[19]

Since October 1792 the Convention and its committees had pieced together a series of emergency measures designed to defeat the invading armies and counter-revolution in all its guises, to address the continuing grievances of urban and rural people, and to control the actions of militants who claimed to represent the people's will. On 5 September 1793 thousands of *sans-culottes*, now at the peak of their power, invaded the National Convention to insist that their 'mandatories' impose radical military and economic measures and demand that the Convention 'make terror the order of the day'. In their own references to the need to intimidate or arouse 'terror' in the minds of counter-revolutionaries, Jacobins were casting back to historical precedent: as recently as the 1770s proponents and opponents of royal power had accused each other of imposing 'terror' in the image of the religious wars of a century earlier.[20]

The decision to terrorize the Revolution's enemies in order to make the Republic safe began the most controversial period of the Revolution. A constant predicament for the Convention and its governing committees was the need to rely on the probity and judgement of deputies-on-mission and army commanders in repressing counter-revolution within the bounds of legality and humanity. Such was the rage against those deemed to be traitors to the Republic that repression frequently spilled over into excess, even atrocity. In the southern Massif Central, one of the centres of revolt was Vabres (today Vabres-l'Abbaye), a village of about seven hundred people that had had the cathedral for a diocese of 130 parishes from 1317 until the reorganization of 1790. In 1793 republican troops devastated the village and its cathedral. Their twenty-three-year-old commander, Jean-Maximilien Lamarque, son of a wealthy deputy from Saint-Sever to the Estates-General, ordered that the marble altar be refashioned into a public monument to Marat.[21]

Some counter-revolutionary enemies were obvious. The Abbé Claude Allier, an instigator of the three 'camps de Jalès' in the period 1790–92, had organized the 'Christian Army of the Midi' in the spring of 1793 with Marc-Antoine Charrier, a former army officer. Designed to harass republican troops en route to the Spanish front, the army seized the small towns of Marvejols and Mende, forcing departmental administrators to flee. Charrier was arrested in June and guillotined the next month; the same fate awaited Allier in August. His younger brother Dominique then took up the counter-revolutionary calling.[22]

Other threats to the safety of the Republic were more insidious. Such were the stakes in the summer of 1793—liberty or death—that the net necessary to ensnare enemies of the Revolution trapped many thousands of people whose only mistake was to be critical of government policy rather than being engaged in armed counter-revolutionary activity. From the outset of the Revolution, denunciation of conspiracy had been the hand-maiden of the new age of virtue and equality. Now the coincidence of foreign invasion, counter-revolution and federalism was compelling proof of the perfidy in the hearts of those unwilling to accept the precepts of the civic virtues.

The Law of Suspects (17 September 1793) was designed to expose the unpatriotic to detention or to intimidate them into inaction. Surveillance committees in every commune made private as well as public behaviour and motives the object of scrutiny. In Rouen, for example, 29 per cent of the 1,158 suspects arrested were nobles, 19 per cent clergy and 7.5 per cent former office-holders; such people were arrested because of who they were, coupled with suspicions of *incivisme*. They were not the only ones arrested: bourgeois comprised 17 per cent of 'suspects' and working people 27 per cent, often charged with anti-revolutionary words and behaviour: among shopkeepers, such behaviour often concerned stockpiling of goods. Almost two-fifths of all 'suspects' were women, particularly from the nobility and clergy, reflecting the tendency for males in these groups to emigrate, and often to fight, leaving women as the focus of suspicion because of their family name and politics.[23]

Nobles were particularly vulnerable. Rousseau's patron, the Enlightenment enthusiast and seigneur the Marquis de Girardin, had tried to accommodate himself to the Revolution, transferring some land to trusted peasants, praising Robespierre, Marat, Desmoulins and the Constitution of 1793, and burning his feudal titles in public on 10 August 1793 to celebrate the anni-versary of the overthrow of the monarchy. Nevertheless, three weeks later he and his family were arrested. Despite his membership of the Cordelier Club, the Marquis, now known simply as René, was accused of 'despotism' by the villagers of Ermenonville, twenty-five miles north-east of Paris, and his château was described as a 'hiding-place for brigands'. In September 1793 the family was imprisoned as 'suspects'. They included Girardin's daughter Sophie, still faithful to the memory of Rousseau, although she had left France with her Prussian diplomat husband in 1789, horrified by the 'hideous scenes' after the taking of the Bastille. She had returned in 1791 in an attempt to safeguard the family property.[24] The family would remain in prison for a year.

But ordinary people could be outraged as well. When a law requiring municipalities to remove symbols of royalism and feudalism was implemented in the small town of Coulommiers, thirty-five miles east of Paris, rumours that Jacobin officials were damaging statuary in the church lit the tinder to community rage, with 'holy women' openly applauding the insurrection in the Vendée and calling on Austrians and Prussians to 'cut the throats of the accursed Jacobins'. Eight people were sentenced to death. One of the two women to die was 'Foi-Franquet' Deltombe, who wrote her last letter to her sister and brother-in-law on 1 February 1794: 'I commend to you my dear husband and my dear child, do not abandon them in these times, you know how sensitive he is, help him to keep his spirits up.'[25]

Military fortunes were mixed. In late June 1793 republican forces won a major victory over the Vendéans at Nantes. There were important consequences: the death of Vendéan leader Jacques Cathelineau from a sniper's shot led to rancorous division about his succession, and the defeat was a blow to those who looked to England's navy to turn Nantes into the capital of the revolt.[26] In July, General Kléber's troops also won an initial victory near Cholet, the military capital of the Vendéan insurrection, but in September his 6,000 troops suffered terrible losses at the hands of the 30,000 troops of the Catholic and Royal Army. Atrocities continued on both sides: at Montaigu captured republican soldiers were thrown into a well.[27]

While many leading federalists were committed republicans, they were doubly compromised: they had repudiated the Convention's authority at a time of the Republic's gravest military crisis, and the support given them by royalists, nobles and priests tarnished them by association. The perception from Paris was that whole communities were either for the unity and indivisibility of the Republic or engaged in a conspiracy with royalists and the coalition armies to overthrow it. It was easy for Jacobins in the Convention to believe that the federalists were in league with the armies of old Europe, which was evident when on 29 August the key Mediterranean naval arsenal of Toulon was handed over by its officers to the English navy blockading the coast.[28]

Nowhere were the consequences of distorting mirrors more tragic than in Lyon. The execution of Joseph Chalier on 17 July convinced Jacobins in the Convention that Lyon was in the hands of counter-revolutionaries looking for liberation from Austrian and Sardinian troops. In fact, both sides were republican, but between governing Jacobins and Lyonnais 'Rolandins' lay a gulf of hatred, panic and fear.

Although self-consciously 'moderate' and legalistic, Lyonnais supporters of rebellion were not counter-revolutionaries, but their actions were seen as such by Jacobins in the Convention, and a ruthless repression was unleashed. On 22 August the deputy-on-mission Edmond Dubois-Crancé announced to the town that

> The cannon are in place, the bombs are ready, the cannon-balls are glowing and flames will devour you. . . . Reflect, Lyonnais, there is still time, tomorrow will be too late. . . . I implore you therefore, to finally open your eyes and obey the laws. . . . The Convention itself will show mercy to the guilty if they can show that they have simply been misled.[29]

Despite his plea, the armed rebellion in Lyon lasted until 9 October. While its origins lay in the increasingly violent hatreds and rhetoric within the city itself, the Lyonnais' decision to repudiate the authority of Paris and to create an army inextricably linked them with the other menaces to the Republic's unity; the Convention had passed a law on 16 December 1792 making armed rebellion against the unity of the nation a capital offence.

The Convention and its committees were determined to make the repression of France's second city exemplary. Barère assured the Convention: 'the town of Lyon will be destroyed: everything belonging to the rich will be destroyed. Only the houses of the poor will be left, those of patriots slaughtered and repressed, buildings used by industry, and monuments to humanity and education.' To oversee the repression, the Committee of Public Safety despatched Jean-Marie Collot d'Herbois, Joseph Fouché, Antoine Albitte and François Laporte. They took the mission seriously, in two days ordering the execution of hundreds of Lyonnais. Initially, those found guilty were to be shot by fusillades from cannon, with those not yet dead finished off by sabres and rifles. Such was the disgust soldiers themselves felt that the authorities resorted to the firing squad and guillotine. On average, forty people were executed each day.

Most Lyonnais had, at least initially, supported the rebellion against local and national Jacobins, but it was the well-to-do who were singled out for punishment.[30] Collot's view was that almost the entire population was culpable, and that 100,000 people would need to be exiled from the city so that it could be razed and depopulated. Couthon went as far as to suggest that the entire city, now called 'Commune Affranchie' ('Emancipated Commune'), be emptied of its inhabitants.

The women of Lyon were particularly culpable, Collot insisted, using all their wiles to seduce his troops while worshipping their patron saint

Charlotte Corday. Much of this was hyperbole designed to impress Paris: there were probably only twenty houses destroyed rather than the 1,600 often referred to, and most of the executions occurred after Collot's recall to Paris. But in the end it has been estimated that 1,867 people were executed, with a similar number acquitted. When the Prussian deserter and now *sans-culotte* Frédéric-Christian Laukhard arrived in Lyon in January 1794, he was astonished by the 'misery and destruction. Whole rows of houses, always the finest, were burned. Churches, convents, all the residences of the former patricians were in ruins. When I reached the guillotine, the blood of those executed a few hours earlier was still running on the square.'[31] Collot would find that he was the person to bear the full responsibility, when none of the Committee criticized him directly at the time.[32]

Further south an artillery captain named Napoleon Bonaparte, who had just turned twenty-four, was involved in the recapture of Avignon from federalist forces. On 28 July he was in Beaucaire, on the last day of its annual fair. He shared dinner, drinks and debate with merchants from Marseille, Montpellier and Nîmes, and afterwards penned a pamphlet, *Le Souper de Beaucaire*, in which he, as 'a soldier', put the Jacobin argument to southern merchants for solidarity in securing the Revolution's victory: 'shake off the yoke of the small number of scoundrels who lead you to counter-revolution, re-establish your constituted authorities, accept the Constitution, and give the representatives their liberty, so that they can go to Paris to intercede for you'. The National Convention was delighted with its contents and ordered the pamphlet to be printed.

In other federalist centres repression was also extreme but not of the same magnitude as in Lyon. In Marseille, now renamed 'Sans Nom' ('Nameless Town'), 499 of the 975 suspects tried by the Revolutionary Tribunal were found guilty, of whom 289 were executed. Others, like the twenty-six-year-old clerk Jean-Louis Laplane, fled Marseille into exile in mid-September 'pursued', in his later words, 'by this barbarian horde who then covered France with blood and mourning'.[33] In Bordeaux the Jacobin Jean-Lambert Tallien's repressive zeal seems to have been softened by the political skills of the twenty-year-old Thérésia Cabarrus with whom he had become infatuated. Cabarrus, born to a wealthy financier in Spain and married to a French noble at age sixteen, had taken advantage of the Revolution's divorce laws; she also took advantage of Tallien to intervene on behalf of nobles seeking to emigrate south from Bordeaux or to avoid the repression of the federalists.[34]

In contrast with zones of bloodily punitive civil war, there were many regions where relative calm prevailed, for example, the rural departments of the south-west. Here local administrations, led by the more able of the deputies-on-mission—such as Jean Bon Saint-André, Joseph Lakanal, Jean-Baptiste Bô, Gilbert Romme and Pierre Roux-Fazillac—sought to make a reality of the Jacobin ideology expressed in the Declaration of Rights and Constitution of 1793. The central element of this view of the world was that social rights took precedence over individual rights: that is, that legitimate rights of free enterprise and trade, of freedom of expression and belief, had to be exercised within the constraints of the rights of others to safety and sustenance.[35]

The legislative programme of the Jacobin-dominated Convention, even at a time of military crisis, was dense and reveals a distinctive ideology of egalitarianism, civic virtue and patriotic zeal. The creation of a harmonious society of citizens equal in dignity and rights would necessarily require government initiatives in education, public works and social welfare. Robespierre's consistency in articulating this ideology had won him the highest respect as the embodiment of these values, but there were scores of thousands of individual Jacobins across the country who acted in accordance with them. Across 1793 Robespierre made almost four long speeches a week—101 in the Convention and 96 to the Jacobin Club—on the themes of patriotism, sacrifice and the virtues, and their mortal enemies, greed, conspiracy and egotism. On 25 September he defended the need for uncompromising repression of the Revolution's opponents:

> over two years a hundred thousand men have been slaughtered through treachery and weakness; it is weakness towards traitors which is destroying us. People feel sorry for the greatest criminals, for those who are giving the homeland up to the enemy's swords; as for me, I can pity only … a generous people who are being slaughtered with so much wickedness.[36]

Patriots needed to avoid any suggestion that they had private or factional interests at odds with those of 'le peuple'. Those who had flattered to deceive—Lafayette, Mirabeau and Dumouriez among them—were a warning against placing one's hopes in great men. The lesson of Mirabeau was that it was safer to have busts in the Convention of heroes from antiquity, although Marat and Lepeletier were immortalized in busts after their assassinations, and David's paintings of them were hung in the Convention, behind the speaker's rostrum. David and his school expressed in their art the virile and masculine virtues of Jacobinism, those of a republican brotherhood contrasted with the emasculated monarchy and effete aristocracy of the *ancien régime*. But Jacobin language was also suffused with Christian messianism: while the term 'Montagne' became commonplace in reference to Jacobins who occupied the higher benches in the chamber, it was often bracketed with 'Holy', an allusion to Mount Sinai, to imply that the Convention had an almost divine capacity to pass just laws and to punish enemies.[37]

These months were the pinnacle both of popular involvement in the Revolution and of popular opposition to it. Ever since 1789 the symbolic representation of liberty, equality and finally of the Republic itself, had been female figures, both because the names of the classical virtues are female in French and in imitation of the representation of the Catholic virtues by the Virgin Mary. Late in 1793 the female allegory of the Republic, even the Republic itself, was often referred to derisively by opponents as 'Marianne', a common peasant name that denoted 'of the people'. As had been the case with the epithet *sans-culottes*, republicans then adopted the name with pride.[38]

Physical symbols of the new regime, particularly busts and paintings of the goddesses of equality and fraternity, replaced the markers of status of the past: the Bourbon lily, coats of arms and religious statuary. 'Patriot' Palloy, the man who had won the contract to demolish the Bastille in 1789, had sent the eighty-three departments a model of the fortress carved from its stones; he had also sent them a carving of Louis XVI. The latter was now an embarrassment, and Palloy replaced it with a Bastille stone carving of the new Declaration of the Rights of Man and Citizen, with a promise of others of Brutus, Lepeletier and Marat. The Council of the Department of Loiret met in Orléans on 10 September to hear a passionate address from the deputy-on-mission Jacques-Léonard Laplanche, who assured them that the sight of the new stone would 'electrify spirits'. Just as the Ten Commandments had been generated 'in the midst of thunder and lightning on Mount Sinai', so the new Declaration had issued 'from the summit of the Mountain in the midst of storms'. The Council was enthusiastic, one member successfully proposing that 40,000 individual copies of the Declaration be printed for families, plus 10,000 public posters. Laplanche talked him out of another idea, that every house in Orléans should have 'Terror is the order of the day' painted above the front door 'so that all aristocrats would tremble'.[39]

As the first anniversary of the proclamation of the Republic approached, even traditional perceptions of time were revolutionized. The first 'inventor' of a revolutionary calendar was the playwright, atheist and political activist Sylvain Maréchal, but it was the Montagnard deputy and mathematician— and former tutor to the Russian nobility—Gilbert Romme who presented a project to the Convention on 17 September 1793. Fabre d'Églantine then added the visual dimension, and named the months and days with the assistance of André Thouin, gardener at the Jardin des Plantes. The calendar was designed to highlight epochal, revolutionary regeneration and the cult of nature rather than Christianity: 22 September marked both the birth of the Republic and the autumn equinox.[40] The new calendar, implemented from 24 October 1793, combined the rationality of decimal measurement (twelve months of thirty days, each with three *décadi* of ten days) with a total repudiation of the Gregorian calendar. Saints' days and religious festivals were replaced by names drawn from plants, the seasons, work implements and the virtues (see 'The Revolutionary Calendar',). The calendar was adopted across the country, but it clashed with the older rhythms of Sunday worship and weekly markets and never fully replaced them.

It was proposed that the great anniversaries of 14 July, 10 August, 21 January and 21 September would ultimately be supported by thirty-six national festivals, one each *décadi*. The festivals organized by the government were lofty affairs elevating the Revolution with evocations of nature, as evidenced in the verses penned by the deputy-on-mission Léonard Bourdon for local patriots who gathered before dawn for the Festival of Nature on a bridge across the Adour at Tarbes in the south-west:

Ye of little faith
Who would see and hear the Supreme Being,
May do so, with morality in your hearts,
But you must go out into the fields,
Two by two, bearing a flower.
There, by pure waters,
One hears a God in one's heart,
As one sees him in Nature.[41]

The crisis of mid-1793 was financial and economic as well as military. Successive meetings of the National Convention had chosen not to cancel the national debt, even though they had abolished noble status, venal office and corporate privilege. The Convention continued to pay the debts of the *ancien régime* just as it compensated former holders of offices now abolished. Now in August 1793 the Jacobin Convention took radical action. It consolidated all state debts into a 'Great ledger of the public debt', guaranteeing creditors 5 per cent interest. This was the work of the influential Finance Committee of the Convention, led by Joseph Cambon, Dominique-Vincent Ravel, François-René Mallarmé, François Chabot and Joseph Delaunay. The new system took months to bed down; in the meantime international financiers were sailing in a stormy sea, needing to arrange loans to the government from within hostile foreign powers. Men such as the Dutch banker Jean-Baptiste Vandenyver, the British banker Walter Boyd and the Belgian Jacobin the Comte de Proly were linked to the ambiguous figure of the Baron de Batz, once head of the National Assembly's committee on the national debt and now a suspected counter-revolutionary intriguer.[42]

But how could public credit be stabilized when the value of *assignats* continued to fall? So the Convention acted to meet *sans-culotte* demands by decreeing the 'general maximum' of 29 September, which pegged the prices of thirty-nine commodities at 1790 levels plus one-third, and set wages at 150 per cent of 1790 levels. The Convention was also impelled to respond to the waves of rural unrest that had affected two-thirds of all departments since 1789. While advocating the subdivision of large estates, or the 'agrarian law', was made a capital offence in March 1793, the Convention took a series of measures designed to win over the rural masses. On 17 July former seigneurs were left with only those 'rents and charges which are purely on land and non-feudal'. The feudal regime was at last dead. To celebrate the final abolition of seigneurial titles, as well as the anniversary of the overthrow of the monarchy, the festival of 10 August in Orléans included the burning of eighteen carriages laden with feudal titles.[43]

The issue of common lands had been contentious for rural people since long before 1789. To whom did they belong? Could individual families take their share? Or would the interests of the rural poor best be secured by keeping them in common? On 14 August 1792 the Legislative Assembly had issued a brief decree directing communes to divide non-forested commons. On 10 June 1793 the Convention replaced this law with one that was more radical and contentious, one of the most ambitious attempts of the revolutionary government to meet the needs of the rural poor. The legislation required communes to proceed to a division if this was the wish of one-third of adult men; the land was then to be divided on the basis of an equal share to every man, woman and child. While many communities opted to keep commons intact in the interests of those with livestock, elsewhere ways were found to divide them equally and fairly.

In the south-west near Montauban, in Verdun-sur-Garonne, the land was divided between the 681 adults; in the tiny village of Marignac efforts were made to ensure the 267 lots were 'comparable'; while Pazayac in the department of Dordogne auctioned its lands and distributed the proceeds equally between males and females.[44] In the north-east some communes in the district of Pont-à-Mousson were pleased to convoke a meeting of all citizens to divide the commons by head, including children born since 10 June, while other communes simply noted that they had decided against division: Rogeville only had a small wood; Mamey used its commons for pastures; Griscourt's commons were nothing but rock. In contrast, some villages decided that it was in their interests to divide their commons: Landremont proceeded to divide its commons into 253 plots and Lixières into 217; Bayonville divided its commons into 223 sections of 'mountain' and 196 sections of 'slopes', the 446 inhabitants receiving a little of each.[45] In the southern department of Gard, in contrast, only eighteen of 361 communes used the law of 10 June 1793 to partition the land, with almost all deciding that the stony *garrigues* were best suited to grazing village livestock in common. In many communes, however, the poor had already seized parts of the commons to eke out a subsistence, in defiance of the law and wealthier locals.[46]

The seigneurial regime had been finally abolished, and common land divided or retained, but it was to take far longer to resolve the associated questions of control of collective economic resources, hunger for land and illegal clearances. In a report written from Lagrasse in Languedoc in December 1793, the playwright and Jacobin official Jean-François Cailhava reported in blunt fashion that the district 'was formerly covered in coppices, mostly in green oak; but with the Revolution every individual treated them like the cabbages in his garden'. In the district of Narbonne there was a terrible shortage of wood 'because of the disdain the inhabitants show for trees which give only shade. . . . People are ready to undertake new clearances, and there is much to fear from this thoughtless passion of turning all the land into fields.'[47]

While attitudes to the Revolution varied sharply across the countryside, underpinning attitudes in most rural areas was hostility both to the *ancien régime* and to laws about private property that seemed to benefit the well-to-do. In Neulise, near Roanne in central France, armed youths who gathered for the conscription ballot of 1793 conducted their own choice for the fifteen men the commune had to supply: the constitutional priest and fourteen bourgeois 'patriots' seen to have profited most from the Revolution.[48] Many rural communities used a variety of strategies to sidestep or openly oppose the demands of central government and its local agents: non-payment of taxes, the avoidance of the general maximum levied on prices of essential consumer items and wages, and an unwillingness to use *assignats*.[49]

Every rural district had its share of ardent Jacobins who read Parisian and local papers or belonged to Jacobin clubs and popular societies. The *Feuille villageoise*, aimed specifically at a rural audience, sold up to 16,000 copies but, because newspapers were commonly passed around or read aloud in rural communities, its audience may have been 250,000 people in 1793. The administration in Auch subscribed to a copy for each of the 599 communes in the department of Gers.[50]

In 'patriotic' towns and villages the distinctive mix of civic virtues that should identify true *sans-culottes* was articulated, for example, by Antoine Bonnet, a café owner and secretary to the surveillance committee in Belley, in the eastern department of Ain: 'men with more common sense than education, virtuous, sensitive, humane; men outraged by the slightest whisper of injustice; intrepid, energetic men who desire the common good, Liberty, Equality or death'.[51] The most important of the Jacobin newspapers, the *Révolutions de Paris*, agreed, defining *sans-culottes* in November 1793 in both social terms (as artisans, once called the 'bonnets de laine' after their woollen work caps or 'the man of the people') but also in moral, political terms: 'he is a patriot strong in mind and body . . . he is the opposite to selfish and dislikes those who are such . . . a republican . . . who has only one passion, the love of order and of equality, of independence and fraternity' (Fig. 22).[52]

Sans-culottes found civic ceremonies more rewarding than church services. In Cézy, on the banks of the Yonne in Burgundy, three liberty trees were planted in symbolic places. One was planted in November 1792 on the spot where a long conflict had finally been resolved over land disputed between the commune and the Princesse de Listenois. (It survived until a storm in 1987, and was replaced.) Another was planted on 10 November 1793 to mark the burning of seigneurial documents at a ceremony attended by officials and 'girls dressed in blue with a tricolour sash, pupils of both sexes, women, the surveillance committee, the popular society'. The same day a third was planted to replace a cross on what was now the Place du Peuple.[53]

Nationally perhaps 6,000 Jacobin clubs and popular societies were created in 1793–94, short-lived though many of them were. Although most common in small towns, in Provence up to 90 per cent of all villages had one, male republican spaces often violently opposed by royalists. At this time of febrile politics and anxiety about war, participation in Jacobin clubs in particular was massive. In the city of Marseille (population 110,000), the Jacobin Club often had 2,000 people at its meetings, and about 6,000 men were members at some point. In its Provençal hinterland almost all adult males were members in some villages: Saint-Zacharie had 195 club members in a population of 1,500; Plascassier had 87 in a village of 226. In provincial Jacobin clubs the number of artisans and shopkeepers had increased since 1789–91 from 39 to 45 per cent and peasants from 1 to 10 per cent. The number of merchants and businessmen had declined from 12 to 8 per cent, while clergy had declined from 7 to 2 per cent. Nobles, amounting to nearly 1 per cent early in the Revolution, had disappeared altogether (Fig. 23).[54]

But Paris was the pulsating, tumultuous centre of the Revolution. The ideology of its *sans-culottes* was democratic and egalitarian, envisaging a more equitable distribution of property at the expense of the idle and the suspect, often lumped together as 'aristocrats'. On 2 September one of the Paris sections—itself named the Section des Sans-Culottes—presented its agenda to the Convention, turning the Revolution's founding principle that 'no-one has the right to do what may harm another' into an attack on profiteering. They called for a purge of former nobles, priests and royal officials from the administration, controls on prices and wages, and for a 'maximum' on property so that individuals could own only one workshop, shop or small farm. 'These measures will restore abundance and tranquility, gradually eliminate the inequalities of fortune that are too great, and increase the number of proprietors.'[55] At times *sans-culotte* egalitarianism went beyond redistribution to a concept of collective ownership. In one statement it was asserted that 'the rich man is less the proprietor than the happy trustee of an excess of fortune intended for the happiness of his co-citizens'.[56]

A distinctive political culture synthesized long-established cultural forms with republican patriotism. Theatre was the core. In October 1793, Maréchal's *Le Jugement dernier des Rois* opened at the Théâtre de la

République, to wild enthusiasm as the tyrants of Europe were banished to an island where the only European was an old man exiled by Louis XV, and were finally swallowed by a volcano. The play would be seen by 100,000 spectators and have a print run of 20,000, of which 6,000 copies were for the army. The most popular scene from the play featured the 'parade of kings' in which *sans-culottes* led the monarchs onto the stage in turn for a burlesque mockery of their crimes. Catherine the Great was depicted in a sexual act with the king of Poland; when performed in Boulogne-sur-Mer, Catherine was played by a hefty and moustachioed man.[57] Royalty was purged in a different way by Philippe Rühl, a Montagnard member of the Committee of General Security, who, while a deputy-on-mission in Reims in October, smashed the Holy Ampulla that contained Clovis's holy oil with which Louis XVI had been anointed in 1775.

The most insistent of the *sans-culottes*, the self-styled Enragés, pressured the Committee of Public Safety and the Convention to take more stringent measures to further revolutionary goals. After Marat's assassination, Hébert had taken up the cudgels for violent revolutionary rhetoric in the *Père Duchesne*. A law clerk from the Norman town of Alençon who had survived on the margins of legality before 1789, Hébert had married the former nun Marie Goupil in 1792 and now found his calling in venomous attacks on priests, nobles and the rich. Like Marat, Hébert targeted internal foes as far more menacing than invading armies, but he used rather more earthy language:

> The rich think only of their interests; they are the Republic's greatest enemy; they despise the Revolution because it has established liberty and equality. . . . Fuck, we've got to finish this off. . . . Shudder then, bastard blood-suckers of the people. . . . The same muscle that pickled the throne of the jackass Capet will fall on you.[58]

Théophile Leclerc, who had succeeded Marat at the *Ami du Peuple*, threatened 'hoarders . . . pitiless blood-suckers, grown fat on the needs of the people . . . speculators . . . suspects . . . egoists': 'take the road either to the frontiers or to the Place de la Révolution where the guillotine awaits you'. The paper also menaced the Convention where there is 'a spirit of moderation, which is hopeless for the public good'.[59]

By September the most militant *sans-culottes*—referred to as Enragés and Hébertistes—were virtually the political masters of Paris. Not only were the most intransigent neighbourhood sections in support of the vitriolic rhetoric of Hébert and others, but they controlled key positions in the administration: the Paris Commune, where Jean-Nicolas Pache was the mayor, Pierre-Gaspard Chaumette the chief legal officer (*procureur*), with Hébert his deputy; the National Guard under François Hanriot; and even the Ministry of War, where François-Nicolas Vincent was general secretary.

The Convention was also under pressure from militant women. The mobilization for war created work in Paris and other cities, but the practice of subletting to private contractors was resented by some of the women workers producing clothing: one hostile petition to the Convention in late August had 4,675 signatures. Later in the year women objected to the lack of heating in workshops employing 'the Sovereign People' while 'its agents were abundantly supplied with it'.[60] Working women like them were, however, far more likely to support the subsistence and military goals of the popular movement as a whole than the individual advocates of women's rights such as Olympe de Gouges and Etta Palm, now dead or discredited because of their political conservatism. Indeed, in May 1793, Théroigne de Méricourt, who supported the Girondins, was subject to a beating by Jacobin women from which she never recovered.

The Revolutionary Republican Citizenesses, led by Claire Lacombe and Pauline Léon, bridged this gap between women's rights and subsistence politics by organizing as an autonomous women's group and campaigning for women's rights to public office and to bear arms, while remaining linked to the Enragés (Fig. 24).[61] 'All the members of the society,' read the rules of the Citizenesses, 'are nothing else than a family of sisters.' The Society, with perhaps 170 members, saw its mission as to 'instruct themselves, to learn well the Constitution and laws of the Republic, to attend to public affairs, to succor suffering humanity, and to defend all human beings who become victims of any arbitrary acts whatever. They want to banish all selfishness, jealousies, rivalry and envy ...'. The Society met in the ossuary of the former church of Saint-Eustache, and claimed as many as 3,000 supporters.[62] A constant tension was whether its primary objective was to support the Convention and its committees or to treat them as obstacles to reform. A delegation was permitted to address the Convention on 26 August 1793: while Lacombe appealed to the principle of unity—'never forget that, without the virtues of Veturia, Rome would never have had the great Coriolanus'—she menaced the Convention for its moderation, and teased Robespierre as 'monsieur' rather than 'citizen'.[63]

Several of the men's section meetings now admitted women as members, and a visiting delegation of men from the Droits de l'Homme Section praised the Society of Revolutionary Republican Citizenesses:

> You have broken one of the links in the chain of prejudice. The one which confined women to the narrow sphere of their households, making a half of all individuals into passive and isolated beings, no longer exists for you. You want to take your place in the social order; apathy offends and humiliates you . . .[64]

But on 16 September the Jacobin Club attacked the Citizenesses, with Chabot questioning whether they were in fact counter-revolutionaries in the disguise of ultra-patriots: 'it is these counter-revolutionary *bougresses* (sluts) who cause all the riotous outbreaks, above all over bread. They made a revolution over coffee and sugar, and they will make others if we don't watch out.' He was referring to an invasion of the Convention on 1 May, which had resulted in a maximum price on grain and flour.[65]

In these months the political participation of Parisian working people reached its zenith. While only about 10 per cent of men regularly attended section meetings, this was a remarkable level of participation at a time of long working days and food queues. Across the nation there was an unprecedented levelling in the social composition of local government: in Paris, for example, one-third of the Commune councillors were from the *menu peuple*, as were four-fifths of the 'revolutionary committees' elected in each of the forty-eight sections of the city. The forty 'popular societies' had about 6,000 members, of whom 86 per cent were artisans and wage-earners.[66] In major provincial towns such as Amiens, Bordeaux, Nancy and Toulouse, bourgeois still dominated local government, but artisans and shopkeepers now comprised 18–24 per cent of councillors in all four cities. In villages, too, the years 1792–94 were a time of social levelling, with poorer peasants and even labourers represented for the first time on councils.

The Republic of 1793 was a demanding regime: the language of patriotism, virtue and citizenship was mixed with one of sacrifice, requisitioning and conscription. It was a regime whose local representatives refused anything smacking of *ancien régime* presumptions and threatened the recalcitrant. In the words of one southern official: 'the time of ridiculous pretensions has passed. . . . The Convention honours and recognizes talents and virtues. . . .

The tree of the Republic will be shaken and the caterpillars which are gnawing it will fall down.'[67]

By the late autumn of 1793 the military tide seemed to be turning. Victories were won in September in the charge of generals Jean-Nicolas Houchard and Jean-Baptiste Jourdan over Hessian and Hanoverian troops under the Duke of York at Hondschoote near Dunkirk; in the south, republican forces under generals Eustache d'Aoust and Jacques Goguet won a major victory over the Spanish on 17 September at Peyrestortes, north of Perpignan. Then on 16 October a victory under generals Jourdan and Carnot over the Austrians at Wattignies, near Maubeuge, stemmed the invasion in the north-east. These victories lifted hopes that the young Republic, fresh from celebrating its first anniversary by inaugurating a new calendar, might just survive the threat of the European coalition.

War against the internal counter-revolution was also being waged without quarter. On 17 October, the morrow of the victory at Wattignies, republican forces won a major battle against the Vendéan army, near Cholet. The federalists of Lyon had just capitulated and would be dealt with as harshly as the rebels in the west. The end to the internal and external wars was not yet in sight, however, and republican administrators faced daunting challenges in conscripting and supplying 700,000 soldiers. Relations between armies and civilians were everywhere of critical importance if troops were to be supplied and battles won, and everywhere the menace of privation, defeat and retribution hung over soldiers and civilians alike. At the same time the Convention was smarting from its intimidation by militant *sans-culottes* in September. Could the Republic survive? And who was to decide when the Revolution had achieved its goals?

CHAPTER TWELVE

SAVING A REPUBLIC OF VIRTUE, OCTOBER 1793–APRIL 1794

ON 10 OCTOBER 1793 THE CONVENTION DECREED THAT 'THE provisional government of France is revolutionary until the peace': all government bodies and the army were placed under the control of the Committee of Public Safety, which had to report weekly to the Convention.[1] No quarter was to be given to the Revolution's enemies, but at the same time the friends of the Revolution were warned that the Convention and its committees were the sole source of political initiative. The twin imperatives of 'virtue and terror' would save the Republic from invasion, counter-revolution and the backsliders, and create a virtuous citizenry worthy of the Revolution.

Deputies-on-mission were given sweeping powers to impose discipline in the armies, backed by the threat of execution for the timid. During the year of greatest military crisis, in 1793–94, eighty-four generals were executed and more than 350 officers dismissed. Military tribunals were kinder to the rank and file: of 122 soldiers accused of desertion in the Army of Italy, for example, almost half were acquitted, and the average prison term of the guilty was less than two years; even so, thirty-six were executed. Revolutionary officials and deputies-on-mission made plain their intolerance of indiscipline and 'excess, either towards their superiors or towards the inhabitants'. Desertion, especially to enemy lines, was punished in deliberately exemplary fashion to 'terrify the cowards and traitors'.[2] The measures taken by deputies-on-mission could be draconian. They reached a peak in the Basque country: when there were mass desertions from the army there in early 1794, thousands of inhabitants of the border villages of Ascain, Itxassou, Sare and many others were deported sixty miles or more from the border in an attempt to prevent flight to the enemy.[3]

No resource was spared from the war effort. The bells of churches and monasteries closed in 1791 were seized, and on 23 July 1793 the Convention decreed that parishes could have only one bell: the metal from others was to be used for weapons or, if unsuitable, for coinage. In many parishes the removal of bells was angrily contested. In Chassy, west of Auxerre in Burgundy, villagers surrounded the authorities in December, shouting 'the bells will not be brought down!' and that 'they did not give a damn' about the local administration. At Marolles-les-Braults near Le Mans in the department of Sarthe, 250 soldiers with artillery were needed to take down the two bells in October 1793. The inhabitants of Plappeville, near Metz, managed to bury their great bell in the cemetery. All precious metals were seized. In the village of Frouard, near Nancy, there were just two chalices, a ciborium for holding the sacrament, a sun, three little unction boxes and 'a head on a little plate', silver in all weighing about seven pounds. But elsewhere the material was considerable, objects in gold and silver alone weighing forty pounds from the synagogue and fifty-two pounds from the cathedral in Nancy. Nationally, up to 100,000 bells from 60,000 church towers were melted down: about 50,000 tons of metal were thereby appropriated for the war effort.[4]

The Jacobin régime had many local faces. In most provincial towns repression had its own rhythm and targets, and it did not wait for a militant Jacobin deputy-on-mission to arrive from Paris. In Dijon locals had arrested more than four hundred 'suspects' from among well-known refractory clergy, former *parlementaires* and pre-revolutionary officials. The arrival of a deputy-on-mission was the occasion for the trial and execution of the most notorious, in all twenty-three.[5] In seven of the eighty-three departments no one was executed in 1793–94; in thirty-one others fewer than ten. For every local autocrat motivated by rage and revenge there were many others dedicated to impartial administration and capable of an extraordinary range of duties. One of these was Polycarpe Pottofeux, the most influential Jacobin in Laon, capital of the Picard department of Aisne. Born in 1763 into a family of carpenters in Saint-Quentin, Pottofeux was elected the department's chief administrator ('procureur-général-syndic') in September 1792 by 359 of the 369 voters. His adroit administration was a key reason why a frontier region characterized by extremes of wealth, and vulnerable to panic as a key route for armies and grain shipments, remained relatively calm.[6]

The Convention had proclaimed that its repression of counter-revolutionaries would be pitiless, and meant it. From the inception of the

Paris Revolutionary Tribunal in March 1793 until September, only 66 of 260 'suspects' had been found guilty of a capital offence; in the final three months of the year this was the fate of 177 of 395 accused. On 16 October, the day of the battle of Wattignies, Marie-Antoinette went to the guillotine, with remarkable stoicism. She had been deluged with accusations, some of them sexual, at her trial, but was finally found guilty of treason and conspiracy with the enemy. Her tumbril passed under Jacques-Louis David's studio window at the Louvre: he rapidly sketched her as he watched on with Rosalie Jullien, wife and mother of other prominent Jacobins. The same day his monumental *Death of Marat* was made available for public viewing. The contrast between the stark pen-and-ink drawing of the gaunt and humiliated former queen and the richly symbolic canvas of the martyred 'friend of the people' could not have been greater.[7]

Marie-Antoinette was followed to the guillotine by twenty-one of the Girondin deputies expelled in June, including Brissot, then by Bailly and Barnave. By succeeding in lifting Marat's parliamentary immunity in April 1793 so that he could be tried before the Revolutionary Tribunal, the Girondins had opened up a precedent that was to be fatal for many of them, for deputies accused before the Tribunal were rarely found innocent, unlike Marat himself. From the perspective of the Convention, the federalist movement was a criminal act of sabotage at a time of the Revolution's greatest challenge, and the Girondins who had been expelled from the Convention on 2 June were guilty of treachery once provincial towns rebelled in their name. Many others accepted the necessity of the Girondins' deaths. For example, the patriotic priest of Saint-Denis-en-Val south of Orléans reported without emotion in his diary that on 21 October a metal rooster and liberty cap had been placed on top of his steeple; ten days later he noted that twenty-one deputies had been guillotined 'for wanting to betray the Convention and the whole of France'.[8]

Marie-Jeanne Roland was found guilty of conspiring with other Girondins against the 'unity and indivisibility of the Republic'. She went to the guillotine with great dignity on 8 November, although her famous last words—'O Liberty, what crimes are committed in your name!'—may be apocryphal. Her husband was devastated by the news. He left his refuge with friends in Rouen and stabbed himself to death in a country lane. When his body was found on 11 November, he had several suicide notes in his pocket. 'Would that my country could at last abhor so many crimes and return to human and social sentiments,' he lamented; 'I learnt that they were going to cut my wife's throat; and I do not wish to remain any longer on an earth which is covered in crimes.'[9] From his hiding place near Saint-Émilion, close to Bordeaux, Jérôme Pétion wrote a final letter to his twelve-year-old son expressing similar views: 'the greatest torment for me would be to think that so many heinous crimes might go unpunished; vengeance is now the most sacred of duties. Forgiveness would be the most criminal of acts.'[10]

Some of those examined by the Revolutionary Tribunal were found guilty by association rather than for having explicitly advocated counter-revolution. Earlier, the actress Olympe de Gouges, a strong supporter of Marie-Antoinette as well as the author of the Declaration of the Rights of Women and Citizenesses, continued to have greater courage than political acumen. While Robespierre and the Girondin Jean-Baptiste Louvet had squared off in the Convention in October 1792 over who was responsible for the 'September massacres', she had signed and pasted up posters in Paris supporting Louvet. After the expulsion of the leading Girondins on 2 June 1793, she wrote an open letter in their defence that was read out in the Convention, and called for a plebiscite on whether France should be a centralized Republic, a federation or a constitutional monarchy. She was executed two days after Brissot and his colleagues.[11]

The revolutionaries repudiated what they saw as the essentials of power in the *ancien régime*: self-interest, duplicity, intrigue and insincerity. But sincerity could be impossible to prove, as the author and actors in François de Neufchâteau's adaptation of Samuel Richardson's novel *Pamela, or Virtue Rewarded* found in September 1793, when Collot d'Herbois ordered their arrest as likely 'counter-revolutionaries' because of the play's English origins and allegedly aristocratic values. The closing couplet indeed seemed an appeal for clemency for counter-revolutionaries:

Ah! Persecutors are the most condemnable
And the most tolerant are the most reasonable.[12]

Private motivations became as potent a proof of conspiracy as criminal behaviour—but animated protestations of patriotism could be interpreted as duplicity. When the prominent Jacobin Jacques-Alexis Thuriot adduced his revolutionary record as evidence of his innocence of 'conspiracy', the journalist and Paris Commune official Jacques-René Hébert retorted 'what is proved by services rendered to the Revolution? Conspirators always adopt this method. In order to deceive the people, one has to have served it; one has to gain its confidence the better to abuse it.'[13] Thuriot was fortunate to survive.

How could one survive such logic? It helped if a character witness was a child. As a man named Petit was being denounced to the Jacobin Club in Paris, a member noticed his son crying in a corner. The minutes recorded that 'young Petit, aged twelve, rushes forward to the rostrum and declares that his father is a good patriot and has raised him in the purest principles of the Revolution'. Thus exonerated, Petit was made a member and his boy given an entry ticket to proceedings.[14] Denunciations could be motivated by personal ill will and rumour as much as by patriotic duty. What was the surveillance committee of Cécile Montagnarde (formerly Sainte-Cécile) near Orange in the south-east to make of a claim that 'Mathieu said that Pierre Four had told him that citizeness Rougier had said to her spouse that the older Saussac had said in Rougier's shop "please to God that the Convention is overthrown"'?[15]

But nowhere was the cost of counter-revolution higher than in the Vendée. By late December 1793 the Catholic and Royal Army had been reduced to about 12,000 members, of whom only half were in a position to fight. They retreated to Savenay, from where the terrified townspeople had fled: in March the constitutional priest and other officials had been murdered by the rebels. The republican troops under General Westermann who attacked Savenay pursued the remnants of the counter-revolutionary army relentlessly in and around the town, and finally through the forest of Gavre, where they had fled. In all about 6,000 would die, including prisoners judged and executed on the spot by a military commission. In a notorious report Westermann exulted that 'the Vendée is no more':

It died under our swords, with its women and children. I've just buried it in the swamps and woods of Savenay. . . . I don't have any prisoners to reproach myself for. I exterminated the lot. . . . The broadsides continue ceaselessly at Savenay, because brigands are arriving all the time presuming that they will be made prisoners. . . . We're not taking prisoners, as it would be necessary to give them the bread of liberty and pity is not revolutionary.[16]

As generals Westermann, Turreau and others conducted punitive purges through the countryside, the Vendéan leader François de Charette responded as best he could, for example ordering seven hundred republicans to be executed when he retook the little town of Legé in February 1794.

The republican troops were in no mood for sympathy. One of them was Corporal François-Xavier Joliclerc, born in 1766 in the village of Froidefontaine in the eastern Jura mountains. A committed revolutionary, he had volunteered as early as 1791, and had fought in the victories in the east in late 1793. By January 1794 he was in the army crushing the rebels in the western departments. On 6 Pluviôse Year III, or 25 January ('slave style', as he usually dubbed the Gregorian calendar), he wrote to his mother from Cholet:

> We will use steel and flames, a rifle in one hand, a burning torch in the other. Men and women, all will feel the end of our swords. All have to die, except small children. These departments must be an example to others which want to revolt. We've already burnt through about seven leagues.

On 4 March, however, he was wounded during an insurrection at nearby Vezins on the day of Carnival, which left fifty-two of his fellows dead, 'all with heads smashed in or with bodies run through with bayonets'. He admitted to his mother that, 'if I recounted to you the cruelties committed in the Vendée by both sides, your hair would stand on end, but I think this war will soon be finished'.[17]

Ultimately, the civil war in the Vendée was to claim perhaps as many as 200,000 lives, including those of 30,000 soldiers. Between December 1793 and May 1794, after the insurrection had been crushed, General Turreau's 'infernal columns' conducted a 'scorched-earth' revenge on 773 communes declared outside the law: 117,000 people (15 per cent of the population) died in these communities. To the Minister of War, Jean-Baptiste Bouchotte, Turreau reported that all rebels and suspected rebels of all ages and both sexes would be bayonetted; 'all villages, farms, woods, heathlands, generally anything that will burn, will be set on fire'. Even the little town of Bressuire (Deux-Sèvres), a republican bastion against the insurgents, was emptied and burned.[18]

Further up the Loire, Nantes had been surrounded by rebel forces for most of the period since March 1793; provisions were almost exhausted. As well as the 83,000 inhabitants, there were 7,000 refugees, thousands of wounded soldiers in ten military hospitals, scores of thousands of soldiers in garrisons, and up to 10,000 prisoners. Sacrificial victims were at hand in the persons of non-juring clergy who had supported the rebels. On 26 Brumaire (16 November), self-styled *sans-culottes* of the popular society of Vincent-la-Montagne in Nantes 'cleansed' the church of Sainte-Croix of 'fanaticism and the priesthood, whose imbecile ministers or imposters, spread out across the globe for the misfortune of the human race, mark their steps by ruination and pious assassinations'. But now the *sans-culottes* would purify 'the temple of madness and the pulpit of lies'. The anti-clerical rage encouraged the deputy-on-mission Jean-Baptiste Carrier to order that ninety-four priests held on the ship *La Gloire* be drowned in the Loire. There were furious Nantais prepared to encourage Carrier in successive mass drownings and shootings, in all of about 1,800 people, but his dictatorial style and penchant for excess and vulgarity would finally alienate even them. The arrival of Robespierre's special envoy, the brilliant young 'Jules' Jullien, just eighteen years old, would result in Carrier's recall from Nantes in February 1794.[19]

Robespierre and others in the Convention became consumed with the threat of the 'foreign plot' to the point where foreigners in general were seen as suspect. The ranks of foreigners living in France had been swollen by refugees from Liège and elsewhere in the north-east and deserters from invading armies; now, at a time of war with a Europe-wide coalition, foreigners were particularly vulnerable. Article 120 of the 1793 Constitution, under which the 'French people offered asylum to those banished for the cause of liberty', had been suspended with the rest of the Constitution. Earlier in 1793 the Ministry of War had ordered that deserters from the enemy were to receive payments when entering the French army; in the winter of 1793–94 they were instead put to work on public works or in agriculture to defray the costs of feeding them, especially in the east where conscription had exacerbated labour shortages. They were no longer to be admitted to the French army.[20] Among those temporarily in prison was the British writer and revolutionary sympathizer Helen Maria Williams. After the September Massacres of 1792 she had allied herself with the Girondins; and she hosted Mary Wollstonecraft, Tom Paine and the South American army officer Francisco de Miranda at her salon. She was imprisoned with her mother, her sister, her lover and her lover's wife in October 1793, and on her release fled to Switzerland.[21]

On 27 Brumaire (17 November), Robespierre delivered a 'Report on the Political Situation of the Republic' to the Convention on behalf of the Committee of Public Safety. The English government above all was singled out. It was accused of everything from wanting to replace Louis XVI with the Duke of York to seeking to drive the south of France into a federation just as in the United States. Robespierre regretted the lack of strong support from other nations, for which he blamed the malevolence of earlier Girondin diplomat appointees to the United States and English manoeuvres in Turkey, 'the useful and faithful ally of France'. Austria had plans to annex Lorraine, Alsace and French Flanders if France was defeated; elsewhere, Robespierre claimed, 'Roussillon, French Navarre and the departments bordering Spain have been promised to His Catholic Majesty.' On 15 Frimaire (5 December), Robespierre again inveighed against Prime Minister William Pitt and the British for their venal values: 'your deputies are industrial commodities, like the wool of your sheep and the steel of your factories ... and you dare speak of morality and freedom!' The nation that he had once admired for its fierce defence of liberty had become the cradle in which all foreign plots were born.[22]

The 'foreign plot' ensnared many. There was no more potent accusation against opponents than that their vices were venal, particularly if 'English gold' was involved. In the aftermath of the consolidation of the national debt from the maze of private loans that had made the *ancien régime*'s finances a tangle of expensive special arrangements, some of the international financiers and unscrupulous Jacobins sought to profit from the liquidation of the government's East India Company through manipulation of share prices. Among the latter were the Jacobins François Chabot, Claude Basire and men close to Danton, such as Fabre d'Églantine, playwright and illustrator of the revolutionary calendar. A denunciation of Chabot at the Jacobin Club in Paris in November ranged from his financial dealings to his marriage to the sister of the wealthy Austrian-Jewish bankers, the Frey brothers. Chabot's categorical denial and attempt to reverse the attack onto the 'calumniators' was pointless: another club member countered that 'that is the kind of thing conspirators always say'.[23]

Among those caught up in the accusations was the most radical of eighteenth-century political cosmopolitans, the Prussian Anacharsis Cloots, who had advocated the abolition of all existing states and the establishment of a single world state, a worldwide 'republic of united individuals'.[24] One of those made a French citizen in September 1792 and elected to the Convention, Cloots was under a cloud because of alleged dealings with the Vandenyvers, bankers condemned to death for criminal corruption by the Revolutionary Tribunal on 17 Frimaire (7 December). Robespierre fulminated against Cloots at the Jacobin Club a few days later, demanding successfully 'the exclusion from the Jacobin Club of all nobles, priests, bankers and foreigners'. 'Can we regard a German baron as a patriot? Can we regard a man with an income of more than one hundred thousand *livres* as a *sans-culotte*?'[25]

Despair at the venality and lack of virtue of such men convinced the Jacobins that military success was not enough. While the overarching aim of the Convention's emergency measures was the survival of the Republic in the face of foreign and internal enemies, the Jacobins who dominated the Convention and its governing committees were committed to creating a regenerated society worthy of the grandeur of the Enlightenment and the Revolution. This was to arise from a secular and republican education system, a national programme of social welfare and a cultural policy to inculcate the virtues.

The Bouquier Law of December 1793 proposed a system of free, compulsory education for children six to thirteen years old, with a curriculum emphasizing republican virtues, the simplification of formal French, physical activity, field-study and observation, and the place of the school in civic festivals. Gabriel Bouquier had no time for the lax attitude to instruction permitted by the parish priests under the *ancien régime*: parents who neglected their responsibilities would lose their citizenship rights for ten years, as would children who failed to learn 'a science, art or trade useful to society'.[26] The new system would require republican reading materials: some seven hundred new titles were produced across the revolutionary decade, two-fifths of them published in 1793–94. Five issues of 'Collections of Heroic and Civic Acts of French Republicans', the third with a print run of 150,000 copies, were sent to schools to replace catechisms.

New, republican heroes could instil the correct patriotic values. Recognition of the triumvirate of 'martyrs of the Revolution' (Marat, Chalier, Lepeletier) was accompanied by the celebration of the heroism of Joseph Bara (aged fourteen) and Joseph-Agricol Viala (aged twelve), both killed fighting counter-revolution. Bara had died at Jallais, near Cholet, on 7 December after refusing to hand over horses to counter-revolutionary rebels. On 28 December, Robespierre claimed that Bara had shouted 'Vive la République!' in defiance at his captors' insistence that he shout 'Vive Le Roi!', and David was commissioned to paint his portrait for primary schools.[27] But primary-school education was in a state of disarray with the departure of so many priests, and few children attended school during this year. In the city of Clermont-Ferrand, for example, only 128 pupils attended school from a population of 20,000 people.

The Constitution of 1793 had made an unprecedented commitment to social rights as the foundation stone of the Republic of virtue. On 4 July 1793 abandoned children became a state responsibility; on 2 November children born outside marriage were guaranteed equal inheritance rights with their siblings. In June and July the Convention had passed laws seizing *émigré* property, while the law of 13 September, giving the poor interest-free loans of 500 *livres* for twenty years, offered peasants the chance to acquire a plot. In the district of Tours there were 112 sales; in Ardèche an estimated 109. By the end of 1793 some 1,546 landless families around Versailles had been allotted an *arpent* (about one acre) of land from the former royal domain, but these plots were not large enough to be viable, and almost all were sold off within a few years.[28]

This was a time of chronic food shortages in towns, as supplies to the army took precedence. Some of the deputies-on-mission, such as Pierre Paganel in Aveyron and Gilbert Romme in Dordogne, established food stores and rationing. In the towns of the south-west during the spring of 1794 the daily bread ration for men was reduced from 24 to 16 ounces, for women from 16 to 8 ounces (except for the pregnant), and for children from 16 to 4 ounces.[29] As with education policy, Jacobin commitment to eradicating poverty foundered because of the financial demands of the war. The Convention recoiled from Saint-Just's remedy for poverty, the draft laws of Ventôse (February–March 1794), which were to seize 'suspects'' property to 'indemnify the poor'; this would have amounted to punishment without trial.

In cities and towns, supporters of the Revolution among working people developed a distinctive *sans-culotte* ideology which was more vengeful than that of the Jacobin leadership. They envisaged a world in which artisans and peasants would be rewarded for the dignity and usefulness of their labour, in a world free of priests, the condescension of the high-born, and the competition of wealthy entrepreneurs. The people's enemies were stigmatized in vitriolic terms. The ideology was expressed through local neighbourhood societies and political clubs, where the forms of meetings borrowed from those of religious services, but with patriotic songs replacing hymns, readings from soldiers' letters instead of the Gospels, and orations on the virtues instead of sermons. The inculcation of republican, virtuous behaviour in the new citizenry drew on the catechism as the model of instruction; but loyalty to the *patrie* replaced the worship of God in these 'republican catechisms'.[30] Good patriots wore the *bonnet rouge*, or liberty cap, to show they were no longer 'slaves'; from late 1793 the slightly different Phrygian cap referring to Greek slaves became more common. Militants used the familiar 'tu' in their social dealings rather than the polite 'vous' formerly required towards their superiors: in the words of a petition of 31 October 1793 to the Convention, 'from this will come less pride, fewer distinctions, less ill-feeling, more obvious familiarity, a greater sense of fraternity: consequently more equality'.[31]

The tumult of political strife, war and counter-revolution generated a spate of neologisms. There were more than 1,350 such innovations in the decade after 1789, most of them during the period 1792–94. The most prominent neologism was 'sans-culottes'; other political labels drawn from individuals were more short-lived: 'robespierriste', 'pittiste', 'maratiste'. Some expressed vindictive mockery of the victims of the guillotine, who would 'boire à la grande tasse' ('drink a large cup') and be subject to 'déportation verticale', in reference to the mass drowning of priests at Nantes. In riposte, those deemed to have acquiesced in the September 1792 massacres in Paris were 'buveurs de sang' ('drinkers of blood') or 'septembriseurs'.[32]

Despite their contempt for 'superstition' and the violence of their threats to counter-revolutionaries, the radical Jacobins of the capital were often self-consciously moralistic, damning what they described as 'loose morals' as smacking of ancien régime laxity and corruption. On 2 October 1793 the Commune of Paris decreed:

> It is forbidden to all girls and women of bad morals to parade on the streets, promenades, public squares, and to encourage licentiousness there. . . . The general council calls to its aid for the implementation and maintenance of its decree republicans who are austere and lovers of good morals . . . invites old people, as ministers of morality, to see that these morals are not outraged . . .[33]

Prostitution itself was banned on 21 Nivôse Year II (10 January 1794), seen by the Commune as an ancien régime vice and in any case unnecessary when there was work in war industries. However, it remained a clandestine last resort for up to 20,000 young women in Paris.

The Jacobins and their supporters created a new symbolic universe to replace what they dismissed as defunct ornaments of oppression. For the first time in history common soldiers who fell in battle were honoured alongside generals. The scale and solidity of the memorials varied markedly:

from a pyramid replacing a statue of Louis XV in Reims, and a stone pedestal in Auch erected with the names of the dead in large letters, to a wooden obelisk in Belleville on the northern edge of Paris, and a simple tree in the Provençal village of Cucuron.[34] In architecture, too, the impulse was to create buildings that represented a unified society. Jean-Jacques Lequeu offered a design of a new city gate for Paris featuring a gigantic colossus wearing a liberty cap and holding a club seated across two small copies of the customs houses destroyed in 1789. Robespierre wondered aloud how national unity might be better captured in terms of political participation if the Convention had a space for 12,000 spectators.[35] But the Jacobins were not to have the time to implement their grandiose plans for massive revolutionary monuments to supplant those of the *ancien régime*.

The 'cultural revolution' of the Year II was expressed most powerfully through popular songs and theatre. For several reasons, including the dire economic situation and the menacing political climate, only 371 new books were published in 1794, compared with over one thousand annually before 1789. One book that was now hugely popular was Rousseau's *Social Contract*: it had not been reprinted since 1772, but there were thirteen new editions in the period 1792–95, including a pocket-sized version for soldiers. In contrast, 1792–94 was a great age of political songs. The number of new songs climbed accordingly: 116 in 1789; 325 in 1792; 590 in 1793; and 701 in 1794. Most of these were exhortations to courage, and mockery of monarchs and aristocrats:

> They have returned to the shadows,
> Those great kings, cowardly and licentious,
> Infamous drinkers, famous hunters,
> Playthings of the vilest harlots. [repeat]
> Oh you, who are discouraged by nothing!
> True lovers of Liberty!
> Establish equality
> On the debris of slavery.[36]

Theatres in Paris were subsidized if they offered a free performance each week. Most of the plays performed in 1793–94 were written before 1789, but it was judicious for directors to rewrite passages that might imply nostalgia for the *ancien régime*. Some old favourites remained popular: during 1793–94 three-quarters of the 17,000 performances were of non-political plays, and the most performed playwright during the Revolution, as before, remained Robineau de Beaunoir, a priest who had worked in the Bibliothèque Royale before emigrating. Other dramas used a mixture of bawdiness and patriotism to appeal to an audience: one of the most popular plays in Paris in this period was *Les Visitandines*, the ribald adventures of two drunken rogues mistaking a convent for an inn.

Political sensitivities were skin deep. In early 1794 the Grand Théâtre in Bordeaux had decided to perform Calderón's seventeenth-century play *La Vida es sueño* (*Life is a Dream*) and, when the actor Arouch delivered his line 'Long live our noble king!', spectators angrily denounced the cast. The Military Commission arrested all eighty-six members of the troupe; ultimately, Arouch was guillotined, allegedly still insisting 'But it was in my part!' The issue was fraught—why had the company chosen to perform that play at that moment?—and the governing committees were plainly more comfortable when a performance was obviously 'patriotic'.[37]

High culture was particularly vulnerable. The Royal Paris Opéra, at the pinnacle of the culture of the *ancien régime*, lost its monopoly in the capital and its directors Louis-Joseph Francoeur and Jacques Cellerier fell under political suspicion: the latter emigrated to England, while the former was imprisoned as a 'suspect'. On 8 October 1793 the Committee of Public Safety approved a loan to the Opéra on condition that it purged its repertoire to perform only 'patriotic' works, that it seek to employ relatives of soldiers, and that 'each week it will give a free and patriotic performance of, by and for the people'. So in 1794 it put on *La Réunion du 10 août*, a five-act celebration of 1792 described as a 'sans-culottide dramatique'. Like those responsible for the Jardin du Roi, the king's personal gardens, the leaders of the Opéra managed ultimately to adapt to the values of the Revolution to reposition their great institution as an exemplar of civic and national pride.[38]

The combination of a surge in patriotism and fury at counter-revolution also generated an explosion of visual expression in a society where imagery remained the most potent form of communication. The restricted world of the Paris Salon was thrown open on the initiative of Jacques-Louis David: only sixty-three painters and sculptors had been invited to exhibit at the Salon of 1787, but now 318 of them displayed 883 works at that of 1793. The government gave 442,000 *livres* in prizes. David, a member of the Committee of General Security, threw himself into the war effort by publishing his ribald cartoons mocking the counter-revolution while, across the Channel, James Gillray depicted the *sans-culottes* as cannibals nourishing their children with the bodies of priests and nobles.

Together with new ways of marking time through the revolutionary calendar, 'patriots' sought to remove all traces of the *ancien régime* by renaming places whose names had 'aristocratic' or Christian connotations. Some of these changes were imposed as a result of military repression—most infamously in Lyon and Marseille—but most of the 3,000 changes were local initiatives. So Saint-Izague became Vin-Bon, Saint-Bonnet-Elvert became Liberté-Bonnet-Rouge; Montmartre was renamed Mont-Marat, while Villedieu took the name La Carmagnole. In the district of La Rochelle, Saint-Ouen became Marat, Saint-Rogatien was changed to Égalité, Saint-Soule to Rousseau and Saint-Vivien to Sans-Culottes. Scores of communes in the department of Gard changed their names, frequently by simply deleting the prefix 'Saint', but often with more imagination: Saint-Gilles on the Camargue took the name of the Greek island and famous battle of Héraclée, Sainte-Eulalie became Canteperdrix ('song of the partridge'), and Saint-Médiers became Vivacité.[39] As in Paris, the streets of La Rochelle were renamed, honouring heroes such as Benjamin Franklin or Jean Calas. The neighbourhood sections of Orléans were renamed after the virtues (Liberté et Egalité, Unité et Indivisibilité, La Loi), the predecessors (Brutus, Rousseau) or the icons of Revolution (Sans-culottes, Jemappes, 1789 et 1792, Lepeletier, Les Piques, Les Fédérés).[40]

Patriot parents gave their newborn children names in keeping with the revolutionary times. In Poitiers, for example, only 62 of 593 babies born in the Year II were named after saints in the *ancien régime* manner. Instead, given names reflected the contrasting sources of political inspiration: 55 per cent of the 430 names adopted in the department of Seine-et-Marne east and south of Paris drew on nature or the new calendar (Rose, Laurier, Floréal), 24 per cent on republican virtues (Liberté, Victoire, La Montagne), 12 per cent on antiquity (Brutus, Mucius Scaevola), and 9 per cent on new heroes (Lepeletier, Marat). One little boy was called Travail ('Work'), another Fumier ('Manure-heap'). In the Alps the Lacau parents gave their daughter the name Phytogynéantrope, Greek for a woman giving birth only to warrior sons; a couple from Châlons-sur-Marne named their son Faisceau Pique Terreur. Revolutionaries sometimes changed their own names: a Jacobin from the Catalan port of Collioure, Jean-Baptiste Berge, adopted that of the profuse local herb Romarin ('Rosemary').[41] In many rural areas the phenomenon was infrequent: only 20 per cent of the

133 communes in the district of Villefranche-en-Beaujolais had any such first names at all. There was also great variation between cities: in early 1794 at least 60 per cent of children received revolutionary names in Marseille, Montpellier, Nevers and Rouen, but not a single child in the more devout towns of Riom and Saint-Étienne in the mountains of central France.[42]

Invoking Rousseau's name had become a powerful rhetorical device. Robespierre, among many, cited Rousseau as his master but he parted company with him on representative government. While Robespierre had justified popular insurrection as an expression of the general will as late as the purge of the Girondins in June 1793, he was profoundly ill at ease with such intimidation, particularly at a time of military crisis. He soon insisted that the Convention was in line with the general will—that is, that insurrection was no longer necessary—and by late 1793 was arguing that representative government was the best expression of democracy.[43]

Accordingly, popular initiative that might intimidate the Convention was to be curtailed. Among the first targets of the Committee of Public Safety were the most radical of the *sans-culottes*, the Enragés, including the militants from the Revolutionary Republican Citizenesses. Claire Lacombe had confronted the Convention on 8 October 1793:

> Our sex has produced only one monster [Charlotte Corday], while for four years we have been betrayed, assassinated, by monsters without number of the masculine sex. Our rights are those of the people and, if we are oppressed, we will know how to provide resistance to oppression.

On 24 October a group of Citizenesses was severely beaten by market women, in part because of the group's insistence that all women wear a tricolour cockade. The Convention had had enough: on 29 October it decreed that 'no person of either sex may constrain another citizen or citizeness to dress in a particular way, each being free to wear whatever clothing and arrangement is felt suitable'.[44] André Amar, from the Committee of General Security, called on the Convention to close the society of Revolutionary Republican Citizenesses by appealing to the imperatives of nature's order:

> Each sex is called to that kind of occupation which is proper to it, its action is circumscribed within a circle which cannot be broken, since

nature, which has placed these limitations on mankind, imperiously commands.... If we reflect that the political education of man is still at its dawning, that the principles are not developed, and that we still stutter over the word 'liberty', how much less are women, whose political education is almost nil, enlightened in those principles.

Another Jacobin, Louis-Joseph Charlier, protested against Amar on 30 October: 'Unless you are going to question whether women are part of the human species, can you take away from them this right which is common to every thinking being?' But the desire to dampen down menacing agitation won out, and women's clubs were closed, including about sixty in the provinces.[45]

At the heart of divisions between the most militant of the deputies and *sans-culottes* and the dominant Jacobins in the government was the extent to which the creation of a secular republican culture should purge France of physical traces of the *ancien régime*. There was often a tension between popular symbolic physical destruction of religious statuary, paintings and other signs of the *ancien régime* and Jacobin concern for what Abbé Grégoire called 'vandalism'.[46] An impulse to curtail the excesses of popular retribution was reflected in the Convention's cultural policy towards libraries and heritage. In the spirit of Grégoire, the Jacobin composer and poet Marie-Joseph Chénier vigorously opposed suggestions that offensive counter-revolutionary or royalist literature be destroyed: he insisted to the Convention that 'we owe the French Revolution [to books].... There are very republican books that are dedicated to princes.'[47]

In some regions, however, even the physical existence of the Church was seen as suspect and retrograde. Requisitioning of most church bells and useful metals had silenced large parts of a countryside that had been abandoned by its clergy at a time when the invading coalition claimed to be fighting a holy war. Deputies sent to the provinces as deputies-on-mission, such as Joseph Fouché at Nevers in Burgundy and Claude Javogues in the departments around Lyon, took the initiative in closing churches.[48] Where they were 'cleansed' and turned into 'temples of reason', there was large-scale destruction of statuary, still visible around the entry of many provincial churches today (Fig. 25). There were parts of the country where local people were predisposed to join in this 'dechristianization' or even to initiate it; elsewhere, however, it was bitterly resented. Anti-clerical ceremonies had a carnival and cathartic atmosphere, often utilizing the 'promenade des ânes [donkeys]', used in the *ancien régime* to censure violators of community norms of behaviour, but now with someone dressed as a priest sitting backwards on a donkey. At Tulle in the department of Corrèze, for example, there was a burial of a coffin containing the remains of 'superstition' and crowned with a pair of ass's ears and a missal; saints' statues were flogged.

In Auxerre in Burgundy, 'Cadet' Roussel, a militant in the popular society and the subject of a sardonic marching-song, was charged with organizing the Festival of Reason on 10 Nivôse Year II (30 December 1793) in which the statue of Saint-Étienne on the altar in the cathedral was replaced by 'a Goddess of Liberty, a young woman lightly clad in the Greek fashion, wearing a Phrygian cap'. A 'Hymn to Liberty' asked her to

Descend, oh Liberty, daughter of Nature,
The People has recognized its immortal power;
On the pompous debris of ancient imposture,
Its hands raise up your altar ...

She did descend and decorated oxen pulled her cart around the town. Roussel himself represented Time, dressed in flesh-coloured robes with two huge cardboard wings and a flowing white beard. The monsters of Despotism, Fanaticism and Federalism were ridiculed.[49] No doubt Roussel's choreography was a source of amusement for the onlookers, but for many people across the nation the Republic's new festivals were poor compensation for the absence of the Catholic ceremonies with which they had grown up.

The 'dechristianization' campaign was often linked with the activities of forty-five 'armées révolutionnaires' (in all, 30,000–40,000 men) operating in fifty-six departments by the autumn of 1793. These bands of *sans-culottes* militants, mixed with men on the run from the law and others who simply enjoyed the rough camaraderie, had as their mission the requisitioning of food for cities and the armies from well-off farmers whom they accused of hoarding, the purging of counter-revolutionaries, the seizure of metals from churches and the maintenance of revolutionary zeal. The size of these bands ranged from small groups of ten to democratically run armies of up to 7,000 in the southern Massif Central. Their confrontational behaviour often outraged devout locals, whatever their politics. A Protestant from

Anduze in the southern Cévennes mountains complained that

> the ultra-revolutionary patriots are more dangerous than the aristocrats; at St-Jean-du-Gard, they are trying to force the people to observe the *décadi* and work on Sundays, they ripped and burnt the Huguenot minister's vestments. ... I fear now that this most patriotic of areas might become the most fanatical.[50]

Tension over food shortages could combine with despair at the absence of priests: on 8–9 Ventôse Year II (27–28 February 1794) a huge crowd led by two prominent farmers in the south-western town of Rabastens shouted 'Bread and religion, down with cockades, down with the patriots!' before seizing the state granary and returning stocks to the farmers.[51]

The surviving, 'patriotic' clergy were in an invidious position: did their faith imply that Christ was 'the first republican' or instead that they were mired in superstition? Forty clerical deputies in the Convention abdicated the priesthood, including seven of the sixteen constitutional bishops. Some even became ardent dechristianizers, turning churches into revolutionary temples, as did deputies-on-mission Paganel at Toulouse, Joseph Lakanal at Bergerac and Claude-Alexandre Ysabeau at Bordeaux.[52] Popular initiative, at times encouraged by these deputies-on-mission, pressured the constitutional clergy to resign and marry as a sign of patriotism. In all, about 20,000 priests abdicated their calling. There were wide variations in the number of such resignations: there were only twenty in the southern department of Lozère but, of the 868 constitutional clergy in the former diocese of Sées in Normandy, 734 left the priesthood during the Year II.[53] There were many motives for such decisions, ranging from fear of reprisals to fury with the papacy. On 24 Brumaire Year II (14 November 1793) the priest of Rosières-aux-Salines, near Nancy, the self-styled *sans-culotte* Joseph Langries, went to his municipality to announce his intention to resign and marry, and repudiated the 'ignorance and superstition' created by 'eighteen centuries of despotism'.[54] However, for many other priests—and their parishioners—these were desperate times, in which the institutional forms of religion collapsed almost completely.

Between 6 Brumaire (27 October 1793) and 28 Floréal (17 May 1794), 268 priests resigned their position in the department of Gard, and 233 communities requested of the deputy-on-mission Jean Borie that their church become a temple of reason. In the month of Ventôse

(February–March 1794) alone 169 priests resigned. Pierre-Joseph Estornel, parish priest of Aiguesmortes, described himself as

> Aged about fifty years, a priest for twenty-five, responsible for fifteen years for six young orphaned nephews, of whom three have been on the frontiers since the beginning of the Revolution to repel the despots' satellites, absolutely devoid of property and wealth, all that I can offer at this time to the homeland is the story of a difficult and laborious life, my *sans-culottisme* at all times, and my devotion to the public good. . . . Long live philosophy! The Mountain! The Republic![55]

In all, some 6,000 priests married during the Revolution, 5,000 of them in the Year II. Priests married for all sorts of reasons. One from the north-east announced that, 'to prove ostensibly that I was a man and a citizen, I married, two months ago, a true *sans-culotte* of my former parish, twenty-two years old, poor in fortune but rich in wisdom and in virtue'. He gave further proof of his civic virtue by abdicating the priesthood and turning to teaching. The republican family was seen as central to virtuous civic life. When the young Jacobin 'Jules' Jullien was sent on mission to the west in the autumn of 1793 to 'enlighten the people', he organized a festival in Rochefort featuring a parade of married couples carrying a banner 'Celibacy is a social crime. To be a good citizen, one must be a good son, a good husband, and a good father.'[56]

In Paris services in the parish of Saint-Sulpice ended on 15 October 1793. The chalices were seized to be melted down, then three parish priests came with their wives and burned their ordination letters. They insisted that 'they had never believed a word of what they preached, which had served only to deceive the people'. Militants lit a bonfire of clerical vestments and sacred books. On 23 October *sans-culottes* removed the images of kings on the facade of Notre-Dame. Then on 7 November the Archbishop of Paris, Jean-Baptiste Gobel, who had already permitted clerical marriage, came to the Convention with eleven of his priests, removed his mitre and replaced it with a liberty cap. Soon Abbé Grégoire, the Bishop of Blois, was the only deputy in clerical garb in the Convention.[57]

The high point of dechristianization was on 10 November 1793, when Notre-Dame was turned into a 'temple of reason'. For Robespierre and others, however, dechristianization was seen as a needless affront to the religious sensibilities of good patriots: one could be a good Christian and a good republican. On 21 November he delivered a speech at the Jacobin Club attacking atheism, and the Convention passed a decree on 6 December affirming the principle of freedom of worship. But the conflict over the place of dechristianization in the construction of the regenerated citizenry would not be resolved quickly. The militant Jacobin deputy-on-mission Antoine Albitte, fresh from organizing the repression of federalism in Lyon, was sent to the neighbouring department of Ain and on 26 January 1794 launched the vandalism that would earn him the nickname of 'the Tiger of Ain'. Among his decisions was to pull down up to eight hundred steeples and many château towers 'whose height is an outrage to the egalitarian principles of all true republicans'.[58]

Ultimately, the exigencies of national mobilization reversed the decentralization of power of the early years of the Revolution and smothered such local initiative. The civil wars of 1793 had served to underline the dangers of local autonomy, just as the *armées révolutionnaires*, the surge of radical women's demands and dechristianization highlighted the challenge of popular initiative. Two days before its law affirming religious freedom, the Convention passed a major decree asserting the pre-eminence of central government at the expense of popular participation and initiative. Article I of the Law of 14 Frimaire (4 December) insisted that 'the National Convention is the sole centre of government initiative'. The 'anarchic' terror of June–November 1793 was over.[59]

The military achievements of the 'popular alliance' of the Year II were astonishing. By the end of 1793 a series of victories had stopped the advance of foreign armies in the north-east and south, and had crushed armed internal counter-revolution. A siege imposed in September to retake Toulon from the English succeeded on 17 December. The young captain Napoleon Bonaparte played a critical role in this success, although he was no longer in the port city when the deputies-on-mission Louis-Stanislas Fréron and Paul Barras oversaw the execution of perhaps eight hundred collaborators in the renamed 'Port-la-Montagne'. The Vendéan rebellion had been contained and the federalist revolt crushed, both at a huge cost in lives. Although the 'general maximum' on prices and wages had not been fully implemented, the economic slide had been reversed and the purchasing power of the *assignat* stood at 48 per cent of its face value.

For many people the governing committees now represented increasingly arbitrary repression, whatever their role in securing military victories. The journalist and deputy Louis-Sébastien Mercier was imprisoned in

October 1793 for speaking out against the purge of the Girondins. For Mercier, the Mountain was a 'sulphurous and fetid crater where sit men of blood and mud, stupid and ferocious beasts'.[60] The Jacobins whom he detested, however, did not see themselves as men of 'blood and mud', but rather as the people's representatives entrusted with saving the Republic and creating a society worthy of it.

Others were convinced by the victories of the Republic's armies that some at least of the Terror's controls could be relaxed. 'Moderate' Jacobins such as Danton and Desmoulins urged an end to the imprisonment of 'suspects' and executions, and the implementation of the Constitution of 1793. On 20 December they interrogated the Committee of Public Safety in Desmoulins' new newspaper, the *Vieux Cordelier*:

> You want to remove all your enemies by means of the guillotine! Has there ever been such great folly? Could you make a single man perish on the scaffold, without making ten enemies for yourself from his family or his friends? . . . I think quite differently from those who tell you that terror must remain the order of the day.[61]

Danton returned to the theme in the Convention on 23 January 1794, reminding it that the committees were established to confront the federalist menace: 'it is still necessary to maintain them in all their strength; but be wary of the two shores upon which we could wreck ourselves'. One shore was an excess of justice: 'we might give ourselves over to moderation, and arm our enemies'. But the other was the repression of liberty: it would be 'better to exaggerate liberty and the Revolution than to give our enemies the slightest hope of turning back'. His anxiety was that justice must be preserved wherever it did not damage the 'public good'.[62]

The problem for Danton and Desmoulins was that the Republic in fact was not yet safe: there were foreign troops still on French soil along all the borders. In the Caribbean, republican troops were engaged in a particularly bloody three-cornered struggle with England and Spain on the one hand and armed, rebellious slaves on the other. On 29 August 1793 the deputy-on-mission Léger-Félicité Sonthonax had made a rallying cry to black insurgents to join with French troops in the war against *ancien régime* Europe, but black resistance was based on their longing for emancipation rather than the deputy's republican civic rhetoric. A key figure in the rebellion was Toussaint Louverture, born a slave, with an Arada father from west Africa. Toussaint was freed over a decade before the Revolution and had briefly owned a slave and managed a plantation. In September, Sonthonax held elections for three new deputies to the Convention from Saint-Domingue, and Louis Dufay, Jean-Baptiste Mills and Jean-Baptiste Belley were elected. The 'tricolour' delegation reached Paris on 23 January 1794 and, after attempts to thwart them by the colonial lobby, appeared before the Convention on 3 February. Slavery was abolished the next day (16 Pluviôse Year II) in Saint-Domingue, Guadeloupe and Guiana.[63]

Robespierre was not in the Convention when slavery was abolished, although he supported the decision. He was preparing his most significant speech, a 'Report on the Principles of Political Morality', delivered on 17 Pluviôse (5 February). 'What is the goal towards which we are heading?', he asked the Convention in a veiled retort to Danton and Desmoulins. The goal was clear—'the peaceful enjoyment of liberty and equality'—but this would necessitate a moral revolution. Robespierre's vision of a regenerated, virtuous and self-abnegating society was, for him, the very *raison d'être* of the Revolution, a society in which 'commerce is the source of public wealth rather than solely the monstrous opulence of a few households . . . where the country secures the welfare of each individual, and each individual proudly enjoys the prosperity and glory of his country'. He drew on a speech familiar to him from his schoolboy years, Cicero's second oration against Lucius Catilina. Like Cicero, who had contrasted the virtues of the Roman Republic—honour, modesty, chastity, equity, temperance, fortitude, prudence, piety—with the vices of tyranny—wantonness, sordidness, fraud, wickedness, baseness, lust—so Robespierre insisted that

> We wish to substitute in our country . . . the empire of reason for the tyranny of custom . . . a people magnanimous, powerful and happy for a people lovable, frivolous and wretched—that is to say, all the virtues and miracles of the Republic for all the vices and puerilities of the monarchy.[64]

The greatest dangers, he emphasized, were now internal: the Republic was under siege from both the 'indulgent', like Desmoulins, Danton and their supporters, and 'ultra' revolutionaries who were contesting the authority of the committees and the Convention in their zeal for equality. In contrast to the mounting calls for a relaxation of controls, Hébert and his allies called for another popular rising like the *journée* of 5–6 September 1793—when the *sans-culottes* had last imposed their will on the National

Convention—in order to push the Revolution still further. In the process they provided the pretext for the Committee of Public Safety to move against them, accused of planning insurrection against the Convention and of disrupting food supplies. The smothering of popular initiative in Paris and elsewhere was consummated in the execution of the Hébertistes, including Anacharsis Cloots, on 24 March. A police observer reported that 'general opinion' was so indignant against them that there should be a special punishment:

> 'That would be against the Constitution,' retorted one citizen, 'the Constitution allows only one form of punishment.' 'That's true,' replied a *sans-culotte*, 'but the dangers of the fatherland don't allow us to enjoy all the advantages of the Constitution yet.'

The *sans-culotte* called for 'revolutionary punishments for all the scoundrels who want to murder the people'.[65]

Members of the governing committees now turned on the 'Indulgents'. As charges and counter-changes swirled through political circles across the winter of 1793–94, there was mounting evidence that some of the Jacobin leaders, perhaps Danton himself, had sought to line their own pockets—the epitome of uncivic behaviour. They were linked to men like the British bankers Walter Boyd and John Ker, denounced on 16 March by Amar as being part of the British conspiracy in his report to the Convention on the East India Company. The bankers had long since fled the country, but their French agent Antoine Géneste was guillotined on 18 April. His home was found to be full of letters from across the continent, essential in the world of international finance but fatal in the fires of war. As in the trial of the Hébertistes, prominent foreigners were added to prove guilt by association: the Dutch banker de Kock, the Belgian Proli, the Moravian Frey brothers, their Danish secretary Diederichsen, the Spanish Guzman. They bore the stigma of being bankers, speculators and political adventurers, and on the wrong side.

When Danton's first wife had died in February 1793, Robespierre had written a beautiful letter to his friend, assuring him that he was 'a loving and devoted friend ... I love you more than ever and until death'. But by March 1794, Robespierre's allegations against his former friend and ally went beyond charges of financial corruption to moral impropriety, accusing him of sneering over dinner that virtue was what 'he practised every night with his wife'. Similarly, in December 1790, Robespierre had been a witness to the marriage of Camille and Lucile Desmoulins, but now not even his memory of holding their son Horace on his knee could save Camille, or Lucile herself. After weeks of hesitation, Robespierre agreed to support the arrest of these giants of the Revolution on 30 March 1794.

Danton, Desmoulins and others were charged with 'a conspiracy aiming at the re-establishment of the monarchy and the destruction of the national representation and the republican government'. The charges were egregious. When Danton spotted another Montagnard, Joseph Cambon, among the witnesses for the prosecution, he mocked: 'Do you believe that we're conspirators? Look, he's laughing! He doesn't believe it. Write down that he laughed.' On the other hand, Robespierre's doctor Joseph Souberbielle, a member of the Revolutionary Tribunal, later recalled that, 'during the trial of Danton, who was a friend of mine, I dared not meet his eyes, for I was determined to condemn him, because I possessed absolute proof that he was planning the overthrow of the Republic'.[66] They went to the guillotine on 5 April 1794.

CHAPTER THIRTEEN

TERROR, VICTORY AND COLLAPSE, APRIL–JULY 1794

THE HÉBERTISTES AND 'INDULGENTS' WERE FAR FROM THE ONLY revolutionaries to have been judged guilty by the Revolutionary Tribunal of undermining the unity of the nation's response to military crisis. But the executions within a fortnight of prominent revolutionaries to the right and left of the dominant Jacobins were the most obviously political trials of the period. They made it plain that open criticism of the governing committees was tantamount to giving succour to the nation's enemies, even to being counter-revolutionary.

The confrontation with Danton and Desmoulins had consumed Robespierre's emotional and physical resources over the winter of 1793–94. He had defended them in public for months, and by the time he had felt forced to the conclusion that they were just as much a threat to the victory of the Revolution as were the Hébertistes he was exhausted to the point of collapse. He never fully recovered. Shortly after they were executed on 5 April he could no longer appear in public, and did not do so again until 7 May.[1] His political triumph and the achievements of the republican armies prefigured the collapse of his capacities and of the entire Jacobin regime.

Robespierre was only one of twelve members of the Committee of Public Safety and had no specific role, but from July 1793 he was seen as the moral compass of the Revolution itself. He was a frail and ascetic man who had thrown himself with extraordinary energy into the role of articulating the meaning and destiny of the Revolution. He had made hundreds of speeches to the Revolution's assemblies and to the Jacobin Club, as well as producing a lengthy newspaper in 1791–92.[2] He had admitted on several occasions that 'my strength and my health are not great enough'; in the aftermath of political crises he had repeatedly needed absences to recuperate. His entry onto the Committee of Public Safety increased the pressure inexorably. By March 1794 acute nervous and physical exhaustion had made him incapable of effective strategic decision-making in order to 'promptly terminate the Revolution to the benefit of the people', as he had written in his notebook late in 1793.[3] Henceforth his capacity for leadership was at odds with his reputation.

The dominant Jacobins and their supporters were walking a narrow political path between the majority in the Convention and the militant sans-culottes outside. On the one hand, for the former members of the 'Plain' and many others in the Convention, the primary goal of the revolutionary government was the attainment of peace, and the sweeping economic and political controls were temporary measures to achieve military safety. The regular extension of the powers of the Committee of Public Safety was in recognition of its extraordinary achievements and the continuing war crisis, but not a measure of support for the Jacobin ideology of regeneration of a virtuous citizenry. On the other hand, the more militant of the sans-culottes had developed a radically different vision of a more egalitarian society created by property redistribution, accompanied by continuing purges of old elites and the surveillance of elected officials. The law on local government of 14 Frimaire (4 December 1793) had repudiated the legitimacy of direct popular pressure on the elected government; now the silencing of the most prominent critics of government policy made it clear to all that it was the Convention and its executive committees that would determine when the nation was safe enough for a return to constitutional government.

An immediate consequence of the execution of the Hébertistes was that, in the three weeks after 16 April 1794, thirty-seven popular societies in Paris were closed (three-quarters of the total) on the grounds that their activities threatened the unity of revolutionary government.[4] Another consequence was that the Convention now had a freer hand to resolve the economic crisis in Paris, where the militants who controlled the Paris Commune had been loath to impose wage controls while selling on the black market continued to force up prices. The government started to encourage selling on the open market by lifting profit margins. Coupled with the imposition of the fixing of wages at September 1793 levels, this dealt a severe blow to wage-earners. Prices of essentials rose and the purchasing power of the assignat once again declined, from 48 per cent of its 1790 face value in December 1793 to 36 per cent by July 1794.

The ruling Jacobins resorted to attempts to mould public opinion in the name of a revolutionary will and morality they claimed to monopolize. Saint-Just, for example, drew on Rousseau's insistence that the 'general will' was not simply an amalgam of opinion but an uncorrupted knowledge of the public interest: in Robespierre's words, 'une volonté une' ('a single will'). On 26 Germinal (15 April 1794), Saint-Just expressed his preference for a politics of 'public conscience ... composed of the penchant of the people for the common good'. Unfortunately, so he believed, this 'penchant' was perverted by the 'evil intent' of former allies: Saint-Just's speech was made only days after the execution of the Hérbertistes and the 'Indulgents', and the day before the arrest of Pauline Léon and Claire Lacombe from the Revolutionary Republican Citizenesses as sympathizers of Hébert.

It is not that criticism of and opposition to the Jacobins were totally cowed: the governing committees and their supporters in the Convention may have been intransigent, but this was not a dictatorship with totalitarian controls. There was vociferous debate in Jacobin clubs across the country. Members of the Convention and the committees were swamped by letters of both denunciation and criticism. Robespierre himself was besieged in person by his oldest friends, Antoine and Charlotte Buissart from Arras, begging him to intervene to stop the ruthless repression that the deputy-on-mission Joseph Le Bon had unleashed in the town.[5]

Theatre remained a way in which the courageous could voice opposition under the guise of performing plays containing ambiguous innuendo. From late 1793, 150 plays had been censored by rewriting or outright banning. By March 1794 ancien régime plays by Corneille and Racine had disappeared from the stage; Antoine-Marin Lemierre rewrote *William Tell*, his 1786 play about the medieval Swiss rebel, before it opened in May 1794 as *Les Sans-culottes suisses*. A vigorous debate ensued about whether non-revolutionary plays were inherently 'unpatriotic'. In defending the production of the pantomime *Adèle de Sacy* against the accusation that it was counter-revolutionary, the director of the Lycée des Arts argued: 'The good republican does not dread denunciations, for they are the touchstone of citizenship; but every denunciation must be examined, tested to its depths; this is the duty of surveillance, and it is only then that public esteem brings justice to the accuser.' In May, Robespierre intervened to allow ancien régime plays to be performed unedited; but the debate continued as to whether all stage representations should be didactic and 'authentic'.[6]

Others complained in private about the atrocities they observed. In the autumn of 1793 the retired Le Havre merchant Toussaint Bonvoisin, horrified by the September massacres of 1792 and what he saw as the spiritual destruction wrought by the Revolution, decided to start a diary with press clippings in order to instruct his children. He entitled it 'Summary of the Revolution relating to Louis XVI. Respect for the King and the Authorities'. He would keep it throughout 1794, adding later reflections and articles to make a collection of 4,000 pages. His daily notes were studded with personal remarks such as 'my pen falls from my hands and refuses to continue with such barbarity', 'I cannot allow myself to transcribe the full odiousness' and 'the indignation of posterity'.[7] A greater risk was taken by a seventy-year-old priest imprisoned with many others in the Limousin region of central France who in May wrote to his nephew, the former noble Joseph de Pradel de Lamase, now in the Prince de Condé's *émigré* army, that the lack of food and bedding was not the worst scourge they suffered. His priestly pen would not allow him to describe the rapes, but he claimed that 'no-one's honour is safe and total brutes sometimes ravish them in front of their husbands and mothers'.[8]

Across the country, however, there was a network of Jacobins who supported the Convention and its committees, and willingly participated in the creation of the new republican world. The networks of about 6,000 Jacobin clubs grouped together those who extolled civic virtue and revolutionary patriotism as their creed. Patriotic expressions were often musical. Far from Paris, in the southern mountains of Auvergne, well over one hundred new songs were composed for festivals. The most common songs celebrated the Republic's military victories, but also the virtues of the 'republican family'.[9] In the east, even though priests in the German-speaking countryside around the little border town of Sarreguemines had almost unanimously rejected the church reforms, in the town itself the priest Nicolas-Antoine Baur remained in place and played a key role in the popular Jacobin Club that included women as well as men, and he cracked down on external signs of both Christianity and Judaism. The French language was promoted in the name of national unity. Baur himself abdicated his clerical functions in February 1794 after having been expelled from the club as a priest, and married the cousin who had been his housekeeper. In May he became the town's librarian, building an impressive collection in part from *émigré* property: the books from the Benedictine monastery of Saint-Avold alone filled twenty carts. 'The establishment of libraries is for posterity one of the greatest benefits of the Convention,' stated a town councillor, 'since it should efface the remains of ignorance and superstition and perpetuate the reign of Reason.'[10]

Local Jacobins continued to respond to the Convention's decrees on requisitioning, especially near war zones. In April 1794 the Jacobin Club of Lunéville east of Nancy (population 11,700) estimated that it had collected more than 108,000 *francs* in addition to a huge number of items of clothing (including 429 pairs of shoes and boots, 671 shirts, 181 pairs of pants and 397 pairs of stockings) and weaponry (seventeen sabres, forty-six breast-plates and fifty-five cartridge boxes). In the villages of the district of Nancy, people did what they could: Lanfroicourt could only send twenty-two shirts, two pairs of woollen stockings, two combs made of cow-horn, a blanket and a pair of shoes. Other people gave money: the village of Custines, with six hundred inhabitants, had ninety donors.[11]

The leaders of revolutionary armies further developed tactics used by Frederick II's troops in the Seven Years War, in which the 'ordre mince' of thin lines of infantry and the 'ordre profond' of deep columns of attack were fused into a flexible 'ordre mixte', whereby troops could be switched from one to the other. The revolutionary troops were far more disciplined than the popular images of furious hordes of revolutionary rabble common in foreign descriptions.[12] But the experience of war remained horrific despite the turning of the tide of battle. At times the logistical challenges of supplying troops were insurmountable: soldiers garrisoned in Phalsbourg north of Strasbourg pillaged the market there on 24 Prairial Year III (12 June 1794).[13] Privation was recalled vividly by Jean Conan, born in 1765 into a poor family of Breton textile workers near Guingamp. In his old age he wrote an extraordinary epic poem of 7,054 lines in Breton, a mixture of mystical religiosity and republicanism in which he saw his courage and survival as a soldier as divinely assured. Conan recalled of his service in the republican army:

> We had only raw turnips and chunks of potato . . .
> Our clothing was ragged and dirty, we were
> Without shoes, our hands and faces black with dirt . . .
> And all this time we fought night and day.[14]

News of victories fuelled uplifting rhetoric in the Convention, but for the soldiers in the field the reality was also mired in homesickness, filth and fear. As one young man on the eastern front wrote home on 2 Floréal Year III (21 April 1794): 'Our sergeant then gave us some brandy; he told us not to be afraid, to take our courage in both hands; but when I then saw him fall to the ground, I was not singing; I waited my turn, I saw the shells and the bullets coming straight at us.'[15]

There are two durable, but contradictory, images of the Jacobin regime of 'terror until peace'. One is of a government unable to provide its citizens with the essentials of life during a year of misery. The second is of a repressive, even totalitarian regime. Both are misleading. The first ignores all those villages and towns across the country where local officials were able both to meet military requisitions and to ensure an equitable distribution of foodstuffs at a time of acute shortages. The second misses the ways in which men and women continued to criticize and disobey. There were still more than fifty newspapers available in Paris in June 1794, many judiciously critical of government policies.[16] The unremitting sacrifices for war, coupled with confusion at the executions of erstwhile patriots, generated public bewilderment and occasional hostility. A worker in an armaments factory was heard to have announced that 'We've had it! (*C'est foutu!*) . . . We're going to die of hunger. We're being fooled by fine words.' A police informant reported that a woman shouted on the Place de Grève: 'Vive le Roi! The Republic can get fucked! I shit on the Nation!' Another heard that a 'true *sans-culotte*', while listening to a child recite a few articles of the Constitution, 'said that he preferred a bottle of wine to all that. What support can the Republic expect from such men?' he lamented.[17]

Even though the 'general maximum' of September 1793 had been imposed on wages as well as consumer goods, in regions of large-scale agriculture the vulnerability of farmers when young men were in the armies enabled harvesters and labourers to strike for higher pay. The district of Montpellier complained that 'the workers involved in agricultural labour form themselves into groups ['se coalisent'], threaten, aggress and force the landowner to pay a day's labour at a rate far above that fixed by the law'. Close to the eastern front the requisitioning of oxen and draft-horses for military transport exacerbated the labour shortage. In Heudicourt and other communes of the department of Somme, labourers confronted farmers with demands that bags of wheat be added to their salaries, holding placards reading: 'Unity is strength—to the harvester of good wil—to harvest at that price—republicans have had enough. All citizens will come at two o'clock for a festival . . . to dance around the tree of fraternity.'[18]

In mid-June 1794 the justice of the peace of the southern village of Durban was complaining similarly of the parlous state of agriculture: 'because of the lack or exorbitant price of labour, the law of the Maximum of 29 September last (old style) is ignored by labourers, merchants and tradesmen'. Labourers once paid a *livre* or two for a day's work were now expecting five or six, or refusing to work and letting crops spoil. The local military commander Jean-Louis Cros, now calling himself 'Rosemary' in line with the Jacobin cult of nature, concluded that 'they would prefer to do nothing rather than work for the Maximum'.[19]

These labour movements were a continuation of ancient forms of collective action known in the north as 'bacchanals', and they were still marked by a carnivalesque tone. Their incidence led the Convention to pass two decrees before the 1794 harvests: the Law of 11 Prairial (30 May) requisitioning citizens for harvests and setting wages and conditions, and the amnesty of 21 Messidor (9 July) freeing labourers being held as 'suspects' so they could work in the fields. In the district of Saint-Flour in the Massif Central, authorities conscripted a workforce of one thousand harvesters and their families. Available soldiers in camps were despatched to work in the fields, such as 4,000 of the 10,000 soldiers camped at Launac near Montpellier.[20]

Across the nation a triangular battle was being played out between the military needs of the Republic, the large-scale producers of grain crops in particular, and urban populations determined both to avoid paying very high prices for bread and to ensure that there was enough for local consumption. The diaries of two artisan women of Orléans, Jeanne-Victoire Delzigue and Marie-Anne Charpentier, make clear that this was essentially a period of fearful shortages for which the elaborate festivals of local Jacobins seemed meagre alternatives to older religious rituals. Another local diarist, the patriotic priest of Saint-Denis-en-Val across the Loire from Orléans, recorded that 'there was no bread to be had at the bakers. It was the greatest misery that anyone had ever seen, since a number of people went several days without eating.' He seems to have felt more for them than for his fellow priest Pierre Porche, a non-juror found hiding in his uncle's wardrobe and guillotined.[21]

This parish was fortunate to have a priest. By Easter 1794, when only about 150 churches openly celebrated mass, most parishes were devoid of a priest, and there were few church bells, the countryside must have been disconcertingly quiet. There were different noises now, as around the massive former abbey of Prémontré in the north-east, which was sold off to a glass manufacturer for more than 223,000 *livres* and converted into a potassium and saltpetre factory, including the sanctuary.[22] Apart from bands of those who had deserted from the army or who were evading conscription, there were no young men in the fields and forests. Fortunate but rare were the minority of villages like Gabian, near Pézenas in the southern department of Hérault, which had both a priest and a lay school-teacher in 1793–94.[23]

Across the nation there were perhaps 80,000 'suspects' being held in detention. Until June 1794 most never appeared before the Revolutionary Tribunal and, of those who did, 40 per cent were acquitted. Among those who were not, however, there were many who were found guilty by association. The seventy-two-year-old Malesherbes, the defender of Louis XVI at his trial, had retreated to his estate near Pithiviers, south of Paris. But in December 1793 he was arrested with his daughter Aline, his son-in-law Lepeletier de Rosanbo and his grandchildren. Rosanbo had drafted a protest from members of his former *parlement* in October 1790, that they still regarded the National Assembly as illegal and as 'despoiling the clergy and bringing about a contempt for religion, by destroying the nobility . . . . by the depredation of royal majesty'. Rosanbo was guillotined on 2 Floréal (21 April 1794); two days later it was the turn of Malesherbes himself, his daughters Antoinette and Aline, and Aline's in-laws the Chateaubriands.[24]

There were many other apparently needless deaths in these months, although none so wasteful as that of Antoine Lavoisier. Lavoisier was the son of a wealthy bourgeois who had bought a noble title, and in 1768 became a private tax-farmer. He was also the most brilliant scientist of his age, the author of the seminal *Traité élémentaire de la chimie*, published in 1789. He undermined ancient certainties that air, water, fire and earth were indivisible elements, devising instead quantitative methods for defining chemical elements and the system for naming chemical compounds. He demonstrated that water is a compound of hydrogen and oxygen, and the chemical processes of combustion. After 1789, Lavoisier had thrown his energies into the Revolution, acting as a senior administrator in armaments during the war and on the commission that devised the metric system, while continuing his experiments.

Lavoisier had a powerful enemy in Jean-Paul Marat, whose scientific theories he had exposed as bogus when Marat attempted to join the Royal Academy of Science. In 1791 Marat denounced him as a 'contemptible little man' responsible for the new tax-collecting *barrières* built around Paris in the 1780s: 'would to heaven he had been strung up from the nearest lamp-post'. In November 1793 charges were laid against all former tax-farmers. Robespierre intervened to save the life of one of them, but Jacques-Louis David, who signed more than four hundred arrest warrants as a member of the Committee of General Security, apparently made no effort to save the man whose luminous portrait he had painted with his wife Marie-Anne in 1788. Lavoisier and the other former tax-farmers were brought to trial on 5 May 1794. Lavoisier wrote a last letter to his wife Marie-Anne before being executed on 8 May:

> I have had quite a long career and, above all, a happy one, and I believe my memory will be accompanied with some glory. What more could I wish for? The events in which I find myself caught up will probably spare me the inconveniences of old age. I shall die in perfect health . . .[25]

More fortunate than Lavoisier was Claude-Nicolas Ledoux, who had designed the majestic neo-classical Parisian customs houses that had made Lavoisier's fortune: Ledoux was imprisoned for 'aristocratie' on 29 November 1793, but never brought to trial.[26]

Those who were found guilty faced the agonies of premature death and farewells to loved ones. In October 1793, Marie-Madeleine Coutelet, who worked at a hemp-spinning mill in Paris, was arrested because of letters found in her room that criticized the government (she insisted in vain that they were ironic mockery). Her last letter was to her family:

> Farewell, I embrace you for the last time, I that am the most loving of daughters, the most affectionate of sisters. I find this day the most beautiful given me by the Supreme Being. . . . I embrace my friends and am grateful to all those who have been so good as to speak in my defence. Farewell for the last time, may our children be happy, that is my last wish.[27]

Her sister was executed five months later.

The insurrection in the Vendée and the last traces of federalism had been crushed, but no quarter was shown to open opposition to the Jacobin Convention. The sweeping powers of deputies-on-mission made communities and individuals vulnerable to the personal weaknesses and obsessions of powerful individuals, no more so than in the little Provençal town (population 2,000) of Bédoin, on the slopes of Mont Ventoux. Formerly part of the papal territory of Comtat-Venaissin, the town was notorious for its opposition to the Revolution and for sheltering refractory clergy. On the night of 12–13 Floréal (1–2 May 1794), the liberty tree was cut down and its red cap thrown in a well, and posters of the Convention's decrees were destroyed. When the deputy-on-mission Étienne Maignet and republican troops failed to convince locals to surrender those responsible, a court was convened that found sixty-three people guilty: thirty-five were guillotined and twenty-eight shot on 28 May. The following week the five hundred houses and eight chapels of the town were set on fire and destroyed.[28]

Jacobin leaders pondered why so many people were slow to recognize the benefits of republican regeneration, of civic virtue and sacrifice. On 20 April, Jacques-Nicolas Billaud-Varenne reported to the Convention on behalf of the Committee of Public Safety that what was needed 'is to recreate the people one wants to return to liberty . . . strong action is needed therefore, a vehement impulse, appropriate for developing civic virtues and repressing the passions of greed, intrigue and ambition'.[29] Robespierre believed that public festivals, inspired by those of the classical world, would both educate participants and avoid the anarchic improvisation of impromptu public display. In particular, a new official Cult of the Supreme Being which he outlined on 7 May would ensure that 'this delightful (*délicieuse*) land that we inhabit . . . is made to be the land of liberty and happiness':

> Nature tells us that Man is born for freedom, and the experience of the centuries shows us Man enslaved. His rights are inscribed in his heart, and his humiliation in history. . . . Sparta shines like a flash of lightning amid vast shadows . . .
>
> Everything in the physical order has changed; everything must change in the moral and political order. Half of the revolution has already occurred; the other half must also be accomplished. . . .
>
> How different is the God of Nature from the God of priests! . . . The priests have created God in their image: they have made Him jealous, capricious, greedy, cruel, implacable. . . . They have relegated Him to Heaven as if to a palace, and have called Him to Earth only to ask for tithes, riches, honours and the pleasures of power for themselves.[30]

The decree established the revolutionary cult—'the French People acknowledge the existence of the Supreme Being and the immortality of the soul'—and guaranteed freedom of worship to all. To festivals celebrating the great revolutionary days—14 July 1789, 10 August 1792, 21 January 1793, 31 May 1793—would be added thirty-six others on each *décadi*, at the end of the ten-day weeks of the revolutionary calendar. These would honour the Revolution's goals (Liberty, Equality, the Republic, World Freedom, Happiness), the revolutionary virtues (Truth, Justice, Modesty, Friendship, Frugality, Courage), and Robespierre's idealized family characteristics: Love, Conjugal Fidelity, Paternal Love, Maternal Tenderness and Filial Piety.

Along with the Convention's educational programme, the Cult of the Supreme Being represented Robespierre's attempt to resolve the central conundrum in his understanding of the Revolution. On the one hand, his conviction was unshakeable that the people's impulses were good, and the Republic would be based on civic virtue; on the other hand, he had realized that the masses were vulnerable to seduction by the malevolent, and evidence of corruption and self-seeking was everywhere. The cult was to be Robespierre's way of finally achieving the regeneration he had craved since 1789 and which the corrupters of the public spirit—whether royalists, backsliders or the factions—had contrived to thwart. Instead of the cruel God of the Catholic religion, this would be a people's cult with its own martyrs and values that reflected the birth of a new era, the era of equality.

In preparation for the great 'Festival of the Supreme Being' on 20 Prairial (8 June 1794), teachers from the Institut National de Musique spread out across Paris to teach citizens lines from François-Joseph Gossec's 'Hymne à l'Être Suprême'.[31] The festival was a brilliant display choreographed by Jacques-Louis David. Robespierre, at that time the elected president of the Convention, led the procession in his favourite light-blue coat and holding a posy of blue flowers. The crowds were massive. For the seventeen-year-old seamstress Marie Monnard, no enthusiast for the Revolution and who went there with her mother and sisters, 'nothing could be compared to the beauty of this festival'.[32] It was a vast and apparently popular gathering, but the evident lack of spontaneous celebration confirmed Saint-Just's fear that 'the Revolution has frozen over'.

The Cult of the Supreme Being had profound resonances outside Paris, too, and the Convention was flooded with letters and messages of congratulation from provincial Jacobin clubs (Fig. 26). Auguste Couet, the parish priest of the tiny village of Orville, north of Orléans, was one of many who were enthusiastic about the cult. He was also a passionate supporter of the Revolution, delivering sermons on the virtues and writing letters to the

Feuille Villageoise. The Festival enabled him to give full voice to his passion, describing in intricate detail how the celebrations would proceed in the district capital of Montargis, including 'groups of women carrying bouquets of roses, groups of girls dressed in white with tricolour ribbons, carrying baskets of flowers, groups of fathers leading their sons, all of them holding branches of oak so as to form a circle around the authorities'. Banners would be carried, one promising that 'The words poor and indigent will be effaced forever from the annals of the Republic'. Among the many verses sung would be:

> Montargis! We see that glory is still in the countryside,
> This field of honour on which the English were vanquished.
> From the Jacobins and the Mountain
> We have the Temple of Virtue . . .
> Adore the eternal being, imitate his clemency
> Be sensitive, human, supporting the indigent,
> Magnanimous French, that is the sole trait
> Of children of Liberty.[33]

In Robespierre's great speech of 5 February 1794 he had defined the imperative of revolutionary government as 'to lead the people by reason and the people's enemies by terror':

> If the mainspring of popular government in peacetime is virtue, amid revolution it is at once *virtue* and *terror:* virtue, without which terror is fatal; terror, without which virtue is impotent. Terror is nothing but prompt, severe, inflexible justice . . .[34]

In the first fortnight of June he and his allies made a dramatic bid to bring to a pinnacle both public instruction in virtue and the use of terror against its enemies. In policies outlining the content and purpose of public festivals, culminating in the Festival of the Supreme Being, Robespierre had set out the meaning of 'virtue' and how to inculcate it in the people (Fig. 27). At the same time he and his allies sought to complete the necessary work of eradicating the enemies of the public good.

The Jacobin government had eliminated its most obvious challengers to right and left in Paris, but when would it be safe to wind down the machinery of terror against such enemies? The mounting evidence of atrocities in

Lyon, Nantes and elsewhere could not be ignored, nor could the excessive practices of special military courts in Arras, Cambrai, Rochefort and elsewhere. On 27 Germinal (16 April) it was decreed that all conspiracy cases would henceforth be tried in Paris: most of the special provincial courts were closed. A new Bureau of General Policing was established on 23 April, including Robespierre, Saint-Just and Georges Couthon.[35] The judicial terror was to be centralized and expedited. Was this a signal that the dominant Jacobins were seeking a way of concentrating control in order to end the repression, or rather to use it more effectively against hostile factions?

The Law of 22 Prairial (10 June) was the culmination of the use of 'terror' against the Republic's enemies. It dramatically expanded definitions of 'counter-revolutionary':

> Article 6. The following are deemed enemies of the people: those who ... have sought to disparage or dissolve the National Convention ... have sought to inspire discouragement ... have sought to mislead opinion ... to impair the energy and the purity of revolutionary and republican principles ...

Just as startlingly, it narrowed the range of punishments:

> Article 7. The penalty provided for all offences under the jurisdiction of the Revolutionary Tribunal is death.

The emergency measures put in place since March 1793 had been a patchwork of responses, attempts by deputies to impose control over the swirling emotions of fear and suspicion and the erratic, often arbitrary, violence that such emotions triggered. Behind the Law of 22 Prairial lay a desire to terminate counter-revolution once and for all by centralizing the dispensation of revolutionary justice in Paris and making the court's powers and decisions terrifyingly simple.[36]

On 8 June the Festival of the Supreme Being had been celebrated on the Place de la Révolution, now no longer appropriate as the site of the guillotine. The implementation of the Law of 22 Prairial two days later would create further, logistical problems. A week after the passage of the law, about sixty people alleged to be linked to an attempt to assassinate Robespierre on 24 May were executed as a group, all wearing the red shirt of parricide: had they tried to kill the 'father' of the Republic? On 9 June the guillotine was moved to the Place de la Bastille, then, such were the problems of disposing of the quantity of blood, on 13 June it was finally moved to the Barrière du Trône Renversé, now the Place de la Nation, in the distant east of the city.[37]

While the military threat remained, so could the practice of terror be justified. In the month of Prairial (20 May–18 June), 183 of the 608 decrees of the Committee of Public Safety concerned supply and transport matters signed by Robert Lindet; 114 were to do with munitions and were initiated by Prieur de la Côte-d'Or; and 130 were decrees from Lazare Carnot about the army and navy. By June 1794, however, the execution of popular revolutionaries to the right and left of the dominant Jacobins, and the escalation of the Terror at a time of military success, had alienated the hard-headed administrators like Lindet. Such was his stature that, when he turned down a request to add his name to the charges against Desmoulins and Danton in April by allegedly quipping that 'I am here to protect citizens, and not to murder patriots', he was regarded as untouchable.[38] Those preoccupied with the war effort found the talk of regeneration and virtue tiresome: at a stormy joint meeting of the Committee of Public Safety and the Committee of General Security on 11 Messidor (29 June) Carnot was alleged to have shouted at Saint-Just that he and Robespierre were 'ridiculous dictators'.[39]

The geographic incidence of executions during the Terror had been concentrated in departments where the military threat had been greatest, but now, as the threat receded, the number of executions for political opposition increased dramatically. The ultimate punishment seemed to be used for new purposes: from March 1793 to 10 June 1794, 1,251 people were executed in Paris; following the law of 22 Prairial, 1,376 were guillotined in just six weeks. Ten times as many people were going to the guillotine each day. Those imprisoned as suspects ranged from a hero of 1789 and 1792, the brewer Santerre, to the composer of the 'Marseillaise', Rouget de l'Isle, and France's greatest poet, André Chénier. The most patriotic of sans-culottes were bewildered: for Jacques-Louis Ménétra, an active member of a Parisian neighbourhood section, these months conjured up images of cannibalism, murder, barbarism and unnecessary death—at least in hindsight.[40]

Ultimately, military success released the spring of the tension that held together the twin imperative of 'virtue and terror'. The revolutionary armies finally expelled Spanish forces across the Pyrenees and won a string of crucial victories in the north, especially at Tourcoing (18 May) and Tournai (22 May), even though they had no particular advantage in terms of numbers.

On 8 June the armies of the Moselle and Ardennes came together under General Jourdan as the army of the Sambre-et-Meuse. Four times it failed to take Charleroi. Then, on 25 June, the 75,000 French troops again crossed the river, confronting 52,000 Austrians under Prince Frederick of Saxe-Coburg. Information gathered from a hot-air balloon, the *Entreprenant*, provided precious statistics about enemy movements. So intense was the artillery barrage that fighting occurred in the smoke of wheatfields on fire. Finally, victory was secured near the Belgian village of Fleurus on 26 June, with Saxe-Coburg ordering a retreat. Among the French troops were members of the Arnould family, Joseph, François and their cousin Léger. The Arnoulds were the sons of the innkeepers in Le Ménil-Mitry, a tiny village near the Moselle river. They had volunteered at different times since 1791, and years of fighting had taken them as far as Brussels, Dusseldorf and Kaiserslautern. Somehow they had survived.[41]

The triumph at Fleurus—finally ending the threat of Austrian troops on French soil—exposed the tensions in the popular alliance of the Year II. But the coincidence of successive assassination attempts on Robespierre and his anxieties prevented him and his closest associates from being able to see the victory as the signal that explicit undertakings could be given to indicate the crisis was almost over. The achievements of the Convention and its committees were astounding: civil wars fought by Vendéans and federalists had been defeated while the Republic simultaneously had waged successful campaigns to expel a European military coalition. But the failure of those in government to indicate when a Republic safe for virtuous citizens could be achieved by encouragement rather than intimidation was to prove fatal. Instead of a pathway back to peacetime, constitutional government, the deputies of the Convention were presented with a daily roll call of plots and executions.

In the spring and summer of 1794 many of the Paris sections organized impromptu public 'banquets', where locals brought what they could to tables in the street. There, according to one newspaper, 'all distinctions disappear entirely; there, the rich mix with the poor and, as they eat a simple meal, they learn the lessons of equality'. To others, this was obligatory, uncomfortable 'fraternization', while to the committees the gatherings suggested a resurgence of local militancy under the pretext of celebrating military victory.[42] Therefore the fraternal banquets celebrating Fleurus were banned as likely to expose the Convention once again to popular pressure. Paris had been disproportionately generous in its sacrifices for the war effort, but ever since the purge of the Girondins those in power were determined that never again would elected representatives be intimidated by menacing crowds of *sans-culottes*.

Others urged in public that it was finally safe to return to peacetime, constitutional government, that the tight screws of virtue and terror could be loosened. One of them was the young Parisian lawyer Jean-Baptiste Billecocq, an enthusiast for the Revolution, but who had preferred the constitutional monarchy and made the mistake in 1794 of signing a petition for the implementation of the 1793 Constitution. He was arrested on 1 July and held as a suspect. For a man of means like him, prison was a bizarre nightmare, with the guillotine hanging over him as he ate well with friends from food brought by his family, read and played cards, sang and played musical instruments.[43]

But how could the controls be relaxed when deadly factionalism was evident at the highest levels of government? The duplicity of Mirabeau and the perjury of the king in 1791 had long convinced Jacobins of the need for civic integrity, of proof of the 'authenticity' of their fellows' claim to be real patriots.[44] From the spring of 1793 fear of death at the hands of counter-revolutionaries or foreign invaders made sincerity an imperative, a matter of life or death. David's portraits of Lepeletier and Marat hanging behind the speaker's podium in the Convention were a constant reminder to deputies that their lives were at stake.

The twin imperatives for deputies were emotional honesty and political transparency. These were seen as two sides of the same coin, but came from different intellectual threads: the natural virtues of sentiments expressed as sincerity, loyalty and sympathy, and the political virtues of transparency, sacrifice and modesty associated with classical republicanism. But the two threads could form a tight web from which protestations of patriotism were not grounds for escape. Public and private virtue was the antidote to insincerity and duplicity, but how could it be demonstrated in the face of denunciation?

Carnot, Lindet and Prieur—those responsible on the Committee of Public Safety for the war, supplies and subsistence, and munitions—found themselves in a minority of 'experts' exhausting themselves by overwhelming workloads and impatient with the factional fighting that was preoccupying others.[45] It may also be that, as evidence mounted of victories in the north-east, these military men on the Committee became focused on the possibility of extending the Republic to its 'natural' frontier of the

Rhine. But all the members of the committees and their bureaucracies were exhausted, and the Committee of Public Safety in particular was fractured by recrimination. And, as already noted, after the Festival of the Supreme Being and the passage of the Law of 22 Prairial, Robespierre had succumbed to nervous and physical exhaustion and was rarely present at the Committee and less voluble at the Jacobin Club.

In the swirl of news of military victories and rumours of conspiracies at the heart of power, government somehow went on. The Convention also sought to resolve the ongoing problem of foreign refugees: there were many thousands of Belgian and Liégois refugees after the Austrian occupation of 1793, and hundreds of Germans from the Rhineland. Many were offered employment in the French administration, and the Convention supplied emergency aid, but their situation was made precarious after the law of 26–27 Germinal (15–16 April), which ordered the expulsion of foreigners from Paris, major ports and frontier towns. On 8 Thermidor (26 July), nevertheless, the Convention decided to allocate a specific sum for every foreign man, woman and child refugee.[46]

Those in the Convention on 8 Thermidor were anticipating a far more momentous discussion. As Robespierre had slowly recovered his strength during July 1794, he began to prepare a breakthrough speech to be delivered to the Convention. At last it seemed that the terrifying uncertainty about the winding down of emergency controls would be resolved. He began by referring to his exhaustion and absence: 'for the last six weeks, at least, my so-called dictatorship has ceased to exist, and I have exercised no sort of influence on the government. ... Has the country been any happier?' He decided to erase a confession of despair from this speech: 'but for my conscience, I should be the unhappiest man alive'.[47]

Drawing again on Cicero, he insisted that 'our enemies retreat, but only to leave us to our internal divisions'. He claimed repeatedly that 'there is a criminal conspiracy', yet named only three deputies apart from vague assertions that conspiracy reached into the Convention and even the governing committees. Again and again he denied that he was responsible for throwing innocents into prison or sending them to the guillotine, while noting that his enemies' rallying cry was 'it's all Robespierre's doing!' The rambling, emotional speech of almost two hours was vague to the point of incoherence, because by then almost everyone was suspected of conspiring: Robespierre even confessed to 'doubting this virtuous republic whose image I had traced for myself'; he seemed to be courting martyrdom.

One of those he had named was Pierre-Joseph Cambon, and Robespierre had made a tactical error by impugning a man of high standing. The son of a wealthy cotton merchant from Montpellier, Cambon was admired for his initiative in 1792 in combining all state debts, including those from before 1789, in a 'Great ledger of the public debt', and in seeking to impose financial regularity during the chaos of war. He had already earned Robespierre's suspicion for proposing the separation of Church and State; now his public targeting signalled to many in the Convention that Robespierre's addled mind threatened everybody.

Robespierre's vague threat to unnamed deputies provided the motivation for reaction. Among those who plotted his overthrow were Fouché, Collot d'Herbois, Fréron and Barras, fearful that Robespierre intended to call them to account for their bloody repression of federalism in Lyon, Toulon and Marseille. While Robespierre that evening, 26 July, received rapturous support from those at the Jacobin Club delighted to have their most admired 'Incorruptible' back among them, those with most to fear organized against him. In particular, those most involved in the vicious bloodletting of June–July, such as Billaud-Varenne and Collot from the Committee of Public Safety, and Vadier and Amar from the Committee of General Security, had Robespierre in their sights. As the Jacobin deputy Marc-Antoine Baudot later reflected, 'the struggle of 9 Thermidor wasn't a question of principles, but of killing ... the death of Robespierre had become a necessity'.[48] On 9 Thermidor (27 July), Collot was president of the Convention and refused Robespierre the floor until it was too late (Fig. 28). When he rose to speak he was howled down. The Jacobin regime had collapsed.

While Robespierre and his allies were placed under arrest, prison authorities refused to incarcerate them, and they then took shelter in the Town Hall. But they could not look for support to the *sans-culottes'* movement, shattered by the death of its leaders and the alienation of wage-earners. Only seventeen of the forty-eight sections responded to calls to save Robespierre, but they soon dispersed. Robespierre was shot in the jaw, either by a police official or in an attempt to commit suicide. He went to the guillotine in agony on 10 Thermidor (28 July) with twenty-one of his closest associates. A police agent reported that, as Robespierre's head fell, a group of brush-makers shouted 'there goes the maximum into the basket', and the next day struck for a one-third increase in wages.[49] Seventy-one 'co-conspirators' from the Paris Commune were executed on 11 Thermidor; others followed over the next few months.

Provincial Jacobin clubs were often disconcerted by the news that Robespierre and the governing Jacobins had been 'conspirators' rather than the guiding 'patriots'. For example, despite the hostility to the Republic in Brittany, the small towns of the regions had their isolated knots of republicans. In the little port of Auray, for instance, a Jacobin club with 70–100 members had survived through the Terror, ending meetings with 'Vive la République! Vive la Montagne! Vive les sans-culottes!' They insisted initially that the overthrow of Robespierre was the work of 'infamous traitors' and a 'horde of scoundrels'.[50] In general, however, the execution of Robespierre and his closest supporters was welcomed at the time as symbolizing the end of large-scale executions. People rushed to repudiate what they now called 'Robespierre's Terror', and for all sorts of reasons.[51]

The overthrow of Robespierre and his associates was far more than the ousting of a governing coterie that had outlived its purpose. It was also the end of a regime that had cherished the twin aims of saving the Revolution and creating a new society. It had achieved the former, at great cost, but the vision of the virtuous, self-abnegating civic warrior embodying the new society had palled. For those mindful of the magnitude of the counter-revolution, it was a triumphant emergency regime, even though too many excesses had been committed. Others were horrified by what they saw as the unnecessary violence used against the Revolution's opponents, particularly as the military crisis receded.

The men in the Convention who rejoiced at Robespierre's downfall were his old enemies who had been intimidated into silence, joined by those of his erstwhile supporters who rushed to absolve their acquiescence in the Terror by emptying their consciences into his grave. The 'Reign of Terror' was labelled and excoriated, and Robespierre became its convenient scapegoat. Deputies who had kept their heads down through fear or cowardice now rushed to inform their constituents of the events and their meaning. Julien Mazade, a Girondin deputy from the south-west who had written letters home glowing with praise for Robespierre, now felt able to express other opinions: 'the tyrant is no more. He was on the point of slaughtering the Convention, our lives hung by a thread. ... Never attach yourselves to any individual. Idolize only the principles of the homeland.' Robespierre was also spurned by his oldest and closest friends: Charlotte Buissart wrote home to her husband Antoine in Arras that 'I cannot describe my surprise when I found out all the horrors that this Maximilien had ordered'; similarly, Rosalie Jullien now claimed that the 'infamous' Robespierre had 'duped' republicans (Fig. 29).[52]

One of the observers of the scapegoating was Captain Watkin Tench, recently returned to England after taking one of the first vessels of British convicts to Australia. Then in November 1794 he was captured off Quimper in Brittany and held in the prison ship the *Marat*. Tench, an intelligent and keen observer, was curious to note that those who had 'prostrated themselves like reptiles' before Robespierre now blamed him for 'all the assassinations and misery': 'it is impossible to pronounce the word *guillotine*, without associating with it its grand mover Robespierre'. Tench, a man who, like Robespierre, had had a classical education, described him as 'that modern Procrustes', drawing on the story of the blacksmith from Attica who stretched or shortened people to force them to fit his iron bed. But Tench was also scathing about Robespierre's erstwhile allies: 'to screen themselves from odium, all the subordinate tyrants fix upon him, and attribute to his orders, the innumerable butcheries and acts of oppression which they have perpetrated'.[53]

While there was a positive popular memory of Robespierre that would survive Thermidor, this was swamped by a wave of vitriol, much of it motivated by the same scapegoating that repelled Tench. It suited all sides to identify Robespierre personally with the atrocities that had been committed; even for most Jacobins this became the easiest way to explain away the excesses that others had committed. A preposterous 'légende noire' about Robespierre was rapidly created and still remains the dominant image of the young republican today.[54]

The overthrow of the Robespierrists did not end the civil war, but certainly attenuated it. The Committee of Public Safety, supported by the Convention and the network of administrations and Jacobin clubs across the country, had saved the Revolution by repelling foreign invasion and repressing counter-revolution. The cost in human life was massive. In the Year II there had been perhaps 170,000 deaths of Vendéans and 70,000 of soldiers in the armies fighting them and the invading armies. But many thousands of others had also been executed in the repression of federalism (about 1,800 executed in Lyon, 800 in Toulon, hundreds in Marseille and Bordeaux). To these must be added the deaths of several thousand counter-revolutionaries during risings in Brittany, the Massif Central and Provence, for example the Provençal town of Bédoin.[55] Probably as many as 40,000 people had been executed after trial: 85 per cent were from the old Third Estate, particularly peasants and urban workers. Those executed were overwhelmingly accused of armed rebellion in the counter-revolution or of federalism, but one in eleven were effectively political executions of those accused with more or less proof of counter-revolutionary activities at a time of war. The Convention itself was not spared. In the sixteen months between March 1793 and July 1794 the Convention purged 144 of its 749 members; sixty-seven were executed, committed suicide or died in prison.[56]

The pattern of repression mirrored the map of internal counter-revolution and foreign invasion. The executions were concentrated in eighteen departments, in each of which there were more than one hundred executions after trials, mostly along the borders and in the west, and in Paris and Lyon. But across almost half the country the deadly menace of repression was limited. This was not only the result of distance from the killing-fields along the frontiers, where personal choice was often fatal; in many departments the local administrators and the deputy-on-mission were judicious and relatively tolerant. But others were utterly uncompromising, at times to the point where opposition to the Revolution was defined as vaguely as its punishment was lethal.

Was it counter-revolution that had made the Revolution violent or was the revolutionary violence of 1793–94 the result of intolerance and obsession with counter-revolutionary conspiracy? It is true that there were elements in revolutionary—as in counter-revolutionary—rhetoric of violent verbal imagery that vilified opponents as conspirators, traitors and enemies to be killed. Such imagery drew on a political culture rich in lessons from classical antiquity, the *ancien régime* court culture of cabals and the Enlightenment vision of virtuous sentiments. But the Terror was not simply the result of paranoid obsession about an 'other' to be exterminated. The repression of counter-revolution was a response to the actual, linked threats of external invasion and violent internal opposition. It was the counter-revolution and the mixed emotions of panic, outrage, pride and fear that it aroused that fostered a willingness to believe that enemies were omnipresent. Then the outbreak of war transformed political divisions into matters of life and death.

The year of 'terror until peace' is best explained by an explosive combination of circumstances and convictions: the profound belief that the virtues inherent in the Revolution were self-evident and to be defended at all costs; the actuality of internal counter-revolution and external invasion, especially after the schism in the Church and the declaration of war; and the difficulty of creating a legitimate central authority that both militant *sans-culottes* and fractured political groupings would accept. All of these created intense emotions of fear and suspicion, which led to the majority in the Convention supporting the suspension of peacetime civil liberties and constitutional government, and to the centralization of authority.[57] The government would be 'revolutionary until the peace'—but who could say when peace had been achieved? Ultimately the Convention did so in Thermidor, but by then the web of suspicion and punishment had been so tightly drawn that few of those in power were content simply to enjoy a return to peacetime government. Scores had to be settled.

CHAPTER FOURTEEN

SETTLING SCORES
THE THERMIDORIAN REACTION, 1794–95

THE THERMIDORIANS WERE HARDENED MEN WHO HAD LIVED through fifteen months of fearful apprehension, and they were determined that their experience would not be repeated.[1] These men, the new majority in the Convention, were former Girondins, the 'Plain', and the anti-Robespierrist Jacobins. Their 'Thermidorian regime' in place from July 1794 was certainly republican, but driven above all else by the need to end the Revolution, most obviously by suppressing the sources of instability represented by the Jacobins and *sans-culottes*. In seeking to end revolutionary upheaval, they unleashed ferocious reaction against those blamed for the perceived excesses of what was now called 'the Terror', and a counter-reaction from those seeking to protect what had been won by sacrifice and virtue in 1793–94. It was a time of retribution, despair and some optimism for a settled future (Fig. 30).

One of the first new members of the Committee of Public Safety was Jean-Lambert Tallien, among those most active in the overthrow of the Robespierrists, and under suspicion for having been too influenced in Bordeaux by his lover, the former noblewoman Thérésia Cabarrus. Tallien, when just twenty-six years old, had instigated with Claude-Alexandre Ysabeau a bloodily punitive repression of federalism in Bordeaux in August 1793, but now he appealed to the Convention one year later to dismantle all the evils of the Terror: 'this was Robespierre's system; he was the one who put it into practice with the help of a few subordinates. . . . The Convention was a victim of it, never an accomplice.' Those who suggested that the Convention should take some responsibility were in fact guilty of sharing in the 'monster' Robespierre's 'infernal system'.[2] Tallien arranged for the release of Cabarrus from prison; they married in December 1794 and Thérésia gave birth to a daughter, named Thermidor. Indeed, Thérésia herself was often called 'Notre Dame de Thermidor'. Those closest to Robespierre, such as Rosalie Jullien, whose young son Jules had confronted Tallien in Bordeaux when an agent for the Committee of Public Safety, now had to appeal obsequiously to Cabarrus as a mother and a woman linked by 'the natural sensitivity of our sex' to secure Jules' release from prison.[3]

Robespierre had almost immediately become the personification of the Terror across France and the subject of preposterous claims and rumours. The seamstress Jeanne-Victoire Delzigue of Orléans wrote solemnly in her diary on 2 August 1794:

> the good fortune for those who had been imprisoned as suspects was that as soon as Robespierre was dead all the prisons of France were opened. . . . Robespierre had said before his death that my head is going to be cut off but they won't cut off my *queue* (penis), which is much worse . . .[4]

Delzigue was certainly correct that the overthrow of the Robespierrists would be the signal for the release of most of the suspects in the prisons of Paris. On 14 Thermidor (1 August) the Law of 22 Prairial was repealed, and the scope of the Revolutionary Tribunal was narrowed to consider only those who had actually taken up arms against the Republic. There were few executions after August: only forty in Paris in the last five months of 1794. The Tribunal was finally abolished in May 1795, after the execution of Antoine-Quentin Fouquier-Tinville, public prosecutor in the Year II, and Martial Herman, an old lawyer friend of Robespierre from Arras who had been president of the Revolutionary Tribunal during the trials of Marie-Antoinette, the Girondins, Hébertistes and Dantonistes.

But the release of suspects was a haphazard process, contingent on them and their families using networks of influence to bring their cases to the notice of authorities. One of the fortunate ones was Marie-Rose de Beauharnais, released from Les Carmes prison in Paris on 19 Thermidor (6 August), again on the intervention of Tallien. Her husband Alexandre was not so fortunate: an army officer, he had been tried on a charge of conspiring with the enemy during the defeat at Mainz in July 1793, and was executed on 5 Thermidor, five days before Robespierre. Marie-Rose, the daughter of the owner of a sugar plantation on the Caribbean island of

Martinique, had been in favour of the Revolution, and seems to have been comfortable with being addressed as 'tu' and 'citoyenne'; nevertheless, her name had made her suspect in the murderous spring of 1794. Like Thérésia Cabarrus, she would now flourish in the new world of post-Thermidorian Paris.[5]

Among others released quickly was the writer François de Neufchâteau: well known for his anti-Jacobinism, he had been arrested on 2 September 1793 for his play *Pamela, or Virtue Rewarded*, based on the novel by Samuel Richardson. On 14 Fructidor (31 August) it was the turn of Sophie de Bohm, the daughter of Rousseau's patron the Marquis de Girardin. After having seen to the release of her parents, she fled to an isolated farmhouse where slowly 'I recovered my health, I regained the strength and courage to complete the drama of my life, as God wishes'.[6] Her father, too, found gardening finally a more peaceful and predictable pastime than politics.

Among the 'suspects' released after Thermidor were many *sans-culottes*, including François-Noël Babeuf, imprisoned early in 1793 for falsifying property registers in order to distribute nationalized church land to the poor. While in prison he had dropped his earlier adopted name 'Camille' for 'Gracchus', a second-century-BC Roman land reformer, and had developed a critique of private property as inimical to the achievement of genuine equality. Gracchus Babeuf was one of a number of militants who imagined that the end of 'the Terror' would allow the implementation of the Constitution of 1793 and a return to popular initiative which might enable him to realize his programme. There were other militant *sans-culotte* critics of Jacobin dominance in the Year II who were now released. Pauline Léon, one of the leaders of the Revolutionary Republican Citizenesses, had been arrested with her Enragé husband Théophile Leclerc on 3 April 1794; they were released on 22 August. It was probably while awaiting release that she described how, from 1789, 'I experienced the greatest enthusiasm and although a woman I did not remain idle; you could see me from morning to evening animating citizens against the tyrants ... barricading streets and encouraging cowards to leave their houses'. But she and Leclerc now quietly exited political life.[7] Her colleague Claire Lacombe had to wait another year for her release, in August 1795.

Some of those who now shifted blame onto Robespierre for the Terror's excesses had in fact been instrumental in them. Some were remarkably successful in distancing themselves from their roles in repressing counter-revolution and federalism, in particular Tallien, Fouché, Fréron, Barras, and even the destroyer of Bédoin in Provence, Étienne Maignet, who went into hiding. But others were so vulnerable to charges of atrocity that their pasts finally caught up with them. In September a group of alleged federalists from Nantes brought before the Revolutionary Tribunal were acquitted, and during the trial the details emerged of the horrors overseen by Jean-Baptiste Carrier in the town during the winter of 1793–94. By November the Convention had resolved to remove his parliamentary immunity; he was executed on 16 December.

At the local level, authority was again in the steady hands of the better-off farmers and professional men, for whom the end of the controls and threats of the Year II represented a return to stability. Scapegoating Robespierre served to expiate discomfort about excesses in the emergency measures that had won the war in 1794. Trees of liberty planted during the Year II were ripped out or felled. In January 1795 the surveillance committee of Lagrasse, south of Carcassonne, even though the centre of a district where there had been no executions and few 'suspects', celebrated the end of the Terror in an address to the Convention:

> The Revolution of 9 Thermidor ... has seen the rebirth of calm and serenity in the hearts of the French, who, released from the errors into which terrorism had led them, and having broken the iron sceptre under which the scoundrel Robespierre held them subject, are enjoying the fruits of your sublime works, marching with joy along the paths of virtue.... Formerly the men of blood slaughtered innocent victims selected by envy, and destiny led to the scaffold how many hardworking and suffering citizens, confounded with the guilty.... France is free, happy and triumphant.[8]

Coinciding with a return to constitutional government and the release of suspects, the Convention and its agents across the country launched a sweeping purge of those tainted by association with the regime of the Year II. Within a month of Robespierre's fall about two hundred provincial Jacobin clubs had complained angrily to their Parisian 'mother club' about the unexpected repercussions. All over the country the year after 9 Thermidor was a time of settling of scores, if not by killing, then by denunciation.

Those who had been the local face of the Year II were either purged from office or had to manoeuvre skilfully to preserve their freedom. The 'popular society' of Bergerac in Dordogne, for example, had shown a remarkable capacity to align its public views with the direction of the Revolution, welcoming the arrest of Louis XVI at Varennes in 1791, then his overthrow in 1792, and quickly detaching itself from federalism in June 1793. Now its smaller, more affluent membership welcomed the crackdown on 'the drinkers of blood' and 'the partisans of anarchy' who wanted to 'resuscitate the reign of Terror'.[9] One who narrowly escaped the purges was the most influential Jacobin militant and administrator in the department of Aisne, Polycarpe Pottofeux. After Thermidor his enemies rounded on 'this Robespierre of Aisne, this petty subaltern tyrant who practised perfectly, in our department, the views and maxims of his master'. Pottofeux would be pursued relentlessly after July 1794, and occasionally detained, but such was the integrity of his long administration that not even the vengeful courts of the Thermidorian reaction would convict him. By 1796 he had had enough and would throw himself into the sugar-beet industry, which would revolutionize Picardy in a different way.[10]

The politics of revenge suffused the dismantling of the network of section assemblies and popular societies that had been the foundation of Jacobin rule. On 22 Brumaire Year III (12 November 1794) the Convention announced the closure of the Jacobin Club itself, the backbone of political life throughout the Revolution. Six months later, on 28 Floréal (17 May 1795), the Convention decreed that the club's premises, just across the rue Honoré from the Manège, where the Convention had met until 9 May 1793, would be demolished to make way for a new market to be called '9 Thermidor'.

The wars were not over, and so surveillance committees continued their work, but after the reform of 7 Fructidor Year II (24 August 1794) as 'comités révolutionnaires' in district capitals and other major towns rather than in villages. Just as the political choices made by people reflected their family background and the social relationships in their village or neighbourhood, so the decision to denounce 'suspects' to the local committee reflected enmities that might be of long-standing. In the south in particular the contest for power had often been so visceral that even families could be permanently divided. So, on 16 Fructidor (2 September 1794), Marguerite Chaix denounced her uncle and his son to the committee in Aix-en-Provence because they had earlier denounced her husband, who had been guillotined by the federalists.[11]

The well-to-do could again breathe easily, as wealth of itself was no longer 'suspicious'. They self-consciously began to use 'Monsieur' and 'Madame' instead of 'Citizen', and 'vous' rather than 'tu'. Their sons and daughters expressed sartorial contempt for the 'honorable mediocrity' favoured by Jacobins by instead parading as dandies (*muscadins* and *merveilleuses*). Aggressive young Parisians dubbed 'gilded youth' (*jeunesse dorée*) patrolled the streets spoiling for the chance to take physical revenge on *sans-culottes*. Stanislas Fréron, putting aside his bloody repression of Toulon in 1793, now used his newspaper, the *Orateur du peuple*, to incite revenge on 'terroristes'. Some *jeunesse dorée* complied, at one point burning a Jacobin in effigy, then going to the Jacobin Club to place the ashes in a chamber pot, in which they were carried to the Montmartre sewer with an inscription referring to the 'September massacres':

> To get rich on 2 September
> I took the name of Jacobin
> My urn was a chamber pot
> And this sewer my Panthéon.[12]

Among the *jeunesse dorée* was the young Louis-Mathieu Molé, from an ancient and eminent noble family, who was taken into exile in 1791. His father subsequently decided to return to Paris to protect the family's property—a fatal decision, which cost him his life during the Terror. In later life Louis-Mathieu would recall how, from the age of fourteen, he went to the Café des Chartres at the Palais-Royal with a knotty stick and pistols in each pocket to listen with other *jeunesse dorée* to table-top orations preaching revenge:

> Families reunited, fortunes were remade . . . great freedom was the rule in ideas, speech and writing. . . . The misfortunes of the Revolution and those of emigration had given us the habit and taste for extreme independence. We did whatever we liked. We spent our money for our own pleasure. It was a question of how to forget our suffering most quickly.[13]

The 'Thermidorian reaction', as it came to be called, was expressed through forms of popular culture as well as politics. The gilded youth's favourite song was 'Le Réveil du Peuple' ('The Reawakening of the People'), with the vengeful words by Pierre Gaveau first sung by him at the Guillaume-Tell section meeting on 30 Nivôse Year III (19 January 1795):

> You suffer while a hideous horde
> Of assassins and brigands

Fouls with its ferocious breath
The land of the living.
All these drinkers of human blood!
War on all the agents of crime!
Pursue them to the death!
Share the horror which drives me!
They won't escape us![14]

The song was popular among resurgent royalists elsewhere. In mid-1795, for example, young people crowded the Grand Théâtre in Bordeaux to hoot and catcall the anti-clerical play *Jean Calas*, demanding that the actors sing instead 'Le Réveil du Peuple'.[15] By May 1796 the town council of Bourg on the other side of the country had despaired of the young men who had failed to register for military service, who delighted in the 'murderous words' of 'Le Réveil du Peuple' while whistling and catcalling when the 'Marseillaise' was sung, and who, they believed, had felled the liberty tree.[16] Such was the song's popularity that it was banned after the government became concerned that its bloody call for revenge would act as a stimulus for a royalist revival.

When the portraitist of the royal family Adélaïde Labille-Guiard returned to Paris from the country home she had bought twelve miles east of the capital in 1792 to escape the turmoil, most of the fourteen revolutionary leaders she had painted in 1791 were dead—among them Robespierre and Barnave. The Revolution's opening up of the art world had endured, however: in 1795 there were hundreds of exhibitors and 534 paintings at the Paris Salon (Fig. 31).[17] The new regime's attempt to define its nature—both republican and anti-Jacobin—was bound to create a space for division to be expressed in the creative arts. The Institut National de Musique gave a concert on the second anniversary of the execution of Louis XVI on 21 January 1795, during which a Jacobin deputy interrupted to ask whether the soft melody suggested that the death was to be regretted. The conductor François-Joseph Gossec replied that it was to express 'the gentle emotions stirred in sensitive souls by the happiness of being delivered from a tyrant', but the orchestra nevertheless felt it politic to launch into the 'Ça ira!'[18]

The reaction was also played out in the theatres. After 113 years of existence, the Comédie-Française had been closed in September 1793 for playing a 'moderate' piece, the *Ami des Lois* by Jean-Louis Laya. After Thermidor the release of its actors deemed 'suspects' accentuated the desire to perform anti-Jacobin plays and to target those who had continued to act during the Terror. One of those was François-Joseph Talma, the most famous actor of the day and a friend of Danton and Desmoulins. Now targeted as a Jacobin, Talma was forced to stop a performance to announce that 'The Reign of Terror cost me many tears, all my friends died on the scaffold.' Crowds of young people came to the Variétés Montansier in Ventôse Year III to applaud the lines in a play 'tyrant, thief, assassin, that can be stated in a single word, and that word is Jacobin!'[19]

The cultural reaction was not only a popular expression of opposition to the constraints of the Year II: it was also official policy. The cultural revolution of the Year II was over. The Abbé Grégoire delivered a report to the Convention on 17 Vendémiaire Year II (5 October 1794), which advocated a deliberate policy of inculcating the right cultural and political values, a sort of 'cultural Thermidor'. Authors had been freed from the controls of the privileged guild of Parisian publishers in 1789, and enjoyed years of unprecedented liberty of expression until the sharp political curbs after 1792. In 1795 authors were again to deal with publishers as free contracting agents. The number of new novels doubled—largely sentimental tales and mysteries. Now, however, the regime was to offer subsidies to its literary supporters.[20]

The Thermidorians also sought to embed their own version of the republican virtues through commemoration. The 'Marseillaise' became the official national anthem on 14 July 1795.[21] Rousseau's name, first seen as too closely associated with the democratic extremism of Robespierre and Saint-Just, was now rehabilitated by the Thermidorians into that of the prophet of the natural virtues. His body was moved from the Île des Peupliers at Ermenonville to the Panthéon on 18 Vendémiaire Year II (15 October 1794), via the little town of Émile (formerly Montmorency). It was here in 1761 and 1762 that the great man had composed his finest works—*Émile*, *The Social Contract* and *La Nouvelle Héloïse*. Music for the occasion was composed by Marie-Joseph Chénier, brother of the poet André guillotined on 25 July 1794.[22]

The cultural reaction was evident in personal behaviour, too. Whereas Montagnards had worn their hair long, straight and often left quite oily, the fashion for middle-class Parisian men now became 'à la Titus', short, washed and lightly curled.[23] The practice of giving revolutionary names to children ceased abruptly, and parents reverted judiciously to using neutral names for their infants. During the Year II almost 11 per cent of babies in the Breton port of Brest had been given 'patriotic' names—most commonly

Brutus, Unité and Marat, but also Abricotine, Égalité and Olympiade. Now first names were more traditional or expressed a longing for a happy future, as in the choice made on 22 Frimaire Year III (12 December 1794) by the parents of Constance Amitié Confiance Amour Bedon.[24]

The Jacobin regime of the Year II had continued state subsidies to 'patriotic' and often beleaguered ministers of religion. The Thermidorians were less tolerant. At the end of the Year II (18 September 1794) the Convention had ended all subsidies to religion; then the law of 3 Ventôse Year III (21 February 1795) restricted the use of bells to national festivals and the *décadi*. Communities resisted, protested or resorted to improvisation. In the village of Castries, north-east of Montpellier, a child was sent through the streets blowing a horn before church services; elsewhere, children were sent down the streets with small hand-held bells. At times the issue provoked open friction. In Caraman, east of Toulouse, in October 1795 parishioners broke down doors, cut the chains and commenced ringing the bells; when the municipal officers appeared in their sashes of office, they were intimidated into retreat. Whether or not the insistence on bell-ringing reflected religious outrage or simply community irritation at inconvenience, silence rankled with rural folk. Indeed, a senior official in Somme concluded that 'there is no disputing the fact that what hit the people hardest in the Revolution was being deprived of their bells'.[25] A petition from nine hundred 'Catholics and republicans' in the northern border district of Bousbecque demanded the reopening of their church in March 1795, with a menacing reference to the Constitution of 1793: 'We declare to you ... We will celebrate our divine mysteries in our church on 1 Germinal if our priest does not flee, and if he does flee, we will find another one. Remember that insurrection is a duty for the people when their rights are violated.'[26]

The Thermidorians also expressed their commitment to a distinctive republican conservatism in their education policy. On 27 Brumaire Year III (17 November 1794) the Convention at last implemented a decree on education, establishing boys and girls classes in a school in every commune, and basing their instruction on reading, writing and arithmetic, with as core texts the Declaration of the Rights of Man and Citizen and the Constitution. Pupils were to be taught 'the miscellany of heroic deeds and triumphal songs'. The language of instruction everywhere was to be French: 'the local idiom may be used only as an auxiliary device'. Ultimately, however, the zeal to edify the young through education had dissipated: on the eve of the dissolution of the National Convention, the more elitist

Daunou Law of 3 Brumaire Year IV (25 October 1795) decreed that teachers would be paid from pupils' fees, that girls would be taught 'useful skills' in separate schools, and that there need only be a school in each canton rather than in every commune.

The Convention was equally concerned to restore and refashion elite education. *Ancien régime* secondary schools and academies were to be replaced by specialist central schools, *conservatoires* of arts and crafts and music, and training schools for the public services—engineering, navigation, mines, roads and bridges. In 1794 these training schools became the École Centrale des Travaux Publics, then in September 1795 the École Polytechnique.[27] Mechanization and new technologies were now to be encouraged by a Conservatoire des Arts et Métiers. In October 1795 the five *ancien régime* academies, abolished in August 1793 as corporate and elitist, were re-established under one umbrella as the Institut de France, celebrating the achievements of a new elite of talent and progress.[28]

The men of the Convention prided themselves on an outlook that was enlightened, progressive and patriotic, and the war gave them impetus to innovate further in the areas of measurement and communications. On 18 Germinal Year III (7 April 1795) the Convention extended the decree of 1 August 1793 on weights and measures, using the litre, gram, metre and hectare, and introducing the decimal *franc* and *centimes* in place of the *livre*, *sous* and *deniers*. Centuries of regional variation was swept away, although it would be 1799 before accurate prototypes of the new measures were distributed throughout the country.[29]

The war also led to the adoption of a brilliant invention by Claude Chappe, son of a baron from Brûlon, near Le Mans in Normandy. Chappe had held a sinecure as the titular head of an abbey; this was abolished in 1789 and the young man (born 1763) turned his talents to his passion, invention. He devised a semaphore system of telegraph stations six to ten miles apart, close enough for telescopes to observe the long arms, and had the good fortune to have a brother, Ignace, in the Legislative Assembly to push his case. The young innovators now running the country were impressed. But it was above all the war that made the men of the Convention receptive, and on 1 April 1793 funds were secured for a first telegraph line, from the Ménilmontant hill in the north-east of Paris north to Saint-Martin-du-Tertre, near Pontoise. When Condé-sur-l'Escaut, on the border north of Valenciennes, was recaptured by the republican armies on 15 August 1794, the Convention learned of it almost immediately, thanks to the completion one month earlier of Chappe's Paris—Lille telegraph line. In return, the Convention was able to inform the citizens of Condé the very same day that their town was now to be known as Nord-Libre.[30]

The release of social restraints on displays of wealth now permitted ostentatious consumption, notably balls at which the wealthy demonstrated their antipathy to the Terror—and symbolized their recent fears—by appearing with shaved necks and thin red ribbons around their throats. Prostitutes soliciting wealthy customers reappeared at the Palais-Royal in Paris. These deliberate displays of wealth and social reaction took on a particularly aggressive edge with the abolition of the 'maximum' on prices and wages in December 1794. This unleashed rampant inflation and, by April 1795, the general level of prices was about 750 per cent above that of 1790. The position of the poor and marginal became desperate at the same time as governments turned their backs on the social promises of the Jacobins. The Church was in no position to provide charity.

The winter of 1795 would remain infamous as 'nonante cinq', the worst since 1709: the Seine froze over, the soil hardened to a depth of two feet, and packs of wolves appeared on the outskirts of Paris. There were cases of people dying of hunger in the streets, and a peak in suicides.[31] Across the country, the hunger of the winter caused an increase in the incidence of criminal bands on the highways but also in food-rioting. On 13 February 1795 hungry women confronted the deputy-on-mission Gilles Porcher in Orléans wanting to know whether they all had to die of hunger and shouting 'Vive Louis XVII! May the nation go to the devil with its republic!'[32] So meagre were food supplies in the town by May that the artisan Marianne Charpentier wrote in her diary that 'those who see these writings will shudder at the great misery their fathers and mothers suffered during this cruel revolution and seeing their poor children asking for bread without being able to give them any'.[33]

There was shocking evidence of the settling of scores through privation. Louis-Sébastien Mercier, who had made his living as a writer before 1789, notably of the utopian novel L'An 2440, had been elected to the Convention. However, having espoused Girondin sympathies, Mercier had been imprisoned during the Terror and released only in December 1794. He dubbed Robespierre a 'sanguinocrat' (a 'ruler in blood'), but was equally scathing towards the counter-revolution and all those who sought to take advantage of the inevitable disorder of revolution. He observed how, late in 1794, well-to-do farmers around Paris delighted in extorting precious objects from wealthy Parisians in return for food. 'Now you could see silk-covered furniture and mahogany tables alongside the ploughs, horses, manure-heaps and tools of the farm.' In the popular neighbourhoods of Paris, on the other hand, crowds of hollow-cheeked workers waited in the cold outside bakeries for their rations.[34] Through the bitter winter months, reports flooded in from places such as Amiens, Lille and Mâcon of bands of famished labourers moving from farm to farm looking for or extorting food. The clock-maker Mâlotain of Dieppe reported that it would take him a week to describe 'the hatred the farmers have always had for the inhabitants of the towns, but what do you expect of uncultured people, who've never known anything but their own greed, and if limits aren't placed we'll see the townspeople die of misery'. The economic reaction of the large farmers was sweetened by their revenge on supporters of the Jacobin Republic.[35]

Some Parisian working women had preserved a positive memory of Robespierre. In January 1795 police reported that the female baker Pommier had been denounced by customers for saying that 'since Robespierre, recognized by all good patriots as a good republican, had been assassinated, the counter-revolution had taken place'. In February others were reported as saying that he had been 'sacrificed as a victim who had no other intention but to bring happiness to France and to deliver it from the tyrants who govern it today'. It was 'impossible that a single man could have oppressed seven hundred' deputies.[36] Pommier was among the *sans-culottes* who made a final desperate attempt to force their views on the Convention, through insurrection on 12–13 Germinal (1–2 April) and 1–4 Prairial (20–23 May). After weeks of rumblings about food shortages and prices, demonstrators burst into the Convention on 1 April, shouting 'Bread and the Constitution of '93!' Paris was placed under military lock-down and order was restored, temporarily.

In May (Prairial) in particular women took the initiative, forcing local administrators to accompany them (and to provide legitimacy), and entering workshops to encourage or force women to march with them. As one police observer wrote, 'bread is the foundation of the insurrection physically speaking, but the Constitution [of 1793] is the soul'. The slogans and cries of the insurgents identified as enemies 'merchants and *muscadins*'.[37] The citeness Gonthier recounted how she found herself surrounded by a group of women in the Faubourg Montmartre, one saying 'come Gonthier, come if you're a good citizeness, come with us. Look at me, instead of milk my child gets nothing but blood from my breast.' A police commissioner reported that 'Hotheads poured out invective and extremely seditious statements against the constituted authorities; the women were especially impatient and seemed to be much more agitated; they stirred the men citizens up to disorder . . .'. In response the *muscadins* were shouting 'Vive la Convention! Vive la République! Down with the Jacobins and drinkers of blood!'[38]

When the neighbourhood sections of the Faubourg Saint-Antoine arrived at the Convention on 20 May, they had slogans on their hats reading 'Bread and the Constitution of 1793'. With them was a journeyman locksmith named Jean Tinelle, who had carried the head of the subsistence official Jean-Bertrand Féraud through the streets on a pike. (Féraud had had to introduce daily bread rationing, at 4 ounces per adult.)[39] Van Heck, the commander of the Cité Section, warned the Convention: 'the citizens for whom I am speaking want the Constitution of 1793; they are tired of spending nights at the bakers' doors. . . . We ask liberty for several thousands of fathers of patriot families, who have been incarcerated since 9 Thermidor.' He was supported by a handful of Jacobin deputies.[40]

On the morning of 22 May the Faubourg Saint-Antoine was surrounded by army units bolstered by National Guards from western Paris and groups of *jeunesse dorée*, but an incursion by the latter was repelled and one of the murderers of Féraud on his way to execution was seized from the police. But such were the armed forces against it that the *faubourg* surrendered the next day. The popular movement was crushed, and spirits seemed broken. Police reported that 'the men just look on, the women say nothing'. A military commission was immediately set up to try 132 prisoners; thirty-four insurgents were condemned to detention, eighteen to deportation and thirty-six to death (including six deputies).[41]

The failure of the May 1795 insurrection unleashed more wide-ranging reaction. Over 4,000 Jacobins and *sans-culottes* were subsequently arrested, and 1,700 were stripped of all civil rights. Prison camps were established in the Seychelles and Guiana, the latter dubbed 'the dry guillotine' because of the harshness of its conditions. Apart from the 'Day of the Black Collars' in July 1795, when *sans-culottes* and some soldiers used the sixth anniversary of the storming of the Bastille to take a short-lived, violent revenge on *jeunesse dorée*, the Parisian popular movement was silenced. This was a major turning point in a Revolution achieved initially by popular insurrection, and a key victory in the Thermidorians' quest for order.

In the mopping-up operation after the Prairial insurrection police compiled dossiers on some of the women most involved. One of them was Marie-Pierre Deffaut, born forty years earlier in the northern town of

Charleville. She made a living from a small-goods stall on the Quai du Louvre, near the home she shared with her husband, a skilled worker in precious metals, also arrested in 1795. They were denounced by their neighbours for their 'atrocious' opinions. Marie-Pierre wore portraits of Marat and Robespierre, and admitted she 'had wept over the fall (of Robespierre) because she believed him to be an honest man'. She abused women wearing green ribbons saying that they were 'Charlotte Corday' and hissed at houses where her denouncers lived that 'this stinks of Fréron'. During the Prairial insurrection she had shouted that they must have 'the Constitution of 1793 at once.... We must crush the moderate toads ... the guillotine will be called *muscadin* from now on ... we must have the traitors' blood'. As well as being imprisoned for six years, she was humiliated by being exposed in public for two hours on three successive days, on the Place du Palais-Égalité (formerly Palais-Royal), the Place de Grève and the Place de la Révolution.[42]

The despair felt by militant *sans-culottes* was shared by some of the Jacobins in the Convention. Philippe Rühl, a deputy for Bas-Rhin in Alsace, committed suicide in May 1795 after being placed under house arrest for his participation in the Prairial insurrection. Rühl had been a member of the Committee of General Security during the Terror and while a deputy-on-mission had demonstrated his zeal by breaking the vessel containing the sacred oil for anointment of the French kings at Reims. Rühl's suicide was a precursor to the suicides and attempted suicides on 29 Prairial Year IV (17 June 1795) of the six deputies dubbed 'martyrs of Prairial' (Romme, Goujon, Bourbotte, Duquesnoy, Duroy and Soubrany), arrested for supporting the insurrection. From his prison Jean-Marie Goujon, aged twenty-nine, wrote to his family for the last time on 14 June:

> I have lived for liberty, I've always done what I believed to be right, just and useful for my homeland. ... May the French people keep their constitution of equality that they voted for in their electoral assemblies. I swore to defend it and die for it. ... It is better that I die rather than betray the homeland. Too many good people are in tears, please don't complain if I share their lot. ... it's better to die.[43]

Another deputy caught up in the Prairial insurrection was Nicolas Maure, a devoted Robespierrist whose repeated roles as a deputy-on-mission had been characterized by a willingness to release large numbers of 'suspects' where the evidence was thin, and to allow churches to stay open. Maure had explained that 'I love the Republic because it is based on eternal justice. . . . I would risk my life to support it, but I have never used violence.' After Thermidor he was subject to wild accusations. Now, on 3 June, he scratched a brief note—'I am not a wicked man, I was just led astray'—and shot himself.[44] In the three months between April and July 1795 the Convention purged eighty of its members accused of being too closely associated with the Robespierrists. Among them, Barère, Billaud-Varenne, Collot and Vadier were sentenced to deportation to Guiana: however, only Collot, who died there in 1796, and Billaud-Varenne, who managed to survive until 1819, were finally transported to 'the dry guillotine'.[45]

The repression in Paris following the insurrection of Prairial triggered a further round of reprisals in the provinces. In the south in particular, many villages and towns had been wracked in 1790–94 by violent political division based on social friction, personal enmities and, at times, religious rivalries. Long traditions of strong local government in the big towns had made the 'federalist' option against Paris particularly attractive, especially to the commercial and professional elites who resumed power. The zeal of deputies-on-mission and local Jacobins in punishing federalists and royalists only entrenched more deeply the desire for revenge. Following the recapture of their city in the Year II, the Revolutionary Tribunal of Marseille had tried 887 people, sentencing 289 to death; a Commission Militaire then executed 123 of the 218 people it judged; and another 332 were sentenced to death by the Commission in Orange. In reprisal, in the spring of 1795 Jacobins were hunted down and killed in many communities. Where they were already in prison, the convenience was irresistible: in Marseille bands of counter-revolutionaries known as 'égorgeurs' ('cut-throats') invaded the prison at the Fort Saint-Jean on 5 June and massacred 127 Jacobins being held there; others survived by barricading themselves in their cells. On 4 May crowds also invaded the prisons of Lyon and up to 120 of the inmates were hacked to death.[46]

This 'White Terror', as it came to be called, was a punitive response of local elites to the menaces, controls and losses they had suffered during the Year II. In the small town of Aubagne, near Marseille, a murderous gang took revenge for the pro-revolutionary violence of 1792–94 by killing fourteen Jacobins in six weeks in the summer of 1795. Here, as in similar outbreaks of violence in the south-east, enmities between factions based on wealth, locality and personal networks had festered into open hatreds as control of local power and resources was contested after 1789. Whereas the savagery of the Terror had been carried out in public, as a violent expression of a will to punish opponents of the Revolution, from 1795 reprisals were undertaken at night, in secluded places, with witnesses intimidated into silence. The punishments were spectacularly brutal, the display of mutilated bodies a warning to others.[47]

Where deadly hatreds ran so deep, the earnest hopes that public life could be calmed by the pacific objectivity of due legal process were bound to fail, for the judges—let alone the juries—were politically scarred as well. Ultimately, 109 persons (including just two women) were arrested for four prison massacres carried out between May and July 1795 in Aix, Tarascon and Marseille; but by the time the trials had concluded in 1801, just six would be found guilty. In all, up to 30,000 'terroristes' may have been murdered during the 'White Terror', almost as many as were executed during the Terror itself.[48]

The atmosphere of political reaction raised royalist hopes, if not for a return of the *ancien régime*, at least for constitutional monarchy. Despite a law of 2 Prairial Year II (21 May 1795), whereby only the tricolour cockade was permitted as a sign of political affiliation, in Bordeaux the royalist *jeunesse dorée* delighted in wearing the white cockade and in beating *sans-culottes* whom they encountered in the streets.[49] Once the dauphin, now styled Louis XVII, died aged ten in prison on 8 June 1795—sadly, of scrofula, 'the king's evil'—his uncle, the Comte de Provence, assumed the title of Louis XVIII. He was certain that his loyal subjects had now seen through the 'impious and factious men' who had brought down on France 'a torrent of calamities'. Now the 'hypocritical despots' of Thermidor had replaced the 'sanguinary despots' of the Terror. Louis was sure that his people would return peaceably to him through their love and regret; if they did not, he assured them, he would not hesitate to conquer 'his rights' through military means.[50] On 25 June, from his exile in Verona, he issued an intransigent declaration that ensured there could be no return to the Constitution of 1791 as a way of stabilizing the Revolution. Indeed, he spoke as if the Revolution of 1789 had never occurred, referring to the restoration of the three Estates and their 'rights', and of the position of the Catholic Church. Those who pined for a return to pre-revolutionary certainties could never agree on just how far a compromise with revolutionary change should go. In any case, given the depths of hatred between republicans and royalists by 1795, a return to the constitutional monarchy of 1791 would not have been possible without military defeat and further civil war. Louis' declaration offered hope only to the most recalcitrant royalists dreaming of a return to the *ancien régime*.[51]

Louis' declaration coincided with an attempt to bring together *émigré* troops and the remnants of the Vendéan rebels (*chouans*), with British support. The Peace of Mabilais on 2 Floréal Year III (21 April 1795) had offered freedom of religion and a full amnesty for deserters and *chouans* in the west if they surrendered. But now, on 28 June, the British navy landed 6,000 troops on the peninsula of Quiberon, west of Vannes in Brittany. On the beach, Urbain-René de Hercé, the elderly *émigré* bishop of the abolished bishopric of Dol, blessed the thousands of locals who rushed to join them. From the outset, however, deep mistrust divided the local Breton *chouan* forces commanded by the constitutional monarchist turned Girondin, Joseph Puisaye, and the uncompromising aristocratic arrivals under Comte Louis Charles Hervilly. As republican troops under General Lazare Hoche cut off access to the peninsula, Hervilly refused to mobilize his forces to avoid sharing the credit for victory with Puisaye in a battle he mistakenly assumed would be won. The *chouan* forces were repelled near Vannes and Puisaye went into hiding with the survivors. Hundreds were arrested.[52]

In 1795, after the failure of the Quiberon landing, and a summary trial by a military commission made up of townsmen, about 750 people were shot, many on what became known as 'Martyrs' Field' near Auray. Among those executed were the majority of the noble officers, in all 366 of those executed.[53] Enraged, the local royalist leader François de Charette ordered three hundred republican prisoners to be killed while he celebrated mass. Charette himself was later captured while fighting in the Vendée and executed by firing squad in Nantes on 29 March 1796.[54]

The crushing of counter-revolution inside France coincided with a debate about foreign policy that was to have far-reaching, Europe-wide consequences. The mantra of the Jacobin regime of the Year II had been 'terror until the peace', but the victories of the early summer of 1794 had exposed a deep tension between Robespierre and Saint-Just on the one hand and Carnot and Lindet on the other, namely about the territorial objective. Was the aim simply to purge the territory of the Republic of invading troops and their collaborators or should the Republic's north-eastern border be extended, even to the Rhine? The issue became particularly acute after the victory at Fleurus on 26 June, which opened up the plains to the north.

Carnot, Lindet and Dubois-Crancé were of the view in December 1794 that the River Meuse was the appropriate border for France, with 'sister republics' being encouraged further east, but there was a noisy clamour in the Convention for the old idea of the Rhine frontier to be realized. Now the initial rationale for war voiced by Brissot and Vergniaud in 1792—that this was a defensive war against tyrannical aggression which would naturally become a war of liberation joined by Europe's oppressed—would develop into a war of territorial expansion. In 1795 a vigorous annexation campaign was launched, with a collection of arguments published under the title *La Rive gauche du Rhin, limite de la République française*, referring to natural geographical limits but also to history dating back to Caesar's Gaul. One of the proponents, Merlin de Douai, argued that incorporating Belgium into France would be the best buffer against Austrian hostility.[55] The acceptance of this point of view was a seminal moment.

War spread further north into the Netherlands against the Stadtholder Prince William V and the Orangists, who were allied with Britain. Early in 1795, William fled to Britain, and the Dutch 'patriots' proclaimed the Batavian Republic, effectively a 'sister republic' of France. Occasionally, the promise of the French Revolution was welcomed. In the town of Zaltbommel on the Rhine, the Reformed Church pastor Joost Kist welcomed the French presence after August 1794, despite the constant fighting across the river with English and Hessian troops. In January 1795 he celebrated in his diary the capitulation of the English:

> 13 January: Some of the citizens decided to plant a tree of liberty. They went to Gameren to cut a big pine tree. Hauled it up the dike and loaded it on a wagon to bring it to the city.
> 14 January: Around 3 the young girls of the city danced around the tree of liberty, and drummers went through all the streets. At night there were celebrations in the town hall.
> 9 March: At 9 the cannon fired salutes and it was proclaimed that all over the city the Declaration of the Rights of Man and Citizen would be read aloud. People dressed in their finest clothes.

For their part, the deputies-on-mission sought to reassure Batavians of their intentions in liberating them from the Stadtholder:

> The blood of the founders of the Republic of the United Provinces still flows through your veins. . . . We have not come to conquer you; the French nation will respect your independence. . . . Practice of any

religion of choice will not be hindered. The laws and customs of the country will be maintained.[56]

The Batavian Republic, first of the 'sister republics', was proclaimed on 19 January 1795. The Treaty of Basle with Prussia on 5 April effectively ceded the left bank of the Rhine to France. Although there were certainly Dutch patriots who welcomed the idea of 'liberation' by France as a 'sister republic', there was neither the same level of support as in Belgium nor the same sense in France that the Netherlands were inherently revolutionary and republican. So the Batavian Republic was treated rather as a conquered territory, required to pay an enormous war indemnity and to pay for the upkeep of the occupying army of 25,000 soldiers.

Just as powerful as groups of 'patriots' were the forces of popular reaction against the French menace. Across the continent, ruling regimes drew legitimacy from a popular backlash against the Revolution. In areas where French troops had invaded, their assumptions about the universality of attraction to 'rational' French systems of administration and social organization were often rejected openly or through sabotage and duplicity. Again and again, the Republic had to confront insurgents motivated by the same bitterness as the Vendéans, but further aggravated by a gulf of language.[57]

Belgian lands were subject to the harshest aspects of military rule. The 283,000 French soldiers essentially lived off the land of a population of fewer than three million, creating shortages, rebellion and crime. It was reported that between three and four thousand people were living rough in a forest between Brussels and Nivelles and were pillaging any cart that passed through.[58] Conditions were scarcely any better in the French armies. Twenty-year-old Charles Lefel wrote home often to his wine-grower parents in Chives, near Soissons in the Aisne department, where his father was mayor. Charles was a hardy young man but during the attack on Maastricht in the winter of 1794–95 even he was led to complain of being 'bare-footed and badly dressed'. Being barefooted on night-watch on the Rhine must have been excruciating. The soldiers were lodged in a ruined château open to the elements, going without bread for three or four days at a time. They survived by digging up carrots, potatoes and turnips from the frozen fields.[59]

When the war expanded across the border, difficulties of supply became more acute as farmers in France resisted requisitioning. Such were the prices producers could command after the harvest failure of 1794 that supplying the armies was less attractive than selling to desperate buyers on domestic markets. Farmers continued to evade requisitions of food, fodder and animals. On 18 Vendémiaire (9 October 1794) the officer in charge of stores of fodder at Trèves berated his colleague at Langres in Lorraine. 'I am being tormented,' his colleague complained, because of the lack of supplies. 'Tremble!,' the officer warned, 'the loss of your position will be the least of the penalties that weighs on your head.'[60] With hundreds of thousands of men still at the front, rural workers could continue to profit from the shortage of labour at harvest time to insist on higher wages. At Attichy, north of Paris near Compiègne, for example, harvests in August 1795 were disrupted by strikes by itinerant harvesters insisting on higher payments.[61]

By late 1794 the transport situation was so difficult on the eastern frontier that members of the Committee of Public Safety—Cambacérès, Carnot, Dubois-Crancé, Boissy and others—were forced to reissue decrees from the Terror, warning that the penalty for opposing the Convention was death, the government was still 'revolutionary until the peace', and supplies were urgent 'considering . . . the success of our armies on enemy territory, the necessity of continuing and maintaining our conquests and the need to continue the current campaign. . . .'[62] Even then, however, owners of means of transport sought to take advantage of the demand by insisting on higher prices. Between January and April 1795 the price of a quintal of wheat in Langres rose from 60 to 193 *livres*, of barley from 37 to 139 *livres*, while the prices of other grains, hay and straw also escalated. By then, the Army of the Moselle, now at Luxembourg, warned that it would be forced to turn back unless administrators and citizens continued to cooperate. The officer in charge of supplies warned those at Langres that 'we are at a desperate point where, through your barbaric selfishness and your cowardly ingratitude, we will lose the precious fruits of five years of difficulty, torment and work'.[63]

Those fruits were about to ripen. A series of treaties in 1795 achieved the key goals of the Convention, removing three powers from the anti-revolutionary coalition: the first Treaty of Basle with Prussia (5 April); the Treaty of The Hague with the Batavian Republic ceding territories to France (16 May); and the second Treaty of Basle with Spain (22 July). South of the Pyrenees there was not the same resolve to incorporate territory as in the Low Countries, and local resistance was in any case more threatening. But the revolutionary advance was a shock: a Madrid priest reported that, 'in the taverns and fashionable salons, all one hears is battles, Revolution, convention, national representation, Liberty, equality. Even the whores ask you about Robespierre.'[64]

Further away, the Convention was powerless to assist its allies. In Poland, where Catherine of Russia had launched a pre-emptive strike against Jacobinism with an invasion in 1792 and partition, patriots rose in March 1794 against the occupying Russian army in Cracow under the slogan of 'Liberty, Integrity, Independence'. Tadeusz Kosciuszko had visited Paris in January 1793, and promised Poles civic rights and the abolition of serfdom. In Warsaw there were bloody reprisals against Russians and their supporters. Tricolour flags festooned towns; Polish translations appeared of the 'Marseillaise' and 'Ça ira!' Despite a 'levée en masse' of 72,000 men, however, the Poles were powerless to prevent renewed Russian invasion; in November 1794, Russian troops killed up to 20,000 Polish civilians in a single day in Warsaw's suburb of Praga. In January 1795, Poland would again be partitioned between Russia, Prussia and Austria.[65]

The wars continued far from Europe. Concern with what the French and patriot victory in the Netherlands would mean for its commercial and colonial interests led Britain to propose that the foundering Dutch East India Company, in control of the Cape of Good Hope since 1652, should cede control to it. At the brief but highly significant Battle of Muizenberg near the Cape in September 1795, a British fleet brushed aside Dutch colonial resistance and seized the Cape, creating the basis for a century of British rule and a far longer anglophone cultural dominance.[66] The war continued in the Caribbean, too, with the retaking of Guadeloupe from Britain in December 1794 and the execution (by guillotine and shooting) of over five hundred French men and women who had fought with the British.[67]

At the same time that the regime had resolved on a foreign policy of expanding the Republic's borders and creating 'sister republics' beyond them, the political challenge at home for the men of Thermidor was how to construct an internal regime which would be immune to the radicalism and popular menace of the Year II but equally robust against resurgent royalism. In the words of the Convention's president, Boissy d'Anglas, 'We have lived through six centuries in six years' (Fig. 32). The new political agenda was made plain by him on 5 Messidor Year III (23 June 1795):

> We should be governed by the best among us; the best are the most highly educated, and those with the greatest interest in upholding the laws; save for the rarest exceptions, you will only find such men among those who, by reason of their owning property, are devoted to the land in which it is situated. . . . If you were to grant unlimited political rights

to men without property ... they would levy or permit the levying of taxes fatal to trade and agriculture ...[68]

In the Convention on 21 Messidor (9 July), Jean Denis Lanjuinais agreed, ridiculing the conceit of equal political rights, which would enfranchise not only 'crass ignorance, the basest greed, and crapulous drunkenness' among men but also 'the mad, idiots, women, children and foreigners'. Women could be intelligent, no doubt, but ideally formed a single entity with their husbands. In any case, they had a higher calling: 'to form, from the cradle, souls in which would shine all the republican virtues; the mother of the Gracchi is their model'.[69]

So the new Constitution of 5 Fructidor (22 August) restricted participation in electoral assemblies by wealth, age and education as well as by sex. Political life was to be the act of voting: petitions, political clubs and even unarmed demonstrations were banned. The social rights promised in the Constitution of 1793 were stripped away; the meaning of equality was now to be sharply restricted to equality before the law:

Article 3. Equality is a circumstance in which the law is the same for all ...

Article 8. The cultivation of land, all production, every means of labour, and the entire social order are dependent on the maintenance of property ...[70]

Only those with an adequate stake in society could be trusted to govern: that is, wealthy, educated, middle-aged and married males. Certainly, voting rights were guaranteed to all male taxpayers, but electoral colleges were to be limited to the wealthiest 30,000 among them, about half the number of 1791. The mass of the population was asked to put their trust in those who knew best. The emphasis was on avoiding the possibility of abrupt political shifts: only one-third of the Council of Five Hundred would be elected at a time; for the first time there would be an Upper House, a Council of Elders (of 250 men over forty years who were married or widowed) who would approve legislation; and one of the executive of five Directors, chosen by the Elders from a list submitted from the Five Hundred, would be replaced annually. In proposing the law, the deputy Pierre-Louis-Charles Baudin argued that this would 'conquer the passions' and allow a transition from 'a revolutionary state to a constitutional order'.[71]

The revolutionaries of 1789 had expressed their optimism in a declaration of rights, the conviction that with the liberation of human creativity all could aspire to the exercise of their capabilities. Freedom would be limited only by the obligation to respect the 'natural and inalienable' rights of others: 'liberty, property, security and resistance to oppression'. The Constitution of 1793 had gone further, adding equality and defining 'resistance to oppression' as not only 'the most sacred of rights' but 'the most indispensable of duties' when oppression was evident. Now the Constitution of 1795 maintained a commitment to 'liberty, equality, security and property' as the core rights of man, but deleted any reference to the right to resist oppression, and appended a Declaration of Duties, above all obedience to the law.[72]

The Constitution was put to a referendum: perhaps 1.3 million men voted in favour, considerably fewer than for its predecessor in 1793. But only 208,000 cast a vote in favour of the Two-Thirds Decree, and there was evident anger that the price of social order was to be limited democracy. A section of voters in Limoges complained that 'We are deeply disturbed to see the wealthy supplanting all other categories of citizen.'[73]

France was again to be governed by representative, parliamentary government based on a property qualification and the safeguarding of economic and civil liberties. In those ways it was a return to the essential principles of the Constitution of 1791. But the Constitution of 1795 and its regime of the Directory were to be republican, not monarchical, and religious divisions were now to be resolved by separating Church and State: 'no one may be forced to contribute to the expenses of a religion. The Republic does not pay for any.'

This would be a regime based on individual rights and responsibilities, on respect for the law and private property, and on political and economic liberalism. Save for professions in health and security, the new Constitution reaffirmed the abolition of controls on entry into occupations, 'of commerce, or of the practice of industry or arts of any kind'. The Convention believed it had brought the Revolution to an end. But, after six years of violent conflict, popular participation and sacrifice, could the exclusions and limitations imposed by these pragmatic, chastened republicans succeed in achieving stability against both resentful urban and rural working people and resurgent royalists?

CHAPTER FIFTEEN

MEN WITH A STAKE IN
SOCIETY, 1795–97

THE MEN OF THE DIRECTORY WERE GRAPPLING WITH AN ACUTE political conundrum, for by 1795 divisions among French citizens were not simply about who was best equipped to represent an electorate but what type of regime best suited the nation. The stakes were high: in all, ninety-six deputies had died prematurely, through execution, assassination or suicide, in the years 1793–95.[1] How could a liberal system be constructed that both protected the Republic against the royalist chimera and yet also insulated it against popular demands and Jacobin excess? The response was a republic based on 'capacity' and a stake in society, but the combination of political exclusion and a commitment to economic liberalism inevitably gave the regime the character of class rule: the 'extreme centre' of a 'bourgeois republic'.[2]

For the better-off all over France the new regime of the Directory put in place on 11 Brumaire Year IV (2 November 1795) represented the essentials of what they wanted: both the guarantee of the main revolutionary achievements and the smothering of the threat of popular intimidation. The return to substantial property-owning as the basis of political power and social eminence facilitated the increasing confidence of the landed proprietors and farmers, such as the 'fermocratie' on the large estates of Artois and Picardy.[3] The political intention of those who had framed the Constitution of the Year III was clear: the heady, uncertain days of popular political initiative were over, and power was to reside in the hands of those with a substantial stake in society. Just as the universalist 'fraternity' of the early years had been narrowed in 1792–94 to mean the fraternal unity of patriots against the counter-revolution, now the dominant republicans of the Directory excluded both 'anarchists', as militant *sans-culottes* were now often called, and royalists. At the same time the regime sought to avoid a strong executive and its Robespierrist connotations through rotation of executive authority among the five Directors.

The vitality of grass-roots political life was deliberately sapped. In the capital, the assemblies in the neighbourhood section were replaced by fewer, larger *arrondissements*, while in the countryside communes were grouped into 'municipalities' at the cantonal level for electoral and local government purposes. As soon as the nation went to the polls for the first time to elect one-third of the members of the Council of Five Hundred, it was evident that the regime could at best look for acquiescence, but not enthusiasm. Even among the 30,000 men with sufficient property to be electors rather than just voters, only about 15 per cent went to the polls, and for the most part they elected royalists.

The men of the Directory had firm convictions that their particular type of republicanism—parliamentary, economically *laissez-faire*, but socially conservative—was that best suited to stabilize the country, but they were never able to feel confident that they acted with the willing support of most citizens. The combination of a narrow social base and internal instability forced the regime to resort to the repression of opposition, even by the use of military force. Hence the Directory declared advocacy of the democratic 1793 Constitution to be a capital offence, and in February called upon Napoleon Bonaparte to use his troops to forcibly close the Panthéon Club in Paris, which had attracted 3,000 Jacobins since its foundation the previous November. In March 1796 the regime sharply restricted freedom of the press and association.

Political repression added to resentment at conscription and shortages of essentials in towns. The summary written to a fellow priest in exile in December 1795 by Chévrier, the former *curé* of Réchicourt in the diocese of Metz, was incisive:

> ... the peasants don't seem poorer than before. As all the matters of prime necessity are in their hands, and sell for very high prices in coin, they are getting by ... [but] the people of Nancy and Lunéville are suffering greatly: no work, no money, no food. . . . Meat is so rare that it is given only to hospitals. . . . No candles. Salt is exchanged for wheat. . . . Throughout November, troops did not stop deserting. There was not a village or 'cense' [large farm] where you couldn't see several pass each day, saying they were ready to die on the spot rather than return to the army.

Those known to have supported the Terror in Nancy were often confronted by young men 'armed with knotty clubs that they call "justices of the peace", who strike them hard across the shoulders'. Chévrier despaired about the impact of the collapse of the Church on morality and religious practice: more and more people saw religion as irrelevant or simply a matter of periodic mass.[4]

A little further east along the frontier, another former *curé*, this time one who had abdicated the priesthood and married, feared for his life. Nicolas-Antoine Baur, a Jacobin activist who had created a public library from seizures of *émigré* property in Sarreguemines, had learned from books why he needed to renounce his calling: 'when I first read the historians who show the shame of the religion of Jesus Christ,' he despaired, 'the burnings in St-Dominique, the conversions of native Americans, the St-Barthélemy massacres ... I took these atrocities for exaggerations'. Now he was expecting to be 'mutilated and killed for having sworn loyalty to the homeland and for having preferred the status of father of a family to that of a priest'. At nearby Hombourg another married ex-priest had effectively been starved to death, his body dragged through the streets during four days before being buried outside the cemetery walls. When in 1796 Baur had the chance to take up a position outside Lorraine, he gave the papers of the Jacobin Club to his successor as librarian, who destroyed them. By the end of the nineteenth century the library had entirely disappeared, too.[5]

Many of those who had spent years in revolutionary activism now left public life out of despair, fear or exhaustion. The furniture-maker Chamouillet, known in Orléans as 'the Patriarch of the *sans-culottes*', had been, among other things, a police commissioner, municipal councillor, president of the departmental administration, president of his section and club, before being imprisoned. On New Year's Day in 1796 he posted a notice on the city walls that he was no longer going to be involved in politics and was putting his carpenter's apron back on.[6]

The political and social atmosphere of the Directory opened up a pathway to power for other citizens, among them a group of talented women. The Jacobins of the Year II had encouraged women to demonstrate their patriotism as 'citizenesses', while closing women's political clubs; now in his *Journal de Paris* the prominent deputy Pierre-Louis Roederer argued in June 1796 that there was no such thing as a 'citizeness': 'the title of citizen is thus a political title. But a woman is only a member of the family. She has no political right in the State. She must not bear any political title.'[7] Instead, some women found other ways of exercising power.

By late 1795, Thérésia Cabarrus had become estranged from her husband Tallien—in part perhaps because of his role in the execution of royalist aristocrats captured at Quiberon in May 1795—and had become the mistress of Paul Barras, former viscount turned Jacobin and now a Director in the new regime. Cabarrus, Juliette Récamier and Marie-Rose de Beauharnais, who married Napoleon Bonaparte on 9 March 1796, would play influential roles as fashionable and activist anti-Jacobin *merveilleuses*. But Bonaparte would later forbid his wife to remain friends with Cabarrus, that 'disreputable and loathsome woman'.[8]

All regimes after 1789 had sought uplifting symbols and festivals to replace those of the *ancien régime*, now moribund with the destruction of its pillars of monarchy, nobility and state religion. The Jacobins had used the heroism of boys like Joseph Bara and Joseph-Agricol Viala to stimulate the patriotic virtues of children. Now the Directory found a more suitable hero. The Paris Salon of 1796 featured a painting by Pierre-Nicolas Legrand entitled *A Kind Deed is Never Forgotten*, celebrating the behaviour of Joseph Cange, the messenger of La Force prison in Paris during the Terror. Cange had been moved by the misery of a prisoner's family to whom he delivered a message, and resolved to help them despite his own poverty. He did the same for the prisoner, both sides believing he was simply the go-between for material support. Only later was the truth discovered, and Cange's kindness was celebrated in portraits and plays, one of them by Marin Gamas, author of the 1792 play *Émigrés in the Austral Lands*.

One of Cange's other virtues was that three of the six children he was raising belonged to a brother-in-law killed at the front. To the authorities he represented a combination of the values of patriotic republicanism, patience and generosity ideal for underpinning the new regime. These were the values that it sought to inculcate through its own official festivals that replaced the Jacobin festivals of Reason and Nature. There were now five 'national festivals', to commemorate 14 July, 10 August, the proclamation of the Republic on 22 September, the execution of Louis XVI on 21 January, and the overthrow of the Robespierrists on 9 Thermidor. In October 1795 the Convention added five 'moral festivals', to celebrate Youth, Old Age, Spouses, Thanksgiving and Agriculture. Typical of the last of them was that celebrated in the north-eastern village of Wassigny in June 1797, when

> citizen Augustin Boulogne, a farmer in the commune of Vénérolles
> (responsible for a family of 13 children, one of whom has died for the

Republic), because of his intelligence, good conduct and activity was proposed as a good example, his name was announced, and he sat next to the president throughout the ceremony.[9]

More spirited, no doubt, was the ceremony in the eastern border town of Thionville on 22 September 1796, the fourth anniversary of the proclamation of the Republic, when a fine stone 'altar of the homeland' was unveiled to commemorate the proclamation of the National Convention on 4 December 1792 that 'Thionville has deserved well of the homeland' for its resistance to Prussian invasion. The altar is the only one of many thousands erected that is still standing today (Fig. 33).

But in general these festivals seemed soulless, earnest affairs and lacked both the cultural resonance of abandoned religious festivals and the spontaneous enthusiasm of the early years of the Revolution. Claude Bailly, a saddle-maker from Chinon in the Loire valley, took pleasure in recording in his diary for 28 April 1796 (he used the Christian calendar): 'A festival took place called the festival of spouses. You go with your wife to the temple of Reason to listen to a speech, give wreaths to the newly married and to sing songs. But the only people there were the municipal officers and a detachment of soldiers.'[10] The Directory needed to resort to compulsion to impose its particular brand of republicanism: in January 1796, for example, a government decree required the 'Marseillaise' to be sung in all theatres before the curtain went up. Political culture had ossified.

The head of the Orléans municipal administration told a silent audience at the Festival of Youth on 10 Germinal Year IV (30 March 1796) that the Revolution, while necessary, had meant that 'the arts were forgotten and ignored; science and urbanity had disappeared in the face of the crudest and most disgusting ignorance; anarchy, religious and political fanaticism, and atheism had led to killings, and made the whole of France a place of prisons and scaffolds.'[11] Similar themes were taken up in successive monthly festivals, whether of Agriculture or Old Age. At the Festival of Liberty and Equality four months later a hymn reminded its audience that the price of liberty was respect for the law and probity. Equality meant the sharing of rights and responsibilities and should not be the path to 'taking from the worker the rich deserts of long industry'. The audience were reassured that, happily, the Constitution of the Year III had suppressed anarchy and restored order and justice.

Despite such reassurances, so difficult were economic circumstances, particularly in towns whose economies had collapsed with the decline of overseas trade, that many working people had come to regret the relative certainties of the past, if not the *ancien régime* itself. By 1795, La Rochelle, for example, was so impoverished that the municipality had to suspend coach and mail services because it no longer had the funds to purchase horse-feed. Commerce had slowly picked up after the hiatus of 1792–94: in 1796 ninety-nine ships arrived in the port, compared with just twenty-five in 1792, including shipments of maize, tobacco, cotton and sugar from the United States. It is not surprising, however, that in the context of economic collapse due to continued warfare and the abolition of slavery, there were many Rochellais openly advocating the return of the monarchy.[12] There were many other towns and regions where economic and social instability fostered nostalgia for previous certainties.

The results of the referendum on the new Constitution were announced on 1 Vendémiaire Year IV (23 September 1795). On 5 October royalists in Paris sought to profit from the popular rejection of the provision that two-thirds of the deputies would not need to stand for re-election by calling for insurrection. A few thousand armed royalists and *jeunesse dorée* were repressed without compromise by the army under Napoleon Bonaparte, leaving several hundred dead. The coup also failed because Parisian working people, no matter how resentful towards the new Republic, refused to respond to appeals from the royalists. The failure of the Vendémiaire uprising put an end to the power of the *jeunesse dorée* as well. The *sans-culotte* challenge had been suppressed in May 1795; now the street power of the *muscadins* became another menace to be dispensed with. More than 35,000 people lost civic rights as the neighbourhood sections were purged. Police agents reported that 'women of the people' were shouting at arrested *muscadins*, 'There you go, you little fanatics, it's your turn now!'[13]

Bonaparte's star had dimmed after the fall of the Jacobins in July 1794, and became fainter with his avoidance of service in the grim mopping-up operations in the Vendée in 1794–95. Now his repression of the royalist insurrection in the streets of Paris had given him the chance of rehabilitation in the eyes of the Directory. Thirty-six hours after his marriage to Marie-Rose de Beauharnais in March 1796, Bonaparte departed as commander-in-chief of the Army of Italy. He pined for the woman he called Joséphine (from Marie-Rose's middle name, Josephe), and begged her to join him as he began accumulating victories: 'You will come, won't

24. The painter Chérieux expresses his horror of a women's club, perhaps the Revolutionary Republican Citizenesses, meeting in a former church in 1793. There were about sixty women's clubs in Paris and the provinces before their forced closure in October 1793.

25. The physical destruction of religious statuary during the 'dechristianization' of late 1793 is still visible on many churches today, as here at Moulins.

26. The parish church of Houdan, forty miles west of Paris, still carries above its doorway the inscription from the 1794 Cult of the Supreme Being: 'The French People recognize the existence of the Supreme Being and the immortality of the soul.'

27. Nicolas Henri Jeaurat de Bertry's allegory, c.1794, is replete with symbols of the new political culture under the watchful gaze of Rousseau and the all-seeing eye of revolutionary vigilance.

28. This powerful sketch was made of Robespierre during the tumult of 9 Thermidor by François-Auguste de Parseval-Grandmaison, a former student of David.

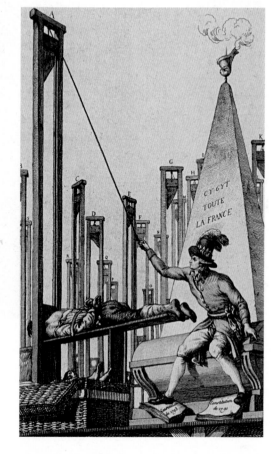

29. The image of Robespierre having to guillotine the executioner because everyone else was dead quickly became a common Thermidorian cliché. Robespierre is here shown trampling underfoot the constitutions of 1791 and 1793. The caption identifies separate guillotines for all groups in French society, from Girondins, nobles and priests to 'the elderly, women and children'.

30. The Swiss painter Jean-François Sablet was a member of the Revolutionary Commune des Arts in 1793. He painted this portrait of Daniel Kervégan (Christophe-Clair Danyel de Kervégan) in 1794, when the former mayor of Nantes in 1789–91 may have just been released from prison. Kervégan, who had made his fortune from colonial commerce and the slave trade, had enjoyed very strong support from 'active' citizens. He was mayor again briefly in 1797, and made a brilliant career under the First Empire.

31. Jean-Baptiste Regnault had begun *The Genius of France between Liberty and Death* in 1793 but its message was reviled when exhibited in 1795, when memories were potent of a year in which liberty and death had been companions rather than alternatives. The Genius of France, with tricolour wings, here gestures to Liberty, with her symbols of equality, the red cap of liberty and the fasces from classical Rome indicating unity.

32. The Protestant lawyer François-Antoine Boissy d'Anglas was a key participant in post-Thermidor politics and the articulation of the principles embedded in the Constitution of 1795.

F. A. DE BOISSY D'ANGLAS.
Député de la Sénéch.ᵉ d'Annonay.

33. Joseph Sicre, the non-juring priest of the frontier community of Saint-Laurent-de-Cerdans, used this tiny chapel of Saint-Cornélis, just across the River Muga in Spain, to baptize and marry hundreds of the faithful from 1796.

34. Despite the wars which swept through the town of Thionville on the Moselle near the Luxembourg border, and repeated enemy occupations, the town has kept its 'altar of the fatherland' at which civic ceremonies were conducted. It was probably erected for the fourth anniversary of the proclamation of the Republic, in 1796, and is the only complete one in existence.

35. Anne-Louis Girodet, who returned to France in 1795, painted this luminous portrait of Jean-Baptiste Belley, the Sénégal-born former slave, elected to the Convention and Council of Five Hundred, but who lost his seat in 1797. The anti-slavery *philosophe* Raynal, who had died in 1796, is also commemorated.

36. André-François Miot (b.1762) was Minister of Foreign Affairs in November 1794, then, after the peace treaty with Tuscany, was appointed Plenipotentiary Minister in Florence in 1795–96. Here Miot is pictured in the colours of the Republic, standing apart from his brother, his wife and his children. Miot is pictured beside a bust of Lucius Junius Brutus, the founder of the Roman Republic. In the background is Minerva, the Roman goddess of wisdom and the arts.

37. Probably from the period of the Directory is a plate proclaiming its owner to be 'Jaque Guillon', from Faremoutiers (Fig. 23), 'a good farmer and a good republican' – the ideal social backbone of the new France.

38. Some of France's most distinguished scientists were involved in the long process, completed in 1799, of designing an exact, decimal set of measures for weight, size, distance, volume and coinage.

39. In 1792 French forces occupied Savoy in the Alps, then part of the Kingdom of Sardinia. The Jacobin former mayor of Montmartre, Félix Desportes, was sent to Geneva as the official resident and in 1796 he commissioned the erection of a hospice and a 'Temple de la Nature' near Sallanches, still commanding breathtaking views of the Mer de Glace on Mont Blanc today. It was restored in 1923.

40. *La Maraichère*, an arresting portrait of a peasant woman or market-gardener by an unknown artist, c.1795, exemplifies the radical shift in the subjects of portraiture.

41. Noël Pinot, the non-juring parish priest of Le Louroux, west of Angers, went into hiding after 1791. He was arrested in 1794. This fresco in the parish church of Saint-Aubin shows his execution in Angers, and was probably completed to mark his beatification in 1926.

you? You will be with me, on my heart, in my arms, on my lips. . . . A kiss on your heart, and then another a little lower, much, much lower.' He underlined the last two words so feverishly that his nib tore the paper. Joséphine demurred; she had met the love of her life, a younger, more amusing and sophisticated soldier, Hippolyte Charles.[14]

Bonaparte's armies would achieve brilliant successes against Austrian forces across the Alps in Lombardy. One reason was the skill of General Alexandre Dumas, son of a slave from Saint-Domingue and now commander-in-chief of the Army of the Alps, who made a name for himself by his daring initiatives (the Austrians called him *der schwarze Teufel*—'the black devil'). Dumas befriended Bonaparte, albeit temporarily.[15] Bonaparte's victories resulted in the creation of 'sister republics'—among them the Cispadane Republic on 25 Vendémiaire Year V (16 October 1796), and the Cisalpine Republic on 11 Messidor (29 June 1797)—and the occupation of the Venetian Republic on 27 Floréal (15 May 1797) (Fig. 34). At the same time, civilian insurrection against the occupying troops was repressed pitilessly: in June 1796, Bonaparte unleashed three days of killing and pillaging in Pavia and Binasco, south-west of Milan; perhaps 10,000 civilians were killed in Verona. His army also slaughtered massive numbers of hostile civilians in and around Nice after its conquest in 1797.[16] National glory came at a huge expense in lives.

Bonaparte's victories against Piedmontese and Austrian forces in northern Italy in 1796 enabled him to impose requisitions on conquered territories. He also expanded the practice commenced in the Austrian Netherlands in 1795 of confiscating art for the Louvre. This provoked a heated debate in Paris in which the question of the ethics of confiscation was a proxy for the debate about the expansionist foreign policy, and also for internal manoeuvring for position among the artist community. Charles-Joseph Trouvé, editor of the newspaper *Moniteur Universel* and for a time secretary to the Directory, inveighed against the 'royalists' wanting to return art, claiming that they will 'declare that there was a French plot against Germany and Italy and that as a result not only artistic monuments but also weapons, pecuniary contributions, and towns [whose seizure] rewarded French valour must be returned—and that, most importantly, the republican government must be destroyed'.[17]

Practising artists needed to be cautious about their politics. Jacques-Louis David had been a lucky man. Arrested in Thermidor for his involvement with the Robespierrists and the Committee of General Security, he, like so many others, claimed that 'my heart is pure, only my head was wrong'. He was released, then rearrested and imprisoned in May 1795, and released again as his health deteriorated. Marguerite Charlotte, who had divorced David in 1793, in part because of her outrage at his vote for Louis XVI's death, supported him while in prison, and the couple remarried in November 1796. David returned to his pre-revolutionary profession of portraiture, among them of Dutch representatives of the Batavian Republic in Paris.[18]

One of David's earlier pupils, Anne-Louis Girodet, had had a protracted stay in Italy after 1789 as winner of the Prix de Rome, then eighteen months in penniless exile in Naples after anti-revolutionary students sacked the French Academy in Rome. When Girodet returned to Paris in 1795, he was too disoriented by the changed France he encountered and the need to safe-guard family property in the Orléanais to resume painting immediately. Not until the Salon of 1798 did he exhibit, a brilliant three-quarter-length portrait of Jean-Baptiste Belley, the Sénégal-born former slave, elected to the Convention and Council of Five Hundred, but who lost his seat in 1797. Belley was the first former slave to be elected to a European parliament (he was born on the island of Gorée in Sénégal in 1746 or 1747). He had made his maiden speech the day the abolition of slavery was passed by acclamation in 1794. Girodet depicted him as a member of the Convention, with his sashes; in the background was a bust of Guillaume Raynal, one of the few *philosophes* to challenge slavery, who had died in March 1796 (Fig. 35).[19]

Scientists, too, had absorbed conflicting messages from the Revolution. One message was that 1789 had opened the way to a fuller appreciation of what the rational application of scientific knowledge could achieve in every domain; the other was the necessity of strong authority in quelling social unrest. Inevitably, the fertile scientific life of these years, and the new institutions that were created, bore the marks of both lessons. Among the most brilliant scientists of his generation was Georges Cuvier, born in 1769 into a Protestant family in Montbéliard, part of the Duchy of Württemburg until its absorption into France in October 1793. In 1795, Cuvier became assistant to Jean-Claude Mertrud, chair of comparative anatomy at the Jardin des Plantes in Paris. There Cuvier met the geologist Faujas de Saint-Fond, author of the remarkable *Recherches sur les volcans éteints du Vivarais et du Velay* (1778); Saint-Fond had survived being the King's Commissioner to factories, armories and royal forests to become in 1793 the first professor of geology at the Jardin des Plantes. The next year, at the age of twenty-seven,

Cuvier stunned his audience at the École Centrale du Panthéon by demonstrating, using mammal fossils, that some animals had become extinct. Meanwhile he was devising a detailed system of paleontological classification, including human races, paralleled by his conviction that the Revolution had demonstrated the need for social order, hierarchy and responsibilities.[20]

The Directory had inherited a massive religious problem. Most priests had refused the oath of allegiance to the Civil Constitution of the Clergy in 1791, or had soon retracted, and the subsequent exile, imprisonment or execution of these priests had created a vengeful, embittered clerical army on France's borders. In many areas constitutional clergy had been unable to overcome local resentment at the departure of the 'bons curés'. In any case they were simply too few to minister to spiritual needs: by 1796 there were perhaps only 15,000 priests for France's 40,000 parishes. The defeat of the European coalition against France had shattered the hopes among the *émigré* clergy for triumphal return, but there was a profound longing in parts of the country for a reconstitution of parish life.

When the *émigré* priest of Franconville became secretary to his former Bishop of Nancy, de La Fare, now the agent of the royal pretender the Comte de Provence at the court in Vienna, he compiled a register of the lot of the diocese's non-jurors. Two hundred were in exile, chiefly in Bavaria and Austria; 113 were in prison in Nancy; there were thirty whose whereabouts the priest did not know. Twenty-three had been sent to Rochefort, where most died in a shipwreck that killed 543 of the 763 prisoners on board.[21] One of the priests in exile from the diocese of Nancy wrote to his parishioners in 1795 regretting what he felt was their lot: 'extravagant maxims, deceitful doctrines, corrupting and erroneous principles ... Rebellion and licence emboldened by impunity. Hatred, greed, persecution, outrages and vexations are now the lot of good people.' He called on them to be true to the maxims in which he had inculcated them while awaiting his return, but failed to recognize the material benefits they had realized from the end of seigneurialism or, indeed, of the tithe paid to the Church.[22]

The intransigence of many of the *émigré* clergy was the major obstacle to reconciliation and the reconstruction of parish life, for how could they be invited to return home seething with such hostility to the changes wrought by the Revolution? French bishops exiled in Switzerland in 1795 had held out an olive branch to some of the constitutional clergy, stating publicly that not all of them were equally guilty and that many could be pardoned and reintegrated, especially if they had avoided 'intruder' bishops.

In contrast, reflecting on how the constitutional clergy ('the brigands') should be treated, the *émigré* priest who was secretary to Bishop de La Fare at the Viennese court drew a comparison with the pillage of the Goths at the time of the emperor Gallien:

> All the usurpers of the positions of others must be banished from the Church. At a time of enemy incursion, to imagine that the time of common ruin could be a time of profit, only the impious and enemies of God could think such a thing. So it is resolved to excommunicate them all, for fear of the wrath of God descending on all the people, and especially on prelates who do not do the right thing.

This was no idle threat: 'We are your soldiers, Lord, but servants of God. . . . We have weapons in our hands, and we won't resist using them: for we would rather die innocent than live with guilt.'[23]

In some parts of the country the recalcitrance of the *émigré* clergy was aligned with the views of local people. The anti-revolutionary guerrilla warfare (*chouannerie*) that had emerged in 1792–93 became endemic in Brittany after 1795. It did not have the military structure of the insurrection in the Vendée, nor was it explicitly counter-revolutionary so much as a rejection of all those people who had disrupted rural life since 1789: local 'patriots' who had bought up church property; 'intruder' priests who had taken posts left vacant by trusted locals; officials determined to meet targets of conscripts and taxes; and the managers of large estates who continued the exploitative rental practices of *domaine congéable*. Priests had traditionally provided the spiritual cohesion for large communities of Breton speakers, many of them farmers whose Sunday worship was the moment when they experienced the community of souls.[24] Armed *chouannerie* used the same hiding places, pathways and ruses as had the legendary salt-smugglers before the Revolution along the borders of Brittany and the provinces of Maine and Anjou.[25] *Chouannerie* had its heroes and victims to act as symbols, such as Éléonor d'Amphernet, arrested in December 1795 and executed the following January. He was an early counter-revolutionary, writing to the municipality of Quimperlé in March 1790 that he and his family were retiring to the country: 'I no longer regard myself as a citizen of this town and will no longer pay taxes.' He had emigrated early in 1791 but returned to fight the Revolution the next year. He died in peace, he reassured his wife, and sure that 'God will reunite us in his holy paradise'.[26]

For the men of the Directory, the religious problem was above all one of public order: they were mistrustful of 'fanaticism' but conscious of a widespread yearning for a reconstitution of the spiritual community. *Émigré* priests were permitted to return under the decree of 7 Fructidor Year IV (24 August 1796), but only on condition that they took a civic oath. Religious observance was to be a purely private matter: bells and outward signs of religiosity remained forbidden, and the regime continued the Convention's separation of Church and State. The Church was to be sustained by the offerings of the faithful. Instead, these years were remarkable for a construction from below of a new Catholicism, as devout women in particular took the initiative in rebuilding a shattered Catholic Church. This was at its strongest in the rural areas (such as parts of the west, Normandy and the south-west) where huge proportions of priests had emigrated, and in provincial towns and cities such as Arles, Laon, Mende, Rouen and Toulouse where the destruction of the institutions of the *ancien régime* had left women particularly vulnerable to unemployment and destitution.

The structures of the Catholic Church had been shattered. The Church had lost its privileged position as the official religion; its property had been seized and sold; and its extensive seigneurial privileges had been abolished. Its many hundreds of monasteries and convents were closed and their religious, like former parish priests, were in exile or had left their calling to sit out the tempest or, in many cases, to take up positions in the revolutionary administration. The pre-revolutionary certainties of church schooling and the rituals of the daily and annual ecclesiastical calendar were gone: the countryside was a quiet place, devoid of the sound of bells and the call to worship. Most children had no school to attend; most parishes had no pastor to intercede for them; and young men were in the secular world of the army. Instead it was women, impatient at the refusal of *émigré* clergy to compromise with the new regime, who took the initiative, and expressed a religiosity that was profound and self-reliant. Local authorities were intimidated into reopening churches, as were some of those who had bought them as national property; venerable lay people said 'messes blanches' (unofficial church services) while midwives baptized the newborn. Sundays were observed as the day of rest rather than the revolutionary calendar's *décadi*, and emptied church treasuries were filled with relics and objects of devotion that had been hidden from the requisitioning *armées révolutionnaires* in 1793.

Elsewhere, people found different ways of sustaining religious practice. When Jacobin armies retook the eastern Pyrenean town of Saint-Laurent-de-Cerdans from the Spanish in May 1794, there was massive emigration of local Laurentins who had fought against the Republic, and the town itself narrowly escaped deliberate physical destruction. The priest Joseph Sicre had already left Saint-Laurent in September 1792 in what he called 'las circumstancias calamitosas de la Iglesia de la frança'. He probably returned to his parish with the invading Spanish army in 1793–94, then left with it as the army retreated. From 11 September 1796, the date of the benediction of the tiny chapel of Saint-Cornélis, Sicre once again began to play a vital role in the lives of his parishioners. The chapel was built in a field just across the border four miles away, along the River Muga, at that point no more than a stream, and became a sacred place for hundreds of the faithful who walked for hours along the rough mountain tracks to marry or to bring a baby for baptism (Fig. 36). Until his return to Saint-Laurent in December 1800, Sicre baptized 331 babies at the chapel of Saint-Cornélis, many of them brought to him by their fathers on the day of their birth, as was the practice before the Revolution, and performed 158 marriages involving Laurentins. His presence there became widely known: he also performed 124 marriages and 281 baptisms of people from other villages near Saint-Laurent and from as far away as the lowlands around Perpignan forty miles to the north-east.[27]

The regime's philosophy of individual responsibility and *laissez-faire* was also applied in social welfare. The Directory reversed the Convention's policy of nationalized hospitals and state responsibilities for welfare; in the Year V local hospital boards were given responsibility for administration, and welfare again became based on private charity. The regime seemed deaf to the pleas of the hospitals that they no longer had the endowments of the Church and nobility, or the labour of nuns, which had formerly sustained them.

One area of social policy where the regime was willing to compromise its assumption of individual responsibility was in control of prostitution, where it reintroduced *ancien régime* measures. Prostitution had remained an occupation of last resort for scores of thousands of urban women, often migrants from rural hinterlands. After 1789 the principle of individual liberty had been extended to prostitution: in July 1791 new municipal regulations in Paris simply made no reference to prostitution and its policing. While many women were thereby freed from the repressive constraints of religious reformatories to which they were sent under the *ancien régime*, it was now assumed that prostitution and its side effects were an individual choice and responsibility. The Directory reversed that policy and required prostitutes to register with the police, to work in closed and discrete brothels to control the spread of syphilis, and to make public thoroughfares more 'respectable'. But no such restrictions were placed on their clients.[28]

The abandonment of price controls in December 1794 had unleashed dramatic inflation. In 1795 landlords had been authorized to take half their rents in kind rather than cash, and the salaries of the Directors and public officials were expressed in measures of grain rather than money. In February 1794 there had been 4,960 million *livres* of *assignats* in circulation; a year later there were 7,350 million, and by the time the printing plates for the *assignats* were destroyed, in February 1796, there were more than 34 billion *livres* of *assignats* in print. The paper currency was now all but worthless. By October 1795 the purchasing power of the *assignat* stood at only 0.75 per cent of its face value; by the following February, when it was abandoned, it was just 0.25 per cent. An attempt to replace *assignats* with 'territorial mandates' backed by the value of unsold national lands also failed, and in February 1797 the use of paper money was terminated altogether.[29]

The difficulties for urban wage-earners created by unchecked price rises were worsened by harvest failure in many regions in the autumn of 1795, followed by another severe winter. The subsistence crises of 1795 and 1796 intensified the volatility of popular responses to the Directory. Women queuing outside shops in February 1796 were reported as muttering, 'it's a fine bugger of a republic for robbers, first they guillotine us, now they make us die of hunger. What's more, Robespierre didn't let us waste away, he only brought death to the rich; this lot are letting us die every day!'[30] The years 1795 and 1796 were probably the hardest of the revolutionary decade for urban wage-earners, and the vulnerable suffered most. In the eastern town of Bourg, for example, there were 523 deaths in these years from a population of 6,500, and 144 of them were of infants under one year of age.[31]

These were hard years for urban wage-earners, but not necessarily for all their rural counterparts. Renters of large farms were able to take advantage of the escalating prices paid for their produce to buy land, clear taxes and pay off leases. Many peasants who had borrowed money to acquire an extra plot during the sale of *émigré* land in 1793–94 were also able to take advantage of rampant inflation to pay back their loan. But a continuing source of friction in the countryside was the insistence of the poor in many areas on seizing, clearing and cultivating patches of commons or forests in defiance both of the government and of neighbours for whom the commons were best used for grazing livestock. Forty-five laws and fifty decrees concerning forests had been passed in the period 1790–95 with little impact on illegal tree-felling. In a series of reports the former priest turned Jacobin, Jacques-Michel Coupé, argued that southern France was now as denuded as other parts of the Mediterranean coast from Spain to the Near East. In the region of Narbonne,

> Even in living memory, people believe that the climate has changed; vines and olives suffer from frosts now, they perish in places where they used to flourish, and people give the reason: the hillsides and peaks were formerly covered with clumps of woods, bushes, greenery . . . the greedy fury of clearances arrived; everything has been cut down without consideration; people have destroyed the physical conditions which conserved the temperature of the region.[32]

The Directory was as powerless as its predecessors, despite the energetic attempts of local authorities to prosecute the illegal land seizures. What the regime did seek to do, however, was to facilitate agrarian individualism and the rights of private property over ancient communal rights or access to forest resources, gleaning, commons, use of uncultivated land, and rights over access across private land. The Directory asserted the rights of the individual owner of private property in forests and on harvested or uncultivated land, and encouraged the sale of common lands by auction. On 21 Prairial Year IV (9 June 1796), it suspended the decree of 10 June 1793 dividing common lands by head.

The Directory had the misfortune of having to establish itself during years of subsistence crisis. But by its religious, military, economic and social policies, the regime further alienated large numbers of people already excluded from legal forms of voicing grievances through the abolition of the right of collective petitioning. The Directory was not only restricted in terms of those who could exercise power, but its policies and ideology were narrowly class-based as well. In response, it had to contend with a resurgence of popular protest, ranging from indignant insistence on the right to worship to clandestine plans for more radical social change.

In many areas there was a deep division between the hard-headed anticlericalism of the local well-to-do and officials and the contrasting desires of others for a return to the cultural richness of ancient religious rituals. In the Norman town of Bayeux in April 1796, for example, a crowd of furious women invaded the cathedral—converted into a 'temple of reason' during the Terror—and dashed a bust of Rousseau to the floor with cries of 'When the good Lord was there we had bread!' In many regions there were overtones of royalism in such actions, but this was not always the case: in the department of Yonne in Burgundy, the devout insisted that they were republicans exercising constitutional guarantees of religious freedom. Petitioners from Chablis claimed that 'we wish to be Catholics and republicans, and we can be both one and the other'.[33] In the small town of Collioure on the Mediterranean border with Spain, on 13 Germinal Year V (2 April 1797), a large crowd of women returning from mass in a nearby village threatened the officer of a grain store located in a former Dominican chapel, demanding both bread and the reopening of the chapel. While most Colliourencs had supported the Revolution and the retaking of the town from Spain by the Jacobin armies in May 1794, religious life had been shattered: Collioure's ten priests and monks had all emigrated with the retreating Spanish army. Jacques Xinxet, the mayor and local notary, had no sympathy for the women: 'fanaticism, the primary source of all our problems' was to blame for the trouble, 'let's cut the evil at the roots if we want to have internal calm'.[34]

At the same time the trial was taking place hundreds of miles away to the north in the town of Vendôme, located in the department of Loir-et-Cher, of 'Gracchus' Babeuf and forty-eight of his associates, accused of having plotted to overthrow the government by insurrection.[35] Babeuf, a mostly self-educated son of impoverished Picard peasants, had by 1795 developed a political and social programme that sought to take power by insurrection and to impose social equality by seizing property in the name of 'the national community'. Babeuf had concluded that neither the Jacobins' social welfare nor the *sans-culottes'* demands for property distribution would resolve the sharp inequalities which made the democracy promised by the 1793 Constitution impossible to realize. Babeuf's trenchant critique of the Directory appealed to a range of the disaffected, from frustrated Jacobins to resentful soldiers, but his programme of collective ownership, even collective work and distribution, had limited resonance in a society dominated by the dream of landowning. His political challenge was indeed threatening to the regime, however, and he was sentenced to death on 27 May 1797. Among others on trial with him, Marc Vadier, one of those who had plotted against Robespierre, was acquitted; and Jean-Baptiste Drouet, the post-master who had recognized the fleeing Louis XVI near Varennes in June 1791, escaped and found his way to Tenerife in the Canary Islands, where he helped repel a British invasion under Horatio Nelson in July 1797.

Huge numbers of people were engaged in some form of rebellion against the Directory in these years; however, it was not the Republic as such that was being spurned, but rather the class politics of its self-perpetuating elite. Some of the most terrifying challenges to the regime had no clear political overtones. On 19 Vendémiaire Year III (11 October 1795) a band of twenty-one men and women from Orléans bound a farmer and tortured him to reveal the whereabouts of his money. His farm workers were beaten or garrotted.[36] Two of the band were guillotined. But for the next two years the region of the Beauce between Orléans and Paris was to be terrorized by the much larger 'bande d'Orgères', an organized, aggressive subculture of perhaps 150 men and women of all ages whose violent forays resulted in seventy-five murders.[37] When finally arrested in 1798, twenty-two of the band were executed. Stories of the band's humiliation and violation of their victims, and of their subsequent orgies, horrified polite society, as did those of the 'chauffeurs' of the south, so-called because they roasted their victims' feet to extract information.

Changes to national borders facilitated such crimes. The expansion of the Republic into the nine new departments created once Belgium was formally annexed on 9 Vendémiaire Year IV (1 October 1795) enabled gangs to range more readily across old borderlands. In March 1797 the twenty-four-year-old Dinah Jacob shocked the criminal court in Tournai by listing details of what she called 'la bande juive' of about eighty people, mainly Jewish, which overlapped with another, the notorious 'bande à Salambier' operating between Antwerp, Ghent, Amiens and Paris. She later claimed that 'la bande juive' was hundreds strong, and led by her husband Kotzo-Picard and her relatives. They utilized old networks of trade and kin, in this case Jewish pedlar itineraries. The band fabricated passports and birth certificates to avoid conscription and enable them to move easily across the border. From September 1795 they robbed isolated farmhouses, often with spectacular cruelty, and benefited from the disarray in the Catholic Church in the new Belgian departments to ransack churches. François-Marie Salambier and his gang also specialized in highway robbery before his capture late in 1796. The leaders of the 'bande juive' were executed; Salambier and twenty-one accomplices were hanged in Bruges in September 1798.[38]

Underpinning much of the popular resentment towards the Directory was resistance to the conscription on which the regime's armies were based. While these were smaller than those of the Year II—382,000 in 1797 compared with 732,000 in August 1794—they were engaged in soul-destroying repression in Brittany and the west when not on foreign soil far from home. Gone was the camaraderie generated by fighting foreign troops on French soil in defence of the Revolution.[39] The Convention had spoken in terms of a war between peoples and tyrants; now the Directory's peace treaties were couched in terms that assumed the coexistence of sovereign states. The creation of 'sister republics' signalled the transition from a war of revolutionary survival to one of expansion and negotiation. All traces of cosmopolitanism seemed to have evaporated: the welcome extended to 'enlightened' foreigners in 1792 had given way under the Terror to surveillance and expulsion; now a series of laws codified the rights of the state over the right of free entry and asylum.[40]

While Bonaparte's armies achieved some famous victories in northern Italy, other foreign policy initiatives were dismal failures, such as the invasion fleet sent to Ireland on 25 Frimaire Year V (15 December 1796) that was scattered in wild weather or seized by British forces three weeks later. The Directory remained convinced that Britain's Achilles heel was the resentment felt by its Celtic minorities. In Wales, where 90 per cent of the population of 590,000 spoke only Welsh, there had been support for the messages of self-determination and religious freedom in the Revolution of 1789, particularly among the educated. As elsewhere in Britain, however, support had waned after the outbreak of war. In London the Welshman Siamas Wynedd defended the 1794 trial for treason of members of the London Corresponding Society, assuring the 'vipers' that 'in Hell you may burn for all eternity with the dark Devil'. In February 1797 a force of 1,400 French troops (800 of them deserters and prisoners) was successfully landed at Fishguard, on the north coast of Wales. The force was commanded by a veteran of the American War of Independence, Colonel William Tate, an Irish-American from South Carolina. The invasion rapidly disintegrated into ill-discipline, drunkenness and defeat, but it generated an anti-French panic and strengthened sentiments of Britishness.[41]

If in France the 1790s was the decade of revolution, in many parts of Europe this was a time of reaction against the threat of revolution. In June 1794 a Breton, Balthesar Haquet, had delivered a revolutionary address at a political banquet in the mining town of Malužiná in the Kingdom of Hungary (today Slovakia), lauding the French war effort, the temples of reason and Maximilien Robespierre. Haquet was working as a doctor in the mines and teaching anatomy and surgery in Lemburg (Lviv) in the western Ukraine. Austrian officials arrested him but none of his audience was prepared to testify against him and he was simply told to go home.[42] But now, as French troops moved eastwards across the borders, repression intensified in the Austrian Empire. In 1795, Hungarian courts sentenced eighteen local 'Jacobins' to death; others were sentenced to death or prison in Vienna.[43] There were setbacks across the Atlantic as well. The 1794 Jay Treaty between England and the United States had severed old bonds with France, and negative attitudes towards France were a factor in John Adams' victory in the November 1796 presidential elections.[44]

One reason for reaction against the message of the French Revolution in occupied lands was that French troops were often reduced to pillaging in order to survive or as retribution against resentful local populations. As the Army of Sambre-et-Meuse retreated after defeats by Austrians at Wurzburg in September 1796, troops resorted to depredations. In the words of one gunner, 'some soldiers, unworthy of the name, engulfed the houses to break into barrels of wine, to steal, and to rape the women, while the true soldiers were hacked about as they protected the retreat'.[45] In Italy a citizen of Villafranca complained in May 1797 that soldiers forced open his house and 'chose the wine they liked best, took bacon, sausage, cheese and bread and ate and drank as long as they pleased'. Such infractions were judged less harshly than desertion: of about 350 cases in Italy in Years IV–V, the average punishment was about six years in prison and only eight soldiers were shot.[46] A new elite of professional officers had to deal with mutinies in Belgium, Holland and Italy, and problems of supply caused officers to turn a blind eye to stealing by troops. By late 1796, however, measures were slowly being put in place for more efficient and reliable systems of transportation of supplies for the army in the form of grains, hay and straw, and for prompt payment to suppliers.[47]

The daily situation of troops in the French armies was miserable, whether inside or outside France. Even a militant revolutionary like François-Xavier Joliclerc, who had calmly described the necessary slaughter of Vendéan rebels in 1794, was reduced to begging material assistance from his stern and grudging mother at home at Froidefontaine in the Jura mountains. On 21 Pluviôse Year IV (10 February 1796) he wrote from near the Breton port of Lorient, explaining that the collapse in the value of the *assignat* was a disaster and provisions were inedible:

... most of the time we are reduced to eating a pound and a half of poor quality rye bread which passes through our stomachs like gruel in twenty-four hours. As for clothing, the majority of soldiers are barefoot. ... So decide which path you want to take, to let me die in misery or to help me. ... I am your son, not too full of food; but it is indeed Ash Wednesday.

Wounded once again shortly afterwards, Joliclerc finally returned home to his mother in Froidefontaine, where he died aged sixty-five in 1832.[48]

Across the decade every institution of public life—civil, judicial, military—had become an arena of conflict over power, which had suffused private relations as well. In the south smouldering animosities were expressed in direct attacks on the persons and property of Jacobins or the local agents of the new regime. The latter were often wealthy purchasers of church and *émigré* property, especially if they were Protestants.[49] In June 1796 the garrison commander at Privas in Ardèche reported the murder of a wealthy Protestant farmer near Florac to the Minister of the Interior:

Attacks on individuals in the department of Lozère are multiplying in alarming fashion, and always ... on patriots, patriots of 89, the good and virtuous, and above all, wealthy Protestants. The fanatics ... want to recreate the old wars of fanaticism in the Cévennes.[50]

The spectacular violence in the Midi was the febrile expression of a political culture of cycles of repression and reaction. The region was 'hyperpolitical', and the loosening of public constraints after Thermidor unleashed accumulated hatreds. The cycle of reactions against former power-holders became ingrained into political life with increasing violence, to the point where it proved virtually impossible to establish a judicial process above factional interests.[51] Political accusations were employed to denigrate local enemies, whatever the issue. For example, in Mornas north of Orange soldiers were accused by local authorities of being 'terrorists' and 'anarchists' who were menacing peaceable civilians; in return the soldiers claimed they were being attacked by 'royalists' and 'chouans'.[52]

In deeply divided southern cities, where eight years of bitterly disputed local power had aggravated long-standing divisions of neighbourhood, clientele and class, a single act of violence could ignite a bloody conflagration. As republicans in Avignon celebrated on 12 February 1797 news of the military victory of French forces under Napoleon over the Austrian garrison at Mantua, one of them was stabbed. The next evening a republican gendarme was murdered. By 26 February the army had moved in, but the royalist neighbourhood of La Fusterie had also armed itself. It was from there that wild crowd violence was launched. Although local republicans, led by Agricol Moureau—the uncle of the boy Viala—cooperated with the army in ensuring that the ensuing bloodshed was limited, the army used the unrest as a pretext to round up hundreds of 'anarchists' and to send about fifty for trial.[53]

Most of the men who dominated politics at both the national and local level after 1795 were sincere republicans desperate to find a way of entrenching representative government and secular civic life. They had been scarred by the costs of making the Republic safe in 1794 and were determined that they would never again be terrified. So in their internal politics they repudiated both the recriminatory nostalgia of hard-line royalists and the menacing egalitarianism of Jacobins and *sans-culottes* recalling the glory days of 1793. The safest external policy was to ensure that foreign invasion could not be a way back either to the *ancien régime* or a new Terror. So the way forward seemed to be a policy mixture of peace with neighbours such as Spain and Austria, direct incorporation of the lands west of the Rhine, and the creation by Bonaparte of 'sister republics'.

As the elections of the Year V loomed in March–April 1797, the Directory passed a law requiring all electors to take an oath swearing hatred of both monarchy and anarchy. Nevertheless, only eleven of the more than 230 retiring deputies were re-elected, and about 180 of those chosen were royalists of various nuances. The change in the political temper of the Council of Five Hundred was reflected in the repeal in August of laws passed against non-juring clergy in 1792 and 1793, as well as several against *émigrés*.

In her diary Marianne Charpentier of Orléans expressed her joy at the reopening of churches at Easter 1797: 'all right-thinking people were delighted to see churches open which had been so soiled by a group of scoundrels who had committed so many ignominious acts in all the temples consecrated to God'. But she was scathing that markets continued to follow the revolutionary calendar, which she refused to use in her diary. Sometimes a market day even fell on a Sunday: 'those who follow their religion mocked this abomination'.[54] The climate of tolerance permitted refractory clergy to re-emerge in the west. Yves-Michel Marchais, the militant anti-revolutionary priest of La Chapelle-du-Genêt south-west of

Angers, had been imprisoned during the uprising in the Vendée. Marchais worked tirelessly to build an image of the rebels as devout Catholics, and now looked forward to a time when priests in exile, like the saints Athanase, Hilaire and Chrysostome, could return.[55] In dismay, an official reported of the countryside around Bayeux on 11 July 1797 that 'fanatics and bandits are stronger than the law: the trees of liberty topple in this canton and are replaced with anti-civic crowns, symbolic of the worship of a couple of old saints of the town and the work of the apostolic mob'. Two hundred people had gathered in Saint-Vigor 'to make a pilgrimage to a saint that used to work miracles'.[56]

As rumours swirled of possible army intervention led by General Lazare Hoche against the rising tide of royalist sentiment, three of the Directors—Jean-François Reubell, Paul Barras and Louis-Marie de La Révellière-Lépeaux—pushed through what amounted to a *coup d'état* with the military investiture of Paris on 17–18 Fructidor (3–4 September). On 19 Fructidor the other Directors, Lazare Carnot and François-Marie Barthélemy, were removed from the Directory; forty-nine departmental elections were annulled, 177 deputies removed, and Carnot, Jean-Charles Pichegru and sixty-three others were deported. Military commissions sentenced almost three hundred individuals to death, one-third of them nobles and clerics deemed to be actively involved in attempts to overthrow the Republic. The Directory dismissed thirty-eight generals accused of royalist sympathies, mostly with internal military commands and alleged to have failed to stem the royalist surge or indeed to have welcomed it. One report stated: 'If they were not guilty of clear involvement in the conspiracy, at the least they knew about it, and were awaiting its outcome.'[57]

The deputies and journalists who were exiled to Guiana encountered the sad remnants of the almost two hundred 'Robespierrists' who in 1794 had been sent to a colony regarded as almost uninhabitable because of tropical diseases and the violent resistance of the indigenous people. Only 54 of the 193 Jacobin exiles had survived: eleven of them had escaped, and the rest had died of diseases. One of the very few new exiles who managed to escape Guiana was the former republican general Pichegru, hero of the invasion of the Netherlands, who had thrown in his lot with royalists before Fructidor. He escaped to London, where he joined General Aleksandr Rimsky-Korsakov's campaign against France in 1799.

The Fructidor coup of September 1797 represented the end of an attempt to make moderate republicanism work. It was the key moment in the shift of emphasis of the Directory from seeking to end the Revolution by the practice of liberal constitutionalism to a resolution to end it through what may be described as 'liberal authoritarianism'. From now on the 'Second Directory' would not hesitate to pervert the constitutional process, and increasingly resorted to armed force and bureaucratic control in its confrontation with persistent counter-revolution, brigandage, tax evasion and avoidance of conscription. It immediately reimposed exile on non-juring clergy. The final sermon of Yves-Michel Marchais spoke of 'the anger of the Lord which again threatens us because we have irritated him again'. He once more refrained from active priesthood, and died the following year.[58] The law of 7 Vendémiaire (28 September) now required religious services to be held indoors.

Just a fortnight after the coup, the republican general Hoche died of consumption at Wetzlar in the Rhineland in September 1797, aged just twenty-nine. Hoche was the orphaned son of a kennel-keeper at Versailles, and had joined the army aged sixteen. A passionate democrat and Jacobin, he was a major player in the defence of Thionville in 1792, made a general in 1793 (aged twenty-five), and then was instrumental in the defeat of royalist forces in the west, notably at Quiberon, in 1794–95. He had also been chosen to play a major role in the disastrous invasion in support of the United Irishmen in December 1796. His death in 1797 may have come as something of a relief for the conservative elite of the Directory; it certainly did for a more ambitious general of the same age, Napoleon Bonaparte.

Napoleone Buonaparte and Marie-Rose ('Joséphine') de Beauharnais had risen to increasing prominence in this atmosphere of popular resentment and political instability. Both had been marginal in the finely graded aristocratic society of the *ancien régime*. She was the daughter of a noble who had mismanaged his slaves and sugar plantation in Martinique; Napoleon (as he gallicized his name) had been born to minor Corsican nobles in 1769 and, when sent to military school in France as a ten-year-old, the studious, diminutive boy smarted under his peers' taunts at his accent and name. Neither Marie-Rose nor Napoleon was particularly attractive, but both could be charming, and they were bonded by passion and a relentless ambition for power. The revolutionary wars offered Napoleon and other brilliant young soldiers the opportunity for rapid promotion unimaginable before 1789: in 1793 his role in the recapture of the port of Toulon from Britain had catapulted him from captain to brigadier-general.

In July 1793, Bonaparte had published *Le Souper de Beaucaire* in which he exclaimed: 'Marat and Robespierre! These are my saints!'[59] By the time of the Directory, however, he had sloughed off such revolutionary rhetoric and concentrated on military power. His standing had been bolstered with the ruthless repression of the royalist Vendémiaire insurrection in October 1795 and again when, late in 1796, French forces retook Corsica after its twenty-eight months as the 'Anglo-Corsican Kingdom'. Bonaparte's rise in popular repute is clear from the songs of the period, for example those performed in Le Caveau, a small gastronomic society founded in Paris in 1726 whose members contributed gently satiric 'vaudeville' songs as well as the cost of their meals. In 1796, Le Caveau recreated itself as the Dîners du Vaudeville and adopted a constitution that excluded political themes from its members' contributions. Nevertheless, many of the songs were marked by expressions of nationalism, and in 1797 one of them eulogized the young Napoleon:

> Hail to our soldiers' leader,
> Who, courageous as well as wise,
> Leads the French into combat
> Or restrains their bravery.
> Of Europe, the victor,
> And the pacifier.
> Glory to the able warrior,
> Who, not yet thirty years old,
> Joins the valour of Achilles,
> And the virtues of Nestor.[60]

For more than two years continued civil strife had been played out in violence in streets and fields as much as in local politics while the regime sought in vain to create a viable polity that would exclude radical Jacobins, *sans-culottes* and royalists. The coup of Fructidor in itself was recognition of that impotence and henceforth central governments would intervene far more readily to impose security and order. Years of being caught between the Scylla of counter-revolution and the Charybdis of Jacobin militancy convinced the 'republican centre' to shy away from both extremes down the path of republicanism without democracy. Prominent intellectuals—such as Benjamin Constant, Louis-Marie de La Révellière-Lépeaux, Pierre-Louis Roederer, Emmanuel-Joseph Sieyès and Germaine de Staël—articulated the regime's ideals of secularism and liberalism shorn of the menace of *sans-culotte* populism and redistribution of property. But this would lead the regime into measures against both evangelical clergy and army deserters that made the use of armed force necessary. Already by 1797 a type of 'liberal authoritarianism' had emerged—the 'security state'—which was vulnerable to its ultimate expression, the autocratic rule of a popular general.[61]

CHAPTER SIXTEEN

THE GREAT NATION AND ITS ENEMIES, 1797–99

THE ELEVEN VOLUMES AND SIX HUNDRED CHAPTERS OF LOUIS-Sébastien Mercier's *Tableau de Paris* (1781–88) offer unparalleled insights into the pre-revolutionary metropolis by a man who became deeply embroiled in the Revolution.[1] Mercier was a Girondin sympathizer in the National Convention, was briefly imprisoned under the Terror, and was fiercely anti-Jacobin thereafter. He was elected to the Council of Five Hundred for the department of Nord in October 1795. Mercier recognized how difficult it was to achieve stability after 1794: 'fear has played such a big part in our revolution, its arena has been so vast, that one has often attributed to politics, to ambition, to deep strategy, that which was done only to disconcert an enemy and to impress on him also fear and terror'.[2]

According to Mercier, the way to eradicate fear was to bring economic and political capacity back into alignment. If the *ancien régime* had functioned for so long, it was because the nobility who dominated every form of power—from the Church to the armed forces—were also seigneurs of the agrarian economy. The republican publicist Charles-Guillaume Théremin agreed: the folly of the Jacobins was that they had tried to impose an ancient, classical form of government on top of a modern economy:

When one wants to give a new form of government to a people, it is necessary to leave untouched their way of subsisting, that is, their system of political economy. One must establish the new form of government on this system, or at least put the two in the greatest possible harmony. ... The political system, as it was conceived during the Terror, was transmitted to us by different hands than was our system of political economy.

In other words, just as Boissy d'Anglas had said when proposing the new Constitution of 1795, there needed to be a new alignment of those who possessed economic power with those who were entrusted with political power.[3]

The Directory and its supporters across the country envisaged a path to progress between the thickets of, on the one side, *sans-culotte* and Jacobin militancy and, on the other, royalism and counter-revolution. The path would lead to a stable, harmonious land of prosperous farms and vigorous commerce, free from both the menace of egalitarianism and noble and clerical nostalgia for the good old days. They practised a cultural politics of rewarding civic virtue and enterprise, inculcating respect for social order, while avoiding Catholic renewal, for which they expressed a dismissive tolerance. The regime would be defended by a functional, professional bureaucracy and the armed forces. A new order based on standing in society would therefore be more stable and have less recourse to violence than the government of the Year II. So, for example, an official in Auch in the south-west made a speech in 1798 recalling that the guillotine had been on the central Place de la Liberté during the Terror 'to make an impression on wicked counter-revolutionaries'. But, now that 'we exist under a gentler and happier government', he hoped that any future executions could be more discreet.[4]

Across the country, prosperous landowners, now free both of Jacobin exactions and the condescension of their noble neighbours, asserted their unprecedented local authority as men of substance (Fig. 37). The consent of these local notables was pivotal to the government's hopes for a new national unity. They refused it, for example, when the Directory despatched François-Yves Besnard into the west to provide moderate, expert administration in Le Mans and its divided region in September 1797. Despite his well-to-do family background, this educated, cultured former priest, who had welcomed the Civil Constitution of the Clergy and abdicated his clerical functions in November 1793, was now rejected by the great landowners as too tarnished by his radical past. Besnard had earlier been rejected by parishioners in Saint-Laud in Anjou, who locked the bell cords high in the bell tower, dampened the candles and sewed up the sacramental garments.[5]

The men of the Directory were committed to the practical virtues of agriculture and commerce. The Jacobin government had sought to establish a regime of public finances based on a consolidated public debt, low interest rates, and stable wages and prices. The Directory, in its opposition to political controls on the economy, took a radically different path. By 1797 it had simply cancelled two-thirds of the public debt, returned to a metallic currency in an attempt to deal with hyper-inflation, and relied increasingly on indirect taxes and the spoils of war. The virtues of self-sufficient farmers were extolled by one of the regime's most eloquent spokesmen, François de Neufchâteau. On 30 Pluviôse Year V (18 February 1797), as the Directory's commissioner for the eastern department of Vosges, he wrote to a senior administrator in Paris to empathize with him on the experience of being imprisoned during the Terror. He also targeted the revolutionary calendar, which he was pleased to report had been scorned by farmers: only public servants were conversant with it and the result was economic lethargy and confusion.[6] But the Revolution had freed men of the land from feudalism, and for the Festival of Agriculture on 11 Messidor Year V (29 June), Neufchâteau composed new words for the 'Marseillaise':

> You will no longer do forced labour,
> Exhaust yourself for a seigneur.
> Your produce is no longer taken
> By an exactor, from under your eyes.
> The plough, in the eyes of France,
> Today is restored to honour,
> It assures you, and with happiness,
> True independence . . .[7]

Among the supporters of the Directory were prominent agronomists, doctors and other medical men who hoped that recognition of those best equipped to rule by virtue of their education, wealth, sex and standing could forge a way between Jacobin levelling and aristocratic exclusiveness. So, even though France was at war with England, the discovery there by Edward Jenner that cowpox vaccination sharply reduced the chances of catching the disease was enthusiastically received and propagated in France.[8] This conviction that the regime represented social and economic progress was reflected similarly in the determination to complete the massive work of establishing precise prototypes for the new uniform metric measures. The imperative of national organization and planning gave a boost to work begun in May 1790 by a Commission on Weights and Measures, including the eminent scientists Monge, Lavoisier, Laplace and Condorcet. In August 1793 the Convention had introduced a comprehensive system based on the earth's meridian and decimal measures: the metre, hectare and litre. The task of surveying exactly the meridian arc to measure metres and kilometres took years, but was eventually completed in 1799 by using two sections of straight road, near Melun and north of Perpignan (Fig. 38).[9]

The values of the men in power during the Directory were evident, too, in educational policies, where they continued the retreat from mass, publicly funded primary schooling for both girls and boys. Education for boys and parental preparedness to pay now mattered most. The revolutionary reforms to education in 1793–94 had opened up possibilities for some women to become schoolteachers. They were not as well paid as men—1,000 *livres* annually as opposed to 1,200 *livres*—and when the Directory turned to student fees as the basis of salaries after October 1795 their position became more precarious. Women were also vulnerable to the political climate. Citizeness Thomet from Vourles, south of Lyon, was lauded in the Year VII for arriving at the Festival of Youth with a large number of children behind a drummer; in contrast, two former religious, Tempié and Pradier, told the inspectors in the south-western town of Tonneins in the Year VI that 'it outraged their consciences to give the Constitution to their pupils', and had their schools closed as a result.[10]

Just as it was no longer fashionable—or wise—for parents to give their babies 'political' names after 1795, so the governing atmosphere of a return to 'normality' was evident in the preference of local authorities to rename public spaces. In November 1797 the municipal authorities of Orléans considered the twenty-four names of streets and other places that had been 'revolutionized' in April–May 1793. It made sense to them to go back to pre-revolutionary names in some cases: the Rue des Assignats again became the Rue Vieille-Monnaie and, rather surprisingly, the Rue de Voltaire again became the Rue d'Angleterre. But these authorities were still republican anti-clericals, so the Faubourg Marat now became the Faubourg Vincent (rather than the Faubourg Saint-Vincent), and the Rue de la Montagne became the Rue du Bonheur (rather than the Rue du Paradis). There was no question of the Rue Égalité resuming its name of the Rue Royale or the Rue J.-J. Rousseau again becoming the Rue de l'Évêché.[11]

Some old institutions had survived the Terror and now prospered. The Jardin du Roi, a jewel in the crown on the left bank of the Seine, far from being destroyed or sold off, became on 10 June 1793 the centre of the Muséum d'Histoire Naturelle, with claims by 1800 to be the world's finest centre of natural history.[12] The garden survives today as the Jardin des

Plantes. Even the Royal Paris Opéra, at the pinnacle of the high culture of the *ancien régime*, survived a revolution intent on eradicating every vestige of aristocratic exclusivity to become a cultural treasure. Like those responsible for the Jardin du Roi, the leaders of the Opéra managed to adapt to the values of the Revolution to reposition their great institution as an exemplar of civic and national pride.[13]

The framers of the Constitution of 1795 had hoped that by separating Church and State the deadly divisions might finally be healed: the Church could run its own affairs as long as its clergy obeyed the law. The constitutional Church now sought to establish itself as an independent Church free of state ties, under the leadership of the Abbé Grégoire and the 'united bishops'. Grégoire's particular target was married priests: despite his loyalty to the Revolution, he had always argued that the way forward for the priesthood was to return to the discipline and simplicity of the Church's origins rather than to prove patriotism by abdication and marriage. His stance proved polarizing, and he was inundated with letters variously questioning his patriotism or from priests begging absolution and annulment of their marriages.[14] The problem for the regime was that the non-juring clergy had no intention of compromising. Many of them had returned in hope after the 1797 elections, but their open opposition to the Revolution again landed them in trouble. The intransigent Abbé Nicolas-François Faligant from Rennes, for example, had spent most of the years 1792–94 in prison and, when freed in January 1795, was repeatedly arrested for his royalist activism. In January 1796 he was appointed chaplain to the 'Army of the Chouans'. The anticlerical reaction after the coup of 18 Fructidor made him a target once again as a member of the *aristo-calotinocratie* ('aristocratic and clerical fanatics'), as local republicans dubbed it, and he was arrested as 'an instigator of the murder of defenders of the homeland and of revolt against the law'. This time he would be held on the Île de Ré, off La Rochelle, for four years.[15]

Shaken by the widespread and often violent contestation of the civic authority held by local representatives of the regime, the Directory attempted in 1798 to intimidate 'disloyal' priests into hiding, but with negligible impact on a religiosity that was less general but more intense than a decade earlier. Devout women in particular found ways to rebuild a Church that had been shattered by a decade of revolution. There were huge numbers of non-juring clergy among the *émigrés* on France's borders and unnerving electoral signs that many of those eligible to vote for deputies were open to a return of monarchy. The Jacobin armies had succeeded in expelling counter-revolutionary armies from French soil, but the war—and with it the problem of the *émigrés*—continued. Ecclesiastical leaders in exile had trouble containing the punitive desires of priests in exile since 1791 or 1792 to re-enter France as soon as possible. The former Bishop of Nancy, La Fare, counselled one such in January 1798 to temper his zeal with prudence, for the former 'is a type of error which may pervert even virtue'.[16]

The commitment by the men of the Directory to hold true to the middle path between revolution and reaction always exposed them to the temptation of interfering with political choice, even that of the narrow electorate they had constructed. In Fructidor Year V their concern had been the resurgence of royalism, and scores of elections had been annulled. By the time of the elections of Floréal Year VI (April 1798), no fewer than 437 seats had to be filled. This time the lurch to the left by the electorate—seventy-one Jacobins who had voted for the death of Louis XVI in 1793 were elected—led to a purge of a different kind. A new coup by the Directors on 22 Floréal (11 May) prevented 127 Jacobin deputies from taking their seats and only forty-seven of ninety-six departments had their results left untouched. Alleged Jacobins were purged from the Ministry of War.

There was greater consistency in the Directory's foreign policy. The insistence in 1790 that the new France would never seek to impose its will on other nations jarred with the view, expressed trenchantly by Danton in March 1793, that France's 'natural borders' in the north-east were along the Rhine, and in the east and south-east the Alps. So Nice and Savoy had been annexed in 1792–93, followed by Belgium in 1795. 'Sister republics' were created, starting in the Netherlands (Batavian Republic, May 1795), and now along the left bank of the Rhine (Cisrhenian Republic, August 1797), and in Switzerland (Helvetic Republic, March 1798) (Fig. 39).[17]

The Directory had placed Bonaparte at the head of its campaign against Austria in Piedmont and Lombardy in March 1796. Over the next year his forces won a series of battles, creating sister republics, exacting huge ransoms (estimated at 46 million *livres*), and turning a blind eye to pillage. Anti-French rebellions were bloodily repressed. By late 1797 the Directory's foreign successes were reflected in a rhetoric increasingly referring to the 'Grande Nation' rather than to 'sister republics', assuming a 'civilizing' mission to take the Republic eastwards. This was a pivotal and durable shift in the relationship between revolutionary France and its neighbours.

The Treaty of Campo Formio with Austria, signed by Bonaparte on 27 Vendémiaire Year VI (18 October 1797) recognized a *fait accompli* and formally ceded to France most of Belgium, several islands in the Mediterranean, and part of Venetia. Austria recognized France's 'sister' Cisalpine Republic, centred on Milan: 'the French Republic acquired it by right of conquest. She renounces dominion over it on this day, and the Cisalpine Republic is now free and independent. . . . From a military regime, the Cisalpine people must therefore pass to a constitutional regime.' The treaty also accepted the extension of the borders of France up to the Rhine, the Nette and the Roer rivers: the Cisrhenian Republic was now simply absorbed into extended French administrative departments. Bonaparte himself intervened in political debate in Paris to oppose Carnot's wish for a compromise peace settlement with Austria rather than total surrender: the young general was now as much a political as a military player.

In Italy the hopes of emancipation and self-determination, in this case away from Austrian rule in the north and domination by aristocracies elsewhere, were to be dashed. In February 1798, General Louis-Alexandre Berthier entered Rome and proclaimed the Roman Republic: Pope Pius VI, who had been in the Vatican since 1775, would end his record reign as pontiff a virtual prisoner of the Republic in the town of Valence, on the Rhône, where he died in August 1799. Piedmont and Tuscany were simply added to areas directly occupied by France earlier (Belgium, Savoy, the Comté de Nice and the Comtat-Venaissin). The 'enlightened' urban middle classes, in particular, had looked to French invasion with great hopes, and saw in the creation of 'sister republics' the chance for progressive reform, even for Italian national unity. Religious minorities were enthusiastic. But the imposition of French institutions and the abolition of tithes and feudal dues were inadequate compensation for rural populations, in particular, whose experience was the destruction of familiar church structures and the imposition of requisitioning and conscription. Resentment was particularly acute in the south, where the Parthenopean Republic proclaimed at Naples in January 1799 was overwhelmed by the 'Christian Army of the Holy Faith' led by the Calabrian Cardinal Ruffo. The Cardinal was to be horrified by the plundering and bloodletting that his army unleashed in the city in June.[18]

The extension of the war beyond France confronted authorities with the issue of how to treat the cultural property of conquered lands. Experts were appointed to travel to Belgium and the Rhineland in 1794, Holland in 1795, the north of Italy in 1796–98, Mannheim in 1798, and Egypt in 1798–99. Arguments in favour were readily at hand: these were spoils of war, and seizure was a long-established practice, and France would in any case look after humanity's patrimony better. The fourth anniversary of Robespierre's fall, in 1798, was celebrated in part with the arrival in Paris of a massive, third convoy of cultural property from Rome and Venice.[19] Much of the plunder was more basic in intent. Captain Gilbert Favier, who had volunteered in 1791 and had returned to the army despite two years of captivity in England from 1793 to 1795, rejoiced in learning Italian and going to the theatre in occupied Brescia: on 30 Vendémiaire Year VIII (21 October 1799) he wrote to his brother, who had been incapacitated by a wound suffered near Tourcoing in May 1794, 'the theatre is very beautiful, but the actors are poor'. But he was bothered that 'among our generals and many subalterns there is so much vulgarity and brigandage that one is often embarrassed to be the companions of such individuals'.[20]

In occupied territories most of the population resented or openly opposed French rule, which quickly took the form of military occupation rather than revolutionary emancipation, and which relied on beleaguered minorities of pro-French reformers. While French law and representative institutions were established, the latter were often used as forums to contest the levies of men and money and the destruction of ancient systems of administration, religion and law.

In the Batavian Republic the institutions of the French Republic were adopted with relative acquiescence, in part because of Batavia's long indigenous democratic tradition; and, despite resentment at the exactions and limits to trade, the alternative of a return to rule by the Stadtholder William V was far more unattractive.[21] In Belgium, in contrast, direct incorporation and the application of the laws of religion—dissolution of monasteries, sales of church property, separation of Church and State— were as unpopular in rural areas as in the west of France. A rebellion in the name of 'land and religion' was brutally suppressed, with 5,600 casualties. Such was the local antipathy that only about 5,000 of the 22,000 men conscripted in 1799 presented for service. In the German-speaking Palatinate west of the Rhine, direct incorporation into the Republic in 1798 secured the Girondin dream of France's 'natural' boundaries, but there never seems to have been a social base of support for the revolutionary reforms, and the experience of the Rhineland was simply one of territorial occupation and exactions.

The French reaction to resistance to occupation was often xenophobic, in stark contrast to the universalism of the early Revolution. The administrator of the department of Forêts (Luxembourg) in 1798 described the locals as 'vile slaves ... Grovelling when they are weaker, relentless, brazen, and unbridled when they are—or believe themselves to be—the stronger .... these people will not be able to appreciate the benefits of our revolution until several generations have passed ...'.[22] The xenophobia generated through war was often the same on both sides, even if the emotional and religious patriotism was frequently more local than national: Mantuan or Catalan as opposed to Italian or Spanish. Hostile popular reactions to French occupation often took on a religious mantle, particularly in Italy, and targeted those minorities that had been given greater civic freedoms under French law. In 1799, Jewish residents in Siena were slaughtered by Catholic militants. In parts of Germany, however, Protestants united with Catholics in hostility to 'the unholy enemies of the state and religion'.[23]

Almost everywhere it seemed that, where direct French rule remained in 'sister republics', the experience was one of resentment, rejection and resistance, even in lands with deep traditions of popular sovereignty like Switzerland. Here French troops invaded in January 1798 and proclaimed a new constitution on 12 April, not just for the French-speaking Pays de Vaud but for the entire country. The assumption that representative democracy, the abolition of feudalism and unified national institutions could simply be imposed on another land was to result in hostility and rejection. Despite initial sympathy in francophone areas, the imposition of uniform revolutionary legislation on the Church and administration triggered violent resistance, particularly in German-speaking Catholic areas. Whereas the Catholic peasants of Savoy had been part of France since 1792 and had experienced the revolutionary élan of the abolition of feudalism, the Republic, and the successful defence of the Republic against the invaders, the Protestant and middle-class Genevans who became French in 1798 were fiercely independent. They had been exempted from conscription until 1803, and the experiment in imposed national unity would collapse the same year.[24]

On the peripheries of Europe, in contrast, the message of the French Revolution for those who longed for self-determination would continue to fire dreams of freedom, as it had in Poland in 1793–94, then in Ireland in 1798. In both cases, however, imperial armies would succeed in crushing revolutionary hopes.[25] Hopes of diverting English naval attention led the

Directory into engagement with Irish patriots. Sympathy for France remained strong among the United Irishmen, a clandestine organization of Protestants and Catholics founded in 1791 and united in opposition to the powers of the British government over the Irish Parliament and the dominance of the Anglican Church over both Irish Catholics and the large number of Presbyterians in the north. In 1798 there were risings against English rule, in particular in Wexford in the south-east, where a republic was proclaimed, slogans of 'Liberty, Equality, Fraternity' were painted on walls, and the revolutionary calendar was adopted. The Directory sought to take advantage of the widespread unrest in Ireland by sending a force under General Humbert in August. Over one thousand troops landed at Killala in Mayo in north-western Ireland but, after some early victories, surrendered in September. Among them was the leader of the United Irishmen, Wolfe Tone, who committed suicide before he could be executed. The killing of ninety pro-English Protestants held as hostages in Wexford ignited a fierce repression of Irish rebels. In a matter of weeks about 30,000 Irish died in punitive killings, about the same number as were executed in the year of the Terror in France, a country with six times the population.[26]

Further afield, the flame of French inspiration was more rapidly extinguished. On the Balkan Peninsula, the Greek patriot Rigas Velestinlis translated the Jacobin Constitution of 1793 into Greek in 1797 to support the movement for liberation from the Ottoman Empire. Velestinlis was subsequently arrested by Austrian police in Trieste with three boxes of a poster headed 'Liberty, Equality, Fraternity' in Greek, and was tortured and murdered in 1798 before he could come to trial.[27] Across the Atlantic, tales of the Terror led Americans to believe that, despite the extent of emigration by loyalists and of killing during the War of Independence, theirs had been the peaceful, benign and successful revolution. The abolition of slavery in the French Caribbean terrified the plantation owners of the Southern states. Attempts by the Foreign Minister Talleyrand in 1798 to construct an alliance with the United States at the price of bribes and loans—the 'XYZ Affair' (the initials referring to French negotiators)—strengthened the political backlash against France. The 1798 Alien and Sedition Act was aimed at those with lingering affection for the French Revolution.[28]

Conflict with Britain continued and, while peace with Austria had been signed at Campo Formio in October 1797, hostilities recommenced in Italy. By September 1798 the French army had more than halved in size to about 327,000 from its peak of 732,000 four years earlier; this convinced the

Directory that irregular army levies had to be replaced by an annual conscription of single men, through the Jourdan Law of 19 Fructidor Year VI (5 September 1798). The law, making all young men aged twenty to twenty-five eligible to be conscripted by ballot for up to five years, sharply intensified the resentment of compulsory military service that had been latent or open since 1793, because it increased the numbers of healthy young men removed from the pool of household labour to fight on foreign soil in wars of territorial expansion. The resentment was the more acute because the law introduced a system of 'replacements' whereby wealthy conscripts could buy a substitute from the poor or unemployed who had missed the ballot, contradicting the principle of universality.[29] The saddle-maker from Chinon, Claude Bailly, recorded in his diary in 1798 that military conscription 'is very hard for the young men and for fathers and mothers who need their children. That has plunged us into a great sadness.' Their departure 'causes a lot of tears when it is time to quit family and friends'. His town was divided, with 'patriots' guarding the liberty tree day and night in case counter-revolutionary 'chouans' tried to cut it down as they had in nearby towns.[30]

Resistance to conscription was particularly common in regions far from the capital where the presence of the royal, then revolutionary, administrations had been weakest, and where there was a strong sense of local linguistic and religious identity (such as parts of Brittany and the west, the Pyrenees, and parts of the Massif Central). The beleaguered local authorities of the Directory became mired in endemic conflict with those refusing the demands of the state just as they were in occupied territories across the borders.[31]

In Brittany in particular, *chouannerie*, a potent mix of royalism, religion and banditry, proved to be almost ineradicable. It was fuelled by anger over the reinstatement of the rights of large landowners renting farms to *colons* under the long-term restrictive leases of *domaine congéable*. In Lower Brittany peasants had responded to government hesitation on their status much as peasants elsewhere had responded to that on the final abolition of feudal dues. But whereas the latter was finally settled by laws in 1792–93, in Brittany the issue of compensation for landowners dragged on until the law of 9 Brumaire Year VI (30 October 1797), which reinstated the rights of owners as in 1791, and offered them compensation for the rents the *colons* had refused to pay.[32] The hostility of tenant-farmers was now further entrenched.

In areas far from Paris, *insoumission* (refusal of conscripts to join the army) became endemic, often with the tacit approval of most of the community: *insoumis* continued to live and work as before, disappearing only when police appeared. Young men also sought to avoid conscription by self-mutilation or by arranged marriages. In rural areas, where officials and the dwindling number of supporters of the regime were likely to be involved in agriculture, the use of personal threats, arson and other destruction of their property could intimidate them into inaction. By 1798 parts of the west, Massif Central and Pyrenees were virtually ungovernable.

The endemic protest of these years involved both males and females, and in many areas linked resentment at the absence of the rituals and personnel of religion in community life with hostility towards conscription. Almost everywhere, attempts to control patterns of bell-ringing continued to be challenged. In Montier-en-l'Isle, in the Champagne region, the bell was rung for four hours in the afternoon of All Saints' Day, 'in an altogether brazen, insolent, and scandalous fashion'.[33] On 7 Brumaire Year VII (28 October 1798) twenty-five girls employed in a spinning-works at the hospice of La Rochelle refused to work because it was a Sunday. The same year forty-four people, mostly women aged between fifteen and seventy-five, were arrested after an illegal mass said by a *sabot* seller, Baptiste Chain. Others protested by avoiding conscription or encouraging others to do so. A poster in the town in 1798 warned:

> Conscripts, if you leave you are cowards. Can you accept that your mothers and fathers have their arms snatched away by you enrolling for the field of glory, to fight for whom? For men thirsty for your blood and your bones. These are the men you are off to fight for. Yes, join together, but let that be to exterminate a government which is odious to all European powers, even the most barbarous.[34]

But most young men did not evade conscription or desert, and many made a career from the army. Louis Godeau, a schoolteacher from the Loire valley, may have lost his fervent republican zeal of the Year II, but living on the run was hardly attractive. The regime steadily became more zealous and effective in tracking down and punishing deserters, evaders and their families. In October 1799, Godeau responded to family entreaties to him to desert: 'each letter that you write to me breaks my heart,' he admitted, but did they want him to flee like other men he knew? 'As soon as they return home, they are continually harassed and forced to hide in the forests.'[35]

Many others felt like the peasants west of Paris, of whom an administrator reported early in 1799 that they

> are not in the least partisans of royalty, the memory of tithes and rents being odious to them. They are quite happy that their harvests should have doubled since the extinction of game rights, they recognize and greatly value the possession of equality. Many of them have bought national lands and all have improved their position.

But, he added perceptively, that was further away than the memory of upheaval and sacrifice: the armies' victories were being bought with their sons' blood and the constant call to exercise their civic rights had left the peasants jaded.[36]

The politics of the Directory had made many people deeply cynical. Now Bonaparte's string of victories in Italy and the hope that the Treaty of Campo Formio presaged a general peace created a frenzy of adulation. To celebrate the victories in Italy and the treaty, the municipal administration of Orléans erected a pyramid in Bonaparte's honour at a festival on 25 Pluviôse VI (13 February 1798). A priest composed a quatrain to be placed at its foot:

> There he is, this heroic lover of the homeland,
> His valour has broken Italy's chains.
> The god of combat, the new thunder of warfare
> He is ripping the seas from England's control.

Young royalists from the richest families of the city had taken to wearing their powdered hair in long tresses as a symbol of support for Bonaparte.[37] Far from Orléans, in the small centre of Aurillac in the southern Massif Central, the hero of Campo Formio was again celebrated in song:

> Oh, you magnanimous warrior
> Wise, humane Buonaparte . . .
> Receive the homage
> Of a triumphant people![38]

In Paris, in contrast, a police agent reported on 14 November 1798 that as one of the Directors, Paul Barras, passed along the Rue Charenton in his carriage, men and women muttered 'Look at that thief there. He would happily drive over us ...'.[39]

Through the Treaty of Campo Formio, France had gained seven formerly Venetian-ruled islands west of Albania and Greece and now treated them as integral to France. Bonaparte announced that 'the Turkish Empire is collapsing day by day, and possessing these islands will allow us to support it as much as that is possible, or to take our proper share'. He insisted that the islanders looked to the *grande nation* to restore 'the science, the arts, and the commerce they have lost under the tyranny of oligarchs'.[40] Most importantly, with the peace of Campo Formio, the war effort could now be devoted to England.

British naval power in the Channel and the Atlantic was too great for the Directory to contemplate challenging, but the Foreign Minister Talleyrand in particular had the idea that a strong presence in Egypt and an alliance with the Muslim ruler of Mysore, Tipu Sultan, would threaten British trade routes to India, even its entire colonial presence there. Bonaparte's ploy to seize the Suez isthmus and control the overland route to India was warmly welcomed. On 19 May 1798 an army of 35,000 men left from Toulon, financed in part from forced levies from the sister republics.

Bonaparte was just the man for the job, fascinated as he also was by Egyptian civilization. He warned his troops to have the same respect for Muslims as for Jews in France, and his proclamation to the Muslim inhabitants of Alexandria articulated a potent ideology of revolutionary zeal, military crusade and social order. Although the invasion was essentially designed to combat British influence, Bonaparte contrived in his proclamation to the people of Egypt to present it as a civilizing mission, both to bring revolutionary emancipation and to restore legitimate authority:

> People of Egypt, you will be told that I have come to destroy your religion; it is a lie, ... I have come to restore your rights. ... Tell them that all men are equal before God; wisdom, talent and virtue are the only differences between men .... from this day on, no Egyptian will be prevented from acceding to an eminent post: the wisest, the most educated, and the most virtuous will govern, and the people will be happy ...

But a subsequent clause was a salutary reminder of the costs of resisting his mission: 'Any village that takes up arms against the army will be burnt to the ground.'[41]

Egypt was then one of seven provinces in a sprawling, unwieldy Ottoman Empire, itself in a state of flux and upheaval. While French revolutionary ideas had had a resonance in Egypt and to some extent in Palestine, assumptions that, for example, Copts and Melkites as Christian minorities would have a natural affinity with revolutionary principles dissolved in a morass of cultural and political misunderstandings. Napoleonic requirements that local office-holders wear tricolour sashes and cockades were received as symbolizing submission. The aggressive behaviour of tens of thousands of French troops outraged local sensibilities.[42]

The expedition was never serious about its respect for religious freedom. In the disarmingly frank words of one of Bonaparte's most loyal generals, Dominique-Martin Dupuy, the Jacobin son of a baker from Toulouse who had risen through the ranks since volunteering in 1792:

> We are celebrating enthusiastically here the Mohammedan festivals; we are deceiving all the Egyptians by our simulated attachment to their religion, in which Bonaparte and we do not believe any more than the defunct one of Pius. However, whatever anyone says, this land will become priceless for France and, before this ignorant people awakes from its stupour, all colonists will have the time to do their business. We are replacing the scoundrels who leave the people nothing but their shirts, and the imposition of uniform taxation will change things greatly.

There was violent insurrection in Cairo in October, in which Dupuy lost his life, aged thirty-one.[43] In the end, most Egyptians were alienated from the French occupiers and, temporarily, turned back towards an Ottoman Empire from which they had been seeking autonomy.

In early August 1798, just two months after his arrival, the British navy almost obliterated Bonaparte's entire fleet near Alexandria. The ignominious defeat could hardly convince local Muslims, Copts and Melkites of the power of the *grande nation*, especially when imposed republican festivals were resented as hostile to local traditions. Bonaparte was reduced to manoeuvring between rival factions in Egypt and present-day Syria and to imposing order: revolts in Cairo and Jaffa in particular were bloodily repressed. The failure of Napoleon's invasion was compounded by repercussions well beyond Egypt: fears of a resurgence of French competition in India should Egypt remain in French hands caused Britain to launch a successful invasion of Mysore, killing the kingdom's ruler and French ally, Tipu Sultan.[44]

In an atmosphere of political division in France, and military defeat and bubbling rebellion in Egypt, Bonaparte abandoned his troops. He had no orders to return or to leave his army. But, on 24 August 1799, taking advantage of a temporary British naval absence, he set sail for France, leaving his army under the command of General Jean-Baptiste Kléber. On 8 October, Napoleon landed in the south of France.[45]

On his arrival in Paris, Napoleon visited Jacques-Louis David as he was completing a vast (13 x 18 feet) classical painting of the Sabine women intervening in 750 BC to end civil conflict in republican Rome, an allegory of David's despair at the endemic political strife threatening the survival of the Revolution. The painter was awed by the brilliant general, despite his failure in Egypt, as much as Napoleon was impressed by the power of David's brush. Was Napoleon the man who could unite or suppress the factions and take the banner of the Revolution to new glories?[46] David and Napoleon had another connection. While a member of the Committee of General Security, David had signed the arrest warrant for Alexandre de Beauharnais, whose widow Joséphine had then married the restlessly ambitious young general.

Bonaparte had arrived at a chaotic but propitious moment for a general adept at propaganda and with a reputation for military heroism and ruthless repression of rebellion. His return coincided with a renewed eruption of *chouannerie* in the west, in response to extended anticlerical measures by resurgent Jacobins in the Council of Five Hundred. By October 1799 some 10,000 rebels were armed: Le Mans was occupied and sacked, and the city of Rennes menaced. There were also large-scale but uncoordinated royalist— or at least anti-republican—risings in the south-west around Toulouse, hitherto a bulwark of the Revolution unlike other major southern cities. Now liberty trees were felled, purchasers of *biens nationaux* had their heads shaved, tax-offices were destroyed, and *ancien régime* institutions were reintroduced. But having failed to enter Toulouse on 5 August, the army of some 5,000 retreated south towards the Pyrenees. They took the small town of Carbonne, where they killed sixty-eight republicans, but were caught at Montréjeau, near Saint-Gaudens, on 18 August and up to 2,000 were killed. Thousands more were taken prisoner or fled to their villages or to Spain.[47] Bonaparte's presence in Paris was now seen by some as an augury of domestic order.

Underpinning the hopes invested in Bonaparte was also the hope of economic recovery through an end to eight years of war, inflation and trade blockades. Despite a good harvest in 1798, the French economy was in tatters: Strasbourg's department had only 146 master-weavers operating compared with 1,800 in 1790, while the western Pyrenees had only 1,200 people employed in the woollens industry compared with 6,000 at the start of the decade. Once again the narrow electorate turned against the government. The elections of April 1799 returned few royalists, but only 66 of 187 endorsed or 'official' candidates were elected, and the turnout was the lowest of any election; instead most candidates were moderate republicans and one-quarter of them new to the legislature. On 30 Prairial Year VII (18 June 1799), for the third consecutive election, a coup was mounted, this time by an uneasy coalition of Jacobins, generals and others disaffected with the regime, purging the Directors and appointing the Jacobin lawyer Louis-Jérome Gohier, the Jacobin general Jean-François Moulin, the Abbé Sieyès and his ally Roger Ducos. Only Barras survived among the Directors.[48]

Events outside France further strengthened Bonaparte's appeal. Following the Treaty of Campo Formio in October 1797, the Congress of Rastadt had been convened in Baden between France, the Holy Roman Empire and ninety German states to consider compensation for the princes along the left bank of the Rhine. As the Congress concluded in April 1799, the murder of two of the French envoys triggered a new war against French expansion through a Second European Coalition. The window was further opened to the attractions of military rule by a brief turnaround in the fortunes of the army: in September 1799 an Anglo-Russian army was pushed out of Batavia, as were Russians and Austrians from Switzerland. For Sieyès, this was the moment when advantage might be taken to reform the structure of the Directory through military intervention.

In his attempt to seize power Bonaparte was supported by his brother Lucien, aged just twenty-four, then president of the Council of Five Hundred, Sieyès and Talleyrand, two of the architects of revolutionary change in 1789–91, and Joseph Fouché, a former priest from the Vendée turned 'dechristianizer' in 1793, infamous for his role in the repression of Lyon. There was nothing certain about their manoeuvre. Bonaparte's dramatic entry with troops into the Council was a gamble that almost failed: he was on the point of nervous collapse when his brother intervened with troops to overcome resistance. On 19 Brumaire Year VIII (10 November 1799) the furious members of the Five Hundred were driven out by troops and a decade of parliamentary rule was over.

Among those for whom Bonaparte's seizure of power was intolerable were the Lindet brothers: Thomas, former constitutional Bishop of Eure and a member of the Council of Elders from 1795 to 1798; and his younger brother Robert, former member of the Committee of Public Safety in 1793–94. Robert Lindet had opposed many Robespierrist policies, but also the Thermidorian Reaction, and defended Barère, Billaud-Varenne and Collot d'Herbois from the accusations made against them in March 1795. Robert was acquitted of the charge of supporting Gracchus Babeuf in 1796, and was then elected to the Council of Five Hundred (by the departments of Eure and Seine), but was not allowed to occupy his seat. Robert had been appointed Minister of Finance in June 1799, just months before the coup. Another who was outraged was Louis-Sébastien Mercier, a member of the Council of Five Hundred, who later recalled a visit of Bonaparte to the Institut National on 15 Nivôse Year VI (4 January 1798). Mercier enthused about the 'conqueror of Italy': 'all republicans should model themselves on Bonaparte and, since they admire in him both the wise man and the warrior, they should also imitate his self-control and reserve'. Mercier's recollection was not published until several weeks after the *coup d'état* of Brumaire, and by then his admiration for the republican general had been shattered by the latter's seizure of power.[49]

On 24 Frimaire (15 December 1799), Bonaparte, Sieyès and Ducos identified themselves as the three Consuls, directly appealing to the resonance of the title of the highest elected officials in classical Rome. They announced that a new constitution would terminate uncertainty while being based on 'the sacred rights of property, equality, and liberty':

> The powers that it institutes will be strong and stable, as they must be in order to guarantee the rights of citizens and the interests of the State. Citizens, the Revolution is established upon the principles that began it: it is ended.[50]

The First Consul Bonaparte had just turned thirty years of age. The pronouncement was made more in hope than in confidence: many provincial Jacobins shared the deputies' outrage that an elected, republican legislature had been dispersed by the army. In the plebiscite of Nivôse (December 1799–January 1800) on the Constitution of the Year VIII, Bonaparte's younger brother Lucien felt it shrewd to double the 'yes' votes from 1.6 million to more than 3 million; only 1,562 were alleged to have voted 'no'. The Constitution placed power effectively in the hands of the three Consuls: now a Legislative Assembly of three hundred was to vote on legislation without discussion. A Tribunate of a hundred members was to discuss legislation but not vote.

On 28 Pluviôse Year VIII (16 February 1800), just three months after seizing power, Napoleon issued an administrative decree that sharply reduced the powers of local government to just the management of communal finances. The mayors of towns with more than 5,000 people were to be directly appointed by the First Consul, while all others were to be named by Bonaparte's departmental 'prefects'. Prefects had similar powers to the pre-revolutionary *intendants*, and local councils, elected for twenty years on a property qualification, were less democratic and unfettered than they had been since 1789. The court system, already made less accessible in 1795 by being concentrated in the 98 department rather than 547 district capitals, was made more hierarchical under Bonaparte, both in terms of the gravity of procedural tone and in the more formal layout of courtrooms. What did not change, however, was the fundamental assumption of the supposedly impartial application of a uniform set of laws by a professionalized college of magistrates. But these judges were to be appointed, not elected.[51]

The years of the Directory, 1795–99, had been characterized by the increasingly unstable rule of a narrow elite of propertied conservatives who shunned popular participation in politics and embarked on territorial expansion, opening the way for a possible military dictatorship. The Directory was chronically unstable not only because of the narrow base of its politics and the absence of a more powerful *raison d'être* than that of a stake in society; the regime also found it impossible to articulate a convincing and conclusive rationale for its foreign policy. Was it trying to create a continental commercial empire to rival that of England's maritime sphere? Or was its objective to create sister republics that would eventually transform the continent into a republican federation under French tutelage? Or was it just trying to find a way to create a durable balance of power? At various times all three aims were articulated, but the twin objectives of social order at home and victories abroad inevitably made attractive the idea of a strong ruler surmounting parliamentary squabbles.

The regime of the Directory was not doomed to fail; nor were its achievements negligible. These years were an integral part of a revolutionary decade that further embedded the assumptions of popular sovereignty and citizenship, however curtailed, and new property relationships and markets became embedded in the countryside, a 'commercial republicanism'. At the same time the regime slowly became more proficient in dealing with deserters, crime and political insurrection, establishing the bases for a 'new security state'.[52] Paradoxically, however, the men of the Directory, by choosing territorial expansion over social welfare and democracy at home, created a new bureaucratic and military professionalism that Napoleon was to use to replace them after his *coup d'état* of 1799.

Napoleon's standing as the First Consul was reinforced at the Battle of Marengo, near Alessandria in Piedmont, on 14 June 1800, when his army drove Austrian forces from Italy. He was able to contrive to paint this as the decisive victory, rather than that of his rival general Jean-Victor Moreau at Hohenlinden, near Munich, on 3 December that year, a victory that effectively ended the war with Austria. The Treaty of Lunéville was signed with Austria on 21 Pluviôse Year IX (9 February 1801) and that of Amiens with Britain on 5 Germinal Year X (25 March 1802). The end (albeit temporary) of war offered the chance for deserters to be amnestied, and for returning *émigrés* and priests to be reintegrated into their communities in a climate of reconciliation. The calm of the summer of 1802 created the perfect conditions for the plebiscite on the new Constitution of the Year X (1802), by which Napoleon became Consul for life.

Bonaparte had staged a military coup against a republic that had promoted him to general. Within a few years, however, he had moved to address major sources of instability and disaffection. Foremost among them were the tens of thousands of *émigrés*, particularly priests, on France's borders. A decree of 29 Vendémiaire Year IX (20 October 1800) permitted *émigrés* who had not taken up arms to return; then, on 6 Floréal Year X (26 April 1802) the path was opened to all other exiles. With them came most of the non-juring priests, convinced of the foolishness of the First Estate's rallying to secular reform in 1789 and of the burning need, after ten years of divine retribution, for a purified Catholicism to rechristianize France. Napoleon would allow that in the interests of social order, but was dismissive of hopes to recreate a past of tithes, monopoly of public worship and intolerance. On 15 July 1801 a Concordat was signed with the papacy, and on Easter Sunday 1802 the bells of Notre-Dame rang out to celebrate it. This was the signal for unchecked bell-ringing across the Republic, wherever bells still existed. The dissidents to the Convention's war on the aural senses had won, and administrators and bishops were asked to agree on a suitable use of bells in future.[53]

When the diarist Marianne Charpentier of Orléans closed her account in 1804 of 'only what she had seen with her own eyes' since 1788, she was sure that later generations would know that 'their ancestors had suffered during the revolution of that century' and hoped that 'God would show the grace to allow you to pass through theirs more easily'. The Concordat was her great comfort, and she blessed Napoleon for having brought peace to the Church and, after so many victories, peace to France. So, too, did the wine-barrel maker Billard of Saint-Denis, just across the Loire, who noted with pleasure that 'on 3 January 1803, for the first time since the Terror, mass was celebrated on the great altar' of Sainte-Croix cathedral in Orléans. A few months later, thirty-nine boys and twenty-four girls took their first communion in his own parish church of Saint-Denis.[54]

Several times during the revolutionary decade those in power had insisted that the Revolution, having achieved its objectives, was finished: when Louis XVI gave his assent to the key revolutionary legislation in October 1789; when he swore to uphold the Constitution in September 1791; when the Robespierrists were overthrown in July 1794; and when the National Convention implemented the Constitution of the Year III in October 1795. Each time these proved vain hopes as the new status quo proved incapable of preserving itself from the pressures of those for whom the Revolution had yet to meet their needs or those for whom its very existence was intolerable. Now at last Bonaparte had both the broader support and the military power to secure his rule.

The Revolution was over. So too was a decade of fear: of privation, violence and insecurity. Instead of the 'man of virtue' as the embodiment of the highest ideals of the Revolution—civic integrity, personal sacrifice, modesty—Napoleon would offer the 'man of glory'. The strong man also promised peace, freedom and stability, but his dreams of imperial grandeur would cost French people far more than had the securing of their Revolution.

CHAPTER SEVENTEEN

THE SIGNIFICANCE OF THE FRENCH REVOLUTION

IN 1787, HENRIETTE-LUCY DILLON, AGED SEVENTEEN, MARRIED Frédéric, Comte de Gouvernet and later Marquis de La Tour du Pin, an army officer from an eminent and wealthy family. Her liberal-minded father-in-law was Minister for War in 1789–90, but his support for Louis XVI and Marie-Antoinette during their trials would cost him his life, along with his brother, on 28 April 1794. Lucy's own father, General Arthur Dillon, was executed a fortnight earlier, accused of involvement in a 'prison plot'; another army officer relative, Théobald Dillon, had been killed on 29 April 1792 by his own troops, who blamed him for their defeat near Lille. Lucy and her husband fled south to their vast estates at Saint-André-de-Cubzac, on the River Dordogne north of Bordeaux, then emigrated to Boston in 1794. Reflecting in later life on the impact of the Revolution, she focused primarily on the Decree on Feudalism of 4–11 August 1789, which 'ruined my father-in-law, and our family fortunes never recovered from the effect of that night's session. It was a veritable orgy of iniquities.' With the loss of exactions from four other estates, she estimated that the annual income of her husband's family had fallen from 80,000 to 22,000 *francs*.[1]

Lucy and her family were able to return to France under the Directory, and Frédéric would have a distinguished career under both Napoleon and the restored monarchy after 1814. But the France in which they lived in the early nineteenth century was in many ways a radically different land from the one they had fled. Not only had the seigneurial system, the basis of their wealth and social power, been abolished, but assumptions about legitimate political power and the social order, even about family life, had been questioned or overturned.

France would again be a monarchy, first under the restored Bourbons between 1814 and 1830, then under their liberal cousin, Louis-Philippe, and the July Monarchy from 1830 to 1848. But the power and image of monarchy had changed forever. Even when France was on its knees after Napoleon's defeat at the Battle of Waterloo in 1815, Louis XVIII and his advisers knew that the price they had to pay for his return to the throne was acceptance of the central elements of revolutionary change. Despite the hopes of militant royalists—'legitimists', as they came to be called—the restored monarchy in 1815 could not reverse the revolutionary change from royal absolutism to constitutional, representative government. The person of the king had now lost its mystique, evident for example at coronations, when sufferers of scrofula traditionally came forward to be cured of the 'king's evil' by the royal touch. In 1774, 2,400 scrofula sufferers had come forward to be healed by Louis XVI; in 1825 only 121 approached his youngest brother Charles X. The king's touch had lost its potency.[2]

The experience of years of political debate, election campaigns and the exercising of new political rights meant that assumptions of citizenship and popular sovereignty were now deeply ingrained, even if new regimes curtailed their practice. This burgeoning sense of citizenship had been expressed by a decade of participation in elections and political societies, by word of mouth, through the printed word and imagery, and through theatre and song, what may be described as a revolution in 'political culture'.[3]

With that of the early American Republic, the electoral system of revolutionary France, although limited by sex and property, marks the beginning of the history of modern representative democracy. By 1790 an estimated 1.2 million elective public offices had been created, including local councillors, justices of the peace and officers in the National Guard. During the revolutionary decade to 1799, twenty sets of local and national elections and three plebiscites were conducted. In a population of 28 million people, no fewer than 4.3 million men (about 60 per cent of adult males) were enfranchised in 1791 and about 6 million in 1793. In comparison, the English electorate was 17 per cent of adult men in the 1790s and only reached the 1791 levels of France with the Third Reform Act in 1884.

The conundrum of this initial decade of electoral democracy is that participation in elections was remarkably uneven. Across the revolutionary decade, the average levels of participation were only about 20–25 per cent, and in Paris itself only 15 per cent. A key reason for this was that the laborious system of voting for assemblies often required attendance for several days. Nor were there political parties and candidate lists around which to mobilize the voters: indeed, direct persuasion was seen as tantamount to factional interest and not in the interests of the 'general will'.

It was only in 1848 that huge majorities of eligible voters went to the polls in France's next democratic elections: the beginning of mass electoral participation. But the revolutionary decade after 1789 proved to be the beginnings of democratic 'apprenticeship', when unprecedented numbers of people came to assume that public office drew its legitimacy and dignity from the remarkable act of voting rather than the centuries-old practice of appointment. This was the central element of the revolution in political culture at the heart of the French Revolution.

The seismic shift from subject to citizen occurred in various ways and voting was only one of them. Far more common in actuality than the potent images of violent mobs were peaceful demonstrations, petitions, banquets and mass meetings. In Paris only 12 per cent of an estimated 750 protests by sans-culottes resulted in physical violence.[4] There was also mass direct involvement through membership of political clubs. Again, participation varied across the regions. In the south-east as many as one commune in three had a political club during the Revolution; in the department of Yonne in Burgundy only 55 of 408 (one in eight) had one.[5]

Those in government who had taken the initiative in creating the new France after 1789 had been bourgeois men, whether in the professions, bureaucracy, commerce, landowning or manufacturing. With the great noble landed proprietors, they were the new ruling class in the early nineteenth century, the 'notables' at the pinnacle of economic, social and political power. For all the vicissitudes of the revolutionary decade, the Revolution was their triumph. Except for the radical years 1792–95, the electoral process ensured that formal political power was in the hands of men of substantial property. Those who were eligible to actually choose deputies at the final stage of elections—men of greater substance and position—were the new 'political class', whose participation and office continued into the Napoleonic period and beyond, unless they made rash political choices.[6]

After Napoleon encouraged émigrés to return from exile, large landholders, including ancien régime nobles, would hold disproportionate power until the 1880s. But gone were the days of aristocratic dominance and seigneurial appointment of village councils. For the abolition of seigneurialism underpinned a revolutionary change in rural social relations, voiced in political behaviour after 1789. The social authority many nobles retained in their rural communities after 1799 was now based on their direct economic power rather than on traditional claims to deference due to a superior order of society.

The years of revolution and empire also intensified the administrative unity of France. The centralizing impulse went back at least to Jean-Baptiste Colbert and Louis XIV in the seventeenth century, but it was dramatically strengthened by the Revolution and then by Napoleon. The central bureaucracy, with fewer than seven hundred employees before the Revolution, was 6,000 strong by 1793 and would grow ceaselessly, both in the professionalism of the 'bureau' and in numbers. The resonance of 'national unity' was central to the ideal of 'fraternity'. The assumption of the August 1789 Decree on Feudalism and the Declaration of the Rights of Man and Citizen was that all citizens, whatever their social background and residence, were to be judged according to a single uniform legal code, and administered, taxed and regulated in the same way. For the first time the state was also understood as representing a more emotional entity, 'the nation', based on citizenship. Mixed with other young citizens within French national armies, young men were exposed to the language of France, *patrie* and nation. Just as 'patriot' was a political term of pride (or denigration), so 'patriotism' pointed to the virtues of membership of the *patrie* or nation rather than the *pays* or region. The French Revolution was the seedbed of modern nationalism, a classic example of the concept of 'imagined community' as the basis of national identity.[7]

It was a community that made extraordinary demands of its members, most obviously in the decades of war that followed the Brissotins' decision to confront Austria and Prussia in 1792. Perhaps as many as 1 per cent of French people died in the great crisis of 1793–94: up to 200,000 in the Vendée and other parts of the west; at least 40,000 people were executed after trials, and perhaps 50,000 died in the external wars. The civil and foreign wars of 1792–1802 cost perhaps as many as 455,000 lives of republican soldiers: 75,000 killed in combat, 180,000 who died in hospital, and up to 200,000 simply unaccounted for.[8] Under the Napoleonic Empire as much as 4–5 per cent of the population of France and occupied Europe were killed.

The wars accentuated the need for precise statistics of resources, and markers of identity and borders; the modern passport was born in the swirl of anxiety following Louis' attempt to flee in June 1791.[9] The revolutionary wars were the first mass mobilization for ideological as much as territorial ends. Combined with the battlefield flexibility of mixed columns, the revolutionary élan gave the armies a major advantage in the sacrifices conscripts could be expected to make.[10] The experience of 'the Revolution armed' would reinforce the importance of national spirit for the Prussian general Carl von Clausewitz:

> In 1793 such a force as no one had any conception of made its appearance. War had again suddenly become an affair of the people, and that of a people numbering thirty millions, every one of whom regarded himself as a citizen of the State. . . . The element of War, freed from all conventional restrictions, broke loose, with all its natural force . . . this participation arose partly from the effects of the French Revolution on the internal affairs of countries, partly from the threatening attitude of the French towards all Nations.[11]

The Revolution strengthened the meritocratic identification of potential officers, in the period of crisis in 1792–94 in particular. By 1793, 70 per cent of officers were commoners. Without the Revolution, soldiers like Michel Ney, Joachim Murat and Lazare Hoche—not to mention the mulatto Alexandre Dumas—would have had no chance to rise in the ranks to the highest levels.[12] So a powerful military legacy was the fusion of army, nation and republic, which would create a potent sense of the people in arms on which republicans would continue to draw in the wars of the twentieth century. Technological innovation would later turn the people's warfare of 1792–94 into industrial-scale killing in the First World War.[13]

The ideology of 'unity' assumed that all individuals were now first and foremost French citizens, members of the new nation. The Revolution represented an abrupt change in cultural and institutional structures of identity, achieved at the expense of privileged social orders, occupations and localities. France in 1789 was a society in which people's main allegiance had been to their particular region: France had a unity only because of the monarchy's claim that this was its territory and the people its subjects. Most people did not use the French language in daily life and looked to elites in provincial capitals such as Toulouse, Rennes and Grenoble to defend them against the increasing claims of the royal state for taxes and conscripts. On the eve of the Revolution, every aspect of the institutions of public life was still marked by a patchwork of regional exceptions and privileges. Not only were the clergy, nobility and certain corporate bodies such as guilds privileged in law and taxation, but the provinces also had their own law codes, degrees of self-government, levels of taxation, and systems of weights and measures, even currency.

In the period 1789–91 revolutionaries reshaped every aspect of institutional and public life according to principles of rationality, uniformity and efficiency. Underpinning these sweeping, durable reforms was an administrative system of departments, districts, cantons and communes. These eighty-three departments (today ninety-six) were henceforth to be administered in precisely the same way; they were to have an identical structure of responsibilities, personnel and powers. Diocesan boundaries coincided with departmental limits, and cathedrals were usually located in departmental capitals. The uniformity of administrative structures was reflected, too, in the imposition of a national system of weights, measures and currency based on new, decimal measures. This amounted to a profound change across the country. For example, in the southern region of the Corbières, just thirty miles by forty, there had been ten different volumes for which the term *setier* was used (usually about eighty-five litres), and no fewer than fifty different measures of area.[14]

Since the Ordinance of Villers-Cotterêts in 1539, French rulers had sought to make their language that of public administration; after 1789, the French language was assumed to be intrinsic to citizenship, even to be at the core of the Revolution itself.[15] From early in the Revolution political elites expressed the view that French was the language of liberty and equality. The national language bore the name of its nation. On 10 September 1791, Talleyrand expressed his surprise to the National Assembly that

> the national language ... remains inaccessible to such a large number of inhabitants. ... Elementary education will put an end to this strange inequality. In school all will be taught in the language of the Constitution and the Law and this mass of corrupt dialects, these last vestiges of feudalism, will be forced to disappear.[16]

During the great crisis of 1793–94, such attitudes became more punitive. Although himself from the Gascon-speaking Pyrenees, Bertrand Barère inveighed to the Convention on 8 Pluviôse Year II (27 January 1794) against the 'ignorance and fanaticism' of 'people who are badly instructed or who speak a different idiom from that of public education'.[17] A few months later, on 16 Prairial (4 June), the Abbé Gregoire was far more informed in listing thirty dialects and languages spoken by six million citizens, but equally stringent in proposing that a single updated grammar and vocabulary be imposed to teach all children 'the language of liberty'. 'What does it matter that Arabic has three hundred words for snake or horse?' he asked; French would be the language of civic sentiment.[18]

The claim that French was the 'language of liberty' and that minority languages were part of the archaic *ancien régime* which had been overthrown was wide of the mark: popular attitudes to the Revolution among the ethnic minorities who together made up a majority of the population varied from enthusiasm to outright hostility across time and place. Certainly, however, the Revolution had a profound impact on collective identity, on the *francisation* ('Frenchification') of the citizens of a new society, both because of participation in elections and referenda within a national context and because, in the years of revolutionary wars, millions of young men were conscripted to fight for the *patrie*, the safety of the Revolution and the Republic. Members of ethnic minorities came to perceive themselves as citizens of the French nation as well as Bretons, Catalans or Basques. But this new 'double identity' was limited to an acceptance of national institutions and the vocabulary of a new, French politics. French remained the daily language of a minority of people and France a land of great cultural and linguistic diversity. This tension between national unity and regional diversity has been another durable consequence of the Revolution.

Women's participation was a central dimension of the revolutionary decade across the political spectrum. Despite the energetic campaigns of individual feminists in the early years of the Revolution, the intervention of working women in collective action in Paris, and their presence in clubs and societies, however, the great majority of politicians of whatever political persuasion were firmly opposed to women's political rights (Fig. 24). Politicians ranging from royalists to Napoleon would have agreed with the Jacobin Amar, of the Committee of General Security, who justified the banning of the Enragé women's organization, the Revolutionary Republican Citizenesses, to the Convention on 30 October 1793 by describing men as

> strong, robust, born with great energy, audacity and courage . . . destined for agriculture, commerce, navigation, travel, war . . . he alone seems suited for serious, deep thought. . . . Women are unsuited for advanced thinking and serious reflection . . . more exposed to error and an exultation which would be disastrous in public life.[19]

The educated middle-class men who filled the seats of successive assemblies shared an education in the classics from which epic tales of masculine civic virtues resonated with relevance for their own lives. Despite—or rather, because of—the political challenge of radical women, the transition from absolutism—under which all were subjects of the king—to a republican fraternity of male citizens had reinforced the subordinate political position of women. In the process a political ideology of gender articulated the idea of 'household suffrage', where male heads of household were seen to be expressing the will of the family.[20]

Nevertheless, the repudiation of the most fundamental sources of authority in the *ancien régime* inevitably called into question the position of women within the family and society (Fig. 40). A number of pieces of legislation were designed to regenerate family life, deemed to have been hitherto cruel and immoral, like the *ancien régime* itself. Family courts were instituted to deal with family conflict, the age of majority was reduced from twenty-five to twenty-one, and penalties for wife-beating were introduced that were twice as heavy as for assaulting a man. It is doubtful, however, whether patterns of male violence changed, despite the exhortations of revolutionary legislators to a peaceful, harmonious family life as the basis of the new political order.

What did change was the legal position of women through the 1792 divorce law. Nationally, perhaps 30,000 divorces were decreed under this legislation, especially in towns: in Paris there were nearly 6,000 in 1793–95. In Rouen, for example, 71 per cent of divorce proceedings were initiated by women, 72 per cent of them textile workers with some economic independence, unlike most rural women. For every eight marriages in Rouen, one divorce was decreed and an equal number were resolved by family mediation. The divorce law challenged domestic relationships at a fundamental level. The law was sharply curtailed in 1804 by Napoleon: henceforth a wife could only sue for divorce if her husband's mistress was brought into the marital home, whereas the simple act of a wife's adultery sufficed for a husband to sue, and the adulterous woman was liable to imprisonment for up to two years. The law was finally abolished altogether in 1816.[21]

More durable was the impact of the abolition of the right of primogeniture in laws of 15 March 1790 and 8 April 1791. Then, in a law on inheritance passed by the National Convention on 7 March 1793, this principle was extended to all wills, requiring all children to inherit equally, extended later in the year to children born outside wedlock. After 1790 the rights of daughters became a family issue, just as the divorce law temporarily empowered wives—this was the most significant shift in the status of women in these years. In Normandy its impact was explosive and women took legal action for redress. One complained to the court in 1795: 'I was married in 1773 "for a bouquet of roses", to use the Norman expression. That was how girls were married then. Greed was in the air and one often sacrificed the daughters for the happiness of one son.' Forty women from Falaise in Normandy petitioned in 1795 that 'from birth nature gave us equal rights to the succession of our fathers'.[22]

For Basque, Occitan and Catalan peasants in the Pyrenees, in contrast, the principle of equal inheritance undermined the central element of the continuity of the extended family and its home (the *exte, ostal* or *mas*). In these areas parents sought ways to sidestep revolutionary legislation, but its principles were a permanent challenge.[23] The effects of the new inheritance law and the abolition of seigneurialism may well have meant that women were both better nourished and in a stronger position within the family, even if the inferior political status of women had, if anything, been consolidated. On 4 Germinal Year VIII (25 March 1800) a law was passed introducing a 'disposable portion' that a parent might leave to a favoured child in order to increase the inheritance. The new regime's sympathy for the rights of fathers and of private property as the basis of the social order was enshrined in Napoleon's Civil Code of March 1804, which also ended the claims of children born outside marriage: henceforth they were entered in birth registers as 'born of an unknown father' and without rights to initiate claims of paternity. However, no subsequent regime would tamper with the principle of equal inheritance.

There was no more dramatic social impact than for the slaves of the Caribbean. The Declaration of the Rights of Man and Citizen and the revolutionary wars had opened up a breach in the ideological certainties behind the Code Noir, which had legitimized the endemic violence of plantation society. Once 'free men of colour' were admitted to citizenship in 1791, then the core principle—that Africans were inherently capable of practising active participation in the polity—had been admitted. The 465,000 slaves of Saint-Domingue—most of France's 700,000 slaves—had won their freedom in 1794. After Napoleon announced the reimposition of the Code Noir and slavery in 1802, they then defended it at a terrible cost in lives before the new nation of Haiti was born in 1804. As many as 100,000 of the colony's total population of 530,000 had died violently by then; almost all the 30,000 whites were dead or had fled.[24] But the experience was mixed for other slave colonies: slavery was never abolished in the Indian Ocean colonies—Réunion, the Seychelles, the Île Maurice—and was either never abolished or was reimposed in Guadeloupe, Martinique and Guiana. On Réunion the Directory's agents were chased from the island by angry planters, and the army subsequently proved unwilling to impose the 1794 law of emancipation in the face of a united front of planters and mulattoes. By 1810 slave numbers had passed 65,000, double what they had been before the Revolution.[25] Nevertheless, the great majority of slaves had won their freedom, even if the slave trade would not be abolished until 1818.

The Revolution and protracted wars had a crippling effect on the economy of coastal cities, while providing a stimulus for other branches of industry.[26] In particular, the uncertainties caused by wars and blockades and the abolition of slavery in 1794 hit overseas trade hard. Between 1790 and 1806 the downturn in trade caused the population of Bordeaux to fall from 110,000 to 92,000. That of Marseille declined from 120,000 to 99,000; that of Nantes from about 90,000 to 77,000. By 1815, French external trade was only half its 1789 volume and did not regain pre-revolutionary levels until 1830.[27] Hinterlands suffered, too. East of Bordeaux the small town of Tonneins had had 1,000 rope-makers for shipping in 1789: there were just 200 in 1800. In other inland cities the effects were not always as dramatic, and it is estimated that industrial output was still about 60 per cent of its 1789 levels a decade later. The cotton, iron and coal industries were stimulated by France's protection from British imports. Certain branches of the textile industry fared well: Bédarieux and Lodève were two small southern textile towns that survived and at times prospered through army contracts, despite the loss of trade with the Middle East.[28]

Most urban work continued to be done in small workplaces, where master craftsmen worked side by side with three or four skilled workers and apprentices. Many decades would pass before a substantial minority of wage-earners were employed in large, mechanized workshops of the type starting to become common in the new industrial cities in the north of England. But from 1789 there was a series of institutional, legal and social changes creating the environment within which capitalist industry and agriculture would later thrive.[29] The free enterprise and free trade (*laissez-faire, laissez-passer*) legislation of the Revolution guaranteed that manufacturers, farmers and merchants could commit themselves to the market economy secure in the knowledge that they could trade without the imped-iments of internal customs and tolls, differing systems of measurement, and a multitude of law codes. Even though the Bonapartist state would deepen the long tradition of state 'dirigisme', or intervention in the economy, the abolition of guilds and workers' associations in 1791 on the one hand and the introduction of internal free trade and uniform economic regulations on the other would create far more fertile terrain for business than the thickets of privilege, preferment and exemption of the *ancien régime*.[30]

Towns and cities that had been centres of ecclesiastical and noble power under the *ancien régime* had endured a decade of turbulent adjustment to the new realities. In Paris the Revolution had a direct impact on the urban landscape. There were now thirty-three rather than fifty parishes and more than two hundred religious houses had been closed. Huge tracts of church property had been sold. While there were still 400 priests in 1796, in the 1760s there had been 3,000, in addition to more than 4,000 members of religious orders. That was one reason why the population of the capital declined from about 650,000 to fewer than 550,000 in 1801. But some new opportunities were created as well: there were 223 printing works in 1799, compared with thirty-six before 1799, the result of hundreds of new news-papers and the labours of the assemblies and their bureaucracies. Paris entered the nineteenth century a more secular and fluid yet more sharply divided city than before: the new markers of hierarchies of wealth, profes-sion and gender were clearer and sharper than within the old maze of status and privilege.[31]

Urban working people had sacrificed most for the Revolution and gained least. The *sans-culottes* of Paris in particular had been the backbone of the Revolution, but they won few tangible benefits. A major grievance of Parisians in 1789, the taxes (*octroi*) levied on consumption goods brought into the city, had been reintroduced in 1798 and customs houses ringing other cities and towns were re-erected. The position of employers was strengthened by the Le Chapelier law and by the reintroduction under Napoleon of the *livret*, an *ancien régime* practice requiring workers to carry a booklet detailing their employment record and conduct. Memories of 1792–94 were to be cold comfort for dashed expectations of real social change. It would be the grandsons of the urban and rural working people of the Revolution who would finally achieve the suffrage in 1848; it would be their great-grandchildren who would win the right to strike in 1864 and to form unions twenty years later, along with guarantees of free and secular education. By then, repeated republican electoral victories in 1876 and 1877 had finally consolidated the democratic republic as the preferred form of regime of most people. The 'Marseillaise' became the national anthem in 1879, and 14 July the national day in 1880. But not until the twentieth century would the Jacobin commitment to social welfare be accepted as a state responsibility; and the voices of the women who campaigned for political rights in 1793 were but a faint echo when female suffrage was at last introduced in 1944.

The Constitution of 1793 had been the first to codify public responsibilities for social welfare and education, but it had never been put into effect. The destitute continued to constitute a major urban and rural underclass swollen in times of crisis by poorer labourers and workers. In 1791 the National Assembly had removed the church's capacity to dispense charity when it abolished the tithe and sold off church property. The realization by the Assembly that local government could not provide adequate poor relief generated a series of work schemes and temporary relief measures that were always piecemeal and never adequately financed by governments preoccupied with war. The hungry years after 1794, when the collapse of economic regulation coincided with harvest failure and inflation, exposed the poor to shortages against which the charity of parish clergy with fewer resources could never be adequate protection.

The Catholic Church never again had the material resources to minister to the needs of the poor even in the limited way it had before 1789. For the Revolution was a watershed in rural–urban relations. In many ways the towns that were centres of *ancien régime* institutions had been parasitic on the countryside. In provincial centres such as Arras, Angers and Toulouse the revenue from feudal dues and tithes was expended by cathedral chapters, religious orders and resident nobles on the employment of domestic servants, purchases from skilled trades, especially in luxury goods, and in provision of charity. As a direct result of the Revolution, the countryside largely freed itself from such exactions from towns, leaving marketing of produce and administration as the remaining links. This caused the impoverishment of those formerly dependent for employment on clerical and noble elites, and made the lot of the urban destitute quite desperate. In the countryside around Angers, for example, the Benedictine abbey of Ronceray had formerly owned five manors, twelve barns and wine-presses, six mills and forty-six farms, bringing into the town 27,000 *livres* annually. Some of it employed lawyers in the fifty-three courts and tribunals who were charged with ensuring that the countryside met its obligations; the rest supported servants, artisans and the poor. All this property was sold during the Revolution.[32]

While most nobles were pragmatic enough to withdraw from public life and accept, however grudgingly, the institutional changes of the Revolution, their losses too were massive. An estimate is that, in real terms, an average provincial noble family's annual income fell from 8,000 to 5,200 francs. While many noble families survived with their lands intact, some 12,500— one-half of all families—lost some land, and a few virtually all.[33] The final abolition of feudal dues in 1793 implied that nobles' income from property would henceforth be based on rents charged to tenants and sharecroppers or on direct exploitation of noble holdings by farm managers employing labourers. Whereas 5 per cent at most of noble wealth were taken by state taxes before 1789, thereafter the uniform land tax was levied at approximately 16 per cent of the land's annual value. Efficient use of landed resources rather than control over persons was now the basis of rural wealth. Moreover, nothing could compensate for the loss of judicial rights and power—ranging from seigneurial courts to the *parlements*—or the incalculable loss of prestige and deference generated by the practice of legal equality. The *émigré* noble returned to a transformed world, of litigation by creditors and peasants, the collapse of mystique, and the exigencies of running an estate as a business.

Like the Directory, Bonaparte sought to base the social order on the solid foundation of 'men of granite', local notables with a stake in society. But their dominance was not accepted dutifully. As the prefect of Aisne in the north-east wrote to him in 1811, 'the principles subversive of all public order which were popular during the Revolution cannot be easily erased'. Similarly, during a protracted battle with the mayor Urbain de Fleury, who had inherited the noble properties at Rennes-les-Bains, south of Carcassonne, locals petitioned the prefect that they regarded him simply as the mayor and 'not their former seigneur armed with feudal power, the arbitrary dispenser of the product of their sweat'.[34]

This collapse of deference infuriated old elites, but nobles remained at the pinnacle of landholding, and landholding remained the major source of wealth. France in 1799 was still a sharply inegalitarian, hierarchical society, one in which most *ancien régime* nobles continued to be eminent. There were about 25,000 noble families in France: from these, almost 14,000 male nobles over twelve years of age had emigrated. In all, 1,158 noble men and women were executed during the Terror, about 10 per cent of adult nobles. Virtually every noble family was directly affected by emigration, imprisonment or death. But the majority sat out the Revolution, albeit in fear and resentment, choosing to keep their estates at the price of sacrificing fiscal and seigneurial privileges and status. Those nobles who steered clear of political trouble and kept their lands intact during the Revolution could continue to play a leading economic and political role into the nineteenth century. Across half of the country a majority of the wealthiest landowners surveyed in 1802 were nobles, and they dominated the wealthiest areas, such as the Paris basin, the valley of the Rhône, Burgundy, Picardy and Normandy.[35] Despite these continuities, however, the source of economic power, social eminence and political legitimacy had changed radically. The wealthy survivors of the landholding elite of the *ancien régime* were now only part of a far broader elite that included all of the wealthy, whatever their social background, and embraced notables in agriculture, business and administration.

France remained essentially a rural society dominated by small farm units on which households used ancient methods and techniques to produce mainly for their own survival. There are contrary examples, particularly in northern France, of the ways in which land sales facilitated capitalist agriculture, based on large-scale ownership or renting of land and the employment of labour. But, across much of the country, subsistence agriculture would persist well into the nineteenth century. With few exceptions agricultural production remained at similar levels in 1800 or 1820 as in 1780. Farming techniques were unchanged by the Revolution, and the household basis of rural production would dominate French rural society for many decades to come.

Decisions taken by successive assemblies, under massive peasant pressure in 1792–93, to finally abolish compensation due to seigneurs for the end of feudal dues and to make *émigré* land available in small plots at low rates of repayment, encouraged peasant owners to stay on the land.[36] The 1791 and 1793 partible inheritance laws ensured that farms would be constantly threatened by subdivision (*morcellement*). But those peasants who owned their own land were the direct and substantial beneficiaries of losses by the nobility and the Church, for their land was now free of seigneurial charges and tithes.[37] The amount of these exactions had varied enormously across the kingdom, but a total weight of 20–25 per cent of the produce of peasant proprietors (not to mention the *corvée*, seigneurial monopolies and irregular payments) was common outside the west of France. As the observant English agronomist Arthur Young commented at the start of 1792, 'small proprietors, who farm their own lands, are in a very improved and easy situation.'[38]

The extent and social incidence of land sales were significant in most areas. About 8.5 per cent of all land changed hands as a result of the expropriation of the Church (about 6.5 per cent) and *émigrés*. Church land in particular was usually of prime quality, sold in large lots by auction, and purchased by urban and rural bourgeois—and more than a few nobles— with the capital to thereby expand pre-existing holdings. Provincial towns dominated by the former privileged orders saw massive sales: 49 per cent of Toulouse changed hands.[39] The sale of *émigré* property benefited the peasantry more, since it was subdivided into small lots and could be paid off in instalments. Overall, peasants bought up perhaps 1.5 million hectares of nationalized land: by 1800 the sum of peasant holdings had increased from perhaps one-third to two-fifths of the total. In all, there were up to 700,000 purchasers: about one family in six bought some land.[40]

Whilst it is difficult to generalize about the impact of the Revolution on standards of living, the inflation aggravated by the decision to deal with state indebtedness by the printing of *assignats* made the decade of revolution a time of chronic difficulty for wage-earners. Nevertheless, the purchasing power of wages from 1790 to 1810 increased between 10 and 20 per cent.[41] One class of people who certainly were significantly better off were the elite of farmers—*laboureurs* and *fermiers*—who in the hyper-inflation under the Directory were able to buy up *émigré* land, pay off their rents or loans in *assignats*, and sell their produce for hard currency.

The improvements in the peasants' standard of living were attested to by Charles-Joseph Trouvé, a highly intelligent young man from an artisan family, who in 1803 became Baron Trouvé, Napoleon's chief administrator of the southern department of Aude:

> The suppression of feudal dues and the tithe, the high price of food-
> stuffs, the division of the large estates, the sale in small lots of national-
> ized lands, the ending of indebtedness by [the inflation in the value of]
> paper currency, gave a great impulse to the industry of the peasantry. . . .
> Although the Revolution had an impact on the diet of the people of the
> countryside, this impact was even more marked on clothing. . . . In the
> old days, rough woollen cloth, or homespun linen, was their finest

apparel; they disdain that today, cotton and velveteen cloth are the fabrics they desire, and the large landholder is often confused with his sharecroppers because of the simplicity of his clothing.[42]

The English Quaker and farmer Morris Birkbeck agreed with Trouvé in his *Notes on a Journey through France*, from Dieppe to the Pyrenees, including Trouvé's department, in 1814:

> Everyone assures me that agriculture has been improving rapidly for the last twenty-five years ... and that vast improvement has taken place in the condition and character of the common people.... I ask for the wretched peasantry of whom I have heard and read so much; but I am always referred to the revolution: it seems they vanished then.[43]

The abolition of the seigneurial system was the single most significant social change brought by the Revolution. With the abolition of dues, peasants retained an extra portion of their output that was often directly consumed by a better-fed population. There were direct physical consequences: in 1792 only one in seven of the army recruits from the impoverished mountain village of Pont-de-Montvert (Lozère) had been the requisite 1.63 metres (5´4˝) or taller; by 1830 that was the average height of conscripts.[44] Elsewhere, in areas close to cities or good transport, the retention of a greater share of produce increased the safety margin for middling and larger peasant landholders, and facilitated contemplating the risks of market specialization.[45] This was particularly the case in parts of Normandy and Languedoc. In the countryside around Bayeux, the heavy, damp soils were quickly converted to cattle-raising once the Church ceased exacting a fixed tithe in grain. On the lowlands of Languedoc, in contrast, peasants started extending their vineyards into fields formerly used for growing grain to pay tithes and dues. Wine-growers were producing one-third more wine by 1812 compared with the years before the Revolution.[46] In the words of the farmer David Nicolas from near Béziers in May 1799, farmers 'have embraced changes and innovations which may be fruitful for them. They have abandoned the routine practices of our grandfathers.'[47]

Some of this wine-growing was on uncultivated land belonging to the commune as commons or to former seigneurs. Previously used for grazing livestock, these 'wastelands' or *vacants* were placed under extreme pressure as the rural poor cleared them for cultivation. The revolutionary years exacerbated long-term stresses on the environment: by 1801 perhaps one-quarter of France's forests had been felled illegally, and in many regions vast areas of commons had been cleared for agriculture.[48] Only the Napoleonic regime succeeded in re-establishing a centralized forests policy along similar lines to that of Colbert in 1669, a reversal of the liberalism of the early years of the Revolution, when owners of private forests had been explicitly authorized to use their resources as they wished. Forests belonging to communes were placed under the same controls as state forests.[49]

In contrast, tenants and sharecroppers experienced limited material improvements from the Revolution. In regions like the Vannetais in Lower Brittany the failure to reform the long-term leases of *domaine congéable* in favour of tenants soon soured the countryside against the Revolution.[50] Like every other group in the rural community, however, tenants and share-croppers had been affected by seigneurial *banalités* (monopolies of mills, ovens, wine- and oil-presses) and, with rural labourers, had been those most vulnerable to the often arbitrary justice of the seigneur's court. Its replacement by a system of elected justices of the peace was one of the most valued innovations of the revolutionary period, providing villagers and towns-people with a way of resolving minor grievances that was prompt, cheap, less partial, and accessible.[51]

For virtually all the 140,000 priests, monks and nuns the revolutionary decade was a turbulent, terrifying and, for many, a tragic experience. Among the 3,000 violent clerical deaths in these years were at least 920 clergy who were publicly executed as counter-revolutionaries. The Church had also lost its extensive property, privileges, and—because of its role in the emigration, counter-revolution and wars—much of its authority and prestige. There were bitter internal divisions between those who had lived through the storms of civil strife to sustain parish life and those now returning with a zeal to rechristianize and punish. One of the targets was the courageous constitutional priest Michel Moulland, who had been imprisoned briefly after refusing to resign his calling during the Terror, but sustained a church presence in Bayeux through the 1790s only to be despatched after the Concordat to a small parish church in the shadow of the imposing château of Balleroy; from there he wrote self-justifying pleas to his bishop for the next twenty-five years.[52]

As many priests refused to accept the 1790 reforms to the Church, thousands of villages found themselves without a priest and church education. Once war was declared in 1792, the support given by the Pope to the counter-revolutionary armies made the Church an object of suspicion, even hatred, for revolutionaries. The Catholic Church was devastated during the height of the war in 1793–94. Probably 30,000–40,000 (up to 25 per cent) of all clergy had emigrated. The number of resignations was nearly the same as that of the constitutional clergy, leaving some regions almost devoid of priests; indeed, many thousands of parishes had no priest for up to a decade after 1791. It would be decades before the Church recovered its pre-revolutionary presence, and there were never again quite so many priests. By 1850 there was one priest for every 750 people; before 1789 there had been one for every 480.

But the laity—especially women—had proved their religious commitment in large areas of the countryside; from women, too, would come a widening stream of recruits to religious orders in the nineteenth century: 15,000 in 1815 and 66,000 in 1850.[53] Like revolutionaries before and since, Jacobins were to find that the attempt to forge a new, revolutionary culture, which would replace the religious dimensions of the *ancien régime* as surely as the Republic had replaced the monarchy, would founder on popular attachment to the rituals of belief. Despite the richness of revolutionary culture, it could not replace a Catholicism that seemed to many people deeper in substance and promise. This was to be a key cause of the violence of the revolutionary decade.

For Protestants and Jews the legislation of 1789–91 represented legal emancipation, civil equality and the freedom to worship. Protestant towns and villages rejoiced in being able to construct their 'temples'. Emancipation guaranteed that most Protestants and Jews supported the Revolution even if, during the Terror, temples and synagogues were closed. The Empire imposed close state control on Jewish communities: some of them would regret that the price of emancipation had been pressure to assimilate by subordinating their religious identity into a wider Frenchness. When from 1831 rabbis were now paid by the state like priests and pastors, Jewish leaders in Nancy felt that the price of citizenship had been the dissolution of the solidarity of the faithful, and just a few wealthy households in the city were now maintaining the synagogue and hospital.[54]

The nature of the marriage ceremony—as of baptism and burial—also changed. Now the mayor entered these rites in a 'civic register', with the priest performing only an optional blessing if indeed a priest was available at all. Religious strictures against marriage in Advent, Lent, on Fridays and Sundays were often ignored. Never again could the Catholic Church claim pre-revolutionary levels of obedience or acceptance among its flock. Consequently, most priests were to become implacably opposed to republicanism and secularism. Nor was the Church ever to regain its old monopoly of morality; for example, Napoleon continued the revolutionary abolition of laws against homosexuality, even though police continued to harass homosexuals using other charges, such as 'outraging moral decency'.

The decline in the social authority of the Church was reflected in a decline in the birth rate from 38.8 per thousand in 1789 to 32.9 in 1804; the average interval between births increased from 19–30 months to 31–48 months, a further indication of the deliberate limitation of family size. This was a phenomenon unique in Europe, directly linked to the consequences of the Revolution in the countryside: land sales, fiscal equity, the removal of seigneurial dues and the tithe, higher wages for agricultural labourers and greater incentives to increase production. Above all, it was the response of the peasantry to the Revolution's inheritance laws requiring children to inherit equally. Given the desire and need to keep small family holdings intact, rural people responded by deliberately limiting family size, usually by coïtus interruptus.[55]

Despite the losses in war and the sharp decline in the birth rate, it is estimated that the population increased by about 2.5 million by 1814 compared with 1789, the result above all of a decline in the mortality rate and an increase in life expectancy from the 1780s to the 1820s: for women from 28.1 to 39.3 years and for men from 27.5 to 38.3 years. The single most important reason for such a dramatic increase was that most of the peasantry were better fed now that much more of what they produced remained with the household to consume.

Except in places where the rural economy had changed abruptly, for example, to more market-oriented wine-growing, or where a branch of urban work had collapsed, most people worked in 1799 as they had in 1789. The nature of their work—manual, skilled, repetitive—remained the same.[56] Even in areas where land use continued unchanged, however, the Revolution had gone to the heart of community and family life. The practices of daily life were changed forever, as were the markers in the mental universe that gave meanings to people about who they were and how the world might be. The Revolution was profoundly transformative. It represented the end of an ancient political and social system based on hierarchical appointment, corporate privilege, exemptions and preferment, and the 'rights' of seigneurs over communities and their land. The Revolution was a triumph for most rural landowners, and for sections of the urban middle classes, with important consequences for the economy, the environment and even family relationships. Sweeping changes to institutional structures and to a national system of laws and measurement underpinned a decisive transition in individual and regional identities.

The Revolution's political legacy was innovative and profound but also unstable and contested. French people would always be divided about which political system was best able to reconcile authority, liberty and equality. Should the head of government be a king, an emperor or an elected executive? Should 'liberty' mean simply political and civic freedoms or a free-enterprise economy as well? And how was 'equality' to be understood: as equality before the law, of political rights, of social status, of economic well-being, of the races, of the sexes? Such questions were at the heart of the political and social divisions during the Revolution; they remain unresolved today.

The Revolution left a legacy of multiple and conflicting memories to both inspire and terrify.[57] For radicals, the violent divisions after 1790 had been caused by the tenacity of the old power-holders and the rigidity of the new social elite determined to entrench the power of property. For many political liberals, the rule of a strong man had been made necessary by the depravity of the 'mob' and its Jacobin sponsors. For conservatives, like Joseph de Maistre, François-René de Chateaubriand and the Abbé Bonald, the revolutionary upheaval and its Napoleonic sequel were incontrovertible demonstration of the folly of meddling with the wisdom of custom in the name of reason and equality. For some, the suffering of so many was the punishment of an angry God.

The most powerful image has always been the legacy of 1789 and the Declaration of the Rights of Man and Citizen, seen to exemplify the highest aspirations for a society based on popular sovereignty, freedom of expression and opportunity, and respect for the rights of others. The surge of 'the nation in arms' called to defend its Revolution in 1792 has formed part of that narrative. At times of national crisis, most notably in 1914 and 1940, those most determined to resist invasion looked to '1792' for inspiration. In August 1914, for example, the most potent historical reference points in the call to arms were to the *patrie en danger* of 1792 and the victorious battles of Valmy and Jemappes.[58]

The contrary, second image is that of 1789 as unnecessary popular excess that degenerated into destructive, bloody civil war. This image has been one of loss: of tradition, of respect for religion and authority, and of the rich tapestry of provincial institutions and cultures. Blame for the fall has been variously attributed to the irresponsible claims of the Enlightenment, to demagoguery and the 'mob'. So in 1797 a Toulouse royalist wrote a tract on the 'true causes' of the Revolution: 'a puerile curiosity for all the fables and rhapsodies that it pleased the philosopher-jugglers to yield up' to a credulous people, bringing down the wrath of God in the form of the 'cannibals' and 'butchers' of the Terror.[59] Among those who still feel a resentful nostalgia for 'the world we have lost' or others who, for example, have never fully accepted the place of Protestants and Jews in public life, the image of the Revolution has been thoroughly negative.

The gulf in popular imagery between these positive and negative images of the Revolution of 1789 has been narrowed by common acceptance of a third image, that of a Revolution which degenerated into intolerance, civil war and arbitrary punishment. Across the political spectrum it has been easiest to explain 'the Terror' as the result of ideological obsessions and the brutality of the ruling Jacobins. Above all it has been convenient to see Maximilien Robespierre as responsible for all that is regrettable, despite the evidence to the contrary. Inside and outside France the trope of 'Robespierre's Terror' remains the most convenient way of explaining the uncomfortable details of repression in 1793–94. The 'Incorruptible', as his admirers called him, is still today the least esteemed figure in French history.

Those with a wider perspective knew that there was far more to the revolutionary upheaval than the vices and virtues of individuals, even when their own families had borne the full force of the punitive violence. One of them was Alexis de Tocqueville, born in 1805 into a family and social milieu deeply scarred by the Revolution. His parents, Hervé, Comte de Tocqueville, formerly an officer of the Constitutional Guard of Louis XVI, and Louise Madeleine Le Peletier de Rosanbo, had married in 1793; the following year they barely escaped the guillotine. Louise's grandfather Malesherbes (Louis XVI's minister and defence lawyer) and both her parents were condemned to death, as were her elder sister and her husband, a brother of Chateaubriand, who had emigrated to North America in 1791 and later became one of the most celebrated royalist romantic writers and politicians of post-revolutionary France. In 1831, aged twenty-six, Tocqueville was commissioned with Gustave de Beaumont by the July Monarchy to study the penitentiary system of the United States, and his *Democracy in America*, finally published in 1835, was a reflection on the age of revolutions as much as an incisive study of the history and culture of the new Republic. In his conclusion, he reflected:

> The world that is rising into existence is still half encumbered by the remains of the world that is waning into decay; and amid the vast perplexity of human affairs none can say how much of ancient institutions and former customs will remain or how much will completely disappear. . . . The nations of our time cannot prevent the conditions of men from becoming equal, but it depends upon themselves whether the principle of equality is to lead them to servitude or freedom, to knowledge or barbarism, to prosperity or wretchedness.[60]

Under the July Monarchy (1830–48) and Second Republic (1848–51), Tocqueville personally sought to embed the practices of constitutional government in French political life, as a parliamentary deputy and minister, before abandoning public life after Bonaparte's nephew Louis Napoléon seized power with the army in December 1851. Tocqueville then devoted himself to writing *The Old Régime and the Revolution*, a historical masterpiece published in 1856. In it he advanced the thesis that in broad terms the Revolution had continued the centralizing and modernizing impulses of the French monarchy since Louis XIV. The violence of the revolutionary changes had also shattered the ancient social order, exposing class distinctions and conflicts more sharply than ever before in the world in which he now lived.[61]

These dramatic and contrasting images have always made the Revolution fertile ground for creative works, from prose and poetry to paintings and film.[62] Two of Balzac's novels, *Les Chouans* (1829) and *Les Paysans* (written in the 1840s), were among the first to capture the potency of memory. The latter, which Balzac claimed to be his most important work, featured old Niseron, 'strong as iron, pure as gold':

> Bent by toil, with pallid face and silvery hair, the old vinedresser, now the sole representative of civic virtue in the community, had been, during the Revolution, president of the Jacobin Club at Ville-aux-Fayes, and a juror in the revolutionary tribunal of the district . . .'[63]

Another novel was inspired by the story of the brilliant black general Thomas-Alexandre Dumas, who had been Bonaparte's commander of cavalry in Egypt and who decided to follow his leader back to France in March 1799. His unseaworthy ship *La Belle Maltaise* had to make landfall in Taranto, Italy, where Dumas spent twenty months interned by the Kingdom of Naples. Earlier, when fighting on the north-eastern frontier in 1792, Dumas had married the daughter of the innkeeper with whom he was billeted in Villers-Cotterêts. Their son Alexandre, born in 1802, would turn his father's twenty months of internment into fourteen years of imprisonment in one of the best-selling novels of the nineteenth century, *The Count of Monte Cristo*.[64]

The decade of political upheaval and division left potent memories, both bitter and sweet, and a legacy of conflicting ideologies that has lasted until our own times. The Revolution was a rich seedbed of ideologies on a spectrum ranging from militant royalism through liberal constitutionalism and social democracy to the first articulation of communism. One of the most potent of the ideologies would be a myth, that of the 'saviour', the strong man who could stand above petty squabbles and deliver social order, prosperity and national glory.[65] The memory of Napoleon Bonaparte would cast a long shadow of the strong man who had restored order and stability but at the cost of military rule and almost continuous war. The period of Jacobin rule remained attractive in hindsight for its emphasis on democracy and social equality and its heroic defence of the Revolution in 1792–94, but it also conjured up negative images of the Terror and controls on civil liberties. On the other hand, attempts to establish constitutional monarchy based on a property suffrage in 1815–48 would fail in part because it could claim the legitimacy neither of the absolutist Bourbon tradition nor of republican democracy.

There were many 'French Revolutions', depending on a person's social background, sex, place of residence and, above all, their individual decisions. Some prominent lives ended sadly: the constitutional bishop Thomas Lindet would try to return to a quiet life in his home town of Bernay in Normandy in 1799, but his apostasy in 1792 then marriage in 1793 would not be forgiven and he would be denied a full Christian burial in 1823. Other lives were tragic: the Protestant textile manufacturer André Guizot of Nîmes welcomed the Revolution, but his active role in federalism cost him his life aged thirty, leaving behind a devastated, brilliant little boy aged six years, named François. This child would become France's first Protestant Prime Minister in 1840–48.[66] Unlike Lindet or Guizot, of course, there were many adroit men who managed to accommodate themselves to every change of regime.

Every individual had a tale to tell, not just the well-known. The impact of the Revolution was felt at every level, in social interactions and family relations as much as in political and economic life. The goals of the revolutionaries in 1789—popular sovereignty, constitutional government, equality before the law, an end to corporate privilege and seigneurialism—had been achieved, but at an enormous cost of life and disruption. No one in the heady days of 1789–90 could have anticipated that the price of 'regeneration' and national unity would be religious schism and civil war, invasion and mass conscription, economic dislocation and cycles of retribution.

Every family and community had its narratives of the Revolution. Mass conscription of young men—as well as emigration, civil war and violent repression in some regions—meant that every family had been touched directly by the Revolution, often to the extent of the premature death of a family member. Experiences of the decade of Revolution were consequently etched deep into the memories of individuals, families and communities. In areas of the south with significant Protestant populations the deadly political divisions of 1793–95 had often followed denominational lines, leaving a legacy of hatred which henceforth ensured that Protestants would support left-wing, secular political parties. A century later a Protestant rural labourer, Jean Fontane from Anduze (department of Gard), recalled that 'if a majority of us were republicans, it was in memory of our beautiful Revolution of 1793, of which our fathers had inculcated the principles which still survive in our hearts. Above all, we were children of the Revolution.'[67]

In contrast, such had been the extent of killing in the Vendée, Brittany and parts of the south that apologists for the *ancien régime* have ever since been able to present the Revolution as the war of the Enlightenment and freemasonry on Christianity, monarchy and feudal traditions supposedly beloved of peasants.[68] The many local 'patriots' are dismissed as collaborators in cultural and religious destruction. In the Vendéan village of Chanzeaux, for example, the church built in the nineteenth century on the ruins of the old one burned in 1794 features stained-glass windows added in 1955 listing the names of the dead of 1793 and visual images which teach villagers that the rising was one of devout peasants defending beloved priests and nobles. The discovery of masses of bones in Les Lucs-sur-Boulogne by the parish priest in 1860 was to result in another myth, still potent today, of the 'Bethlehem of the Vendée', according to which 564 women, 107 children and many men were massacred on a single day, on 28 February 1794.[69] More than two hundred years later, the insurrection remains the central element in the collective identity of the people of the west of France (Fig. 41). Indeed, in 2013, the Front National and other right-wing deputies signed a petition calling on the National Assembly to recognize the repression of the Vendée uprising as 'genocide'.[70]

Despite low levels of electoral participation, there were already signs in the elections under the Republic in the period 1792–99 of the broad regional traditions that were to be a continuity in political life until the 1980s: a conservative north, an anti-republican west, a republican centre and south-west, and a divided south-east.[71] When the grandsons of the revolutionary generation were able to express their political preferences in France's first elections by direct and universal manhood suffrage under the Second Republic in April 1848 and May 1849, one of the crucial determinants in their choice between republicans and parties of Order would be the political attitudes they had absorbed 'with their mother's milk'. In the elections of 1849 the anti-republican Party of Order won 144 of the 148 seats in Brittany and the west, in part by consistently feeding fears that a vote for republicans threatened a return to the Terror. In regions of the centre and south, in contrast, left 'démocrate-socialiste' candidates were often successful; here, memories of the Revolution were often positive.[72]

Ultimately, the changes wrought by the Revolution endured because they addressed some of the deepest grievances of the bourgeoisie and peasantry in their *cahiers de doléances* of 1789: popular sovereignty, civil equality, careers open to 'talent', and the abolition of the seigneurial system. But those who celebrated with such fervour and optimism the first anniversary on 14 July 1790 of the seizure of the Bastille could not have known that the ultimate price for securing those changes would be years of civil war and foreign invasion, massive loss of life and personal insecurity. While in 1790 they were confident that they were in the avant-garde of humanity's progress, so contested as well as so inspiring was the progress they promised that the consequences of the Revolution continue to reverberate, globally as well as in France itself.

The French Revolution had been born in the heat of a global imperial crisis. This was a clash of great empires—the British, French and Spanish in particular, but also the Ottoman and Mughal—for territory and commercial advantage, and for the military power necessary to defend them. The costs of the warfare necessary to defend a sprawling North American empire had proved too great for the French monarchy after 1756; then the temptation to intervene on the side of Britain's North American colonists after 1778 was too great to resist, but success came at an enormous financial cost. The political repercussions would prove too awkward for Louis XVI and his ministry.

France was the epicentre of the global crisis. The shock waves of its radical revolution were felt throughout Europe, and beyond. They reverberated across the Atlantic to the Americas, especially the Caribbean, along the shores of the Mediterranean, reaching as far as South Asia and even South Africa and the South Pacific.[73] Other European powers—from Austria and Prussia to Britain and Spain—were so antipathetic to what they believed the upheavals threatened for their own societies and the international order that they were prepared to form a military alliance to crush them. Their coalition finally succeeded in returning France's pre-revolutionary family to the throne in 1815, but at a massive price in lives lost and only after a compromise with the main changes wrought by the Revolution.

The French Revolution was a turning point in world history—or 'world-historical'—and its origins and consequences have to be understood both as global and 'internal'. As the cauldron in which modern nationalism and nationalist wars were born, the Revolution ended the dream of Enlightenment cosmopolitanism, dissipated by international warfare, the establishment of 'sister republics' after 1795, and calls to extend France's natural borders to the mouth of the Rhine.[74] There was always an uneasy tension between the military rhetoric of defending the Revolution and the universal mission of revolutionary change. This was so at the grass roots, too: when the little town of Fontenay-le-Peuple, formerly Fontenay-le-Comte, was retaken from Vendéan rebels in 1793, a brochure entitled 'Liberty, Equality or Death' listed the Ten Commandments of the French Republic, beginning:

1. Frenchmen, you will defend your homeland so you can live in Liberty.
2. You will pursue all tyrants to the other side of Hindustan.[75]

In response to such a threat, one of the most important consequences of the Revolution was the hostile European reaction after 1792, which linked suspicion of radicalism to the strengthening of support for established forms of government and religion.

The outbreak of the Revolution had been welcomed as a harbinger of liberal reform across the continent. European attitudes to France changed dramatically after 1792 because of war, the proclamation of the Republic and the execution of Louis XVI.[76] In 1805, William Wordsworth recalled in 'The Prelude' how he had felt at the age of nineteen in 1789:

Bliss was it in that dawn to be alive,
But to be young was very heaven!—Oh! times,
In which the meagre, stale, forbidding ways
Of custom, law, and statute, took at once
The attraction of a country in romance!
When Reason seemed the most to assert her rights . . .
Not favoured spots alone, but the whole earth,
The beauty wore of promise . . .[77]

By 1805, however, Wordsworth had long ceased to be sympathetic to France and its Revolution because of what he saw as its departure from founding principles after 1793. The hostile political environment in England meant that publication of a revised version of the poem—now seen as his greatest—was delayed until his death in 1850.[78] In Britain and elsewhere there was widespread repression of democrats after 1792 and the unleashing of war propaganda depicting French revolutionaries as blood-thirsty dictators and cannibalistic mobs. A cluster of brilliant young writers—including Samuel Taylor Coleridge, Helen Maria Williams, William Godwin, William Drennan and Wordsworth himself—had their careers blighted or had to make significant political compromises in the context of Prime Minister William Pitt's 'Reign of Alarm'.[79]

There were repercussions even in the South Pacific as Britain and France explored, mapped and seized territory. Bruni d'Entrecasteaux's expedition had been sent to Australia in 1791 in search of the explorer Jean-François La Pérouse, missing since 1788. Its leader dead, the malnour-ished and exhausted expedition straggled into Java in October 1793, where it learned of events earlier in the year. A violent division soon emerged between the expedition's new leader, the royalist Alexandre d'Auribeau, and the naturalist Jacques Labillardière, in the 1760s a classmate in Alençon of Jacques Hébert, now a prominent Enragé in Paris. At the same time in 1793 leaders of Scottish reformism were on their way to Botany Bay in Australia as political prisoners.[80]

Just as there had been revolutionary precedents before 1789—most notably in North America, Corsica, Geneva and the United Provinces (Netherlands)—so the French Revolution encouraged revolutionaries across the continent. In Poland, after partition in 1792 (between Russia, Prussia and Austria), nationalist rebellion in 1794 temporarily succeeded under the lead-ership of Tadeusz Kosciuszko. It was crushed uncompromisingly, as was the

United Irishmen rebellion against Britain in 1798. The reception of news of the French Revolution was profound but varied around the Mediterranean, and in parts of South Asia. As a revolution for liberty, equality and fraternity it would inspire others as diverse as the leader of Latin American struggles for national independence, Simón Bolívar (who attended Napoleon's coronation in 1804),[81] and one of the early Indian nationalists of the 1830s, Ram Mohun Roy.

The full impact of the French Revolution is best understood within this international, even global perspective, that of the long history of the struggles within Europe and its colonies for self-determination, representative government and individual liberties against entrenched hierarchies of social orders, corporate privilege and autocracy.[82] But it was also unique. Only in France were the fullest consequences of Revolution carried through: popular sovereignty, equality before the law, the abolition of seigneurialism and of slavery, and equality of inheritance. Other reforms were enacted, then repudiated: universal manhood suffrage, the separation of Church and State, the right to divorce among others. Only in France was a democratic Republic able to mobilize its forces to defeat a European coalition intent on its destruction. That is why this 'age of revolutions' was first and foremost the age of the French Revolution in the minds of contemporaries.

Celebrations of the bicentenary of the Revolution in 1989 in Paris occurred in the aftermath of the crushing of student protests in Beijing and the collapse of the Soviet Union. Right-wing commentators rushed to assert that the French Revolution was 'over' and no longer of importance in public life or even among historians. They were wrong. Indeed, the two great waves of revolutionary change since 1989—the overthrow of regimes in eastern and south-eastern Europe and the 'Arab spring'—have served to revivify our interest in the world-changing upheavals of two centuries and more ago. Public interest in the Revolution no less than academic research continues to find it a time of questions that still resonate.[83] How had the golden expectations of 1789 descended into civil war and terror by 1793? Why had attempts to create an electoral and constitutional regime been superseded by the rule of a strong man by 1799? At a time of terrorism and 'wars on terror', the meanings of 1789 continue to serve as a marker for principles underpinning public life. For example, witness the response to the killing of twelve journalists working for the satirical weekly *Charlie Hebdo* in January 2015, when an estimated 3.7 million people marched across France in defence of liberties seen to stretch back to the French Revolution.

After more than 225 years, the fundamental questions posed and probed by the French Revolution remain at the heart of all democratic political life everywhere. Is the quest for equality inimical to liberty or is a measure of social equality the precondition for genuine freedom? Are healthy societies best created by interventionist governments acting for what they see as the public good or by freeing people's entrepreneurial urges? The French Revolution was never 'over'. Its achievements and triumphs—like its deceptions and atrocities—were of a scale that has made its stature unique. Its reverberations were felt across the globe after 1789—and they live with us still.

CHRONOLOGY

1756–63   Seven Years War

1778   Franco-American alliance; war with Britain

1783
3 September   Peace of Paris

1787
22 February   Meeting of the Assembly of Notables
June–August   Refusal of Parlement of Paris to register royal reforms; exile of *parlementaires* of Paris and Bordeaux

1788
8 May   Lamoignon's reforms to reduce power of *parlements*
7 June   'Journée des Tuiles' at Grenoble
8 August   Estates-General convened for 5 May 1789
24–26 August   Brienne resigns; Necker reappointed
5 October–   Second Assembly of Notables
12 December
27 December   Royal Council decree doubling the number of the Third Estate's representatives

1789
February   Sieyès publishes *Qu'est-ce que le Tiers État?*
February–June   Elections to the Estates-General
27–28 April   Réveillon riots in Paris

THE ESTATES GENERAL

(5 May–27 June 1789)

5 May	Opening of the Estates-General at Versailles
17 June	Declaration of the National Assembly
20 June	Tennis Court Oath
23 June	King's Declaration concerning the Estates-General

THE NATIONAL CONSTITUENT ASSEMBLY

(28 June 1789–30 September 1791)

1789

11 July	Dismissal of Necker
14 July	Taking of the Bastille
Late July–early August	Municipal revolutions, peasant revolts, Great Fear
4–11 August	August Decree on feudalism
10 August	Decree establishing National Guards
26 August	Declaration of the Rights of Man and Citizen
11 September	National Assembly grants suspensive, rather than absolute, veto to king
5–6 October	March of the Parisian women on Versailles; royal family brought back to Paris
21 October	Decree on martial law
2 November	'Nationalization' of church property
14 December	Decree establishing municipal government
19 December	First issue of *assignats* (revolutionary currency)
24 December	Grant of religious liberty to Protestants

1790

28 January	Sephardi Jews granted equal rights
13 February	Decree prohibiting monastic vows in France
26 February	Decree dividing France into departments
15 March	Inheritance law introducing equality for sons and daughters
10 May	Sectarian violence in Montauban
22 May	National Assembly renounces wars of conquest

10 June	Request from Avignon for annexation into France
13 June	Sectarian violence in Nîmes
19 June	Decree abolishing hereditary nobility and titles
12 July	Civil Constitution of the Clergy
14 July	Fête de la Fédération
18 August	First counter-revolutionary assembly at Jalès
31 August	Mutiny in garrison at Nancy
29 October	Revolt of slaves and black freemen in Saint-Domingue
31 October	Decree providing for uniform tariffs
27 November	Decree requiring the clerical oath

1791

2 March	Suppression of guilds
2 April	Death of Mirabeau
13 April	Papal Bull *Charitas*
15 May	Children of free blacks in colonies granted equal rights
14 June	Le Chapelier Law
20 June	King's flight and Declaration
5 July	Padua Circular
16–17 July	Petition and 'massacre' of the Champ de Mars
14 August	Slave rebellion in Saint-Domingue
27 August	Declaration of Pillnitz
14 September	Louis XVI accepts the new constitution
14 September	Annexation of Avignon and Comtat-Venaissin
28 September	Ashkenazi Jews granted equal rights

THE LEGISLATIVE ASSEMBLY

(1 October 1791–20 September 1792)

9 November	Decree against *émigrés* (vetoed by the king 12 November)
29 November	Priests refusing to take oath to constitution suspended from functions (vetoed by the king 19 December)

1792

9 February	Decree nationalizing *émigré* property
20 April	Declaration of war on Austria

25 April	First execution by guillotine
27 May	Decree on deportation of non-juring priests (vetoed 19 June)
12 June	Dismissal of Girondin ministers
13 June	Prussia declares war
20 June	Invasion of the Tuileries by Parisian *sans-culottes*
11 July	Declaration of the 'patrie en danger'
25 July	Publication of the Brunswick Manifesto
10 August	Storming of the Tuileries and suspension of the king
19 August	Defection of Lafayette to Austrians
2 September	Fall of Verdun to Prussians
2–6 September	'September massacres' in Paris and provinces
20 September	Decrees on divorce and civil ceremonies

THE FIRST PHASE OF THE NATIONAL CONVENTION

(20 September 1792–2 June 1793)

20 September	First session of the National Convention
20 September	Victory at Valmy
22 September	Proclamation of the Republic
6 November	Victory at Jemappes
27 November	French annexation of Savoy
11 December	First appearance of Louis XVI before the Convention

1793

January	The king's trial
21 January	Execution of Louis XVI
1 February	French declaration of war on England and Holland
24 February	Decree for a levy of 300,000 men
7 March	Declaration of war on Spain
10 March	Creation of special Revolutionary Tribunal
10 March	Creation of Surveillance Committees
10–11 March	Massacres at Machecoul and start of Vendéan insurrection
19 March	Decree on public relief
28 March	Decree against *émigrés*
4 April	Defection of Dumouriez to the Austrians
6 April	Decree on the formation of a Committee of Public Safety

9 April	Decree establishing 'deputies on mission'
13–24 April	Trial and acquittal of Marat
29 April	Federalist insurrection in Marseille
4 May	The first law of the Maximum
30 May	Chalier Jacobins overthrown in Lyon
31 May–2 June	Invasion of Convention by Paris sections; fall of Girondins
7 June	Federalist revolts in Bordeaux and Caen

THE SECOND PHASE OF THE CONVENTION: THE TERROR

(3 June 1793–28 July 1794)

24 June	Constitution of 1793
13 July	Assassination of Marat
17 July	Execution of Chalier and Federalist revolt in Lyon
17 July	Final abolition of feudalism
27 July	Robespierre appointed to Committee of Public Safety
1 August	Decree establishing a uniform system of weights and measures
23 August	Decree establishing the *levée en masse*
25 August	Recapture of Marseille by revolutionary armies
27 August	Toulon surrenders to the British navy
5–6 September	Popular 'journée' pressures the Convention into radical measures; 'terror until peace'
8 September	Victory over British forces at Hondschoote
17 September	Law of Suspects
17 September	Victory over Spanish forces at Peyrestortes
22 September	Beginning of Year II
29 September	Law of the General Maximum
5 October	Decree establishing the French Era (14 Vendémiaire Year II)
9 October	Suppression of Federalist insurrection in Lyon
10 October	Declaration of Revolutionary Government (19 Vendémiaire Year II)
16 October	Execution of Marie-Antoinette
17 October	Victory over Austrian forces at Wattignies
31 October	Execution of the Girondin leaders

4 December	The Constitution of the Terror (Law of 14 Frimaire Year II)
8 December	Decree concerning religious liberty (18 Frimaire Year II)
19 December	Decree concerning public education (29 Frimaire Year II)
19 December	Recapture of Toulon
23 December	Defeat of Vendéan forces at Savenay

1794

4 February	Abolition of slavery in French colonies
3 March	Ventôse decrees on suspects' property (13 Ventôse Year II)
13–24 March	Arrest and execution of Hébertistes
30 March–5 April	Arrest and execution of Dantonists
8 June	Festival of Supreme Being in Paris
10 June	Law of 22 Prairial Year II
26 June	Victory at Fleurus
23 July	Introduction of wage regulation in Paris
27 July	Overthrow of Robespierrists (9 Thermidor Year II)
28–29 July	Execution of Robespierre, Saint-Just and associates
1 August	Repeal of Law of 22 Prairial
12 November	Closure of Jacobin Club
17 November	Decree on primary schools (27 Brumaire Year III)
24 December	Abolition of General Maximum

THE THIRD PHASE OF THE CONVENTION: THE THERMIDORIAN REACTION

(29 July 1794–26 October 1795)

28 December	Decree reorganizing the Revolutionary Tribunal (8 Nivôse Year III)

1795

March	Arrest of Billaud-Varenne, Collot d'Herbois, Barère, Fouquier-Tinville
1 April	Germinal: popular *journée* in Paris

5 April	Treaty of Basle with Prussia (16 Germinal Year III)
7 April	Decree on weights and measures (18 Germinal Year III)
April–May	'White Terror' in southern France
16 May	Treaty of The Hague (27 Floréal Year III); Batavian Republic
20 May	Invasion of Convention by Parisian crowd (Prairial Year III)
31 May	Abolition of Revolutionary Tribunal
8 June	Death of Louis XVII; Comte de Provence becomes pretender to French throne (Louis XVIII)
21 July	Defeat of royalist invasion at Quiberon
22 July	Peace signed with Spain
22 August	Constitution of the Year III (5 Fructidor Year III)
30 August	Decree of the two-thirds (13 Fructidor Year III)
29 September	Decree on the exercise of worship (7 Vendémiaire IV)
1 October	Annexation of Belgium (9 Vendémiaire Year IV)
5 October	Royalist rising in Paris (13 Vendémiaire Year IV)
25 October	Decree concerning the organization of public education (3 Brumaire Year IV)
26 October	Dissolution of Convention

THE DIRECTORY

(2 November 1795–10 November 1799)

16 November	Panthéon Club opened
10 December	Forced loan (19 Frimaire Year IV)

1796

19 February	Abolition of *assignats* (30 Pluviôse Year IV)
27 February	Panthéon Club closed
2 March	Bonaparte appointed General-in-Chief of the Army in Italy (12 Ventôse Year IV)
29 March	Vendéan leader Charette executed
11 April	Invasion of Italy (22 Germinal Year IV)
10 May	Conspiracy of the Equals; Babeuf arrested (21 Floréal Year IV)

23 May	Insurrection in Pavia
12 June	Invasion of papal territory (24 Prairial Year IV)
5 August	Alliance with Spain (18 Thermidor Year IV)
16 October	Cispadane Republic proclaimed (25 Vendémiaire Year V)
15–17 November	Battle of Arcole (25–27 Brumaire Year V)
15 December	Departure of fleet for Ireland (25 Frimaire Year V)

1797

6 January	Withdrawal of Irish expedition (18 Nivôse Year V)
2 February	Capture of Mantua (14 Pluviôse Year V)
4 February	Abolition of *assignats*; return to metallic currency
19 February	Babeuf's trial begins
March–April	Royalist successes in legislative elections
15 May	Venetian Republic occupied (27 Floréal Year V)
27 May	Execution of Babeuf
29 June	Cisalpine Republic proclaimed (11 Messidor Year V)
25 July	Political clubs closed
24 August	Laws against clergy repealed
4 September	*Coup d'état* against royalist deputies (18 Fructidor Year V)
5 September	Carnot and Barthélemy removed from Directory (19 Fructidor Year V)
17 October	Treaty of Campo Formio (26 Vendémiaire Year VI)

1798

11 May	Removal from office of many republican deputies (22 Floréal Year VI)
19 May	Bonaparte leaves for Egyptian campaign
21 May	Uprising in Ireland
1 August	Battle of the Nile; French fleet defeated
5 September	First general conscription law (19 Fructidor Year VI)

1799

March	War of the Second Coalition
April	Year VII legislative elections favour neo-Jacobins
23 August	Bonaparte embarks for France

9 October	Bonaparte's return to France
18 October	Decree on francs and *livres* (26 Vendémiaire Year VIII)
10 November	Overthrow of Directory (19 Brumaire Year VIII)
13 December	Constitution of the Year VIII (22 Frimaire Year VIII)
28 December	Churches reopened for worship on Sundays

THE REVOLUTIONARY CALENDAR

The calendar was introduced to mark the first anniversary of the proclamation of the Republic on 22 September 1792. The 'Decree establishing the French Era' and the calendar's introduction were passed on 14 Vendémiaire Year II (5 October 1793). The calendar represented a repudiation of the Gregorian calendar and its saints' names; instead, there would be 'rational' months of thirty days, each with three *décades*, and every day would have a name drawn from nature: in Nivôse, for example, clay, slate and sandstone. The *décadi*, or tenth days, were named after farm implements. The calendar lasted until New Year's Day 1806.

Autumn:	Vendémiaire	(month of vintage)	22 September–21 October
	Brumaire	(month of fog)	22 October–20 November
	Frimaire	(month of frost)	21 November–20 December
Winter:	Nivôse	(month of snow)	21 December–19 January
	Pluviôse	(month of rain)	20 January–18 February
	Ventôse	(month of wind)	19 February–20 March
Spring:	Germinal	(month of budding)	21 March–19 April
	Floréal	(month of flowers)	20 April–19 May
	Prairial	(month of meadows)	20 May–18 June
Summer:	Messidor	(month of harvest)	19 June–18 July
	Thermidor	(month of heat)	19 July–17 August
	Fructidor	(month of fruit)	18 August–16 September

Sans-culottides: 17–21 September inclusive plus extra day in leap years.

NOTES

Abbreviations

AD	Archives départementales
AM	Archives municipales
AN	Archives nationales
AP	*Archives parlementaires*
AHR	*American Historical Review*
AHRF	*Annales Historiques de la Révolution Française* (Note: The *AHRF* changed from volumes to individual issue numbers from 1977.)
Annales	*Annales. Histoire, Sciences Sociales*
CNRS	Éditions du Centre National de la Recherche Scientifique
CTHS	Éditions du Comité des Travaux Historiques et Scientifiques
ÉHÉSS	Éditions de l'École des Hautes Études en Sciences Sociales
EHR	*English Historical Review*
FH	*French History*
FHS	*French Historical Studies*
HJ	*Historical Journal*
JMH	*Journal of Modern History*
MU	*Moniteur Universel*
P&P	*Past and Present*
PUF	Presses Universitaires de France
SH	*Social History*
SÉR	Société des Études Robespierristes

Introduction

1. Michel Biard and Pascal Dupuy, *La Révolution française. Dynamique et ruptures, 1787–1804*, 2nd edn. Paris: Armand Colin, 2008, p. 21.
2. Comte de Courchamps, *Souvenirs de la marquise de Créquy de 1710 à 1803*, 10 vols. Paris: Garnier Frères, 1865, vol. 9, pp. 144–45.
3. Recent historiographical trends are charted and discussed in a special issue of *FHS*, 32 (2009). Two recent collections bring together current scholarship: David Andress (ed.), *The Oxford Handbook of the French Revolution*, Oxford: Oxford University Press, 2015; Peter McPhee (ed.), *A Companion to the French Revolution*, Oxford: Wiley-Blackwell, 2013.
4. There are many surveys of the historiography of the Revolution, including William Doyle, *Origins of the French Revolution*, 3rd edn., Oxford and New York: Oxford University Press, 1999; Alan Forrest, *The French Revolution*, Oxford: Oxford University Press, 1995; Gwynne

Lewis, *The French Revolution: Rethinking the Debate,* London and New York: Routledge, 1993; Peter J. Davies, *The Debate on the French Revolution,* Manchester: Manchester University Press, 2006; and, most recently and successfully, Paul R. Hanson, *Contesting the French Revolution,* Malden, MA, and Oxford: Wiley-Blackwell, 2009.

5. Mao Tse-Tung, *Selected Works,* vol. 1, Peking: Foreign Languages Press, 1961, p. 28.

6. *Oeuvres de Maximilien Robespierre,* 11 vols, Ivry: SER, 1912–2007, vol. 9, pp. 77–78, 86–91.

7. This assumption underpins, for example, D. M. G. Sutherland, *The French Revolution and Empire: The Quest for a Civic Order,* Oxford: Blackwell, 2003, p. 387; Richard Cobb, *Reactions to the French Revolution,* London: Oxford University Press, 1972, p. 125.

8. Rolf Reichardt and Hubertus Kohle, *Visualising the Revolution: Politics and the Pictorial Arts in Late Eighteenth-Century France,* translated by Corinne Atwood and Felicity Baker, London: Reaktion Books, 2008; Annie Jourdan, *Les Monuments de la Révolution, 1770–1804: une histoire de représentation,* Paris: Champion; Geneva: Slatkine, 1997; Richard Taws, *The Politics of the Provisional: Art and Ephemera in Revolutionary France,* Philadelphia, PA: Pennsylvania State University Press, 2013.

Chapter 1   Patchworks of Power and Privilege: France in the 1780s

1. Ambrogio A. Caiani, *Louis XVI and the French Revolution, 1789–1792,* Cambridge: Cambridge University Press, 2012, pp. 221–22. The panels were burned in 1794, although one survived to be found in Switzerland in the 1990s.

2. Fernand Braudel, *The Identity of France,* translated by Sian Reynolds, vol. 1, London: Collins, 1988, pp. 91–97; Graham Robb, *The Discovery of France,* London: Picador, 2007; Daniel Roche, *France in the Enlightenment,* translated by Arthur Goldhammer, Cambridge, MA: Harvard University Press, 1998, chs 1, 2 and 6, pp. 488–91.

3. The best detailed overview of France in the 1780s is Roche, *France in the Enlightenment.* Expert summaries are in William Doyle, *The Oxford History of the French Revolution,* 2nd edn., Oxford and New York: Oxford University Press, 2002, ch. 1; and the contributions to Doyle (ed.), *The Oxford Handbook of the Ancien Régime,* Oxford and New York: Oxford University Press, 2012.

4. P. M. Jones, *The Peasantry in the French Revolution,* Cambridge: Cambridge University Press, 1988, ch. 2.

5. Maurice, Denise and Robert Bréant, *Menucourt. Un village du Vexin français pendant la Révolution, 1789–1799,* Menucourt: Mairie de Menucourt, 1989.

6. Peter McPhee, *Une communauté languedocienne dans l'histoire: Gabian 1760–1960,* Nîmes: Lacour, 2001, ch. 1.

7. On rural France in general, see Roche, *France in the Enlightenment,* ch. 4; Jones, *Peasantry,* ch. 1. Case studies of contrasting regions include Liana Vardi, *The Land and the Loom: Peasants and Profit in Northern France, 1680–1800,* Durham, NC, and London: Duke University Press, 1993; and D. M. G. Sutherland, *The Chouans: The Social Origins of Popular Counter-Revolution in Upper Brittany, 1770–1796,* Oxford: Oxford University Press, 1982.

8. Michael Kwass, *Privilege and the Politics of Taxation in Eighteenth-Century France,* Cambridge: Cambridge University Press, 2000, pp. 33–68.

9. Robert Forster, *The Nobility of Toulouse in the Eighteenth Century: A Social and Economic Study,* Baltimore, MD: Johns Hopkins University Press, 1960, pp. 185–88; Robert Forster, *The House of Saulx-Tavanes: Versailles and Burgundy, 1700–1830,* Baltimore, MD: Johns Hopkins University Press, 1977, pp. 140–41; Kwass, *Privilege and Politics,* ch. 2.

10. Joël Cornette (ed.), *Atlas de l'histoire de France, 481–2005,* Paris: Belin, 2012, pp. 304–05.

11. On Paris, see Richard Mowery Andrews, 'Paris of the Great Revolution: 1789–1796', in Gene Brucker (ed.), *People and Communities in the Western World,* vol. 2, Homewood, IL: Dorsey Press, 1979, pp. 56–112; Daniel Roche, *The People of Paris: An Essay in Popular Culture in the Eighteenth Century,* translated by Marie Evans, Berkeley and Los Angeles, CA: University of California Press, 1987; David Garrioch, *Neighbourhood and Community in Paris, 1740–1790,* Cambridge: Cambridge University Press, 1986; Arlette Farge, *Fragile Lives: Violence, Power, and Solidarity in Eighteenth-Century Paris,* translated by Carol Shelton, Cambridge, MA: Harvard University Press, 1993. An indispensable contemporary source is Louis-Sébastien Mercier, *Tableau de Paris,* 12 vols, Amsterdam: n.p., 1784–87; a selection is

Mercier, *Panorama of Paris: Selections from Tableau de Paris*, translated by Helen Simpson and Jeremy D. Popkin, University Park, PA: Pennsylvania State University Press, 1999.

12. David Garrioch, *The Making of Revolutionary Paris*, Berkeley and Los Angeles, CA, and London: University of California Press, 2002, p. 66 and ch. 3.
13. Garrioch, *Making of Revolutionary Paris*, pp. 42–43, 159, 298 and ch. 6.
14. Peter McPhee, *Robespierre: A Revolutionary Life*, New Haven, CT, and London: Yale University Press, 2012, p. 20; Hervé Leuwers, *Robespierre*, Paris: Fayard, 2014, ch. 1.
15. Garrioch, *Making of Revolutionary Paris*, p. 39.
16. Alain Nolibos, *Arras: de Nemetucam à la communauté urbaine*, Lille: La Voix du Nord, 2003, pp. 86–101; McPhee, *Robespierre*, ch. 1.
17. Augustin Deramecourt, *Le Clergé du diocèse d'Arras, Boulogne et Saint-Omer pendant la Révolution (1789–1802)*, 4 vols, Paris: Bray et Retaux; Arras: Imprimerie du Pas-de-Calais, 1884–86, vol. 1, especially pp. 50–55, 148–54, 452–53, 482–86.
18. Roche, *France in the Enlightenment*, pp. 159, 167.
19. Garrioch, *Making of Revolutionary Paris*, pp. 103–08, 121, 309–10.
20. Roche, *France in the Enlightenment*, ch. 12.
21. George D. Sussman, *Selling Mothers' Milk: The Wet-Nursing Business in France, 1715–1914*, Urbana, IL: University of Illinois Press, 1982, chs 2–4.
22. Among the important studies of the grain trade are Steven Kaplan, *Provisioning Paris: Merchants and Millers in the Grain and Flour Trade during the Eighteenth Century*, Ithaca, NY: Cornell University Press, 1984; Cynthia Bouton, *The Flour War: Gender, Class, and Community in late Ancien Régime French Society*, University Park, PA: Pennsylvania State University Press, 1993; Judith Miller, *Mastering the Market: The State and the Grain Trade in Northern France, 1700–1860*, Cambridge and New York: Cambridge University Press, 1998.
23. McPhee, *Gabian*, ch. 1.
24. For the Church in the eighteenth century, see Roche, *France in the Enlightenment*, ch. 11; and the outstanding survey by John McManners, *Church and Society in Eighteenth-Century France*, vol. 1, Oxford and New York: Oxford University Press, 1998.
25. Olwen Hufton, 'Women in Revolution, 1789–1796', *P&P*, 53 (1971), pp. 90–108; John McManners, *French Ecclesiastical Society under the Ancien Régime: A Study of Angers in the Eighteenth Century*, Manchester: Manchester University Press, 1960; McManners, *Church and Society*, ch. 4.
26. Cornette (ed.), *Atlas de l'histoire de France*, pp. 356–57. This 'line' is based on the research of Louis Maggiolo in the 1870s.
27. Ralph Gibson, *A Social History of French Catholicism, 1789–1914*, London and New York: Routledge, 1989, pp. 24, 27.
28. Patrice L. R. Higonnet, *Pont-de-Montvert: Social Structure and Politics in a French Village, 1700–1914*, Cambridge, MA: Harvard University Press, 1971; McManners, *Church and Society*, ch. 46.
29. David Garrioch, *The Huguenots of Paris and the Coming of Religious Freedom, 1685–1789*, New York: Cambridge University Press, 2014.
30. Christian Pfister, *Histoire de Nancy*, vol. 3, Paris: Éditions du Palais Royal; Nancy: Éditions Berger-Levrault, 1974, pp. 320–28; Julie Kalman, *Rethinking Antisemitism in Nineteenth-Century France*, New York: Cambridge University Press, 2010, p. 52.
31. Nigel Aston, *Religion and Revolution in France, 1780–1804*, Basingstoke: Macmillan, 2000, pp. 14–15.
32. A fine overview is Jay M. Smith, 'Nobility', in Andress (ed.), *Oxford Handbook*, ch. 3. See also Smith, *Nobility Reimagined: The Patriotic Nation in Eighteenth-Century France*, Ithaca, NY, and London: Cornell University Press, 2005; Rafe Blaufarb, *The Politics of Fiscal Privilege in Provence, 1530s–1830s*, Washington, DC: The Catholic University of America Press, 2012.
33. Alan Forrest, *Soldiers of the French Revolution*, Durham, NC: Duke University Press, 1990, p. 36; Rafe Blaufarb, *The French Army, 1750–1820: Careers, Talent, Merit*, Manchester and New York: Manchester University Press, 2002.
34. Garrioch, *Making of Revolutionary Paris*, p. 87 and ch. 4.
35. Forster, *House of Saulx-Tavanes*, p. 126; Roche, *France in the Enlightenment*, p. 407.
36. Robert Forster, 'The Survival of the Nobility during the French Revolution', *P&P*, 37 (1967), pp. 71–86.

37. Simon Schama, *Citizens: A Chronicle of the French Revolution*, New York: Alfred A. Knopf, 1989, pp. 71–79, 313.
38. Iain A. Cameron, *Crime and Repression in the Auvergne and the Guyenne, 1720–1790*, Cambridge: Cambridge University Press, 1981, pp. 154–75; Nicole Castan, 'Summary Justice', in Robert Forster (ed.), *Deviants and the Abandoned in French Society*, Baltimore, MD: Johns Hopkins University Press, 1978, pp. 111–56; Richard Mowery Andrews, *Law, Magistracy and Crime in Old Regime Paris, 1735–1789*, vol. 1, *The System of Criminal Justice*, Cambridge: Cambridge University Press, 1994.
39. Olwen Hufton, 'Women and the Family Economy in Eighteenth-Century France', *FHS*, 9 (1975), pp. 1–22; Roche, *France in the Enlightenment*, ch. 7, pp. 287–99; Schama, *Citizens*, p. 75.
40. Peter McPhee, *Revolution and Environment in Southern France: Peasant, Lords, and Murder in the Corbières, 1780–1830*, Oxford: Clarendon Press, 1999, p. 37.
41. McPhee, *Revolution and Environment*, pp. 36–39; Olwen Hufton, 'Attitudes towards Authority in Eighteenth-Century Languedoc', *SH*, 3 (1978), pp. 281–302; Georges Fournier, *Démocratie et vie municipale en Languedoc du milieu du XVIIIe au début du XIXe siècle*, 2 vols, Toulouse: Les Amis des Archives, 1994; Nicole Castan, *Les Criminels du Languedoc: les exigences d'ordre et les voies du ressentiment dans une société pré-Révolutionnaire (1750–1790)*, Toulouse: Université de Toulouse-Le Mirail, 1980. Bazin de Bezons, born in 1701, was Archbishop of Carcassonne from 1730 to 1778.

Chapter 2 A World of Intellectual Ferment

1. Maximilien Robespierre, *Oeuvres de Maximilien Robespierre*, 11 vols, Paris: SÉR, 1912–2007, vol. 2, pp. 129–224; Jessica Riskin, *Science in the Age of Sensibility: The Sentimental Empiricists of the French Enlightenment*, Chicago, IL, and London: University of Chicago Press, 2002, ch. 5; Marie-Hélène Huet, *Mourning Glory: The Will of the French Revolution*, University Park, PA: University of Pennsylvania Press, 1997, pp. 10–21.
2. Peter McPhee, *Robespierre: A Revolutionary Life*, New Haven, CT, and London: Yale University Press, 2012, pp. 34–35; Robespierre, *Oeuvres*, vol. 11, pp. 11–15. Within a year, however, Vissery had died and the municipality demolished his contraption: Riskin, *Science in the Age of Sensibility*, p. 186.
3. Robespierre, *Oeuvres*, vol. 3, p. 29; McPhee, *Robespierre*, pp. 34–35. The significance of Franklin and the American experience has been strongly restated by Annie Jourdan, *La Révolution, une exception française?*, Paris: Flammarion, 2004, part 2, ch. 4; and David Andress, *1789: The Threshold of the Modern Age*, London: Little, Brown, 2008, ch. 1.
4. An extensive survey is Jonathan I. Israel, *Democratic Enlightenment: Philosophy, Revolution, and Human Rights, 1750–1790*, Oxford: Oxford University Press, 2012. Lucid summaries of the Enlightenment are by Dorinda Outram, *The Enlightenment*, Cambridge: Cambridge University Press, 1995; Daniel Roche, *France in the Enlightenment*, translated by Arthur Goldhammer, Cambridge, MA: Harvard University Press, 1998, part 3.
5. Translated from Denis Diderot, *Oeuvres complètes*, 20 vols, Paris: Garnier, 1875–77, vol. 20, p. 28.
6. Diderot, *Lettres à Sophie Volland*, in *Oeuvres complètes*, vol. 19, pp. 138–41.
7. Liana Vardi, *The Physiocrats and the World of the Enlightenment*, Cambridge and New York: Cambridge University Press, 2012.
8. Clare Haru Crowston, *Credit, Fashion, Sex: Economies of Regard in Old Regime France*, Durham, NC, and London: Duke University Press, 2013; William H. Sewell Jr., 'Connecting Capitalism to the French Revolution: The Parisian Promenade and the Origins of Civic Equality in Eighteenth-Century France', *Critical Historical Studies*, 1 (2014), pp. 5–46; Colin Jones, 'Bourgeois Revolution Revivified: 1789 and Social Change', in Colin Lucas (ed.), *Rewriting the French Revolution*, Oxford: Clarendon Press, 1991, ch. 4; and 'The Great Chain of Buying: Medical Advertisement, the Bourgeois Public Sphere, and the Origins of the French Revolution', *AHR*, 101 (1996), pp. 13–40.
9. Marisa Linton, *The Politics of Virtue in Enlightenment France*, Basingstoke: Palgrave Macmillan, 2001; Jay M. Smith, *Nobility Reimagined: The Patriotic Nation in Eighteenth-Century France*, Ithaca, NY, and London: Cornell University Press, 2005.
10. Jones, 'Bourgeois Revolution Revivified'; Jones, 'The Great Chain of Buying'; Charles Walton, *Policing Public Opinion in the French Revolution: The Culture of Calumny and the*

Problem of Free Speech, Oxford and New York: Oxford University Press, 2009, chs 1–3; Will Slauter, 'A Trojan Horse in Parliament: International Publicity in the Age of the American Revolution', in Charles Walton (ed.), *Into Print: Limits and Legacies of the Enlightenment. Essays in Honor of Robert Darnton*, University Park, PA: Pennsylvania State University Press, 2011; Arlette Farge, *Subversive Words: Public Opinion in Eighteenth-Century France*, translated by Rosemary Morris, Oxford: Polity Press, 1994.

11. David Garrioch, *The Formation of the Parisian Bourgeoisie, 1690–1830*, Princeton, NJ: Harvard University Press, 1996, p. 278; Roche, *France in the Enlightenment*, p. 199.

12. Simon Burrows and Mark Curran, 'How Swiss was the Société Typographique de Neuchâtel? A Digital Case Study of French Book Trade Networks', *Journal of Digital Humanities*, 1 (2012), see http://journalofdigitalhumanities.org/1-3/how-swiss-was-the-stn-by-simon-burrows-and-mark-curran; Simon Burrows, 'Books, Philosophy, Enlightenment', in David Andress (ed.), *The Oxford Handbook of the French Revolution*, Oxford: Oxford University Press, 2015, ch. 5.

13. Mary Ashburn Miller, *A Natural History of Revolution: Violence and Nature in the French Revolutionary Imagination, 1789–1794*, Ithaca, NY, and London: Cornell University Press, 2011.

14. Lynn Hunt, *Inventing Human Rights: A History*, New York: W. W. Norton, 2007; Paul Friedland, *Seeing Justice Done: The Age of Spectacular Capital Punishment in France*, Oxford: Oxford University Press, 2012, ch. 8.

15. Kenneth Loiselle, *Freemasonry and Male Friendship in Enlightenment France*, Ithaca, NY: Cornell University Press, 2014; Margaret Jacob, *Living the Enlightenment: Freemasonry and Politics in Eighteenth-Century Europe*, Oxford: Oxford University Press, 1991.

16. Jeremy L. Caradonna, *Enlightenment in Practice: Academic Prize Contests and Intellectual Culture in France, 1670–1794*, Ithaca, NY: Cornell University Press, 2012.

17. On the 'spaces' of public life, see Thomas E. Crow, *Painters and Public Life in Eighteenth-Century Paris*, New Haven, CT, and London: Yale University Press, 1985; Joan B. Landes, *Women and the Public Sphere in the Age of the French Revolution*, Ithaca, NY: Cornell University Press, 1988, ch. 1; Jack Censer and Jeremy Popkin (eds), *Press and Politics in Pre-Revolutionary France*, Berkeley, CA: University of California Press, 1987; Dena Goodman, *The Republic of Letters: A Cultural History of the French Enlightenment*, Ithaca, NY, and London: Cornell University Press, 1994; Jacob, *Living the Enlightenment*; and Roche, *France in the Enlightenment*, ch. 13.

18. John Shovlin, *The Political Economy of Virtue: Luxury, Patriotism, and the Origins of the French Revolution*, Ithaca, NY, and London: Cornell University Press, 2006, pp. 177–78 and chs 4–5.

19. Julian Swann and Joël Félix (eds), *The Crisis of the Absolute Monarchy: France from Old Regime to Revolution*, published for The British Academy, Oxford: Oxford University Press, 2013, p. 319.

20. McPhee, *Robespierre*, pp. 42–43.

21. Sophie de Bohm, *Prisonnière sous la Terreur. Mémoires d'une captive en 1793*, Paris: Cosmopole, 2001, pp. 6–7; R. B. Rose, *Tribunes and Amazons: Men and Women of Revolutionary France, 1789–1871*, Sydney: Macleay Press, 1998, ch. 1.

22. Roche, *France in the Enlightenment*, ch. 11; Dale K. Van Kley, *The Religious Origins of the French Revolution: From Calvin to the Civil Constitution, 1560–1791*, New Haven, CT, and London: Yale University Press, 1996.

23. Jean-Jacques Rousseau, *A Discourse on the Origins of Inequality* (1755), in *The Social Contract and Discourses* (1762), translated by G. D. H. Cole, London: J. M. Dent and Sons, 1913, pp. 166–67. See Jean Bloch, *Rousseauism and Education in Eighteenth-Century France*, Oxford: Voltaire Foundation, 1995.

24. Jean-Jacques Rousseau, *Émile, or On Education* (1762), translation and introduction by Allan Bloom, New York: Basic Books, 1979, p. 460.

25. A vigorous debate around Robert Darnton's conclusions centres on the digital resource *The French Book Trade in Enlightenment Europe, 1769–1794*, which suggests much less 'innovation' in readers' tastes. See Simon Burrows, 'French Banned Books in International Perspective, 1770–1789', in David Andress (ed.), *Experiencing the French Revolution*, Oxford: Voltaire Foundation, 2013, pp. 19–46; Robert Darnton, *Reviews in History*, review of *The French Book Trade in Enlightenment Europe, 1769–1794* (review no. 1355, 2012): http://www.history.ac.uk/reviews/review/1355. Date accessed: 7 August 2014.

26. Robert Darnton, *The Forbidden Best-Sellers of Pre-Revolutionary France*, New York and London: W. W. Norton, 1995, ch. 4. On Mercier, see Geneviève Boucher, *Écrire le temps: les tableaux urbains de Louis-Sébastien Mercier*, Montreal: Les Presses de l'Université de Montréal, 2014.

27. Robert Darnton, *The Literary Underground of the Old Regime*, Cambridge, MA: Harvard University Press, 1982, p. 200; Roche, *France in the Enlightenment*, p. 671. The cultural origins of the French Revolution are successfully explored in the 1989 film version of Choderlos de Laclos' 1782 novel *Dangerous Liaisons*, and in the 1996 film *Ridicule*.

28. Antoine de Baecque, *The Body Politic: Corporeal Metaphor in Revolutionary France, 1770–1800*, translated by Charlotte Mandell, Stanford, CA: Stanford University Press, 1997, pp. 31–51. A discussion of the sexual incompatibility of the king and queen is by Simone Bertière, *Les Reines de France au temps des Bourbons, vol. 4. Marie-Antoinette, l'insoumise*, Paris: Éditions de Fallois, 2002.

29. David Garrioch, *The Making of Revolutionary Paris*, Berkeley and Los Angeles, CA, and London: University of California Press, 2002, p. 169 and ch. 7.

30. Jacques-Louis Ménétra, *Journal of My Life*, translated by Arthur Goldhammer, New York: Columbia University Press, 1986; Roche, *France in the Enlightenment*, pp. 342–46, ch. 20.

31. Charly Coleman, *The Virtues of Abandon: An Anti-Individualist History of the French Enlightenment*, Stanford, CA: Stanford University Press, 2014.

32. R. R. Palmer, *The School of the French Revolution: A Documentary History of the College of Louis-le-Grand and its Director, Jean-François Champagne, 1762–1814*, Princeton, NJ: Princeton University Press, 1975, pp. 16–18, 27–29; McPhee, *Robespierre*, ch. 2.

33. 'Second Oration against Lucius Catalina: Addressed to the People', *M. Tullius Cicero: The Orations of Marcus Tullius Cicero, literally translated by C. D. Yonge, B.A.*, London: Henry G. Bohn, 1856; Thomas E. Kaiser, 'Conclusion: Catalina's Revenge-Conspiracy, Revolution, and Historical Consciousness from the Ancien Régime to the Consulate', in Peter R. Campbell, Thomas E. Kaiser and Marisa Linton (eds), *Conspiracy in the French Revolution*, Manchester: Manchester University Press, 2007, pp. 191–92, 200. See the important overview by Linton, *Politics of Virtue*.

34. Simon Schama, *Citizens: A Chronicle of the French Revolution*, New York: Alfred A. Knopf, 1989, p. 174.

35. Simon Lee, *David*, London: Phaidon, 1999, ch. 2; Richard Wittman, *Architecture, Print Culture, and the Public Sphere in Eighteenth-Century France*, New York and London: Routledge, 2007.

36. Robespierre, *Oeuvres*, vol. 3, pp. 22–23; William Doyle, 'Dupaty (1746–1788): A Career in the Late Enlightenment', *Studies on Voltaire and the Eighteenth Century*, 230 (1985), pp. 7–14, 35.

37. Paul Cheney, *Revolutionary Commerce: Globalization and the French Monarchy*, Cambridge, MA: Harvard University Press, 2010.

38. Laurent Dubois, *Avengers of the New World: The Story of the Haitian Revolution*, Cambridge, MA: Belknap Press of Harvard University Press, 2004, pp. 20–21; Trevor Burnard, 'The British Atlantic World', in Jack P. Greene and Philip D. Morgan (eds), *Atlantic History: Critical Appraisals*, Oxford and New York: Oxford University Press, 2009, ch. 16; Frédéric Régent, 'Slavery and the Colonies', in Peter McPhee (ed.). *A Companion to the French Revolution*, Oxford: Wiley-Blackwell, 2013, ch. 24.

39. Abel Louis, *Les Libres de couleur en Martinique*, 3 vols, Paris: L'Harmattan, 2012, vol. 2; Karl Noël, *L'Esclavage à l'Ile de France (Ile Maurice) de 1715 à 1810*, Paris: Éditions Two Cities ETC, 1991, chs 2, 10.

40. Alan Forrest, *Society and Politics in Revolutionary Bordeaux*, Oxford: Oxford University Press, 1975, ch. 1.

41. Jean-Michel Deveau, *La Traite rochelaise*, Paris: Karthala, 1990; Roche, *France in the Enlightenment*, ch. 5; James F. Searing, *West African Slavery and Atlantic Commerce: The Senegal River Valley, 1770–1860*, Cambridge: Cambridge University Press, 1993; Robert-Louis Stein, *The French Slave Trade in the Eighteenth Century*, Madison, WI: University of Wisconsin Press, 1979; Stewart R. King, *Blue Coat or Powdered Wig: Free People of Color in Pre-Revolutionary Saint Domingue*, Athens, GA: University of Georgia Press, 2001.

42. Armel de Wismes, *Nantes et le temps des négriers*, Paris: Éditions France-Empire, 1983; Robert Stein, 'The Profitability of the Nantes Slave Trade, 1783–1792', *Journal of Economic History*, 35 (1975), pp. 779–93.

43. The concept of an 'Atlantic', 'western' or 'democratic' revolution was first articulated in the 1950s by Jacques Godechot and R. R. Palmer: see Palmer, *The Age of the Democratic Revolution: A Political History of Europe and America, 1760–1800*, 2 vols, Princeton, NJ: Princeton University Press, 1959, 1964; Jacques Godechot, *France and the Atlantic Revolution of the Eighteenth Century, 1770–1799*, translated by Herbert H. Rowen, New York: The Free Press, 1965. It has been rejuvenated by, among others, Jourdan, *La Révolution, une exception française?*; David Armitage and Sanjay Subrahmanyam (eds), *The Age of Revolutions in Global Context, 1760–1840*, Basingstoke and New York: Palgrave Macmillan, 2010; Suzanne Desan, Lynn Hunt and William Max Nelson (eds), *The French Revolution in Global Perspective*, Ithaca, NY and London: Cornell University Press, 2013; and Pierre Serna, Antonino De Francesco and Judith A. Miller (eds), *Republics at War, 1776–1840: Revolutions, Conflicts, and Geopolitics in Europe and the Atlantic World*, Basingstoke: Palgrave Macmillan, 2013.

44. Martine Acerra, 'Marine militaire et bois de construction. Essai d'évaluation (1779–1789)', in Denis Woronoff (ed.), *Révolution et espaces forestiers. Colloque des 3 et 4 juin 1987*, Paris: L'Harmattan, 1988, p. 114; C. A. Bayly, *The Birth of the Modern World, 1780–1914: Global Connections and Comparisons*, Oxford: Blackwell, 2004, ch. 3.

45. Lynn Hunt, 'Globalizing the French Revolution', in Desan, Hunt and Nelson (eds), *French Revolution in Global Perspective*.

46. Doina Pasca Harsanyi, 'How to Make a Revolution without Firing a Shot: Thoughts on the Brissot-Chastellux Polemic (1786–1788)', *FH*, 22 (2008), pp. 197–216.

Chapter 3 Mismanaging Crisis, 1785–88

1. Joan Haslip, *Marie-Antoinette*, London: Weidenfeld & Nicolson, 1987, chs 22–23; Sarah Maza, 'The Diamond Necklace Affair Revisited', in Lynn Hunt (ed.), *Eroticism and the Body Politic*, Baltimore, MD: Johns Hopkins University Press, 1991.

2. Sarah Maza, *Private Lives and Public Affairs: The Causes Célèbres of Pre-Revolutionary France*, Berkeley, CA: University of California Press, 1993, pp. 242–55; William Doyle, 'Dupaty (1746–1788): A Career in the Late Enlightenment', *Studies on Voltaire and the Eighteenth Century*, 230 (1985), pp. 82–106.

3. David Garrioch, *The Formation of the Parisian Bourgeoisie, 1690–1830*, Cambridge, MA: Harvard University Press, 1996, p. 1; Maza, *Private Lives and Public Affairs*; Sarah Maza, 'Luxury, Morality, and Social Change: Why There Was no Middle-Class Consciousness in Pre-Revolutionary France', *JMH*, 69 (1997), pp. 199–229.

4. David A. Bell, *Lawyers and Citizens: The Making of a Political Elite in Old Regime France*, Oxford and New York: Oxford University Press, 1994, ch. 6 and Conclusion.

5. Michel Figeac, 'The Crisis of the Nobility at the Twilight of the Monarchy', in Julian Swann and Joël Félix (eds), *The Crisis of the Absolute Monarchy: France from Old Regime to Revolution*, published for The British Academy, Oxford: Oxford University Press, 2013, p. 289.

6. On the pre-revolutionary crisis, see the classic analysis by Georges Lefebvre, *The Coming of the French Revolution*, translated by R. R. Palmer, Princeton, NJ: Princeton University Press, 1947; and recent surveys by Peter Campbell (ed.), *The Origins of the French Revolution*, Basingstoke: Palgrave Macmillan, 2006; Thomas E. Kaiser and Dale K. Van Kley (eds), *From Deficit to Deluge: The Origins of the French Revolution*, Stanford, CA: Stanford University Press, 2011; William Doyle, *The Oxford History of the French Revolution*, 2nd edn., Oxford and New York: Oxford University Press, 2002, chs 4–5.

7. See the chapters by Michael Rapport and Olivier Chaline in Swann and Félix (eds), *Crisis of the Absolute Monarchy*; James C. Riley, *The Seven Years War and the Old Regime in France: The Economic and Financial Toll*, Princeton, NJ: Princeton University Press, 1986; Francois R. Velde and David R. Weir, 'The Financial Debt Market and Government Debt Policy in France, 1746–1793', *Journal of Economic History*, 52 (1992), pp. 1–39; Lynn Hunt, 'The French Revolution in Global Context', in David Armitage and Sanjay Subrahmanyam (eds), *The Age of Revolutions in Global Context, 1760–1840*, Basingstoke and New York: Palgrave Macmillan, 2010, ch. 2; Joël Félix, 'The Monarchy', in David Andress (ed.), *The Oxford Handbook of the French Revolution*, Oxford: Oxford University Press, 2015, ch. 4.

8. Stephen Miller, 'Venal Offices, Provincial Assemblies and the French Revolution', *FH*, 28 (2014), pp. 343–65. More generally on the reforms of 1787 and the 'noble revolt', see P. M. Jones, *Reform and Revolution in France: The Politics of Transition, 1774–1791*,

Cambridge: Cambridge University Press, 1995; Jean Égret, *The French Pre-Revolution, 1787–1788*, translated by W. D. Camp, Chicago, IL: Chicago University Press, 1977; Vivian R. Gruder, *The Notables and the Nation: The Political Schooling of the French, 1787–1788*, Cambridge, MA, and London: Harvard University Press, 2007; John Hardman, *Overture to Revolution: The 1787 Assembly of Notables and the Crisis of France's Old Régime*, Oxford: Oxford University Press, 2010.

9. Doyle, *Oxford History*, p. 73 and ch. 3; Simon Schama, *Citizens: A Chronicle of the French Revolution*, New York: Alfred A. Knopf, 1989, pp. 227–38.

10. John Hardman, *Louis XVI*, New Haven, CT, and London: Yale University Press, 1993, p. 126; David Andress, *1789: The Threshold of the Modern Age*, London: Little, Brown, 2008, chs 1, 3.

11. Annie Jourdan, 'Tumultuous Contexts and Radical Ideas (1783–89): The "Pre-Revolution" in a Transnational Perspective', and Thomas E. Kaiser, 'The Diplomatic Origins of the French Revolution', in Andress (ed.), *Oxford Handbook*, chs 6–7.

12. *AP*, 19 November 1787, series 1, vol. 1, pp. 265–69.

13. Gruder, *Notables and the Nation*, pp. 212, 292.

14. The Museum of the French Revolution is today housed in Périer's former château at Vizille.

15. One advertisement in the *Affiches de Toulouse* in December 1788 was for 'véritables pastilles à la Neckre [*sic*]': patriotic 'cough-drops for the public good': see Colin Jones, 'Bourgeois Revolution Revivified: 1789 and Social Change', in Colin Lucas (ed.), *Rewriting the French Revolution*, Oxford: The Clarendon Press, 1991, ch. 4, and Jones, 'The Great Chain of Buying: Medical Advertisement, the Bourgeois Public Sphere, and the Origins of the French Revolution', *AHR*, 101 (1996), pp. 13–40. On Necker's ministry, see John Hardman, 'The View from Above', in Andress (ed.), *Oxford Handbook*, ch. 8.

16. Arthur Young, *Travels in France during the Years 1787, 1788 and 1789*, New York: Anchor Books, 1969, pp. 97–98.

17. Maximilien Robespierre, *Oeuvres de Maximilien Robespierre*, 11 vols, Paris: SÉR, 1912–2007, vol. 3, pp. 22–23; Maza, *Private Lives and Public Affairs*, pp. 246–55; Doyle, 'Dupaty'; Barry M. Shapiro, *Revolutionary Justice in Paris, 1789–1790*, Cambridge, MA, and New York: Cambridge University Press, 1993, p. 8.

18. Robespierre, *Oeuvres*, vol. I, pp. 160–81; Peter McPhee, *Robespierre: A Revolutionary Life*, New Haven, CT, and London: Yale University Press, 2012, pp. 51–52.

19. Laura Mason and Tracey Rizzo (eds), *The French Revolution: A Document Collection*, Boston, MA, and New York: Houghton Mifflin, 1999, pp. 46–48.

20. Richard Mowery Andrews, 'Paris of the Great Revolution: 1789–1796', in Gene Brucker (ed.), *People and Communities in the Western World*, vol. 2, Homewood, IL: Dorsey Press, 1979, p. 59.

21. Daniel Roche, *France in the Enlightenment*, translated by Arthur Goldhammer, Cambridge, MA: Harvard University Press, 1998, pp. 669–72.

22. Rolf Reichardt and Herbert Schneider, 'Chanson et musique populaires devant l'histoire à la fin de l'Ancien Régime', *Dix-huitième siècle*, 18 (1986), pp. 117–42.

23. Michael Sonenscher, *Before the Deluge: Public Debt, Inequality, and the Intellectual Origins of the French Revolution*, Princeton, NJ: Princeton University Press, 2007.

24. Tim Blanning, 'William "Bill" Doyle and the *Origins of the French Revolution*', in Swann and Félix (eds), *Crisis of the Absolute Monarchy*, pp. 311–23; Kenneth Margerison, *Pamphlets and Public Opinion: The Campaign for a Union of Orders in the Early French Revolution*, West Lafayette, IN: Purdue University Press, 1998, ch. 3.

25. *AP*, 12 December 1788, series 1, vol. 1, pp. 487–89.

26. Gail Bossenga, *The Politics of Privilege: Old Regime and French Revolution in Lille*, Cambridge: Cambridge University Press, 1991, pp. 90–102, 204.

27. Rafe Blaufarb, *The Politics of Fiscal Privilege in Provence, 1530s–1830s*, Washington, DC: The Catholic University of America Press, 2012, ch. 5.

28. Michael Kwass, *Privilege and the Politics of Taxation in Eighteenth-Century France*, Cambridge: Cambridge University Press, 2000, pp. 268, 276, 285 and chs 4, 6; Égret, *The French Pre-Revolution*.

29. Peter Campbell, 'Introduction: The Origins of the French Revolution in Focus', in Campbell (ed.), *Origins*, p. 31.

30. Timothy Tackett, 'Paths to Revolution: The Old Regime Correspondence of Five Future Revolutionaries', *FHS*, 32 (2009), pp. 531–54.

31. Joël Cornette, *Histoire de la Bretagne et des Bretons*, vol. 2, Paris: Éditions du Seuil, 2005, ch. 42; Jacques Godechot, *The Taking of the Bastille, July 14th, 1789*, translated by Jean Stewart, London: Faber and Faber, 1970, pp. 128–29.

32. Emmanuel Sieyès, *What is the Third Estate?*, translated by M. Blondel, London: Pall Mall Press, 1963. See, too, Jay M. Smith, 'Social Categories, the Language of Patriotism, and the Origins of the French Revolution: The Debate over *noblesse commerçante*', *JMH*, 72 (2000), pp. 339–74; William H. Sewell Jr, *A Rhetoric of Bourgeois Revolution: The Abbé Sieyès and 'What is the Third Estate?'*, Durham, NC: Duke University Press, 1994.

33. Antoine de Baecque, *The Body Politic: Corporeal Metaphor in Revolutionary France, 1770–1800*, translated by Charlotte Mandell, Stanford, CA: Stanford University Press, 1997, p. 139.

34. Emmet Kennedy, *A Cultural History of the French Revolution*, New Haven, CT, and London: Yale University Press, 1989, pp. 35–47. Roger Chartier doubts the practice of reading aloud in *Cultural History: Between Practices and Representations*, translated by Lydia Cochrane, Cambridge: Cambridge University Press, 1988, ch. 7.

35. Jean-François Henry de Richeprey, *Journal des voyages en Haute-Guienne*, vol. 1, Rodez: H. Guilhamon, 1952, p. 70; Hilton L. Root, *Peasant and King in Burgundy: Agrarian Foundations of French Absolutism*, Berkeley, CA: University of California Press, 1987; Robert Forster, *The House of Saulx-Tavanes: Versailles and Burgundy, 1700–1830*, Baltimore, MD: Johns Hopkins University Press, 1977, ch. 2.

36. For an overview, see John Markoff, 'Peasants and their Grievances', in Campbell (ed.), *Origins*, ch. 9; P. M. Jones, *The Peasantry in the French Revolution*, Cambridge: Cambridge University Press, 1988, pp. 53–58.

37. Patricia Taylor, *Thomas Blaikie: The 'Capability' Brown of France, 1751–1838*, East Linton: Tuckwell, 2001, p. 115 and ch. 11.

38. Peter McPhee, *Revolution and Environment in Southern France: Peasants, Lords, and Murder in the Corbières, 1780–1830*, Oxford: Clarendon Press, 1999, p. 40.

39. A contrary argument that 'feudalism' was dead by the 1780s was put most famously by Alfred Cobban, *The Social Interpretation of the French Revolution*, Cambridge: Cambridge University Press, 1964; then by Emmanuel Le Roy Ladurie, in Georges Duby and Armand Wallon (eds), *Histoire de la France rurale*, Paris: Le Seuil, 1975–76, vol. 2, esp. pp. 554–72.

40. The classic Marxist formulations of the origins of the crisis of 1789 were by Lefebvre, *Coming of the French Revolution*, and Albert Soboul, *The French Revolution, 1787–1799: From the Storming of the Bastille to Napoleon*, translated by Alan Forrest and Colin Jones, New York: Vintage Books, 1975, pp. 25–113. A recent contribution is Lauren R. Clay, 'The Bourgeoisie, Capitalism, and the Origins of the French Revolution', in Andress (ed.), *Oxford Handbook*, ch. 2. This approach has been contested by William Doyle, *Origins of the French Revolution*, 3rd edn., Oxford and New York: Oxford University Press, 1999; Doyle, *Oxford History*, ch. 1; and T. C. W. Blanning, *The French Revolution: Aristocrats versus Bourgeois?*, London: Macmillan, 1987. The argument for the continuity of the reformist impulse during 1774–91 is eloquently stated by Peter Jones in *Reform and Revolution in France*; Jonathan Israel, *Revolutionary Ideas: An Intellectual History of the French Revolution from The Rights of Man to Robespierre*, Princeton, NJ: Princeton University Press, 2014, dwells on the Enlightenment as 'the one major cause'.

41. Julian Swann, 'Introduction: The Crisis of the Absolute Monarchy', in Swann and Félix (eds), *Crisis of the Absolute Monarchy*.

Chapter 4 The People's Revolution, 1789

1. AD Loiret J 557, 2J 1983; Paul Guillaume, 'La Vie dans l'Orléanais de 1788 à 1818, d'après le journal inédit d'une famille', unpublished ms, Orléans c.1960.

2. Jacques Godechot, *The Taking of the Bastille, July 14th, 1789*, translated by Jean Stewart, London: Faber and Faber, 1970, pp. 124–33; Donald Sutherland, 'Urban Crowds, Riot, Utopia, and Massacres, 1789–92', in Peter McPhee (ed.), *A Companion to the French Revolution*, Oxford: Wiley-Blackwell, 2013, p. 233.

3. P. M. Jones, *The Peasantry in the French Revolution*, Cambridge: Cambridge University Press, 1988, pp. 60–81; P. M. Jones, *Reform and Revolution in France: The Politics of Transition, 1774–1791*, Cambridge: Cambridge University Press, 1995, pp. 166–74, 180–83; Godechot,

Taking of the Bastille, ch. 6; Georges Lefebvre, *The Great Fear of 1789: Rural Panic in Revolutionary France*, translated by Joan White, New York: Vintage Books, 1973, ch. 4; David Andress, *1789: The Threshold of the Modern Age*, London: Little, Brown, 2008, pp. 205–07.

4. Godechot, *Taking of the Bastille*, p. 129; John Markoff, *The Abolition of Feudalism: Peasants, Lords, and Legislators in the French Revolution*, University Park, PA: Pennsylvania State University Press, 1996, p. 226.

5. John Hall Stewart (ed.), *A Documentary Survey of the French Revolution*, New York: Macmillan, 1951, pp. 29–30.

6. On the *cahiers*, see Gilbert Shapiro and John Markoff, *Revolutionary Demands: A Content Analysis of the Cahiers de Doléances of 1789*, Stanford, CA: Stanford University Press, 1998; Markoff, *Abolition of Feudalism*; Pierre-Yves Beaurepaire, 'The View from Below: The 1789 cahiers de doléances', in David Andress (ed.), *The Oxford Handbook of the French Revolution*, Oxford: Oxford University Press, 2015, ch. 9; Philippe Grateau, *Les Cahiers de doléances: une relecture culturelle*, Rennes: Presses Universitaires de Rennes, 2001. Several thousand parish *cahiers* were published in the first half of the twentieth century under the auspices of the Ministère de l'Instruction Publique as the *Collection de documents inédits sur l'histoire économique de la Révolution française*. This series is outlined in Shapiro and Markoff, *Revolutionary Demands*, pp. 117–19.

7. *Cahiers de doléances du bailliage de Bourges et des bailliages secondaires de Vierzon et d'Henrichement pour les Etats-Généraux de 1789*, Bourges: Tardy-Pigelet, 1910.

8. *Cahiers de doléances du bailliage de Bourges.*

9. Paul Beik (ed.), *The French Revolution*, London: Macmillan, 1971, pp. 56–63.

10. Michael P. Fitzsimmons, *The Remaking of France: The National Assembly, the Constitution of 1791 and the Reorganization of the French Polity*, Cambridge and New York: Cambridge University Press, 1994, pp. 28–32; Régine Robin, *La Société française en 1789: Semur-en-Auxois*, Paris: Plon, 1970.

11. Jeffry Kaplow (ed.), *France on the Eve of Revolution*, New York: Wiley, 1971, pp. 161–67; Richard Cobb and Colin Jones (eds), *Voices of the French Revolution*, Topsfield, MA: Simon & Schuster, 1988, p.42; 'Doléances particulières des marchandes bouquetières fleuristes chapelières en fleurs de la Ville et faubourgs de Paris', in Charles-Louis Chassin, *Les Elections et les cahiers de Paris en 1789*, 4 vols, Paris: Jouaust et Sigaux, 1888–89, vol. 2, pp. 534–37.

12. Jeffry Kaplow, *Elbeuf during the Revolutionary Period: History and Social Structure*, Baltimore, MD: Johns Hopkins University Press, 1964, pp. 192–205.

13. On the limitations to the usefulness of the *cahiers*, see Jones, *Peasantry*, pp. 58–67; Markoff, *Abolition of Feudalism*, pp. 25–29.

14. Shapiro and Markoff, *Revolutionary Demands*, pp. 136–40.

15. Marcelle Richard (ed.), *1789. Doléances et élections dans le futur Morbihan*, 2nd edn., Vannes: AD du Morbihan, 1988, pp. 15–27.

16. Jones, *Peasantry*, pp. 94–98.

17. Maurice, Denise and Robert Bréant, *Menucourt. Un village du Vexin français pendant la Révolution, 1789–1799*, Menucourt: Mairie de Menucourt, 1989, pp. 45–46.

18. Jones, *Peasantry*, pp. 58–67; Peter McPhee, '"The misguided greed of peasants"? Popular Attitudes to the Environment in the Revolution of 1789', *FHS*, 24 (2001), pp. 247–69.

19. Étienne Frénay (ed.), *Cahiers de doléances de la province de Roussillon (1789)*, Perpignan: AD des Pyrénées-Orientales, 1979; McPhee, *Revolution and Environment in Southern France: Peasants, Lords, and Murder in the Corbières, 1780–1830*, Oxford: Clarendon Press, 1999, p. 49.

20. McPhee, *Revolution and Environment*, p. 42.

21. Philip Dawson (ed.), *The French Revolution*, Englewood Cliffs, NJ: Prentice Hall, 1967, pp. 16–18, 30–32.

22. 'Cahier des plaintes et demandes de la ville de Rhuis aux États-Généraux', AD Morbihan, Bibliothèque R 2748. See Godechot, *Taking of the Bastille*, pp. 128–29; T. J. A. Le Goff, *Vannes and its Region: A Study of Town and Country in Eighteenth-Century France*, Oxford: Clarendon Press, 1981, chs 11–12; *La Bretagne. Une province à l'aube de la Révolution. Colloque de Brest, 28–30 septembre 1988*, Brest and Quimper: Centre de Recherche Bretonne et Celtique, 1989.

23. Anatoli Ado, *Paysans en Révolution. Terre, pouvoir et jacquerie, 1789–1794*, Paris: SÉR, 1996, p. 114.

24. On the elections of 1789, see Malcolm Crook, *Elections in the French Revolution: An Apprenticeship in Democracy, 1789–1799*, Cambridge and New York: Cambridge University Press, 1996, ch. 1; Jones, *Peasantry*, pp. 28, 62–64; Micah Alpaugh, 'A Personal Revolution: National Assembly Deputies and the Politics of 1789', in Andress (ed.), *Oxford Handbook*, ch. 11.

25. Jones, *Peasantry*, pp. 65–67; Lefevbre, *Great Fear*, p. 39. A regional study is Clay Ramsay, *The Ideology of the Great Fear: The Soissonnais in 1789*, Baltimore, MD, and London: Johns Hopkins University Press, 1992.

26. Peter McPhee, *Robespierre: A Revolutionary Life*, New Haven, CT, and London: Yale University Press, 2012, pp. 50–61.

27. On the composition of the Estates-General, see Timothy Tackett, *Becoming a Revolutionary: The Deputies of the French National Assembly and the Emergence of a Revolutionary Culture (1789–1790)*, Princeton, NJ: Princeton University Press, 1996, ch. 1.

28. Jean-René Suratteau and François Gendron (eds), *Dictionnaire historique de la Révolution française*, Paris: PUF, 1989, p. 47. Le Floc'h was killed in front of his children by Vendéan rebels in November 1793.

29. T. C. W. Blanning, 'Doyle and the *Origins*', in Julian Swann and Joël Félix (eds), *The Crisis of the Absolute Monarchy: France from Old Regime to Revolution*, published for The British Academy, Oxford: Oxford University Press, 2013, p. 319.

30. On Grégoire, see Joseph F. Byrnes, *Priests of the French Revolution: Saints and Renegades in a New Political Era*, University Park, PA: Pennsylvania State University Press, 2014, ch. 1; Alyssa Goldstein Sepinwall, *The Abbé Grégoire and the French Revolution: The Making of Modern Universalism*, Berkeley and Los Angeles, CA, and London: University of California Press, 2005.

31. Godechot, *Taking of the Bastille*, pp. 133–51; David Garrioch, *The Making of Revolutionary Paris*, Berkeley and Los Angeles, CA, and London: University of California Press, 2002, ch. 11.

32. Antoine Caillot, *Mes vingt ans de folie, d'amour et de bonheur, ou mémoires d'un abbé petit-maître*, Paris: À la Librairie Économique, 1808, vol. 3, pp. 177–78.

33. Madame de La Tour du Pin, *Memoirs: Laughing and Dancing our Way to the Precipice*, translated by Felice Harcourt, London: Harvill Press, 1999, pp. 103–04, 112–14.

34. D. Lottin, *Recherches historiques sur la Ville d'Orléans*, 8 vols, Orléans: Imprimerie Alexandre Jacob, 1836–45, vol. 3, pp. 47–50.

35. J. M. Thompson (ed.), *English Witnesses of the French Revolution*, Oxford: Oxford University Press, 1938, p. 58; Aileen Ribeiro, *Fashion in the French Revolution*, London: Batsford, 1988, p. 46.

36. John Hardman, *Louis XVI*, New Haven, CT, and London: Yale University Press, 1993, p. 21.

37. Dale K. Van Kley, *The Religious Origins of the French Revolution: From Calvin to the Civil Constitution, 1560–1791*, New Haven, CT, and London: Yale University Press, 1996, p. 349.

38. *Gazette Nationale ou le Moniteur Universel*, no. 10, 20–24 June 1789, vol. 1, p. 89.

39. S. A. Bent (ed.), *Familiar Short Sayings of Great Men*, Boston, MA: Ticknor and Co., 1887. His actual words are unknown.

40. Micah Alpaugh, *Non-Violence and the French Revolution: Political Demonstrations in Paris, 1787–1795*, Cambridge: Cambridge University Press, 2014. Others prefer to emphasize the violence of urban crowds: D. M. G. Sutherland, 'Urban Violence in 1789', in Andress (ed.), *Oxford Handbook*, ch. 16; Haim Burstin, *Révolutionnaires. Pour une anthropologie de la Révolution française*, Paris: Vendémiaire, 2013, pp. 312–27.

41. George Rudé, *The Crowd in the French Revolution*, Oxford: Oxford University Press, 1959, p. 46; Alpaugh, *Non-Violence*; Gérard Bonn, *Camille Desmoulins, ou la plume de la liberté*, Paris: Éditions Glyphe, 2006.

42. Momcilo Markovic, 'La Révolution aux barrières: l'incendie des barrières de l'octroi à Paris en juillet 1789', *AHRF*, 372 (2013), pp. 27–48. Four of the *barrières* are still standing, the most imposing of them the Rotonde de la Villette.

43. Rudé, *Crowd in the French Revolution*, ch. 4.

44. *Women in Revolutionary Paris, 1789–1795. Selected Documents Translated with Notes and Commentary by Darline Gay Levy, Harriet Branson Applewhite and Mary Durham Johnson*, Urbana and Chicago, IL: University of Illinois Press, 1980, pp. 29–30.

45. Godechot, *Taking of the Bastille*, pp. 259–60; Laura Auricchio, *The Marquis: Lafayette Reconsidered*, New York: Alfred A. Knopf, 2014, ch. 12.

46. Simon Schama, *Citizens: A Chronicle of the French Revolution*, New York: Alfred A. Knopf, 1989, p. 446; Burstin, *Révolutionnaires*, pp. 312–27; *Les Révolutions de Paris*, no. 1, 12–18 July 1789, pp. 17–19, no. 2, 18–25 July 1789, pp. 18–25. An excellent collection of newspaper articles is J. Gilchrist and W. J. Murray (eds), *The Press in the French Revolution: A Selection of Documents Taken from the Press of the Revolution for the Years 1789–1794*, Melbourne: Cheshire; London: Ginn, 1971.

47. Lynn Hunt, *Revolution and Urban Politics in Provincial France: Troyes and Reims, 1786–1790*, Stanford, CA: Stanford University Press, 1978; Lefebvre, *Coming of the French Revolution*, ch. 8.

48. Arthur Young, *Travels in France during the Years 1787, 1788 and 1789*, New York: Anchor Books, 1969, p. 144.

49. Jacques Bernet (ed.), *Le Journal d'un maître d'école d'Île-de-France (1771–1792): Silly-en-Multien de l'Ancien Régime à la Révolution*, Villeneuve-d'Asq: Centre d'Histoire de la Région du Nord et de l'Europe du Nord-Ouest, Université Charles de Gaulle-Lille III, 2000, pp. 189, 195–96. The commune is today Silly-le-Long.

50. Eugène Dubois, *Histoire de la Révolution dans l'Ain*, vol. 1, *La Constituante (1789–1791)*, Bourg-en-Bresse: Brochot, 1931, pp. 60–68; Louis Trenard, 'Le "vandalisme révolutionnaire" dans les pays de l'Ain: faits matériels et motivations', in Simone Bernard-Griffiths, Marie-Claude Chemin and Jean Ehrard, *Révolution française et 'vandalisme révolutionnaire'. Actes du colloque international de Clermont-Ferrand, 15–17 décembre 1988*, Paris: Universitas, 1992, pp. 252–53.

51. Ted W. Margadant, 'Summary Justice and the Crisis of the Old Regime in 1789', *Historical Reflections/Réflexions historiques* 29 (2003), pp. 495–528.

52. Claude Muller, 'Religion et Révolution en Alsace', *AHRF*, 337 (2004), p. 70; Timothy Tackett, 'Collective Panics in the Early French Revolution', *FH*, 17 (2003), pp. 149–58.

53. Claudia Ulbrich, 'Sarreguemines en révolution ou l'histoire d'un "caméléon politique"', *Annales de l'Est*, 44 (1992), pp. 16–17.

54. A. Racinet, *Histoire de Mortagne* (1899), Paris: Res Universis, 1988, pp. 73–76. Lamberdière would be tried for sedition, sentenced on 2 October, and hanged in Alençon, as local authorities desperately tried to restore order.

55. Lefebvre, *Great Fear*, p. 40.

56. *AHRF*, 1955, pp. 161–62; Philip Dwyer and Peter McPhee (eds), *The French Revolution and Napoleon: A Sourcebook*, London and New York: Routledge, 2002, pp. 22–23.

57. *Moniteur universel*, no. 40, 11–14 August 1789, vol. 1, pp. 332–33; Michael P. Fitzsimmons, *The Night the Old Regime Ended: August 4, 1789 and the French Revolution*, University Park, PA: Pennsylvania State University Press, 2003; Jones, *Peasantry*, pp. 81–85; Markoff, *Abolition of Feudalism*, ch. 8. An interesting discussion of conflicting emotions at play is by Jon Elster, 'The Night of August 4, 1789: A Study of Social Interaction in Collective Decision-Making', *Revue européenne des sciences sociales*, 45 (2007), pp. 71–94.

58. Timothy Tackett, *The Coming of the Terror in the French Revolution*, Cambridge, MA, and London: The Belknap Press of Harvard University Press, 2015, p. 60.

59. Eric Thompson, *Popular Sovereignty and the French Constituent Assembly, 1789–1791*, Manchester: Manchester University Press, 1952, ch. 1.

60. 'Cahier de doléances et réclamations des femmes par Mme. B . . . B. . . ., 1789', in *Cahiers de doléances des femmes et autres textes*, Paris: Des Femmes, 1981, pp. 47–59.

61. David Andress, *The French Revolution and the People*, London: Hambledon and London, 2004, p. 103; Rudé, *Crowd in the French Revolution*, pp. 47, 209.

Chapter 5 Regenerating the Nation, 1789–90

1. David Andress, *1789: The Threshold of the Modern Age*, London: Little, Brown, 2008, ch. 12; Simon Lee, *David*, London: Phaidon, 1999, ch. 3; Thomas E. Crow, *Emulation: David, Drouais, and Girodet in the Art of Revolutionary France*, New Haven, CT, and London: Yale University Press, 2006, pp. 117–19. Like David, Antoine Lavoisier had married a woman half his age: Marie-Anne was just fourteen when she married the twenty-eight-year-old Antoine.

2. Timothy Tackett, *Becoming a Revolutionary: The Deputies of the French National Assembly and the Emergence of a Revolutionary Culture (1789–1790)*, Princeton, NJ: Princeton University Press, 1996, pp. 188–95.

3. T. C. W. Blanning, 'Doyle and the *Origins*', in Julian Swann and Joël Félix (eds), *The Crisis of the Absolute Monarchy: France from Old Regime to Revolution*, published for The British Academy, Oxford: Oxford University Press, 2013; Michel Biard and Pascal Dupuy, *La Révolution française. Dynamique et ruptures, 1787–1804*, 2nd edn., Paris: Armand Colin, 2008, pp. 50–53.

4. Rabaut St-Étienne, *Réflexions sur la nouvelle division du Royaume et sur les privilèges et les assemblées des provinces d'états*, reprinted in M. J. Madival (ed.), *Archives parlementaires*, Paris, 1878, vol. 10, pp. 37–38; Ted W. Margadant, *Urban Rivalries in the French Revolution*, Princeton, NJ: Princeton University Press, 1992, p. 84; Suzanne Desan, *The Family on Trial in Revolutionary France*, Berkeley and Los Angeles, CA, and London: University of California Press, 2004, p. 72.

5. Colin Lucas, 'The Theory and Practice of Denunciation in the French Revolution', *JMH*, 68 (1996), p. 770.

6. Peter R. Campbell, Thomas E. Kaiser and Marisa Linton (eds), *Conspiracy in the French Revolution*, Manchester: Manchester University Press, 2007; Dale K. Van Kley. 'Conspiracy Theories and Theories of Conspiracy: A Review Essay', *H-France Review*, 10 (2010), no. 11. http://www.h-france.net/vol10reviews/vol10no11kley.pdf. Recent explorations of revolutionary 'psychology' in 1789 are Timothy Tackett, *The Coming of the Terror in the French Revolution*, Cambridge, MA, and London: The Belknap Press of Harvard University Press, 2015, ch. 2; Haim Burstin, *Révolutionnaires. Pour une anthropologie de la Révolution française*, Paris: Vendémiaire, 2013.

7. Alessandro Galante Garrone, *Gilbert Romme: histoire d'un révolutionnaire, 1750–1795*, translated from the Italian by Anne and Claude Manceron, Paris: Flammarion, 1971. Romme's decision to introduce Pavel to the Jacobin Club in 1790 seems to have been the catalyst for his father to order him home to Russia.

8. [Edmond Géraud], *Journal d'un étudiant pendant la Révolution, 1789–1793*, Paris: Plon, 1910, pp. 23–25.

9. AD Loiret 2J 1983; D. Lottin, *Recherches historiques sur la ville d'Orléans*, 8 vols, Orléans: Imprimerie Alexandre Jacob, 1836–45, vol. 3, pp. 59–60; Luc Rojas, '"Les forgeurs et les limeurs" face à la machine: la destruction de l'atelier de Jacques Sauvade (1er et 2ème septembre 1789)', *AHRF*, 376 (2014), pp. 27–52.

10. Tackett, *Becoming a Revolutionary*, pp. 195–206; George Rudé, *The Crowd in the French Revolution*, Oxford: Oxford University Press, 1959, p. 69 and ch. 5; Micah Alpaugh, *Non-Violence and the French Revolution: Political Demonstrations in Paris, 1787–1795*, Cambridge: Cambridge University Press, 2014.

11. John Hardman, *Louis XVI*, New Haven, CT, and London: Yale University Press, 1993, p. 171.

12. Arlette Farge, *Subversive Words: Public Opinion in Eighteenth-Century France*, translated by Rosemary Morris, Oxford: Polity Press, 1994, pp. 117–21.

13. There is no evidence of an expression of Marie-Antoinette's contempt for the masses inherent in her purported snort, 'The peasants have no bread? Then let them eat cake.' The remark first seems to have been attributed to her in a German children's book in 1931. See Véronique Campion-Vincent and Christine Shojaei Kawan, 'Marie-Antoinette et son célèbre dire: deux scénographies et deux siècles de désordres, trois niveaux de communication et trois modes accusatoires', *AHRF*, 327 (2002), pp. 29–56.

14. *Réimpression de l'Ancien Moniteur, seule histoire authentique et inaltérée de la Révolution française, depuis la réunion des Etats-Généraux jusqu'au Consulat*, 32 vols, Paris, 1847, vol. 2, 1789, p. 544; Richard Cobb and Colin Jones (eds), *Voices of the French Revolution*, Topsfield, MA: Simon & Schuster, 1988, p. 88.

15. Rudé, *Crowd in the French Revolution*, p. 79.

16. Michael Kennedy, *The Jacobin Clubs in the French Revolution: The First Years*, Princeton, NJ: Princeton University Press, 1982.

17. Élisabeth Vigée-Lebrun, *Memoirs of Mme Vigée Lebrun*, translated by Lionel Strachey, New York: G. Braziller, 1989, pp. 55–56.

18. Michael Rapport, 'The International Repercussions of the French Revolution', in Peter McPhee (ed.), *A Companion to the French Revolution*, Oxford: Wiley-Blackwell, 2013, p. 383.

19. See, in general, R. R. Palmer, *The Age of the Democratic Revolution: A Political History of Europe and America, 1760–1800*, 2 vols, Princeton, NJ: Princeton University Press, 1959,

1964; Jacques Godechot, *France and the Atlantic Revolution of the Eighteenth Century, 1770–1799*, translated by Herbert H. Rowen, New York: The Free Press, 1965.

20. Ambrogio A. Caiani, *Louis XVI and the French Revolution, 1789–1792*, Cambridge: Cambridge University Press, 2012, pp. 65–67.

21. Mona Ozouf, 'La Révolution française et la perception de l'espace national: fédérations, fédéralisme et stéréotypes régionaux', in Ozouf, *L'École de la France: essais sur la Révolution, l'utopie et l'enseignement*, Paris: Gallimard, 1984, p. 33.

22. In general, see Alan Forrest, 'Reimagining Space and Power' in McPhee (ed.), *Companion*, ch. 6; P. M. Jones, *Reform and Revolution in France: The Politics of Transition, 1774–1791*, Cambridge: Cambridge University Press, 1995, ch. 6; Peter McPhee, *Living the French Revolution, 1789–99*, London and New York: Palgrave Macmillan, 2006, ch. 3; Michael P. Fitzsimmons, *The Remaking of France: The National Assembly and the Constitution of 1791*, Cambridge and New York: Cambridge University Press, 1994; Malcolm Crook, 'The New Regime: Political Institutions and Democratic Practices under the Constitutional Monarchy, 1789–1791', in David Andress (ed.), *The Oxford Handbook of the French Revolution*, Oxford: Oxford University Press, 2015, ch. 13.

23. On Brittany, see T. J. A. Le Goff, *Vannes and its Region: A Study of Town and Country in Eighteenth-Century France*, Oxford: Clarendon Press, 1981; *La Bretagne. Une province à l'aube de la Révolution. Colloque de Brest, 28–30 septembre 1988*, Brest and Quimper: Centre de Recherche Bretonne et Celtique, 1989; Joël Cornette, *Histoire de la Bretagne et des Bretons*, vol. 2, Paris: Éditions du Seuil, 2005; Roger Dupuy, *La Bretagne sous la Révolution et l'Empire (1789–1815)*, Rennes: Éditions Ouest-France, 2004.

24. Martyn Lyons, *Revolution in Toulouse: An Essay on Provincial Terrorism*, Bern, Frankfurt am Main and Las Vegas: Peter Lang, 1978.

25. Margadant, *Urban Rivalries*, pp. 263–64; McPhee, *Living*, p. 81.

26. Arthur Young, *Travels in France during the Years 1787, 1788 and 1789*, New York: Anchor Books, 1969, p. 226.

27. Comte de Courchamps, *Souvenirs de la marquise de Créquy de 1710 à 1803*, 10 vols, Paris: Garnier Frères, 1865, vol. 9, pp. 107–08.

28. Jill Maciak Walshaw, *A Show of Hands for the Republic: Opinion, Information, and Repression in Eighteenth-Century Rural France*, Rochester, NY: Rochester University Press, 2014, ch. 3.

29. P. M. Jones, *The Peasantry in the French Revolution*, Cambridge: Cambridge University Press, 1988, p. 209.

30. Bibliothèque Municipale, Nancy, ms 1412.

31. Nigel Aston, *Religion and Revolution in France, 1780–1804*, Basingstoke: Macmillan, 2000, p. 133; Tackett, *Becoming a Revolutionary*, pp. 203–04.

32. Scattered research on the sales of *biens nationaux* is synthesized in Bernard Bodinier and Éric Teyssier, *L'Événement le plus important de la Révolution: la vente des biens nationaux en France et dans les territoires annexés, 1789*–1867, Paris: SÉR, 2000; Bernard Bodinier, 'La Vente des biens nationaux: essai de synthèse', *AHRF*, 315 (1999), pp. 7–19; Jones, *Peasantry*, pp. 154–61; Joël Cornette (ed.), *Atlas de l'histoire de France, 481–2005*, Paris: Belin, 2012, p. 316.

33. Peter McPhee, *Revolution and Environment in Southern France: Peasants, Lords, and Murder in the Corbières, 1780–1830*, Oxford: Clarendon Press, 1999, ch. 3.

34. Aimé Coiffard, *La Vente des biens nationaux dans le district de Grasse (1790–1815)*, Paris: Bibliothèque nationale, 1973, pp. 94–103.

35. Michel Péronnet, Robert Attal and Jean Bobin, *La Révolution dans l'Aisne, 1789–1799*, Le Coteau: Horvath, 1988, p. 109; Michel Bur (ed.), *Histoire de Laon et du Laonnois*, Toulouse: Privat, 1987, p. 199.

36. S. E. Harris, *The Assignats*, Cambridge, MA: Harvard University Press, 1930.

37. William Doyle, *The Oxford History of the French Revolution*, 2nd edn., Oxford and New York: Oxford University Press, 2002, p. 124.

38. Lottin, *Orléans*, vol. 3, pp. 77–79. In general, see Malcolm Crook, *Elections in the French Revolution: An Apprenticeship in Democracy, 1789–1799*, Cambridge and New York: Cambridge University Press, 1996; Melvin Edelstein, *The French Revolution and the Birth of Electoral Democracy*, Farnham, Surrey, and Burlington, VT: Ashgate, 2014.

39. Dominique Godineau, *The Women of Paris and their French Revolution*, translated by Katherine Streip, Berkeley, CA: University of California Press, 1998, pp. 76–77.

40. Anthony Crubaugh, *Balancing the Scales of Justice: Local Courts and Rural Society in Southwest France, 1750–1800*, University Park, PA: Pennsylvania State University Press, 2001.

41. Katherine Taylor, 'Geometries of Power: Royal, Revolutionary, and Post-Revolutionary French courtrooms', *Journal of the Society of Architectural Historians*, 72 (2013), pp. 434–74.

42. Michael Sibalis, 'The Regulation of Male Homosexuality in Revolutionary and Napoleonic France, 1789–1815', in Jeffrey Merrick and Bryant T. Ragan (eds), *Homosexuality in Modern France*, New York: Oxford University Press, 1996, pp. 80–101.

43. Paul Friedland, *Seeing Justice Done: The Age of Spectacular Capital Punishment in France*, Oxford: Oxford University Press, 2012, chs 9–10; Daniel Arasse, *The Guillotine and the Terror*, translated by Christopher Miller, London: Penguin, 1989, pp. 11–14.

44. Friedland, *Seeing Justice Done*, pp. 247–48; Arasse, *Guillotine and the Terror*, pp. 26–30.

45. Christian Pfister, *Histoire de Nancy*, vol. 3, Paris: Éditions du Palais Royal; Nancy: Éditions Berger-Levrault, 1974, pp. 328–32.

46. *Moniteur universel*, no. 46, 15 February 1790, vol. 2, pp. 368–69; Gary Kates, 'Jews into Frenchmen: Nationality and Representation in Revolutionary France', in Ferenc Fehér (ed.), *The French Revolution and the Birth of Modernity*, Berkeley, CA: University of California Press, 1990, pp. 103–16.

47. Abraham Spire, *Le Journal révolutionnaire d'Abraham Spire*, translated by Simon Schwarzfuchs, Paris: Institut Alain de Rothschild/Verdier, 1989, pp. 120–22.

48. Roger Dupuy, 'Les Émeutes anti-féodales de Haute-Bretagne (janvier 1790 et janvier 1791): meneurs improvisés ou agitateurs politisés?', in Jean Nicolas (ed.), *Mouvements populaires et conscience sociale, XVI–XIXe siècles. Actes du colloque de Paris, 24–26 mai 1984*, Paris: Maloine, 1985, pp. 453–54.

49. Jean Boutier, 'Jacqueries en pays croquant: les révoltes paysannes en Aquitaine (décembre 1789–mars 1790)', *AHRF*, 34 (1979), p. 765; *Campagnes en émoi. Révoltes et Révolution en Bas-Limousin, 1789–1800*, Treignac: Éditions les Monédières, 1987; Jones, *Peasantry*, pp. 105–17; Mona Ozouf, *Festivals and the French Revolution*, translated by Alan Sheridan, Cambridge, MA: Harvard University Press, 1988, pp. 37–38, 232–43.

50. Christiane Constant, *Journal d'un bourgeois de Bégoux. Michel Célarié (1771–1836)*, Cahors: Le Stum, 1992, pp. 146–48. On the rural revolution, see Jones, *Peasantry*, pp. 67–85; John Markoff, *The Abolition of Feudalism: Peasants, Lords, and Legislators in the French Revolution*, University Park, PA: Pennsylvania State University Press, 1996, chs 5–7; Anatoli Ado, *Paysans en Révolution. Terre, pouvoir et jacquerie, 1789–1794*, Paris: SÉR, 1996, chs 4–6; the chapters by Jean Bart and Jean-Pierre Jessenne in Michel Biard (ed.), *La Révolution française, une histoire toujours vivante*, Paris: Tallandier, 2009; McPhee, *Living*, ch. 3.

51. Bryant T. Ragan, 'Rural Political Equality and Fiscal Activism in the Revolutionary Somme', in Bryant T. Ragan and Elizabeth A. Williams (eds), *Re-creating Authority in Revolutionary France*, New Brunswick, NJ: Rutgers University Press, 1992, p. 46; Ozouf, *Festivals*, pp. 37–39.

52. P. Sagnac and P. Caron, *Le Comité des droits féodaux et de législation et l'abolition du régime seigneurial, 1789–1793*, Paris: Imprimerie Nationale, 1907, p. 252. In general, see McPhee, *Living*, ch. 3; Noelle Plack, 'Challenges in the Countryside, 1790–2', in Andress (ed.), *Oxford Handbook*, ch. 20.

53. Josef Konvitz, *Cartography in France, 1660–1848: Science, Engineering, and Statecraft*, Chicago, IL: University of Chicago Press, 1987.

54. Courchamps, *Souvenirs de la marquise de Créquy*, vol. 9, pp. 107–08, 145.

55. Jacques Godechot, *The Taking of the Bastille, July 14th, 1789*, translated by Jean Stewart, London: Faber and Faber, 1970, pp. 263–66; Héloïse Bocher, *Démolir la Bastille. L'édification d'un lieu de mémoire*, Paris: Vendémiaire, 2012; Hans-Jürgen Lüsebrink and Rolf Reichardt, *The Bastille: A History of a Symbol of Despotism and Freedom*, Durham, NC: Duke University Press, 1997.

56. Lottin, *Orléans*, vol. 3, pp. 120–50.

57. Micah Alpaugh, 'Les Émotions collectives et le mouvement des fédérations (1789–1790)', *AHRF*, 372 (2013), pp. 49–80.

58. F.-A. Mignet, *Histoire de la Révolution française depuis 1789 jusqu'en 1814*, London: David Nutt, 1882, p. 88.

59. Pascal Dupuy (ed.), *La Fête de la Fédération*, Rouen: Publications des Universités de Rouen et du Havre, 2012, p. 132. On revolutionary festivals in general, see Ozouf, *Festivals*; Jean

Ehrard and Paul Viallaneix (eds), *Les Fêtes de la Révolution. Colloque de Clermont-Ferrand (juin 1974)*, Paris: SÉR, 1977.

60. Rebecca L. Spang, *The Invention of the Restaurant: Paris and Modern Gastronomic Culture*, Cambridge, MA: Harvard University Press, 2000, pp. 99–100.

61. Alain Corbin, *Village Bells: Sound and Meaning in the 19th-Century French Countryside*, translated by Martin Thom, New York: Columbia University Press, 1998, pp. xix, 8, 95–96, 301.

62. Fitzsimmons, *Remaking of France*; pp. 209–10; Ozouf, *Festivals*, p. 51.

63. Ozouf, *Festivals*, p. 51; Aileen Ribeiro, *Fashion in the French Revolution*, New York: Holmes and Meier, 1988.

Chapter 6 The Revolution Triumphant, 1790

1. Peter McPhee, *Robespierre: A Revolutionary Life*, New Haven, CT, and London: Yale University Press, 2012, p. 102.

2. Antoine Casanova and Ange Rovère, *La Révolution française en Corse: 1789–1800*, Toulouse: Privat, 1989; Philip Dwyer, *Napoleon: The Path to Power, 1769–1799*, London: Bloomsbury, 2007.

3. Ian Coller, 'The Revolutionary Mediterranean', in Peter McPhee (ed.), *A Companion to the French Revolution*, Oxford: Wiley-Blackwell, 2013, ch. 25.

4. Greg Burgess, *Refuge in the Land of Liberty: France and its Refugees, from the Revolution to the End of Asylum, 1787–1939*, Basingstoke and New York: Palgrave Macmillan, 2008, pp. 7–24; Michael Rapport, *Nationality and Citizenship in Revolutionary France: The Treatment of Foreigners, 1789–1799*, Oxford: Clarendon Press, 2000, ch. 2; Coller, 'Revolutionary Mediterranean'.

5. Emmet Kennedy, *A Cultural History of the French Revolution*, New Haven, CT, and London: Yale University Press, 1989, ch. 8; Lucie Favier, *La Mémoire de l'État: histoire des Archives nationales*, Paris: Fayard, 2004.

6. William Doyle, *The Oxford History of the French Revolution*, 2nd edn., Oxford and New York: Oxford University Press, 2002, pp. 160–64.

7. Jacques Godechot, *France and the Atlantic Revolution of the Eighteenth Century, 1770–1799*, translated by Herbert H. Rowen, New York: The Free Press, 1965, p. 131.

8. Pierre Devanthey, *La Révolution bas-valaisanne de 1790*, Martigny: Imprimerie Pillet, 1972.

9. Michael Rapport, 'The International Repercussions of the French Revolution', in McPhee (ed.), *Companion*, p. 385; Adrian Carton, *Mixed-Race and Modernity in Colonial India: Changing Concepts of Hybridity across Empires*, London and New York: Routledge, 2012.

10. Laurent Dubois, 'Slavery in the Age of Revolution', in Gad Heuman and Trevor Burnard (eds), *The Routledge History of Slavery*, London: Routledge, 2011, pp. 267–80; Pierre Boulle, 'In Defence of Slavery', in Frederick Krantz (ed.), *History from Below: Studies in Popular Protest and Popular Ideology*, Oxford and New York: Blackwell, 1988, pp. 221–41.

11. Jean-Michel Deveau, *Le Commerce rochelais face à la Révolution. Correspondance de Jean-Baptiste Nairac (1789–1790)*, La Rochelle: Rumeur des âges, 1989; Claudy Valin, *La Rochelle-la Vendée, 1793. Révolution et Contre-Révolution*, Paris: Le Croît vif, 1997, parts 1 and 2; Lynn Hunt (ed. and trans.), *The French Revolution and Human Rights: A Brief Documentary History*, Boston, MA, and New York: Bedford/St. Martin's Press, 1996, pp. 109–11.

12. AD Loire-Atlantique, L366.

13. Ted W. Margadant, *Urban Rivalries in the French Revolution*, Princeton, NJ: Princeton University Press, 1992.

14. Michael P. Fitzsimmons, *From Artisan to Worker: Guilds, the French State, and the Organization of Labor, 1776–1821*, New York: Cambridge University Press, 2010, ch. 1; Steven L. Kaplan, *La Fin des corporations*, Paris: Fayard, 2001.

15. Peter McPhee, *Revolution and Environment in Southern France: Peasants, Lords, and Murder in the Corbières, 1780–1830*, Oxford: Clarendon Press, 1999, ch. 3.

16. Daniel Morvan, 'L'Oeil du maître. Rosanbo, une seigneurie au quotidien', *Skol Vreizh*, 24 (1992), pp. 1–83.

17. AD Charente-Maritime L 147, 739; Peter McPhee, *Living the French Revolution, 1789–99*, London and New York: Palgrave Macmillan, 2006, p. 63; Anthony Crubaugh, *Balancing the Scales of Justice: Local Courts and Rural Society in Southwest France, 1750–1800*, University Park, PA: Pennsylvania State University Press, 2001, pp. 55–56.

18. Peter McPhee, '"The misguided greed of peasants"? Popular Attitudes to the Environment in the Revolution of 1789', *FHS*, 24 (2001), p. 247.

19. Georges Bourgin, *Le Partage des biens communaux; documents sur la préparation de la loi du 10 juin 1793*, Paris: Imprimerie Nationale, 1908, pp. 22–23.

20. McPhee, *Revolution and Environment*, p. 60.

21. Jacques Bernet (ed.), *Le Journal d'un maître d'école d'Île-de-France (1771–1792): Silly-en-Multien de l'Ancien Régime à la Révolution*, Villeneuve-d'Asq: Presses Universitaires du Septentrion, 2000, pp. 214–15.

22. Malcolm Crook, *Elections in the French Revolution: An Apprenticeship in Democracy, 1789–1799*, Cambridge and New York: Cambridge University Press, 1996; Timothy Tackett, *Becoming a Revolutionary: The Deputies of the French National Assembly and the Emergence of a Revolutionary Culture (1789–1790)*, Princeton, NJ: Princeton University Press, 1996. This 'political culture' is explored in the four volumes of Keith Michael Baker, Colin Lucas, François Furet and Mona Ozouf (eds), *The French Revolution and the Creation of Modern Political Culture*, Oxford: Oxford University Press, 1987–94; Michael Kennedy, *The Jacobin Clubs in the French Revolution: The First Years*, Princeton, NJ: Princeton University Press, 1982: Mona Ozouf, *Festivals and the French Revolution*, translated by Alan Sheridan, Cambridge, MA: Harvard University Press, 1988.

23. All that survives today of the immense Cordeliers convent in the Latin Quarter is the refectory, the rest becoming part of the École de Medicine.

24. AP, 15 March 1790, p. 173.

25. Siân Reynolds, *Marriage and Revolution: Monsieur and Madame Roland*, Oxford: Oxford University Press, 2012, pp. 138–43.

26. D. Lottin, *Recherches historiques sur la ville d'Orléans*, 8 vols, Orléans: Imprimerie Alexandre Jacob, 1836–45, vol. 3, pp. 201–02.

27. John R. Cole, *Between the Queen and the Cabby: Olympe de Gouges's Rights of Woman*, Montreal, Quebec; Kingston, Ontario; London; and Ithaca, NY: McGill-Queen's University Press, 2011; Joan Landes, *Women and the Public Sphere in the Age of the French Revolution*, Ithaca, NY: Cornell University Press, 1988, pp. 93–129.

28. Jack R. Censer, *Prelude to Power: The Parisian Radical Press, 1789–1791*, Baltimore, MD, and London: Johns Hopkins University Press, 1976, pp. 8–11.

29. Rolf Reichardt, 'The Politicization of Popular Prints in the French Revolution', in Ian Germani and Robin Swales (eds), *Symbols, Myths and Images: Essays in Honour of James A. Leith*, Regina, Saskatchewan: University of Regina, 1998, p. 17.

30. Laura Auricchio, *Adélaïde Labille-Guiard: Artist in the Age of Revolution*, Los Angeles, CA: J. Paul Getty Museum, 2009, pp. 73–79.

31. Nicole Pellegrin, *Les Vêtements de la Liberté: Abécédaire des pratiques vestimentaires en France de 1780 à 1800*, Aix-en-Provence: Éditions Alinéa, 1989, p. 159.

32. Timothy Tackett, 'Conspiracy Obsession in a Time of Revolution: French Elites and the Origins of the Terror', *AHR*, 105 (2000), pp. 691–713.

33. Marcel Lecoq, *La Conspiration du marquis de Favras, 1789–1790*, Paris: Foliguet et Rigot, 1955.

34. Gwynne Lewis, *The Second Vendée: The Continuity of Counter-Revolution in the Department of the Gard, 1789–1815*, Oxford: Clarendon Press, 1978, p. 19 and ch. 1; Alan Forrest, *Conscripts and Deserters: The Army and French Society during the Revolution and Empire*, Oxford: Oxford University Press, 1989, p. 155.

35. Munro Price, 'Mirabeau and the Court: Some New Evidence', *FHS*, 29 (2006), pp. 37–75.

36. Adrian O'Connor, 'Between Monarch and Monarchy: The Education of the Dauphin and Revolutionary Politics, 1790–91', *FH*, 27 (2013), pp. 176–201; John Hardman, *Louis XVI*, New Haven, CT, and London: Yale University Press, 1993, ch. 13.

37. Rapport, 'International Repercussions', p. 386; and Thomas E. Kaiser, 'A Tale of Two Narratives: The French Revolution in International Context', in McPhee (ed.), *Companion*, ch. 10.

38. On the impact of the Revolution on the armed forces, see Jean-Paul Bertaud, *The Army of the French Revolution: From Citizen-Soldiers to Instrument of Power*, translated by R. R. Palmer, Princeton, NJ: Princeton University Press, 1988, ch. 1; Alan Forrest, *Soldiers of the French Revolution*, Durham, NC: Duke University Press, 1990, ch. 2; Alan Forrest, 'Military Trauma', in David Andress (ed.), *The Oxford Handbook of the French Revolution*, Oxford: Oxford University

Press, 2015, ch. 22; William S. Cormack, *Revolution and Political Conflict in the French Navy, 1789–1794*, Cambridge: Cambridge University Press, 1995.

39. Éric Hartmann, *La Révolution française en Alsace et en Lorraine*, Paris: Perrin, 1990, ch. 8.
40. J. Gilchrist and W. J. Murray (eds), *The Press in the French Revolution: A Selection of Documents Taken from the Press of the Revolution for the Years 1789–1794*, Melbourne: Cheshire; London: Ginn, 1971, p. 15.
41. Marcel David, *Fraternité et Révolution française, 1789–1799*, Paris: Aubier, 1987, pp. 69–71, 247.

Chapter 7 Fracturing Christ's Family: Religious Schism and the King's Flight, 1790–91

1. *Mémoires de la Comtesse de Boigne, née d'Osmond*, 4 vols, Paris: Plon, 1908, vol. 1, p. 137; Madame de La Tour du Pin, *Memoirs: Laughing and Dancing our Way to the Precipice*, translated by Felice Harcourt, London: Harvill Press, 1999, pp. 153–55.
2. AD Meurthe-et-Moselle, L 479. In general, see Gemma Betros, 'Liberty, Citizenship and the Suppression of Female Religious Communities in France, 1789–90', *Women's History Review*, 18 (2009), pp. 311–36.
3. AD Meurthe-et-Moselle, L 1720.
4. D. Lottin, *Recherches historiques sur la ville d'Orléans*, 8 vols, Orléans: Imprimerie Alexandre Jacob, 1836–45, vol. 3, p. 227.
5. Eric Thompson, *Popular Sovereignty and the French Constituent Assembly, 1789–1791*, Manchester: Manchester University Press, 1952, p. 119; William Doyle, *The Oxford History of the French Revolution*, 2nd edn., Oxford and New York: Oxford University Press, 2002, pp. 137–39.
6. Edward J. Woell, 'Religion and Revolution', in David Andress (ed.), *The Oxford Handbook of the French Revolution*, Oxford: Oxford University Press, 2015, pp. 266–67. On the Civil Constitution of the Clergy, see Timothy Tackett, *Religion, Revolution, and Regional Culture in Eighteenth-Century France: The Ecclesiastical Oath of 1791*, Princeton, NJ: Princeton University Press, 1986; P. M. Jones, *The Peasantry in the French Revolution*, Cambridge: Cambridge University Press, 1988, pp. 191–204; Dale K. Van Kley, *The Religious Origins of the French Revolution: From Calvin to the Civil Constitution, 1560–1791*, New Haven, CT, and London: Yale University Press, 1996, pp. 349–67.
7. Michael P. Fitzsimmons, *The Remaking of France: The National Assembly and the Constitution of 1791*, Cambridge and New York: Cambridge University Press, 1994, pp. 209–10; Ted W. Margadant, *Urban Rivalries in the French Revolution*, Princeton, NJ: Princeton University Press, 1992, pp. 263–64; Peter McPhee, *Living the French Revolution, 1789–99*, London and New York: Palgrave Macmillan, 2006, p. 81.
8. Martyn Lyons, *Revolution in Toulouse: An Essay on Provincial Terrorism*, Bern, Frankfurt am Main and Las Vegas: Peter Lang, 1978.
9. *MU*, no. 150, 30 May 1790; no. 151, 30 May 1790, pp. 498–99.
10. Dale Van Kley, 'The *Ancien Régime*, Catholic Europe, and the Revolution's Religious Schism', in Peter McPhee (ed.), *A Companion to the French Revolution*, Oxford: Wiley-Blackwell, 2013, ch. 8. The Assembly's viewpoint is expertly analyzed by Rodney Dean, *L'Assemblée constituante et la réforme ecclésiastique, 1790: la Constitution civile du clergé du 12 juillet et le serment ecclésiastique du 27 novembre*, Paris: Picard, 2014.
11. R. Hervé de La Bauche, *Protestation de cent cinq curés de la Bretagne contre la nouvelle organisation civile du clergé, adressée à l'Assemblée nationale*, 1790.
12. Marcel Coquerel, 'Le Journal d'un curé du Boulonnais', *AHRF*, 46 (1974), p. 289. On priests' reactions in general, see Tackett, *Religion, Revolution, and Regional Culture*, chs 3–4.
13. AD Meurthe-et-Moselle, L 1713.
14. Gaël Rideau, 'De l'Impôt à la sécularisation: reconstruire l'église. Les Doléances religieuses dans les cahiers de doléances du bailliage d'Orléans', *AHRF*, 345 (2006), pp. 3–29.
15. AD Loiret, 2J 1978.
16. François-Pierre Julliot, *Souvenirs d'un prêtre réfractaire du diocèse de Troyes publiés par Octave Beuve*, Arcis-sur-Aube: Société d'Histoire Départementale, 1909.
17. Augustin Theiner, *Documents inédits rélatifs aux affaires religieuses de la France*, Paris: Firmin Didot frères, 1857, pp. 75, 85, 88.
18. Lottin, *Orléans*, vol. 3, pp. 314–15.

19. Tackett, *Religion, Revolution, and Regional Culture*, ch. 11.

20. *Correspondance de l'abbé Rousselot, constituant, 1789–1795*, Besançon: Annales Littéraires de l'Université de Besançon, 1992, pp. 128, 146.

21. Marcel David, *Fraternité et Révolution française, 1789–1799*, Paris: Aubier, 1987, pp. 69–71, 247.

22. Dean, *Assemblée constituante et réforme ecclésiastique*, pp. 707–09; Dominique Soulas de Russel, *Un Révolutionnaire normand fidèle aux siens, à son terroir et à ses convictions: Thomas Lindet, à travers sa correspondance familiale de 1789 à 1799*, Luneray: Bertout, 1997.

23. Bertrand Frélaut, *Les Débuts de la contre-révolution en Bretagne. L'Attaque de Vannes (13 février 1791)*, Nantes: Ouest Éditions; Rennes: Institut Culturel de Bretagne, 1989; Joël Cornette, *Histoire de la Bretagne et des Bretons*, Paris: Éditions du Seuil, 2005, vol. 2, p. 158; Marcelle Richard (ed.), *Le Morbihan pendant la Révolution, 1789–1795*, 2nd edn., Vannes: AD Loire-Atlantique, 1988, pp. 10–14, 29; Joseph-Marie Le Mené, *Histoire archéologique, féodale et religieuse des paroisses du diocèse de Vannes*, 2 vols, Vannes: Imprimerie Galles, 1891–94.

24. AD Morbihan, L 134.

25. AD Morbihan, Archives communales de St-Nolff, 3ES 231/4, 27 March 1790, 19 December 1790, 28 January 1791.

26. Michel Péronnet and Yannick Guin, *La Révolution dans la Loire-Inférieure*, Le Coteau: Horvath, 1989, pp. 96–101.

27. AD Loire-Atlantique, L 1366. Among the terms of abuse were 'foutu trousse couillon', 'fripon' and 'coquin'.

28. Laura Mason, *Singing the French Revolution: Popular Culture and Politics, 1787–1799*, Ithaca, NY: Cornell University Press, 1996, p. 50.

29. Jean-Marie Carbasse, 'Un des premiers cas de résistance populaire à la Révolution: l'émeute du 25 janvier 1791 à Millau', *Bulletin d'histoire économique et sociale* (1984–85), pp. 57–72; Timothy Tackett, 'Women and Men in Counterrevolution: The Sommières Riot of 1791', *JMH*, 59 (1987), pp. 680–704.

30. *Women in Revolutionary Paris, 1789–1795. Selected Documents Translated with Notes and Commentary by Darline Gay Levy, Harriet Branson Applewhite and Mary Durham Johnson*, Urbana and Chicago, IL: University of Illinois Press, 1980, pp. 66–67, 72–74; R. B. Rose, *The Enragés: Socialists of the French Revolution?*, Melbourne: Melbourne University Press, 1965, ch. 5.

31. Richard Cobb and Colin Jones (eds), *Voices of the French Revolution*, Topsfield, MA: Simon & Schuster, 1988, p. 110.

32. Alan Forrest, *Conscripts and Deserters: The Army and French Society during the Revolution and Empire*, Oxford: Oxford University Press, 1989, p. 155; Stephen Clay, 'Camps de Jalès', in Jean-Clément Martin (ed.), *Dictionnaire de la contre-révolution XVIIIe–XXe siècle*, Paris: Perrin, 2011, pp. 319–21; Gwynne Lewis, *The Second Vendée: The Continuity of Counter-Revolution in the Department of the Gard, 1789–1815*, Oxford: Oxford University Press, 1978; François de Jouvenel, 'Les Camps de Jalès (1790–1792), épisodes contre-révolutionnaires?', *AHRF*, 337 (2004), pp. 1–20.

33. J. Gilchrist and W. J. Murray (eds), *The Press in the French Revolution: A Selection of Documents Taken from the Press of the Revolution for the Years 1789–1794*, Melbourne: Cheshire; London: Ginn, 1971, p. 268.

34. AD Meurthe-et-Moselle, MS SAL 480; Timothy Tackett, *The Coming of the Terror in the French Revolution*, Cambridge, MA, and London: The Belknap Press of Harvard University Press, 2015, pp. 140–41 and ch. 4.

35. Malcolm Crook, 'The New Regime: Political Institutions and Democratic Practices under the Constitutional Monarchy, 1789–1791', in Andress (ed.), *Oxford Handbook*, pp. 227–28.

36. Monique Cubells, 'La Société populaire d'Éguilles, en Provence: histoire d'une scission', in Christine Le Bozec and Éric Wauters (eds), *Pour la Révolution française. En hommage à Claude Mazauric*, Rouen: Publications de l'Université de Rouen, 1998, p. 231.

37. The king's flight is expertly narrated and analyzed by Timothy Tackett, *When the King Took Flight*, Cambridge, MA: Harvard University Press, 2003; a shorter account is by John Hardman, *Louis XVI*, New Haven, CT, and London: Yale University Press, 1993, ch. 14.

38. *AP*, 21 June 1791, pp. 378–83. Two very different, but equally brilliant, cinematic presentations of the king's flight are Ariane Mnouchkine's 1974 film of *1789*, a Théâtre du Soleil play, and Ettore Scola's *La Nuit de Varennes* (1982).

39. Georges Lefebvre, 'The Murder of the Comte de Dampierre (June 22, 1791)', in Jeffry Kaplow (ed.), *New Perspectives on the French Revolution: Readings in Historical Sociology*, New York: John Wiley, 1965, pp. 277–86.

40. Laurent Brassart, *Gouverner le local en Révolution. État, pouvoirs et mouvements collectifs dans l'Aisne (1790–1795)*, Paris: SÉR, 2013, pp. 85–87.

41. Tackett, *When the King Took Flight*, pp. 151–55; Henri Texier et al. (eds), *La Révolution française 1789–1799 à Saintes*, Poitiers: Projets Éditions, 1988, p. 88.

42. Munro Price, *The Road from Versailles: Louis XVI, Marie Antoinette, and the Fall of the French Monarchy*, New York: St. Martin's Press, 2003. Price uses the revealing archives of Louis' confidants held in Austria and Stockholm as well as France.

43. William J. Murray, *The Right-Wing Press in the French Revolution: 1789–1792*, London: Royal Historical Society, 1986, pp. 126–28, 289.

44. Gilchrist and Murray (eds), *Press in the French Revolution*, pp. 132–33.

45. AD Loiret, J 557.

46. Henri Labroue, *La Société populaire de Bergerac pendant la Révolution*, Paris: Société de l'Histoire de la Révolution Française, 1915, pp. 139–49.

47. *MU*, no. 166, 15 June 1791, p. 662.

48. Anatoli Ado, *Paysans en Révolution. Terre, pouvoir et jacquerie, 1789–1794*, Paris: SÉR, 1996, pp. 236–37; McPhee, *Living*, p. 92; Jacques Bernet, 'Les Grèves de moissonneurs ou "bacchanals" dans les campagnes d'Ile-de-France et de Picardie au XVIIIe siècle', *Histoire et sociétés rurales*, 11 (1999), pp. 153–86.

49. Bernard Richard, *Cloches et querelles de cloches dans l'Yonne. La Cloche entre maire et curé, XVIIIe–XXe*, Villeneuve-sur-Yonne: Les Amis du Vieux Villeneuve, 2010.

50. *AP*, 15 July 1791, pp. 326–34. In 1792–93, Barnave wrote one of the first histories of the Revolution: see Emanuel Chill (ed. and trans.), *Power, Property and History: Barnave's Introduction to the French Revolution and other Writings*, New York: Harper and Row, 1971.

51. *Révolutions de Paris*, 16–23 July 1791, pp. 53–54, 60–61, 64–65. The original petition was destroyed in the destruction by fire of the Hôtel de Ville in Paris in 1871.

52. David Andress, *Massacre at the Champ de Mars: Popular Dissent and Political Culture in the French Revolution*, Woodbridge, Suffolk: The Royal Historical Society, 2000, pp. 221–22; George Rudé, *The Crowd in the French Revolution*, Oxford: Oxford University Press, 1959, ch. 6.

53. *MU*, no. 201, 20 July 1791, vol. 10, p. 170.

54. Rudé, *Crowd*, pp. 85–86. She may have been related to Catherine Évrard, wife of Jean-Paul Marat's typesetter, and to Simone Évrard, by then living with Marat, who married her on 1 January 1792 'with as witness to the eternal fidelity he swears to her the creator who hears them'; Peter McPhee, *Robespierre: A Revolutionary Life*, New Haven, CT, and London: Yale University Press, 2012, pp. 92–93.

55. Edna Hindie Lemay, 'Poursuivre la Révolution: Robespierre et ses amis à la Constituante', in Jean-Pierre Jessenne et al. (eds), *Robespierre: de la nation artésienne à la République et aux nations. Actes du Colloque, Arras, 1–2–3 Avril 1993*, Villeneuve d'Asq: Centre d'Histoire de la Région du Nord et de l'Europe du Nord-Ouest, Université Charles de Gaulle-Lille III, 1994, pp. 139–56. On the Feuillant split, see Michael Kennedy, *The Jacobin Clubs in the French Revolution: The First Years*, Princeton, NJ: Princeton University Press, 1982, ch. 15.

56. Nicole Felkay and Hervé Favier (eds), *En prison sous la Terreur. Souvenirs de J.-B. Billecocq (1765–1829)*, Paris: SÉR, 1981, pp. 73–75.

57. James H. Johnson, *Listening in Paris: A Cultural History*, Berkeley and Los Angeles, CA, and London: University of California Press, 1995, pp. 110–11.

58. Jean-Pierre Jessenne and Edna Hindie Lemay (eds), *Deputé-paysan et fermière de Flandre en 1789. La Correspondence des Lepoutre*, Lille: Université Charles de Gaulle-Lille 3, 1998, Introduction, pp. 431, 524.

59. Doyle, *Oxford History*, pp. 170–73.

60. Antoine de Baecque, *The Body Politic: Corporeal Metaphor in Revolutionary France, 1770–1800*, translated by Charlotte Mandell, Stanford, CA: Stanford University Press, 1997, pp. 51–63.

61. De Baecque, *The Body Politic*, pp. 63–75.

62. Cf. William Reddy, 'Sentimentalism and its Erasure: The Role of Emotions in the Era of the French Revolution', *JMH*, 72 (2000), pp. 109–52; and William Reddy, *The Navigation of*

Feeling: A Framework for the History of Emotions, Cambridge: Cambridge University Press, 2001, p. 326, for whom revolutionaries 'had great difficulty distinguishing between reasonable dissent and evil, dissembling opposition'.

63. F.-A. Mignet, *Histoire de la Révolution française depuis 1789 jusqu'en 1814*, London: David Nutt, 1882, p. 88.

Chapter 8 Fear and Fury, 1791–92, and a Second Revolution

1. This is the argument of Michael P. Fitzsimmons, *The Remaking of France: The National Assembly and the Constitution of 1791*, Cambridge and New York: Cambridge University Press, 1994, against the following: the Marxist critique of Albert Soboul, *Comprendre la Révolution: problèmes politiques de la Révolution française (1789–1797)*, Paris: F. Maspero, 1981, translated by April A. Knutson as *Understanding the French Revolution*, New York: International Publishers, 1988; and the accusation of Terror incipient in majority rule by François Furet, *Interpreting the French Revolution*, translated by Elborg Forster, Cambridge and Paris: Cambridge University Press and Éditions de la Maison des Sciences de l'Homme, 1981, pp. 52–54.

2. Rila Mukherjee, 'Creating a New Century? Truth, Liberty, Nightmare and Corrective Discipline in the Bernstein Collection', *The Michael Bernstein Collection and Studies on the French Revolution*, Tokyo: Senshu University, 2008, pp. 1–10.

3. R. B. Rose, 'Jacquerie at Davenescourt in 1791', in *Tribunes and Amazons: Men and Women of Revolutionary France, 1789–1871*, Sydney: Macleay Press, 1998, ch. 2, and *Gracchus Babeuf: The First Revolutionary Communist*, London: Edward Arnold, 1978, chs 5–7.

4. P. M. Jones, *Reform and Revolution in France: The Politics of Transition, 1774–1791*, Cambridge: Cambridge University Press, 1995, p. 237.

5. On Robespierre, see the special issue of *AHRF*, no. 371 (2013); Michel Biard and Philippe Bourdin (eds), *Robespierre: portraits croisés*, Paris: Armand Colin, 2012; and the two most recent, and contrasting, biographies in English and French, by McPhee and Leuwers: Peter McPhee, *Robespierre: A Revolutionary Life*, New Haven, CT, and London: Yale University Press, 2012; and Hervé Leuwers, *Robespierre*, Paris: Fayard, 2014.

6. Jean-Jacques Rousseau, *The Social Contract and Discourses*, translated by G. D. H. Cole, London: J. M. Dent and Sons, 1913, especially pp. 19, 22–23, 30–31, 44–45; Marisa Linton, *Choosing Terror: Virtue, Friendship, and Authenticity in the French Revolution*, Oxford: Oxford University Press, 2013, chs 3–4; McPhee, *Robespierre*, ch. 7.

7. Jacques-Pierre Brissot and Étienne Clavière, *Nouveau Voyage dans les États-Unis de l'Amérique septentrionale*, 3 vols, Paris: Buisson, 1791.

8. Noelle L. Plack, *Common Land, Wine and the French Revolution: Rural Society and Economy in Southern France, c.1789–1820*, Farnham, Surrey, and Burlington, VT: Ashgate, 2009, ch. 2; Peter McPhee, *Revolution and Environment in Southern France: Peasants, Lords, and Murder in the Corbières, 1780–1830*, Oxford: Clarendon Press, 1999, ch. 5.

9. Alain Le Bloas, 'La Question du domaine congéable', *AHRF*, 331 (2003), pp. 1–27; *Cahiers de doléances des sénéchaussées de Quimper et de Concarneau pour les États-Généraux de 1789*, Rennes: Imprimerie Oberthur, 1927, p. 37; Léon Dubreuil, *Les Vicissitudes du domaine congéable en Basse-Bretagne à l'époque de la Révolution*, 2 vols, Rennes: Imprimerie Oberthur, 1915, vol. 1, pp. 22–26.

10. Françoise Fortunet, 'Le Code rural ou l'impossible codification', *AHRF*, 247 (1982), pp. 95–112.

11. *MU*, no. 136, 16 May 1791, vol. 8, p. 404; Robert Forster, 'Who is a Citizen? The Boundaries of "La Patrie": The French Revolution and the People of Color, 1789–91', *French Politics & Society*, 7 (1989), pp. 50–64; Bernard Gainot and Marcel Dorigny (eds), *La Société des amis des noirs, 1788–1799. Contribution à l'histoire de l'abolition de l'esclavage*, Paris: Éditions UNESCO/EDICEF, 1998.

12. Laurent Dubois, *Avengers of the New World: The Story of the Haitian Revolution*, Cambridge, MA: The Belknap Press of Harvard University Press, 2004; Laurent Dubois, 'Slavery in the Age of Revolution', in Gad Heuman and Trevor Burnard (eds), *The Routledge History of Slavery*, London: Routledge, 2011, pp. 267–80; Jeremy D. Popkin, *You Are All Free: The Haitian Revolution and the Abolition of Slavery*, New York: Cambridge University Press, 2010, chs 3–4; David Patrick Geggus, *Haitian Revolutionary Studies*, Bloomington, IN: Indiana

University Press, 2002, chs 4–5. The numbers are very difficult even to estimate: see Jeremy D. Popkin, *A Concise History of the Haitian Revolution*, Oxford: Wiley-Blackwell, 2012, ch. 2.

13. AD Loire-Atlantique, L 1630.

14. Armitage and Subrahmanyam (eds), *Age of Revolutions in Global Context*, p. xxiii.

15. R. R. Palmer, *Age of the Democratic Revolution: A Political History of Europe and America, 1760–1800*, 2 vols, Princeton, NJ: Princeton University Press, 1959, 1964, vol. 1, p. 2.

16. Michael Rapport, 'The International Repercussions of the French Revolution', in Peter McPhee (ed.), *A Companion to the French Revolution*, Oxford: Wiley-Blackwell, 2013, p. 384.

17. Ian Coller, 'Egypt in the French Revolution', in Suzanne Desan, Lynn Hunt and William Max Nelson (eds), *The French Revolution in Global Perspective*, Ithaca, NY, and London: Cornell University Press, 2013, pp. 120–22; Bernard Lewis, *The Muslim Discovery of Europe*, New York: W. W. Norton, 2001, p. 52.

18. Barry M. Shapiro, ' "The Case against the King", 1789–1793', in McPhee (ed.), *Companion*, ch. 7.

19. Hervé le Bévillon, *Comment la Bretagne est devenue française. Des origines à la naissance de la république*, Fouesnant: Yoran Embanner, 2010, pp. 124–31, 163–200.

20. Michael Kennedy, *The Jacobin Club of Marseilles, 1790–1794*, Ithaca, NY, and London: Cornell University Press, 1973, p. 180.

21. René Moulinas, *Les Massacres de la Glacière: enquête sur un crime impuni, Avignon 16–17 octobre 1791*, Aix-en-Provence: Édisud, 2003, and *Histoire de la Révolution d'Avignon*, Avignon: Aubanel, 1986.

22. Melvin Edelstein, *The French Revolution and the Birth of Electoral Democracy*, Farnham, Surrey, and Burlington, VT: Ashgate, 2014.

23. C. J. Mitchell, *The French Legislative Assembly of 1791*, Leiden: E. J. Brill, 1988; Michel Biard and Pascal Dupuy, *La Révolution française. Dynamique et ruptures, 1787–1804*, 2nd edn., Paris: Armand Colin, 2008, pp. 81–82.

24. Jeremy Whiteman, *Reform, Revolution and French Global Policy, 1787–1791*, Aldershot and Burlington, VT: Ashgate, 2002; Thomas E. Kaiser, 'A Tale of Two Narratives: The French Revolution in International Context, 1787–93', in McPhee (ed.), *Companion*, ch. 10.

25. Samuel F. Scott, *The Response of the Royal Army to the French Revolution: The Role and Development of the Line Army, 1787–93*, Oxford: Oxford University Press, 1978, pp. 109–10.

26. The depth of conspiratorial belief at this point is explored superbly by Timothy Tackett, *The Coming of the Terror in the French Revolution*, Cambridge, MA, and London: The Belknap Press of Harvard University Press, 2015; and Linton, *Choosing Terror*, ch. 4.

27. Colin Lucas, 'The Theory and Practice of Denunciation in the French Revolution', *JMH*, 68 (1996), p. 770.

28. *MU*, no. 313, 9 November 1791, vol. 10, p. 325.

29. Patricia Chastain Howe, *Foreign Policy and the French Revolution: Charles-François Dumouriez, Pierre LeBrun, and the Belgian Plan, 1789–1793*, Basingstoke: Palgrave Macmillan, 2008.

30. Maximilien Robespierre, *Oeuvres de Maximilien Robespierre*, 11 vols, Paris: SÉR, 1912–2007, vol. VIII, pp. 47–64. Note the comments of Alan Forrest, 'Robespierre, the War and its Organisation', in Colin Haydon and William Doyle (eds), *Robespierre*, Cambridge and New York: Cambridge University Press, 1999, pp. 128–30; Maxime Rosso, 'Les Réminiscences spartiates dans les discours et la politique de Robespierre de 1789 à Thermidor', *AHRF*, 349 (2007), pp. 51–77. For the debates on the origins of the war, see Georges Michon, *Robespierre et la guerre révolutionnaire, 1791–1792*, Paris: M. Rivière, 1937; Michael Kennedy, *The Jacobin Clubs in the French Revolution: The Middle Years*, Princeton, NJ: Princeton University Press, 1988, ch. 9; Marc Belissa, 'War and Diplomacy (1792–1795)', in David Andress (ed.), *The Oxford Handbook of the French Revolution*, Oxford: Oxford University Press, 2015, ch. 24; Frank Attar, *Aux Armes citoyens! Naissance et fonctions du bellicisme révolutionnaire*, Paris: Éditions du Seuil, 2010.

31. Robespierre, *Oeuvres*, vol. VIII, pp. 74–93.

32. Robespierre, *Oeuvres*, vol. VIII, pp. 178–80.

33. Anatoli Ado, *Paysans en Révolution. Terre, pouvoir et jacquerie, 1789–1794*, Paris: SÉR, 1996, pp. 292–302.

34. François Rouvière, *Histoire de la Révolution française dans le département du Gard*, 4 vols, Nîmes: Librairie Ancienne A. Catélan, 1887–89, vol. 2, ch. 4.

35. On the Simonneau killing and its wider context, see Sukla Sanyal, 'The 1792 Food Riot at Étampes and the French Revolution', *Studies in History*, 18 (2002), pp. 23–50; R. B. Rose, 'The

"Red Scare" of the 1790s and the "Agrarian Law"', in *Tribunes and Amazons*, ch. 6; David Hunt, 'The People and Pierre Dolivier: Popular Uprisings in the Seine-et-Oise Department, 1791–1792,' *FHS*, 11 (1979), pp. 184–214; Maurice Dommanget, *1793: les Enragés contre la vie chère-les curés rouges, Jacques Roux-Pierre Dolivier*, Paris: Spartacus, 1976; Anon., *Étampes en Révolution, 1789–1799*, Le Mée-sur-Seine: Éditions Amatteis, 1989, ch. 5.

36. Robespierre, *Ouvres*, vol. VIII, pp. 250–53; Warren Roberts, *Jacques-Louis David and Jean-Louis Prieur, Revolutionary Artists: The Public, the Populace, and Images of the French Revolution*, Albany, NY: State University of New York Press, 2000, pp. 139–44.

37. Francisco Dendena, 'A New Look at Feuillantism: The Triumvirate and the Movement for War in 1791', *FH*, 26 (2012), pp. 6–33.

38. *Procès-Verbal (Assemblée législative)*, vol. 7, p. 355; *MU*, no. 143, 23 May 1790, vol. 4, p. 432.

39. Edward James Kolla, 'The French Revolution, the Union of Avignon, and the Challenges of National Self-Determination', *Law and History Review*, (31) 2013, pp. 717–47.

40. Gabriel-Isidore Blondin d'Abancourt, *Onze ans d'émigration. Mémoires . . . publiés par son petit-neveu Blondin de Saint-Hilaire . . . et suivis d'un historique de la Compagnie des Cent-Suisses depuis Charles VIII*, Paris: Alphonse Picard et fils, 1897, p. 12.

41. AD Aude, Antoine de Fournas de la Brosse, 'Une Famille française sous la Révolution, l'Empire et la Restauration' (n.p., n.d. [1979]); and 'Correspondance de Blaise de Fournas de la Brosse', vol. 1, '1761–1809'.

42. Elizabeth Rapley, ' "Pieuses Contre-Révolutionnaires": The Experience of the Ursulines of Northern France, 1789–1792', *FH*, 2 (1988), pp. 453–73.

43. Jacques Godechot, *France and the Atlantic Revolution of the Eighteenth Century, 1770–1799*, translated by Herbert H. Rowen, New York: The Free Press, 1965, p. 131.

44. Rouvière, *Révolution française dans le Gard*, vol. 2, pp. 359–65, 488–99.

45. Elisabeth Roudinesco, *Madness and Revolution: The Lives and Legends of Théroigne de Méricourt*, translated by Martin Thom, London and New York: Verso, 1991, p. 95; Dominique Godineau, *The Women of Paris and their French Revolution*, translated by Katherine Streip, Berkeley, CA: University of California Press, 1998.

46. Siân Reynolds, *Marriage and Revolution: Monsieur and Madame Roland*, Oxford: Oxford University Press, 2012, pp. 223–29.

47. R. B. Rose, *The Making of the 'sans-culottes': Democratic Ideas and Institutions in Paris, 1789–92*, Manchester: Manchester University Press, 1983, p. 106; Antoine de Baecque, *The Body Politic: Corporeal Metaphor in Revolutionary France, 1770–1800*, translated by Charlotte Mandell, Stanford, CA: Stanford University Press, 1997; Raymonde Monnier, *Le Faubourg Saint-Antoine (1789–1815)*, Paris: SÉR, 1981, ch. 5; Michael Sonenscher, *Sans-Culottes: An Eighteenth-Century Emblem in the French Revolution*, Princeton, NJ: Princeton University Press, 1989. A long-standing debate about the nature of the *sans-culottes* is well summarized by David Andress, 'Politics and Insurrection: The *sans-culottes*, the "Popular Movement" and the People of Paris', in Andress (ed.), *Oxford Handbook*, ch. 23.

48. The origins of the vituperative attacks on Marie-Antoinette are studied by Lynn Hunt, *The Family Romance of the French Revolution*, London: Routledge, 1992; Chantal Thomas, *The Wicked Queen: The Origins of the Myth of Marie-Antoinette*, translated by Julie Rose, New York: Zone Books, 1999; and Thomas E. Kaiser, 'Who's Afraid of Marie-Antoinette? Diplomacy, Austrophobia and the Queen', *FH*, 14 (2000), pp. 241–71.

49. William J. Murray, *The Right-Wing Press in the French Revolution: 1789–1792*, London: Royal Historical Society, 1986, chs 11–12; Emmet Kennedy, *A Cultural History of the French Revolution*, New Haven, CT, and London: Yale University Press, 1989, chs 5, 9–10; Laura Mason, *Singing the French Revolution: Popular Culture and Politics, 1787–1799*, Ithaca, NY: Cornell University Press, 1996.

50. Charles Walton, *Policing Public Opinion in the French Revolution: The Culture of Calumny and the Problem of Free Speech*, Oxford and New York: Oxford University Press, 2009.

51. Ambrogio A. Caiani, *Louis XVI and the French Revolution, 1789–1792*, Cambridge: Cambridge University Press, 2012, pp. 113, 119.

52. Caiani, *Louis XVI*, pp. 217–18 and ch. 7.

53. Jefferson to James Madison, 30 January 1787, in Julian P. Boyd et al. (eds), *The Papers of Thomas Jefferson*, Princeton, NJ: Princeton University Press, 1950–, vol. 11, p. 95.

54. *MU*, 12 July 1792, vol. 13, p. 108.

55. Jean-Paul Rothiot, 'Armée et nation dans la France de l'Est', in Annie Crépin, Jean-Pierre Jessenne and Hervé Leuwers (eds), *Civils, citoyens-soldats et militaires dans L'État-nation (1789–1815). Actes du colloque d'Arras (7–8 novembre 2003)*, Paris: SÉR, 2006, pp. 31–44.

56. Stephen Clay, 'Les Camps de Jalès', in Jean-Clément Martin (ed.), *Dictionnaire de la contre-révolution, XVIIIe–XXe siècle*, Paris: Perrin, 2011, pp. 319–21.

57. *MU*, no. 216, 3 August 1792, vol. 13, pp. 305–06.

58. Elizabeth Cross, 'The Myth of the Foreign Enemy? The Brunswick Manifesto and the Radicalisation of the French Revolution', *FH*, 25 (2011), p. 197. Cross minimizes the actuality of the threat.

59. Leigh Whaley, 'Political Factions and the Second Revolution: The Insurrection of 10 August 1792', *FH*, 7 (1993), pp. 205–24; Tackett, *Coming of the Terror*, ch. 7.

60. George Rudé, *The Crowd in the French Revolution*, Oxford: Oxford University Press, 1959, ch. 7.

61. *MU*, no. 241, 23 August 1792, vol. 13, p. 540.

62. *Gazette Nationale ou le Moniteur Universel*, no. 241, 23 August 1792, vol. 13, pp. 540–41; Suzanne Desan, 'Foreigners, Cosmopolitanism, and French Revolutionary Universalism', in Desan, Hunt and Nelson (eds), *The French Revolution in Global Perspective*, ch. 6.

63. John Markoff, *The Abolition of Feudalism: Peasants, Lords, and Legislators in the French Revolution*, University Park, PA: Pennsylvania State University Press, 1996, pp. 426, 497–98, ch. 8; P. M. Jones, *The Peasantry in the French Revolution*, Cambridge: Cambridge University Press, 1988, pp. 70–74; Ado, *Paysans en Révolution*, ch. 2.

64. Dubreuil, *Vicissitudes du domaine congéable*, vol. 1, pp. 22–26, 32–33.

65. AN D XLII 5: a list in November 1792 detailed the deaths of 1,079 prisoners of a total 2,616. The standard work on the killings is Pierre Caron, *Les Massacres de septembre*, Paris: Maison du Livre Français, 1935; an excellent overview is David Andress, *The Terror: Civil War in the French Revolution*, London: Little, Brown, 2005, ch. 4.

66. Colin Lucas, 'The Crowd and Politics between *Ancien Régime* and Revolution in France', *JMH*, 60 (1988), p. 438; M. J. Sydenham, *The French Revolution*, New York: Capricorn Books, 1966, p. 122.

67. Nicolas Restif de la Bretonne, *Les Nuits de Paris*, part XVI, Paris: Hachette, 1960. Restif's description may be based on hearsay rather than observation.

68. [Edmond Géraud], *Journal d'un étudiant pendant la Révolution, 1789–1793*, Paris: Plon, 1910, pp. 290–95.

69. Rosalie Jullien and Édouard Lockroy, *Journal d'une bourgeoise pendant la Révolution, 1791–1793*, Paris: Calmann Levy, 1881, pp. 287–94. The Julliens' story is well told by Lindsay A. H. Parker, *Writing the Revolution: A French Woman's History in Letters*, Oxford and New York: Oxford University Press, 2013.

70. D. Lottin, *Recherches historiques sur la ville d'Orléans*, 8 vols, Orléans: Imprimerie Alexandre Jacob, 1836–45, vol. 3, pp. 360–406.

71. AD Loiret 2J 1983; Georges Lefebvre, *Études orléanaises*, 2 vols, Paris: Commission d'Histoire Économique et Sociale de la Révolution, 1962, vol. 2, pp. 62–67.

72. W. D. Edmonds, *Jacobinism and the Revolt of Lyon, 1789–1793*, Oxford: Oxford University Press, 1990, pp. 123–30.

73. AD Aisne, 'Mémoires de Nicolas-Joseph Grain', pp. 156–57; *La Révolution vue de l'Aisne, en 200 documents*, Laon: Archives Départementales de l'Aisne, 1990, pp. 153–54.

74. Simon Schama, *Citizens: A Chronicle of the French Revolution*, New York: Alfred A. Knopf, 1989, p. 637; Norman Hampson, *Prelude to Terror: The Constituent Assembly and the Failure of Consensus, 1789–1791*, Oxford and New York: Blackwell, 1988; François Furet, *The French Revolution, 1770–1814*, translated by Antonia Nevill, Oxford: Blackwell, 1992. Jonathan I. Israel, *Revolutionary Ideas: An Intellectual History of the French Revolution from* The Rights of Man *to Robespierre*, Princeton, NJ: Princeton University Press, 2014, pp. 271–73, sides with the Brissotins in their claim that Robespierre, Marat and their allies organized the massacres, even though he notes the lack of evidence.

Chapter 9 Republicans at the Crossroads, 1792–93

1. William Doyle, *The Oxford History of the French Revolution*, 2nd edn., Oxford and New York: Oxford University Press, 2002, p. 193.

2. When Brunswick moved his army forward towards Valmy, he used as his headquarters the Château de Hans, where the Comte de Dampierre had been born and lived before his murder in June 1791 (see ch. 7).

3. Peter McPhee, *Living the French Revolution, 1789–99*, London and New York: Palgrave Macmillan, 2006, p. 114; William S. Cormack, *Revolution and Political Conflict in the French Navy, 1789–1794*, Cambridge: Cambridge University Press, 1995, pp. 147–48.

4. Étienne-Louis Borrel, *Histoire de la Révolution tarentaise et de la réunion de la Savoie à la France en 1792. D'après des documents originaux*, Moutiers: Ducloz, 1901, chs 4, 8.

5. Denis Richet, 'Natural Borders', in François Furet and Mona Ozouf (eds), *Critical Dictionary of the French Revolution*, translated by Arthur Goldhammer, Cambridge, MA: Harvard University Press, 1989, pp. 754–62.

6. Laura Mason, *Singing the French Revolution: Popular Culture and Politics, 1787–1799*, Ithaca, NY: Cornell University Press, 1996, pp. 93–103.

7. Ronald Schechter, 'Translating the "Marseillaise": Biblical Republicanism and the Emancipation of Jews in Revolutionary France', *P&P*, 143 (1994), pp. 128–55.

8. Pierre Pinsseau, *Cadet Roussel (1743–1807)*, Paris: Clavreuil, 1945.

9. Bernard Richard, *Les Emblèmes de la République*, Paris: CNRS, 2012, pp. 79–81.

10. We know virtually nothing about Gamas except that he wrote three other plays around this time. The text was published by the 'citizeness Toubon' in 1794. See Patricia Clancy, *The First 'Australian' Play: Les Émigrés aux terres australes (1792) by Citizen Gamas*, Melbourne: Monash University, 1984.

11. Richard, *Emblèmes*, p. 43 and chs 1–2.

12. Ly-Hoang Thien, 'La Bibliothèque nationale sous la Révolution', *Dix-huitième siècle*, 14 (1982), pp. 75–88; Emmet Kennedy, *A Cultural History of the French Revolution*, New Haven, CT, and London: Yale University Press, 1989, pp. 212–20.

13. Lynn Hunt, *Politics, Culture, and Class in the French Revolution*, Berkeley, CA: University of California Press, 1984, pp. 150–51. There were no political parties in the modern sense during the Revolution, and the identification of political and social tendencies within the Convention is complicated: see Alison Patrick, *The Men of the First French Republic: Political Alignments in the National Convention of 1792*, Baltimore, MD; Johns Hopkins University Press, 1972; Michael Sydenham, *The Girondins*, London: Athlone Press, 1961; and the forum in *FHS*, 15 (1988), pp. 506–48.

14. Patrick, *Men of the First French Republic*, pp. 247–52; Stéphane Le Moal, 'Pierre Faure, entrepreneur, homme public et publiciste havrais', *À travers la Haute-Normandie en Révolution, 1789–1800. Études et recherches*, Rouen: Comité Régional d'Histoire de la Révolution Française, 1992, pp. 419–21.

15. Siân Reynolds, *Marriage and Revolution: Monsieur and Madame Roland*, Oxford: Oxford University Press, 2012.

16. Maximilien Robespierre, *Oeuvres de Maximilien Robespierre*, 11 vols, Paris: SÉR, 1912–2007, vol. VIII, pp. 74–93; Lindsay A. H. Parker, *Writing the Revolution: A French Woman's History in Letters*, Oxford and New York: Oxford University Press, 2013, p. 93; Carol Blum, *Rousseau and the Republic of Virtue: The Language of Politics in the French Revolution*, Ithaca, NY, and London: Cornell University Press, 1986, pp. 153–62; Peter McPhee, *Robespierre: A Revolutionary Life*, New Haven, CT, and London: Yale University Press, 2012, pp. 107–08, 115; Marisa Linton, 'The Man of Virtue: The Role of Antiquity in the Political Trajectory of L. A. Saint-Just', *FH*, 24 (2010), pp. 393–419. A tragic coincidence would be the death of Mary Wollstonecraft, author of a famous 1792 critique of Rousseau, from puerperal fever nine days after giving birth in 1797.

17. These statements of Girondin and Jacobin attitudes are taken from Mason, *Singing the French Revolution*, p. 82; Albert Soboul, *A Short History of the French Revolution, 1789–1799*, translated by Geoffrey Symcox, Berkeley, CA: University of California Press, 1977, pp. 86–90; Soboul, *French Revolution*, pp. 273–82, 303–13.

18. Simon Schama, *Citizens: A Chronicle of the French Revolution*, New York: Alfred A. Knopf, 1989, pp. 96–103, 655–64.

19. *MU*, no. 218, 6 August 1791, vol. 9, pp. 312–20; no. 348, 13 December 1792, vol. 14, pp. 720–21. On the king's trial, see Patrick, *Men of the First French Republic*, chs 3–4; David Jordan, *The King's Trial: The French Revolution vs. Louis XVI*, Berkeley, CA: University of California Press, 1979; Michael Walzer (ed.), *Regicide and Revolution: Speeches at the Trial of Louis XVI*, Cambridge: Cambridge University Press, 1974.

20. Robert Saut, *Les Quatre saisons du conventionnel Cassanyes*, Perpignan: Éditions Rivages des Arts, 1983, p. 62.

21. Huntley Dupre, *Two Brothers in the French Revolution: Robert and Thomas Lindet*, Hamden, CT: Archon Books, 1967.

22. Schama, *Citizens*, p. 663.

23. AD Gironde 12L 19. On provincial women's clubs, see Suzanne Desan, '"Constitutional Amazons": Jacobin Women's Clubs in the French Revolution', in Bryant T. Ragan and Elizabeth A. Williams (eds), *Re-creating Authority in Revolutionary France*, New Brunswick, NJ: Rutgers University Press, 1992, ch. 1.

24. John Hardman, *Louis XVI*, New Haven, CT, and London: Yale University Press, 1993, pp. 232–34. Louis is described in this sympathetic biography as 'fairly intelligent and fairly hard-working', p. 234; Paul Friedland, *Seeing Justice Done: The Age of Spectacular Capital Punishment in France*, Oxford: Oxford University Press, 2012, pp. 249–50; Daniel Arasse, *The Guillotine and the Terror*, translated by Christopher Miller, London: Penguin, 1989, pp. 48–72.

25. Alan Forrest, *Soldiers of the French Revolution*, Durham, NC: Duke University Press, 1990, pp. 50–52.

26. Jeremy Black, *European Warfare, 1660–1815*, New Haven, CT, and London: Yale University Press, 1994, p. 170.

27. Rafe Blaufarb, *The French Army, 1750–1820: Careers, Talent, Merit*, Manchester and New York: Manchester University Press, 2002, ch. 3.

28. L. Duchet (ed.), *Deux volontaires de 1791. Les frères Favier de Montluçon. Journal et lettres*, Montluçon: A. Herbin, 1909, pp. 13, 80, 93–94, 97; Patricia Chastain Howe, *Foreign Policy and the French Revolution: Charles-François Dumouriez, Pierre Lebrun, and the Belgian Plan, 1789–1793*, New York: Palgrave Macmillan, 2008, p. 176 and ch. 10. On Lafayette's defection, see Laura Auricchio, *The Marquis: Lafayette Reconsidered*, New York: Alfred A. Knopf, 2014, ch. 17.

29. Peter McPhee, *Revolution and Environment in Southern France: Peasants, Lords, and Murder in the Corbières, 1780–1830*, Oxford: Clarendon Press, 1999, p. 97.

30. There were many complaints from landowners about shortages of labour: see, for example, AD Meurthe-et-Moselle, ms SAL 480.

31. Michel Ragon, *1793: l'insurrection vendéenne et les malentendus de la liberté*, Paris: Albin Michel, 1992, p. 180. Among studies of the Vendée, see Charles Tilly's pathbreaking *The Vendée*, Cambridge, MA: Harvard University Press, 1964; Timothy Tackett, 'The West in France in 1789: The Religious Factor in the Origins of the Counterrevolution', *JMH*, 54 (1982), pp. 715–45; Claude Petitfrère, 'The Origins of the Civil War in the Vendée', *FH*, 2 (1988), pp. 187–207.

32. Charles Tilly, 'Local Conflicts in the Vendée before the Rebellion of 1793', *FHS*, 2 (1961), p. 231.

33. Edward J. Woell, *Small-Town Martyrs and Murderers: Religious Revolution and Counter-Revolution in Western France, 1774–1914*, Milwaukee, WI: Marquette University Press, 2006, esp. ch. 4.

34. AD du Morbihan, Lz831; Émile Souvestre, *Mémoires d'un sans-culotte bas-breton*, Brussels: Wouters, Raspoet, 1843.

35. Cf. Dan Edelstein, *The Terror of Natural Right: Republicanism, the Cult of Nature, and the French Revolution*, Chicago, IL: University of Chicago Press, 2009, pp. 142–46, for whom the law signifies the terroristic construction of a category of 'others' to be exterminated.

36. Émile Gabory, 'La Guerre de Vendée–soldats paysans', *Mémoires de la Société d'histoire et d'archéologie de Bretagne*, 6 (1925), p. 312.

37. J. Gilchrist and W. J. Murray (eds), *The Press in the French Revolution: A Selection of Documents Taken from the Press of the Revolution for the Years 1789–1794*, Melbourne: Cheshire; London: Ginn, 1971, pp. 276–77; Pierre-René Choudieu, *Mémoires et notes*, Paris: Plon, 1897, p. 360.

38. Of the 1,500 men in the battalion of Confolens, for example, 334 would die in hospitals in Thouars and Parthenay: Gaston Blandin, 'L'Hospitalisation pendant la guerre de Vendée', *Annales de Bretagne et des pays de l'ouest*, 97 (1990), p. 486.

39. Quoted by D. M. G. Sutherland in *H-France Forum*, 5 (2010) http://www.h-france.net/forum/forumvol5/sutherland5.pdf.

40. A. Lallié, *Les Sociétés populaires à Nantes pendant la Révolution*, 2nd edn., Nantes: L. Durance, 1914.

41. D. Lottin, *Recherches historiques sur la ville d'Orléans*, 8 vols, Orléans: Imprimerie Alexandre Jacob, 1836–45, vol. 3, pp. 429–31.

42. AD Loiret 2J 1983; Jacques Debal, *Orléans. Une ville, une histoire*, 2 vols, Orléans: x-nova, 1998, vol. 2, p. 81; Michael J. Sydenham, *Léonard Bourdon: The Career of a Revolutionary*, Waterloo, ON: Wilfred Laurier Press, 1999, ch. 7.

43. Lottin, *Orléans*, vol. 4, pp. 64–66, 77.

44. Lottin, *Orléans*, vol. 4, pp. 79–84, 96–101.

45. Michel Vovelle, *De la Cave au grenier: un itinéraire en Provence au XVIIIe siècle. De l'histoire sociale à l'histoire des mentalités*, Aix-en-Provence: Édisud, 1980.

46. Jean-Paul Rothiot, 'Comités de surveillance et Terreur dans le département des Vosges de 1793 à l'an III', *AHRF*, 314 (1998), pp. 621–68.

47. Anatoli Ado, *Paysans en Révolution. Terre, pouvoir et jacquerie, 1789–1794*, Paris: SÉR, 1996, pp. 345–48.

48. Michael Rapport, 'The International Repercussions of the French Revolution', in Peter McPhee (ed.), *A Companion to the French Revolution*, Oxford: Wiley-Blackwell, 2013, pp. 390–93.

49. On admiration for England early in the Revolution, see, for example, Steve Pincus, *1688: The First Modern Revolution*, New Haven, CT, and London: Yale University Press, 2009, p. 11.

50. Dorothy Carrington, 'The Corsican Constitution of Pascal Paoli', *EHR*, 88 (1973), pp. 481–503; Jean Defranceschi, *La Corse française, 30 novembre 1789–15 juin 1794*, Paris: SÉR, 1980.

51. Ian Coller, 'The Revolutionary Mediterranean', in McPhee (ed.), *Companion*, pp. 426–29.

52. Rapport, 'International Repercussions', p. 385.

53. Michael Rapport, *Nationality and Citizenship in Revolutionary France: The Treatment of Foreigners, 1789–1799*, Oxford: Clarendon Press, 2000, p. 203 and ch. 4.

54. Richard, *Emblèmes*.

55. Peter Morgan, 'Republicanism, Identity and the New European Order: Georg Forster's Letters from Mainz and Paris, 1792–1793', *Journal of European Studies*, 22 (1992), p. 88.

56. Sophie Wahnich, *In Defence of the Terror: Liberty or Death in the French Revolution*, translated by David Fernbach, London and New York: Verso, 2012, pp. 61–63.

57. Richard Mowery Andrews, 'Paris of the Great Revolution: 1789–1796', in Gene Brucker (ed.), *People and Communities in the Western World*, vol. 2, Homewood, IL: Dorsey Press, 1979, pp. 56–112.

58. Rosalie Jullien and Édouard Lockroy, *Journal d'une bourgeoise pendant la Révolution, 1791–1793*, Paris: Calmann Lévy, 1881; Parker, *Writing the Revolution*, ch. 4; Marisa Linton, *Choosing Terror: Virtue, Friendship, and Authenticity in the French Revolution*, Oxford: Oxford University Press, 2013, pp. 162–64.

59. Soboul, *French Revolution*, p. 309. On this *journée*, see George Rudé, *The Crowd in the French Revolution*, Oxford: Oxford University Press, 1959, ch. 8; Morris Slavin, *The Making of an Insurrection: Parisian Sections and the Gironde*, Cambridge, MA, and London: Harvard University Press, 1986.

60. Among the many studies of 'Federalism', see Alan Forrest, *Society and Politics in Revolutionary Bordeaux*, Oxford: Oxford University Press, 1975, ch. 5; W. D. Edmonds, *Jacobinism and the Revolt of Lyon, 1789–1793*, Oxford: Oxford University Press, 1990; Paul R. Hanson, *The Jacobin Republic under Fire: The Federalist Revolt in the French Revolution*, University Park, PA: Pennsylvania State University Press, 2003; Paul R. Hanson, *Provincial Politics in the French Revolution: Caen and Limoges, 1789–1794*, Baton Rouge, LA, and London: Louisiana State University Press, 1989; Paul R. Hanson, 'From Faction to Revolt', in David Andress (ed.), *The Oxford Handbook of the French Revolution*, Oxford: Oxford University Press, 2015, ch. 25.

61. For Marseille politics during the Revolution, see also William Scott, *Terror and Repression in Revolutionary Marseilles*, London: Macmillan, 1973; Jacques Guilhaumou, *Marseille républicaine (1791–1793)*, Paris: Presses de la Fondation Nationale des Sciences Politiques, 1992; and Hanson, *Jacobin Republic under Fire*, pp. 154–60.

62. Guillaume Mazeau, 'La Répression du "fédéralisme" pendant l'été 1793: histoire d'une "réussite"', in Bernard Gainot and Vincent Denis (eds), *Un Siècle d'ordre public en Révolution*, Paris: SÉR, 2010, pp. 47–70; Hanson, *Provincial Politics*; Hanson, *Jacobin Republic under Fire*, pp. 12, 72–74.

63. Edmonds, *Jacobinism and the Revolt of Lyon*, chs 6–7.

64. Mona Ozouf, 'Federalism', in Furet and Ozouf, *Critical Dictionary*, pp. 54–64.

65. Timothy Tackett, *The Coming of the Terror in the French Revolution*, Cambridge, MA, and London: The Belknap Press of Harvard University Press, 2015; Linton, *Choosing Terror*.

Chapter 10 Liberty or Death: Choosing Sides in Violent Times, 1793

1. Léon Dufour, *À travers un siècle (1780–1865), science et histoire: souvenirs d'un savant français*, Paris: J. Rothschild, 1888, pp. 8–9.
2. Good general discussions of choice are by Timothy Tackett, *Religion, Revolution, and Regional Culture in Eighteenth-Century France: The Ecclesiastical Oath of 1791*, Princeton, NJ: Princeton University Press, 1986, ch. 11; Peter M. Jones, 'Choosing Revolution and Counter-Revolution', in Peter McPhee (ed.), *A Companion to the French Revolution*, Oxford: Wiley-Blackwell, 2013, ch. 17; Michel Vovelle, *La Découverte de la politique. Géopolitique de la Révolution française*, Paris: Éditions la Découverte, 1993; Laurent Brassart, '"Plus de vingt paysanneries contrastées en révolution". De la pluralité des dynamiques sociales du politique en milieu rural pendant la Révolution', *AHRF*, 359 (2010), pp. 53–74.
3. D. M. G. Sutherland, *Murder in Aubagne: Lynching, Law, and Justice during the French Revolution*, Cambridge and New York: Cambridge University Press, 2009.
4. Henri Labroue, *La Société populaire de Bergerac pendant la Révolution*, Paris: Société de l'Histoire de la Révolution Française, 1915, pp. 258–66.
5. Peter McPhee, *The Politics of Rural Life: Political Mobilization in the French Countryside, 1846–1852*, Oxford: Clarendon Press, 1992, ch. 5; Mona Ozouf, 'Fédérations, fédéralisme et stéréotypes régionaux', in Ozouf, *L'École de la France: essais sur la Révolution, l'utopie et l'enseignement*, Paris: Gallimard, 1984, pp. 39–45.
6. Vovelle, *Découverte de la politique*.
7. See, for example, Helen Davies, *Émile and Isaac Pereire: Bankers, Socialists and Sephardic Jews in Nineteenth-Century France*, Manchester: Manchester University Press, 2014, ch. 2.
8. Régine Crossuard, *La Révolution dans le district de Vitré, 1789–1795*, Rennes: Rue des Scribes, 1989, pp. 215–19; Tackett, *Religion, Revolution, and Regional Culture*, pp. 257–83.
9. The account that follows draws on records in the AM La Rochelle and the AD Charente-Maritime, and Claudy Valin, *Autopsie d'un massacre. Les journées des 21 et 22 mars 1793 à La Rochelle*, St-Jean-d'Angély: Éditions Bourdessoules, 1992.
10. Christine Peyrard, *Les Jacobins de l'ouest. Sociabilité et formes de politisation dans le Maine et la Basse-Normandie (1789–1799)*, Paris: Publications de la Sorbonne, 1996, pp. 159–76.
11. Olivier Paradis, 'De la difficulté à vivre ses choix politiques. Les jeunes officiers de l'armée, du service du roi à celui de l'empereur', in Annie Crépin, Jean-Pierre Jessenne and Hervé Leuwers (eds), *Civils, citoyens-soldats et militaires dans L'État-nation (1789–1815). Actes du colloque d'Arras (7–8 novembre 2003)*, Paris: SÉR, 2006, pp. 135–47.
12. Comte Régis de L'Estourbeillon de La Garnache, *Les Familles françaises à Jersey pendant la Révolution*, Nantes: Imprimerie Vincente Forest et Émile Grimaud, 1886.
13. François-Pierre Julliot, *Souvenirs d'un prêtre réfractaire du diocèse de Troyes publiés par Octave Beuve*, Arcis-sur-Aube: Société d'Histoire Départementale, 1909, pp. 49–50.
14. Jean Vidalenc, *Les Émigrés français, 1789–1825*, Caen: Associations des Publications de la Faculté des Lettres et Sciences Humaines de l'Université de Caen, 1963; Jacques Godechot, *The Counter-Revolution: Doctrine and Action, 1789–1804*, translated by Salvator Attanasio, London: Routledge & Kegan Paul, 1972, ch. 9; Bette W. Oliver, *Surviving the French Revolution: A Bridge Across Time*, Lanham, MD: Lexington Books, 2013.
15. John G. Gallaher, *General Alexandre Dumas: Soldier of the French Revolution*, Carbondale and Edwardsville, IL: Southern Illinois University Press, 1997; Tom Reiss, *The Black Count: Glory, Revolution, Betrayal, and the Real Count of Monte Cristo*, New York: Crown, 2012.
16. Chancellor Pasquier, *Memoirs (1767–1815)*, translated by Douglas Garman, London: Elek, 1967, p. 31. Pasquier would be a prominent administrator under Napoleon, and was made Chancelier de France by Louis-Philippe in 1837.
17. Suzanne Desan, *The Family on Trial in Revolutionary France*, Berkeley and Los Angeles, CA, and London: University of California Press, 2004, ch. 3.
18. Marie-Victoire Monnard, *Souvenirs d'une femme du peuple, 1777–1802*, Creil: Bernard Dumerchez, 1989, pp. 86–87. The bonds of religious commitment are emphasized in two important articles by Olwen Hufton, 'Women in Revolution, 1789–1796', and 'Women in Revolution', *French Politics and Society*, 7 (1989), pp. 65–81.

19. Suzanne Desan, '"Constitutional Amazons": Jacobin Women's Clubs in the French Revolution', in Bryant T. Ragan and Elizabeth A. Williams (eds), *Re-creating Authority in Revolutionary France*, New Brunswick, NJ: Rutgers University Press, 1992, ch. 1. Male attitudes to the suffrage are explored by Anne Verjus, *Le Bon mari: une histoire politique des hommes et des femmes à l'époque révolutionnaire*, Paris: Fayard, 2010; Anne Verjus, 'Gender, Sexuality, and Political Culture', in McPhee (ed.), *Companion*, ch. 12.

20. Ted W. Margadant, *Urban Rivalries in the French Revolution*, Princeton, NJ: Princeton University Press, 1992, pp. 316–18.

21. AD Aisne, L 1502, 1505, 'Affaires ecclésiastiques: correspondance générale', June–November 1790; May–December 1791; AM Laon, SRL 99, Culte catholique; Michel Péronnet, Robert Attal and Jean Bobin, *La Révolution dans l'Aisne, 1789–1799*, Le Coteau: Horvath, 1988, p. 88.

22. AM Laon, SRL 1, Délibérations de la commune de Laon, June–December 1790; Peter McPhee, *Living the French Revolution, 1789–99*, London and New York: Palgrave Macmillan, 2006, p. 81.

23. Kieko Matteson, *Forests in Revolutionary France: Conservation, Community, and Conflict, 1669–1848*, Cambridge: Cambridge University Press, 2014, pp. 177–87.

24. Christine Le Bozec, *Boissy d'Anglas, un grand notable libéral*, Privas: Fédération des Oeuvres Laïques de l'Ardèche, 1995.

25. Charles Walton, '*Les Graines de la discorde:* Print, Public Spirit, and Free Market Politics in the French Revolution', in Walton (ed.), *Into Print: Limits and Legacies of the Enlightenment: Essays in Honor of Robert Darnton*, University Park, PA: Pennsylvania State University Press, 2011, ch. 10.

26. R. R. Palmer, *From Jacobin to Liberal: Marc-Antoine Jullien, 1775–1848*, Princeton, NJ: Princeton University Press, 1993, ch. 1.

27. Peter McPhee, 'Counter-Revolution in the Pyrenees: Spirituality, Class and Ethnicity in the Haut-Vallespir, 1793–1794', *FH*, 7 (1993), pp. 313–43.

28. Peter McPhee, *Collioure et la Révolution française, 1789–1815*, Perpignan: Le Publicateur, 1989.

29. David M. Hopkin, *Soldier and Peasant in French Peasant Culture, 1766–1870*, Woodbridge, Suffolk: Boydell Press, 2003, p. 248; Jean-Paul Rothiot, 'Armée et nation dans la France de l'Est', in Crépin, Jessenne and Leuwers (eds), *Civils, citoyens-soldats et militaires*, pp. 31–44.

30. *Journal de marche d'un volontaire de 1792 (journal du Sergent Fricasse)*, Paris: J. Dumoulin, 1882, p. 4.

31. Palmer, *Marc-Antoine Jullien*, pp. 4–5; Marisa Linton, *Choosing Terror: Virtue, Friendship, and Authenticity in the French Revolution*, Oxford: Oxford University Press, 2013, p. 137, and ch. 5; Marisa Linton, 'Friends, Enemies, and the Role of the Individual', in McPhee (ed.), *Companion*, ch. 16.

32. P. Delarue, *Un Aumônier des Chouans, l'abbé Nicolas-François Faligant, 1755–1813*, Rennes: Plihon and Hommay; Nantes: Durance, 1910. When Vendéan insurgents stormed Mont-St-Michel and freed Faligant and other priests in November 1793, he wrote exultantly to his sister that 'the white flag was flying over Mont-St-Michel yesterday, the Royal and Catholic Army is master of all this part of the Manche'. But his expectation that he would soon be on Jersey was to be disappointed.

33. Philippe Bourdin, *Le Noir et le Rouge. Itinéraire social, culturel et politique d'un prêtre patriote (1736–1799)*, Clermont-Ferrand: Presses Universitaires Blaise-Pascal, 2000, pp. 154, 451, 486, 494.

34. Joël Cornette, *Un Révolutionnaire ordinaire. Benoît Lacombe, négociant, 1759–1819*, Seyssel: Champ Vallon, 1986. By 1816, Lacombe would be a firm adherent of throne and altar.

35. AD Morbihan, 1Q; L 1424; Lz 501.

Chapter 11 'Terror until the peace', July–October 1793

1. Laura Mason and Tracey Rizzo (eds), *The French Revolution: A Document Collection*, Boston, MA, and New York: Houghton Mifflin, 1999, pp. 201–03; Ian Germani, *Jean-Paul Marat: Hero and Anti-hero of the French Revolution*, Lewiston, NY, Queenston, ON and Lampeter, Wales: The Edward Mellon Press, 1992, pp. 36–37.

2. Germani, *Marat*, pp. 43–45; David L. Dowd, *Pageant-Master of the Republic: Jacques-Louis David and the French Revolution*, Freeport, NY: Libraries Press, 1969. A sympathetic reading of Marat is by Clifford D. Connor, *Jean-Paul Marat: Tribune of the Revolution*, London: Pluto Press, 2012.

3. In general on the crisis of 1793, see Albert Soboul, *Comprendre la Révolution: problèmes politiques de la Révolution française (1789–1797)*, Paris: F. Maspero, 1981; translated by April A. Knutson as *Understanding the French Revolution*, New York: International Publishers, 1988, part 2, ch. 3; Timothy Tackett, *The Coming of the Terror in the French Revolution*, Cambridge, MA, and London: The Belknap Press of Harvard University Press, 2015, chs 10–11.

4. AP, 24 June 1793, vol. 67, pp. 143–50.

5. Malcolm Crook, *Elections in the French Revolution: An Apprenticeship in Democracy, 1789–1799*, Cambridge and New York: Cambridge University Press, 1996, ch. 5.

6. Suzanne Desan, *The Family on Trial in Revolutionary France*, Berkeley and Los Angeles, CA, and London: University of California Press, 2004, ch. 3; Roderick Phillips, *Family Breakdown in Late Eighteenth-Century France: Divorces in Rouen, 1792–1803*, Oxford: Oxford University Press, 1980.

7. André Burguière, 'Politique de la famille et Révolution', in Michael Adcock et al. (eds), *Revolution, Society and the Politics of Memory*, Melbourne: University of Melbourne, 1997, pp. 72–73; Desan, *Family on Trial*.

8. The names are in 'Liste des citoyens envoyés à Paris, par les assemblées primaires, à la fête nationale de l'unité et de l'indivisibilité de la République du 10 août 1793', Paris: Imprimerie Nationale, 1793. http://gallica.bnf.fr/ark:/12148/bpt6k41089m. On the festival, see Mona Ozouf, *Festivals and the French Revolution*, translated by Alan Sheridan, Cambridge, MA: Harvard University Press, 1988, ch. 4.

9. [Edmond Gēreaud], *Journal d'un étudiant pendant la Révolution, 1789–1793*, Paris: Plon, 1910, p. 323.

10. James H. Johnson, *Listening in Paris: A Cultural History*, Berkeley and Los Angeles, CA, and London: University of California Press, 1995, pp. 99–103.

11. See Jacques Guilhaumou, 'Fragments of a Discourse of Denunciation (1789–1794)', in Keith Michael Baker (ed.), *The French Revolution and the Creation of Modern Political Culture*, vol. 4, *The Terror*, Oxford: Pergamon Press, 1994, p. 147; Jean-Clément Martin, *Violence et Révolution: essai sur la naissance d'un mythe national*, Paris: Éditions du Seuil, 2006; Roger Dupuy, *La République jacobine. Terreur, guerre et gouvernement révolutionnaire*, Paris: Seuil, 2005, ch. 6; Dan Edelstein, 'What was the Terror?', and Marisa Linton, 'Terror and Politics', in David Andress (ed.), *The Oxford Handbook of the French Revolution*, Oxford: Oxford University Press, 2015, chs 26–27. Jean-Clément Martin has argued that the term 'the Terror' should no longer be applied to the period, for example, in 'Violences et justice', in Michel Biard (ed.), *Les Politiques de la Terreur, 1793–1794: actes du colloque international de Rouen, 11–13 janvier 2007*, Paris: SÉR, 2008, pp. 129–40.

12. A good starting point for this central question is Paul R. Hanson, *Contesting the French Revolution*, Malden, MA, and Oxford: Wiley-Blackwell, 2009, ch. 9. The most recent and convincing analyses are Tackett, *Coming of the Terror*, and Marisa Linton, *Choosing Terror: Virtue, Friendship, and Authenticity in the French Revolution*, Oxford: Oxford University Press, 2013. For other perspectives, see Mona Ozouf, 'War and Terror in French Revolutionary Discourse (1793–1794)', *JMH*, 56 (1984), pp. 579–97; Dan Edelstein, *The Terror of Natural Right: Republicanism, the Cult of Nature, and the French Revolution*, Chicago, IL: University of Chicago Press, 2009; Annie Jourdan, 'Les Discours de la terreur à l'époque révolutionnaire (1776–1798): étude comparative sur une notion ambiguë', *FHS*, 36 (2013), pp. 51–81; and Michel Biard and Hervé Leuwers (eds), *Visages de la Terreur. L'exception politique de l'an II*, Paris: Armand Colin, 2014.

13. Alan Forrest, *Conscripts and Deserters: The Army and French Society during the Revolution and Empire*, Oxford: Oxford University Press, 1989, pp. 94–95; Félix Mourlot, *Recueil des documents d'ordre économique contenus dans les registres de délibérations des municipalités du district d'Alençon, 1788–An IV*, Alençon: Imprimerie Veuve Félix Guy, 1907, p. 404.

14. R. R. Palmer, *Twelve who Ruled: The Year of the Terror in the French Revolution*, Princeton, NJ: Princeton University Press, 1969, p. 108.

15. *MU*, 25 August 1793, vol. 17, p. 478. On the military mobilization, see Forrest, *Conscripts and Deserters*; Howard Brown, *War, Revolution, and the Bureaucratic State: Politics and Army Administration in France, 1791–1799*, Oxford: Clarendon Press, 1995, chs 3–5.

16. Alan Forrest, *Soldiers of the French Revolution*, Durham, NC: Duke University Press, 1990, pp. 27–36.

17. Forrest, *Soldiers of the French Revolution*, p. 160; see, too, Jean-Paul Bertaud, *The Army of the French Revolution: From Citizen-Soldiers to Instrument of Power*, translated by R. R. Palmer, Princeton, NJ: Princeton University Press, 1988; John A. Lynn, *The Bayonets of the Republic: Motivation and Tactics in the Army of Revolutionary France, 1791–94*, Urbana, IL: University of Chicago Press, 1984. A taste of the *Père Duchesne* may be found in Richard Cobb and Colin Jones (eds), *Voices of the French Revolution*, Topsfield, MA: Simon & Schuster, 1988, pp. 184–85, and J. Gilchrist and W. J. Murray (eds), *The Press in the French Revolution: A Selection of Documents Taken from the Press of the Revolution for the Years 1789–1794*, Melbourne: Cheshire; London: Ginn, 1971.

18. Laurent Brassart, *Gouverner le local en Révolution. État, pouvoirs et mouvements collectifs dans l'Aisne (1790–1795)*, Paris: SÉR, 2013, pp. 270–72.

19. Jill Maciak Walshaw, *A Show of Hands for the Republic: Opinion, Information, and Repression in Eighteenth-Century Rural France*, Rochester, NY: Rochester University Press, 2014, appendix.

20. George Armstrong Kelly, 'Conceptual Sources of the Terror', *Eighteenth Century Studies*, 14 (1980), pp. 18–36. See, too, Jourdan, 'Discours de la terreur'; Dan Edelstein, 'Do We Want a Revolution without Revolution? Reflections on Political Authority', *FHS*, 35 (2012), pp. 269–89.

21. Lamarque became a general under Bonaparte, and his Paris funeral in 1832 was the occasion for the insurrection that forms the backdrop to Hugo's *Les Misérables*.

22. Valérie Sottocasa, *Mémoires affrontées. Protestants et catholiques face à la Révolution dans les montagnes du Languedoc*, Rennes: Presses Universitaires de Rennes, 2004.

23. Gilles Fleury, 'Analyse informatique du statut socioculturel des 1,578 personnes déclarées suspectes à Rouen en l'an II', in *Autour des mentalités et des pratiques politiques sous la Révolution française*, Paris: CTHS, 1987, vol. 3, pp. 9–23.

24. Sophie de Bohm, *Prisonnière sous la Terreur. Mémoires d'une captive en 1793*, Paris: Cosmopole, 2001, pp. 7–9, 25; R. B. Rose, *Tribunes and Amazons: Men and Women of Revolutionary France, 1789–1871*, Sydney: Macleay Press, 1998, ch. 7. A final blow to the Girardins was the transfer of Rousseau's remains from Ermenonville to the Panthéon in October 1794. The marquis abandoned his politics, if not his love of landscape.

25. Olivier Blanc, *Last Letters: Prisons and Prisoners of the French Revolution, 1793–1794*, translated by Alan Sheridan, New York: Michael di Capua Books; Farrar, Straus & Giroux, 1987, pp. 160–67.

26. Yannick Guin, *La Bataille de Nantes, 29 juin 1793. Un Valmy dans l'ouest*, Laval: Siloë, 1993.

27. Michel Péronnet and Yannick Guin, *La Révolution dans la Loire-Inférieure*, Le Coteau: Horvath, 1989.

28. Malcolm Crook, *Toulon in War and Revolution: From the Ancien Régime to the Restoration, 1750–1820*, Manchester: Manchester University Press, 1991.

29. Michel Biard, *1793, le siège de Lyon. Entre mythe et réalités*, Clermont-Ferrand: Lemme Éditions, 2013; Paul Chopelin, *Ville patriote et ville martyre. Une histoire religieuse de Lyon pendant la Révolution (1788–1805)*, Paris: Letouzey and Ané, 2010.

30. Colin Lucas, 'The Theory and Practice of Denunciation in the French Revolution', *JMH*, 68 (1996), p. 768.

31. Frédéric-Christian Laukhard, *Un Allemand en France sous la Terreur: souvenirs de Frédéric-Christian Laukhard, professeur d'université saxon et sans-culotte français, 1792–1794*, Paris: Perrin, 1915, p. 271.

32. Michel Biard, *Collot d'Herbois. Légendes noires et révolution*, Lyon: Presses Universitaires de Lyon, 1995, pp. 137–48; W. D. Edmonds, *Jacobinism and the Revolt of Lyon, 1789–1793*, Oxford: Oxford University Press, 1990, chs 7–10.

33. Jean-Louis Laplane, *Journal d'un Marseillais, 1789–1793*, Marseille: J. Laffitte, 1989, p. 177. Laplane returned in 1795 and died in 1845.

34. Christine Adams, '"Venus of the Capitol": Madame Tallien and the Politics of Beauty under the Directory', *FHS*, 37 (2014), pp. 599–629. Ultimately Tallien was recalled from Bordeaux and Cabarrus was herself imprisoned in Paris on 30 May 1794.

35. On Jacobin ideology and practice, see Jean-Pierre Gross, *Fair Shares for All: Jacobin Egalitarianism in Practice*, Cambridge and New York: Cambridge University Press, 1997;

Patrice L. R. Higonnet, *Goodness beyond Virtue: Jacobins during the French Revolution*, Cambridge, MA: Harvard University Press, 1998.

36. Maximilien Robespierre, *Oeuvres de Maximilien Robespierre*, 11 vols, Paris: SÉR, 1912–2007, vol. 10, pp. 116–21; Peter McPhee, *Robespierre: A Revolutionary Life*, New Haven, CT, and London: Yale University Press, 2012, p. 170.

37. Thomas E. Crow, *Emulation: David, Drouais, and Girodet in the Art of Revolutionary France*, New Haven, CT, and London: Yale University Press, 2006; Ronald Schechter, 'The Holy Mountain and the French Revolution', *Historical Reflections*, 40 (2014), pp. 78–107; Linton, *Choosing Terror*, pp. 174–75.

38. Maurice Agulhon, *Marianne into Battle: Republican Imagery and Symbolism in France, 1789–1880*, translated by Janet Lloyd, Cambridge: Cambridge University Press, 1979, pp. 32–33.

39. AD Loiret, 2J 1899.

40. Sanja Perovic, *The Calendar in Revolutionary France*, Cambridge and New York: Cambridge University Press, 2012, ch. 3; Matthew Shaw, *Time and the French Revolution: The Republican Calendar, 1789-Year XIV*, Woodbridge and Rochester, NY: Boydell & Brewer, 2011; Noah Shusterman, *Religion and the Politics of Time: Holidays in France from Louis XIV through Napoleon*, Washington, DC: Catholic University of America Press, 2010.

41. Ozouf, *Festivals*, p. 117; Michael Sydenham, *Léonard Bourdon: The Career of a Revolutionary, 1754–1807*, Waterloo, ON: Wilfred Laurier University Press, 1999.

42. Hunt, 'Globalizing the French Revolution', in Suzanne Desan, Lynn Hunt and William Max Nelson (eds), *The French Revolution in Global Perspective*, Ithaca, NY, and London: Cornell University Press, 2013; Jean Bouchary, *Les Manieurs d'argent à Paris à la fin du XVIIIe siècle*, vol. 1, Paris: Marcel Rivière, 1939.

43. AD Loiret, J 557.

44. Gross, *Fair Shares for All*, pp. 102–18.

45. AD Meurthe-et-Moselle, L 1876; Robert Parisot, *Histoire de Lorraine*, vol. 2, Paris: Auguste Picard, 1924, p. 171.

46. Noelle L. Plack, 'Agrarian Individualism, Collective Practices and the French Revolution: The Law of 10 June 1793 and the Partition of Common Land in the Department of the Gard', *EHR*, 35 (2005), pp. 39–62.

47. Peter McPhee, *Revolution and Environment in Southern France: Peasant, Lords, and Murder in the Corbières, 1780–1830*, Oxford: Clarendon Press, 1999, p. 134.

48. P. M. Jones, *The Peasantry in the French Revolution*, Cambridge: Cambridge University Press, 1988, p. 225.

49. See the innovative study of the attitudes to the *assignat* by Rebecca L. Spang, *Stuff and Money in the Time of the French Revolution*, Cambridge, MA: Harvard University Press, 2015.

50. Melvin Edelstein, *'La Feuille villageoise': communication et modernisation dans les régions rurales pendant la Révolution*, Paris: Bibliothèque Nationale, 1977, ch. 6.

51. Giles MacDonogh, *Brillat-Savarin: The Judge and his Stomach*, London: John Murray, 1992, p. 103. On rural political tendencies, see David Hunt, 'Peasant Politics in the French Revolution', *SH*, 9 (1984), pp. 277–99; Jones, *Peasantry*, pp. 206–40; Rose, *Tribunes and Amazons*, chs 2, 4, 6; Laurent Brassart, ' "Plus de vingt paysanneries contrastées en révolution". De la pluralité des dynamiques sociales du politique en milieu rural pendant la Révolution', *AHRF*, 359 (2010), pp. 53–74.

52. Gilchrist and Murray (eds), *Press in the French Revolution*, pp. 199–202.

53. Bernard Richard, 'Les Arbres de la liberté dans le département de l'Yonne sous la Révolution et l'Empire', in Claude Farenc and Christine Lamarre (eds), *Emblèmes et symboles de la Révolution en Côte-d'Or*, Dijon: AD Côte-d'Or, 2013.

54. Michael Kennedy, *The Jacobin Clubs in the French Revolution, 1793–1795*, New York: Berghahn Books, 2000; Michael Kennedy, *The Jacobin Club of Marseilles, 1790–1794*, Ithaca, NY, and London: Cornell University Press, 1973, pp. 150–52.

55. Mason and Rizzo (eds), *French Revolution*, pp. 199–201.

56. William H. Sewell, *Work and Revolution in France: The Language of Labor from the Old Regime to 1848*, Cambridge: Cambridge University Press, 1980, p. 112 and ch. 5.

57. Perovic, *Calendar*, pp. 141–48.

58. Mason and Rizzo (eds), *French Revolution*, pp. 204–06.

59. Gilchrist and Murray (eds), *Press in the French Revolution*, pp. 282–84.
60. Dominique Godineau, *The Women of Paris and their French Revolution*, translated by Katherine Streip, Berkeley, CA: University of California Press, 1998, pp. 72–75.
61. Claude Guillon, 'Pauline Léon, une républicaine révolutionnaire', *AHRF*, 344 (2006), pp. 147–59.
62. Darline Gay Levy, Harriet Branson Applewhite and Mary Durham Johnson, *Women in Revolutionary Paris, 1789–1795: Selected Documents Translated with Notes and Commentary*, Urbana and Chicago, IL: University of Illinois Press, 1980, pp. 161–65 and ch. 4.
63. Annie K. Smart, *Citoyennes: Women and the Ideal of Citizenship in Eighteenth-Century France*, Newark, DE: University of Delaware Press, 2011, p. 153 and ch. 5.
64. Rose, *Tribunes and Amazons*, pp. 246–48. Rose's argument may be compared with Olwen Hufton, 'Women in Revolution', *French Politics and Society*, 7 (1989), and Madelyn Gutwirth, *The Twilight of the Goddesses: Women and Representation in the French Revolutionary Era*, New Brunswick, NJ: Rutgers University Press, 1992, ch. 7.
65. Godineau, *Women of Paris*, p. 162 and chs 6–7; Olwen H. Hufton, *Women and the Limits to Citizenship*, Toronto: University of Toronto Press, 1992, pp. 28, 35. Other contrasting approaches are by Jean-Clément Martin, *La Révolte brisée. Femmes dans la Révolution française et l'Empire*, Paris: Armand Colin, 2008; Élizabeth G. Sledziewski, *Révolutions du sujet*, Paris: Méridiens Klincksieck, 1989.
66. The classic study of the *sans-culottes* in the Year II is Albert Soboul, *The Parisian Sans-Culottes and the French Revolution, 1793–4*, translated by Gwynne Lewis, Oxford: Oxford University Press, 1964.
67. McPhee, *Revolution and Environment*, p. 111.

Chapter 12 Saving a Republic of Virtue, October 1793–April 1794

1. John Hall Stewart (ed.), *A Documentary Survey of the French Revolution*, New York: Macmillan, 1951, pp. 479–81.
2. Ian Germani, 'Terror in the Army: Representatives on Mission and Military Discipline in the Armies of the French Revolution', *Journal of Military History*, 75 (2011), pp. 733–68.
3. Alan Forrest, *The Revolution in Provincial France: Aquitaine 1789–1799*, Oxford and New York: Oxford University Press, 1996, pp. 234–35.
4. Alain Corbin, *Village Bells: Sound and Meaning in the 19th-Century French Countryside*, translated by Martin Thom, New York: Columbia University Press, 1998, pp. 12–23; Bernard Richard, *Cloches et querelles de cloches dans l'Yonne. La Cloche entre maire et curé, XVIIIe–XXe*, Villeneuve-sur-Yonne: Les Amis du Vieux Villeneuve, 2010; AD Meurthe-et-Moselle, L 3132, 3133.
5. Lee Baker, 'The French Revolution as Local Experience: The Terror in Dijon', *Historian*, 67 (2005), pp. 694–711.
6. Laurent Brassart, *Gouverner le local en Révolution. État, pouvoirs et mouvements collectifs dans l'Aisne (1790–1795)*, Paris : SÉR, 2013, pp. 393–97; *La Révolution vue de l'Aisne, en 200 documents*, Laon: Archives Départementales de l'Aisne, 1990, pp. 195–96; Donald Greer, *The Incidence of the Terror during the French Revolution: A Statistical Interpretation*, Cambridge, MA: Harvard University Press, 1935, pp. 161–64.
7. T. J. Clark, 'Painting in the Year Two', *Representations*, 47 (1994), pp. 13–63.
8. AD Loiret, J 557.
9. Siân Reynolds, *Marriage and Revolution: Monsieur and Madame Roland*, Oxford: Oxford University Press, 2012, pp. 282–88.
10. Paul R. Hanson, *The Jacobin Republic under Fire: The Federalist Revolt in the French Revolution*, University Park, PA: Pennsylvania State University Press, 2003, p. 243.
11. Olympe de Gouges, *Écrits politiques, 1788–1791*, preface by Olivier Blanc, Paris: Côté-Femmes, 1993, pp. 21–24.
12. Cecilia Feilla, *The Sentimental Theater of the French Revolution*, Farnham, Surrey, and Burlington, VT: Ashgate, 2013, pp. 160–66 and ch. 4; F. W. J. Hemmings, *Theatre and State in France, 1760–1905*, Cambridge: Cambridge University Press, 1994, pp. 83–86.
13. Cited by Colin Lucas, 'The Theory and Practice of Denunciation in the French Revolution', *JMH*, 68 (1996), p. 784.
14. Lucas, 'Theory and Practice of Denunciation', pp. 782–85.

15. Jacques Guilhaumou and Martine Lapied, 'Femmes et comités de surveillance', in Danièle Pingué and Jean-Paul Rothiot (eds), *Les Comités de surveillance. D'une création citoyenne à une institution révolutionnaire*, Paris: SÉR, 2012, p. 130.

16. The claim of genocide in Reynald Secher, *A French Genocide: The Vendée*, translated by George Holoch, Notre Dame, IN: University of Notre Dame Press 2003, is contested by Hugh Gough, 'Genocide and the Bicentenary: The French Revolution and the Revenge of the Vendée', *Historical Journal*, 30 (1987), pp. 977–88; and Jean-Clément Martin, 'Dénombrer les victimes de la Terreur. La Vendée et au-delà', in Michel Biard and Hervé Leuwers (eds), *Visages de la Terreur. L'Exception politique de l'an II*, Paris: Armand Colin, 2014, pp. 155–65.

17. Étienne Jolicler, *Joliclerc, volontaire aux armées de la Révolution. Ses lettres (1793–1796)*, 4th ed., Paris: Perrin, 1905, pp. 154–63.

18. Richard Cobb and Colin Jones (eds), *Voices of the French Revolution*, Topsfield, MA: Simon & Schuster, 1988, p. 206. See Anne Rolland-Boulestreau, *Les Colonnes infernales*, Paris: Fayard, 2015; Charles Merle, *La Révolution française à Bressuire, 1789–1799*, Poitiers: Projets Éditions, 1988.

19. Michel Péronnet and Yannick Guin, *La Révolution dans la Loire-Inférieure*, Le Coteau: Horvath, 1989, pp. 127–31; A. Lallié, *Les Sociétés populaires à Nantes pendant la Révolution*, 2nd edn., Nantes: L. Durance, 1914, pp. 133–66.

20. AD Meurthe-et-Moselle, L 1661; BM Nancy, ms 1540/1, 4 Fructidor II. On the tension between the Revolution's 'universalism' and national military interests, see Albert Mathiez, *La Révolution et les étrangers: cosmopolitisme et défense nationale*, Paris: La Renaissance du Livre, 1918; Greg Burgess, *Refuge in the Land of Liberty: France and its Refugees, from the Revolution to the end of Asylum, 1787–1939*, Basingstoke and New York: Palgrave Macmillan, 2008, pp. 22–30; Sophie Wahnich, *L'Impossible citoyen. L'Étranger dans le discours de la Révolution française*, Paris: Albin Michel, 1997; Michael Rapport, *Nationality and Citizenship in Revolutionary France: The Treatment of Foreigners, 1789–1799*, Oxford: Clarendon Press, 2000, pp. 202–03, 224–39.

21. Helen Maria Williams, *Letters containing a sketch of the politics of France: from the thirty-first of May 1793, till the twenty-eighth of July 1794, and of the scenes which have passed in the prisons of Paris*, Dublin: J. Chambers, 1795.

22. Peter McPhee, *Robespierre: A Revolutionary Life*, New Haven, CT, and London: Yale University Press, 2012, pp. 172–74; Michael Rapport, 'Robespierre and the Universal Rights of Man, 1789–1794', *FH*, 10 (1996), pp. 323–24; Laurent Petit, 'Robespierre et le discours sur l'étranger: buts et limites d'une modélisation des nationalités', in Jean-Pierre Jessenne et al. (eds), *Robespierre: de la nation artésienne à la République et aux nations. Actes du Colloque, Arras, 1–2–3 Avril 1993*, Villeneuve d'Asq. Centre d'Histoire de la Région du Nord et de l'Europe du Nord-Ouest, Université Charles de Gaulle-Lille III, 1994, pp. 315–36.

23. Lucas, 'Theory and Practice of Denunciation', pp. 782–85; Lynn Hunt, 'Globalizing the French Revolution', in Suzanne Desan, Lynn Hunt and William Max Nelson (eds), *The French Revolution in Global Perspective*, Ithaca, NY, and London: Cornell University Press, 2013.

24. In *La République universelle ou adresse aux tyrannicides*, Paris: n.p., 1792; *Bases constitutionelles de la république du genre humain*, 1793, Paris: Imprimerie Nationale, 1793. See François Labbé, *Anarchasis Cloots, le Prussien francophile. Un philosophe au service de la Révolution française et universelle*, Paris: L'Harmattan, 1999.

25. McPhee, *Robespierre*, pp. 175–76; William Doyle, *Aristocracy and its Enemies in the Age of Revolution*, Oxford University Press, Oxford, 2009, pp. 290–91; Sophie Wahnich, *L'Impossible citoyen: l'étranger dans le discours de la Révolution française*. Paris: Albin Michel, 1997, pp. 185–200.

26. *MU*, 21 December 1793, vol. 19, p. 6. On education policy, see Emmet Kennedy, *A Cultural History of the French Revolution*, New Haven, CT, and London: Yale University Press, 1989, pp. 353–62; R. R. Palmer, *The Improvement of Humanity: Education and the French Revolution*, Princeton, NJ: Princeton University Press, 1985, chs 4–5.

27. Rachel Jaeglé, 'Bara: un enfant de Palaiseau entre dans l'histoire', in Serge Bianchi (ed.), *Héros et héroïnes de la Révolution française*, Paris: CTHS, 2012, pp. 333–42.

28. Éric Teyssier, 'Appliquer une loi sociale en France sous la Convention. La mise en oeuvre de la loi du 13 septembre 1793', *AHRF*, 312 (1998), pp. 265–83; Peter Jones, 'Agrarian Radicalism during the French Revolution', in Alan Forrest and Peter Jones (eds), *Reshaping*

France: Town, Country and Region during the French Revolution, Manchester: Manchester University Press, 1991, pp. 137–51.

29. Jean-Pierre Gross, *Fair Shares for All: Jacobin Egalitarianism in Practice*, Cambridge and New York: Cambridge University Press, 1997, pp. 85–87.

30. Adrian Velicu, *Civic Catechisms and Reason in the French Revolution*, Farnham, Surrey, and Burlington, VT: Ashgate, 2010.

31. John Hardman (ed.), *French Revolution Documents*, Oxford: Oxford University Press, 1973, vol. 2, pp. 132–33. On popular ideology in Paris, see Albert Soboul, *The Parisian Sans-Culottes and the French Revolution, 1793–4*, translated by Gwynne Lewis, Oxford: Oxford University Press, 1964, chs 1–3; William H. Sewell, *Work and Revolution in France: The Language of Labour from the Old Régime to 1848*, Cambridge: Cambridge University Press, 1980, ch. 5.

32. Max Frey, *Les Transformations du vocabulaire français à l'époque de la Révolution (1789–1800)*, Paris: PUF, 1925.

33. Hardman (ed.), *French Revolution Documents*, vol. 2, pp. 127–28.

34. Joseph Clarke, 'Cenotaphs and Cypress Trees: Commemorating the Citizen-Soldier in the Year II', *FH*, 22 (2008), pp. 217–40.

35. Richard Wittman, *Architecture, Print Culture, and the Public Sphere in Eighteenth-Century France*, New York and London: Routledge, 2007, pp. 213–17.

36. *Les Républicaines: chansons populaires des révolutions de 1789, 1792 et 1830*, 3 vols, Paris: Pagnerre, 1848, vol. 1, pp. 34–36. On the 'cultural revolution', see Serge Bianchi (ed.), *La Révolution culturelle de l'an II*, Paris: Aubier, 1982, esp. ch. 5; Aileen Ribeiro, *Fashion in the French Revolution*. New York: Holmes and Meier, 1988; Kennedy, *Cultural History*, ch. 9, Appendix A.

37. James H. Johnson, *Listening in Paris: A Cultural History*, Berkeley and Los Angeles, CA, and London: University of California Press, 1995, pp. 116–27; Kennedy, *Cultural History*, pp. 168–85.

38. Victoria Johnson, *Backstage at the Revolution: How the Royal Paris Opera Survived the End of the Old Regime*, Chicago, IL, and London: University of Chicago Press, 2008, pp. 186–93; Mark Darlow, *Staging the French Revolution: Cultural Politics and the Paris Opera, 1789–1794*, New York: Oxford University Press, 2012. Francoeur survived imprisonment under the Terror, being released a fortnight after Robespierre's death, to be reappointed an administrator to the debt-ridden Opéra in April 1798, when he was reunited with Cellerier.

39. François Rouvière, *Histoire de la Révolution française dans le department du Gard*, 4 vols, Nîmes: Librairie Ancienne A. Catélan, 1887–89, vol. 4, pp. 377–81. Saint-Gilles still boasts its Hôtel Héraclée.

40. Jacques Debal, *Orléans. Une ville, une histoire*, 2 vols, Orléans: x-nova, 1998, vol. 2, p. 82

41. Peter McPhee, *Collioure et la Révolution française, 1789–1815*, Perpignan: Le Publicateur, 1989, p. 136; Bianchi (ed.), *La Révolution culturelle*.

42. See the special issue of *AHRF*, 322 (2000), on revolutionary place names.

43. Bernard Manin, 'Rousseau', in François Furet and Mona Ozouf (eds), *Critical Dictionary of the French Revolution*, translated by Arthur Goldhammer, Cambridge, MA: Harvard University Press, 1989, pp. 829–43.

44. Nicole Pellegrin, *Les Vêtements de la Liberté: Abécédaire des pratiques vestimentaires en France de 1780 à 1800*, Aix-en-Provence: Éditions Alinéa, 1989, pp. 48–49, 111–12.

45. Laura Mason and Tracey Rizzo (eds), *The French Revolution: A Document Collection*, Boston, MA, and New York: Houghton Mifflin, 1999, pp. 232–36. This episode in the history of women's political participation is discussed by Suzanne Desan, '"Constitutional Amazons": Jacobin Women's Clubs in the French Revolution', in Bryant T. Ragan and Elizabeth A. Williams (eds), *Re-Creating Authority in Revolutionary France*, New Brunswick, NJ: Rutgers University Press, 1992, ch. 1; Scott H. Lytle, 'The Second Sex (September, 1793)', *JMH*, 26 (1955), pp. 14–26; Joan Landes, *Women and the Public Sphere in the Age of the French Revolution*, Ithaca, NY: Cornell University Press, 1988, pp. 140–45, 160–68; Marie Cerati, *Le Club des citoyennes républicaines révolutionnaires*, Paris: Éditions Sociales, 1966; R. B. Rose, *The Enragés: Socialists of the French Revolution?* Melbourne: Melbourne University Press, 1965, chs 5–6.

46. Vitriolic denunciations of the supposedly omnipresent vandalism of the Revolution are by Louis Réau, *Histoire du vandalisme. Les Monuments détruits de l'art français*, Paris: Robert

Laffont, 1994; François Souchal, *Le Vandalisme de la Révolution*, Paris: Nouvelles Éditions Latines, 1993.

47. David Gilks, 'Attitudes to the Displacement of Cultural Property in the Wars of the French Revolution and Napoleon', *HJ*, 56 (2013), p. 118.

48. Colin Lucas, *The Structure of the Terror: The Example of Javogues and the Loire*, Oxford: Oxford University Press, 1973.

49. Pierre Pinsseau, *Cadet Roussel (1743–1807)*, Paris: Clavreuil, 1945, pp. 57–67.

50. Richard Cobb, *The People's Armies*, translated by Marianne Elliott, New Haven, CT, and London: Yale University Press, 1987, p. 728.

51. Anatoli Ado, *Paysans en Révolution. Terre, pouvoir et jacquerie, 1789–1794*, Paris: SÉR, 1996, pp. 405–15.

52. Ruth Graham, 'The Secularization of the Ecclesiastical Deputies to the National Convention, 1792–1794', *Consortium on Revolutionary Europe, 1750–1850*, 3 (1974), pp. 65–79.

53. Pierre Flament, *Deux mille prêtres normands face à la Révolution, 1789–1801*, Paris: Perrin, 1989, p. 156; Bianchi (ed.), *La Révolution culturelle*, pp. 89–91. General discussions of the effects on the Church are Ralph Gibson, *A Social History of French Catholicism, 1789–1914*, London and New York: Routledge, 1989, ch. 2; Nigel Aston, *Religion and Revolution in France, 1780–1804*, Basingstoke: Macmillan, 2000, chs 8–10; Michel Vovelle, *The Revolution against the Church: From Reason to the Supreme Being*, translated by Alan Jose, Cambridge: Cambridge University Press, 1991.

54. AD Meurthe-et-Moselle, L 1712.

55. Rouvière, *Révolution dans le Gard*, vol. 4, pp. 381–600.

56. Claire Cage, '"Celibacy is a social crime": The Politics of Clerical Marriage', *FHS*, 36 (2013), pp. 601–28.

57. Timothy Tackett, *The Coming of the Terror in the French Revolution*, Cambridge, MA, and London: The Belknap Press of Harvard University Press, 2015, pp. 316–17; William Doyle, *The Oxford History of the French Revolution*, 2nd edn., Oxford and New York: Oxford University Press, 2002, p. 261.

58. Louis Trenard, 'Le "vandalisme révolutionnaire" dans les pays de l'Ain: faits matériels et motivations', in Simone Bernard-Griffiths, Marie-Claude Chemin and Jean Ehrard (eds), *Révolution française et 'vandalisme révolutionnaire'. Actes du colloque international de Clermont-Ferrand, 15–17 décembre 1988*, Paris: Universitas, 1992, pp. 251–58.

59. Jean-Clément Martin, *Violence et Révolution: essai sur la naissance d'un mythe national*, Paris: Éditions du Seuil, 2006.

60. Ribeiro, *Fashion*, p. 143.

61. *Le Vieux Cordelier*, no. 4, 30 Frimaire Year II (20 December 1793).

62. Mason and Rizzo (eds), *French Revolution*, pp. 236–38.

63. Jeremy D. Popkin, *You Are All Free: The Haitian Revolution and the Abolition of Slavery*, New York: Cambridge University Press, 2010, ch. 10; David Geggus, 'The Caribbean in the Age of Revolution', in David Armitage and Sanjay Subrahmanyam (eds), *The Age of Revolutions in Global Context, 1760–1840*, Basingstoke and New York: Palgrave Macmillan, 2010, ch. 5; Manuel Covo, 'Race, Slavery and Colonies in the French Revolution', in David Andress (ed.), *The Oxford Handbook of the French Revolution*, Oxford: Oxford University Press, 2015, ch. 17. Slavery was never abolished during this period in the Indian Ocean, where planters successfully insulated the islands from news of reforms.

64. McPhee, *Robespierre*, pp. 185–86. The drama of the confrontation between Robespierre and Danton—and of the struggle for power in Poland in the early 1980s—is evoked in Andrzej Wajda's 1982 film *Danton*, based on a 1930s' play by Stanislawa Przybyszewska.

65. Paul Friedland, *Seeing Justice Done: The Age of Spectacular Capital Punishment in France*, Oxford: Oxford University Press, 2012, p. 259.

66. Marisa Linton, 'Do you Believe that we're Conspirators? Conspiracies Real and Imagined in Jacobin Politics, 1793–94', in Peter R. Campbell, Thomas E. Kaiser and Marisa Linton (eds), *Conspiracy in the French Revolution*, Manchester: Manchester University Press, 2007, p. 143; Marisa Linton, *Choosing Terror: Virtue, Friendship, and Authenticity in the French Revolution*, Oxford: Oxford University Press, 2013, ch. 8; Poumiès de la Siboutie, *Recollections of a Parisian Doctor under Six Sovereigns, Two Revolutions and a Republic (1789–1863)*, translated by Theodora Davidson, London: John Murray, 1911, ch. 2.

Chapter 13 Terror, Victory and Collapse, April–July 1794

1. Peter McPhee, *Robespierre: A Revolutionary Life*, New Haven, CT, and London: Yale University Press, 2012, pp. 194, 207–08, chs 11–12. The most recent French biography prefers to emphasize Robespierre's physical health but increasing political isolation: Hervé Leuwers, *Robespierre*, Paris: Fayard, 2014, chs 22, 24. A hostile recent view is Jonathan I. Israel, *Revolutionary Ideas: An Intellectual History of the French Revolution from* The Rights of Man *to Robespierre*, Princeton, NJ: Princeton University Press, 2014; for example, pp. 21–22, 449, in which Robespierre is vilified as an anti-liberal, anti-intellectual and xenophobic authoritarian who suffered from 'megalomania, paranoia and vindictiveness'.

2. See the remarkable list of speeches in Gérard Walter, *Robespierre*, 2 vols, Paris: Gallimard, 1961, vol. 2, pp. 191–322.

3. Maximilien Robespierre, *Oeuvres de Maximilien Robespierre*, 11 vols, Paris: SÉR, 1912–2007, vol. 11, pp. 397–415; J. M. Thompson, *Robespierre*, Oxford: Blackwell, 1935, pp. 387–402.

4. Raymonde Monnier, *L'Espace publique démocratique. Essai sur l'opinion à Paris de la Révolution au Directoire*, Paris: Éditions Kimé, 1994, pp. 177–87.

5. McPhee, *Robespierre*, p. 195.

6. James H. Johnson, 'Revolutionary Audiences and the Impossible Imperatives of Fraternity', in Bryant T. Ragan and Elizabeth A. Williams (eds), *Re-creating Authority in Revolutionary France*, New Brunswick, NJ: Rutgers University Press, 1992; Marvin A. Carlson, 'The Citizen in the Theater', in Renée Waldinger, Philip Dawson and Isser Woloch (eds), *The French Revolution and the Meaning of Citizenship*, Westport, CT: Greenwood Press, 1993.

7. Éric Saunier, '"Lire pour résister, lire pour instruire". La Revue de presse de Toussaint Bonvoisin', *AHRF*, 373 (2013), pp. 123–44.

8. Paul and Martial de Pradel de Lamase, *Nouvelles notes intimes d'un émigré . . . officier à l'armée de Condé. Les grandes journées révolutionnaires*, Paris: Émile-Paul Frères, 1914, pp. 196–202.

9. Frédéric Derne, 'La Chanson, "arme" révolutionnaire et chambre d'écho de la société en Auvergne', *AHRF*, 341 (2005), pp. 25–51.

10. Claudia Ulbrich, 'Sarreguemines en révolution ou l'histoire d'un "caméléon politique"', *Annales de l'Est*, 44 (1992), pp. 20–26. In Alsace, Jewish men were expected to cut off their beards: Claude Muller, 'Religion et Révolution en Alsace', *AHRF*, 337 (2004), pp. 63–83.

11. René Ducret, *Les Sans-culottes de Lunéville*, Nancy: Imprimerie Bastien, 1967, p. 27; Patrice L. R. Higonnet, *Goodness beyond Virtue: Jacobins during the French Revolution*, Cambridge, MA: Harvard University Press, 1998, p. 174; AD Meurthe-et-Moselle, L 1668.

12. Annie Crépin, 'The Army of the Republic: New Warfare and a New Army', in Pierre Serna, Antonino De Francesco and Judith A. Miller (eds), *Republics at War, 1776–1840: Revolutions, Conflicts, and Geopolitics in Europe and the Atlantic World*, Basingstoke: Palgrave Macmillan, 2013, pp. 136–38.

13. AD Meurthe-et-Moselle, L 2151.

14. Joël Cornette, *Histoire de la Bretagne et des Bretons*, vol. 2, Paris: Éditions du Seuil, 2005, ch. 48.

15. Alan Forrest, *Soldiers of the French Revolution*, Durham, NC: Duke University Press, 1990, p. 166.

16. Jean-Paul Bertaud, 'An Open File: The Press under the Terror', in Keith Michael Baker (ed.), *The French Revolution and the Creation of Modern Political Culture*, vol. 4, *The Terror*, Oxford: Pergamon Press, 1994, ch. 16.

17. See the remarkable police reports in AN F7 3821–22; Marc Bouloiseau, *The Jacobin Republic, 1792–1794*, translated by Jonathan Mandelbaum, Cambridge: Cambridge University Press; Paris: Éditions de la Maison des Sciences de l'Homme, 1983, p. 195.

18. Anatolï Ado, *Paysans en Révolution. Terre, pouvoir et jacquerie, 1789–1794*, Paris: SÉR, 1996, pp. 416–23; R. Legrand, *La Révolution dans la Somme*, Abbeville: F. Paillart, 1988, p. 262. The argument that the Terror was designed to contain this popular protest as much as to crush counter-revolution is put by Sophie Wahnich, *In Defence of the Terror: Liberty or Death in the French Revolution*, translated by David Fernbach, London and New York: Verso, 2012.

19. Peter McPhee, *Revolution and Environment in Southern France: Peasants, Lords, and Murder in the Corbières, 1780–1830*, Oxford: Clarendon Press, 1999, p. 116.

20. Yvonne Crebouw, 'Les Salariés agricoles face au maximum des salaires', in *La Révolution française et le monde rural. Actes du colloque tenu en Sorbonne les 23, 24 et 25 octobre 1987*, Paris: CTHS, 1989, pp. 120–21; Nathalie Alzas, 'Les Rapports entre civils et militaires à l'arrière

pendant la Révolution dans les départements du Midi', in Annie Crépin, Jean-Pierre Jessenne and Hervé Leuwers (eds), *Civils, citoyens-soldats et militaires dans L'État-nation (1789–1815). Actes du colloque d'Arras (7–8 novembre 2003)*, Paris: SÉR, 2006, p. 73; Jacques Bernet, 'Les Grèves de moissonneurs ou "bacchanals" dans les campagnes d'Ile-de-France et de Picardie au XVIIIe siècle', *Histoire et sociétés rurales*, 11 (1999), pp. 153–86.

21. AD Loiret J 557, 2J 1983; Paul Guillaume, 'La Vie dans l'Orléanais de 1788 à 1818, d'après le journal inédit d'une famille', unpublished ms, Orléans c.1960; Georges Lefebvre, *Études orléanaises*, 2 vols, Paris: Commission d'Histoire Économique et Sociale de la Révolution, 1962.

22. Martine Plouvier, 'L'Abbaye de Prémontré au XVIIe et XVIIIe siècles', thèse de troisième cycle, Université de Paris-I, 1982, pp. 358–59.

23. Peter McPhee, *Une Communauté languedocienne dans l'histoire: Gabian 1760–1960*, Nîmes: Lacour, 2001, ch. 2.

24. George Armstrong Kelly, *Victims, Authority and Terror: The Parallel Deaths of d'Orleans, Custine, Bailly, and Malesherbes*, Chapel Hill, NC: University of North Carolina Press, 1982, ch. 16; Simon Schama, *Citizens: A Chronicle of the French Revolution*, New York: Alfred A. Knopf, 1989, pp. 822–27. Malesherbes' other daughter, Louise, would be the mother of Alexis de Tocqueville.

25. Olivier Blanc, *Last Letters: Prisons and Prisoners of the French Revolution, 1793–1794*, translated by Alan Sheridan, New York: Farrar, Straus & Giroux, 1987, pp. 190–91; Stephen Jay Gould, 'The Passion of Antoine Lavoisier', in Gould, *Bully for Brontosaurus: Reflections in Natural History*, New York and London: W. W. Norton and Co., 1991, ch. 24; Arthur Donovan, *Antoine Lavoisier: Science, Administration, and Revolution*, Oxford: Blackwell, 1993. Marie-Anne organized the posthumous circulation of copies of Lavoisier's final memoirs, *Mémoires de physique et de chimie*.

26. Daniel Rabreau, *Claude Nicolas Ledoux*, Paris: Monum, 2005, pp. 83–86. Ledoux was released on 13 January 1795.

27. Blanc, *Last Letters*, p. 134.

28. Jacques Guilhaumou and Martine Lapied, 'La Mission Maignet', *AHRF*, 300 (1995), pp. 283–94.

29. John M. Burney, 'The Fear of the Executive and the Threat of Conspiracy: Billaud-Varenne's Terroristic Rhetoric in the French Revolution, 1788–1794', *FH*, 5 (1991), p. 162.

30. Robespierre, *Oeuvres*, vol. 10, pp. 442–65. On the Cult of the Supreme Being and Robespierre's repudiation of the 'materialism' of the *philosophes*, see Michel Vovelle, 'The Adventures of Reason, or From Reason to the Supreme Being', in Colin Lucas (ed.), *Rewriting the French Revolution*, Oxford: Clarendon Press, 1991, pp. 132–50; Carol Blum, *Rousseau and the Republic of Virtue: The Language of Politics in the French Revolution*, Ithaca, NY, and London: Cornell University Press, 1986, ch. 13.

31. James H. Johnson, *Listening in Paris: A Cultural History*, Berkeley and Los Angeles, CA, and London: University of California Press, 1995, pp. 116–27; Emmet Kennedy, *A Cultural History of the French Revolution*, New Haven, CT, and London: Yale University Press, 1989, pp. 168–85.

32. Marie-Victoire Monnard, *Souvenirs d'une femme du peuple, 1777–1802*, Creil: Bernard Dumerchez, 1989, pp. 89–91.

33. AD Loiret, J 557, L 6(4).

34. Robespierre, *Oeuvres*, vol. 10, pp. 350–66.

35. Arne Ording, *Le Bureau de police du Comité de salut public. Étude sur la Terreur*, Oslo: Skrifter utgitt av det Norske Videnskaps, Academi i Oslo, no. 6, 1931.

36. Cf. Dan Edelstein, *The Terror of Natural Right: Republicanism, the Cult of Nature, and the French Revolution*, Chicago, IL: University of Chicago Press, 2009, ch. 5, for whom the Law of 22 Prairial was to be instead a durable foundation of a 'natural republic'.

37. Daniel Arasse, *The Guillotine and the Terror*, translated by Christopher Miller, London: Penguin, 1989, pp. 107–09.

38. On Lindet, see François Pascal, *L'Économie dans la Terreur: Robert Lindet, 1746–1825*, Paris: SPM, 1999; Huntley Dupre, *Two Brothers in the French Revolution: Robert and Thomas Lindet*, Hamden, CT: Archon Books, 1967; Amand Montier, *Robert Lindet*, Paris: Félix Alcan, 1899.

39. Albert Mathiez, *The Fall of Robespierre, and Other Essays*, New York: A. M. Kelley, 1968, chs 8–9.

40. Jacques-Louis Ménétra, *Journal of My Life*, translated by Arthur Goldhammer, New York: Columbia University Press, 1986, pp. 219–20.

41. AD Meurthe-et-Moselle, 49J 15: Philippe Arnould, 'Quatre volontaires lorrains'.

42. Rebecca L. Spang, *The Invention of the Restaurant: Paris and Modern Gastronomic Culture*, Cambridge, MA: Harvard University Press, 2000, pp. 109–12; McPhee, *Robespierre*, p. 210.

43. Jean-Baptiste Billecocq, *En Prison sous la Terreur. Souvenirs de Jean-Baptiste Billecocq, 1765–1829*, Paris: SÉR, 1981, pp. 36–40.

44. Marisa Linton, *Choosing Terror: Virtue, Friendship, and Authenticity in the French Revolution*, Oxford: Oxford University Press, 2013; Harold T. Parker, *The Cult of Antiquity and the French Revolutionaries: A Study in the Development of the Revolutionary Spirit*, New York: Octagon, 1965.

45. R. R. Palmer, *Twelve who Ruled: The Year of the Terror in the French Revolution*, Princeton, NJ: Princeton University Press, 1969, p. 364.

46. Robespierre, *Oeuvres*, vol. 10, pp. 430–31; P. Raxhon, 'Les Réfugiés Liégeois à Paris: un état de la question', in Michel Vovelle (ed.), *Paris et la Révolution. Actes du Colloque de Paris I, 14–16 avril 1989*, Paris: Publications de la Sorbonne, 1989, pp. 212–24; Greg Burgess, *Refuge in the Land of Liberty: France and its Refugees, from the Revolution to the end of Asylum, 1787–1939*, Basingstoke and New York: Palgrave Macmillan, 2008, pp. 24–30; Michael Rapport, *Nationality and Citizenship in Revolutionary France: The Treatment of Foreigners, 1789–1799*, Oxford: Clarendon Press, 2000, ch. 4.

47. Robespierre, *Oeuvres*, vol. 10, pp. 543–76. Two detailed documentary accounts of the events of late July are Gérard Walter, *La Conjuration du Neuf Thermidor, 27 July 1794*, Paris: Gallimard, 1974, and Richard Bienvenu, *The Ninth of Thermidor: The Fall of Robespierre*, New York: Oxford University Press, 1968.

48. Françoise Brunel, *Thermidor, la chute de Robespierre*, Brussels: Éditions Complexe, 1999, p. 7.

49. George Rudé, *The Crowd in the French Revolution*, Oxford: Oxford University Press, 1959, ch. 9; Colin Jones, 'The Overthrow of Maximilien Robespierre and the "Indifference" of the People', *AHR*, 119 (2014), pp. 689–713; Haim Burstin, *Révolutionnaires. Pour une anthropologie de la Révolution française*, Paris: Vendémiaire, 2013, pp. 352–64.

50. Michel Péronnet and Yannick Guin, *La Revolution dans la Loire-Inférieure*, Le Coteau: Horvath, 1989, pp. 144–46.

51. AN F7 7904/4561; W 79, liasse 1; Jacques Bernet, 'La Perception de Robespierre dans les clubs de Jacobins de Champagne et de Picardie (1791–1795)', in Jean-Pierre Jessenne, Gilles Derégnaucourt, Jean-Pierre Hirsch and Hervé Leuwers (eds), *Robespierre: de la nation artésienne à la République et aux nations. Actes du Colloque, Arras, 1–2–3 Avril 1993*, Villeneuve d'Asq. Centre d'Histoire de la Région du Nord et de l'Europe du Nord-Ouest, Université Charles de Gaulle-Lille III, 1994; Michael Kennedy, *The Jacobin Clubs in the French Revolution, 1793–1795*, New York: Berghahn Books, 2000, ch. 17; Peter McPhee, *Living the French Revolution, 1789–99*, London and New York: Palgrave Macmillan, 2006, pp. 163–68. Letters of denunciation and interrogations are to be found, for example, in AN F7 4432, plaque 2, 4433, plaques 3 and 4, and in the Committee of General Security files in AN F7 4577–4775.

52. See Louis Jacob, *Robespierre vu par ses contemporains*, Paris: A. Colin, 1938, pp. 63, 101, 125, 136–37, 181–87; Louis Jacob, 'Un Ami de Robespierre: Buissart (d'Arras)', *Revue du Nord*, 20 (1934), pp. 287–93; Lindsay A. H. Parker, *Writing the Revolution: A French Woman's History in Letters*, Oxford and New York: Oxford University Press, 2013, pp. 116–18. Buissart subsequently retired from public life, until becoming a municipal councillor under the Restoration. He died aged eighty-three in 1820.

53. Watkin Tench, *Letters Written in France, to a Friend in London, Between the Month of November 1794, and the Month of May 1795*, Whitefish, MO: Kessinger Publishing, 2009, pp. 67, 191–92, 194–95, 198; Gavin Edwards (ed.), *Watkin Tench: Letters from Revolutionary France*, Cardiff: University of Wales Press, 2001, Introduction.

54. See, for example, Antoine de Baecque, *Glory and Terror: Seven Deaths under the French Revolution*, translated by Charlotte Mandell, New York and London: Routledge, 2001, pp. 145–72; McPhee, *Robespierre*, Epilogue; Hervé Leuwers, 'Robespierre, la Terreur incarnée? Aux origines d'une personnification de l'an II', in Michel Biard and Hervé Leuwers (eds), *Visages de la Terreur. L'Exception politique de l'an II*, Paris: Armand Colin, 2014, pp. 197–210; Marc Belissa and Yannick Bosc, *Robespierre. La Fabrication d'un mythe*, Paris: Ellipses, 2013.

55. Jean-Clément Martin, 'La Vendée. Enquête sur les crimes de la Révolution', *Histoire*, 377 (2012), pp. 40–61; Jean-Clément Martin, 'Dénombrer les victimes de la Terreur. La Vendée et au-delà', in Biard and Leuwers (eds), *Visages de la Terreur.*

56. Michel Biard, *La Liberté ou la Mort. Mourir en député (1792–1795)*, Paris: Tallandier, 2015; Mette Harder, 'A Second Terror: The Purges of French Revolutionary Legislators after Thermidor', *FHS*, 38 (2015), pp. 33–60.

57. This conclusion is largely in agreement with Timothy Tackett, *The Coming of the Terror in the French Revolution*, Cambridge, MA, and London: The Belknap Press of Harvard University Press, 2015, Conclusion. For alternative views, see, for example, Patrice Gueniffey, *La Politique de la Terreur: essai sur la violence révolutionnaire*, Paris: Fayard, 2000; William M. Reddy, 'Sentimentalism and its Erasure: The Role of Emotions in the Era of the French Revolution', *JMH*, 72 (2000), pp. 109–52; Arno J. Mayer, *The Furies: Violence and Terror in the French and Russian Revolutions*, Princeton, NJ: Princeton University Press, 2000.

Chapter 14 Settling Scores: The Thermidorian Reaction, 1794–95

1. On the Thermidorian regime, see Laura Mason, 'Thermidor and the Myth of Rupture', in David Andress (ed.), *The Oxford Handbook of the French Revolution*, Oxford: Oxford University Press, 2015, ch. 30; Bronislaw Baczko, *Ending the Terror: The French Revolution after Robespierre*, translated by Michael Petheram, Cambridge: Cambridge University Press; Paris: Éditions de la Maison des Sciences de l'Homme, 1994.

2. Laura Mason and Tracey Rizzo (eds), *The French Revolution: A Document Collection*, Boston, MA, and New York: Houghton Mifflin, 1999, pp. 263–68.

3. Christine Adams, '"Venus of the Capitol": Madame Tallien and the Politics of Beauty under the Directory', *FHS*, 37 (2014), pp. 599–629; Lindsay A. H. Parker, *Writing the Revolution: A French Woman's History in Letters*, Oxford and New York: Oxford University Press, 2013, pp. 118–19.

4. AD Loiret, 2J 184. On the obsession with Robespierre's *queue* (tail or penis), see Antoine de Baecque, *Glory and Terror: Seven Deaths under the French Revolution*, translated by Charlotte Mandell, New York and London: Routledge, 2001, pp. 160–65; Howard G. Brown, 'Robespierre's Tail: The Possibilities of Justice after the Terror', *Canadian Journal of History*, 45 (2010), pp. 303–35.

5. Evangeline Bruce, *Napoleon and Josephine: An Improbable Marriage*, New York: Scribner, 1995.

6. Sophie de Bohm, *Prisonnière sous la Terreur. Mémoires d'une captive en 1793*, Paris: Cosmopole, 2001, p. 143.

7. Claude Guillon, 'Pauline Léon, une républicaine révolutionnaire', *AHRF*, 344 (2006), pp. 147–59; Darline Gay Levy, Harriet Branson Applewhite and Mary Durham Johnson, *Women in Revolutionary Paris, 1789–1795: Selected Documents Translated with Notes and Commentary*, Urbana and Chicago, IL: University of Illinois Press, 1980, p. 271.

8. Peter McPhee, *Revolution and Environment in Southern France: Peasants, Lords, and Murder in the Corbières, 1780–1830*, Oxford: Clarendon Press, 1999, p. 120.

9. Henri Labroue, *La Société populaire de Bergerac pendant la Révolution*, Paris: Société de l'Histoire de la Révolution Française, 1915, pp. 379–89.

10. Laurent Brassart, *Gouverner le local en Révolution. État, pouvoirs et mouvements collectifs dans l'Aisne (1790–1795)*, Paris: SÉR, 2013, pp. 393–97, 421–22.

11. Jacques Guilhaumou and Martine Lapied, 'Femmes et comités de surveillance', in Danièle Pingué and Jean-Paul Rothiot (eds), *Les Comités de surveillance. D'une création citoyenne à une institution révolutionnaire*, Paris: SÉR, 2012, p. 129.

12. François Gendron, *The Gilded Youth of Thermidor*, translated by James Cookson, Montreal and Kingston, ON, London, Buffalo, NY: McGill-Queen's University Press, 1993, p. 54.

13. Louis-Mathieu Molé, *Souvenirs de jeunesse, 1793–1803*, Paris: Mercure de France, 1991, pp. 75–76, 91–92.

14. Gendron, *Gilded Youth*, pp. 70–71.

15. Alan Forrest, *The Revolution in Provincial France: Aquitaine 1789–1799*, Oxford and New York: Oxford University Press, 1996, p. 334.

16. AD Ain, AC Bourg, Registre des délibérations du Conseil Général, 10 Germinal, 30 Floréal, 11 Prairial An IV.

17. Laura Auricchio, *Adélaïde Labille-Guiard: Artist in the Age of Revolution*, Los Angeles, CA: J. Paul Getty Museum, 2009, ch. 5.

18. Gendron, *Gilded Youth*, pp. 53–54.

19. Gendron, *Gilded Youth*, pp. 69–76.

20. Carla Hesse, *Publishing and Cultural Politics in Revolutionary Paris, 1789–1810*, Berkeley and Los Angeles, CA: University of California Press, 1991.

21. The 'Marseillaise' only lasted as the anthem until 1804; it was reintroduced under the Third Republic in 1879. Bastille Day became the national day in 1880.

22. Carol Blum, *Rousseau and the Republic of Virtue: The Language of Politics in the French Revolution*, Ithaca, NY, and London: Cornell University Press, 1986, pp. 278–81.

23. Nicole Pellegrin, *Les Vêtements de la Liberté: Abécédaire des pratiques vestimentaires en France de 1780 à 1800*, Aix-en-Provence: Éditions Alinéa, 1989, p. 175.

24. Annie Heywood, 'Étude des prénoms à Brest pendant la Révolution (1789–1799)', *Les Cahiers de l'Iroise*, 35 (1988), pp. 145–60.

25. Alain Corbin, *Village Bells: Sound and Meaning in the 19th-Century French Countryside*, translated by Martin Thom, New York: Columbia University Press, 1998, pp. 23–32.

26. Suzanne Desan, *Reclaiming the Sacred: Lay Religion and Popular Politics in Revolutionary France*, Ithaca, NY: Cornell University Press, 1990, p. 162.

27. John Hall Stewart (ed.), *A Documentary Survey of the French Revolution*, New York: Macmillan, 1951, pp. 616–19.

28. Michael P. Fitzsimmons, *From Artisan to Worker: Guilds, the French State, and the Organization of Labor, 1776–1821*, New York: Cambridge University Press, 2010, ch. 2.

29. Stewart (ed.), *Documentary Survey*, pp. 555–60; Josef Konvitz, *Cartography in France, 1660–1848: Science, Engineering, and Statecraft*, Chicago, IL: University of Chicago Press, 1987.

30. The telegraphs linked the major cities of France by the 1830s before being replaced by electric telegraphs. See Rollo Appleyard, *Pioneers of Electrical Communication*, London: Macmillan, 1930.

31. Richard Mowery Andrews, 'Paris of the Great Revolution: 1789–1796', in Gene Brucker (ed.), *People and Communities in the Western World*, vol. 2, Homewood, IL: Dorsey Press, 1979, pp. 98–111; Dominique Godineau, *S'Abréger les jours. Le suicide en France au XVIIIe siècle*. Paris: Armand Colin, 2012.

32. AD Loiret, J 557.

33. AD Loiret, 2J 1983.

34. Louis-Sébastien Mercier, *Paris pendant la Révolution (1789–1798) ou le nouveau Paris*, Paris: Livre Club du Librairie, 1962, pp. 204–07.

35. Richard Cobb, *The Police and the People: French Popular Protest, 1789–1820*, Oxford: Oxford University Press, 1970, pp. 299–300.

36. Dominique Godineau, *The Women of Paris and their French Revolution*, translated by Katherine Streip, Berkeley, CA: University of California Press, 1998, p. 300 and chs 13–14.

37. Godineau, *Women of Paris*, pp. 310–45; George Rudé, *The Crowd in the French Revolution*, Oxford: Oxford University Press, 1959, ch. 10.

38. Gendron, *Gilded Youth*, ch. 4.

39. Philip Dawson (ed.), *The French Revolution*, Englewood Cliffs, NJ: Prentice-Hall, 1967, pp. 172–74.

40. Dawson (ed.), *French Revolution*, pp. 152–53. On these *journées*, see Rudé, *Crowd*, ch. 10; Gendron, *Gilded Youth*; Jean-Paul Bertaud, *The Army of the French Revolution: From Citizen-Soldiers to Instrument of Power*, translated by R. R. Palmer, Princeton, NJ: Princeton University Press, 1988, ch. 12.

41. Michel Biard and Pascal Dupuy, *La Révolution française. Dynamique et ruptures, 1787–1804*, 2nd edn, Paris: Armand Colin, 2008, p. 125; Raymonde Monnier, *Le Faubourg Saint-Antoine (1789–1815)*, Paris: SÉR, 1981, pp. 138–46; Gendron, *Gilded Youth*, pp. 159–63; Rudé, *Crowd*, pp. 154–56.

42. Godineau, *Women of Paris*, pp. 376–99.

43. Françoise Brunel and Sylvain Goujon, *Les Martyrs de Prairial. Texte et documents inédits*, Geneva: Georg, 1992.

44. Jacques Pimoulle, *Le Conventionnel Nicolas Maure, 1743–1795*, Auxerre: Imprimerie Moderne, 1989, pp. 215–16; Michel Biard, *Missionnaires de la République*, Paris: CTHS, 2002.

45. Mette Harder, 'A Second Terror: The Purges of French Revolutionary Legislators after Thermidor', *FHS*, 38 (2015), pp. 33–60. Barère would emerge as a secret agent under Bonaparte, but would be exiled after 1815 as a regicide.

46. Michael Kennedy, *The Jacobin Club of Marseilles, 1790–1794*, Ithaca, NY, and London: Cornell University Press, 1973, pp. 220–21.

47. D. M. G. Sutherland, *Murder in Aubagne: Lynching, Law, and Justice during the French Revolution*, Cambridge and New York: Cambridge University Press, 2009.

48. Stephen Clay, 'Vengeance, Justice and the Reactions in the Revolutionary Midi', *FH*, 23 (2009), pp. 22–46; Colin Lucas, 'Themes in Southern Violence after 9 Thermidor', in Gwynne Lewis and Colin Lucas (eds), *Beyond the Terror: Essays in French Regional and Social History, 1794–1815*, Cambridge: Cambridge University Press, 1983, pp. 152–94.

49. Forrest, *Revolution in Provincial France*, p. 334; Mason, *Singing the French Revolution*, ch. 5.

50. Mason and Rizzo (eds), *French Revolution*, pp. 275–77.

51. On the links between internal and external counter-revolution, see Maurice Hutt, *Chouannerie and Counter-Revolution: Puisaye, the Princes and the British Government in the 1790s*, 2 vols, Cambridge: Cambridge University Press, 1983; William Fryer, *Republic or Restoration in France? 1794–1797: The Politics of French Royalism*, Manchester: Manchester University Press, 1965; Harvey Mitchell, *The Underground War against Revolutionary France: The Missions of William Wickham, 1794–1800*, Oxford: Oxford University Press, 1965.

52. Roger Dupuy, *La Noblesse entre l'exil et la mort*, Rennes: Éditions Ouest-France, 1989, pp. 102–09.

53. AD Morbihan, L1476. In 1829 the bones were exhumed and deposited in the vault of a memorial chapel at the Auray monastery, on what is now called the Champ des Martyrs. A plaque on a wall in the park of La Garenne in Vannes commemorates those shot there, including Hercé.

54. Michel Péronnet and Yannick Guin, *La Révolution dans la Loire-Inférieure*, Le Coteau: Horvath, 1989, pp. 144–46.

55. Daniel Nordman, 'Le Sacré du territoire sous la Révolution', in Raymonde Monnier (ed.), *Citoyens et citoyenneté sous la Révolution française*, Paris: SÉR, 2006, pp. 103–14.

56. Kindly translated by Margreet de Brie from the *Amsterdamse Courant*, 22 January 1795; and the town archives of Zaltbommel: 20 Archieven van de stad Zaltbommel (1293) 1327–1815; 20/1162 Dagboek van Joost Gerard Kist, predikant te Zaltbommel, 21 September 1794–17 June 1795. See Simon Schama, *Patriots and Liberators: Revolution in the Netherlands, 1780–1813*, New York: Vintage Books, 1977; Jonathan Israel, *The Dutch Republic: Its Rise, Greatness and Fall, 1477–1806*, Oxford: Oxford University Press, 1995.

57. Michael Rapport, 'The International Repercussions of the French Revolution', in Peter McPhee (ed.), *A Companion to the French Revolution*, Oxford: Wiley-Blackwell, 2013, pp. 390–94.

58. Michael Rapport, 'Belgium under French Occupation: Between Collaboration and Resistance, July 1794 to October 1795', *FH*, 16 (2002), pp. 53–82.

59. 'Lettres d'un jeune soldat des armées révolutionnaires à ses parents (1793–1795)', *Fédération des sociétés d'histoire et d'archéologie de l'Aisne*, 23 (1978), pp. 96–127.

60. Jacques Bernet, 'Les Grèves de moissonneurs ou "bacchanals" dans les campagnes d'Ile-de-France et de Picardie au XVIIIe siècle', *Histoire et sociétés rurales*, 11 (1999), pp. 153–86.

61. BM Nancy, ms 1540/1.

62. BM Nancy, ms 1540/1.

63. BM Nancy, ms 1540/2.

64. William Doyle, *The Oxford History of the French Revolution*, 2nd edn., Oxford and New York: Oxford University Press, 2002, ch. 9. On the cosmopolitan and republican impulse of the Directory in foreign policy, see Pierre Serna (ed.), *Républiques sœurs: le Directoire et la Révolution atlantique*, Rennes: Presses Universitaires de Rennes, 2009.

65. Rapport, 'International Repercussions', p. 388.

66. C. A. Bayly, *The Birth of the Modern World, 1780–1914: Global Connections and Comparisons*, Oxford: Blackwell, 2004, ch. 3. The Cape was briefly returned to the Netherlands in 1804–06.

67. Laurent Dubois, *A Colony of Citizens: Revolution and Slave Emancipation in the French Caribbean, 1787–1804*, Chapel Hill, NC: University of North Carolina Press, 2004, p. 201.

68. *MU*, 11 Messidor Year III (29 June 1795), vol. 25, pp. 81, 92; Albert Soboul, *Comprendre la Révolution: problèmes politiques de la Révolution française (1789–1797)*, Paris: F. Maspero, 1981; translated by April A. Knutson as *Understanding the French Revolution*, New York: International Publishers, 1988, pp. 453–55.

69. Yannick Bosc and Sophie Wahnich (eds), *Les Voix de la Révolution. Projets pour la démocratie*, Paris: Documentation Française, 1990, pp. 50–51.

70. Stewart (ed.), *Documentary Survey*, pp. 572–612.

71. Andrew Jainchill, *Reimagining Politics after the Terror: The Republican Origins of French Liberalism*, Ithaca, NY, and London: Cornell University Press, 2008, p. 59.

72. Stewart (ed.), *Documentary Survey*, pp. 113–15, 454–68, 572–612.

73. Malcolm Crook, *Elections in the French Revolution: An Apprenticeship in Democracy, 1789–1799*, Cambridge and New York: Cambridge University Press, 1996, pp. 124–28.

Chapter 15 Men with a Stake in Society, 1795–97

1. Michel Biard, *La Liberté ou la mort. Mourir en député, 1792–1795*, Paris: Tallandier, 2015.

2. See Pierre Serna, *La République des girouettes. 1789–1815 et au-delà, une anomalie politique: la France de l'extrême centre*, Seyssel: Champ-Vallon, 2005; D. M. G. Sutherland, *The French Revolution and Empire: The Quest for a Civic Order*, Oxford: Blackwell, 2003, ch. 8.

3. Jean-Pierre Jessenne, *Pouvoir au village et Révolution: Artois, 1760–1848*, Lille: Presses Universitaires de Lille, 1987.

4. BM Nancy, ms 1853.

5. Claudia Ulbrich, 'Sarreguemines en révolution ou l'histoire d'un "caméléon politique"', *Annales de l'Est*, 44 (1992), pp. 26–29.

6. D. Lottin, *Recherches historiques sur la ville d'Orléans*, 8 vols, Orléans: Imprimerie Alexandre Jacob, 1836–45, vol. 6, pp. 1–2.

7. Jennifer Ngaire Heuer, *The Family and the Nation: Gender and Citizenship in Revolutionary France, 1789–1830*, Ithaca, NY, and London: Cornell University Press, 2005, p. 81.

8. Christine Adams, '"Venus of the Capitol": Madame Tallien and the Politics of Beauty under the Directory', *FHS*, 37 (2014), pp. 599–629.

9. AD Aisne, L 588.

10. Claude Bailly, *Journal d'un artisan tourangeau, 1789–1830*, Chinon: Amis du vieux Chinon, 1989, pp. 51–53.

11. Lottin, *Orléans*, vol. 6, pp. 29, 73–77.

12. Jean-Marie Augustin, *La Révolution française en Haut-Poitou et pays Charentais*, Toulouse: Privat, 1989.

13. François Gendron, *The Gilded Youth of Thermidor*, translated by James Cookson, Montreal and Kingston, ON, London, Buffalo, NY: McGill-Queen's University Press, 1993, ch. 5.

14. Evangeline Bruce, *Napoleon and Josephine: An Improbable Marriage*, New York: Scribner, 1995, pp. 169–70 and chs 10–11; Philip Dwyer, *Napoleon: The Path to Power, 1769–1799*, London: Bloomsbury, 2007, chs 8–9.

15. Tom Reiss, *The Black Count: Glory, Revolution, Betrayal, and the Real Count of Monte Cristo*, New York: Crown, 2012.

16. Jean-Clément Martin, 'La Vendée. Enquête sur les crimes de la Révolution', *Histoire*, 377 (2012), pp. 40–61.

17. David Gilks, 'Art and Politics during the "First" Directory: Artists' Petitions and the Quarrel over the Confiscation of Works of Art from Italy', *FH*, 26 (2012), pp. 53–78.

18. Simon Lee, *David*, London: Phaidon, 1999, ch. 4.

19. Thomas E. Crow, *Emulation: David, Drouais, and Girodet in the Art of Revolutionary France*, New Haven, CT, and London: Yale University Press, 2006, pp. 225–28; Jeremy D. Popkin, *You Are All Free: The Haitian Revolution and the Abolition of Slavery*, New York: Cambridge University Press, 2010.

20. Martin J. S. Rudwick, *Georges Cuvier, Fossil Bones, and Geological Catastrophes*, Chicago, IL: University of Chicago Press, 1997.

21. BM Nancy, ms 1853, Abbé Jacques.

22. BM Nancy, ms 1853.

23. BM Nancy, ms 1853.

24. Roger Dupuy, *De la Révolution à la chouannerie. Paysans de Bretagne, 1788–1794*, Paris: Flammarion, 1988, p. 306; Dupuy, *Bretagne*, pp. 233–34; Jean-Clément Martin, 'The Vendée, Chouannerie, and the State, 1791–99', in Peter McPhee (ed.), *A Companion to the French Revolution*, Oxford: Wiley-Blackwell, 2013, ch. 15.

25. Alain Racineux, 'Du Faux-saunage à la chouannerie, au sud-est de la Bretagne', *Mémoires de la société d'histoire et d'archéologie de Bretagne*, 56 (1989), pp. 192–206.

26. Anne Brillet, 'La Vie tragique d'Éléonor d'Amphernet (1747–1796). Un héros de la chouannerie dans le Sud-Finistère', *Les Cahiers de l'Iroise*, 35 (1988), pp. 43–47.

27. These figures come from a register Sicre brought back with him to Saint Laurent and which is today in the archives of the parish church: Peter McPhee, 'Counter-Revolution in the Pyrenees: Spirituality, Class and Ethnicity in the Haut-Vallespir, 1793–1794', *FH*, 7 (1993), pp. 313–43.

28. Richard Cobb, *The Police and the People: French Popular Protest, 1789–1820*, Oxford: Oxford University Press, 1970, pp. 234–39; Colin Jones, 'Picking up the Pieces: The Politics and the Personnel of Social Welfare from the Convention to the Consulate', in Gwynne Lewis and Colin Lucas (eds), *Beyond the Terror: Essays in French Regional and Social History, 1794–1815*, Cambridge and New York: Cambridge University Press, 1983, pp. 53–91.

29. Christian Aubin, 'Les Assignats sous la Révolution française: un exemple d'hyperinflation', *Revue économique*, 42 (1991), pp. 745–61.

30. William Doyle, *The Oxford History of the French Revolution*, 2nd edn., Oxford and New York: Oxford University Press, 2002, p. 325.

31. AD Ain, État Civil de Bourg-en-Bresse.

32. Peter McPhee, *Revolution and Environment in Southern France: Peasants, Lords, and Murder in the Corbières, 1780–1830*, Oxford: Clarendon Press, 1999, p. 132.

33. Suzanne Desan, *Reclaiming the Sacred: Lay Religion and Popular Politics in Revolutionary France*, Ithaca, NY: Cornell University Press, 1990, p. 146; Olwen Hufton, 'Women in Revolution, 1789–1796', *P&P*, 53 (1971), p. 105; Olwen Hufton, *Bayeux in the Late Eighteenth Century: A Social Study*, Oxford: Oxford University Press, 1967, p. 232. A superb overview is Olwen Hufton, 'The Reconstruction of a Church, 1796–1801', in Lewis and Lucas (eds), *Beyond the Terror*, pp. 21–52.

34. Peter McPhee, *Collioure et la Révolution française, 1789–1815*, Perpignan: Le Publicateur, 1989, pp. 72–73.

35. R. B. Rose, *Gracchus Babeuf: The First Revolutionary Communist*, London: Edward Arnold, 1978; J. A. Scott (ed. and trans.), *The Defense of Gracchus Babeuf before the High Court of Vendôme*, Amherst, MA: University of Massachusetts Press, 1967.

36. Lottin, *Orléans*, vol. 5, p. 413.

37. Richard Cobb, *Reactions to the French Revolution*, London: Oxford University Press, 1972, ch. 5; Michel Vovelle, 'From Beggary to Brigandage: The Wanderers in the Beauce during the French Revolution', in Jeffry Kaplow (ed.), *New Perspectives on the French Revolution: Readings in Historical Sociology*, New York: John Wiley, 1965, pp. 287–304.

38. Richard Cobb, *Paris and its Provinces*, Oxford: Oxford University Press, 1975, ch. 5.

39. On the army under the Directory, see Jean-Paul Bertaud, *The Army of the French Revolution: From Citizen-Soldiers to Instrument of Power*, translated by R. R. Palmer, Princeton, NJ: Princeton University Press, 1988, chs 10–11. The question of how 'liberating' French armies were divides historians: see R. R. Palmer, *The Age of the Democratic Revolution: A Political History of Europe and America, 1760–1800*, 2 vols, Princeton, NJ: Princeton University Press, 1959, 1964, vol. 2; T. C. W. Blanning, *French Revolution in Germany: Occupation and Resistance in the Rhineland, 1792–1802*, Oxford: Oxford University Press, 1983.

40. Michael Rapport, *Nationality and Citizenship in Revolutionary France: The Treatment of Foreigners, 1789–1799*, Oxford: Clarendon Press, 2000.

41. Richard Rose, *The French at Fishguard: Fact, Fiction and Folklore*, London: Transactions of the Honourable Society of Cymmrodorian, 2003. On Wales, see the recent scholarship in M.-A. Constantine and D. Johnston (eds), *Footsteps of Liberty and Revolt: Essays on Wales and the French Revolution*, Cardiff: University of Wales Press, 2013; M. Löffler, *Welsh Responses to the French Revolution: Press and Public Discourse, 1789–1802*, Cardiff: University of Wales Press, 2012.

42. Antoine Vantuch, 'Un Savant Breton prêche la Révolution dans les Carpates', *Annales de Bretagne et des pays de l'ouest*, 96 (1989), pp. 485–89. Haquet was a remarkable polymath, having published multi-volume studies of geology, botany and ethnography in the Carpathians.

43. Michael Rapport, 'The International Repercussions of the French Revolution', in McPhee (ed.), *Companion*, pp. 390–93.

44. Rapport, 'International Repercussions', p. 389; Philipp Ziesche, *Cosmopolitan Patriots: Americans in Paris in the Age of Revolution*, Charlottesville, VA: University of Virginia Press, 2010, ch. 5.

45. Ian Germani, 'Military Justice under the Directory: The Armies of Italy and of the Sambre et Meuse', *FH*, 23 (2009), pp. 47–68.

46. Germani, 'Military Justice under the Directory'.

47. BM Nancy, ms 1540/3.

48. Étienne Jolicler, *Joliclerc, volontaire aux armées de la Révolution. Ses lettres (1793–1796)*, 4th edn., Paris: Perrin, 1905, pp. 241–45.

49. McPhee, *Revolution and Environment*, p. 136. Popular politics in the countryside are studied by Gwynne Lewis, *The Second Vendée: The Continuity of Counter-Revolution in the Department of the Gard, 1789–1815*, Oxford: Oxford University Press, 1978, ch. 3; Colin Lucas, 'Themes in Southern Violence after 9 Thermidor', in Gwynne Lewis and Colin Lucas (eds), *Beyond the Terror: Essays in French Regional and Social History, 1794–1815*, Cambridge: Cambridge University Press, 1983, pp. 152–94; Cobb, *Reactions to the French Revolution*, pp. 19–62; P. M. Jones, *The Peasantry in the French Revolution*, Cambridge: Cambridge University Press, 1988, pp. 240–47.

50. Cobb, *Police and the People*, p. 350.

51. Stephen Clay, 'Les Réactions du Midi: conflits, continuités et violences', *AHRF*, 345 (2006), pp. 55–91.

52. Nathalie Alzas, 'Les Rapports entre civils et militaires', in Annie Crépin, Jean-Pierre Jessenne and Hervé Leuwers (eds), *Civils, citoyens-soldats et militaires dans L'État-nation (1789–1815). Actes du colloque d'Arras (7–8 novembre 2003)*, Paris: SÉR, 2006, p. 70.

53. Christine Peyrard, 'L'Affaire du 26 Pluviôse an II à Avignon ou la tradition révolutionnaire du peuple en armes', in Jacques Bernet, Jean-Pierre Jessenne and Hervé Leuwers (eds), *Du Directoire au Consulat*, vol. 1, *Le Lien politique local dans la grande nation*, Villeneuve d'Ascq: Université Charles de Gaulle—Lille 3, 1999, pp. 55–70.

54. AD Loiret 2J 1983.

55. François Lebrun, *Parole de Dieu et Révolution. Les Sermons d'un curé angevin avant et pendant la guerre de Vendée*, Paris: Éditions Imago, 1988, p. 128.

56. Laura Mason and Tracey Rizzo (eds), *The French Revolution: A Document Collection*, Boston, MA, and New York: Houghton Mifflin, 1999, pp. 322–23.

57. Howard Brown, *War, Revolution, and the Bureaucratic State: Politics and Army Administration in France, 1791–1799*, Oxford: Clarendon Press, 1995, pp. 224–25; Brown, *Ending the French Revolution: Violence, Justice, and Repression from the Terror to Napoleon*, Charlottesville, VA: University of Virginia Press, 2006.

58. François Lebrun, *Parole de Dieu et Révolution. Les Sermons d'un curé angevin avant et pendant la guerre de Vendée*, Paris: Éditions Imago, 1988, p. 130; Joël Cornette, *Histoire de la Bretagne et des Bretons*, Paris: Éditions du Seuil, 2005, vol. 2, pp. 609–10. Only the Concordat with the papacy and the construction of the garrison town of Pontivy in 1802 would quieten the region.

59. Bruce, *Napoleon and Josephine*, p. 97. Accessible accounts of Napoleon's rise are Malcolm Crook, *Napoleon Comes to Power: Democracy and Dictatorship in Revolutionary France, 1795–1804*, Cardiff: University of Wales Press, 1998; Dwyer, *Napoleon: the Path to Power*; and Robert Asprey, *The Rise of Napoleon Bonaparte*, New York: Basic Books, 2000.

60. From Laura Mason, *Singing the French Revolution: Popular Culture and Politics, 1787–1799*, Ithaca, NY: Cornell University Press, 1996, p. 199; Brigitte Level, *À travers deux siècles. Le Caveau: société bachique et chantante, 1726–1939*, Paris: Presses de l'Université de Paris-Sorbonne, 1988.

61. Andrew Jainchill, *Reimagining Politics after the Terror: The Republican Origins of French Liberalism*, Ithaca, NY, and London: Cornell University Press, 2008; Brown, *War, Revolution, and the Bureaucratic State*; Serna, *République des girouettes*.

Chapter 16 The Great Nation and its Enemies, 1797–99

1. Louis-Sébastien Mercier, *Panorama of Paris: Selections from Tableau de Paris*, translated by Helen Simpson and Jeremy D. Popkin, University Park, PA: Pennsylvania State University Press, 1999.
2. James Livesey, *Making Democracy in the French Revolution*, Cambridge, MA, and London: Harvard University Press, 2001, esp. p. 244.
3. Andrew Jainchill, *Reimagining Politics after the Terror: The Republican Origins of French Liberalism*, Ithaca, NY, and London: Cornell University Press, 2008, pp. 114–17. Théremin had been born in Prussia of Huguenots who had fled France after the revocation of the Edict of Nantes in 1685.
4. Paul Friedland, *Seeing Justice Done: The Age of Spectacular Capital Punishment in France*, Oxford: Oxford University Press, 2012, p. 268.
5. Martine Taroni, *Un Prêtre en révolution. François-Yves Besnard, souvenirs d'un nonagenaire*, Rennes: PUF, 2011; François-Yves Besnard, *Souvenirs d'un nonagenaire*, 2 vols, Paris: H. Champion, 1880.
6. BM Nancy, MS 1715.
7. Éric Hartmann, *La Révolution française en Alsace et en Lorraine*, Paris: Perrin, 1990, pp. 482–83.
8. Richard B. Fisher, *Edward Jenner, 1749–1823*, London: André Deutsch, 1991.
9. *MU*, 2 August 1793, vol. 17, 287; John Hall Stewart (ed.), *A Documentary Survey of the French Revolution*, New York: Macmillan, 1951, pp. 503–05; Josef Konvitz, *Cartography in France, 1660–1848: Science, Engineering, and Statecraft*, Chicago, IL: University of Chicago Press, 1987.
10. Caroline Fayolle, 'Des Institutrices républicaines (1793–1799)', *AHRF*, 368 (2012), pp. 87–103.
11. Jacques Debal, *Orléans. Une ville, une histoire*, 2 vols, Orléans: x-nova, 1998, vol. 2, p. 171.
12. E. C. Spary, *Utopia's Garden: French Natural History from Old Regime to Revolution*, Chicago, IL, and London: University of Chicago Press, 2000, for example, p. 152.
13. Victoria Johnson, *Backstage at the Revolution: How the Royal Paris Opera Survived the End of the Old Regime*, Chicago, IL, and London: University of Chicago Press, 2008, especially pp. 191–93.
14. Claire Cage, '"Celibacy is a Social Crime": The Politics of Clerical Marriage', *FHS*, 36 (2013), pp. 623–26; Alyssa Goldstein Sepinwall, *The Abbé Grégoire and the French Revolution: The Making of Modern Universalism*, Berkeley and Los Angeles, CA: University of California Press, 2005.
15. P. Delarue, *Un aumônier des Chouans, l'abbé Nicolas-François Faligant, 1755–1813*, Rennes: Plihon and Hommay; Nantes: Durance, 1910.
16. AD Meurthe-et-Moselle, ms SAL 159.
17. Overviews of foreign policy include William Doyle, *The Oxford History of the French Revolution*, 2nd edn., Oxford and New York: Oxford University Press, 2002, ch. 15; Jacques Godechot, *La Grande Nation: l'expansion révolutionnaire de la France dans le monde de 1789 à 1799*, Paris: Aubier, 1956.
18. Stuart J. Woolf, *A History of Italy*, London: Methuen, 1979; Bernard Gainot, 'War and Citizenship: Central Italy, 1798–1799', in Pierre Serna, Antonino de Francesco and Judith A. Miller (eds), *Republics at War, 1776–1840: Revolutions, Conflicts, and Geopolitics in Europe and the Atlantic World*, Basingstoke: Palgrave Macmillan, 2013.
19. David Gilks, 'Attitudes to the Displacement of Cultural Property in the Wars of the French Revolution and Napoleon', *HJ*, 56 (2013), pp. 113–43.
20. L. Duchet (ed.), *Deux Volontaires de 1791. Les frères Favier de Montluçon. Journal et lettres*, Montluçon: A. Herbin, 1909, pp. 156–57.
21. Michael Rapport, 'The International Repercussions of the French Revolution', in Peter McPhee (ed.), *A Companion to the French Revolution*, Oxford: Wiley-Blackwell, 2013, pp. 387–88. See Raymond Kubben, *Regeneration and Hegemony: Franco-Batavian Relations in the Revolutionary Era, 1795–1803*, Leiden and Boston, MA: Martinus Nijhoff Publishers, 2011; Simon Schama, *Patriots and Liberators: Revolution in the Netherlands, 1780–1813*, New York: Vintage Books, 1977.
22. T. C. W. Blanning, *The French Revolution in Germany: Occupation and Resistance in the Rhineland, 1792–1802*, Oxford: Clarendon Press, 1983, especially pp. 326–29.

23. Rapport, 'International Repercussions', pp. 392–93.
24. Sylvain Sick, 'Les Nouveaux Français et l'armée dans les départements du Léman et du Mont-Blanc', in Annie Crépin, Jean-Pierre Jessenne and Hervé Leuwers (eds), *Civils, citoyens-soldats et militaires dans L'État-nation (1789–1815). Actes du colloque d'Arras (7–8 novembre 2003)*, Paris: SÉR, 2006, pp. 77–86; Mark H. Lerner, 'The Helvetic Republic: An Ambivalent Reception of French Revolutionary Liberty', *FH*, 18 (2004), pp. 50–75; Robert Chagny (ed.), *La Révolution française: idéaux, singularités, influences*, Grenoble: Presses Universitaires de Grenoble, 2002, pp. 131–93.
25. Jean-Pierre Poussou (ed.), *Le Bouleversement de l'ordre du monde. Révoltes et révolutions en Europe et aux Amériques à la fin du 18e siècle*, Paris: Sedes, 2004.
26. Marianne Elliott, *Wolfe Tone*, 2nd edn., Chicago, IL: University of Chicago Press, 2012; Sylvie Kleinman, 'Theobald Wolfe Tone's Mission to France 1796–1798', in Serna, De Francesco and Miller (eds), *Republics at War*.
27. Alexandra Sfini, 'Langages de la Révolution et transferts conceptuels. La Constitution montagnarde en grec', *AHRF*, 347 (2007), pp. 83–92.
28. Philipp Ziesche, *Cosmopolitan Patriots: Americans in Paris in the Age of Revolution*, Charlottesville, VA, and London: University of Virginia Press, 2010, chs 5, 6 and Epilogue.
29. Alan Forrest, *Conscripts and Deserters: The Army and French Society during the Revolution and Empire*, Oxford: Oxford University Press, 1989, pp. 34–36.
30. Claude Bailly, *Journal d'un artisan tourangeau, 1789–1830*, Chinon: Amis du Vieux Chinon, 1989, pp. 73, 78.
31. Alan Forrest, 'Conscription and Crime in Rural France during the Directory and Consulate', in Gwynne Lewis and Colin Lucas (eds), *Beyond the Terror: Essays in French Regional and Social History, 1794–1815*, Cambridge and New York: Cambridge University Press, 1983, pp. 92–120.
32. Léon Dubreuil, *Les Vicissitudes du domaine congéable en Basse-Bretagne à l'époque de la Révolution*, 2 vols, Rennes: Imprimerie Oberthur, 1915, vol. 1, pp. 22–26; vol. 2, p. 276; Alain Le Bloas, 'La Question du domaine congéable dans l'actuel Finistère à la veille de la Révolution', *AHRF*, 331 (2003), pp. 1–27.
33. Alain Corbin, *Village Bells: Sound and Meaning in the 19th-Century French Countryside*, translated by Martin Thom, New York: Columbia University Press, 1998, p. 33.
34. AD Charente-Maritime; Jean-Marie Augustin, *La Révolution française en Haut-Poitou et pays Charentais*, Toulouse: Privat, 1993.
35. Alan Forrest, *Soldiers of the French Revolution*, Durham, NC: Duke University Press, 1990, pp. 158, 170.
36. See J. F. Bosher (ed.), *French Government and Society, 1500–1850: Essays in Memory of Alfred Cobban*, London: Athlone Press, 1973, p. 286.
37. D. Lottin, *Recherches historiques sur la ville d'Orléans*, 8 vols, Orléans: Imprimerie Alexandre Jacob, 1836–45, vol. 6, pp. 154–55.
38. Frédéric Derne, 'La Chanson, "arme" révolutionnaire et chambre d'écho de la société en Auvergne', *AHRF*, 341 (2005), pp. 50–51.
39. Laura Mason and Tracey Rizzo (eds), *The French Revolution: A Document Collection*, Boston, MA, and New York: Houghton Mifflin, 1999, pp. 318–19.
40. Ian Coller, 'Egypt in the French Revolution', in Suzanne Desan, Lynn Hunt and William Max Nelson (eds), *The French Revolution in Global Perspective*, Ithaca, NY, and London: Cornell University Press, 2013, pp. 120–22.
41. Henry Laurens, *L'Expédition d'Égypte, 1798–1801*, Paris: Armand Colin, 1989, pp. 75–77.
42. Ian Coller, *Arab France: Islam and the Making of Modern Europe, 1798–1831*, Berkeley, Los Angeles, CA, and London: University of California Press, 2011, ch. 1; Coller, 'Egypt in the French Revolution'.
43. Coller, 'Egypt in the French Revolution'; Claude Petitfrère (ed.), *Le Général Dupuy et sa correspondance (1792–1798)*, Paris: SÉR, 1962; *La Campagne d'Égypte 1798–1891. Mythes et réalités. Actes du colloque des 16 et 17 juin 1998*, Paris: Éditions In Forma, 1998.
44. Rapport, 'International Repercussions', p. 389; Anon., 'France and the Early Modern Mediterranean', special issue of *FH*, 29 (2015).
45. Evangeline Bruce, *Napoleon and Josephine: An Improbable Marriage*, New York: Scribner, 1995, chs 15–19; Philip Dwyer, *Napoleon: The Path to Power, 1769–1799*, London: Bloomsbury, 2007, chs 14–21; Coller, *Arab France*, ch. 1.

46. Simon Lee, *David*, London: Phaidon, 1999, ch. 4.
47. Jacques Godechot, *La Révolution française dans le Midi toulousain*, Toulouse: Éditions Privat, 1986, ch. 6; Martyn Lyons, *Revolution in Toulouse: An Essay on Provincial Terrorism*, Bern: Lang, 1978.
48. Howard Brown, *War, Revolution, and the Bureaucratic State: Politics and Army Administration in France, 1791–1799*, Oxford: Clarendon Press, 1995, chs 8–9; Brown, 'The Politics of Public Order, 1795–1802', in David Andress (ed.), *The Oxford Handbook of the French Revolution*, Oxford: Oxford University Press, 2015, ch. 31.
49. Louis-Sébastien Mercier, *Paris pendant la Révolution (1789–1798) ou le nouveau Paris*, Paris: Livre Club du Librairie, 1962, pp. 307–09; Jean-René Suratteau and François Gendron (eds), *Dictionnaire historique de la Révolution française*, Paris: PUF, 1989.
50. Stewart (ed.), *Documentary Survey*, p. 780.
51. Katherine Taylor, 'Geometries of Power: Royal, Revolutionary, and Post-Revolutionary French Courtrooms', *Journal of the Society of Architectural Historians*, 72 (2013), pp. 434–74.
52. Livesey, *Making Democracy*, and Brown, *War, Revolution, and the Bureaucratic State*, place contrasting emphasis on these dimensions of the Directory.
53. Corbin, *Village Bells*, pp. 32–40.
54. AD Loiret 2J 1983, J 557, Paul Guillaume, 'La Vie dans l'Orléanais de 1788 à 1818, d'après le journal inédit d'une famille', unpublished ms, Orléans c.1960.

Chapter 17 The Significance of the French Revolution

1. Madame de La Tour du Pin, *Memoirs: Laughing and Dancing our Way to the Precipice*, translated by Felice Harcourt, London: Harvill Press, 1999, pp. 93–94, 243–44. This noblewoman is the heroine of the conclusion to Simon Schama, *Citizens: A Chronicle of the French Revolution*, New York: Alfred A. Knopf, 1989, pp. 861–66. The family had been given its title at Louis' coronation in 1775. It became embroiled in a royalist plot in the Vendée in 1831 and again fled France. Lucy died in Pisa in 1853.
2. Marc Bloch, *The Royal Touch: Sacred Monarchy and Scrofula in England and France*, translated by J. E. Anderson, London: Routledge & Kegan Paul, 1973, first published 1924.
3. These shifts are explored expertly by Carla Hesse, *Publishing and Cultural Politics in Revolutionary Paris, 1789–1810*, Berkeley, CA: University of California Press, 1991; Emmet Kennedy, *A Cultural History of the French Revolution*, New Haven, CT, and London: Yale University Press, 1989.
4. This is the core argument of Micah Alpaugh, *Non-Violence and the French Revolution: Political Demonstrations in Paris, 1787–1795*, Cambridge: Cambridge University Press, 2014. Cf. Schama, *Citizens*, for whom violence was the essence of the Revolution.
5. Léo Hamon (ed.), *La Révolution à travers un département (Yonne)*, Paris: Éditions de la Maison des Sciences de l'Homme, 1990, chs 8–9.
6. Lynn Hunt, *Politics, Culture, and Class in the French Revolution*, Berkeley, CA: University of California Press, 1984, ch. 5; Michael Kennedy, *The Jacobin Club of Marseilles, 1790–1794*, Ithaca, NY, and London: Cornell University Press, 1973; Malcolm Crook, *Elections in the French Revolution: An Apprenticeship in Democracy, 1789–1799*, Cambridge and New York: Cambridge University Press, 1996, pp. 17, 160, Conclusion; Melvin Edelstein, 'Les Maires des chefs-lieux de département de 1789 à 1792: une prise de pouvoir par la bourgeoisie?', in Jean-Pierre Jessenne (ed.), *Vers un Ordre bourgeois? Révolution française et changement social*, Rennes: Presses Universitaires de Rennes, 2007, pp. 199–210.
7. Benedict Anderson, *Imagined Communities: Reflections on the Origin and Spread of Nationalism*, London and New York: Verso, 1983.
8. Jean-Clément Martin, 'Dénombrer les victimes de la Terreur. La Vendée et au-delà', in Michel Biard and Hervé Leuwers (eds), *Visages de la Terreur. L'Exception politique de l'an II*, Paris: Armand Colin, 2014, pp. 155–65; Michel Biard and Pascal Dupuy, *La Révolution française. Dynamique et ruptures, 1787–1804*, 2nd edn., Paris: Armand Colin, 2008, p. 278.
9. Howard Brown, *War, Revolution, and the Bureaucratic State: Politics and Army Administration in France, 1791–1799*, Oxford: Clarendon Press, 1995, ch. 10; Vincent Denis, *Une Histoire de l'identité, France, 1715–1815*, Paris: SÉR, 2008; Serge Aberdam, *Démographes et démocrates. L'Oeuvre du Comité de division de la Convention nationale*, Paris: SÉR, 2004.

10. Annie Crépin, 'The Army of the Republic: New Warfare and a New Army', in Pierre Serna, Antonino De Francesco and Judith A. Miller (eds), *Republics at War, 1776–1840: Revolutions, Conflicts, and Geopolitics in Europe and the Atlantic World*, Basingstoke: Palgrave Macmillan, 2013, expertly synthesizes a vast body of historical research.

11. A. Rapoport (ed.), *Clausewitz: On War*, London: Penguin, 1982, pp. 384–86.

12. John G. Gallaher, *General Alexandre Dumas: Soldier of the French Revolution*, Carbondale and Edwardsville, IL: Southern Illinois University Press, 1997, Conclusion; Ken Alder, *Engineering the French Revolution: Arms and the Enlightenment in France, 1763–1815*, Princeton, NJ: Princeton University Press, 1997; Rafe Blaufarb, *The French Army, 1750–1820: Careers, Talent, Merit*, Manchester and New York: Manchester University Press, 2002, ch. 6 and Conclusion.

13. See David Bell, *The First Total War: Napoleon's Europe and the Birth of Modern Warfare*, Boston, MA: Houghton Mifflin; London: Bloomsbury, 2007; Hervé Drévillon, *Guerres et armées napoléoniennes: nouveaux regards*, Paris: Éditions Nouveau Monde, 2013.

14. Peter McPhee, *Revolution and Environment in Southern France: Peasants, Lords, and Murder in the Corbières, 1780–1830*, Oxford: Clarendon Press, 1999, ch. 1. For another example, see Dominique Flon, 'La Révolution et la fin du particularisme lorrain', in Laurent Versini et al. (eds), *Nancy et la Lorraine sous la Révolution*, Jarville-La Malgrange: Éditions de l'Est, 1990, pp. 47–63.

15. Alan Forrest, *Paris, the Provinces and the French Revolution*, London: Arnold, 2004; Michel de Certeau, Dominique Julia and Jacques Revel, *Une Politique de la langue: la Révolution française et les patois. L'enquête de Grégoire*, Paris: Gallimard, 1975.

16. Ferdinand Brunot, *Histoire de la langue française des origines à 1900*, vol. 9, 1ère partie, Paris: Armand Colin, 1927, pp. 13–14.

17. Cited in Roger Dupuy, *De la Révolution à la chouannerie. Paysans de Bretagne, 1788–1794*, Paris: Flammarion, 1988, pp. 7–8. See Patrice Higonnet, 'The Politics of Linguistic Terrorism and Grammatical Hegemony during the French Revolution', *SH*, 5 (1980), pp. 41–69; Martyn Lyons, 'Politics and Patois: The Linguistic Policy of the French Revolution', *Australian Journal of French Studies*, 18 (1981), pp. 264–81.

18. Yannick Bosc and Sophie Wahnich (eds), *Les Voix de la Révolution. Projets pour la démocratie*, Paris: La Documentation Française, 1990, pp. 187–90.

19. On women's participation in the Revolution, see R. B. Rose, *Tribunes and Amazons: Men and Women of Revolutionary France, 1789–1871*, Sydney: Macleay Press, 1998, chs 14, 15; Joan Landes, *Women and the Public Sphere in the Age of the French Revolution*, Ithaca, NY: Cornell University Press, 1988, ch. 6, Conclusion; Carla Hesse, *The Other Enlightenment: How French Women Became Modern*, Princeton, NJ: Princeton University Press, 2001; and the special issue of *AHRF*, 'La Prise de parole publique des femmes', 344 (2006). A negative view of the impact of the Revolution on women is Candice E. Proctor, *Women, Equality, and the French Revolution*, Westport, CT: Greenwood Press, 1990.

20. Anne Verjus, *Le Bon mari: une histoire politique des hommes et des femmes à l'époque révolution-naire*, Paris: Fayard, 2010; Lynn Hunt, *The Family Romance of the French Revolution*. London: Routledge, 1992.

21. Suzanne Desan, *The Family on Trial in Revolutionary France*, Berkeley and Los Angeles, CA, and London: University of California Press, 2004; Roderick Phillips, *Family Breakdown in Late Eighteenth-Century France: Divorces in Rouen 1792–1803*, Oxford: Oxford University Press, 1980.

22. Suzanne Desan, '"War between Brothers and Sisters": Inheritance Law and Gender Politics in Revolutionary France', *FHS*, 20 (1997), pp. 624, 628; Desan, *Family on Trial*; Élisabeth G. Sledziewski, 'The French Revolution as the Turning Point', in Geneviève Fraisse and Michelle Perrot (eds), *A History of Women in the West: Emerging Feminism from Revolution to World War*, translated by Arthur Goldhammer, Cambridge, MA: Harvard University Press, 1993; P. Viallaneix and J. Ehrard (eds), *Aimer en France, 1760–1860, Actes du colloque interna-tional de Clermont-Ferrand*, Clermont-Ferrand: Faculté des Lettres et Sciences Humaines, 1980.

23. Jacques Poumarède, 'La Législation successorale', in I. Théry and C. Biet (eds), *La Famille, la loi, l'État. De la Révolution au Code Civil*, Paris: Imprimerie Nationale, 1989; Margaret H. Darrow, *Revolution in the House: Family, Class and Inheritance in Southern France, 1775–1825*, Princeton, NJ: Princeton University Press, 1989; P. M. Jones, *Politics and Rural Society: The*

Southern Massif Central c.1750–1880, Cambridge: Cambridge University Press, 1985, pp. 101–04; Louis Assier-Andrieu, 'Custom and Law in the Social Order: Some Reflections upon French Catalan Peasant Communities', *Law and History Review*, 1 (1984), pp. 86–94.

24. Jeremy D. Popkin, *A Concise History of the Haitian Revolution*, Oxford: Wiley-Blackwell, 2012, p. 141.

25. Abel Louis, *Les Libres de couleur en Martinique*, 3 vols, Paris: L'Harmattan, 2012, vol. 2; Laurent Dubois, 'Slavery in the Age of Revolution'; Karl Noël, *L'Esclavage à l'Ile de France (Ile Maurice) de 1715 à 1810*, Paris: Éditions Two Cities ETC, 1991, chs 2, 13.

26. Historians disagree about the significance and nature of the Revolution's economic impact. Marxist historians have seen it as crucial in accelerating the trend to capitalism: see Albert Soboul in Pierre Léon et al. (eds), *Histoire économique et sociale de la France*, vol. 3, Paris: PUF, 1976; Gwynne Lewis, *The Advent of Modern Capitalism in France, 1770–1840: The Contribution of Pierre-François Tubeuf*, Oxford: Clarendon Press, 1993; Henry Heller, *The Bourgeois Revolution in France, 1789–1815*, New York and Oxford: Berghahn Books, 2006. Others have seen it as destructive: see Florent Aftalion, *The French Revolution: An Economic Interpretation*, translated by M. Thom, Cambridge: Cambridge University Press, 1990. Nuanced overviews are provided by the contributors to Gérard Gayot and Jean-Pierre Hirsch (eds), *La Révolution française et le développement du capitalisme*, Villeneuve d'Ascq: Revue du Nord, 1989; Jeff Horn, 'Lasting Economic Structures: Successes, Failures, and Revolutionary Political Economy', and Jennifer Ngaire Heuer, 'Did Everything Change? Rethinking Revolutionary Legacies', in David Andress (ed.), *The Oxford Handbook of the French Revolution*, Oxford: Oxford University Press, 2015, chs 35–36.

27. Paul Butel, 'The Revolution and the Urban Economy', in Alan Forrest and Peter Jones (eds), *Reshaping France*; *Révolution de 1789: Guerres et croissance économique*, special issue of *Revue économique*, 40 (1989), pp. 939–84.

28. François Crouzet, 'Les Origines du sous-développement économique du sud-ouest', *Annales du Midi*, 71 (1959), pp. 3–21; Denis Woronoff, *L'Industrie sidérurgique en France pendant la Révolution et l'Empire*, Paris: ÉHÉSS, 1984; Christopher H. Johnson, *The Life and Death of Industrial Languedoc, 1700–1920*, New York and Oxford: Oxford University Press, 1995, pp. 13–15.

29. Geneviève Koubi (ed.), *Propriété et Révolution: Actes du colloque de Toulouse, 1989*, Paris: CNRS, 1990.

30. Steven L. Kaplan, *La Fin des corporations*. Paris: Fayard, 2001; William H. Sewell, *Work and Revolution in France: The Language of Labour from the Old Régime to 1848*, Cambridge: Cambridge University Press, 1980; Gail Bossenga, *The Politics of Privilege: Old Regime and French Revolution in Lille*, Cambridge: Cambridge University Press, 1991, Conclusion.

31. David Garrioch, *The Making of Revolutionary Paris*, Berkeley and Los Angeles, CA, and London: University of California Press, 2002, pp. 303, 306–09, Epilogue.

32. John McManners, *French Ecclesiastical Society under the Ancien Régime: A Study of Angers in the Eighteenth Century*, Manchester: Manchester University Press, 1960, chs 1, 12; Olwen Hufton, 'Women in Revolution, 1789–1796', *P&P*, 53 (1971), pp. 90–108.

33. Robert Forster, 'The Survival of the Nobility during the French Revolution', *P&P*, 37 (1967), pp. 71–86; Forster, 'The French Revolution and the "New" Elite, 1800–1850', in J. Pelenski (ed.), *The American and European Revolutions, 1776–1848*, Iowa City, IA: University of Iowa Press, 1980, pp. 182–207.

34. McPhee, *Revolution and Environment*, p. 168.

35. Louis Bergeron, Guy Chaussinand-Nogaret and Robert Forster, 'Les Notables du "Grand Empire" en 1810', *Annales*, 26 (1971), pp. 1,052–75. The standard statistical works on the emigration and executions remain Donald Greer, *The Incidence of the Terror during the French Revolution: A Statistical Interpretation*, Cambridge, MA: Harvard University Press, 1935, and Greer, *The Incidence of the Emigration during the French Revolution*, Cambridge, MA: Harvard University Press, 1951.

36. Georges Lefebvre, 'La Révolution française et les paysans', in Lefebvre, *Études sur la Révolution française*, Paris: PUF, 1954, p. 257; Alfred Cobban, *The Social Interpretation of the French Revolution*, Cambridge: Cambridge University Press, 1964, chs 7, 12, 14; P. M. Jones, 'Agricultural Modernization and the French Revolution', *Journal of Historical Geography*, 16 (1990), pp. 38–50; T. J. A. Le Goff and D. M. G. Sutherland, 'The Revolution and the Rural Economy', in Forrest and Jones (eds), *Reshaping France*.

37. This is the overarching argument of John Markoff, *The Abolition of Feudalism: Peasants, Lords, and Legislators in the French Revolution*, University Park, PA: Pennsylvania State University Press, 1996; Peter McPhee, *Living the French Revolution, 1789–99*, London and New York: Palgrave Macmillan, 2006.

38. Arthur Young, *Travels in France during the Years 1787, 1788 and 1789*, New York: Anchor Books, 1969, p. 351.

39. Bernard Bodinier, 'La Révolution française et la question agraire: un bilan national en 2010', *Histoire et sociétés rurales*, 33 (2010), pp. 7–47; Nicolas Marqué, 'Toulouse, ville à vendre? Saisie et devenir des biens nationaux dans l'ancienne capitale du Languedoc (2 novembre 1789–5 décembre 1814)', *Annales du Midi*, 126 (2014), pp. 439–66.

40. Bernard Bodinier and Éric Teyssier, *L'Événement le plus important de la Révolution: la vente des biens nationaux en France et dans les territoires annexés, 1789–1867*, Paris: SÉR, 2000; P. M. Jones, *The Peasantry in the French Revolution*, Cambridge: Cambridge University Press, 1988, pp. 7–9; Jones, *Liberty and Locality in Revolutionary France: Six Villages Compared, 1760–1820*, Cambridge: Cambridge University Press, 2003, pp. 245–50.

41. Gilles Postel-Vinay, 'À la Recherche de la Révolution économique dans les campagnes (1789–1815)', *Revue économique*, 6 (1989), pp. 1,015–45.

42. Charles-Joseph Trouvé, *États de Languedoc et département de l'Aude*, 2 vols, Paris: Imprimerie Nationale, 1818, vol. 1, pp. 452–53, 563.

43. Cited by Gillian Tindall, *Footprints in Paris: A Few Streets, a Few Lives*, London: Chatto & Windus, 2009, p. 39.

44. Patrice L. R. Higonnet, *Pont-de-Montvert: Social Structure and Politics in a French Village, 1700–1914*, Cambridge, MA: Harvard University Press, 1971, p. 97.

45. Anatoli Ado, *Paysans en Révolution. Terre, pouvoir et jacquerie, 1789–1794*, Paris: SÉR, 1996, p. 6, Conclusion; Florence Gauthier, *La Voie paysanne dans la Révolution française: l'exemple picard*, Paris: François Maspero, 1977; Paul T. Hoffman, *Growth in a Traditional Society: The French Countryside, 1450–1815*, Princeton, NJ: Princeton University Press, 1996; Peter McPhee, 'The French Revolution, Peasants, and Capitalism', *AHR*, 94 (1989), pp. 1265–80; McPhee, *Revolution and Environment*, ch. 7; Noelle L. Plack, *Common Land, Wine and the French Revolution: Rural Society and Economy in Southern France, c.1789–1820*, Farnham, Surrey, and Burlington, VT: Ashgate, 2009; James Livesey, 'Material Culture, Economic Institutions and Peasant Revolution in Lower Languedoc 1770–1840', *P&P*, 182 (2004), pp. 143–73.

46. Olwen Hufton, *Bayeux in the Late Eighteenth Century: A Social Study*, Oxford: Oxford University Press, 1967; Plack, *Common Land*, ch. 6; McPhee, *Revolution and Environment*, ch. 7.

47. Livesey, 'Material Culture', p. 164.

48. Serge Chassagne, 'L'Industrie lainière en France à l'époque révolutionnaire et impériale, 1790–1810', in Albert Soboul (ed.), *Voies nouvelles pour l'histoire de la Révolution française*, Paris: Bibliothèque Nationale, 1978, pp. 143–167; Nadine Vivier, *Propriété collective et identité communale: les biens communaux en France, 1750–1914*, Paris: Publications de la Sorbonne, 1998; Peter McPhee, '"The misguided greed of peasants"? Popular Attitudes to the Environment in the Revolution of 1789', *FHS*, 24 (2001), pp. 247–69.

49. Denis Woronoff (ed.), *Révolution et espaces forestiers. Colloque des 3 & 4 juin 1987, Groupe d'histoire des forets francaises*, Paris: L'Harmattan, 1988; Andrée Corvol (ed.), *La Nature en Révolution. Colloque Révolution, nature, paysage et environnement*, Paris: L' Harmattan, 1993; Kieko Matteson, *Forests in Revolutionary France: Conservation, Community, and Conflict, 1669–1848*, Cambridge: Cambridge University Press, 2014, pp. 187–98.

50. T. J. A. Le Goff, *Vannes and its Region: A Study of Town and Country in Eighteenth-Century France*, Oxford: Clarendon Press, 1981, pp. 343–53.

51. Anthony Crubaugh, *Balancing the Scales of Justice: Local Courts and Rural Society in Southwest France, 1750–1800*, University Park, PA: Pennsylvania State University Press, 2001.

52. Hufton, *Bayeux*, pp. 264–80; Claude Langlois and Timothy Le Goff, 'Les Vaincus de la Révolution: jalons pour une sociologie des prêtres mariés', in Soboul (ed.), *Voies nouvelles*.

53. Claude Langlois, *Le Catholicisme au féminin: les congrégations françaises à supérieure générale au XIXe siècle*, Paris: Cerf, 1984.

54. Jay Berkovitz, 'The French Revolution and the Jews: Assessing the Cultural Impact', *AJS Review*, 20 (1995), pp. 25–86; Christian Pfister, *Histoire de Nancy*, vol. 3, Paris: Éditions du

Palais Royal; Nancy: Éditions Berger-Levrault, 1974, vol. 3, pp. 333–34; AD Meurthe-et-Moselle, ms SAL 430, 159.

55. There is an important article by Paul Spagnoli, 'The Unique Decline of Mortality in Revolutionary France', *Journal of Family History*, 22 (1997), pp. 425–61. See too Jacques Dupâquier, *Histoire de la population française*, vol. 3, Paris: PUF, 1988, ch. 7; Étienne van de Walle, 'Motivations and Technology in the Decline of French Fertility', in R. Wheaton and T. K. Hareven (eds), *Family and Sexuality in French History*, Philadelphia, PA: University of Pennsylvania Press, 1980, pp. 135–78.

56. Jeff Horn, *The Path Not Taken: French Industrialization in the Age of Revolution*, Cambridge, MA: MIT Press, 2006.

57. Among the best, contrasting overviews of how the revolutionary legacy played out over the course of the nineteenth century within France are Maurice Agulhon, *Marianne into Battle: Republican Imagery and Symbolism in France, 1789–1880*, translated by Janet Lloyd, Cambridge and New York: Cambridge University Press, 1981; and François Furet, *Revolutionary France, 1770–1880*, translated by Antonia Nevill, Oxford: Blackwell, 1992. See also Jeremy Jennings, *Revolution and the Republic: A History of Political Thought in France since the Eighteenth Century*, Oxford: Oxford University Press, 2011; Robert Gildea, *The Past in French History*, New Haven, CT, and London: Yale University Press, 1994; Pascal Dupuy, 'The Revolution in History, Commemoration, and Memory', in Peter McPhee (ed.), *A Companion to the French Revolution*, Oxford: Wiley-Blackwell, 2013, ch. 29.

58. Alan Forrest, *The Legacy of the French Revolutionary Wars: The Nation-in-Arms in French Republican Memory*, Cambridge: Cambridge University Press, 2009.

59. Laura Mason and Tracey Rizzo (eds), *The French Revolution: A Document Collection*, Boston, MA, and New York: Houghton Mifflin, 1999, pp. 313–17.

60. Alexis de Tocqueville, *Democracy in America*, translated by Henry Reeve, New York: Alfred A. Knopf, 1945, Section IV, ch. 8.

61. See, for example, André Jardin, *Tocqueville*, New York: Farrar Straus Giroux, 1989.

62. A brilliant example is explored by Guillaume Mazeau, *Le Bain de l'histoire: Charlotte Corday et l'attentat contre Marat, 1793–2009*, Seyssel: Champ Vallon, 2009; See, too, Biard and Leuwers (eds), *Visages de la Terreur*.

63. *Les Paysans*, translated as *Sons of the Soil* by Katharine Prescott Wormeley, Boston: Roberts Brothers, 1891, pp. 240–43.

64. Tom Reiss, *The Black Count: Glory, Revolution, Betrayal, and the Real Count of Monte Cristo*, New York: Crown, 2012. Dumas was the highest-ranking black officer in a European army before or since; in 1802, however, Bonaparte removed black officers from the army. Dumas set the story after 1814.

65. See the recent polemic by former Prime Minister Lionel Jospin, *Le Mal napoléonien*, Paris: Éditions du Seuil, 2014.

66. Charles-Hippolyte Pouthas, *Une Famille bourgeoise française de Louis XIV à Napoléon*, Paris: Librairie Félix Alcan, 1934.

67. Peter McPhee, *The Politics of Rural Life: Political Mobilization in the French Countryside, 1846–1852*, Oxford: Clarendon Press, 1992, p. 161.

68. See, for example, Raymond de Sagazan, 'L'Association bretonne face à la célébration du bicentenaire de la Révolution française', *Bulletin de l'Association Bretonne et Union régionaliste bretonne*, 1990, pp. 41–48; Yves-Marie Salem-Carrière, *Terreur révolutionnaire et résistance catholique dans le Midi*, Bouère and Grez-en-Bouère: D.M. Morin, 1989.

69. Another estimate is that between 300 and 500 people of Luc's 2,320 people were killed in all the fighting during the Vendéen insurrection: Jean-Clément Martin and Xavier Lardière, *Le Massacre des Lucs-Vendée 1794*, Geste Editions: Vouillé, 1992. On Chanzeaux, see Lawrence Wylie, *Chanzeaux: a Village in Anjou*, Cambridge, MA: Harvard University Press, 1966.

70. A key historical text for these deputies is Reynald Secher, *A French Genocide: The Vendée*, translated by George Holcch. Notre Dame, IN: University of Notre Dame Press, 2003. René Sedillot, *Le Coût de la Révolution française*, Paris: Librairie Académique Perrin, 1987, pp. 24–25, makes the preposterous claim that the repression of the Vendée was a more intense genocide than the Holocaust.

71. Hunt, *Politics, Culture and Class*, p. 147 and ch. 4; Vovelle, *Découverte de la politique*.

72. McPhee, *Politics of Rural Life*, chs 4–5. Other studies of nineteenth-century political choice include Ted W. Margadant, *French Peasants in Revolt: The Insurrection of 1851*, Princeton, NJ: Princeton University Press, 1979.

73. On the global context of the Revolution, see David Armitage and Sanjay Subrahmanyam (eds), *The Age of Revolutions in Global Context, 1760–1840*, Basingstoke and New York: Palgrave Macmillan, 2010; Suzanne Desan, Lynn Hunt and William Max Nelson (eds), *The French Revolution in Global Perspective*, Ithaca, NY, and London: Cornell University Press, 2013; C. A. Bayly, *The Birth of the Modern World, 1780–1914: Global Connections and Comparisons*, Oxford: Blackwell, 2004; Serna, De Francesco and Miller (eds), *Republics at War, 1776–1840*; Joseph Klaits and Michael H. Haltzel (eds), *The Global Ramifications of the French Revolution*, New York: Cambridge University Press, 1994; Wim Klooster, *Revolutions in the Atlantic World: A Comparative History*, New York: New York University Press, 2009. Note the critical review by David A. Bell, 'Questioning the Global Turn: The Case of the French Revolution', *FHS*, 37 (2014), pp. 1–24.

74. Daniele Conversi, 'Cosmopolitanism and Nationalism', in Athena Leoussi and Anthony D. Smith (eds), *Encyclopaedia of Nationalism*, New Brunswick, NJ, and London: Transaction Publishers, 2001, pp. 34–39; Mary Helen McMurran, 'The New Cosmopolitanism and the Eighteenth Century', *Eighteenth-Century Studies*, 47 (2013), pp. 19–38.

75. Philippe Bonetti, *Montaigu en Révolution: la force du destin*, Maulévrier: Hérault Éditions, 1990, p. 127.

76. Haydn Trevor Mason and William Doyle (eds), *The Impact of the French Revolution on European Consciousness*, Stroud: Sutton, 1989; Ehrhard Bahr and Thomas Saine (eds), *Internalized Revolution: German Reactions to the French Revolution, 1789–1989*, New York: Garland, 1992; Mike Rapport, 'Jacobinism from Outside', and David A. Bell, 'Global Conceptual Legacies', in Andress (ed.), *Oxford Handbook*, chs 29, 37.

77. 'The Prelude', in William Wordsworth, *The Complete Poetical Works*, London: Macmillan and Co., 1888.

78. See Kenneth R. Johnston, *The Hidden Wordsworth: Poet, Lover, Rebel, Spy*, New York: W. W. Norton, 1998.

79. Kenneth R. Johnston, *Unusual Suspects: Pitt's Reign of Alarm and the Lost Generation of the 1790s*, Oxford: Oxford University Press, 2013; James Epstein, *Radical Expression: Political Language, Ritual, and Symbol in England, 1790–1850*, New York: Oxford University Press, 1994.

80. Edward Duyker, *Citizen Labillardière: A French Naturalist in New Holland and the South Pacific*, Melbourne: Melbourne University Press, 2003; Michael Rapport, 'The International Repercussions of the French Revolution', in McPhee (ed.), *Companion*, p. 391.

81. The impulse for independence in South America came largely from the Creole population, and this impulse rarely extended further to a measure of social equality for slaves and indigenous inhabitants.

82. Annie Jourdan puts the argument against the 'French exception' most powerfully in *La Révolution, une exception française?*, Paris: Flammarion, 2004. The importance of the international context has never been recognized in France more than today, exemplified by the recent special issues of the *AHRF*: 'Les Îles britanniques et la Révolution française', 342 (2005); 'L'Amérique du Nord à l'époque de la Révolution française', 363 (2011); 'Lumières et révolutions en Amérique latine', 365 (2011); 'Les Indes orientales au carrefour des empires', 375 (2014).

83. On the vigour of the debates at the time of the bicentenary, see E. J. Hobsbawm, *Echoes of the Marseillaise: Two Centuries Look Back on the French Revolution*, London: Verso, 1990; Steven Laurence Kaplan, *Farewell, Revolution: Disputed Legacies, France 1789/1989*, Ithaca, NY: Cornell University Press, 1995; and Kaplan, *Farewell, Revolution: The Historians' Feud, 1789–1989*, Ithaca, NY: Cornell University Press, 1995.

SELECT BIBLIOGRAPHY

This is a bibliography of those printed sources most useful for this book; other references are cited in the notes, as are references to some of the manuscript material used from archives in Alençon, Bordeaux, Bourg-en-Bresse, Carcassonne, Laon, La Rochelle, Montpellier, Nancy, Nantes, Orléans, Paris, Perpignan and Vannes.

Newspapers

La Feuille villageoise, 1790–95
Le Moniteur Universel, 1789–99
Le Vieux Cordelier, 1793–94

Other Printed Sources

Archives parlementaires. Stanford University Libraries' French Revolution Digital Archive website (FRDA): http://frda.stanford.edu/.

Ayats, Alain, André Balent and Martine Camiade (eds). *Entre Révolution et guerres. Les Mémoires de Pierre Comellas, apothicaire de Perpignan, 1789–1813*. Perpignan: AD des Pyrénées-Orientales, 2005.

Bailly, Claude. *Journal d'un artisan tourangeau, 1789–1830*. Chinon: Amis du Vieux Chinon, 1989.

Barras, Paul. *Memoirs*, translated by Charles E. Roche, 4 vols. London: Osgood, McIlvaine and Co., 1895.

Bernet, Jacques (ed.). *Le Journal d'un maître d'école d'Île-de-France (1771–1792): Silly-en-Multien de l'Ancien Régime à la Révolution*. Villeneuve-d'Asq: Presses universitaires du Septentrion, 2000.

Besnard, François-Yves. *Souvenirs d'un nonagenaire*, 2 vols. Paris: H. Champion, 1880.

Biré, Edmond. *The Diary of a Citizen of Paris during 'the Terror'*, translated by John de Villiers. London: Chatto and Windus, 1896.

Bohm, Sophie de. *Prisonnière sous la Terreur. Mémoires d'une captive en 1793*. Paris: Cosmopole, 2001.

Bosc, Yannick, and Sophie Wahnich (eds). *Les Voix de la Révolution. Projets pour la démocratie*. Paris: La Documentation française, 1990.

Bourgin, Georges (ed.), *Le Partage des biens communaux: documents sur la loi du 10 juin 1793*, Paris: Imprimerie nationale, 1908.

Bourguignon du Perré, Jacques-François le. *Notes d'un détenu de la maison de réclusion des ci-devant Carmélites de Caen pendant la Terreur*. Évreux: Imprimerie de l'Eure, 1903.

Cahiers de doléances pour les États-Généraux de 1789, published from 1906 by the Ministère de l'Instruction Publique as the *Collection de Documents Inédits sur l'Histoire Économique de la Révolution Française*.

Caron, Pierre (ed.). *Rapports des agents du Ministre de l'Intérieur dans les départements (1793 – an II)*, 2 vols. Paris: Imprimerie nationale, 1913–51.

— (ed.). *Paris pendant la Terreur: rapports des agents secrets du Ministre de l'Intérieur*, 6 vols. Paris: Société d'Histoire Contemporaine, 1943–64.

Chill, Emanuel (ed. and trans.). *Power, Property and History: Barnave's Introduction to the French Revolution and other Writings.* New York: Harper & Row, 1971.

Choudieu, Pierre-René. *Mémoires et notes.* Paris: Plon, 1897.

Constant, Christiane. *Journal d'un bourgeois de Bégoux. Michel Célarié (1771–1836).* Cahors: Le Stum, 1992.

Correspondance de l'abbé Rousselot, constituant, 1789–1795. Besançon: Annales Littéraires de l'Université de Besançon, 1992.

Courchamps, comte de. *Souvenirs de la marquise de Créquy de 1710 à 1803*, 10 vols. Paris: Garnier Frères, 1865.

Dawson, Philip (ed.). *The French Revolution.* Englewood Cliffs, NJ: Prentice-Hall, 1967.

Delarue, P. *Un aumônier des Chouans, l'abbé Nicolas-François Faligant, 1755–1813.* Rennes: Plihon and Hommay; Nantes: Durance, 1910.

Duchet, L. (ed.). *Deux volontaires de 1791. Les frères Favier de Montluçon. Journal et lettres.* Montluçon: A. Herbin, 1909.

Felkay, Nicole, and Hervé Favier (eds). *En prison sous la Terreur. Souvenirs de J.-B. Billecocq (1765–1829).* Paris: SÉR, 1981.

Fouché, Joseph. *The Memoirs of Joseph Fouché, Duke of Otranto*, 2 vols. London: H. S. Nicholls, 1896.

Frénay, Étienne (ed.). *Cahiers de doléances de la province de Roussillon (1789).* Perpignan: Direction des Services d'Archives, 1979.

[Géraud, Edmond]. *Journal d'un étudiant pendant la Révolution, 1789–1793.* Paris: Plon, 1910.

Gilchrist, J., and W. J. Murray (eds). *The Press in the French Revolution: A Selection of Documents Taken from the Press of the Revolution for the Years 1789–1794.* Melbourne: Cheshire; London: Ginn, 1971.

Godard, Abbé. *Journal d'une visitandine pendant la Terreur ou Mémoires de la Sœur Gabrielle Gauchat.* Paris: Poussielque-Rusand, 1855.

Gouges, Olympe de. *Écrits politiques, 1788–1791*, preface by Olivier Blanc. Paris: Côté-femmes, 1993.

Jessenne, Jean-Pierre, and Edna Hindie Lemay (eds). *Deputé-paysan et fermière de Flandre en 1789. La correspondence des Lepoutre.* Lille: Université Charles de Gaulle-Lille 3, 1998.

Jolicler, Étienne. *Joliclerc, volontaire aux armées de la Révolution. Ses lettres (1793–1796)*, 4th edn. Paris: Perrin, 1905.

Journal de marche d'un volontaire de 1792 (journal du Sergent Fricasse). Paris: J. Dumoulin, 1882.

Jullien, Rosalie, and Édouard Lockroy, *Journal d'une bourgeoise pendant la Révolution, 1791–1793.* Paris: Calmann Lévy, 1881.

Julliot, François-Pierre. *Souvenirs d'un prêtre réfractaire du diocèse de Troyes publiés par Octave Beuve.* Arcis-sur-Aube: Société d'Histoire Départementale, 1909.

La Tour du Pin, Madame de. *Memoirs: Laughing and Dancing our Way to the Precipice*, translated by Felice Harcourt. London: Harvill Press, 1999.

Laukhard, Frédéric-Christian. *Un Allemand en France sous la Terreur: souvenirs de Frédéric-Christian Laukhard, professeur d'université saxon et sans-culotte français, 1792–1794.* Paris: Perrin, 1915.

'Lettres d'un jeune soldat des armées révolutionnaires à ses parents (1793–1795)', *Fédération des sociétés d'histoire et d'archéologie de l'Aisne*, 23 (1978), pp. 96–127.

Levy, Darline Gay, Harriet Branson Applewhite and Mary Durham Johnson, *Women in Revolutionary Paris, 1789–1795: Selected Documents Translated with Notes and Commentary.* Urbana and Chicago, IL: University of Illinois Press, 1980.

Mason, Laura, and Tracey Rizzo (eds). *The French Revolution: A Document Collection.* Boston, MA, and New York: Houghton Mifflin, 1999.

Ménétra, Jacques-Louis. *Journal of My Life*, translated by Arthur Goldhammer. New York: Columbia University Press, 1986.

Mercier, Louis-Sébastien. *Paris pendant la Révolution (1789–1798) ou le nouveau Paris.* Paris: Livre Club du Librairie, 1962.

Michel, Jean. *Journal de la déportation des ecclésiastiques du département de la Meurthe dans la rade de l'Ile d'Aix, près Rochefort, en 1794 et 1795, par un de ces déportés.* Nancy: Grimblet, Raybois et Cie, 1840.

Molé, Louis-Mathieu. *Souvenirs de jeunesse, 1793–1803.* Paris, 1991.

Monnard, Marie-Victoire. *Souvenirs d'une femme du peuple, 1777–1802.* Creil: Bernard Dumerchez, 1989.

Nodier, Charles. *Séraphine, Amélie, Jean-François les Bas-Bleus; souvenirs de jeunesse.* Paris: Dentu, 1894.

Noël, Joseph-Louis-Gabriel. *Au temps des volontaires: lettres d'un volontaire de 1792.* Paris: Plon, 1912.

Pasquier, Chancellor. *Memoirs (1767–1815)*, translated by Douglas Garman. London: Elek, 1967.

Petitfrère, Claude (ed.). *Le Général Dupuy et sa correspondance (1792–1798).* Paris: SÉR, 1962.

Restif de la Bretonne, Nicolas. *Les Nuits de Paris*, part XVI. Paris: Hachette, 1960.

La Révolution vue de l'Aisne, en 200 documents. Laon: Archives Départementales de l'Aisne, 1990.

Robespierre, Maximilien. *Oeuvres de Maximilien Robespierre*, 11 vols. Paris: SÉR, 1912–2007.

Roederer, Pierre-Louis. *Mémoires sur la Révolution, le Consulat et l'Empire.* Paris: Plon, 1942.

Roland de la Platière, Jeanne-Marie. *An Appeal to Impartial Posterity.* Oxford and New York: Woodstock Books, 1990.

—. *Lettres de Madame Roland*, 2 vols. Paris: C. Perroud, 1900–02.

Rudemare, Jacques-Henri. *Journal d'un prêtre parisien, 1788–1792.* Paris: Gaume, 1905.

Saulx-Tavanes, Aglaé-Marie-Louise. *Mémoires de la Duchesse de Saulx-Tavanes.* Paris: Calmann Lévy, 1934.

Souvestre, Émile. *Mémoires d'un sans-culotte bas-breton.* Brussels: Wouters, Raspoet, 1843.

Spire, Abraham. *Le Journal révolutionnaire d'Abraham Spire*, translated by Simon Schwarzfuchs. Paris: Institut Alain de Rothschild/Verdier, 1989.

Thompson, J. M. (ed.). *English Witnesses of the French Revolution.* Oxford: Oxford University Press, 1938.

Vaxelaire, Jean-Claude. *Mémoires d'un vétéran de l'ancienne armée (1791–1800).* Paris: Charles Delagrave, 1892.

Vigée Lebrun, Élisabeth. *Memoirs of Mme Vigée Lebrun*, translated by Lionel Strachey. New York: G. Braziller, 1989.

Williams, Helen Maria. *Letters containing a sketch of the politics of France: from the thirty-first of May 1793, till the twenty-eighth of July 1794, and of the scenes which have passed in the prisons of Paris.* Dublin: J. Chambers, 1795.

Young, Arthur. *Travels in France during the Years 1787, 1788 and 1789.* New York: Anchor Books, 1969.

Secondary Sources

Aberdam, Serge. 'Deux occasions de participation féminine en 1793: le vote sur la constitution et le partage des biens communaux', *AHRF*, 339 (2005), pp. 17–34.

Adams, Christine. '"Venus of the Capitol": Madame Tallien and the Politics of Beauty under the Directory', *FHS*, 37 (2014), pp. 599–629.

Ado, Anatoli. *Paysans en Révolution. Terre, pouvoir et jacquerie, 1789–1794.* Paris: SÉR, 1996.

Aftalion, Florent, *The French Revolution: An Economic Interpretation*, translated by M. Thom. Cambridge: Cambridge University Press, 1990.

Agulhon, Maurice. *Marianne into Battle: Republican Imagery and Symbolism in France, 1789–1880*, translated by Janet Lloyd. Cambridge and New York: Cambridge University Press, 1981.

Alder, Ken. *Engineering the French Revolution: Arms and the Enlightenment in France, 1763–1815.* Princeton, NJ: Princeton University Press, 1997.

Alpaugh, Micah. *Non-Violence and the French Revolution: Political Demonstrations in Paris, 1787–1795.* Cambridge: Cambridge University Press, 2014.

Andress, David. *Massacre at the Champ de Mars: Popular Dissent and Political Culture in the French Revolution.* Woodbridge, Suffolk: The Royal Historical Society, 2000.

—. *The French Revolution and the People.* London: Hambledon and London, 2004.

—. *The Terror: Civil War in the French Revolution.* London: Little, Brown, 2005.

—. *1789: The Threshold of the Modern Age.* London: Little, Brown, 2008.

— (ed.). *The Oxford Handbook of the French Revolution.* Oxford: Oxford University Press, 2015.

Andrews, Richard Mowery. *Law, Magistracy and Crime in Old Regime Paris, 1735–1789*, vol. 1, *The System of Criminal Justice*. Cambridge: Cambridge University Press, 1994.

—. 'Paris of the Great Revolution: 1789–1796', in Gene Brucker (ed.), *People and Communities in the Western World*, vol. 2. Homewood, IL: Dorsey Press, 1979, pp. 56–112.

Andrieu, Étienne. *La Contre-Révolution en Gévaudan (Aveyron et Lozère). Marc-Antoine Charrier et l'insurrection de l'Armée chrétienne du Midi en 1793*. Évreux: Éditions Guénégaud, 2000.

Arasse, Daniel. *The Guillotine and the Terror*, translated by Christopher Miller. London: Penguin, 1989.

Armitage, David, and Sanjay Subrahmanyam (eds). *The Age of Revolutions in Global Context, 1760–1840*. Basingstoke and New York: Palgrave Macmillan, 2010.

Aston, Nigel. *Religion and Revolution in France, 1780–1804*. Basingstoke: Macmillan, 2000.

Attar, Frank. *Aux armes citoyens! Naissance et fonctions du bellicisme révolutionnaire*. Paris: Éditions du Seuil, 2010.

Auricchio, Laura. *Adélaïde Labille-Guiard: Artist in the Age of Revolution*. Los Angeles, CA: J. Paul Getty Museum, 2009.

Ayoun, Richard. *Les Juifs de France. De l'émancipation à l'intégration (1787–1812)*. Paris and Montreal: L'Harmattan, 1997.

Baczko, Bronislaw. *Ending the Terror: The French Revolution after Robespierre*, translated by Michael Petheram. Cambridge: Cambridge University Press; Paris: Éditions de la Maison des Sciences de l'Homme, 1994.

Baecque, Antoine de. *Glory and Terror: Seven Deaths under the French Revolution*, translated by Charlotte Mandell. New York and London: Routledge, 2001.

—. *The Body Politic: Corporeal Metaphor in Revolutionary France, 1770–1800*, translated by Charlotte Mandell. Stanford, CA: Stanford University Press, 1997.

Baker, Keith Michael. *Inventing the French Revolution: Essays on French Political Culture in the Eighteenth Century*. Cambridge: Cambridge University Press, 1990.

Bastier, Jean. *La Féodalité au siècle des lumières dans la région de Toulouse, 1730–1790*. Paris: Bibliothèque nationale, 1975.

Bayly, C. A. *The Birth of the Modern World, 1780–1914: Global Connections and Comparisons*. Oxford: Blackwell, 2004.

Belissa, Marc, and Yannick Bosc. *Robespierre. La fabrication d'un mythe*. Paris: Ellipses, 2013.

Bell, David A. *Lawyers and Citizens: The Making of a Political Elite in Old Regime France*. Oxford and New York: Oxford University Press, 1994.

—. *The Cult of the Nation in France: Inventing Nationalism, 1680–1800*. Cambridge, MA: Harvard University Press, 2001.

—. *The First Total War: Napoleon's Europe and the Birth of Warfare as we Know it*. Boston, MA: Houghton Mifflin, 2007.

Berkovitz, Jay. 'The French Revolution and the Jews: Assessing the Cultural Impact', *AJS Review*, 20 (1995), pp. 25–86.

Bernard-Griffiths, Simone, Marie-Claude Chemin and Jean Ehrard (eds). *Révolution française et 'vandalisme révolutionnaire'. Actes du colloque international de Clermont-Ferrand, 15–17 décembre 1988*. Paris: Universitas, 1992.

Bernet, Jacques. 'Les Limites de la déchristianisation de l'an II éclairées par le retour au culte de l'an III', *AHRF*, 312 (1998), pp. 285–99.

— (ed.). *Procès-verbaux de la société populaire de Crépy-en-Valois (Oise) (septembre 1793–avril 1795)*. Paris: CTHS, 2007.

Bertaud, Jean-Paul. *Camille et Lucile Desmoulins. Un couple dans la tourmente*. Paris: Presses de la Renaissance, 1986.

—. *La Vie quotidienne en France au temps de la Révolution (1789–1795)*. Paris: Hachette, 1983.

—. *The Army of the French Revolution: From Citizen-Soldiers to Instrument of Power*, translated by R. R. Palmer. Princeton, NJ: Princeton University Press, 1988.

—. *La Révolution culturelle de l'an II*. Paris: Aubier, 1982.

—. *La Révolution et la première république au village. Pouvoirs, votes et politisation dans les campagnes d'Île-de-France, 1787–1800*. Paris: CTHS, 2004.

Bianchi, Serge (ed.). *Héros et héroïnes de la Révolution française*. Paris: CTHS, 2012.

Biard, Michel. *1793, le siège de Lyon. Entre mythe et réalités*. Clermont-Ferrand: Lemme, 2013.

—. *Collot d'Herbois. Légendes noires et révolution*. Lyon: Presses Universitaires de Lyon, 1995.

—. 'The "Jacobin machine", a Historical Fantasy Revisited in the Light of a Local Study: The Popular Society of Honfleur (1791–95)', *FH* 26 (2012), pp. 79–95.

— (ed.). *La Révolution française, une histoire toujours vivante.* Paris: Tallandier, 2009.

— (ed.). *Les Politiques de la Terreur, 1793–1794: actes du colloque international de Rouen, 11–13 janvier 2007.* Rennes: Presses Universitaires de Rennes; Paris: SÉR, 2008.

— and Hervé Leuwers (eds). *Visages de la Terreur. L'Exception politique de l'an II.* Paris: Armand Colin, 2014.

Bienvenu, Richard. *The Ninth of Thermidor: The Fall of Robespierre.* New York: Oxford University Press, 1968.

Blanc, Olivier. *Last Letters: Prisons and Prisoners of the French Revolution, 1793–1794,* translated by Alan Sheridan. New York: Farrar, Straus and Giroux, 1987.

Blanning, T. C. W., *The French Revolution in Germany: Occupation and Resistance in the Rhineland, 1792–1802.* Oxford: Clarendon Press, 1983.

—. *The Origins of the French Revolutionary Wars.* London: Longman, 1986.

— (ed.). *The Rise and Fall of the French Revolution.* Chicago, IL: Chicago University Press, 1996.

Blaufarb, Rafe. *The French Army, 1750–1820: Careers, Talent, Merit.* Manchester and New York: Manchester University Press, 2002.

—. *The Politics of Fiscal Privilege in Provence, 1530s–1830s.* Washington, DC: The Catholic University of America Press, 2012.

Bluche, Frédéric. *Septembre 1792: logiques d'un massacre.* Paris: Robert Laffont, 1986.

Blum, Carol. *Rousseau and the Republic of Virtue: The Language of Politics in the French Revolution.* Ithaca, NY, and London: Cornell University Press, 1986.

Bocher, Héloïse. *Démolir la Bastille. L'édification d'un lieu de mémoire.* Paris: Vendémiaire, 2012.

Bodinier, Bernard, and Éric Teyssier. *L'Événement le plus important de la Révolution: la vente des biens nationaux en France et dans les territoires annexés, 1789–1867.* Paris: SÉR, 2000.

Borrel, Étienne-Louis. *Histoire de la Révolution tarentaise et de la réunion de la Savoie à la France en 1792. D'après des documents originaux.* Moutiers: Ducloz, 1901.

Bossenga, Gail. *The Politics of Privilege: Old Regime and French Revolution in Lille.* Cambridge: Cambridge University Press, 1991.

Bouloiseau, Marc. *The Jacobin Republic, 1792–1794,* translated by Jonathan Mandelbaum. Cambridge: Cambridge University Press; Paris: Éditions de la Maison des Sciences de l'Homme, 1983.

Bourdin, Philippe. *Le Noir et le Rouge. Itinéraire social, culturel et politique d'un prêtre patriote (1736–1799).* Clermont-Ferrand: Presses universitaires Blaise-Pascal, 2000.

Boutier, Jean. *Campagnes en émoi. Révoltes et Révolution en Bas-Limousin, 1789–1800.* Treignac: Éditions les Monédières, 1987.

Brassart, Laurent. *Gouverner le local en Révolution. État, pouvoirs et mouvements collectifs dans l'Aisne (1790–1795).* Paris: SÉR, 2013.

—. '"Plus de vingt paysanneries contrastées en révolution". De la pluralité des dynamiques sociales du politique en milieu rural pendant la Révolution', *AHRF,* 359 (2010), pp. 53–74.

La Bretagne. Une province à l'aube de la Révolution. Colloque de Brest, 28–30 septembre 1988. Brest and Quimper: Centre de Recherche Bretonne et Celtique, 1989.

Brown, Howard. *Ending the French Revolution: Violence, Justice, and Repression from the Terror to Napoleon.* Charlottesville, VA: University of Virginia Press, 2006.

—. *War, Revolution, and the Bureaucratic State: Politics and Army Administration in France, 1791–1799.* Oxford: Clarendon Press, 1995.

Brunel, Françoise. 'Le Jacobinisme, un "rigorisme de la vertu"? "Puritanisme" et révolution', in *Mélanges Michel Vovelle. Sur la révolution, approches plurielles.* Paris: SÉR, 1997.

—. *Thermidor, la chute de Robespierre.* Bruxelles: Éditions Complexe, 1999.

— and Sylvain Goujon. *Les Martyrs de Prairial. Texte et documents inédits.* Geneva: Georg, 1992.

Brunot, Ferdinand. *Histoire de la langue française des origines à 1900,* vol. IX, part I. Paris, 1927.

Burstin, Haim. *Révolutionnaires. Pour une anthropologie de la Révolution française.* Paris: Vendémiaire, 2013.

—. *Une Révolution à l'oeuvre: le Faubourg Saint-Marcel (1789–1794).* Seyssel: Champ Vallon, 2005.

Butel, Paul. 'Succès et decline du commerce colonial français, de la Révolution à la Restauration', *Revue économique,* 6 (1989), pp. 1,079–96.

Buttoud, G. 'Les Projets forestiers de la Révolution (1789–1798)', *Revue forestière française* 35 (1983), pp. 9–20.

Byrnes, Joseph F. *Priests of the French Revolution: Saints and Renegades in a New Political Era.* University Park, PA: Pennsylvania State University Press, 2014.

Cadé, Michel. *Guerre et Révolution en Roussillon, 1793–1795.* Perpignan: Direction des Services d'Archives, 1990.

Cage, Claire. '"Celibacy is a Social Crime": The Politics of Clerical Marriage', *FHS*, 36 (2013), pp. 601–28.

Caiani, Ambrogio A. *Louis XVI and the French Revolution, 1789–1792.* Cambridge: Cambridge University Press, 2012.

La Campagne d'Égypte, 1798–1891. Mythes et réalités. Actes du colloque des 16 et 17 juin 1998. Paris: Éditions In Forma, 1998.

Campbell, Peter R. (ed.). *The Origins of the French Revolution.* Basingstoke: Palgrave Macmillan, 2006.

—, Thomas E. Kaiser, and Marisa Linton (eds). *Conspiracy in the French Revolution.* Manchester: Manchester University Press, 2007.

Caron, Pierre. *Les Massacres de septembre.* Paris: La Maison du Livre Français, 1935.

Castaing, Thomas. 'Histoire d'un patrimoine en revolution: Claude Bonnet de Paillerets, robin de Marvejols en Lozère de 1766 à 1815', *AHRF*, 290 (1992), pp. 517–37.

Censer, Jack R. *Prelude to Power: The Parisian Radical Press, 1789–1791.* Baltimore, MD, and London: Johns Hopkins University Press, 1976.

Certeau, Michel de, Dominique Julia and Jacques Revel. *Une politique de la langue: la Révolution française et les patois. L'enquête de Grégoire.* Paris: Gallimard, 1975.

Chagny, Robert (ed.). *Aux origines provinciales de la Révolution.* Grenoble: Presses universitaires de Grenoble, 1990.

Chartier, Roger. *The Cultural Origins of the French Revolution.* Durham, NC: Duke University Press, 1991.

Cheney, Paul. *Revolutionary Commerce: Globalization and the French Monarchy.* Cambridge, MA: Harvard University Press, 2010.

Cholvy, Gérard. 'Une Révolution culturelle? Le test des prénoms', in *Pratiques religieuses, mentalités et spiritualités dans l'Europe révolutionnaire (1780–1820). Actes du colloque de Chantilly, 27–29 novembre 1986.* Paris: CNRS, 1988, pp. 300–08.

Chopelin, Paul. *Ville patriote et ville martyre. Une histoire religieuse de Lyon pendant la Révolution (1788–1805).* Paris: Letouzey & Ané, 2010.

Ciotti, Bruno. *Du volontaire au conscrit. Les levées d'hommes dans le Puy-de-Dôme pendant la Révolution française.* 2 vols. Clermont-Ferrand: Presses Universitaires Blaise Pascal, 2001.

Clarke, Joseph. *Commemorating the Dead in Revolutionary France: Revolution and Remembrance, 1789–1799.* Cambridge and New York: Cambridge University Press, 2007.

Clay, Stephen. 'Les Réactions du Midi: conflits, continuités et violences', *AHRF*, 345 (2006), pp. 55–91.

—. 'Vengeance, Justice and the Reactions in the Revolutionary Midi', *FH*, 23 (2009), pp. 22–46.

Cobb, Richard. *Paris and its Provinces.* Oxford: Oxford University Press, 1975.

—. *Reactions to the French Revolution.* London: Oxford University Press, 1972.

—. *The People's Armies. The 'armées révolutionnaires': Instrument of the Terror in the Departments, April 1793 to Floréal Year II,* translated by Marianne Elliott. New Haven, CT, and London: Yale University Press, 1987.

—. *The Police and the People: French Popular Protest, 1789–1820.* Oxford: Oxford University Press, 1970.

Cobban, Alfred. *Aspects of the French Revolution.* London: Cape, 1968.

—. *The Social Interpretation of the French Revolution.* Cambridge: Cambridge University Press, 1964.

Coller, Ian. *Arab France: Islam and the Making of Modern Europe, 1798–1831.* Berkeley and Los Angeles, CA, and London: University of California Press, 2011.

Corbin, Alain. *Village Bells: Sound and Meaning in the 19th-Century French Countryside,* translated by Martin Thom. New York: Columbia University Press, 1998.

Cornette, Joël. *Histoire de la Bretagne et des Bretons,* vol. 2. Paris: Éditions du Seuil, 2005.

—. *Un révolutionnaire ordinaire. Benoît Lacombe, négociant, 1759–1819.* Seyssel: Champ Vallon, 1986.

— (ed.). *Atlas de l'histoire de France, 481–2005.* Paris: Belin, 2012.

Corvol, Andrée (ed.). *La Nature en Révolution. Colloque Révolution, nature, paysage et environnement*. Paris: L'Harmattan, 1993.

Crépin, Annie, Jean-Pierre Jessenne and Hervé Leuwers (eds). *Civils, citoyens-soldats et militaires dans L'État-nation (1789–1815). Actes du colloque d'Arras (7–8 novembre 2003)*. Paris: SÉR, 2006.

Crook, Malcolm. *Elections in the French Revolution: An Apprenticeship in Democracy, 1789–1799*. Cambridge and New York: Cambridge University Press, 1996.

—. *Napoleon Comes to Power: Democracy and Dictatorship in Revolutionary France, 1795–1804*. Cardiff: University of Wales Press, 1998.

—, William Doyle, and Alan Forrest (eds). *Enlightenment and Revolution: Essays in Honour of Norman Hampson*. Aldershot: Ashgate, 2004.

Cross, Máire F. and David Williams (eds). *The French Experience from Republic to Monarchy, 1792–1824*. Basingstoke: Palgrave Macmillan, 2000.

Crubaugh, Anthony. *Balancing the Scales of Justice: Local Courts and Rural Society in Southwest France, 1750–1800*. University Park, PA: Pennsylvania State University Press, 2001.

Darlow, Mark. *Staging the French Revolution: Cultural Politics and the Paris Opera, 1789–1794*. New York: Oxford University Press, 2012.

Darnton, Robert. *The Forbidden Best-Sellers of Pre-Revolutionary France*. New York and London: W. W. Norton, 1995.

—. *The Kiss of Lamourette: Reflections in Cultural History*. New York: W. W. Norton, 1990.

—. *The Literary Underground of the Old Regime*. Cambridge, MA: Harvard University Press, 1982.

Darrow, Margaret. *Revolution in the House: Family, Class and Inheritance in Southern France, 1775–1825*. Princeton, NJ: Princeton University Press, 1989.

Dean, Rodney. *L'Assemblée constituante et la réforme ecclésiastique, 1790: la Constitution civile du clergé du 12 juillet et le serment ecclésiastique du 27 novembre*. Paris: Picard, 2014.

Debal, Jacques. *Orléans. Une ville, une histoire*, 2 vols. Orléans: x-nova, 1998.

—, Jean Vassort, and Christian Poitou. *Histoire d'Orléans et de son terroir*, vol. 2. Roanne: Horvath, 1982.

Dendena, Francisco. 'A New Look at Feuillantism: The Triumvirate and the Movement for War in 1791', *FH*, 26 (2012), pp. 6–33.

Denis, Vincent. *Une histoire de l'identité, France, 1715–1815*. Paris: SÉR, 2008.

Desan, Suzanne. *Reclaiming the Sacred: Lay Religion and Popular Politics in Revolutionary France*. Ithaca, NY: Cornell University Press, 1990.

—. *The Family on Trial in Revolutionary France*. Berkeley and Los Angeles, CA, and London: University of California Press, 2004.

—, Lynn Hunt and William Max Nelson (eds). *The French Revolution in Global Perspective*. Ithaca, NY, and London: Cornell University Press, 2013.

DiCaprio, Lisa. *The Origins of the Welfare State: Women, Work, and the French Revolution*. Champaign, IL: University of Illinois Press, 2007.

Dorigny, Marcel (ed.). *The Abolitions of Slavery: From Léger Félicité Sonthonax to Victor Schoelcher, 1793, 1794, 1848*. New York and Oxford: Berghahn Books; Paris: Éditions UNESCO, 2003.

Doyle, William. *Aristocracy and its Enemies in the Age of Revolution*. Oxford: Oxford University Press, 2009.

—. *Jansenism: Catholic Resistance to Authority from the Reformation to the French Revolution*. Basingstoke: Macmillan, 2000.

—. *Origins of the French Revolution*, 3rd edn. Oxford and New York: Oxford University Press, 1999.

—. *The Oxford History of the French Revolution*, 2nd edn. Oxford and New York: Oxford University Press, 2002.

—. 'Dupaty (1746–1788): A Career in the Late Enlightenment', *Studies on Voltaire and the Eighteenth Century*, 230 (1985), pp. 1–125.

—. (ed.) *The Oxford Handbook of the Ancien Régime*. Oxford and New York: Oxford University Press, 2012.

Dubois, Laurent. *A Colony of Citizens: Revolution and Slave Emancipation in the French Caribbean, 1787–1804*. Chapel Hill, NC: University of North Carolina Press, 2004.

—. *Avengers of the New World: The Story of the Haitian Revolution*. Cambridge, MA: Belknap Press of Harvard University Press, 2004.

Dubreuil, Léon. *Les Vicissitudes du domaine congéable en Basse-Bretagne à l'époque de la Révolution*, 2 vols. Rennes: Imprimerie Oberthur, 1915.

Duby, Georges, and Armand Wallon (eds). *Histoire de la France rurale*, vols 2–3. Paris: Éditions du Seuil, 1975–76.

Dumas, G. 'Les "Émotions populaires" dans le département de l'Aisne de la fin de 1790 à l'an IV (1795–1796)', *Société d'histoire et d'archéologie de Senlis* 22 (1977), pp. 38–64.

Dupâquier, Jacques. *Histoire de la population française*, vol. 3. Paris: PUF, 1988.

Dupuy, Pascal (ed.). *La Fête de la Fédération*. Rouen: Publications des universités de Rouen et du Havre, 2012.

Dupuy, Roger. *De la Révolution à la chouannerie. Paysans de Bretagne, 1788–1794*. Paris: Flammarion, 1988.

—. *La Bretagne sous la Révolution et l'Empire (1789–1815)*. Rennes: Éditions Ouest-France, 2004.

—. *La République jacobine. Terreur, guerre et gouvernement révolutionnaire*. Paris: Éditions du Seuil, 2005.

Dwyer, Philip. *Napoleon: The Path to Power, 1769–1799*. London: Bloomsbury, 2007.

Edelstein, Dan. *The Terror of Natural Right: Republicanism, the Cult of Nature, and the French Revolution*. Chicago, IL: University of Chicago Press, 2009.

—. 'Do We Want a Revolution without Revolution? Reflections on Political Authority', *FHS*, 35 (2012), pp. 269–89.

Edelstein, Melvin. *'La Feuille villageoise': communication et modernisation dans les régions rurales pendant la Révolution*. Paris: Bibliothèque Nationale, 1977.

—. *The French Revolution and the Birth of Electoral Democracy*. Farnham, Surrey, and Burlington, VT: Ashgate, 2014.

Edmonds, W. D. *Jacobinism and the Revolt of Lyon, 1789–1793*. Oxford: Oxford University Press, 1990.

Égret, Jean. *The French Pre-Revolution, 1787–1788*, translated by W. D. Camp. Chicago, IL: Chicago University Press, 1977.

Farge, Arlette. *Subversive Words: Public Opinion in Eighteenth-Century France*, translated by Rosemary Morris. Oxford: Polity Press, 1994.

Feilla, Cecilia. *The Sentimental Theater of the French Revolution*. Farnham, Surrey, and Burlington, VT: Ashgate, 2013.

'Femmes, genres, Révolution', special issue of *AHRF*, 358 (2009).

Fitzsimmons, Michael P. *From Artisan to Worker: Guilds, the French State, and the Organization of Labor, 1776–1821*. New York: Cambridge University Press, 2010.

—. *The Night the Old Regime Ended: August 4, 1789 and the French Revolution*. University Park, PA: Pennsylvania State University Press, 2003.

—. *The Remaking of France: The National Assembly and the Constitution of 1791*. Cambridge and New York: Cambridge University Press, 1994.

Flament, Pierre. *Deux mille prêtres normands face à la Révolution, 1789–1801*. Paris: Perrin, 1989.

Forrest, Alan. *Conscripts and Deserters: The Army and French Society during the Revolution and Empire*. Oxford: Oxford University Press, 1989.

—. *Paris, the Provinces and the French Revolution*. London: Arnold, 2004.

—. *Society and Politics in Revolutionary Bordeaux*. Oxford: Oxford University Press, 1975.

—. *Soldiers of the French Revolution*. Durham, NC: Duke University Press, 1990.

—. *The French Revolution and the Poor*. Oxford: Blackwell, 1981.

—. *The Revolution in Provincial France: Aquitaine 1789–1799*. Oxford and New York: Oxford University Press, 1996.

— and Peter Jones (eds). *Reshaping France: Town, Country and Region during the French Revolution*. Manchester: Manchester University Press, 1991.

Forster, Robert. *The House of Saulx-Tavanes: Versailles and Burgundy, 1700–1830*. Baltimore, MD: Johns Hopkins University Press, 1977.

—. 'The French Revolution and the "New" Elite, 1800–1850', in J. Pelenski (ed.), *The American and European Revolutions, 1776–1848*. Iowa City, IA: University of Iowa Press, pp. 182–207.

—. *The Nobility of Toulouse in the Eighteenth Century: A Social and Economic Study*. Baltimore, MD: Johns Hopkins University Press, 1960.

—. 'The Survival of the Nobility during the French Revolution', *P&P*, 37 (1967), pp. 71–86.

Fournier, Georges. *Démocratie et vie municipale en Languedoc du milieu du XVIIIe au début du XIXe siècle*, 2 vols. Toulouse: Les Amis des Archives, 1994.

— and Michel Péronnet. *La Révolution dans l'Aude*. Le Coteau: Horvath, 1989.

Frélaut, Bertrand. *Les Débuts de la contre-révolution en Bretagne. L'Attaque de Vannes (13 février 1791)*. Nantes: Ouest Éditions; Rennes: Institut Culturel de Bretagne, 1989.

Friedland, Paul. *Political Actors: Representative Bodies and Theatricality in the Age of the French Revolution*. Ithaca, NY: Cornell University Press, 2002.

—. *Seeing Justice Done: The Age of Spectacular Capital Punishment in France*. Oxford: Oxford University Press, 2012.

Furet, François. *Interpreting the French Revolution*, translated by Elborg Forster. Cambridge and Paris: Cambridge University Press and Éditions de la Maison des Sciences de l'Homme, 1981.

—. *The French Revolution, 1770–1814*, translated by Antonia Nevill. Oxford: Blackwell, 1992.

— and Mona Ozouf (eds). *Critical Dictionary of the French Revolution*, translated by Arthur Goldhammer. Cambridge, MA: Harvard University Press, 1989.

Gainot, Bernard, and Vincent Denis (eds). *Un Siècle d'ordre public en Révolution*. Paris: SÉR, 2010.

Gallaher, John G. *General Alexandre Dumas: Soldier of the French Revolution*. Carbondale and Edwardsville, IL: Southern Illinois University Press, 1997.

Garrigus, John. *Before Haiti: Race and Citizenship in French Saint-Domingue*. New York: Palgrave Macmillan, 2006.

Garrioch, David. *The Formation of the Parisian Bourgeoisie, 1690–1830*. Cambridge, MA: Harvard University Press, 1996.

—. *The Making of Revolutionary Paris*. Berkeley and Los Angeles, CA, and London: University of California Press, 2002.

Gauthier, Florence. *L'Aristocratie de l'épiderme. Le Combat de la Société des citoyens de couleur, 1789–1791*. Paris: CNRS, 2007.

—. *La Voie paysanne dans la Révolution française: l'exemple picard*. Paris: François Maspero, 1977.

— (ed.). *Périssent les colonies plutôt qu'un principe! Contributions à l'histoire de l'abolition de l'esclavage, 1789–1804*. Paris: SÉR, 2002.

Gayot, Gérard, and Jean-Pierre Hirsch (eds). *La Révolution française et le développement du capitalisme*. Villeneuve d'Ascq: Revue du Nord, 1989.

Geggus, David Patrick. *Haitian Revolutionary Studies*. Bloomington, IN: Indiana University Press, 2002.

Gendron, François. *The Gilded Youth of Thermidor*, translated by James Cookson. Montreal and Kingston, London, Buffalo, NY: McGill-Queen's University Press, 1993.

Germani, Ian. *Jean-Paul Marat: Hero and Anti-hero of the French Revolution*. Lewiston, NY, Queenston, ON, Lampeter, Wales: The Edward Mellon Press, 1992.

—. 'Military Justice under the Directory: The Armies of Italy and of the Sambre et Meuse', *FH*, 23 (2009), pp. 47–68.

—. 'Terror in the Army: Representatives on Mission and Military Discipline in the Armies of the French Revolution', *Journal of Military History*, 75 (2011), pp. 733–68.

Gilks, David. 'Art and Politics during the "First" Directory: Artists' Petitions and the Quarrel over the Confiscation of Works of Art from Italy', *FH*, 26 (2012), pp. 53–78.

—. 'Attitudes to the Displacement of Cultural Property in the Wars of the French Revolution and Napoleon', *HJ*, 56 (2013), pp. 113–43.

Godechot, Jacques. *France and the Atlantic Revolution of the Eighteenth Century, 1770–1799*, translated by Herbert H. Rowen. New York: The Free Press, 1965.

—. *La Révolution française dans le Midi toulousain*. Toulouse: Éditions Privat, 1986.

—. *The Counter-Revolution: Doctrine and Action, 1789–1804*, translated by Salvator Attanasio. London: Routledge & Kegan Paul, 1972.

—. *The Taking of the Bastille, July 14th, 1789*, translated by Jean Stewart. London: Faber and Faber, 1970.

Godineau, Dominique. *S'abréger les jours. Le suicide en France au XVIIIe siècle*. Paris: Armand Colin, 2012.

—. *The Women of Paris and their French Revolution*, translated by Katherine Streip. Berkeley, CA: University of California Press, 1998.

Goodman, Dena. *The Republic of Letters: A Cultural History of the French Enlightenment*. Ithaca, NY, and London: Cornell University Press, 1994.

Gough, Hugh. *The Terror in the French Revolution*, 2nd edn. Basingstoke: Palgrave Macmillan, 2010.

Graham, Ruth. 'The Secularization of the Ecclesiastical Deputies to the National Convention, 1792–1794', *Consortium on Revolutionary Europe, 1750–1850*, 3 (1974), pp. 65–79.

Greer, Donald. *The Incidence of the Emigration during the French Revolution*. Cambridge, MA: Harvard University Press, 1951.

—. *The Incidence of the Terror during the French Revolution: A Statistical Interpretation*. Cambridge, MA: Harvard University Press, 1935.

Gross, Jean-Pierre. *Fair Shares for All: Jacobin Egalitarianism in Practice*. Cambridge and New York: Cambridge University Press, 1997.

Gruder, Vivian R. *The Notables and the Nation: The Political Schooling of the French, 1787–1788*. Cambridge, MA, and London: Harvard University Press, 2007.

Gueniffey, Patrice. *La Politique de la Terreur: essai sur la violence révolutionnaire*. Paris: Fayard, 2000.

—. *Le Nombre et la raison: la Révolution française et les elections*. Paris: ÉHÉSS, 1993.

Guilhaumou, Jacques. *La Langue politique et la Révolution française: de l'événement à la raison linguistique*. Paris: Méridiens Klincksieck, 1989.

— and Martine Lapied. 'La mission Maignet', *AHRF*, 300 (1995), pp. 283–94.

Guillon, Claude. 'Pauline Léon, une républicaine révolutionnaire', *AHRF*, 344 (2006), pp. 147–59.

Guin, Yannick. *La Bataille de Nantes, 29 juin 1793. Un Valmy dans l'ouest*. Laval: Siloë, 1993.

Hamon, Léo (ed.). *La Révolution à travers un département (Yonne)*. Paris: Éditions de la Maison des Sciences de l'Homme, 1990.

Hampson, Norman. *Danton*. Oxford: Blackwell, 1978.

—. 'François Chabot and his Plot', *Transactions of the Royal Historical Society*, 5th series, 26 (1976), pp. 1–14.

—. *Prelude to Terror: The Constituent Assembly and the Failure of Consensus, 1789–1791*. Oxford: Oxford University Press, 1988.

—. *Saint-Just*. Oxford: Blackwell, 1991.

—. *The Life and Opinions of Maximilien Robespierre*. London: Duckworth, 1974.

—. *Will and Circumstance: Montesquieu, Rousseau and the French Revolution*. London: Duckworth, 1983.

Hanson, Paul R. *Contesting the French Revolution*. Malden, MA, and Oxford: Wiley-Blackwell, 2009.

—. *Provincial Politics in the French Revolution: Caen and Limoges, 1789–1794*. Baton Rouge, LA, and London: Louisiana State University Press, 1989.

—. *The Jacobin Republic under Fire: The Federalist Revolt in the French Revolution*. University Park, PA: Pennsylvania State University Press, 2003.

Hardman, John. *Louis XVI*. New Haven, CT, and London: Yale University Press, 1993.

—. *Overture to Revolution: The 1787 Assembly of Notables and the Crisis of France's Old Régime*. Oxford: Oxford University Press, 2010.

Harris, S. E. *The Assignats*. Cambridge, MA: Harvard University Press, 1930.

Hartmann, Éric. *La Révolution française en Alsace et en Lorraine*. Paris: Perrin, 1990.

Haydon, Colin, and William Doyle (eds). *Robespierre*. Cambridge and New York: Cambridge University Press, 1999.

Heller, Henry. *The Bourgeois Revolution in France, 1789–1815*. New York and Oxford: Berghahn Books, 2006.

Hesse, Carla. *Publishing and Cultural Politics in Revolutionary Paris, 1789–1810*. Berkeley, CA: University of California Press, 1991.

—. *The Other Enlightenment: How French Women Became Modern*. Princeton, NJ: Princeton University Press, 2001.

Heuer, Jennifer Ngaire. *The Family and the Nation: Gender and Citizenship in Revolutionary France, 1789–1830*. Ithaca, NY, and London: Cornell University Press, 2005.

Higonnet, Patrice L. R. *Goodness beyond Virtue: Jacobins during the French Revolution*. Cambridge, MA: Harvard University Press, 1998.

—. *Pont-de-Montvert: Social Structure and Politics in a French Village, 1700–1914*. Cambridge, MA: Harvard University Press, 1971.

Hood, James N. 'Protestant–Catholic Relations and the Roots of the First Popular Counter-Revolutionary Movement in France', *JMH*, 43 (1971), pp. 245–75.

Horn, Jeff. *The Path Not Taken: French Industrialization in the Age of Revolution*. Cambridge, MA: MIT Press, 2006.

Houdaille, Jacques. 'Un indicateur de pratique religieuse: la célébration saisonnière des mariages avant, pendant et après la Révolution française', *Population*, 2 (1978), pp. 367–80.

Huet, Marie-Hélène. *Mourning Glory: The Will of the French Revolution*. University Park, PA: University of Pennsylvania Press, 1997.

—. 'Attitudes towards Authority in Eighteenth-Century Languedoc', *SH*, 3 (1978), pp. 281–302.

Hufton, Olwen. *Bayeux in the Late Eighteenth Century: A Social Study*. Oxford: Oxford University Press, 1967.

—. *Women and the Limits to Citizenship*. Toronto: University of Toronto Press, 1992.

—. 'Women in Revolution', *French Politics and Society*, 7 (1989), pp. 65–81.

—. 'Women in Revolution, 1789–1796', *P&P*, 53 (1971), pp. 90–108.

Hunt, David. 'Peasant Movements and Communal Property during the French Revolution', *Theory and Society*, 17 (1988), pp. 255–83.

—. 'Peasant Politics in the French Revolution', *SH*, 9 (1984), pp. 277–99.

—. 'The People and Pierre Dolivier: Popular Uprisings in the Seine-et-Oise Department, 1791–1792,' *FHS*, 11 (1979), pp. 184–214.

Hunt, Lynn. *Inventing Human Rights: A History*. New York: W. W. Norton, 2007.

—. *Politics, Culture, and Class in the French Revolution*. Berkeley, CA: University of California Press, 1984.

—. *The Family Romance of the French Revolution*. London: Routledge, 1992.

— (ed.). *Eroticism and the Body Politic*. Baltimore, MD: Johns Hopkins University Press, 1991.

Ikni, Guy. 'Sur les biens communaux pendant la Révolution française', *AHRF*, 247 (1982), pp. 71–94.

Israel, Jonathan I. *Democratic Enlightenment: Philosophy, Revolution, and Human Rights, 1750–1790*. Oxford: Oxford University Press, 2012.

—. *Revolutionary Ideas: An Intellectual History of the French Revolution from* The Rights of Man *to* Robespierre. Princeton, NJ: Princeton University Press, 2014.

Jacobson, Gavin. 'Caricatures Travel Better than Portraits: On Maximilien Robespierre', *EHR*, 129 (2014), pp. 388–402.

Jainchill, Andrew. *Reimagining Politics after the Terror: The Republican Origins of French Liberalism*. Ithaca, NY, and London: Cornell University Press, 2008.

Jessenne, Jean-Pierre. *Pouvoir au village et revolution: Artois, 1760–1848*. Lille: Presses universitaires de Lille, 1987.

— (ed.). *Vers un ordre bourgeois? Révolution française et changement social*. Rennes: Presses universitaires de Rennes, 2007.

—, Gilles Derégnaucourt, Jean-Pierre Hirsch, and Hervé Leuwers (eds). *Robespierre: de la nation artésienne à la République et aux nations. Actes du Colloque, Arras, 1–2–3 Avril 1993*. Villeneuve d'Asq: Centre d'Histoire de la Région du Nord et de l'Europe du Nord-Ouest, Université Charles de Gaulle-Lille III, 1994.

Johnson, Christopher H. *The Life and Death of Industrial Languedoc, 1700–1920*. New York and Oxford: Oxford University Press, 1995.

Johnson, James H. *Listening in Paris: A Cultural History*. Berkeley and Los Angeles, CA, and London: University of California Press, 1995.

Johnson, Victoria. *Backstage at the Revolution: How the Royal Paris Opera Survived the End of the Old Regime*. Chicago, IL, and London: University of Chicago Press, 2008.

Jollet, Anne. *Terre et société en Révolution: Approche du lien social dans la région d'Amboise*. Paris: CTHS, 2000.

Jones, Colin. 'The Great Chain of Buying: Medical Advertisement, the Bourgeois Public Sphere, and the Origins of the French Revolution', *AHR*, 101 (1996), pp. 13–40.

—. *The Longman Companion to the French Revolution*. London and New York: Longman, 1988.

—. 'The Overthrow of Maximilien Robespierre and the "Indifference" of the People', *AHR*, 119 (2014), pp. 689–713.

Jones, P. M. *Liberty and Locality in Revolutionary France: Six Villages Compared, 1760–1820*. Cambridge: Cambridge University Press, 2003.

—. *Politics and Rural Society: The Southern Massif Central c.1750–1880*. Cambridge: Cambridge University Press, 1985.

—. *Reform and Revolution in France: The Politics of Transition, 1774–1791*. Cambridge: Cambridge University Press, 1995.

—. *The Peasantry in the French Revolution*. Cambridge: Cambridge University Press, 1988.

Jordan, David P. *The King's Trial: The French Revolution vs. Louis XVI.* Berkeley, CA: University of California Press, 1979.

—. *The Revolutionary Career of Maximilien Robespierre.* New York: Free Press, 1985.

Jourdan, Annie. *La Révolution, une exception française?* Paris: Flammarion, 2004.

—. 'Les discours de la terreur à l'époque révolutionnaire (1776–1798): étude comparative sur une notion ambiguë', *FHS*, 36 (2013), pp. 51–81.

Jouvenel, François de. 'Les Camps de Jalès (1790–1792), épisodes contre-révolutionnaires?', *AHRF*, 337 (2004), pp. 1–20.

Kaiser, Thomas E. 'From the Austrian Committee to the Foreign Plot: Marie-Antoinette, Austrophobia, and the Terror', *FHS*, 26 (2003), pp. 579–617.

Kaplan, Steven L. *Farewell, Revolution: Disputed Legacies, France 1789–1989.* Ithaca, NY: Cornell University Press, 1995.

—. *Farewell, Revolution: The Historians' Feud, 1789–1989.* Ithaca, NY: Cornell University Press, 1995.

—. *La Fin des corporations.* Paris: Fayard, 2001.

Kaplow, Jeffry. *Elbeuf during the Revolutionary Period: History and Social Structure.* Baltimore, MD: Johns Hopkins University Press, 1964.

— (ed.). *New Perspectives on the French Revolution: Readings in Historical Sociology.* New York: John Wiley, 1965.

Kelly, George Armstrong. 'Conceptual Sources of the Terror', *Eighteenth Century Studies*, 14 (1980), pp. 18–36.

Kennedy, Emmet. *A Cultural History of the French Revolution.* New Haven, CT, and London: Yale University Press, 1989.

Kennedy, Michael. *The Jacobin Clubs in the French Revolution: The First Years.* Princeton, NJ: Princeton University Press, 1982.

—. *The Jacobin Clubs in the French Revolution: The Middle Years.* Princeton, NJ: Princeton University Press, 1988.

—. *The Jacobin Clubs in the French Revolution, 1793–1795.* New York: Berghahn Books, 2000.

Koubi, Geneviève (ed.). *Propriété et Révolution: Actes du colloque de Toulouse, 1989.* Paris: CNRS, 1990.

Kwass, Michael. *Privilege and the Politics of Taxation in Eighteenth-Century France.* Cambridge: Cambridge University Press, 2000.

Labroue, Henri. *La Société populaire de Bergerac pendant la Révolution.* Paris: Société de l'Histoire de la Révolution Française, 1915.

Landes, Joan. *Women and the Public Sphere in the Age of the French Revolution.* Ithaca, NY: Cornell University Press, 1988.

Lapied, Martine. 'La Place des femmes dans la sociabilité et la vie politique locale en Provence et dans le Comtat Venaissin pendant la Révolution', *Provence historique*, 46 (1996), pp. 457–69.

Larguier, Gilbert et al. (eds). *Cahiers de doléances audois.* Carcassonne: Association des Amis des Archives de l'Aude, 1989.

Laurent, Robert, and Gavignaud, Geneviève. *La Révolution française dans le Languedoc méditerranéen.* Toulouse: Privat, 1987.

Le Bloas, Alain. 'La Question du domaine congéable', *AHRF*, 331 (2003), pp. 1–27.

Le Bozec, Christine. *Boissy d'Anglas, un grand notable libéral.* Privas: Fédération des Oeuvres Laïques de l'Ardèche, 1995.

— and Éric Wauters (eds). *Pour la Révolution française. En hommage à Claude Mazauric.* Rouen: Publications de l'Université de Rouen, 1998.

Lebrun, François. *Parole de Dieu et Révolution. Les Sermons d'un curé angevin avant et pendant la guerre de Vendée.* Paris: Éditions Imago, 1988.

—. 'La guerre de Vendée: massacre ou génocide?', *Histoire*, 78 (1985), pp. 93–99.

Lee, Simon. *David.* London: Phaidon, 1999.

Lefebvre, Georges. *Études orléanaises*, 2 vols. Paris: Commission d'Histoire Économique et Sociale de la Révolution, 1962.

—. *Études sur la Révolution française.* Paris: PUF, 1954.

—. *Les Paysans du Nord pendant la Révolution française.* Bari: Laterza, 1959.

—. *Questions agraires au temps de la Terreur. Documents publiés et annotés.* La Roche-sur-Yon: Potier, 1954.

—. *The French Revolution*, translated by John Hall Stewart and James Friguglietti, 2 vols. London: Routledge & Kegan Paul, 1964–65.

—. *The Great Fear of 1789: Rural Panic in Revolutionary France*, translated by Joan White. New York: Vintage Books, 1973.

—. *The Thermidorians and the Directory: Two Phases of the French Revolution*, translated by Robert Baldick. New York: Random House, 1964.

Le Goff, T. J. A. *Vannes and its Region: A Study of Town and Country in Eighteenth-Century France*. Oxford: Clarendon Press, 1981.

— and D. M. G. Sutherland. 'The Revolution and the Rural Community in Brittany', *P&P*, 62 (1974), pp. 96–119.

Lemarchand, Guy. 'La Féodalité et la Révolution française: seigneurie et communauté paysanne (1780–1799)', *AHRF*, 242 (1980), pp. 536–58.

—. 'Troubles populaires au XVIIIe siècle et conscience de classe: une préface à la Révolution française', *AHRF*, 279 (1990), pp. 32–48.

Lemay, Edna Hindie. *Dictionnaire des constituants, 1789–1791*, 2 vols. Oxford: Voltaire Foundation, 1991.

— and Alison Patrick. *Revolutionaries at Work: The Constituent Assembly, 1789–1791*. Oxford: Voltaire Foundation, 1996.

Lenoël, Pierre, and Marie-Françoise Lévy (eds). *L'Enfant, la famille et la Révolution française*. Paris: Olivier Orban, 1990.

Léon, Pierre et al. *Histoire économique et sociale de la France*, vol. 3. Paris: PUF, 1976.

Lerner, Mark H. 'The Helvetic Republic: An Ambivalent Reception of French Revolutionary Liberty', *FH*, 18 (2004), pp. 50–75.

Leuwers, Hervé. *Robespierre*. Paris: Fayard, 2014.

—, Annie Crépin, and Dominique Rosselle. *Histoire des provinces françaises du nord. La Révolution et l'Empire. Le Nord—Pas-de-Calais entre Révolution et contre-révolution*. Arras: Presses de l' Université d'Artois, 2008.

Lévêque, Jean-Jacques, and Victor R. Brelot. *Guide de la Révolution française*, 2nd edn. Paris: Éditions Horay, 1989.

Lewis, Gwynne. *The Advent of Modern Capitalism in France, 1770–1840: The Contribution of Pierre-François Tubeuf*. Oxford: Clarendon Press, 1993.

—. *The French Revolution: Rethinking the Debate*. London and New York: Routledge & Kegan Paul, 1993.

—. *The Second Vendée: The Continuity of Counter-Revolution in the Department of the Gard, 1789–1815*. Oxford: Oxford University Press, 1978.

— and Colin Lucas (eds). *Beyond the Terror: Essays in French Regional and Social History, 1794–1815*. Cambridge and New York: Cambridge University Press, 1983.

Linton, Marisa. *Choosing Terror: Virtue, Friendship, and Authenticity in the French Revolution*. Oxford: Oxford University Press, 2013.

—. *The Politics of Virtue in Enlightenment France*. Basingstoke: Palgrave Macmillan, 2001.

Livesey, James. *Making Democracy in the French Revolution*. Cambridge, MA, and London: Harvard University Press, 2001.

—. 'Material Culture, Economic Institutions and Peasant Revolution in Lower Languedoc, 1770–1840', *P&P*, 182 (2004), pp. 143–73.

Lottin, D. *Recherches historiques sur la ville d'Orléans*, 8 vols. Orléans: Imprimerie Alexandre Jacob, 1836–45.

Louis, Abel. *Les Libres de couleur en Martinique*, 3 vols. Paris: L'Harmattan, 2012.

Luc, Jean-Noël. *Paysans et droits féodaux en Charente-Inférieure pendant la Révolution française*. Paris: Commission d'Histoire de la Révolution française, 1984.

—. 'The Rules of the Game in Local Politics under the Directory', *FHS*, 16 (1989), pp. 345–71.

Lucas, Colin. *The Structure of the Terror: The Example of Javogues and the Loire*. Oxford: Oxford University Press, 1973.

—. 'The Theory and Practice of Denunciation in the French Revolution', *JMH*, 68 (1996), pp. 768–85.

— (ed.). *Rewriting the French Revolution*. Oxford: Clarendon Press, 1991.

— (ed.). *The French Revolution and the Creation of Modern Political Culture*, 4 vols. Oxford: Oxford University Press, 1987–94.

Lüsebrink, Hans-Jürgen, and Rolf Reichardt. *The Bastille: A History of a Symbol of Despotism and Freedom*. Durham, NC: Duke University Press, 1997.

Lyons, Martyn. *France under the Directory*. Cambridge and New York: Cambridge University Press, 1975.

McManners, John. *Church and Society in Eighteenth-Century France*, 2 vols. Oxford and New York: Oxford University Press, 1998.

—. *French Ecclesiastical Society under the Ancien Régime: A Study of Angers in the Eighteenth Century*. Manchester: Manchester University Press, 1960.

McPhee, Peter. *Collioure et la Révolution française, 1789–1815*. Perpignan: Le Publicateur, 1989.

—. 'Counter-Revolution in the Pyrenees: Spirituality, Class and Ethnicity in the Haut-Vallespir, 1793–1794', *FH*, 7 (1993), pp. 313–43.

—. *Living the French Revolution, 1789–99*. London and New York: Palgrave Macmillan, 2006.

—. *Revolution and Environment in Southern France: Peasants, Lords, and Murder in the Corbières, 1780–1830*. Oxford: Clarendon Press, 1999.

—. *Robespierre: A Revolutionary Life*. New Haven, CT, and London: Yale University Press, 2012.

—. *The French Revolution, 1789–1799*. Oxford: Oxford University Press, 2002.

—. *Une communauté languedocienne dans l'histoire: Gabian 1760–1960*. Nîmes: Lacour, 2001.

—. 'The French Revolution, Peasants, and Capitalism', *AHR*, 94 (1989), pp. 1,265–80.

—. '"The misguided greed of peasants"? Popular Attitudes to the Environment in the Revolution of 1789', *FHS*, 24 (2001), pp. 247–69.

— (ed.). *A Companion to the French Revolution*. Oxford: Wiley-Blackwell, 2013.

Mansfield, Paul. 'The Repression of Lyon, 1793–4: Origins, Responsibility and Significance', *FH*, 2 (1988), pp. 74–101.

Margadant, Ted W. *Urban Rivalries in the French Revolution*. Princeton, NJ: Princeton University Press, 1992.

Markoff, John. *The Abolition of Feudalism: Peasants, Lords, and Legislators in the French Revolution*. University Park, PA: Pennsylvania State University Press, 1996.

Markovic, Momcilo. 'La Révolution aux barrières: l'incendie des barrières de l'octroi à Paris en juillet 1789', *AHRF*, 372 (2013), pp. 27–48.

—. 'Histoire et polémique, les massacres de Machecoul', *AHRF*, 291 (1993), pp. 33–60.

—. *La Révolte brisée. Femmes dans la Révolution française et l'Empire*. Paris: Armand Colin, 2008.

—. 'La Vendée. Enquête sur les crimes de la Révolution', *Histoire*, 377 (2012), pp. 40–61.

Martin, Jean-Clément. *Nouvelle histoire de la Révolution française*. Paris: Perrin, 2012.

—. 'Vendée: les criminels de guerre en procès', *Histoire*, 25 (2004), pp. 82–87.

—. *Violence et Révolution: essai sur la naissance d'un mythe national*. Paris: Éditions du Seuil, 2006.

— (ed.). *La Révolution à l'œuvre. Perspectives actuelles dans l'histoire de la Révolution française*. Rennes: Presses Universitaires de Rennes, 2005.

Mason, Laura. *Singing the French Revolution: Popular Culture and Politics, 1787–1799*. Ithaca, NY: Cornell University Press, 1996.

— and Tracey Rizzo (eds). *The French Revolution: A Document Collection*. Boston, MA, and New York: Houghton Mifflin, 1999.

Massé, Pierre. *Varennes et ses maitres. Un domaine rural, de l'Ancien Régime à la Monarchie de juillet (1779–1842)*. Paris: S.E.V.P.E.N., 1956.

Mathiez, Albert. *After Robespierre: The Thermidorian Reaction*, translated by Catherine Alison Phillips. New York: Grosset and Dunlap, 1965.

—. *Un procès de corruption sous la Terreur: l'affaire de la Compagnie des Indes*. Paris: Félix Alcan, 1920.

Matteson, Kieko. *Forests in Revolutionary France: Conservation, Community, and Conflict, 1669–1848*. Cambridge: Cambridge University Press, 2014.

Maza, Sarah. *Private Lives and Public Affairs: The Causes Célèbres of Pre-Revolutionary France*. Berkeley, CA: University of California Press, 1993.

Mazauric, Claude (ed.). *La Révolution française et l'homme moderne*. Paris: Éditions Messidor, 1989.

Mazeau, Guillaume. *Le Bain de l'histoire: Charlotte Corday et l'attentat contre Marat, 1793–2009*. Seyssel: Champ Vallon, 2009.

Michel, Georges. *Une famille provençale du XVIe siècle au Consulat*. Paris: Éditions Berger-Levrault, 1950.

Miller, Judith. *Mastering the Market: The State and the Grain Trade in Northern France, 1700–1860.* Cambridge and New York: Cambridge University Press, 1998.

Miller, Mary Ashburn. *A Natural History of Revolution: Violence and Nature in the French Revolutionary Imagination, 1789–1794.* Ithaca, NY, and London: Cornell University Press, 2011.

Miller, Stephen. 'Venal Offices, Provincial Assemblies and the French Revolution', *FH*, 28 (2014), pp. 343–65.

Mirouse, Florence (ed.). *François Ménard de la Groye, député du Maine aux États généraux. Correspondance (1789–1791).* Le Mans: Conseil Général de la Sarthe, 1989.

Mitchell, C. J. *The French Legislative Assembly of 1791.* Leiden: E. J. Brill, 1988.

Monnier, Raymonde. *L'Espace public démocratique: essai sur l'opinion à Paris de la Révolution au Directoire.* Paris: Éditions Kimé, 1994.

—. *Le Faubourg Saint-Antoine (1789–1815).* Paris: SÉR, 1981.

—. *Républicanisme, patriotisme et Révolution française.* Paris: Harmattan, 2005.

— (ed.). *Citoyens et citoyenneté sous la Révolution française.* Paris: SÉR, 2006.

Moran, Daniel, and Arthur Waldron (eds). *The People in Arms: Military Myth and National Mobilization since the French Revolution.* Cambridge: Cambridge University Press, 2003.

Morgan, Peter. 'Republicanism, Identity and the New European Order: Georg Forster's Letters from Mainz and Paris, 1792–1793', *Journal of European Studies*, 22 (1992), pp. 71–100.

Moriceau, J.-M., and Gilles Postel-Vinay. *Ferme, entreprise et famille.* Paris: ÉHÉSS, 1992.

Morvan, Daniel. 'L'Oeil du maître. Rosanbo, une seigneurie au quotidien', *Skol Vreizh*, 24 (1992), pp. 1–83.

Moulinas, René. *Histoire de la Révolution d'Avignon.* Avignon: Aubanel, 1986.

—. *Les Massacres de la Glacière: enquête sur un crime impuni, Avignon 16–17 octobre 1791.* Aix-en-Provence: Édisud, 2003.

Muller, Claude. 'Religion et Révolution en Alsace', *AHRF*, 337 (2004), pp. 63–83.

Murray, William J. *The Right-Wing Press in the French Revolution: 1789–1792.* London: Royal Historical Society, 1986.

Nicod, Jean-Claude. 'Les "séditieux" en Languedoc à la fin du XVIIIe siècle', *Recueil de Mémoires et travaux de la Société d'histoire du droit et des institutions des anciens pays de droit écrit*, 8 (1971), pp. 145–65.

Nicolas, Jean (ed.). *Mouvements populaires et conscience sociale, XVI–XIXe siècles. Actes du colloque de Paris, 24–26 mai 1984.* Paris: Maloine, 1985.

Nicolle, Paul. 'Les Meurtres politiques d'août–septembre 1792 dans le département de l'Orne: étude critique', *AHRF*, 62 (1934), pp. 97–118.

Noël, Karl. *L'Esclavage à l'Ile de France (Ile Maurice) de 1715 à 1810.* Paris: Éditions Two Cities ETC, 1991.

Noiriel, Gérard. *Réfugiés et sans-papiers. La République face au droit d'asile XIXe–XXe siècle.* Paris: Hachette, 1998.

Oliver, Bette W. *Surviving the French Revolution: A Bridge Across Time.* Lanham, MD: Lexington Books, 2013.

Ozouf, Mona. *Festivals and the French Revolution*, translated by Alan Sheridan. Cambridge, MA: Harvard University Press, 1988.

—. *L'École de la France: essais sur la Révolution, l'utopie et l'enseignement.* Paris: Gallimard, 1984.

Palmer, R. R. *The Age of the Democratic Revolution: A Political History of Europe and America, 1760–1800*, 2 vols. Princeton, NJ: Princeton University Press, 1959, 1964.

—. *The Improvement of Humanity: Education and the French Revolution.* Princeton, NJ: Princeton University Press, 1985.

—. *Twelve who Ruled: The Year of the Terror in the French Revolution.* Princeton, NJ: Princeton University Press, 1969.

Parisot, Robert. *Histoire de Lorraine*, vol. 3. Paris: Auguste Picard, 1924.

Parker, Harold T. *The Cult of Antiquity and the French Revolutionaries: A Study in the Development of the Revolutionary Spirit.* New York: Octagon, 1965.

Parker, Lindsay A. H. *Writing the Revolution: A French Woman's History in Letters.* Oxford and New York: Oxford University Press, 2013.

Patrick, Alison. *The Men of the First French Republic: Political Alignments in the National Convention of 1792.* Baltimore, MD: Johns Hopkins University Press, 1972.

Pellegrin, Nicole. *Les Vêtements de la Liberté: Abécédaire des pratiques vestimentaires en France de 1780 à 1800.* Aix-en-Provence: Éditions Alinéa, 1989.

Péronnet, Michel, Robert Attal and Jean Bobin. *La Révolution dans l'Aisne, 1789–1799,* Le Coteau: Horvath, 1988.

—, and Georges Fournier. *La Révolution dans l'Aude.* Le Coteau: Horvath, 1989.

—, and Gérard Bourdin. *La Révolution dans l'Orne.* Le Coteau: Horvath, 1988.

—, and Yannick Guin. *La Révolution dans la Loire-Inférieure.* Le Coteau: Horvath, 1989.

Perovic, Sanja. *The Calendar in Revolutionary France.* Cambridge and New York: Cambridge University Press, 2012.

Petitfrère, Claude. *La Vendée et les Vendéens.* Paris: Gallimard, 1981.

—. *Les Vendéens d'Anjou (1793).* Paris: Bibliothèque Nationale, 1981.

—. 'La Vendée en l'an II: défaite et répression', *AHRF,* 300 (1995), pp. 173–87.

—. 'The Origins of the Civil War in the Vendée', *FH,* 2 (1988), pp. 187–207.

Peyrard, Christine. *Les Jacobins de l'Ouest. Sociabilité et formes de politisation dans le Maine et la Basse-Normandie (1789–1799).* Paris: Publications de la Sorbonne, 1996.

Pfister, Christian. *Histoire de Nancy,* vol. 3. Paris: Éditions du Palais Royal; Nancy: Éditions Berger-Levrault, 1974.

Phillips, Roderick. *Family Breakdown in Late Eighteenth-Century France: Divorces in Rouen, 1792–1803,* Oxford: Oxford University Press, 1980.

Pimoulle, Jacques. *Le Conventionnel Nicolas Maure, 1743–1795.* Auxerre: n.p., 1989.

Pingué, Danièle, and Jean-Paul Rothiot (eds). *Les Comités de surveillance. D'une création citoyenne à une institution révolutionnaire.* Paris: SÉR, 2012.

Pinsseau, Pierre. *Cadet Roussel (1743–1807).* Paris: Clavreuil, 1945.

Plack, Noelle L. *Common Land, Wine and the French Revolution: Rural Society and Economy in Southern France, c.1789–1820.* Farnham, Surrey, and Burlington, VT: Ashgate, 2009.

Popkin, Jeremy D. *Revolutionary News: The Press in France, 1789–1799.* Durham, NC, and London: Duke University Press, 1990.

—. *You Are All Free: The Haitian Revolution and the Abolition of Slavery.* New York: Cambridge University Press, 2010.

Postel-Vinay, Gilles. 'À la recherche de la Révolution économique dans les campagnes (1789–1815)', *Revue économique,* 6 (1989), pp. 1,015–45.

Potofsky, Allan. *Constructing Paris in the Age of Revolution.* London: Palgrave Macmillan, 2009.

Pouthas, Charles-H. *Une famille bourgeoise française de Louis XIV à Napoléon.* Paris: Librairie Félix Alcan, 1934.

'Les Prénoms révolutionnaires', special issue of *AHRF,* 322 (2000).

Price, Munro. 'Mirabeau and the Court: Some New Evidence', *FHS,* 29 (2006), pp. 37–75.

—. *The Road from Versailles: Louis XVI, Marie Antoinette, and the Fall of the French Monarchy.* New York. St. Martin's Press, 2003.

Racineux, Alain. 'Du faux-saunage à la chouannerie, au sud-est de la Bretagne', *Mémoires de la Société d'histoire et d'archéologie de Bretagne,* 56 (1989), pp. 192–206.

Ragan, Bryant T., and Elizabeth A. Williams (eds). *Re-creating Authority in Revolutionary France.* New Brunswick, NJ: Rutgers University Press, 1992.

Ramsay, Clay. *The Ideology of the Great Fear: The Soissonnais in 1789.* Baltimore, MD, and London: Johns Hopkins University Press, 1992.

Rapport, Michael. 'Belgium under French Occupation: Between Collaboration and Resistance, July 1794 to October 1795', *FH,* 16 (2002), pp. 53–82.

—. *Nationality and Citizenship in Revolutionary France: The Treatment of Foreigners, 1789–1799.* Oxford: Clarendon Press, 2000.

Reddy, William. *The Navigation of Feeling: A Framework for the History of Emotions.* Cambridge: Cambridge University Press, 2001.

Régent, Frédéric. *La France et ses esclaves. De la colonisation aux abolitions (1620–1848).* Paris: Grasset, 2007.

Reichardt, Rolf, and Herbert Schneider. 'Chanson et musique populaires devant l'histoire à la fin de l'Ancien Régime', *Dix-huitième siècle,* 18 (1986), pp. 117–42.

—. and Hubertus Kohle. *Visualising the Revolution: Politics and the Pictorial Arts in Late Eighteenth-Century France,* translated by Corinne Atwood and Felicity Baker. London: Reaktion Books, 2008.

Reinhardt, Steven G., and Elisabeth A. Cawthorn (eds). *Essays on the French Revolution: Paris and the Provinces*. Arlington, TX: Texas A&M University Press, 1992.

Révolution de 1789: Guerres et croissance économique, special issue of *Revue économique*, 40 (1989).

La Révolution française et le monde rural. Actes du colloque tenu en Sorbonne les 23, 24 et 25 octobre 1987. Paris: CTHS, 1989.

Reynolds, Siân. *Marriage and Revolution: Monsieur and Madame Roland*. Oxford: Oxford University Press, 2012.

Ribeiro, Aileen. *Fashion in the French Revolution*. London: Batsford, 1988.

Richard, Bernard. *Cloches et querelles de cloches dans l'Yonne. La Cloche entre maire et curé, XVIIIe–XXe*. Villeneuve-sur-Yonne: Les Amis du Vieux Villeneuve, 2010.

—. *Les Emblèmes de la République*. Paris: CNRS, 2012.

Richard, Marcelle (ed.). *Le Morbihan pendant la Révolution, 1789–1795*, 2nd edn. Vannes: AD Loire-Atlantique, 1988.

Rideau, Gaël. 'De l'impôt à la sécularisation: reconstruire l'église. Les Doléances religieuses dans les cahiers de doléances du bailliage d'Orléans', *AHRF*, 345 (2006), pp. 3–29.

Riley, James C. *The Seven Years War and the Old Regime in France: The Economic and Financial Toll*. Princeton, NJ: Princeton University Press, 1986.

Riskin, Jessica. *Science in the Age of Sensibility: The Sentimental Empiricists of the French Enlightenment*. Chicago, IL, and London: University of Chicago Press, 2002.

Roberts, Warren. *Jacques-Louis David and Jean-Louis Prieur, Revolutionary Artists: The Public, the Populace, and Images of the French Revolution*. Albany, NY: State University of New York Press, 2000.

Robin, Régine. *La Société française en 1789: Semur-en-Auxois*. Paris: Plon, 1970.

Roche, Daniel. *A History of Everyday Things: The Birth of Consumption in France, 1600–1800*, translated by Brian Pearce. Cambridge: Cambridge University Press, 2000.

—. *France in the Enlightenment*, translated by Arthur Goldhammer. Cambridge, MA: Harvard University Press, 1998.

—. *The People of Paris: An Essay in Popular Culture in the 18th Century*, translated by Marie Evans. Berkeley and Los Angeles, CA: University of California Press, 1987.

Roger-Noël, Isabelle. 'La Révolution aux frontières vue par un volontaire de 1792 à 1796', *Revue historique des armées*, 42 (1986), pp. 3–15.

Rose, R. B. *Gracchus Babeuf: The First Revolutionary Communist*. London: Edward Arnold, 1978.

—. *The Enragés: Socialists of the French Revolution?* Melbourne: Melbourne University Press, 1965.

—. *The Making of the 'sans-culottes': Democratic Ideas and Institutions in Paris, 1789–92*. Manchester: Manchester University Press, 1983.

—. *Tribunes and Amazons: Men and Women of Revolutionary France, 1789–1871*. Sydney: Macleay Press, 1998.

Roudinesco, Elisabeth. *Madness and Revolution: The Lives and Legends of Théroigne de Méricourt*, translated by Martin Thom. London and New York: Verso, 1991.

Rouvière, François. *Histoire de la Révolution française dans le department du Gard*, 4 vols. Nîmes: Librairie Ancienne A. Catélan, 1887–89.

Rudé, George. *The Crowd in the French Revolution*. Oxford: Oxford University Press, 1959.

Sagnac, Philippe, and Pierre Caron. *Les Comités des droits féodaux et de législation et l'abolition du régime seigneurial (1789–1793)*. Paris: Imprimerie Nationale, 1907.

Schama, Simon. *Citizens: A Chronicle of the French Revolution*. New York: Alfred A. Knopf, 1989.

Schechter, Ronald. 'The Holy Mountain and the French Revolution', *Historical Reflections*, 40 (2014), pp. 78–107.

Secher, Reynald. *A French Genocide: The Vendée*, translated by George Holoch. Notre Dame, IN: University of Notre Dame Press, 2003.

Sentou, Jean (ed.). *Révolution et contre-révolution dans la France du Midi (1789–1799)*. Toulouse: Presses Universitaires du Mirail, 1991.

Sepinwall, Alyssa Goldstein. *The Abbé Grégorie and the French Revolution: The Making of Modern Universalism*. Berkeley and Los Angeles, CA: University of California Press, 2005.

Serna, Pierre. *La République des girouettes. 1789–1815 et au-delà, une anomalie politique: la France de l'extrême centre*. Seyssel: Champ-Vallon, 2005.

— (ed.). *Républiques sœurs: le Directoire et la Révolution atlantique*. Rennes: Presses Universitaires de Rennes, 2009.

—, Antonino de Francesco and Judith A. Miller (eds). *Republics at War, 1776–1840: Revolutions, Conflicts, and Geopolitics in Europe and the Atlantic World*. Basingstoke: Palgrave Macmillan, 2013.

Sewell, William H. 'Collective Violence and Collective Loyalties in France: Why the French Revolution Made a Difference', *Politics and Society*, 18 (1990), pp. 527–52.

—. 'Connecting Capitalism to the French Revolution: The Parisian Promenade and the Origins of Civic Equality in Eighteenth-Century France', *Critical Historical Studies*, 1 (2014), pp. 5–46.

—. *Work and Revolution in France: The Language of Labour from the Old Régime to 1848*. Cambridge: Cambridge University Press, 1980.

Shapiro, Barry M. *Revolutionary Justice in Paris, 1789–1790*. Cambridge, MA, and New York: Cambridge University Press, 1993.

—. *Traumatic Politics: The Deputies and the King in the Early French Revolution*. University Park, PA: Pennsylvania State University Press, 2009.

Shapiro, Gilbert, and John Markoff. *Revolutionary Demands: A Content Analysis of the Cahiers de Doléances of 1789*. Stanford, CA: California University Press, 1998.

Shaw, Matthew. *Time and the French Revolution: The Republican Calendar, 1789–Year XIV*. Woodbridge, Suffolk, and Rochester, NY: Boydell and Brewer, 2011.

Sheppard, Thomas. *Lourmarin in the Eighteenth Century: A Study of a French Village*. Baltimore, MD: Johns Hopkins University Press, 1971.

Shovlin, John. *The Political Economy of Virtue: Luxury, Patriotism, and the Origins of the French Revolution*. Ithaca, NY, and London: Cornell University Press, 2006.

Sibalis, Michael. 'The Regulation of Male Homosexuality in Revolutionary and Napoleonic France, 1789–1815', in Jeffrey Merrick and Bryant T. Ragan (eds), *Homosexuality in Modern France*. New York: Oxford University Press, 1996, pp. 80–101.

Slavin, Morris. *The Hébertistes to the Guillotine: Anatomy of a 'Conspiracy' in Revolutionary France*. Baton Rouge, LA, and London: Louisiana State University Press, 1994.

—. *The Making of an Insurrection: Parisian Sections and the Gironde*. Cambridge, MA, and London: Harvard University Press, 1986.

Sledziewski, Élisabeth G. 'The French Revolution as the Turning Point', in Geneviève Fraisse and Michelle Perrot (eds), *A History of Women in the West: Emerging Feminism from Revolution to World War*, translated by Arthur Goldhammer. Cambridge, MA: Harvard University Press, 1993.

Smart, Annie K. *Citoyennes: Women and the Ideal of Citizenship in Eighteenth-Century France*. Newark, DE: University of Delaware Press, 2011.

Smith, Jay M. *Nobility Reimagined: The Patriotic Nation in Eighteenth-Century France*. Ithaca, NY, and London: Cornell University Press, 2005.

Soboul, Albert. *Comprendre la Révolution: problèmes politiques de la Révolution française (1789–1797)*. Paris: F. Maspero, 1981; translated by April A. Knutson as *Understanding the French Revolution*. New York: International Publishers, 1988.

—. *Paysans, sans-culottes et Jacobins*. Paris: Clavreuil, 1966.

—. *Précis d'histoire de la Révolution française*. Paris: Éditions Sociales, 1962; translated by Alan Forrest and Colin Jones as *The French Revolution, 1787–1799: From the Storming of the Bastille to Napoleon*. New York: Vintage Books, 1975.

—. *Problèmes paysans de la Révolution, 1789–1848*. Paris: François Maspero, 1976.

—. *The Parisian Sans-Culottes and the French Revolution, 1793–4*, translated by Gwynne Lewis. Oxford: Oxford University Press, 1964.

— (ed.). *Contributions à l'histoire paysanne de la Révolution française, 1789–1848*. Paris: Éditions Sociales, 1977.

Sonenscher, Michael. *Before the Deluge: Public Debt, Inequality, and the Intellectual Origins of the French Revolution*. Princeton, NJ: Princeton University Press, 2007.

Sottocasa, Valérie. *Mémoires affrontées. Protestants et catholiques face à la Révolution dans les montagnes du Languedoc*. Rennes: Presses Universitaires de Rennes, 2004.

Spagnoli, Paul. 'The Unique Decline of Mortality in Revolutionary France', *Journal of Family History*, 22 (1997), pp. 425–61.

Spang, Rebecca L. *Stuff and Money in the Time of the French Revolution*. Cambridge, MA: Harvard University Press, 2015.

—. *The Invention of the Restaurant: Paris and Modern Gastronomic Culture*. Cambridge, MA: Harvard University Press, 2000.

Spary, E. C. *Utopia's Garden: French Natural History from Old Regime to Revolution*. Chicago, IL, and London: University of Chicago Press, 2000.

Stein, Robert. 'The Profitability of the Nantes Slave Trade, 1783–1792', *Journal of Economic History*, 35 (1975), pp. 779–93.

Suratteau, Jean-René, and François Gendron (eds). *Dictionnaire historique de la Révolution française*. Paris: PUF, 1989.

—. 'Justice and Murder: Massacres in the Provinces, Versailles, Meaux and Reims in 1792', *P&P*, 222 (2014), pp. 129–62.

Sutherland, D. M. G. *Murder in Aubagne: Lynching, Law, and Justice during the French Revolution*. Cambridge and New York: Cambridge University Press, 2009.

—. 'Peasants, Lords, and Leviathan: Winners and Losers from the Abolition of French Feudalism, 1780–1820', *Journal of Economic History*, 62 (2002), pp. 1–24.

—. *The Chouans: The Social Origins of Popular Counter-Revolution in Upper Brittany, 1770–1796*. Oxford: Oxford University Press, 1982.

—. *The French Revolution and Empire: The Quest for a Civic Order*. Oxford: Blackwell, 2003.

Swann, Julian, and Joël Félix (eds). *The Crisis of the Absolute Monarchy: France from Old Regime to Revolution*, published for The British Academy. Oxford: Oxford University Press, 2013.

Sydenham, Michael. *The Girondins*. London: Athlone Press, 1961.

Tackett, Timothy. *Becoming a Revolutionary: The Deputies of the French National Assembly and the Emergence of a Revolutionary Culture (1789–1790)*. Princeton, NJ: Princeton University Press, 1996.

—. *Religion, Revolution, and Regional Culture in Eighteenth-Century France: The Ecclesiastical Oath of 1791*. Princeton, NJ: Princeton University Press, 1986.

—. *The Coming of the Terror in the French Revolution*. Cambridge, MA, and London: The Belknap Press of Harvard University Press, 2015.

—. *When the King took Flight*. Cambridge, MA: Harvard University Press, 2003.

—. 'Collective Panics in the Early French Revolution, 1789–1791: A Comparative Perspective', *FH*, 17 (2003), pp. 149–71.

Taws, Richard. *The Politics of the Provisional: Art and Ephemera in Revolutionary France*. Philadelphia, PA: Pennsylvania State University Press, 2013.

Taylor, Katherine. 'Geometries of Power: Royal, Revolutionary, and Post-Revolutionary French Courtrooms', *Journal of the Society of Architectural Historians*, 72 (2013), pp. 434–74.

Thery, Irène, and Christian Biet (eds). *La Famille, la loi, l'État. De la Révolution au Code Civil*. Paris: Imprimerie Nationale Éditions, 1989.

Thien, Ly-Hoang. 'La Bibliothèque Nationale sous la Révolution', *Dix-huitième siècle* 14 (1982), pp. 75–88.

Thomas, Chantal. *The Wicked Queen: The Origins of the Myth of Marie-Antoinette*, translated by Julie Rose. New York: Zone Books, 1999.

Thompson, Eric. *Popular Sovereignty and the French Constituent Assembly, 1789–1791*. Manchester: Manchester University Press, 1952.

Thompson, J. M. *Robespierre*. Oxford: Blackwell, 1935.

Thomson, J. K. J. *Clermont-de-Lodève, 1633–1789: Fluctuations in the Prosperity of a Languedocian Cloth-Making Town*. Cambridge: Cambridge University Press, 1982.

Tilly, Charles. 'The Emergence of Citizenship in France and Elsewhere', *International Review of Social History* 40 (1995), pp. 223–36.

—. *The Vendée*. Cambridge, MA: Harvard University Press, 1964.

Ulbrich, Claudia. 'Sarreguemines en révolution ou l'histoire d'un "caméléon politique"', *Annales de l'Est*, 44 (1992), pp. 15–34.

Valin, Claudy. *Autopsie d'un massacre. Les journées des 21 et 22 mars 1793 à La Rochelle*. St-Jean-d'Angély: Éditions Bordessoules, 1992.

—. *La Rochelle-la Vendée, 1793. Révolution et Contre-Révolution*. Paris: Le Croît vif, 1997.

Van Kley, Dale K. *The French Idea of Freedom: The Old Regime and the Declaration of Rights of 1789*. Stanford, CA: Stanford University Press, 1994.

—. *The Jansenists and the Expulsion of the Jesuits from France*. New Haven, CT, and London: Yale University Press, 1975.

—. *The Religious Origins of the French Revolution: From Calvin to the Civil Constitution, 1560–1791*. New Haven, CT, and London: Yale University Press, 1996.

—. 'The Abolition of the Guilds during the French Revolution', *FHS*, 15 (1988), pp. 704–17.

Vardi, Liana. *The Land and the Loom: Peasants and Profit in Northern France, 1680–1800.* Durham, NC, and London: Duke University Press, 1993.

—. *The Physiocrats and the World of the Enlightenment.* Cambridge and New York: Cambridge University Press, 2012.

Velde, Francois R., and David R. Weir. 'The Financial Debt Market and Government Debt Policy in France, 1746–1793', *Journal of Economic History*, 52 (1992), pp. 1–39.

Velicu, Adrian. *Civic Catechisms and Reason in the French Revolution.* Farnham, Surrey, and Burlington, VT: Ashgate, 2010.

Verjus, Anne. *Le Bon mari: une histoire politique des hommes et des femmes à l'époque révolutionnaire.* Paris: Fayard, 2010.

Viallaneix, Paul, and Jean Ehrard (eds). *Aimer en France, 1760–1860. Actes du colloque international de Clermont-Ferrand.* Clermont-Ferrand: Faculté des Lettres et Sciences Humaines, 1980.

Vidalenc, Jean. *Les Émigrés français, 1789–1825.* Caen: Associations des Publications de la Faculté des Lettres et Sciences Humaines de l'Université de Caen, 1963.

Vinot, Bernard. 'La Révolution au village, avec Saint-Just, d'après le registre des délibérations communales de Blérancourt', *AHRF*, 335 (2004), pp. 97–110.

Vivier, Nadine. *Propriété collective et identité communale. Les Biens communaux en France, 1750–1914.* Paris: Publications de la Sorbonne, 1998.

Voies nouvelles pour l'histoire de la Révolution française. Paris: Bibliothèque Nationale, 1978.

Vovelle, Michel. *Combats pour la Révolution française.* Paris: Éditions la Découverte/SÉR, 1993.

—. *La Découverte de la politique. Géopolitique de la Révolution française.* Paris: Éditions la Découverte, 1993.

—. *La Mentalité révolutionnaire: société et mentalité sous la Révolution française.* Paris: Messidor/Éditions Sociales, 1985.

—. 'Le Tournant des mentalités en France, 1750–1789: la "sensibilité" pré-Révolutionnaire', *SH*, 5 (1977), pp. 605–29.

—. *The Fall of the Monarchy (1787–1792)*, translated by Susan Burke. Cambridge: Cambridge University Press, 1983.

—. *The Revolution against the Church: From Reason to the Supreme Being.* Cambridge: Cambridge University Press, 1991.

— (ed.). *Révolution et République: l'exception française.* Paris: Éditions Kimé, 1994.

Wahnich, Sophie. *In Defence of the Terror: Liberty or Death in the French Revolution*, translated by David Fernbach. London and New York: Verso, 2012.

—. *L'Impossible citoyen: l'étranger dans le discours de la Révolution française.* Paris: Albin Michel, 1997.

Waldinger, Renée, Philip Dawson and Isser Woloch (eds). *The French Revolution and the Meaning of Citizenship.* Westport, CT: Greenwood Press, 1993.

Walshaw, Jill Maciak. *A Show of Hands for the Republic: Opinion, Information, and Repression in Eighteenth-Century Rural France.* Rochester, NY: Rochester University Press, 2014.

Walter, Gérard. *Robespierre*, 2 vols. Paris: Gallimard, 1961.

Walton, Charles. *Policing Public Opinion in the French Revolution: The Culture of Calumny and the Problem of Free Speech.* Oxford and New York: Oxford University Press, 2009.

Walzer, Michael (ed.). *Regicide and Revolution: Speeches at the Trial of Louis XVI.* New York: Columbia University Press, 1974.

Whiteman, Jeremy. *Reform, Revolution and French Global Policy, 1787–1791.* Aldershot and Burlington, VT: Ashgate, 2002.

Williams, David, and Maire Cross (eds). *The French Experience from Republic to Monarchy, 1792–1824: New Dawns in Politics, Knowledge and Culture.* Basingstoke: Palgrave Macmillan, 2000.

Wismes, Armel de. *Nantes et le temps des négriers.* Paris: Éditions France-Empire, 1983.

Wittman, Richard. *Architecture, Print Culture, and the Public Sphere in Eighteenth-Century France.* New York and London: Routledge, 2007.

Woell, Edward J. *Small-Town Martyrs and Murderers: Religious Revolution and Counter-Revolution in Western France, 1774–1914.* Milwaukee, WI: Marquette University Press, 2006.

Woloch, Isser. *The French Veteran from the Revolution to the Restoration.* Chapel Hill, NC: University of North Carolina Press, 1979.

—. *The New Regime: Transformations of the French Civic Order, 1789–1820s.* New York: W. W. Norton, 1994.

Woronoff, Denis. *Histoire de l'industrie en France: du XVIe siècle à nos jours*. Paris: Éditions du Seuil, 1998.

— (ed.). *Revolution et espaces forestiers. Colloque des 3 & 4 juin 1987. Groupe d'histoire des forêts françaises*. Paris: L'Harmattan, 1988.

Wrigley, Richard. *The Politics of Appearances: Representations of Dress in Revolutionary France*. Oxford and New York: Berg Publishers, 2002.

Wylie, Lawrence. *Chanzeaux: A Village in Anjou*. Cambridge, MA: Harvard University Press, 1966.

Ziesche, Philipp. *Cosmopolitan Patriots: Americans in Paris in the Age of Revolution*. Charlottesville, VA, and London: University of Virginia Press, 2010.

INDEX

Abancourt, Gabriel-Isidore Blondin d' 153
Abbeville 5
Aelders, Etta Palm d' 111
agricultural labourers 5, 40, 54, 64, 76, 176,
226, 257, 258, 285, 353, 354, 358, 360,
365
agriculture 3–7, 10, 26, 28, 54, 258, 295, 322,
332, 348, 351, 355, 357, 358
Aisne (department) 89, 133, 134, 162, 171,
196, 211, 229, 278, 292, 354
Aix-en-Provence xiv, 59, 90, 125, 131, 278,
289
Albert, Abbé 2
Albitte, Antoine 215, 247
Alençon 59, 76, 224, 368
Alès 154
Allarde Law, d' 107, 134
Allassac 97
Allier, Abbé Claude 212
Allier (department) 202
Alps (region) 2, 15, 241, 303, 326
Alsace (region) 10, 15, 76, 92, 96, 97, 129,
148, 235, 287
Amelot, Bishop 127
Amelot, Comtesse d' 108
America
  Latin 165, 367, 369
  North 24, 35, 37, 144, 362, 366–8
American
  Republic 24, 35, 38, 81, 87, 99, 144, 159,
  235, 302, 314, 330, 343, 362, 366
  Revolution 80, 159, 385
  War of Independence 24, 38, 41, 43, 56, 72,
  151, 313
Americans 102, 159, 234, 299, 313, 384
Amiens 5, 58, 142, 226, 285, 312
  Treaty of 340
Amis de la Constitution see Jacobin clubs

Amis des Noirs 38, 105
ancien régime xi, 1–22, 55, 80, 88, 89, 93, 96,
97, 107, 111, 148–9, 151, 173, 178, 182,
187, 193, 204, 220–2, 226, 231, 235, 236,
238, 239, 241, 243, 244, 248, 272, 289,
290, 300, 302, 308, 316, 321, 336, 348,
349, 352, 353, 365
Anduze 245, 365
Angers 12, 20, 121, 173, 177–8, 191, 317,
353
Anjou (region) 12, 111, 125, 126, 127, 190,
306, 322
Annonay 197
archives 54, 103, 168
Ardennes (department) 266
Argentan 210
army 9, 14, 15–16, 32, 151, 158, 162,
165–7, 171, 173, 175, 194, 197, 199,
200, 212, 224, 232–3, 237, 248, 252,
256, 261, 275, 283, 286, 290, 292–3,
307–8, 314, 330, 332, 334, 338, 342,
346, 351, 357, 363
  Catholic and Royal – Vendéan 178, 214,
  227, 229, 232, 325
  conscription 176–8, 190, 196, 211, 222,
  226, 234, 259, 298, 312–13, 318, 327,
  329, 331–2, 365
  deserters from 210–11, 228, 234, 259, 298,
  320
  Napoleon and 302–3, 336, 340, 377
  nobles and 15–16, 29, 67, 115, 119, 139,
  153, 175, 183, 194
  republican 179, 183–4, 186, 197, 194,
  210–212, 228–9, 233–4, 237, 256, 265–6,
  316–8
  royal 149, 171, 173, 175
  unrest in 117, 152, 256
  volunteers 160, 173–5, 200, 211, 328

Arras 8–10, 19, 23–4, 29, 102, 142, 254, 264, 270, 275, 353

artisans 5, 7–8, 37, 64, 66, 72, 76, 89, 107, 148, 169, 177, 178, 192, 193, 222–3, 226, 237, 352, 354

Artois, Comte d' 33, 50, 73, 115–16, 139, 149

Artois (province) xiv, 9, 19, 23, 29, 59–60, 65, 66, 89, 297

Ascain 228

assassinations *see* killings, extra-judicial

Assemblée législative *see* Legislative Assembly

Assemblée nationale *see* National Assembly

Assembly of Notables 42–3, 46, 50

assignats xiii, 92–3, 106, 184, 220, 222, 247, 253, 309, 315–5, 356

Atlantic trade 36, 56, 105, 176, 192

Attichy 293

Aubagne 189

Auch 18, 222, 239, 322

Aude (department) *see also* Carcassonne 108, 175, 356

August Decree on Feudalism 77–8, 87, 97–8, 108–9, 139, 144, 148, 342

Auribeau, Alexandre d' 368

Aurillac 151, 333

Australia 181, 271, 368

Austria 86, 139, 150, 153, 156–9, 235, 294, 305, 326, 327, 330, 340, 345, 367, 368

Austrians 32, 44, 86, 104, 154, 162, 165, 166, 174, 175, 214, 227, 266, 268, 291, 303, 314, 316, 330, 337, 340

Autun (diocese) 49, 76, 91, 100, 125

Auvergne (region) 2, 17, 19, 27, 193, 255

Auxerre 167, 229, 244

Aveyron (department) 237

Avignon 15, 19, 90, 96, 120, 124, 147–8, 153, 216, 315

Babeuf, François Noël ('Gracchus') 143, 276, 311, 338

'bacchanals' *see also* strikes 134, 258

Bagarre de Nîmes 115, 130, 154

Bailly, Claude 301, 331

Bailly, Jean-Sylvain 70, 72–3, 85, 115, 152, 230

banalités 17, 63, 65, 358

Bande à Salambier *see* Salambier, Bande à

'bacchanals' *see also* strikes 134, 258

Bara, Joseph 236, 300

Barbaroux, Charles Jean-Marie 155

Barère de Vieuzac, Bertrand 87–8, 209, 210, 215, 288, 338, 347

Barnave, Antoine 68, 106, 114, 136, 138, 152, 200, 230, 280

Barras, Paul 247, 269, 276, 300, 317, 333, 337

Basire, Claude 150, 235

Basque (language) 63, 199

Basques, Pays Basque 2, 89, 228, 348, 350

Bas-Rhin (department) *see also* Alsace 287

Basses-Pyrénées (department) *see also* Pyrenees 89

Bastille 32, 39, 72–6, 85, 86, 93, 99, 100, 102, 104, 108, 135, 148, 200, 213, 218

anniversaries of 14 July 147, 154, 208, 286, 366

Place de la 265

Bayeux 13, 311, 317, 357, 358

Bayonne 15, 18

Bazin de Bezons, Armand 21

Beauce (region) 3, 312

Beaufort-en-Vallée 101

Beaumarchais 29

Beaumont, Chassepot de 3–4

Beaumont, Gustave de 362

Beauvais 7

Beauvais, Abbé de 15

Beccaria, Cesare 28

Bédarieux 4

beggars *see also* poor relief 19, 31, 76, 196

Belley 222, 249

Belley, Jean-Baptiste 304

Bergerac 134, 189, 245, 277

Bernouville 175

Berry (region) 60, 125

Besançon 33, 59

Besse (region) 59

Béziers 4, 65, 357

Bigorre (region) 87–8

Billard (of) Saint-Denis-en-Val 59, 134, 341

Billaud-Varenne, Jean-Nicolas 144, 261, 269, 288, 338

births *see* population

Bizanet 92

Blérancourt 180

Blois 18

bocage 127, 176, 193

Boigne, Adèle d'Osmonde, Comtesse de 119

Boissy d'Anglas, François-Antoine 197–8, 293, 294, 322

Bonaparte, Napoléon xi, 181, 216, 247, 298, 300, 302–3, 313, 316, 318, 319, 326–7, 333–41, 354, 364

Bonnet, Antoine 222

Bonnet Rouge (section) 182

bonnet rouge see also phrygian cap, liberty cap 168, 195, 237, 241

books *see* literature

Bordeaux 6–7, 10, 15, 35–6, 40, 45, 73, 78, 83, 96, 100, 106, 125, 148, 161, 169, 173, 176, 185, 186, 189, 197, 203, 209, 216, 226, 231, 140, 245, 271, 274, 275, 280, 289, 351

Bossuet, Jacques-Bénigne 33

Bouillé, Marquis de 117, 132, 152

Bouillerot, Nicholas 27
Bouisse, Baron Saint Jean de 109
Boulogne, Augustin 300
Boulogne-sur-Mer 27, 123, 224
Bouquier Law 236
Bourdon, Léonard 179, 219
Bourg 76, 280, 309
Bourges 60–1, 121, 184
Bousbecque 282
Boutenac 92
Bresse (region) 75–6
Bressuire 233
Brest 117, 158, 165, 281
Breton, Bretons 52, 64, 66, 68, 85, 89, 101,
    123, 134, 147, 165, 178, 203, 256, 281,
    290, 306, 313, 314, 348
  language 63, 64, 256, 306, 348
Bridaine, Father 13
'brigands' 41, 75–6, 161, 200, 213, 232, 279,
    306
Brissot, Jacques-Pierre 38, 56, 105, 111, 144,
    148, 149, 151, 156, 165, 169, 171, 176,
    200, 230, 231, 291
Brissotins 150, 152–3, 155, 158, 345
Britain 35, 37–8, 111, 181, 291, 294, 313, 318,
    330, 335, 340, 366–8
Brittany (region) 2, 13–14, 19, 20, 45,
    52, 63–5, 75, 77, 89, 93, 97, 108,
    121, 126, 127, 144, 160, 190, 191–4,
    207, 209, 270–1, 290, 306, 313, 358, 3
    65, 366
Brunswick, Duke of 158, 160, 164
  manifesto of 158, 184
Brussels 266, 292
Buissart,
    Antoine 23, 254, 270
    Charlotte 254, 270
Burgundy (region) 4, 10, 16, 19, 54, 125,
    135, 175, 222, 229, 243, 244, 311,
    344, 355
business (sector) see also commerce 162, 197,
    223, 352, 355
Buzot, François 111

Cabarrus, Thérésia 216, 274–6, 300
Caen 185, 190, 197, 205
cahiers de doléances 60–5, 75, 77, 78, 80, 96,
    119, 121, 123, 176, 191, 366
Cahors 97
Cailhava, Jean-François 221
Caillot, Antoine 67
Calméjanne (seigneur) 98
Calonne Charles-Alexandre de 42–3, 53,
    94, 98
Calvados (department) 126, 193
Cambon, Joseph 220, 251, 269
Cambrai 59, 264
Cambrésis (region) 12, 59

'camps de Jalès' 130, 154, 212
Canal du Midi 55
Carbonne 336
Carcassonne 21, 58, 108, 153, 277, 354
Caribbean 10, 35–6, 37, 47, 105, 176, 186,
    248, 275, 294, 330, 350, 367
Cassanyes, Joseph 172
Castelnaudary 70, 107
Cathelineau, Jacques 214
Catalan, Catalans see also language 2, 62, 172,
    198, 199, 241, 329, 348, 350
Catholic Church, Catholicism 1, 2, 3, 8, 9,
    12–14, 18, 30, 61, 91–2, 96, 119, 120–1,
    122, 126, 129, 147, 159, 189, 190, 198,
    203, 236, 244, 282, 289, 307, 309, 312,
    329, 330, 353, 359
  reforms to 119–129, 246–7, 296, 307–8,
    325
cattle 7, 176, 357
Caux, pays de (region) 80
Célarié, Michel 97
Cercle social 111
Cévennes (region) 14, 115, 128, 245, 315
Chabot, François 220, 226, 235
Chalier, Joseph 186, 205, 214, 236
Châlons-sur-Marne 133, 241
Chambéry 165
Champagne (region) 1, 4, 40, 42, 64, 125, 332
Champ de Mars 24, 100, 113
  massacre 136–7, 171
Charente-Inférieure (department) 108
Charitas (Papal Bull) 124
charity see poor relief
Charlier, Louis-Joseph 243
Charon, Joseph 48
Charpentier, Marie-Anne 258, 316, 340
Charrier, Marc-Antoine 212
Chartres 29, 53, 137, 171, 181, 279
Château-Thierry 133, 135
châteaux, destruction of 59, 75, 76, 151, 154,
    247
Chavignon 124
Chénier, André 265, 281
Chénier, Marie-Joseph 113, 135, 243, 281
children see also education, inheritance laws
    xi, 7, 12, 16, 20, 36, 47, 49, 76, 104, 112,
    121, 165, 188, 192, 207, 221, 232, 233,
    236, 241, 282, 284, 295, 300, 331, 349,
    360, 365
  outside wedlock 29, 114, 237,
    349–50
  revolutionary names 114, 241–2, 281
Chinon 301
Cholet 177, 214, 227, 233, 236
Chouans 290, 315, 325, 331, 363
Choudieu, René 173
Cicé, Champion de (Archbishop of
    Bordeaux) 78

citizen(s) 27, 48, 98, 99 128, 134, 137, 139, 152, 154, 155, 165, 166, 167, 172, 174, 180, 181, 182, 186, 204, 205, 207, 217, 221, 223, 235, 246, 257, 262, 265, 276, 277, 278, 284, 286, 291, 293, 296, 297, 298, 299, 306, 314, 338, 344, 345, 346, 348, 349
   active 93–4, 110, 111, 122, 124, 145, 148
   passive 93–4, 136
citizenesses 112, 173, 180, 207, 225–6, 231, 232, 242, 254, 262, 276, 285, 299, 324, 348
citizenship 41, 63–4, 96, 105, 109, 159, 226, 236, 254, 339, 343, 345, 347, 350, 359
Civil Code (1804) 350
Civil Constitution of the Clergy (12 July 1790) 121, 123–5, 128, 131, 135, 153, 156, 177, 191, 197, 198, 201–3, 305
classical antiquity, references to 27, 33–5, 37, 51, 81, 83, 114, 151, 168, 180, 201, 209, 218, 241, 249, 261, 267, 268, 271, 272, 281–2, 291, 321, 336, 338, 349
Clavière, Étienne 38, 111
clergy see also individual religious orders 1, 3, 8, 12–14, 18, 29, 49, 52–3, 60, 61, 63, 67–9, 76, 78, 83, 88, 91, 93, 100, 107, 113, 119, 123, 124, 125, 126, 148, 156, 169, 176–7, 190, 193–8, 213, 223, 243, 259, 320, 325, 340, 346, 353, 358–9
   constitutional 123–9, 159, 246, 202, 245, 305–7
   marriage of 83, 172, 246, 325, 364
   non-juring, refractory 123–9, 131, 139, 150–1, 154, 157, 159, 178, 191–2, 229, 233, 261, 316, 318
Clermont-Ferrand 202, 236
Clermont-Tonnerre, Stanislas, Comte de 81
Cloots, Jean-Baptiste du Val-de-Grâce, Baron de (Anarchasis) 102–3, 159, 165, 235, 250
clothes see dress
Club des Amis de la Constitution
   see also Jacobin clubs, Cordelier club, Feuillant club xii, 110–2, 162, 182, 184, 193, 195, 226, 237, 243, 253, 278, 295, 299, 343, 344, 348
Cluny 76
Coblenz 149, 153
Code Napoléon see Napoleonic Code
Coëtbugat 97
coffee 36, 226
Cohin, Pierre 211
Coigny, Duc de 51
Collioure 199, 241, 311
Collot d'Herbois, Jean-Marie 180, 215–16, 231, 269, 288, 338
Colmar 114
colonies 105

Canada 35, 37
Chandernagore, Pondichéry 35, 181–2
   Guadeloupe 35–6, 249, 294, 351
   Martinique 35–6, 276, 318
   Réunion 36, 351
   Saint-Domingue 35–6, 56, 105, 136, 145–6, 186, 191, 194, 249, 303, 350
   Saint-Lucie 35, 337, 351
   Sénégal 36, 105, 304
comités révolutionnaires see revolutionary committees
commerce see also transport 2, 26, 29, 36, 42, 56, 62, 106, 152, 176, 191, 249, 296, 302, 322, 334, 344, 348
committees 76, 188, 204, 206, 211–15, 225, 228, 236, 240, 247–53, 266, 268, 278,
   of general security 183, 224, 240, 260, 265, 269, 287, 303, 336, 348
   of public safety 183, 208–10, 224, 228, 234, 240, 242, 248, 250, 252–3, 261, 265, 267–9, 271, 274–5, 293, 338
Committee on Feudalism (National Assembly) 98
common land 63, 90, 98, 108–9, 143–5, 220–3, 310, 357–8
communes 88, 93, 94, 98, 108–9, 121, 193, 220–2, 233, 241–2, 257, 298, 347, 358
Commune of Paris (1792–) 179, 184, 225, 231, 238, 253, 269
communication see also newspapers, petitions, transport 90, 115, 149, 210, 218, 231, 240, 283, 299, 330, 332
compagnonnages see guilds
Compiègne 293
Comtat-Venaissin (region) 15, 147, 153, 261, 327
Condé, Prince de 139, 193, 255
Condé-sur-L'Escaut 283–4
Condillac 30
Condorcet, Marie-Jean-Antoine, Marquis de 49, 67, 99, 111, 148, 323
conscription see army
Conspiracy, allegations of 34, 51, 59, 73, 75, 81, 83, 114–5, 117, 136, 140, 143, 149–50, 155, 158, 161, 170, 186–7, 201–2, 205, 213, 214, 217, 230–2, 235, 250, 251, 264, 266, 268, 269–70, 272, 275, 317
Constituent Assembly see National Assembly
constitutions 17, 48, 50, 51, 70, 95, 225, 250, 257, 319, 324, 329, 338, 340, 347
Constitution (1791) 91, 100–1, 117, 131, 136–8, 140, 142–3, 147–9, 152, 159, 165, 171–2, 341
Constitution (1793) 206–7, 209, 213, 216–7, 234, 237, 248, 267, 276, 282, 285, 286–7, 295, 296–8, 311, 330, 353
Constitution of Year III (1795) 295–7, 301, 302, 322, 325, 341

Consuls 338
Conti, Prince de 16, 90
convents *see* religious orders
Cook, Captain James 27, 182
Corbières (region) 54, 108, 165, 347
Corday, Charlotte 205, 216
Cordeliers Club 110, 129, 136, 254
Cornwallis, General 37
corporations *see also* guilds 6, 98, 107, 134
Corsica 18, 37, 102, 148, 181, 319, 368
corruption, allegations of 29, 34, 82, 138, 170, 235, 238, 250, 262, 305
corvée 110, 355
costume *see* dress
cotton 5, 36, 269
Couet, August 262
Coulommiers 214
Coutelet, Marie-Madeleine 260
Couthon, Georges 208, 215, 264
Council of Five Hundred 295, 298, 304, 316, 321, 336–8
counter-revolution 134, 149, 153, 154, 158, 163, 178, 185, 187–9, 196, 198, 205–6, 212–3, 216, 227, 228, 231–2, 236, 238, 240, 243, 247, 252, 254, 264, 271–2, 284, 285, 290, 297, 306, 318, 319, 322, 327, 331, 358–9,
counter-revolutionaries 131, 150, 160, 183, 201, 214, 226, 244, 288, 358
courts 1, 11, 13, 16, 17, 19, 41, 94, 95–6, 98, 107, 117, 160, 196, 244, 264, 278, 314, 349, 353
seigneurial 78, 354
Courville 181
Creil 195
Créquy, Victoire de Froulay de Tessé, Marquise de x, 90, 99
crime(s) *see also* killings, extra-judicial xii, 28, 40, 85, 95, 117, 131, 137, 148, 172, 179, 224, 230, 231, 246, 280, 292, 312, 340
Cromwell, Oliver 37, 151
crops *see* harvests

Damoye, Antoine-Pierre 7, 183–4
Dansard, Claude 111
Danton, Georges-Jacques 110, 163, 165, 169, 170, 183, 235, 248–51, 252, 265, 281, 326
Dantonists 275
Dauch, Martin 70
Dauphiné (region) 43, 46
David, Jacques-Louis 34–5, 81, 103, 113, 152, 205–6, 208, 217–8, 230, 236, 240, 260, 262, 267, 303–4, 336
deaths (violent) *see also* killings, extra-judicial, population 73, 95, 115, 117, 130, 146, 157, 230, 259, 272, 358

dechristianization 243–4, 246–7, 337
Declaration of the Rights of Man and the Citizen 78–80, 82, 84, 86, 87, 93, 96, 102–7, 112, 120, 124, 149, 151, 155, 206, 209, 216–8, 272, 282, 289, 291, 296, 345, 350, 361,
deference 18, 21–2, 85, 345, 354
Delzigue, Jeanne-Victoire 58–9, 258, 275
Demissy, Pierre Samuel 105
Delahaye, Pierre Louis-Nicolas 75, 110
Delaunay, Joseph 220
Desmoulins, Camille 34, 71, 93, 117, 138, 169, 200, 208, 213, 248–9, 251–2, 265, 281
Diamond Necklace Affair 39–40, 42
Diderot, Denis 25, 28, 35
Dieppe 285, 357
Directory 296–320, 322–6, 330–4, 337–42, 351, 354, 356
divorce *see also* women, marriage 111, 195, 208, 216, 304, 349–50, 369
Dole 197
domaine congéable 64, 97, 144, 306, 331, 358
Dordogne (department) 221, 237, 277
River 134, 189, 342
dress
aristocratic 15, 168
peasant 66, 356–7
revolutionary 101, 206, 223, 242, 263, 291
Dubois-Crancé, Edmond 173, 186, 215, 290, 293
Dubois de Fosseux, Ferdinand 29
Ducos, Pierre-Roger 337–8
Dufour, Léon 188, 195
Dumas, Alexandre 194, 303, 346, 363–4
Dumas, René 197
Dumouriez, Charles-François 164, 175, 186, 194, 217
Dunkerque 36
Duport, Adrien 49, 68, 83, 114, 152
Durban 258
Durosoi, Barnabé 131
Duval d'Eprémesnil, Jean Jacques 46, 51

Easter 14, 127, 131, 258, 316, 340
École Polytechique 283
economic liberalism 107–8, 139, 169, 296–7
Eden, William Lord Auckland 174
education *see also* children 13, 30–1, 66, 80, 82, 120, 168, 215, 217, 236–7, 243, 255, 262, 282–3, 295, 307, 324, 347–9, 353
Égalité (section) 241
Effiat, Château 193
Egypt 328, 334–6, 364
Elbeuf 5, 62

elections 42, 50, 66, 68–9, 83, 88, 89, 93–4, 110, 112, 122, 164, 175, 203, 207, 249, 302, 314, 316–7, 325–6, 337, 343–4, 348, 366
   participation 65, 93–4, 109–10, 142, 148, 207, 226, 295, 343–4, 348, 366
élites 18, 48, 56, 99, 152, 159, 170, 185, 194, 197–9, 253, 288, 346, 347, 353, 354–6
émigrés 100, 119, 139, 149–51, 153, 157, 162, 168–9, 183, 188, 193–4, 197, 204, 211, 255, 305, 316, 325–6, 340, 344, 356
empires, colonial 6, 35, 37–8, 55–6, 105, 148, 165, 176, 330, 366
Empire, Holy Roman 39, 314, 337
Empire, Napoleonic 345, 359
Empire, Ottoman 147, 330, 334–5
England see Britain
Enlightenment 24–7, 30, 35, 213, 236, 272, 362, 365, 367
Enragés 224–5, 242
Entrecasteaux, Bruny, d' 368
environmental concerns see also common land, forests 108, 145, 358, 361
Erceville 64
Ermenonville 30, 213, 281
Esgrigny, Chevalier d' 154
Essarts, Nicolas Toussaint des 41
Estates-General 44, 46–73
Eure (department) 126, 172, 193, 337–8
   River 185
Eure-et-Loir (department) 137
Europe xi, 1–2, 6, 20, 24–5, 30, 35, 37, 86–7, 103–5, 116, 131, 138, 144, 148–51, 153–4, 159, 168, 173, 191, 209, 214, 224, 227, 234, 248, 266, 290–1, 294, 305, 313, 319, 329, 332, 337, 345, 360, 367, 369
Évreux 52, 185

Falbaire, Fenouillot de 180
family relationships 3, 7, 16, 188–9, 190, 194–5, 201–3, 207–8, 213, 246, 255, 260, 262, 266, 278, 287, 299, 300, 301–2, 331–2, 342, 349–50, 354–5, 356, 360–1, 365
famine see hunger
Fauchet, Claude Abbé 126
Faure, Pierre 169
Favier, Gilbert-Amable 174–5, 328
Favras, Thomas de Mahy, Marquis de 115
federalism, federalists 185–6, 189, 205, 209, 213, 214–6, 227, 244, 247, 260, 266, 269, 271–2, 274, 276–8, 288, 364
federation movement 99–100
fear 50, 53, 74, 75–6, 77, 138, 139, 140, 142, 146, 149–50, 163, 175, 180, 183, 186–7,

214, 257, 264, 267, 269, 270, 272–3, 274, 284, 299, 321, 341, 355, 366
feminists 111–12, 225–6, 231, 348
Fernig, Félicité and Théophile 175
festivals 53, 101, 118, 129, 152, 207, 219, 220, 236, 246, 255, 257–8, 261–2, 282, 300–1, 323, 324, 333, 335
   Festival of Federation 100, 113, 140, 208
   Festival of Reason 244, 300
   Festival of the Supreme Being 262–4, 268
   Festival of the Unity and Indivisibility of the Republic 206, 208
feudalism see seigneurialism
Feuillants 138, 148–50
Figueur, Marie-Thérèse 175
First Estate see clergy
fiscal crisis 45–6, 49, 51, 55–6, 60, 91, 203
Flanders (region) 10, 154, 235
Flemish (language) 2, 63, 199
Flesselles, Jacques de 73
Fleurus, battle of 266, 290
flight to Varennes 132–4, 140
Florac 315
Fontfroide 92
Fonton, Antoine 181
food 3, 6–7, 9, 11, 13, 31, 51, 59, 60, 75–6, 83, 85, 108, 135, 151, 174, 226, 237, 244–5, 250, 255, 257, 267, 285, 293, 298, 315, 356
   riots 12, 21, 51, 54, 59, 68, 71, 83–4, 171, 226, 284–6
foreign policy, French 18, 37–8, 146–51, 153, 290, 294, 303, 313, 326, 339
forests 4, 108–9, 144–5, 197, 259, 304, 310, 332, 358
Forster, Georg 182–3
Fouché, Joseph 215, 243, 269, 276, 337
Foulon, Joseph 73–4
Fournas de la Brosse, Blaise de 153
Fragonard, Jean-Honoré 209
Fraïsse 109
Franche-Comté (region) 59, 125, 197
Franklin, Benjamin 24, 35, 102, 241
French language see also language 1–2, 34, 63, 91, 191, 198, 255, 282, 292, 345–8
Fréron, Louis-Stanislas 247, 269, 276, 279, 287
Fricasse, Jacques 200
Froment, François 115, 130

Gabian 4–5, 12, 259
Gaillard, Dame 154
Gamas, Marin (citizen) 168, 300
gaols see prisons
Gap 59
Gard (department) 130, 151, 221, 241, 365
Garesché, Daniel 105, 192

Garnier de Saintes, Jacques 179
Gascon language *see also* language 87, 91, 347
Gascony (region) 18, 87, 91, 347
Géneste, Antoine 250
Genoa 37
Gensonné, Armand 155, 169
Géraud, Edmond 86, 161, 209
Gers (department) 222
Girardin, René, Marquis de 29, 213, 276
Gironde (department) 169, 173
Girondins 169–72, 175–6, 179, 183–6, 189, 193, 197–8, 204, 205, 225, 230–1, 234, 242, 248, 274–5
  ideology 169–72, 176, 184, 197, 198, 204
Godeau, Louis 332
Goethe, Johann Wolfgang von 86, 164
Goguet, Jacques 227
Gohier, Jérôme 337
Gorsas, Antoine-Joseph 170–1
Gouges, Olympe de 111–12, 225, 231
Grand-Champ 203–4
Grasse 92
Great Fear 74–7
Grégoire, Abbé Henri 67, 69, 91, 105, 118, 136, 169, 243, 246, 281, 325, 347
Grenoble 45, 56, 86, 136, 346
Grève, Place de 71
Grimaud, Pascal-Antoine 202
Grospierres 109
Grouchy, Sophie de 111
Guéméné 127
guilds 8, 26, 50, 62, 107, 134, 347, 352
guillotine, guillotinings 95, 154, 173, 186, 200, 211, 212, 215–6, 224, 238, 240, 248, 250, 251, 258–9, 261, 265, 267–9, 271, 278, 281, 286, 287–8, 294, 309, 312, 322, 362

Hainaut (region) 59
Hardy, Sébastien 71, 84
harvests *see also* food 3, 4, 5, 7, 12, 17, 51, 53–4, 59, 75, 84, 88, 93, 134–5, 144, 258, 293, 309, 336, 353
Haute-Marne (department) 200
Haute-Saône (department) 157
Hautes-Pyrénées (department) 88
Havre, Le 10, 36, 169, 255
Hébert, Jacques-René 134, 155, 211, 224–5, 231, 249, 254, 268
Hébertists 224, 250, 252–4, 275
hérault (department) 259
hoarders, hoarding 59, 71, 180, 224, 244
Holbach, Baron d' 25, 32, 35
homeland *see patrie*
homosexuality 156, 360
hospitals 15, 72, 188, 298, 308, 359
  military 179, 233, 345

Houdon, Jean-Antoine 81
Huard, Pierre 4
humiliation 75, 132, 163, 177, 179, 192, 230, 261, 287, 312
hunting 43, 59, 63, 65, 66, 77, 90
hunger 12, 13, 21, 47, 51, 54, 58–9, 68, 71, 73, 75, 221, 257, 264, 284, 309

identity 2, 15, 88, 98–9, 185, 331, 344–6, 347–8, 359, 366
India, Indians 35, 37, 102, 104, 181, 334–5
indigo 36
industry 4, 5, 7–8, 9, 10, 11, 13, 26, 29, 54, 56, 58–9, 62, 94, 162, 215, 256, 278, 296, 301, 337, 349, 351, 364
inheritance laws *see also* children 111, 195, 207, 237, 349–50, 355, 360, 369
Ireland 147, 313, 329–30
Italy 25, 228, 302–4, 313–4, 327–9, 330, 333, 338, 340, 364

Jacobin clubs 85, 105, 110–11, 131, 133, 134, 138, 147, 151, 152, 154, 182, 184, 193, 195, 200, 217, 222–3, 226, 232, 235, 247, 252, 254–6, 262, 268, 269, 270–71, 277–79, 299, 363
Jacobins 103, 111, 116, 136, 148, 150, 152, 156–8, 180, 198, 210, 214, 215, 218, 219, 221, 230, 235, 236, 238, 239, 248, 252–5, 263, 265, 267, 271, 274, 279, 284, 286, 298, 300, 311, 314, 315, 319, 321, 326, 337, 359
  Girondin criticism of 169–71, 176, 184, 185, 197
  ideology 149, 170, 172–3, 185, 217–8, 253
  Napoleon and 302, 336
  régional and local 185–6, 196, 197, 215, 217, 222, 256, 258, 288, 338
Jansenism 30
Jaucourt, Louis de 25
Javogues, Claude 243
Jefferson, Thomas 35, 81, 99, 157
Jemappes, battle of 165, 175, 241, 361
Jews 14–5, 96–7, 114, 121–2, 130, 166, 190, 334, 359, 362
Jourdan Law 331
Jourdan, Jean-Baptiste 227, 266
Jourdan, Mathieu ('Coupe-tête') 148
Jullien, Marc-Antoine ('Jules') 184, 198, 200, 234, 246, 275
Jullien, Rosalie 161, 170, 184, 200–1, 230, 270, 275
Julliot, François-Pierre 124, 194

killings, extra-judicial 66–8, 72–4, 115, 136–8, 148, 151–2, 158, 159, 160–3, 171, 178, 204, 205, 261, 277, 288, 290, 301, 330, 336, 342

Kellerman, François-Christophe 164
Kléber, Jean-Baptiste 214, 336

La Tour du Pin, Henriette Lucy Dillon,
    Marquise de 68, 119, 342
Labillardière, Jacques-Julien Houtou
    de 368
Labille-Guiard, Adélaïde 114, 280
Lacau 241
Lacombe, Benôit 202–3
Lacombe, Claire 225, 242, 254, 276
Lacoste 180
Lafaurie, Elisabeth 195–6
Lafayette, Marquis de 37, 49, 67, 72–3, 84, 86,
    100, 113, 115, 117, 137–8, 152, 157, 159,
    173–4, 186, 217
Lagrasse 55, 221, 277
Lakanal, Joseph 217, 245
Lallemand de Sainte-Croix 142
Lally-Tollendal, Marquis de 81
Lamballe 207
Lamballe, Princesse de 160
Lamberdière, François 76
Lameth, Alexandre de 114, 152
Lameth brothers 49, 68
Lamoignon, Chrétien-François de 40, 43,-6,
    55
Lamoignon, Guillaume-Chrétien de
    Malesherbes de 14, 27, 108, 171
land tax 41–3, 46, 51, 54, 63, 222, 295,
    354
language see french also individual languages
    1–2, 24, 34, 45, 48, 63, 64, 68, 91, 112,
    127, 191, 198, 199, 255, 282, 292, 345,
    346–8,
Languedoc (region) 2, 4, 6, 19, 21, 55, 65, 70,
    89, 92, 108, 115, 221, 357
Lannion 108
Laon 89, 92, 101, 121, 124, 196, 207, 229,
    307
Laplanche, Jacques-Léonard 180, 218
La Rochelle 35–6, 105–6, 179, 190, 191–3,
    241, 302, 325, 332
Latierce (mayor) 108
Laukhard, Frédéric-Christian 216
Lauragais (region) 17
Lavabre, Guillaume 167
Lavoisier, Antoine 18, 81, 99, 259–60,
    323
Law of 14 Frimaire Year II 247, 253
Law of 22 Prairial Year II 264–5, 268, 275
Law of General Maximum 220, 222, 247,
    258, 269, 284
Law of Suspects 213, 259, 275
lawyers 13, 23–4, 40–1, 47, 53, 66, 94–5, 99,
    106, 168, 353–4
Le Chapelier, Isaac-René-Guy 134
Le Chapelier Law 134–5

Legislative Assembly 148–150, 152–160, 172,
    183, 203, 208, 283, 338
Lejeune, Sylvain 211
Le Mans 11, 229, 283, 322, 336
Léon, Pauline 129, 138, 155, 159, 225, 254, 276
Lepeletier de Saint-Fargeau, Louis-Michel
    41, 168, 172, 179, 205, 217, 268, 236, 241
Le Peletier de Rosanbo family 55, 208, 259,
    362
Lequinio, Joseph Marie 211
Le Raincy 54
Les Vans 158
'levée en masse' see army (conscription)
liberalism see also economic liberalism 79, 320,
    358, 423, 425–6, 447
liberty cap see also phrygian cap 101, 165, 195,
    230, 239, 246
liberty trees see also trees 98, 101, 165–6, 182,
    222, 277, 317, 336
Liège 44, 234
livrets 8, 352
Lille 6, 42, 50–1, 58, 100, 138, 154, 175,
    284–5, 342
Limousin (region) 255
Limoux 68, 165
Lindet, Robert 172, 185, 210, 265, 267, 290,
    337–8, 364,
Lindet, Thomas 126, 172, 337
Lisle, Rouget de 166
literature 27–9, 31–2, 33, 61, 112, 144, 168,
    239, 243, 246, 255, 299
local government 89, 94, 186, 191, 217, 222,
    226, 253, 257, 266, 277, 288, 298, 319,
    339, 353
Loire (department) 83
Loire (river) 18, 59, 66, 99, 101, 127, 176, 233,
    234, 258, 301, 332, 341
Loiret (department) 99, 179, 218
Longuet, Jean 135
Longwy 159, 164
Lorraine (region) 2, 15, 18, 63, 67, 74, 76, 97,
    120, 129, 198, 235, 293, 299
Louis XIV 32, 208, 224
Louis XV 13, 102, 120, 239
Louis XVI xii, 1–2, 7, 10, 14, 17–18, 41, 43–4,
    46, 49, 56, 58–60, 67–71, 73, 82, 84,
    85, 87, 100, 116, 131–4, 136–40, 142,
    146–50, 155–9, 165, 176, 193, 205, 218,
    224, 234, 259, 278, 326, 341–2172
    trial and death of 171–3, 181, 200
Loustallot, Élysée 73–4, 117
Lunéville 256, 298
Lyon 5, 6, 7, 9, 10, 11, 75, 98, 111, 125, 162,
    176, 186, 197, 205, 214, 216, 243, 288,
    324
    federalism and repression of 185, 209,
    215, 227, 241, 247, 264, 269, 271–2,
    337

Mably 30
Machecoul 178
Mâcon 76, 285
magistrates 16, 23, 27, 49, 50–1, 192, 339
Maignet, Étienne-Christophe 261, 277
Maine (region) 11, 111, 125
Mainz (Mayenne) 139, 166, 182, 275
Malbosc, Louis-Bastide de 130
Malouet, Baron 78, 81
manufacturing see industry
Marat, Jean-Paul 110, 130, 138, 163, 169, 170, 172, 184, 189, 193, 205–6, 212–3, 217–8, 224, 230, 236, 259, 267, 287, 319
Marchais, Yves-Michel 13, 316–8
Marcou (priest) 165
Marie-Antoinette 1, 39, 85, 87, 112, 116, 138–40, 149, 152, 156, 161, 230–1, 342
markets 4, 9, 12, 62, 84, 151, 198, 219, 316, 339
Marne (department) 7
marriage see also clergy, divorce 4, 11, 12–14, 17, 32, 112, 195, 208, 308, 332, 349, 359
Marseillaise 166, 281
Marseille 6–7, 9–10, 36, 59, 147, 158, 166, 186, 189, 197, 211, 216, 223, 241–2, 351
  federalism and repression of 269, 271, 288–9
Martinique 35–6, 276, 318, 351
massacres see killings, extra-judicial
Maure, Nicolas 287
maximum price-controls 135, 220, 222–3, 226, 247, 257, 258, 269, 284
maypoles 97–8
Melun 324
Ménétra, Jacques-Louis 33, 265
Mercier, Louis-Sébastien 31, 48, 128, 247–8, 284, 321, 338
Mercier-Dupaty, Jean-Baptiste 35, 40, 47
Mercy-Argenteau, Comte de 43, 116
Méricourt, Théroigne de 84, 111, 156, 159, 225
Metz 35, 42, 96, 117, 132–3, 166, 229, 298
Meurthe (department) 157
Meurthe-et-Moselle (department) 159
militia 72, 75, 184
Millau 5, 129
Mirabeau, Honoré-Gabriel Riquetti, Comte de 41, 49, 51, 67, 70, 77, 78, 81, 115–7, 143, 217, 267
Miranda, Francisco de 164–5, 234
Miromesnil, Marquis de 39
monarchy x, 1, 3, 6, 18, 28–31, 33, 38, 40–2, 44–5, 48, 50–2, 55–6, 70, 72, 80, 82, 91, 113, 126, 129–30, 147, 158–9, 164–5, 174, 181, 198, 206, 208, 213, 218, 220,

249, 251, 300, 302, 316, 326, 342–3, 346, 359, 362, 363, 365–6
  constitutional 140, 142, 144, 148, 156, 231, 267, 289, 364
Monnard, Marie-Victoire 175, 195, 262
Montautour 191
Montesquiou, General 165
Montmartre 241, 279, 285
Montminot 101
Montmorency 281
Montmorency, Duke of 77
Montmorillon 133
Montmorin, Comte de 44, 116
Montpellier 166, 216, 242, 257–8, 269, 282
Morbihan (department) 127
Mortagne-au-Perche 76
mortality see population 12, 360
Moselle (department) 266, 293
Mounier, Jean-Jacques 81–2
Mountain, The 246, 248, 263
Municipal Law (14 December 1789) 94
murder see crime, killings

names see also children 56, 89, 106, 114, 146, 198, 218–9, 241–2, 281–2, 324
Nancy 117, 120, 123, 180, 226, 229, 245, 256, 298, 299, 305, 359
  Bishop of 305, 326
Nantes 6–7, 10, 36–7, 46–7, 105–6, 127, 133, 146, 179, 191, 214, 233–4, 238, 264, 277, 290, 351
Nanteuil 110
Narbonne 55, 68, 110, 109, 221, 310
National Assembly 69–79, 82–5, 88–105, 114, 116–23, 126–149, 152–9, 168–9, 181, 199, 209, 220, 259, 347, 353
National Convention 162, 164–5, 169, 179, 179–86, 198, 203, 205, 209, 212, 215, 216, 219–20, 223, 225, 229, 235, 236, 239, 247, 249, 255, 262, 264, 281, 282, 286, 293, 300–1, 307, 308, 321, 323, 341, 347, 348, 349
National Guard 84, 89, 94, 99, 101, 116, 117, 130, 133, 134, 135, 137, 154, 158, 198, 211, 225, 286, 343
Necker, Jacques 46, 71, 73, 89, 90, 115–6
Neerwinden, battle of 175
Nemours, Dupont de 49
Neuchâtel 27, 31
Neufchâteau, François de 131, 276, 323
Nevers 242, 243
newspapers (general) 27, 73, 84, 112, 138, 257
  Ami du peuple 130, 224
  Ami du Roi 129
  Courrier de l'Europe 27

Courrier extraordinaire 96
Feuille villageoise 222, 263
Gazette de Leyde 27
Gazette de Paris 131, 134
Charlie Hebdo 369
Journal de la mode et du goût 101
Journal de Paris 34, 35, 299
Journal de santé 27
Magyar Kurir 86
Mercure de France 51
Moniteur Universel 303
Orateur du people 279
Père Duchesne 134, 155, 211, 224
Républicain 173
Révolutions de France et de Brabant 93, 117
Révolutions de Paris 73, 78, 117, 166, 179, 222
Saint Petersburg Gazette 86
Vieux Cordelier 248
Nîmes 5, 14, 82, 90, 115, 130, 143, 158, 216, 364,
Niort 114
nobility, nobles 3, 11, 16, 61, 65, 68, 83, 168, 218, 318, 342, 344, 354–5
Noailles, Louis de 49
Nord (department) 321
Normandie, Louis-Charles, Duc de 116
Normandy (region) 5, 19, 48, 51, 52, 111, 172, 185, 193–4, 210, 245, 283, 307, 350, 355, 357, 364
Notre-Dame (Paris) 126, 246, 340
nuns *see* religious orders
Nusse, J.-F. (priest) 124

Oberkampf, Christophe-Philippe 10
Occitan (language) 2, 4, 63, 167
Occitans 4–5, 12, 199, 350
October Days 1789 84–6
Oise (river) 63
Oisy, Comte de 60
opera 240, 325
Orléans 58, 59, 64, 68, 83–4, 90, 94, 99, 111, 120, 123–5, 134, 162, 179–80, 205, 218, 220, 230, 241, 258, 262, 284, 299, 301, 312, 324, 333, 340–1
Orléans, Louis-Philippe-Joseph, Duc d' 16, 54, 70, 114
Orne (department) 193
orphans *see* children

Paganel, Pierre 237, 245
Pailleterie, Thomas-Alexandre Davy de la 194
Paine, Tom 146, 159, 165, 182, 234
Palloy, Pierre-François 99, 200, 218
Paoli, Pasquale 37, 102, 181,
pamphlets 27, 32, 49, 52, 67,

Paris xii, 3–14, 16, 19, 20, 24, 26–7, 30–1, 33, 35, 38, 41, 48, 58, 59, 66, 71–5, 77, 80, 83–6, 89, 91, 92, 94, 95, 98, 100, 102, 105, 107, 111, 112, 115, 119, 125, 126, 133, 135, 136, 146, 148, 149–51, 155–8, 160–2, 164–9, 172–86, 190, 192, 193, 196–8, 202, 204, 206, 208, 211, 215, 216, 223–6, 229–32, 235, 238, 239, 240–1, 246, 249, 250, 253, 257, 260, 262–6, 268, 269, 272, 275, 276, 279, 300, 302–8, 312, 317, 319, 321, 323, 325, 327–8, 336, 344, 348, 349, 352, 355, 368, 369
Paris, *parlement* of 39–40, 43, 44–5, 49, 108, 144, 194
Paris, *salon* 35, 81, 113, 240, 280, 300, 304
parlements 17, 19, 39, 41, 43–6, 51, 95, 114, 354
Pasquier, Étienne-Dennis 194
patrie 29, 64, 101, 130, 137, 157, 162, 166, 168, 171, 180, 185, 192, 195, 201, 211, 217, 237, 246, 270, 287, 299, 301, 325, 333, 345, 348, 361, 367
patrie en danger, decree 157, 361
Pays de Caux (region) 80
peasants *see also* agricultural labourers 2–6, 12, 28, 59, 63, 64, 66, 75–7, 80, 90, 91, 93, 97, 107, 108, 109, 115, 125, 127, 133, 142, 143, 144, 145, 148, 151, 177, 178, 179, 191, 193, 203, 213, 223, 226, 237, 271, 298, 309, 311, 329, 331, 333, 350, 354, 355–7, 365.
Pelletier, Nicholas-Jacques 95–6
Périer, Claude 46, 56
Périgueux 97
Perpignan 19, 117, 133, 175, 227, 308, 324
Pétion, Jérôme 53, 82, 111, 155, 156, 200, 231
petitions 121, 123, 129, 136–7, 154–5, 180, 193, 225, 238, 267, 282, 295, 310, 311, 344, 350, 354, 366
Peyrat 98
Peyrestortes, battle of 227
Phrygian caps *see also* bonnet *rouge* 168, 238, 244
Picardy (region) 69, 121, 278, 297, 355
Pillnitz 139, 158
Pinaigre, Marguerite 72
Pithiviers (priest) 124, 259
Pitt, William 134, 235, 368
Pius VI, Pope 120, 123–6, 147, 154, 327, 358
'Plain' 169, 176, 183, 253, 274
Ploërmel 77
plots *see* conspiracies
Poitou (region) 69, 125, 194
Pontoise 207, 283
poor relief 1, 11, 13, 55, 94, 120, 129, 183, 196, 284, 308, 353
popular societies *see* clubs

population 3, 5–10, 12, 15, 19, 36, 89, 100, 121, 131, 133, 134, 157, 158, 174, 176, 181, 188, 190, 194, 199, 202, 211, 215, 223, 233, 236, 256, 258, 261, 292, 295, 308, 309, 314, 327, 328, 343, 345, 348, 350, 351, 352, 357, 360, 365,
Poullain de Grandprey, Joseph de 131
Prémontré, abbey of 258–9
press *see* newspapers
prices *see also* maximum price controls 8, 9, 11, 12, 54, 55, 68, 76, 84, 181, 183, 220, 222–3, 235, 247, 253, 258, 284–5, 293, 298, 309, 322
priests *see* clergy
Priestley, Joseph 147, 159, 165, 182
primogeniture *see* inheritance
prisons, prisoners *see also* Bastille 19, 160, 161, 188, 275, 288, 301,
Privas 315
prostitution 9, 11, 31, 156, 238, 284, 308–9
protests *see* food riots, strikes, *taxation populaire*
Provence, Comte de 50, 69, 115, 139, 149, 289, 305
Provence (region) 51, 59, 90, 92, 125, 131, 150, 180, 223, 271, 277,
Provins 142
Prussia 20, 139, 150, 153, 157, 182
Prussians, 102, 156, 159, 161, 162, 165, 213, 214, 216
    army, troops 43, 44, 86, 158, 164, 182, 199, 200
Puylaurens 167
Pyrenees (region) 3, 14, 62, 87, 139, 198–9, 265, 293, 331–2, 336, 337, 347, 350, 357
Pyrénées-Orientales (department) *see also* Perpignan 148, 172, 198–9

Quercy (region) 98, 132
Quesnay 25–6
Quesques and Lottinghen (priest of) 123
Quiberon 290, 300, 318
Quimper 271, 306

Rabaut Saint-Étienne, Jean-Paul 14, 66, 82–3, 90, 120, 122, 143
Raynal, Abbé 30, 35, 304
reading *see also* literature 31, 53, 91, 112, 236, 237, 282
refugees 15, 37, 44, 103, 138, 150, 233, 234, 268
'regeneration' 53, 64, 70, 80–3, 87–8, 98, 114, 118, 128, 149, 163, 208, 219, 253, 261, 262, 265
Reims 1, 224, 239, 287
religious orders 12, 13, 15, 61, 120, 121, 177, 196, 352–3, 359

renaming *see* names
Rennes 201, 325, 336, 346, 354
republic 144, 159, 164–87, 189, 192, 201, 206, 207, 208, 209, 210, 212, 214, 215, 218, 219, 227, 228, 231, 234–7, 246, 249, 251, 255, 257, 258, 262–4, 266–8, 269–71, 275, 284, 285, 288, 294, 296, 297, 300, 330, 340, 346, 348, 353, 359, 363, 366, 369
'sister republics' 291–3, 326–9, 334, 339, 367
republican calendar 219, 227, 235, 241, 262, 307, 316, 323, 330, 380
requisitioning *see* army
Restif de la Bretonne, Nicolas 4, 160–1
restoration 147, 289
Rethel 42
Reubell, Jean-François 96, 317
'Réveil du Peuple, Le', song 279–80
Réveillon, riots 7, 67–8,
revolutionary committees 226, 228, 236, 250, 252–4, 278
revolutionary oath *see* Civil Constitution of the Clergy
Revolutionary Republican Citizenesses *see also* citizenesses 225–6, 242–3, 254, 276, 348
Revolutionary Tribunal 180, 183, 188, 197, 205, 216, 230–1, 235, 251, 252, 259, 264, 275, 277, 288, 363
Rhineland (region) 165–6, 182, 268, 318, 327–8,
Rhône (river) 45, 104, 130, 327, 355
Rime (merchant) 68
Robespierre, Augustin 66, 102
Robespierre, Charlotte 102
Robespierre, Maximilien xii, 8, 23–4, 29, 34, 35, 47, 66, 68, 82, 102, 111, 114, 138, 143, 148, 150–1, 155, 157, 158, 169, 170–1, 172, 197, 200, 206, 210, 213, 217, 225, 231, 234–6, 239, 242, 246, 249–54, 260–6, 268–71, 274–8, 280–1, 284, 285, 287, 290, 293, 309, 312, 314, 319, 328, 362
Rochambeau, Comte de 37
La Rochefoucauld-Liancourt 49
Roland de la Platière,
    Jean-Marie 111, 155, 167, 169–70, 198, 230
    Marie-Jeanne ('Manon') 111, 169–70, 186, 230
Rolandins 214
Rome 18, 33–4, 86, 104, 125, 179, 201, 225, 304, 327–8, 336, 338
Romme, Charles-Gilbert 83, 217, 219, 237, 287
Ronceray 353
Rouen 4, 5, 6, 10, 58, 62, 121, 135, 213, 230, 242, 307, 349

Rougier de la Bergerie, Jean-Baptiste 29
Rousseau, Jean-Jacques 25, 30–3, 35, 83, 143, 170, 213, 239, 242, 254, 276, 281, 311
Roussel, Guillaume ('Cadet') 167, 244
Rousselot, Abbé 125
Roussillon (region) 63, 235
Roux-Fazillac, Pierre 217
royalists 102, 115, 117, 129–31, 134, 140, 153, 156, 162, 166, 185–6, 189, 205, 214, 223, 243, 262, 280, 289, 290, 296, 297–8, 300, 302–3, 315–9, 325, 333, 336–7, 343, 348, 362, 368
Rural Code of 1791 145
Russia 1, 83, 86, 104, 219, 294, 337, 368

Sade, marquis de 180
Sagy 63
Saint-André, Jean Bon 217
Saint-André-de-Cubzac 342
Saint-Antoine, faubourg 7, 67, 72, 183, 286
Saint-Brieuc 191
Saint-Cloud 87, 131
Saint-Denis-en-Val 59, 134, 230
Saint-Dié 157
Saint-Domingue See Colonies
Saint-Émilion 231
Saint-Eulalie 241
Saint-Eustache 225
Saint-Fond, Faujas de 27, 304
Saint-Germain 9, 16
Saint-Gilles 241
Saint-Étienne 14, 66, 84, 242, 244
Saint-Flour 258
Saint-Hilaire 123
Saint-Honoré 16
Saint-Izague 241
Saint-Jean-d'Angély 108
Saint-Just, Louis-Antoine 171–2, 180, 210, 237, 254, 262, 264, 265, 281, 290
Saint-Laud 322
Saint-Laurent-de-Cerdans 198–9, 308
Saint-Lazare 72
Saint-Marcel 27
Saint-Martin-du-Tertre 283
Saint-Médiers 241
Saint-Nicolas-de-la-Grave 207
Saint Nolff 127
Saint-Omer 23
Saint-Ouen 241
Saint Papoul 19, 107
Saint-Paul 58, 107
Saint-Pierre 91
Saint-Quentin 229
Saint-Rogatien 241
Saint-Sever 188, 199, 212
Saint-Sulpice 76, 128, 202, 246,
Saint-Vincent 324
Saint-Zacharie 223

Sainte-Croix 234
Sainte-Menehould 132–3
Saintes 133
Salambier, Bande à 312
salons 28, 111, 234, 293
salt 191, 298, 306
    tax 20, 64, 76, 135
sans-culottes 155, 168, 176, 180, 183–4, 196, 198, 203, 205, 212, 216, 218, 222, 223–4, 227, 233–4, 236, 237–8, 240, 242–6, 249, 250, 253, 254, 257, 267, 269, 270, 272, 274, 276, 279, 285–7, 297, 299, 311, 316, 319, 322, 344, 352
Sans-Culottes (place name) 179, 241
sans-jupons 155
Saône (valley) 76
Sare 228
Sarlat 101
Sarreguemines 76
Sarthe (department) 193, 229
satire 32–3, 140, 156, 167
Saumur 66
Sauveur, Joseph 178
Sauvigny, Louis Bertier de 73
Savenay 232
Savoy (region) 116, 165–6, 226–7, 329
schools see also education 8, 13, 33, 82, 94, 123, 193, 236, 282, 283, 324
school teachers see also education 75, 83, 90, 110, 111, 167, 201, 259, 262, 283, 324
Second Estate see nobility
seigneurialism 17, 41, 51, 63, 65, 75–6, 90–1, 97, 98, 160, 180, 189, 203, 213, 305, 323, 329, 342, 345, 347, 350, 354–5, 357–8, 365, 369
Seine (river) 156, 184, 284, 324, 338
Seine-et-Marne (department) 241
Senez 15, 19
Senozan 76
September Massacres 1792 160–4, 170, 183, 192, 231, 234, 238, 255, 279
Servan, Joseph 167
Sicre, Joseph 308
Sieyès, Emmanuel 29, 52–3, 66, 67, 68, 82, 169, 319, 337, 338
Silly-en-Multien 75, 90, 110
Simonneau (mayor) 151–2
slave
    insurrections 145–6, 186, 350–1
    trade 35–6, 38, 56, 105–6, 136, 142, 145, 191, 248, 318
slavery 32, 80, 105–6, 131, 145–6, 174, 176, 194, 239, 249, 302, 304, 330, 350–1, 369
Society of Friends of the Constitution see Jacobin club
Society of Thirty, Paris 49, 67
Soissons 89, 162–3, 180, 196, 292
soldiers see army

Solliès 59
Somme (department) 142, 257, 282
Sommières 129
Souchet, Chenu de 167
Spain 9, 15, 37, 86, 116, 127, 134, 139, 153, 154, 173, 216, 235, 248, 293, 310, 311, 316, 336, 367
starvation *see* hunger
Strasbourg 7, 15, 100, 256, 337
strikes 134, 136, 151, 258, 293
sugar 36, 56, 145, 191, 226, 275, 302, 318
suspects 148, 184, 202, 211, 213, 216, 224, 229–30, 237, 248, 258, 259, 265, 275–6, 277–8, 280, 287
Switzerland 31, 104, 119, 234, 305, 326, 329, 337

Talleyrand-Périgord, Charles Maurice de 16, 49, 67, 76, 91–2, 100, 114, 125, 330, 334, 337, 347
Talma, François-Joseph 113, 281
Tarascon 289
Tarbes 219
Target, Guy-Jean 95
Tarn-et-Garonne (department) 207
taxation 1–2, 6, 12, 19–20, 42, 61–3, 65, 70, 88, 91, 93, 122–3, 135, 335, 347
    taxation populaire see also food riots 12, 21, 54, 68, 76, 83–4, 85, 151–2, 162, 181, 257–8, 309
taxes
    ancien régime 3, 6, 20, 42, 48, 54, 70, 74, 91, 93, 259–60
    revolutionary 89–93, 94, 105, 107, 122, 127, 135, 177, 222, 309, 318, 323, 354
teachers *see* schoolteachers
terror
    emotion of 45, 51, 76, 109, 151, 160, 163, 175, 274, 284, 290, 321
    regime of 209–12, 213, 217–8, 228, 236, 238–40, 247, 253–4, 257, 260–8, 272
textiles *see* industry
theatre 168, 240, 254, 300
theft *see* crime
Thermidor 280, 286, 288–9, 294, 300, 303
Thermidorians 279, 281–2, 338
Third Estate 5–6, 32, 46, 49–53, 56, 58, 65–73, 75, 77, 80, 103, 105, 121, 137, 180, 190, 201, 271
Thionville 166, 301, 318
Thouret, Jacques Guillaume 95
Tithes 3, 5, 13, 59, 63, 66, 70, 74, 76–8, 93, 261, 327, 333, 340, 353, 355, 357
tobacco 36, 76, 302

Tocqueville, Alexis de 55, 362–3
Tonneins 324, 351
Tosi, Joseph 182
Totes 135
Toulon 117, 131, 133, 197, 214, 247, 269, 271, 279, 318, 334
Toulouse 19, 45, 54, 87, 89, 100, 121, 186, 211, 226, 245, 282, 307, 335–6, 346, 353, 356, 362
Touraine (region) 117
Tournus 76
Tours 190, 237
trade *see* commerce
transport 20, 210, 257, 265, 293, 314, 357
treaties
    Basle 292–3
    Campo Formio 327, 330, 333–4, 337
    Jay 314
    Lunéville 340
    Paris 35, 38
    Pyrenees 9
trees *see also* forests, liberty trees 4, 90, 110, 144, 210
Treilhard, Jean-Baptiste 122
Trouvé, Charles-Joseph 303, 356–7
Troyes 33, 40, 43, 58, 61, 124, 194
Tulle 244
Turgot 8, 25–6, 30
Turreau, Louis-Marie 232–3
Two-Thirds Decree 296, 302

United Kingdom *see* Britain
United States *see* American, America, North
Ursulines 154
Uzès 130, 158

vacants see wasteland
Vadencourt 162
Valenciennes 59, 211, 283
Valmy, battle of 164–5, 175, 198, 361
Vannes 59, 98
Varaize 108
Vatimesnil 62
Vauban 55
Vendée insurrection 176–9, 183–4, 186, 190, 191, 192, 197, 207, 214, 232, 233, 260, 290, 302, 306, 317, 337, 345, 365–6
Verdouble (river) 54
Verdun 160–1, 164, 200, 221
Versailles 2, 6, 7, 10–11, 16, 21, 30, 38, 41, 49, 58, 60, 62, 64–5, 68, 71, 81, 84, 87, 91, 103, 119, 142, 162, 208, 237, 318
Vervins 196
Viala, Joseph Agricola 236, 300, 316
Vienne (department) 133
Vigée Lebrun, Elisabeth 86, 114
Viguier, Antoine 175
Villardebelle 165

Villedieu 241
Villefranche-en-Beaujolais 242
Villers-Cotterêts 2, 347, 364
Villette, Marquis de 156
vineyards *see* wine
violence *see* crime(s), killings
virtue, civic virtues 26, 31–4, 37, 53, 82–3,
    112, 138, 168, 170, 179, 201, 208, 213,
    217–8, 219, 222, 225, 226, 228, 236, 246,
    250, 255, 261–3, 265, 267, 272, 277, 281,
    295, 322, 323, 326, 334, 341, 345, 349,
    362, 363
Vissery de Bois-Valé, Charles Dominique
    de 23
Vizille 46, 56
Volland, Sophie 26
Voltaire 25, 28, 32, 35, 52, 324
volunteers *see* army
vote, voting *see* elections

wages *see also* strikes 9, 11, 54, 67, 71, 220,
    222–3, 247, 253, 257–8, 269, 284, 292–3,
    322, 356, 360
Washington, George 86–7, 159, 182
wasteland 109, 357
weavers, weaving *see* textile industry
weights and measures 1, 20, 99, 283–4, 323, 347

Weis, Nanine 192
wet-nursing 11
Williams, Helen-Maria 103, 234, 268
wine, wine-growing 4, 7, 36, 56, 72, 91,
    142, 183, 191, 257, 314, 353, 357,
    358, 360
women *see also* citizenesses, feminists,
    inheritance laws 28, 52, 61, 62, 67, 76,
    80, 84–5, 93–4, 101, 111–12, 113, 119,
    122, 128–9, 142, 147, 154–5, 158–9,
    162, 175, 180, 183, 195–6, 199, 200, 204,
    207–8, 210, 214, 215, 223, 225–6, 231–2,
    233, 237, 238, 242, 243, 247, 263, 284,
    285–7, 289, 294, 295, 299, 302, 308–9,
    311–12, 314, 324, 332, 334, 336, 348–50,
    353, 355, 360, 365
    and divorce 111, 195, 208, 216, 304,
        349–50, 369
    and religion 13–14, 120, 125, 127, 192, 307,
        325, 359
woods *see* deforestation

Xinxet Lanquine, Jacques 311

Yonne (department) 311, 344
    river 7, 222
Young, Arthur 46–7, 74, 90, 356

Illustration Credits

1. RMN-Grand Palais/Jean-Gilles Berizzi. 2. Suzy Schmitz. 3. Bibliothèque nationale de France. 4. Musée des Beaux-Arts, Ville de Bernay. 5. RMN-Grand Palais/Stéphane Maréchalle. 6. Peter McPhee. 7. Author's collection. 8. Bibliothèque nationale de France. 9. Fornaci Giorgi images library, Via Fornaci Vecchie, 03013 Ferentino Italy. 10. Peter McPhee. 11. Bibliothèque nationale de France. 12. Peter McPhee. 13. Bibliothèque nationale de France. 14. Fronza Woods. 15. Public domain, via Wikimedia Commons. 16. Bibliothèque nationale de France. 17. Bibliothèque nationale de France. 18. RMN-Grand Palais (Chateau de Versailles)/Gérard Blot. 19. Author's collection. 20. Beinecke Rare Book and Manuscript Library. 21. Bibliothèque nationale de France. 22. Bibliothèque nationale de France. 23. RMN-Grand Palais (Chateau de Versailles)/Gérard Blot. 24. Peter McPhee. 25. AD Loire-Atlantique. 26. Bibliothèque nationale de France. 27. Peter McPhee. 28. Peter McPhee. 29. Musée des Beaux-Arts de Lyon. 30. Bridgeman Images. 31. Bibliothèque nationale de France. 32. Bibliothèque nationale de France. 33. National Gallery of Victoria, Melbourne. 34. Peter McPhee. 35. Bibliothèque nationale de France. 36. Bpk, Hamburger Kunsthalle, Hanne Moschkowitz. 37. Peter McPhee. 38. Greg Burgess. 39. National Gallery of Victoria, Melbourne. 40. Bibliothèque nationale de France. 41. Public domain, via Wikimedia Commons. 42. Bibliothèque nationale de France. 43. Peter McPhee.